THE

ILLUSTRATED

HORSE MANAGEMENT

CONTAINING DESCRIPTIVE REMARKS UPON

ANATOMY, MEDICINE, SHOEING, TEETH, FOOD. VICES, STABLES;

LIKEWISE A PLAIN ACCOUNT OF THE

Situation, Nature, and Value of the various Points

TOGETHER WITH COMMENTS ON

GROOMS, DEALERS, BREEDERS, BREAKERS, AND TRAINERS

ALSO ON

CARRIAGES AND HARNESS.

Embellished with more than 400 Engravings, from Original Designs made expressly for this Work.

BY

EDWARD MAYHEW, M.R.C.V.S.

UTHOR OF "THE ILLUSTRATED HORSE DOCTOR," AND OTHER WORKS

W

Published by
Melvin Powers
WILSHIRE BOOK COMPANY
12015 Sherman Road
No. Hollywood, California 91605
Telephone: (213) 875-1711

Printed by

HAL LEIGHTON PRINTING COMPANY
P.O. Box 3952
North Hollywood, California 91605
Telephone: (213) 983-1105

PRINTED IN THE UNITED STATES OF AMERICA

ISBN 0-87980-210-3

PREFACE.

THE reader, after having perused the present volume, may imagine the writer should have been more explicit when advertising the book's intentions, that a mass of speculative novelty should not have been hastily intruded upon the general public. Such, probably, will be the primary impression of most purchasers. The author, however, regrets he is by truth obliged to decline the compliment embodied in such a complaint. Those notions which, hurriedly regarded, appear as original, will, to the matured judgment, show only as an obvious result, worked out by the easy application of a single idea. Common sense embraces every merit in the ensuing pages. Grant this, and there remains no loftier claim to advance. The different chapters contain nothing which is not very superficial and entirely based upon fact. Every statement included in the following articles becomes plain and self-evident to the man who can release his mind from the trammels of conventionality, and will allow his conceptions to be shaped by the habits and the inclinations which are natural to the equine species.

No living creature could be more exposed to the willfulness of perversity than the horse has hitherto been. All around and about the quadruped was moulded by influences which never regard the instincts of the animal. Every incident, directly or remotely concerning its welfare, was misconstrued or misstated. In proof of this is the common belief that Arabia produces the perfection of the tribe. This opinion is not to be substantiated by investigation. It is accepted upon no positive evidence. It is opposed to deductions drawn from a notorious fact. The greater number of Arabian steeds are not much larger than ordinary ponies. The climate dwarfs the stature. Dwindled development is recognized as the established proof of an uncongenial location.

The Arab horse is undoubtedly the most beautiful and the most intelligent specimen of its race. Travelers assure us it lives beside its master. It is the companion of the man and the playmate of the child. The country may not be favorable to its bodily perfection; but the affections and the mental attributes of a dumb intelligence are in that land cultivated and enlarged. Arabia boasts possession of the most civilized race of quadrupeds which are known to mankind. Looking on the creatures of that country, the world can contemplate the money value of kindness, since the indulgence of this emotion can conceal a serious corporal defect!

Probably it may be urged such intimacy between the human being and the beast is compatible only with a wild and a half-savage state of society. But there exist other nations as unrefined; nay, many peoples are known to be more barbarous than are the Arabs. The animal, however, fares as badly with inhabitants of the uncultured as with people of the civilized regions. The absence or the presence of refinement does not influence the welfare of an equine slave. Then gentleness in the Arabian must be a purely responsive emotion. Its presence or its absence is apart from mental status, or the social distinctions of the population to whom it is subjected and by whom it is surrounded.

The horse, in Britain, generally occupies the same house as the groom; but it is not, therefore, regarded with the feeling which is indulged by the inhabitant of the tent. The change from the soil of its birth to the English stable is attended with a total alteration of circumstances. Coldness or brutality, however, cannot banish the spirit which benevolence had fostered. The rebellion provoked by harshness is only more complete. The quietude of content is replaced by the wildness of timidity. Confidence is destroyed; fear assumes the likeness of savagery. The horse becomes a brute; for ignorance will not believe its inferior can be actuated by a reasonable motive.

In India the cavalry are mounted upon half-bred Persian horses. Not a few of the officers, however, bestride chargers of pure Arabian blood. These last are commonly under the charge of European servants, and serve European masters. The animal's nature changes with its location. The alteration, therefore, is independent of heat or of frost. The Arabs of India are as famed for ferocity as the creatures of the desert are notorious for gentleness of disposition.

The English behavior is chiefly shaped by selfishness, based upon a degraded superstition, which insists that every form of inferior existence was created for man's use and relinquished to his pleasure. The author must leave to others the inquiry, whether Christianity invests those who profess to believe its doctrines with any power which can be separated from the potency of charity. It is not for him to decide whether the conduct of a half-savage and a pagan tribe should, in its fruits and in its results, shame the consequences produced by the acts of men who boast of education and worship the exemplification of self-sacrifice and of love.

Would man only be content to base observations upon fact, anatomy has for a sufficient period ascertained a circumstance which should have startled public wonder into exclamation. But, where the horse is involved, centuries of prejudice appear to have generated a slothfulness of comprehension which overpowers all ordinary intelligence. In a bird a similar development has for ages been accepted as the proof of peacefulness of disposition. The pigeon congregates in flocks; it lives on vegetable substances, and it possesses a liver which exhibits no gall-bladder. This deficiency and these habits apply to the horse as literally as to the feathered type of innocence. Perhaps the higher status of the quadruped might be urged as the ground of a primary title to human consideration. Yet the dove-cot would seem to have blinded man to the merits of the stable!

The horse possesses a full-sized liver; still the gland exhibits no receptacle in which any excess of biliary secretion may be retained. The testimony of nature associates the creatures which man views as opposites, or regards as the emblem of peace and as the living embodiment of inveterate vice. Sameness and dissimilarity appear oddly united when both lives are viewed as the creations of the Omniscient. Resemblance in body should direct recognition to a likeness in spirit. Bearing in mind by whose ordinization all facts originate; remembering how life in this world is linked by bonds more difficult to trace than a positive sameness; and admitting that the One Parent had a design in every part of the many forms which He called into existence,—human ignorance must be wrong when it refuses to acknowledge an identity thus plainly emphasized.

That the workings of mortal conception are peculiarly eccentric, or at all events that candid appreciation has not embraced the helpmate of man on earth, is established by every rule of right being perverted when the horse appears upon the scene. The spirit of perversion seems so powerful it involves even the people who act with the animal. When Mr. Rarey came to England, he was hailed as a wonder. Mr. Rarey is now away from these shores, and the persons who formerly acknowledged his genius now speak of the system which he publicly demonstrated, as a flagrant imposture!

Why is this? What causes such contradictory opinions? His present defamers declare Mr. Rarey to be a humbug, because horses, when returned to the former grooms and subjected to the former treatment, resume the former habits. Like causes in other spheres are admitted to produce like results. The animal merely responds to the conduct of those who surround it. Mr. Rarey tames by the exhibition of kindness. He convinces dumb intelligence how futile is resistance, and makes apparent the groundlessness of fear. It is not the spirit which he subdues, but it is the confidence which he gains. All his acts are dictated by a desire to banish distrust. The animal having learned its lesson is restored to its proprietor. But if the owner has not profited by the instruction which he also has witnessed, ought he to be surprised if his inferior should forget the lesson received?

Is there not something remorselessly evil in thus converting the bad conduct of mankind into a reason for denying the operation of an obvious goodness; in refusing to acknowledge the responsive nature of the companion specially given to soften the doom of the human race; and doing this only to warrant the insolence of severity, which would seem to be a failing inherent in mortal breasts? But the doctrines of love and of charity are, by many worthy individuals, supposed to apply only to the conduct of man to man. There, in general belief, begins and ends the lesson. Even at this late period it is often read but never understood that Universal Benevolence looked down and blessed every form of life which the Spirit had created.

To inculcate the Christian theory; to simply illustrate its wisdom, and to demonstrate the folly of verbally acknowledging its teaching, while the acts of its professed believers do not testify to its truth, has been the endeavor of the author. He imagines that possibly he may convince some reader of the loss which the existing customs entail upon society. He does not anticipate to actuate many purchasers; but should a few carry into practice one or two of his suggestions, and such innovations should upon trial prove successful, other experiments will be hazarded, until all meriting adoption are generally recognized.

But numerous readers, after having read the foregoing, may nevertheless be inclined to inquire, "What is the use of this fuss about morality, when the issue only involves *a horse?*" To this interrogatory the writer unhesitatingly replies, that the first and the most difficult teaching of civilization ever concerns man's behavior to his inferiors. Make humanity gentle or reasonable toward animals, and strife or injustice between human beings would speedily terminate. But instruction to be effective should be convincing: therefore, purposely avoiding sentimentality, the author has sought to enlist the feeling only by satisfying the judgment.

Such are the purposes which induced "Horse Management" to be indited. But high as the object may be, the writer, when submitting his labors to the notice of the public, cannot otherwise than feel there is a common phrase, which passes current for criticism, and to which this book is peculiarly exposed. The colloquialism alluded to is the more insidious because it rather appeals to a prejudice than expresses anything absolute or definite. It rests upon a word in general use among the superficial of every profession, and that word is one which, in the public credulity, exalts the individual who abuses it. Let a medical practitioner study to master the rudiments of his calling, and the purpose of his assiduity will be whispered away by insinuations about the student being a most admirable theorist; but, unhappily, not being "a *practical* man."

Another individual shall earn disgrace at college. Yet this man shall start business to knock about the drugs and hack at living flesh, without comprehending the parts he is interfering with or having any knowledge of the medicines which he ventures to administer. This last person, though he neither adorns nor enlarges the sphere in which he acts, invariably attains the lucrative repute of being "a purely *practical* man." The notoriety brings profit to the object who merits no reward, while the absence of such fame acutely increases the sufferings of a deserving gentleman who had dared to brave the thorns which proverbially beset the pathway of desert to the recognition of society.

Against the facts declared in the present pages those who are interested to uphold existing foolish and cruel customs will probably urge their "*favorite phrase.*" To conceal its hollowness and to render acceptable its wholesale condemnation, it may be ushered in by an appearance of candor: thus, "Oh! the book is very pretty—nice reading—very humane—a little weak—rather overdone—too philanthropical, and wholly '*unpractical.*' It teaches nothing which experience could adopt or which the thorough horseman can do more than laugh at. *Entirely unpractical.*"

How long are men to be subjugated by mere verbal assertion? All this world has to boast of—all mighty truths, all great inventions—have originally had to *struggle* against this "*practical*" bugbear, which ignorance sets up to frighten its fellows from those doctrines which aim at the amelioration of mankind. Recently it delayed the realization of railways. It has long opposed all social improvement; and as this is written it is being advanced as a barrier to Practical Christianity itself! Those who can regard the instruction of the Creator as too fine for the creature of his creation, may readily condemn all human promptings!

To deprive this phrase of its abuse and destroy its mysterious signification, let the reader quietly ask himself what is really meant by a thing, a book, or a doctrine being "*practical.*" If the word bears any construction, it obviously must imply that which can be used, or a lesson which is capable of being illustrated by performance. The test of "*practicability*," then, resides in the sincerity of those endeavors which attempt to embody certain instructions. Where no wish to exemplify exists, of course no teaching can be "*practical*." The proof, consequently, generally reposes with the person who advances the accusation, and the accuser is by this prejudice constituted judge of that he has already condemned.

What is there in the present volume or in the "Horse Doctor" which cannot possibly be enacted, supposing an actuating motive to influence the trial? Nothing can be practical if there be wanting the desire to embody particular directions; but to ascertain the value of a current phrase, he to whom it is addressed should ask for the special passage to which this condemnation pointedly alludes. If no specific warrant can be produced, a verdict merely founded upon generalities should never be accepted.

The author, when seeking to accomplish the evident purpose of the volume, deeply regrets those comments which a regard for correctness has compelled him to offer upon the present race of grooms. He can, however, with sincerity deny that the indulgence of dislike, or the gratification of malice, has induced him to travel beyond the limits of his subject. The men in this capacity occupy an unfortunate position. They and their interests range in the foremost rank of existing wrong. It is impossible to amend the regulations of any modern stable without removing some of this calling, or overthrowing some of the abuses, with a perpetuation of which the stable servant and his perquisites are directly involved. An earnest desire for improvement, therefore, compelled the review of that class who, if unassailed, were interested to be the most strenuous advocates of the bad usages which it was desired should be overthrown.

In conclusion, the getting up of the work bespeaks the care bestowed upon the volume by the publishers, to whom the author offers his most fervent acknowledgments. Nor can the writer bid adieu to his patrons without directing attention to the talent exhibited by the numerous artists and engravers whose labors adorn the pages of the present publication.

NORBURY,
LANSDOWNE ROAD, TORQUAY

CONTENTS.

CHAPTER I.

PAGE

The body of the horse anatomically considered 17

CHAPTER II.

Physic—The mode of administering it, and minor operations . . . 58

CHAPTER III.

Shoeing—Its origin, its uses, and its varieties 95

CHAPTER IV.

The Teeth—Their natural growth, and the abuses to which they are liable. 133

CHAPTER V.

Food—The fittest time for feeding, and the kind of food which the horse naturally consumes 168

CHAPTER VI.

The evils which are occasioned by modern stables 200

CHAPTER VII.

The faults inseparable from most present erections which are used as stables. 233

CHAPTER VIII.

The so-called "incapacitating vices," which are the results of injury or of disease 263

CHAPTER IX.

Stables as they should be 297

CHAPTER X.

Grooms—Their prejudices, their injuries, and their duties . . 327

CHAPTER XI.

Horse Dealers—Who they are, their mode of dealing, their profits, their morality, and their secrets 357

CHAPTER XII.

Points—Their relative importance, and where to look for their development. 379

CHAPTER XIII.

Breeding—Its inconsistencies and its disappointments 427

CHAPTER XIV.

Breaking and Training—Their errors and their results . . 449

CHAPTER XV.

Carriages—Their cost, their make, their excellences, and their management. 477

CHAPTER XVI.

Saddlery, Harness, and Stable Sundries—Of what these consist; their application and their preservation 494

INDEX 527

THE

ILLUSTRATED HORSE MANAGEMENT.

CHAPTER I.

THE BODY OF THE HORSE ANATOMICALLY CONSIDERED.

WERE the equine race extinct, nevertheless an anatomist, by studying its bones, might affirm its instincts and assert its uses. Every part declares it to be a creature of speed; while its large cranium and beauti-

STUDENTS DISSECTING AT THE ROYAL VETERINARY COLLEGE, LONDON.

fully-arranged teeth would announce it to have once been connected with civilization by its intelligence, by its uses, and its herbivorous habit. The provision made for the united strength and elasticity of the spine would indicate the care nature had bestowed upon the comfort of a rider; while the mode in which the members were joined to the body, with the reach of limb peculiar to the skeleton, would equally announce that grace and that ease which had characterized the lost animal's movements.

What lamentation would be poured forth over the absence of such a treasure! How would poignant regrets be awakened, as science demonstrated what once were the endowments of an extinct inhabitant of earth! Yet, at the present time, humanity possesses this priceless creature to lighten toil and heighten pleasure. But, how few of mankind have ever reflected upon the marvelous delicacy of the slave's construction! It is lashed unto exhaustion and worked into deformity. Because of the treatment it experiences at the hands of the master, whom it serves, it generally ceases to exist before its body is matured; but short as its life may be, existence is to it only one continued misery!

Even mortal instruments, things of the world's manufacture, are limited in their applications, and capable of being deranged. A spring carriage is, obviously, not a suitable conveyance for a load of paving stones. He would be esteemed mad, who should appropriate such a vehicle to so gross a purpose. The horse's body is more delicately arranged and more nicely balanced than the perfection of human skill can hope to imitate; nevertheless, people expose themselves to no rebuke when they wrench, cripple, or destroy the beauty which is intrusted to their authority.

Yet, the thing constructed by human hands, if injured, can be repaired, and may be thus rendered again equal to its uses. A living animal, however, being damaged, is not, on this earth, to be restored tc its integrity. That has been, and is lost! Mortal science may relieve the wound, but the scar remains, to conjure up thoughts of that deeper seated derangement, which is beyond the reach of this world's medicine. The body may partially recover and the life may be prolonged; but deformity, accompanied by a proportionate loss of function, will testify to the folly that deteriorated the perfection which was given as a helpmate.

Those forms of agony, which a few years ago were more common in England than such are even at the present time, evidently declared that the horse was altogether unequal to increasing wants and growing desires of mankind. Neither the fleetness of the courser nor the strength of the heavier breed embodied the requirements of the age. Something faster and more powerful had become a public necessity; therefore railroads were permitted.

Such persons as can talk of railroads being destined to destroy the breed of horses, must suffer under a confusion of ideas. The breed of horses may be endangered, as this is being written; but the source of peril lies very far removed from the lines of tramway. The objects, capable of being fulfilled by breathing flesh and by steaming iron, are altogether separate and distinct. No living body can aspire to contend, in strength or in speed, with the results of mechanical contrivance. Neither can the forge or the furnace ever hope to produce any combination of springs and wheels which can compare with the ease of motion, the docility of temper, or the intelligence of spirit that should recommend the quadruped to the kindness of its earthly proprietor.

The horse is the associate of man. It is true, the poor animal can be goaded to excessive labor; but the creature becomes degraded when it toils beyond the sphere of mortal sympathy. No living animal should be subjected to the exactions of avarice. Life was not made to be thus debased. What, however, the horse, when properly treated, is capable of performing, remains to be hereafter demonstrated. How much it can enact, and how greatly it can benefit, when justly treated, the present customs refuse the willing drudge a chance of proving. No steed is now permitted to grow till its thews and muscles are matured. Before the season of its utility can come round, the colt is seized upon by the impatience of gain, and the baby limbs are distorted by that early affliction which forbids the natural powers to be developed.

We can, however, even by the inspection of the body, discover that it is admirably adapted for continuous and prolonged exertion. The maintenance of animal motion chiefly depends on the provision made for aerating the blood. In proportion as the vital current can be revivified or oxygenated is health promoted by those efforts, which in most bodies would, assuredly, induce congestion and death. Age becomes very important when the subject is thus considered. Respiration is in youth quicker than during adultism, because there is so much more oxygen needed when the frame is in a growing state. By working the horse before maturity is attained, the animal is obliged to labor when the ordinary velocity of the respiration permits of the less marginal speed for the breathing apparatus to exert upon extraordinary occasions. Nevertheless, that the reader may judge correctly of the care nature had bestowed upon the formation of a creature destined for subserviency to man, the following engraving is appended.

The accompanying illustration exhibits the lungs as of large proportional dimensions; while the stomach will be recognized as of more than an equally diminished capacity. Everybody must have experienced how greatly respiration is impeded by a loaded digestion; and the Common Benefactor, when creating an animal destined to display speed, seems to have anticipated the probability of such a contingency. The intestines, however, are comparatively of large extent. Into these receptacles the horse's food passes, after having perfected the first process of digestion, and there it is subsequently mixed with the fluid secretion of the bowels, whereby the nutritive matter is separated and rendered fit for absorption.

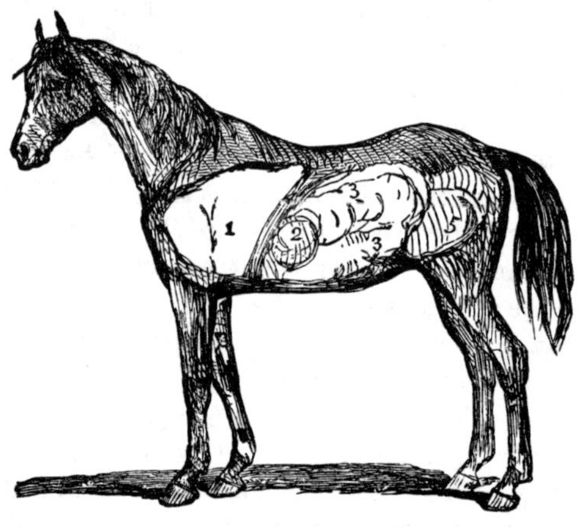

THE FIGURE OF A HORSE, PORTRAYING THE COMPARATIVE IMPORTANCE AND THE RELATIVE SITUATIONS OF SOME INTERNAL ORGANS.

1. The lungs. 2. The stomach. 3. The colon. 4. The diaphragm. 5. The situation of the bladder.

The smallness of the horse's stomach is in itself sufficient evidence that the quadruped was designed to be a frequent feeder. It was not intended to endure prolonged abstinence; for almost in every region which the animal may canter over, its legitimate food abounds. Man, however, frequently starves the creature, that a loaded stomach may not interfere with the activity of the respiration; he, in his ignorance and in his presumption, not being willing to trust to such provision as the *All-wise* had made, anticipatory of this accident. At other times, the quadruped is suffered to over-gorge, its keeper paying no regard to its requirements. After an excessive fast, a quantity of cut food is placed in the manger, and the ravenous horse eats, and eats, till its small stomach, being unequal to the reception of much bolted provender, cracks its walls from excessive repletion. Such a circumstance does not demonstrate that nature was wrong, or that the equine races were formed unequal to their purposes; but it satisfactorily establishes that man cannot, with impunity, cross the designs or run counter to the institutions of Omnipotence.

The horse was created to live off the grass of the field. This habit necessitated that much ground should be traveled before the appetite of so large a body could be appeased; and the distance was the greater as the animal was sent upon the earth a nice feeder—biting oft the juicy tops of the herbage, not tearing up roots and all, like the less scrupulous bovine tribe. The time was also lengthened, by the equine race not being gifted with a power to ruminate. The ox, having filled the mouth, bestows little care upon the comminution of the food; but the jaw being moved twice or thrice, thereby crushing the herbage, so as to form it into a pellet, the mouthful is forwarded at once to the rumen. This receptacle is large, and is somewhat hastily filled. Then the ox retires to a quiet spot and there enjoys its meal; the grass being regurgitated and fully masticated, during which time the animal is said to be "chewing the cud." The horse has no such power. The food it gathers must be prepared by mastication and insalivation before it enters the stomach; consequently, because of the niceness of its appetite, and the absolute necessity for each mouthful being separately comminuted, the horse, in a free state, has to journey far and to feed long before it can lie down and rest.

The equine race were meant to collect their sustenance from the surface of the earth; and, doubtless, the tribe are most at ease when feeding with the head lowered to the necessary position. A dog naturally lowers the mouth when it laps a fluid; but, if this creature be tempted to drink from a saucer held on a level with the ordinary elevation of the head, repeated coughing will interrupt the draught and testify to the inconvenience experienced by the animal. So, in the instance of the horse, we may infer the meal is most relished when the head sinks to its gratification; and, to justify such an inference, anatomy discloses a special provision made to that end. Such a proof is, to the author's mind, of much more weight than any assertion to the contrary of the united British public, as emphasized by the fixed altitude of all the mangers throughout the three kingdoms.

A serious suggestion here forces itself upon the mind of the writer; and it is one the importance of which should recommend it to the consideration of the public. Laryngeal affections are among the most frequent annoyances of every stable, and stand foremost among the most vexatious of the many evils which the veterinary surgeon is expected to eradicate.

However, it is proved that if sustenance be swallowed with the head at a certain elevation, it must interfere with the most irritable organ entering into the composition of the entire body. Then, horse proprietors would do well to reflect upon the fact, and to say, how far constantly-repeated provocation may aggravate or induce the fearful laryngeal maladies to which domesticated horses are peculiarly liable.

The valves existing in the jugular veins are formed by duplicatures of its internal lining membrane; and they are so arranged as to prevent the natural tendency to regurgitate when the fluid within the vessel moves against gravity. When the head is erect, and the venous current, flowing toward the heart, is of course downward or is favored by gravity, then the valves do not act; but the passage of the blood forces the duplicatures of membrane to remain close against the sides of the tube.

The jugulars conduct the dark-colored blood from the brain; and as that important organ cannot endure the smallest pressure, some special provision was imperative to carry away the fluid, and also to anticipate the possibility of its return to oppress the sensorium. When the horse is grazing, the head is lower than the heart, and it naturally occupies that position for the greater portion of the twenty-four hours. During all that time the venous current must mount against the influence of gravitation; and to aid the reader in properly understanding the means by which this is effected, his attention is invited to the following diagrams.

A SKETCH, DISPLAYING THE ACTION OF THE JUGULAR VALVES WHEN THE HEAD IS LOWERED TO FEED OFF THE GROUND.

The elevated crest, therefore, presents a clear channel to the vital current. For that reason, the violent action or the most rapid pace of the animal never produces congestion of its brain. The racer may sink from exhaustion, but does not perish from apoplexy. The head, when depressed, however, shows the same canal divided by numerous intersecting marks. Such lines are intended to represent the venous valves, which assist the blood in its upward journey, and render impossible the slightest pressure upon the sensorium. The first thing which strikes the reader, upon beholding the arrangement depicted above, is the vast number of valves; and this causes him to inquire, where was the necessity for such repeated checks. If the conservation of the brain was the only end to be attained, might not that object have been assured by a single set of valves? Such may seem a feasible objection; but to prevent the return current was, as nature appears to have conceived, best done by repeated assistance of the onward flow; consequently, these numerous valves anticipate the possibility of regurgitation in any degree, and provide repeated checks to pressure from the supported column of heavy venous blood.

There remains, however, another provision to be explained. The return current has hitherto been spoken of, as though the upward flow of fluid was its natural tendency. Still, every person must have perceived the necessity, when liquid was to be propelled in that direction, of something resembling a forcing pump. Such an apparatus nature has provided. The head of a healthy animal is depressed only when eating or when drinking. During the performance of either function, muscles are contracting which compress the soft coats of the veins, and thus help to drive the circulation against gravity.

Thus, during feeding, the head is maintained in a depressed attitude for hours together; and, throughout that space, a most powerful agent is in operation. The lower jaw, while the quadruped chances to be thus engaged, is in constant motion, being opened and closed either in biting or in chewing. When the jaw sinks, the muscles of mastication are relaxed, and the venous blood rushes from the cranium into the sinuses. But when the bone is raised by those strong motor agents which render the bite of a horse so fearful an infliction, the current from the brain is for a moment checked, and the contents of the maxillary sinuses are energetically propelled up the jugulars. During the first half of the action, the valves are in operation, having all the strength necessary for the perfect performance of their allotted function; but, during the latter part, they are forced against the sides of the vessels by the contractive masticatory influence, and cease to act in any way upon the internal current of the blood.

Notwithstanding the strong conviction emphatically asserted by the fixed position of the nation's mangers, the author must be obstinate enough to disregard human authority, when he has an opportunity of studying the living book, written by the unerring hand of nature. Valves, though generally present in veins, are never discovered where the position of the vessel or other reason would render such provisions unnecessary. The Great Creator often makes one thing to serve more than one use; but never creates when *His* work can answer no profitable purpose.

The use of veins is simply that of conduits, to convey the refuse blood back to the heart, whence it is forced into the lungs, and there revivified or rendered equal to its many forms of nutrition. This mighty change is very simply effected. When the thorax expands, air merely enters the lungs to anticipate the vacuum, which otherwise must be occasioned by the enlargement of the chest. The air consists chiefly of two substances in a gaseous state—of oxygen and of nitrogen. The venous blood, being very near to the inhaled air within the lungs, extracts the oxygen from it, and in exchange sends forth a quantity of carbonic acid, which is voided with the expired breath.

This change will take place when blood is extracted from the body. If the contents of some vein are exposed to the atmosphere, they will in time change from a deep modena to a bright scarlet hue. There is,

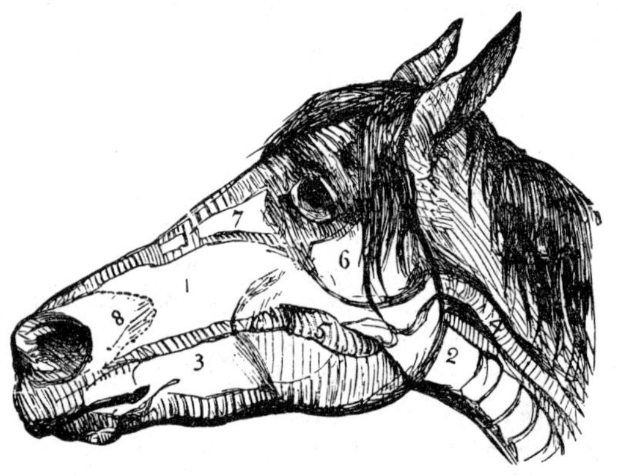

A DIAGRAM, EXPLANATORY OF THE SPECIAL PROVISIONS DISCOVERABLE IN THE HEAD OF A HORSE.

1. The nostril leading direct to—2. The larynx, situated at the commencement of the windpipe. 3. The tongue. 4. The œsophagus or gullet. 5. The soft palate, which lies upon the tongue and affords a resting-place whereon reposes the epiglottis, or the guardian cartilage to the entrance of the larynx (2). 6. The guttural pouches, or large membranous and open sacs, containing nothing but atmospheric air. 7. Nasal or frontal sinuses.

however, this difference which marks the two processes. The alteration, when quickened by vitality, is instantaneous; but the change, when it ensues under human inspection, is slowly, and, as it were, laboriously accomplished. The size of the equine nostrils informs us of the ample draughts of air which the animal is fitted to appropriate; it likewise testifies to the high state of that vitality which could necessitate such a provision. Creatures with small nostrils, for instance ox and dog, are endowed with a limited capacity as respects nasal respiration. Yet, as a recompense, such creatures are formed to inhale through the mouth. The horse, however, requires no such faculty, its nostrils are ample; and, under ordinary circumstances, the mouth is closed by a thick, fleshy screen, which hangs pendulous from the most backward portion of the bony palate.

In the previous diagram, figure 1 indicates the space allotted to the nasal chamber, near the external opening to which will be observed the numeral 8. The dotted lines surrounding the last figure represent the dimensions of a blind pouch, or cul-de-sac, which separates the external from the internal wall of the true nostril. The existence of such a provision has long been a puzzle to physiologists; but, would these gentlemen have given *nature* full credit for that care with which the *Common Parent* studies to preserve the beauty of the higher order of *His* children, and have considered that the horse's necessity for different quantities of air varies with different times and during different occupations, they might have sooner comprehended the utility of the development.

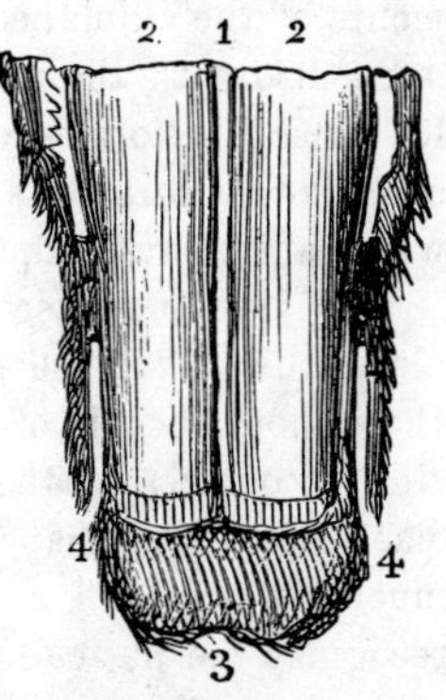

DIAGRAM OF THE FALSE NOSTRILS

1. The septum nasi. 2. The nasal chambers. 3. The upper lip. 4. The false nostrils.

Where the false nostril is placed is the only portion of the nasal chamber which is not inclosed by bone; consequently it is situated at the only place where the cavity admits of distention and of contraction. The animal, in a passive state, breathes very leisurely; at such times the nostrils would sink inward, or be deformed by the unavoidable collapse of the wall, were not the false nostril present to permit its diminution without materially affecting the external form. But subsequent to severe exertion, everybody must have remarked the nostril spasmodically strain, as though each effort would crack the boundaries of the opening. At such times the false nostril offers no stubborn opposition to the violence of respiration, while it serves to soften down the aspect, which, if laid bare, might show too fearfully.

A varied capacity for admitting air also presupposes a varied capacity to alter the dimensions of the passages through which the atmosphere travels to the lungs. If the reader will again refer to the facial diagram, he will perceive a free space, in the center of which is placed the figure 6. These spaces (one on either side of the face) represent what are termed the guttural pouches, they being merely bladders containing air, and communicating separately with each nasal chamber. A bladder with an external opening is of course most readily compressible. That no doubt may be entertained of the use for which these vacant spaces were established, they are placed immediately above the course of the atmosphere to the lungs, and would contract or dilate according to its volume.

Such a condition of parts imagines the windpipe also able to alter its dimensions, so that it may be in accord with other structures; and anatomy discloses facts which amply support such a supposition. The larynx or opening to the windpipe is composed of several pieces of cartilage and of numerous muscles. The presence of the first plastic and highly elastic structure is a proof that the larynx is of no fixed shape, while the division of the organ into distinct parts, together with the internal and external presence of many muscles of motion, is absolute confirmation that the larynx was created not only to assume various forms, but also to exhibit different capacities, according to the requirements of the animal economy.

So also with the windpipe itself, and the tubes which proceed from it; these are formed of distinct rings, or of separate pieces of elastic cartilage so curved as to form rings, but having free overlapping ends, which are operated upon by muscular fiber.

The diagram inserted below accurately represents such a ring; it also shows that the springy cartilage is not made of one thickness throughout, but is of that form which the mechanic of the present time recognizes as that best adapted for the preservation of continued elasticity. The shape and the free ends convinces that such a ring must always have a tendency to expand, and by this perception we recognize the purpose of the muscle, which draws the extremities over each other; thus two opposing forces regulate the capacity of the circle.

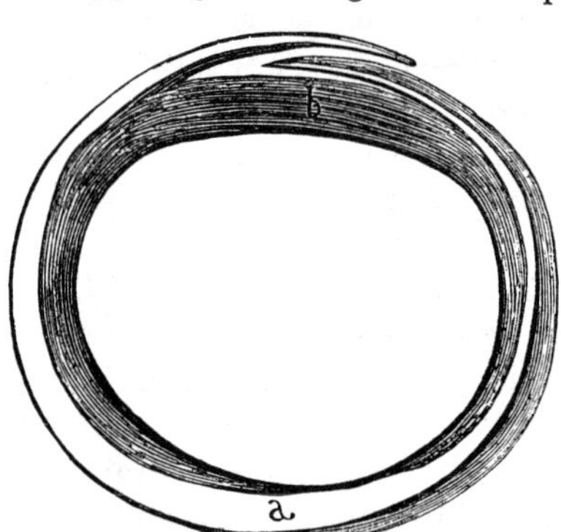

ONE OF THE CARTILAGINOUS RINGS, NUMBERS OF WHICH JOINED TOGETHER FORM THE TRACHEA OR THE WINDPIPE OF THE HORSE.

a One of the cartilages from the trachea of a horse, having free and overlapping extremities.
b The muscular fiber situated within the ring, which regulates the diameter of the circle.

The presence of muscular fiber is always absolute proof of motion. Where muscle exists and morbid circumstances render motion an impossibility, the function being destroyed, the motor organ becomes pallid, or suffers atrophy. The existence, therefore, of such a structure in a healthy condition is always sufficient proof that the function of expansion and of contraction was present during life; thus we reach an absolute certainty that the air-passages of the horse possess a property of adapting themselves to the necessities of the animal.

Then, looking at these structures, we find them not only free, but so composed as to be always open, excepting when the momentary swallowing of the food causes the larynx to close. To breathe is the primary necessity of life. Health cannot be maintained unless the blood is sufficiently oxygenated; this fact makes us doubt the national wisdom, which persists in thrusting the quadruped into stables, rendered close and hot by the products of impurity. Oxygen is always deficient where impurity prevails; and, having seen the necessity of its presence, because it is the primary requirement of existence, and not because of the warmth or oppression which its absence generates, does the author presume to oppose his opinion to the decision apparently approved by the entire British public.

Seeing these provisions made *by nature* to preserve the beauty of her most graceful quadruped, and remarking how profusely, in various forms, loveliness is distributed throughout this earth, we cannot slightingly esteem the attribute which *Perfect Knowledge* has impressed, as an order of merit, upon its creations. Beauty is here spoken of as distinct from gaudiness. The term is employed not to represent the luster of the beetle or the vividness of the tropical bird, but to portray that harmony of parts and deep-seated perfection which is present only in the more elaborate works of the *Creator*, and which renders the horse, even when deprived of its skin, a picture deserving mortal adoration. Viewing the world and its inhabitants, we must confess that nothing was formed without its uses; on such a basis, we may safely assert that the horse was not made the most beautiful of beasts without intention. This quality appeals in a most mysterious and powerful manner to the human sympathies. It should influence the mind even more than it gratifies the eye, and though avarice may blind humanity to its claims, yet even the most hardened cannot witness the destruction of perfection without a poignant pang of regret.

In the head of the animal we discern evidences of the care bestowed to preserve a harmony of form. Above the nasal chambers are certain hollow spaces, indicated by the figure 7. These empty chambers may serve to impart depth to the voice, but as the horse is generally a silent creature, such, obviously, must be only a secondary purpose. To preserve the undulation of the outline was assuredly the primary intent, though at the same time the vacancies aid the reverberation of sound, and with other structures also lighten that part of the body in which they are situated.

The passage of the air to the lungs, and the admirable provisions to admit its ingress and its egress, without destroying the mild and characteristic aspect of the quadruped, having been described, it now becomes the author's duty to dwell upon the extraordinary conditions which conserve the passages of the food. Referring again to the diagram here

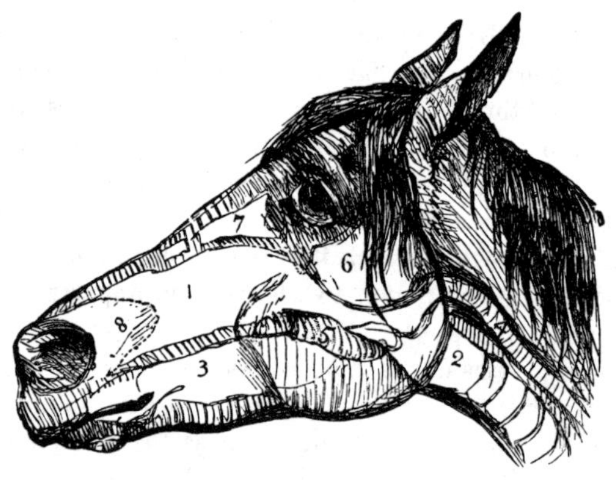

A DIAGRAM, EXPLANATORY OF THE SPECIAL PROVISIONS DISCOVERABLE IN THE HEAD OF A HORSE.

1. The nostril leading direct to—2. The larynx, situated at the commencement of the windpipe. 3. The tongue. 4. The œsophagus or gullet. 5. The soft palate, which lies upon the tongue and affords a resting-place, whereon reposes the epiglottis, or the guardian cartilage to the entrance of the larynx (2). 6. The guttural pouches, or large membranous and open sacs, containing nothing but atmospheric air. 7. Nasal or frontal sinuses.

reproduced, we see the mouth, occupied by the tongue, (figure 3,) on the base of which organ reposes a dark body, particularized by the figure 5. This last is the soft palate, which drops pendulous from the osseous roof of the masticatory orifice. Upon the soft palate lies the most forward of the laryngeal cartilages, which is anatomically spoken of as the epiglottis; while the most backward of the laryngeal cartilages, which are called the aretenoids, repose beneath the roof of the pharynx. This pharynx is the enlarged and muscular commencement of the gullet, the situation and direction of which channel is notified by the number 4.

We thus perceive in its course the food is apparently thrice forbidden to enter the gullet of the horse. In the first place, there is the soft palate, retained firmly in its position by pressure of the epiglottis. The second obstacle we recognize in the opening of the larynx; the third impediment appears in the aretenoids, that seem to bar all entrance to the tube which leads to the stomach. Moreover, the gullet itself being a muscular organ, in the passive state of semi-contraction is closed; thus appearing to oppose a further hinderance to the admission of sustenance into its proper receptacle. However, upon inquiry, the reader will discover these provisions, which appear at first glance to be ranged against the entrance of nutriment, are in reality only so many elaborate protections, all tending to the comfort and well-being of the animal.

The soft palate so effectually closes the posterior of the mouth as to prevent that cavity from being employed to modulate the voice, though such a peculiarity does not distinguish all the equine tribe. Everybody must have remarked the bray distend the jaws of an ass, whereas the neigh flutters only the nostril of the horse, the different channels through which the sound has to emerge fully accounting for the marked contrast which is conspicuous in the voices of the animals. Moreover, the horse does occasionally vomit; but, save when the organization is disturbed by the agonies of death, the voided matter is generally ejected through the nostrils.

However, the reader will perhaps best understand how the apparently closed cavity is rendered subservient to its uses by the process of deglutition being described. A portion of food is bitten off by the incisors; the substance is, by the action of the tongue, next passed to the molars, or is placed between the grinding teeth. There it is thoroughly comminuted. While this is being performed, the saliva is secreted and mingled with the mass, so as to render it quite soft or pultaceous. In this state it is formed into a pellet, and is then pressed by the tongue against the palate or roof of the mouth. The morsel, being now round and soft, is afterward, by a more energetic contraction of the tongue, driven against the pendulous palate, which seemingly closes the posterior of the orifice.

The last organ lies in that direction which enables it to offer a formidable resistance, especially when supported by the base of the tongue, to any substance proceeding *from* the stomach. In the contrary direction it is only held down by the epiglottis; that comparatively feeble body is forced to yield before the greater contractile power of the lingual organ. The epiglottis flies forward, covering the opening to the larynx, in which position the posterior cartilages or the aretenoids also fold over the more forward protector. A secure floor is thus formed, preventing anything from falling into the windpipe, where intrusion of the smallest substance would provoke the most alarming spasm; while a roof to the passage is also made by the raised, soft palate, whereby the nasal chambers are protected from the encroachment of undigested matters.

A safe way being thus provided, the pellet is shot into the pharynx, which, independently of the will, immediately contracts upon any substance coming within its reach, and drives the morsel into the œsophagus or gullet. The tube, surprised by the presence of the morsel, is obliged to separate for its reception; but it immediately closes on the stranger, thereby driving it lower down, when, the contractility of the fiber being again aroused, it is once more driven onward, and this action is continued until the food is safely lodged within the walls of the stomach.

Few persons can comprehend the above explanation without being forcibly impressed by the beauty and the nicety of the whole arrangement. The elevation of the soft palate closes the nostrils, and at the same time provides a floor for the gaping passage to the lungs. The motion of the soft palate nudges the epiglottis, which lies upon it and causes that cartilage to bend over the opening to the larynx. The bowing down of the epiglottis induces the aretenoids also to stoop, thus forming a safe floor to the necessitated passage. Across the chasm, now rendered secure, the food is shot into the pharynx and conveyed to the stomach, the whole process being accomplished in an instant, for the act of swallowing provokes no sensible impediment to the continuance of respiration.

These things, however instructive or amusing they may be when related, nevertheless are too little thought of; nor is the horse itself sufficiently considered. Were the lessons, which its body should teach mankind, properly understood, those abuses, that are at present limited to no class, would instantaneously cease to be practiced. Most people of this country, however, treat the horse as though it were an original inhabitant of the English climate. Rich and poor in this respect are equally faulty, save that those are most to blame who, possessing wealth, can command the leisure requisite for inquiry, and, being blessed with ability to gratify their inclinations, have no excuse for lack of sympathy in the pressure of necessity. The great error, however, consists in a national carelessness about the matter. The slave is accepted as a property; its life is wasted; its body is abused; man sleeps happy in the belief that animals were created for his use. To render them subservient to his pleasure is the amount of all that he conceives to be his duty. The winter's straw yard and the autumn's run are both follies—sadly common, but nevertheless deserving the condemnation of all good or thoughtful men.

The animal carries about its person the signs which testify it once roamed within a warmer climate than our northern region. The certificate of its origin is legibly written in the eye of the quadruped. This organ mutely attests, that the temperate zone was not the birthplace of its progenitors. It has long been a captive in Britain; but the proof of its proper dwelling-place no time can obliterate. The eye of the horse, like that of the camel, displays a special provision, fitting the creature to endure the strongest glare of a tropical sun, even when reflected from a level waste of shining sand; or, in other words, the first parents of the tribe must have careered across some burning desert.

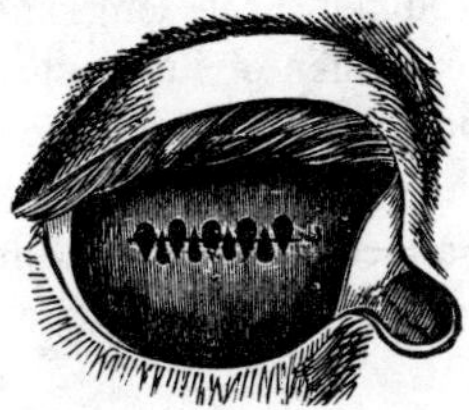
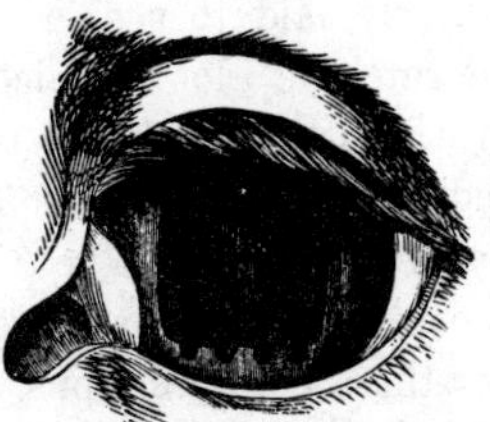

THE PUPIL OF THE HORSE'S EYE IN THE OPPOSITE STATES OF CONTRACTION AND DILATATION, SHOWING THE SITUATION AND THE USE OF THE CORPORA NIGRA.

The corpora nigra, in the eye of the camel, are black bodies, pendent from the margin of the iris. The purpose of so special a provision is not apparent, when darkness occasions the opening to dilate; but when the glare is powerful—so powerful as to induce blindness even in the natives of those lands where a concentrated light is possible—then the intent of its Beneficent Creator becomes apparent.

The pupil of the horse's eye is never circular, being, when much dilated, rather oblong in figure; but, when exposed to the direct rays of the summer's sun, the opening energetically contracts. Then the pupil is best represented by a mere line; for the edges of the iris at such a season seemingly touch each other. In this condition, the uses of the corpora nigra can hardly be mistaken: the little black bodies appear to fit into one another, forming apparently an impenetrable network opposed to the entrance of too strong a glare.

Let the author and the reader, however, temperately consider this matter. The pupil in the eye of the horse is not more distant than two inches from the origin of the optic nerve. When the division to be seen through is so close, and the object to be viewed is exhibited under the strongest natural light, the merest crevice will be equal to all the purposes of perfect vision. The full glare of the sun alone occasioning the horse's pupil to contract, that which causes the opening to almost shut also provides the excess of light, which alone could render useful that narrow division through which objects must be recognized; while the dark bodies, being stationed before the point of sight, answer the purpose of the smoke which lads load upon glass when they are ambitious of gazing at the sun.

The reader must have remarked the pupillary line through which the domestic cat exercises perfect vision during the bright noon of a mid-summer day. The eye of the feline race is, however, possessed of no other protection. The contraction may be the effect of weakness of sight; at all events, the author thinks he may conclude the far-famed eye of the cat to be inferior to that of a horse. The domestic mouser is popularly said to see in the dark; the steed has been long known to penetrate the gloom which sets the strained vision of its master at defiance; but it remains to be granted that both horse and cat are equally fitted to roam by night. The habits of the herbivorous creature would, however, assert it to be possessed of such a faculty; and the anatomist discovers in the visual organ of the animal a provision specially adapting it for these peregrinations.

Upon the upper and forward surface of the inner, dark chamber, and so placed as to catch, to concentrate, and to reflect every stray ray of light upon the optic nerve, the tapidum lucidum is discovered within the globe of the horse's eye. This structure is, after death, very bright or of metallic luster, and, because of its concave form, is admirably adapted to its particular function. That no doubt may remain as to the design of such a provision, the tapidum lucidum is found only within the eyes of those quadrupeds created to roam by night. It is altogether absent in such animals as were destined to move about during daylight.

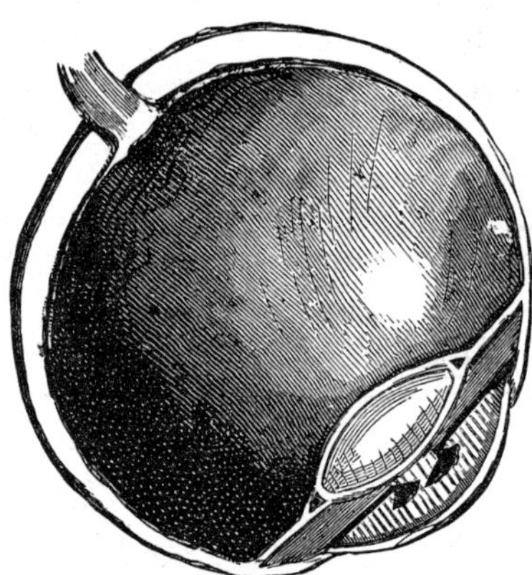

DIAGRAM, EXPOSING THE INTERIOR OF THE HORSE'S EYE, AND DISPLAYING THE SITUATION OF THE TAPIDUM LUCIDUM, OR GLOSSY SURFACE DEVELOPED WITHIN THE ORGAN.

The tapidum lucidum, therefore, viewed in conjunction with the corpora nigra, becomes an inferential proof that the horse originally inhabited some land in which the coolness of the night offered the greatest temptation for pleasant pasturage. The *Mighty Benefactor*, consequently, formed *His* creature to enjoy the bounties among which it was permitted to roam. We know the cat was imported from the tropics; and, seeing that the eyes of both animals, in one marked particular, resemble each other, we may conjecture the horse originally inhabited a warmer climate; while the likeness between the equine race and "the ship of the desert" demonstrates that that locality was the hottest portion of the earth.

The eye of the horse is also provided with a power which could seldom be needed in these Northern climes, where the fleetness of the equine tribe might readily set at defiance the comparative feebleness of all the predatory beasts of prey. Besides, the wooded state of this country must have rendered the presence of telescopic vision unnecessary. Upon the far-stretching level of the desert, however, where larger and more ferocious animals prowl by night, the possession of such a faculty would be a needed protection. Accordingly, we find the interior of the globe to consist chiefly of water, the outward covering being formed of a tough substance, which is easily compressible; while all the hidden portion of the exterior is enveloped by muscular fiber.

Situated directly upon the forward portion of the ball are the two oblique muscles. These are inserted at opposite places, and each pulls in a contrary direction to the other. The two, simultaneously acting, could not move the organ, but would, obviously, tend to fix it or to render the globe stationary. The outer substance of the horse's eyes is composed of a thick and pliable covering, purely tendinous in character. The interior consists of fluid perfectly pure and transparent. At the back of all is placed the optic nerve; while the exterior is enveloped by several thick and straight muscles.

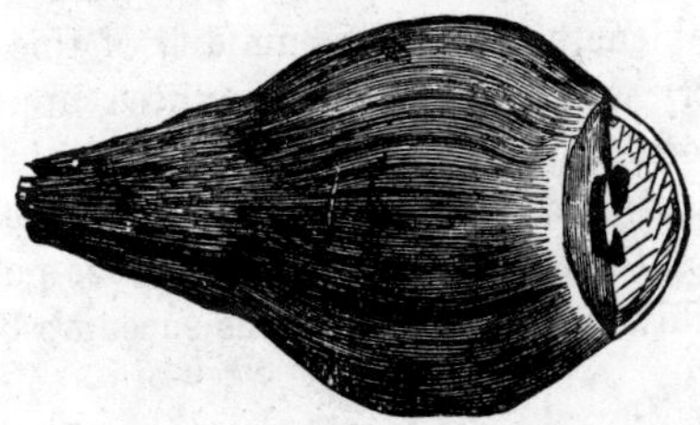

DIAGRAM, DISPLAYING THE COATING OF MUSCULAR FIBER WHICH COVERS THE SOFT GLOBE OF THE HORSE'S EYE.

The motor agents are endowed with an ability to contract or to shorten in their reach. When parts of this nature operate upon a plastic substance, which is filled only with a fluid, they must of necessity tend to alter the shape of that body on which they repose. The oblique muscles act to prevent rotation; the pressure, therefore, can only compress, elongate, and force backward the ball of the eye. By such a capacity that telescopic property is produced which man feebly imitates by a complex and costly machine.

3

Anatomy also discovers another important function proper to the eye of the horse, which equally indicates a sandy plain to have been the original habitat of the tribe.

The soft sand of the Southern region would form a soil over which the equine foot could safely travel. The horn, in an unprotected state, was created to journey over so yielding and so dry a surface. Harder ground is poorly suited to the tread of the animal, a fact well established by the brittle hoof being among the recognized diseases of this country; while a wet soil is by no means advantageous, which circumstance is amply illustrated by the weak horn characteristic of those animals reared on the fens of Lincolnshire. The level of the desert presented that combination of qualities which could render the exhibition of its speed a delight to the unbroken quadruped; while the warmth of the climate would afford the medium in which a lustrous coat testifies to the health of a beautiful body.

In opposition to the above inference is the recorded fact that, when English horses were transported as cavalry into Egypt, the dryness of the climate frequently caused the hoofs so to crack as to render the animals totally useless. This circumstance, when first learned, appears to weigh heavily against the conclusion toward which the author's arguments were tending. In reality, however, it establishes nothing; it fades before rational investigation. A life, after having left its native country, does not necessarily thrive when it revisits the land of its origin. Englishmen, who have spent their youth in India, generally return to the variableness and to the humidity of this climate, and complain of the country which, when it was quitted, appeared to be cursed with no evil properties. Negroes captured by British cruisers, and set free on the far-famed colony of emancipation, are ascertained to perish the more rapidly on their return to Africa. These poor people are said to sink more speedily than even Europeans succumb before the clime of flame.

The speed of the horse would enable the quadruped to travel with comparative ease between those remote spots of verdure which lie scattered throughout the desert. The distance which divides these luxuriant localities could present no insurmountable obstacle to the unburdened steed, since the domesticated animal has carried its rider more than one hundred miles. The horse can endure long fasts, and even sustain severe thirst—the colon being a portion of the bowel generally devoted to the store of liquid nutriment; but the distance must have been accomplished in a cloud of sand sufficiently dense to blind the creature which traveled in the center of a moving herd.

The eye of the horse, however, is by nature provided with a protection against so terrible an affliction, which would expose any wild animal to a fearful death. The outer membrane of the eye is almost limited to covering the more forward or transparent surface, being thence reflected upon the interior of the eyelids. This membrane, when in a single layer, is incapable of communicating to the sensorium more than a feeling of uneasiness. When single, it may be touched, burnt, and cut, without producing actual pain; but the unpleasant sensation provokes a desire to wink, and the instant the lid descends upon the globe, or from the moment when two surfaces of the membrane are in apposition, agony ensues.

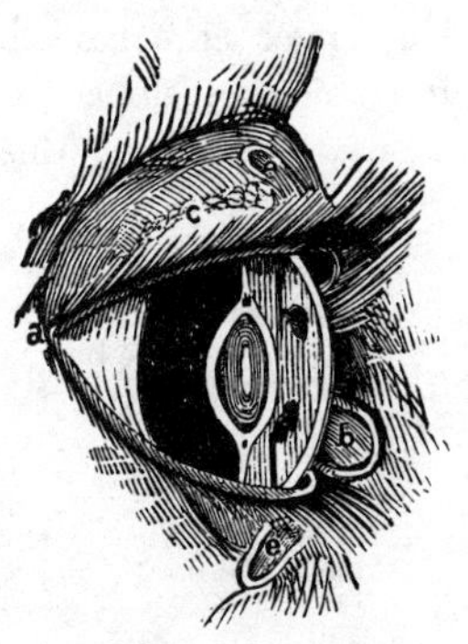

DIAGRAM, EXPLANATORY OF THE SITUATION OF THE LACHRYMAL GLAND, OR THE SOURCE OF TEARS, AND OF OTHER PARTS PROPER TO THE HORSE'S EYE.

a. The outer angle. *b*. The puncta lachrymalis, or round body, situated at the inner angle of the eye. *c*. The lachrymal gland, covered by the upper lid and placed near the outer angle of the eye. *e e*. The position, extent, and doubling of the conjunctiva, or of the investing mucous membrane, which envelops the outer portion of the globe and lines the lids.

The membrane now under consideration renders it an impossibility for any substance to get "into the eye;" the pain present, when such an assertion is commonly made, gives the strongest proof that the foreign body is retained between two surfaces of that delicate structure which is called conjunctiva. Dryness is, however, destructive of the feeling and of the transparency of this membrane. Nature, therefore, has created a special gland for assuring its perpetual moisture. This last body is situated immediately beneath the surface, under the upper lid and toward the outer corner of the eye. It is, on ordinary occasions, stimulated to send forth its secretion by the act of winking; and the outer corner being situated above the inner corner of the horse's eye, the moisture is, by the motion of the lid, instantaneously brushed over the circular globe.

The gland of the horse, however, has a distinct use not shared by any similar provision to be found in the eye of man. In the human being, grief or pain provokes the secretion; these are always accompanied by floods of tears. Some writers assert they have witnessed agony induce tears in the quadruped; but the author has seen fearful operations inflicted on the noble animal—he has heard huge groans testify to the sufferings endured; yet he has never beheld the eye overflow, or seen anything present which approximated to weeping.

Pain, when occasioned by some foreign body between the two layers of membrane, produces not weeping, but a positive overflow of liquid, the purpose of which will be best explained after the reader has been made acquainted with a particular organ situated at the inner angle of the eye.

The lower corner of the organ is characterized by a round body, which, being enveloped in a single layer of membrane, is strictly without sensation. Upon this body the grime of the human eye accumulates, and we shall shortly perceive that its presence in the horse is not without a purpose. Next to the foregoing development, and so placed as to accurately fit the globe, is a structure which anatomists name the cartilago nictitans, or the winking cartilage. The more forward portion of this cartilage possesses a fine edge, while its base presents a broad surface, which reposes upon the fat at the back of the orbit. Now, as fat is not compressible by ordinary force, whenever the muscles draw the globe backward, the adipose matter is driven forward; this last carries with it the cartilago nictitans, which is consequently projected suddenly over the surface of the globe. But when the muscles relax, the fat resumes its original place, and with it the cartilage also retires.

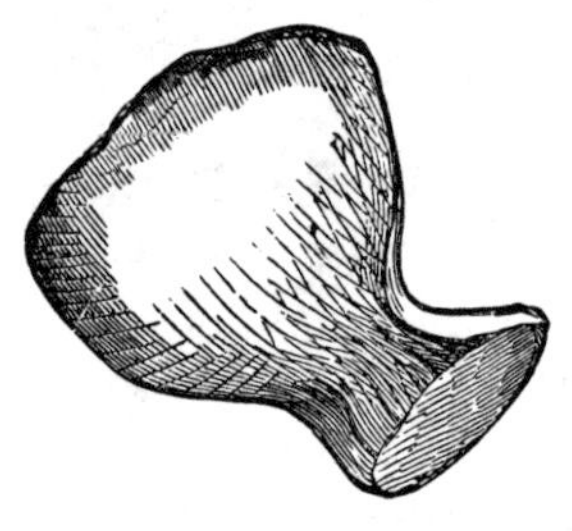

THE CARTILAGO NICTITANS, WHEN REMOVED FROM THE EYE OF A HORSE.

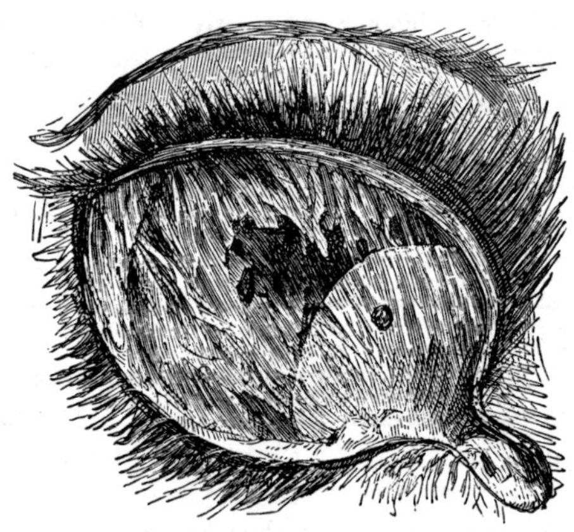

DIAGRAM, TO ILLUSTRATE THE ACTION OF THE CARTILAGO NICTITANS UPON THE HORSE'S EYE.

When any foreign body gets between the two layers of membrane, instant winking results; the gland, stimulated by the motion of the lid, sends forth a gush of liquid. It is not simply a tear or two, but a deluge of fluid is emitted; this flood, aided by the action of the lid, carries the foreign substance in the course of gravity, or from the external toward the internal corner of the globe. While this is taking place, the pain also excites the powerful muscles of the eye to spasmodic activity. With every spasm the fat is displaced, and the cartilage darts from the inner corner partially over the round surface of the eyeball. The process continues until the substance is partly brushed and partly washed to within the range of the fine anterior edge of the cartilage; when, by its withdrawal, the foreign particle is lodged upon the round insensitive body developed at the inner corner of the eye. Toward the last point the tears naturally tend, and any exciting substance, when there placed, is soon floated on to the hair of the cheek.

By joining these many proofs, we gain a moral certainty concerning the region whence the horse originated. The eye is seen to be gifted not only with a special provision against the glare of the desert, but it also possesses a peculiar development fitting the animal to enjoy the cool pasturage of the night. The eye is likewise endowed with a telescopic power suited to sweep the far-stretching horizon of the sandy waste. Moreover, the organ discloses a special apparatus evidently designed to overcome those accidents to which inhabitants of arid plains, when rapidly traveling long distances, and in large herds, were exposed.

The reader, perhaps, somewhat wearied by this lengthened description, may, however, be inclined to exclaim, "So that we possess the horse, what care we whence the beast was derived?" There can be no crumb of knowledge so small, but it is worth man's while to stoop and pick up the treasure. Its uses may not be apparent at the time of its discovery, but its application is certain before long to repay the person who prizes it. Taking the instance just narrated about the horse, an assured knowledge of the land whence the beautiful stranger came enables man the better to feel for its requirements; attention to the welfare of its life will be repaid by more lasting service to the master who claims it as a property. By disregarding this teaching, we subject the quadruped to suffering, which cramps the limbs, limits the utility, and shortens the existence, thus stinting the worth and curtailing the lease of the possession.

When writing the foregoing, the author is aware that gentlemen of known probity have reported the existence of herds of wild horses careering free and unbroken over the plains of Asia. Such was formerly said to be the case, and was also credited as an established fact with regard to Southern America. Subsequent inquiry, however, has shown that the wild animals of the pampas are no more than neglected flocks roaming, apparently without an owner, but which, in reality, are allowed thus to gain a cheap livelihood by a careless proprietor. These American herds are liable to the claim of some man, almost as wild as the animals themselves; so also the reported Asian quadrupeds turn out to be the recognized possession of some wandering Tartar.

However, to leave the consideration of particular parts, and to view the entire body anatomically, the vertebræ or spinal chain, as forming the base of the skeleton, becomes of primary importance. The back-bone of the horse consists of various pieces, so firmly held together by interlacing ligaments and muscles that students, when desirous of dividing the spine of a dead animal, often find it easier to saw the bones asunder than to separate them with the knife. The neck is composed of seven bones; the back is formed by eighteen vertebræ; the loins consist of six pieces, and the sacrum is made up of five distinct parts, although long before adultism all of these last are united by osseous junction.

SOME OF THE DEEP-SEATED MUSCLES IMMEDIATELY INVESTING THE SPINE OF THE HORSE.

1. The hair. 2. The skin. 3. The adipose, or fatty tissue directly under the skin. 4. The bursæ mucosæ, or synovial sacks placed above each dorsal spine. 5. The yellow, elastic ligament connecting the dorsal spines together. 6. The spines of the dorsal vertebræ. 7. The semi-spinalis dorsi muscle. 8. The heads of the ribs. 9. The levatores costarum muscle. 10. The ribs.

The sacrum, therefore, is not reckoned among the true vertebræ, the number of which, however, amounts to thirty-two. Of these many divisions, the bones of the neck alone are not subject to deviations. The lumbar may be five or seven, and the dorsal limitation is either one above or one below the usual amount, neither of which varieties are of very rare occurrence. The links of the back-bone differ in form and in function. The dorsal vertebræ seem, at first sight, to possess no lateral processes; whereas in the lumbar region these developments are so extended as to constitute the principal features of the several parts. So also the two first bones of the neck enjoy great motion, and all the links of the neck are very far from stationary. But the parts of the back, on the contrary, are all but fixed; yet, although each is endowed with a very limited movement, the whole is gifted with an evident elasticity which affords an easy seat to the rider.

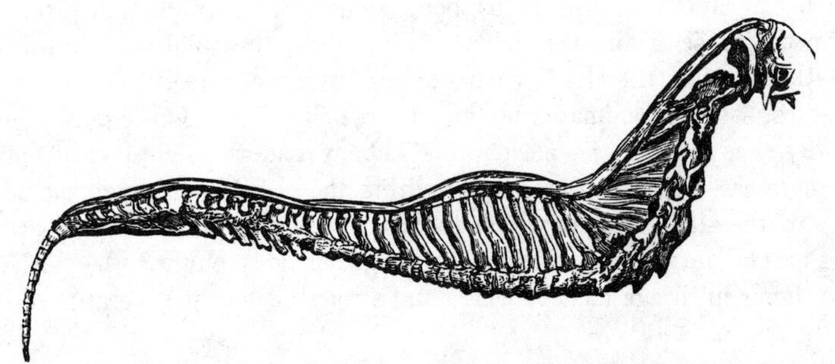

THE SPINE OF THE HORSE, OR THE BASIS OF ITS ANATOMICAL FRAMEWORK.

Along the top of the back-bone runs a strong cord of yellow, elastic fiber, which unites the several parts, holding these firmly together as one whole. The elastic cord, however, passes directly from the last dorsal spine, to be fixed into the back portion of the skull, thus skipping over all the bones of the neck. The fibers of this cord are longitudinally arranged; and however elastic such a substance may be, the dorsal arrangement would not allow of that freedom of motion which was requisite in the neck of an animal which was to crop its food from the surface of the earth.

The necessity, however, was fully met by an elastic cloth being, as it were, thrown over the cord, and extending thence to the bones of the neck. By this arrangement, frequent attachments were avoided and grace of outline was preserved, while no deterioration was made in that provision by means of which the heavy head is supported without apparent strain upon the muscular fiber. One end of the elastic expansion being inserted into the cervical bones, all the ease and beauty of movement is rendered possible by the retractile property of the cloth-like ligament being fully equal to the sustenance of the weight, but not strong enough to resist the action of the muscles when excited. Thus, the muscles situated at the base of the neck serve to depress the head; the elastic cloth answers as a counterpoising force, which steadies the movement; the action of the motor agents near the crest, aided by the ligamentous elasticity of the neck, serve to elevate the part, while the muscular power at the base of the bones regulates and guides the upward motion.

But the reader may be desirous to learn how far the back of the animal is suited to endure the weight of the rider. The bones of the spine, not being joined by osseous union, may give solidity to the part; but it must be self-evident the chain possesses no inherent power to sustain the smallest pressure. Therefore, the body of the rider, when placed upon the back, cannot be upheld by bone alone. The weight must repose upon the muscles and the ligaments by which the solid parts are kept together. Man, therefore, when mounted upon a horse, is seated upon elastic substances, animated by the powers of vitality. This circumstance readily accounts for the pleasurable feelings and the lightness of spirit communicated to the master when within the saddle; although the delicacy of the structures on which the burden is cast should also instruct that an elaborately and a delicately organized body ought to be shielded from labor until age has confirmed and strengthened the several portions of the frame.

When contemplating the uses for which the quadruped was created, we perceive the necessity of that huge mass of muscular fiber with which the back is cushioned. We also recognize the beauty of intention which those numerous supports, called ribs, embody and declare. These props, eighteen on either side, must greatly strengthen the main structure, although each is of a loose texture, and every one is more or less pliable. The innate property of elasticity belonging to the horse's ribs seems to have been long known to country urchins, who, out of these bones, have

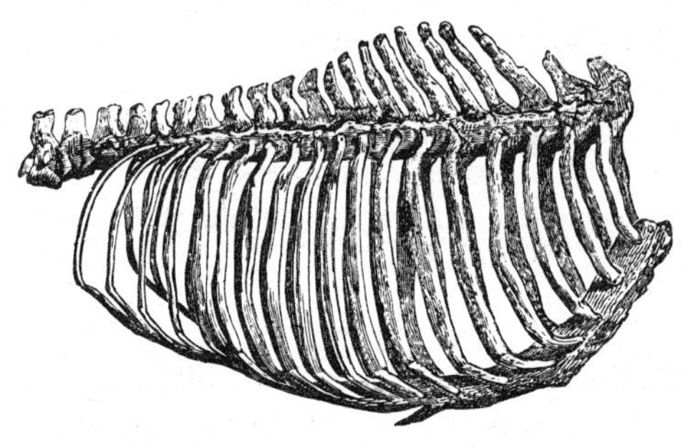

THE THORACIC FRAMEWORK OF THE HORSE.

Showing the manner in which the ribs spring from the spine to unite upon the bone of the breast.

been accustomed to form bows whence to propel juvenile arrows. Nature, however, seems not to have been satisfied with this provision, for the inferior portion of the ribs consists of cartilage, which anatomists speak of as the most elastic substance in the body; this yielding termination rests on the sternum or breast-bone, a structure more than three parts of which are composed of the last-named material.

The manner in which the fore limb is united to the trunk likewise offers matter for the reader's admiration. Considering that the horse is a beast of burden, man, were he designing a creature fitted for such uses, would assuredly have sought to gain strength by the insertion of bone. Bone, however, would have interfered with that agility which, no less than strength, is an attribute of the horse's body. The presence even of a clavicle joining the shoulder to the thorax would have exposed a jumping quadruped to repeated fractures. Nature, therefore, bound the parts together by interlacing fibers. And to afford an idea of the marvelous care bestowed on this arrangement, the following diagram is submitted to the contemplation of the reader.

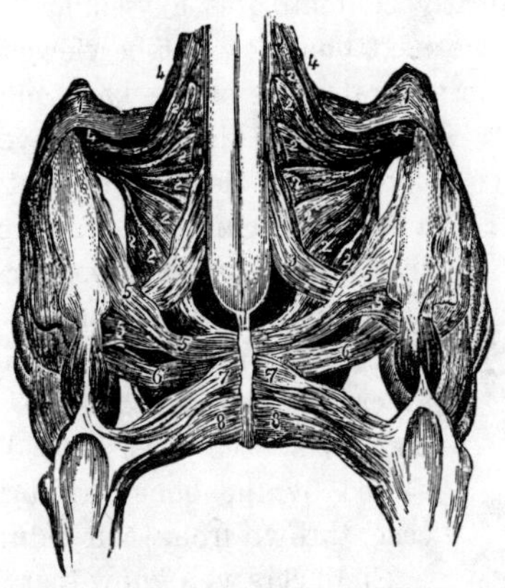

SOME OF THE MUSCLES WHICH ATTACH THE FORE LIMB TO THE TRUNK.

Three muscles have already been removed, viz., the panniculus carnosus, the levator humeri, and the latissimus dorsi.

1. The trapezius. 2. The seratus magnus. 3. The subscapulo hyoideus. 4. The rhomboideus. 5. The pectoralis anticus. 6. The anterior portion of the pectoralis magnus. 7. The pectoralis parvus. 8. The pectoralis transversus.

The rider, therefore, when mounted on a horse, is not only seated upon fleshy and ligamentous fiber, and upheld by pliable bone based upon elastic cartilage, but as the thorax is supported by the anterior extremity, he actually swings upon the strongest and most yielding substance known throughout animated nature. Could mortal ingenuity, by the exercise of any force or duration of thought, have perfected so exquisite a work? But the mind is abased and humbled before the proofs of Superior Wisdom, when we find that all hitherto made known is but a part of the lavish provision bestowed upon the perfection of God's most beautiful gift to man.

The bones within the fore limb are not self-sustaining. Remove their coverings, and they will not retain their several places, but will fall in a heap upon the earth. The fact proves that the osseous framework, although it confers solidity upon the body, is nevertheless upheld by the structures with which it is enveloped. The bony column, however, when united and bound together, exhibits an intention of bestowing elasticity quite as much as of conferring strength. In the first place, the solid column is crowned by a broad but thin plate of cartilage, the yielding property of which has already been dilated upon; so that the trunk not only swings upon living fiber, but the primary weight is endured by what anatomists designate "the most elastic substance in the body," of a shape and form which develops to the uttermost its bending property.

The arrangement of the shoulder-blade and the bone on which it rests being angular, evidently contemplates a yielding to any force coming from above. The two next bones cannot be viewed as meant solely for strength; though the several parts of the knee and shank are slightly columnar in their order, nevertheless the pastern bones again display an intent to yield rather than a design at gaining decided resistance. Yet, even there remains further food for contemplation when viewing these dry bones of a quadruped. The shock, of which the rider complains when doomed to cross the trunk of some poor animal whose body has been disorganized by abuse, is occasioned by the bones having been, through disease, thrown from their natural positions.

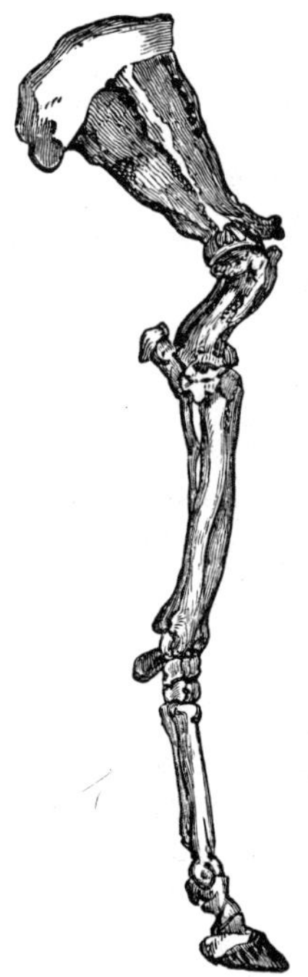

THE BONES OF THE FORE LIMB.

Engineers well know that sand will oppose the force of a cannon ball, the power being rapidly exhausted which has to travel through numerous separated particles. Each grain of sand, therefore, being distinct, a bag of that substance offers a good preventive to the concussion produced by the explosive force of gunpowder. But the reader, when endeavoring to ascertain the provisions instituted by BENEVOLENCE to save the equestrian from concussion, can at once perceive the purpose for which the osseous support of the limb was formed of several pieces, as well as appreciate the beauty and grace of motion which is thereby assured.

Looking at the illustration, we observe that certain of the component solids of the limbs are altogether out of the perpendicular, and consequently must receive other support than is derived from the bone immediately below them. Indeed, no portion of the structure is decidedly columnar in its arrangement. Either the parts are crooked, or they lean in a direction from the plummet line. The angularity of the two topmost pieces can, however, not possibly escape notice; neither can the slanting position of the pastern bones fail to attract attention. Noting these peculiarities, the reader recognizes that the bones of the fore extremity cannot be self-sustaining, but they must be upheld or retained in their relative situations by the structures which surround them in the living subject.

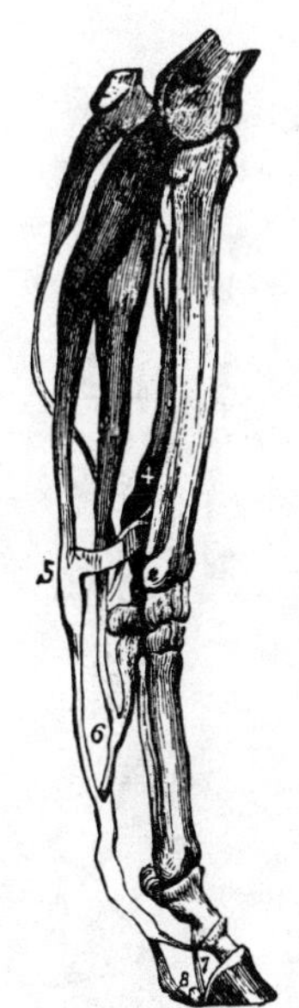

THE PRINCIPAL FLEXOR TENDONS OF THE FORELEG.

1. The perforans. 2. The perforatus. 3, 4. Accessory muscles. 5, 6. Restraining ligaments. 7. The pedal cartilage divided. 8. The navicular bone.

The scapula and humerus, or the two topmost bones, are rendered firm by the joint action of the powerful extensor and flexor muscles appertaining to the shoulder. The pastern bones transfer their weight to the strong tendon which passes immediately under their lower surfaces. The other bones are held in their situations by the energetic contractility of the muscles which embrace them. Hence it is obvious the rider, when seated on the back of a horse, is not upheld by any osseous resistance. His burden reposes upon living fiber. The bone limits the sphere of contractility, and thus gives firmness to the limbs; but it endures no portion of the weight. So exquisitely has nature adapted her creature to its uses, that in the horse man is provided with a means of conveyance remarkable for fleetness, but more wonderful for the elastic and buoyant seat which an admirable body affords to an ungrateful master.

Had weight been cast upon bone, the shock communicated by placing the foot upon the ground would have been so powerful as must have made the saddle a seat of torture. This is no speculative conjecture, but it is a deduction drawn from positive fact. Hard work causes the pastern bones to quit the slant, which is their natural position, and to assume a more upright direction. They very rarely become actually perpendicular; but as they verge toward that attitude, so as partially to transfer their weight from the tendon to one another, the jar communicated to the rider becomes most distressing. The tendons of the foreleg are, therefore, of all importance; the utility of these structures cannot be better illustrated than by appealing to the terrible effects which ensue upon injury to these organs.

However, that the reader may fully appreciate the simplicity and the seeming complexity developed in the various arrangements exposed upon dissection, the next illustration is inserted, against which numerous lines are fixed. Those marks indicate the points where a substance, like to white of egg, is interposed between the extremities of the bones. Each separate bone thus not only rests upon a liquid, but the ends of these formations are likewise tipped with cartilage, thus doubly securing the ease of progression. Nor have the perfection of these various arrangements received full justice, for concussion of the foot has not only to travel through different bones tipped by cartilage and separated by the interposition of a fluid, but it also has to progress through the various structures of which the limb itself is composed, and to travel in different directions.

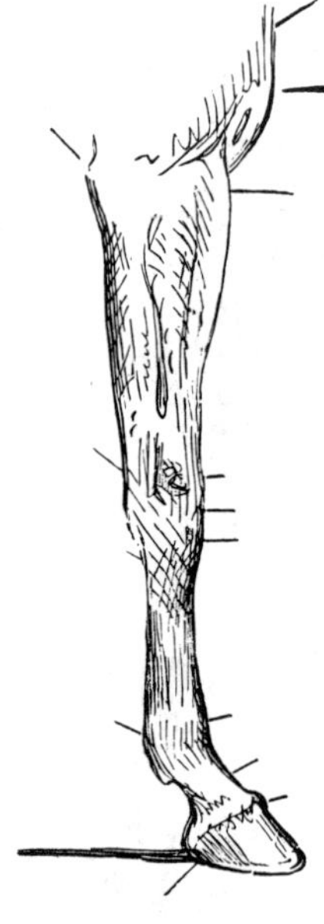

THE ARTIST'S IDEA OF A HORSE'S FORE LIMB.

The lines indicate the places where synovia (or a fluid resembling white of egg) is interposed between the different structures.

So elaborate an arrangement, or one better fitted to answer its intention, no human study could invent. Man has for ages labored to disarrange the parts thus admirably adjusted; when so employed, he has only followed the example of the savage who destroys the product he is incapable of understanding. No injury, no wrong, no cruelty can be conceived which barbarity has not inflicted on the most generous of man's many willing slaves. While this has been going forward, nations, at a vast outlay, have retained expensive establishments to entreat the mercies of a SUPERIOR to be lavished upon themselves, and at the moment these people were boasting aloud of their refined feelings or of their exalted civilization, they have been incapable of sympathizing with the agony which was imprisoned within the walls of their premises.

Looking toward the quarters of the horse, we perceive the spines of the lumbar and sacral bones arranged in so peculiar a manner as to excite remark. Those of the loins bend forward, while those of the haunch incline backward, thus leaving a free space dividing the uppermost bones of two neighboring regions. There must be a reason for so evident a design. Inspecting the last lumbar bone, we ascertain it to be united by its lateral processes, yet it does not touch the first sacral body, all other parts of the chain joining at their centers.

Here is cause for reflection! What takes place at this spot which could render imperative such an arrangement? In what action is the inclination of the trunk so opposite to the position of the quarters as to render imperative such a special provision as is here exemplified in the skeleton? In prancing, in rearing, and in jumping, the hind legs are firmly planted upon the earth; then, by exertion of the powerful muscles of the quarters, the forward trunk is raised. This action could not have been exhibited had the spines of the sacral bones ranged in the same direction as those of the lumbar vertebræ; and to enforce the reason of this evident provision a free space characterizes this particular joint, others being formed by the interposition of cartilage.

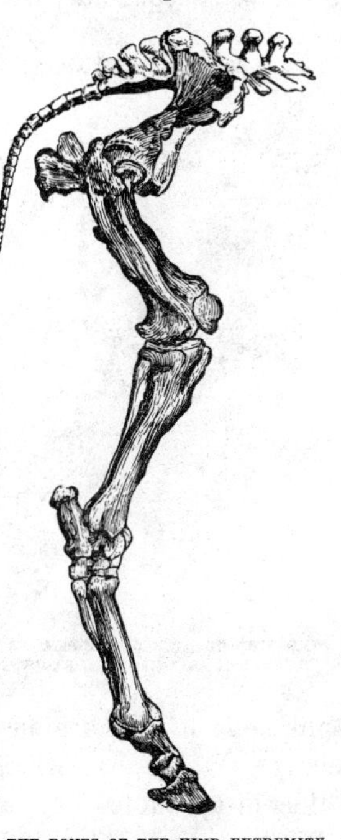

THE BONES OF THE HIND EXTREMITY.

The skeleton of the quarters is characterized by further distinctive peculiarities. The sacral bones are fixed one to another, and joining them at the spine is the huge hip-bone. This is the heaviest of the many weighty pieces which compose the osseous frame of the horse. It is irregular in form, and remarkable for an unusually rugged exterior. An anatomist, by simply inspecting it, could designate its uses, so emphatically is everywhere written the origin and insertion of powerful motor muscles. In every ridge, in every indentation, in every inequality anatomy discovers such a purpose; thus, when "the gnarled and bossy" developments upon this bone are viewed in conjunction with the solid and uneven appearance of the lower osseous supports of the hind limb, no person properly instructed can doubt that the quarters are peculiarly the seat of muscular power in the equine race.

Then the angular arrangement of the bones suggests the immediate purpose of flexion and extension. "Yes," interrupts the reader, "that is true; but supposing the loose bones of the skeleton only to exist, what was to suggest the angularity of arrangement?" Such a fact could be thus readily ascertained. The bodies of other animals would inform the anatomist of the relative situations of the stifle and the elbow joints, while the different lengths and points of bearing in the fore and hind extremities would instruct him concerning all the rest.

But no knowledge could enable the anatomist to infer the gracefulness of form and flow of line which characterizes the body of the horse, even when deprived of its outward investment. Here is a sketch of the quarter after partial dissection. It scarcely awakens the disgust which anatomical labors generally create. The elegance which distinguishes the living creature is hardly lost—certainly it is not entirely destroyed—and the author is acquainted with no other body which could equally endure so harsh a test.

The inferior bones of the subjoined sketch lead to the foot; but as the osseous structure of this part was illustrated in a previous sketch, and as the fore and hind feet of the horse are in the leading particulars alike, the author will not fill valuable space by unnecessary repetition. However, the hind foot of the horse being the point whence all the strain of propulsion must proceed, the part, from such a cause alone, will be liable to certain distortions. The evils engendered by the cruel impatience of mankind, which forces the colt into too early labor, causes the natural position of the member to become altered. The pastern bones grow to be erect, and, should the toil still be enforced, the shank bone afterward projects. If these warnings are disregarded, inhumanity provokes the heels to be drawn upward, and a valuable helpmate is thus incapacitated from assisting man in his earthly task.

THE HIND QUARTER OF A HORSE, FROM WHICH THE SKIN HAS BEEN REMOVED.

While writing of the horse, it should not be forgotten that in this country there is another animal which properly belongs to the equine race, and which is liable to most of the evils as well as worthy of much of the commendation that has been already pronounced, as though these referred only to one specimen of the tribe. The donkey is much misunderstood. Because its name has become a figure of reproach, no writer hitherto has dilated seriously upon its requirements, although several have been ignorantly sentimental, where suffering needed only truth to plead in its behalf. The animal must have its uses, or its breed would not be preserved.

The fact establishes that the creature is of service to mankind, since the life, whose season of utility has expired, like the dodo, soon ceases to exist. It is, however, chiefly the property of those whose feelings are subject to their necessities. The purchase of such a chattel is comparatively easy; the food is the refuse of the stable; but the work is often disproportionately heavy, for the ass too frequently belongs to those whose daily round of toil would tax the strength of the largest horse.

The prejudice which encircles this miserable being appears to be countenanced even in the dissecting rooms of the veterinary profession Anatomy is a science the only merit of which depends upon its being a literal record of facts; yet students, at the before-mentioned places, are fond of alluding to the larynx of the ass, as displaying a peculiar development, which accounts for the difference of voice between the last-named animal and the horse. The author could never discover such a curiosity, nor is any necessary, when the peculiarity of the two sounds is attentively noticed. One is a nasal tone, modulated by the flutter of the nostrils; the other is a harsh, grating noise, produced by energetically inhaling and expelling the atmosphere through the extended pipe of the animal's trachea.

The donkey labors, however, beyond the care of its enslaver and without the region of human sympathy. Be its toil exhaustive, let it work without cessation throughout the day and far into the night, no eye regards its fatigue with commiseration. It is an object only to laugh at. The popular belief is, that the tribe is so peculiarly hardy as to be altogether removed from the necessities, the liabilities, or the accidents common to every other form of life. All grades of existence which men please to neglect, they generally designate as "hardy." Human beings, however, notoriously become less "hardy" as knowledge is enlarged and as life becomes better cared for. Will the time ever arrive when perception can embrace that which we now view only as an object of fun, and when the donkey will be regarded as entitled to share the consideration bestowed upon all the other inhabitants of earth?

The country is not secure, the people are not released from barbarism, while the pressure of want can blind the nation to the lawful needs of the lives which surround and which serve it. Civilization must be far from perfected, when an inquiry concerning the man who has beheld a dead donkey can make a large assemblage laugh. The author has, however, known poor families to be plunged into deep distress because the assinine form of existence was *not* immortal. His experience may, probably, be peculiar, but it is opposed to the stale jest of our theaters; for when he was demonstrator at the Royal Veterinary College, he used to dispute with the man who supplied donkeys for the pupils to dissect, whether the institution should or should not bear the loss of such as died before their lives were required by the school. These creatures were bought at Smithfield, and brought to Saint Pancras for animals enjoying health; they were wanted to endure but a few days; yet the author has seen three carcasses anticipate this brief interval of permitted existence.

The author can further testify that, among the scores of carcasses which he has dissected, he never examined the body of a donkey, however young it might have been, that he did not encounter appalling proofs of internal injuries—injuries which had resulted in change of structure, and which would have consigned the horse to the knacker's yard. Yet the animals thus maimed were working up to the date of purchase; the inability to move was attributed to the obstinacy which is generously supposed to characterize the ill-treated animal, and the blows fell heavier in proportion as its actual condition should have appealed to human forbearance.

STABLED FOR THE NIGHT.

To properly comprehend the sufferings of the quadruped, we must know the country whence it is derived, and be acquainted with the soil it is fitted to inhabit. The wild ass delights in the sandy desert of a tropical region, and for the products of such a locality a taste is, by the English representative, retained. It lives and thrives upon the spontaneous herbage of the arid waste. The heat, under which other forms of life appear to languish, fills the donkey with animation. The comparative size of its intestines fit it to store away that amount of water which in the land of its nativity is proverbially scarce.

The donkey in England is dragged into a wintry climate, rendered more inhospitable by the low temperature which is the most prominent characteristic of the country. In cold and in wet, the native of a tropical soil must lead a miserable existence. In Britain, however, it breathes and breeds; but it is here on the limits of even its power to endure. In Scotland the tribe is all but unknown. Where it can live, however, no one thinks of its real condition; no mortal is so weak as to waste pity upon its suffering. Its toil is without other limit than the pleasure of its master; when the day's work is done, the nearest lane is the only stable ready to receive it.

The author has often, when passing down some narrow and unfrequented highway, during the early part of December, encountered a miserable group of beings endeavoring to afford each other a little warmth by crowding close together. The weather at this season is piercing cold. The ground is squashy, and moisture loads the atmosphere. The fierce wind bends the bare twigs of the adjacent hedge, and the temperature is of that kind which heralds the Christmas frost. It is not yet so low as to numb sensation; but it leaves the edge of feeling unblunted, that sense may fully appreciate the heavy misery, before whose wildness all nature moans and crouches. In such a place, and at such a season, the author has been made sad by the living anguish which the preceding illustration feebly depicts.

The donkey, in this country, is very unfortunate in the class whom it principally serves. The lower order, though with impulses untainted by politeness, yet, in the struggle for life, have little leisure to quicken their perceptions or to cultivate their feelings. Their own necessities forbid them to be generous, and render somewhat rude their intercourse. They exist not within the amenities, but upon the borders of society; the law, under whose protection the affluent breathe in comfort, is to them a cruel institution, which forces them to endure, which they recognize only as a restraint, and with which they are powerless openly to contend.

In towns, the homes of such a race are without attractions. The very poor are ignorant of domesticity. They eat and live abroad, and seek their lodgings only when utter weariness makes them heedless where they rest. If the lodging be large enough to conceal, it possesses all the requirements poverty demands. To be larger is to be colder; for the ignorant study rather to drag on existence from day to day than think to promote the health, which is their only real possession.

When such a people rise in their sphere of contention, and can afford to discard the hand-barrow for the donkey-tray, the inferior animal can expect no separate lodging. That will hardly be provided for a beast which the master was too abased to conceive necessary for the members of his family.

The donkey is hailed as a new possession; and for security, not from any loftier consideration, it has to share the proprietor's home. No hole can be too narrow, too dark, or too stifling for the animal's abode, so that it provides the safe keeping for which it is sought. Humanity shudders as it pictures the strange places which poverty may view as the fitting homes of its dependants!

The young horse may be stinted in its food, but it is spared from work until a certain period has arrived. All classes have their stated ages when the colt should first begin to labor; but the ass has no recognized season of rest, even for its immaturity. It is forced to work so soon as need can see in the growing body a capacity to assist. Foals are often to be seen dragging loaded trays about the streets of London, and the day's toil is lengthened or shortened by the quickness or the slowness of the day's sale. The food is, during this time, the refuse of the stock; seldom can the owner spare from his earnings that which will purchase fodder for the life which is the partner of his fatigues.

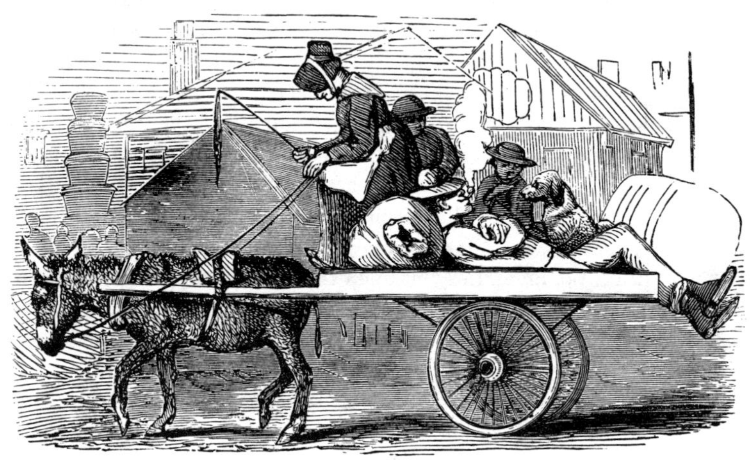

THE DONKEY'S PREPARATION FOR THE LABOR OF THE DAY.

The donkey is harnessed for the early market. The costermonger rides with his family to make his bargains for the day; and the stock-in-trade being procured, he and they ride with it back again. The very poor never walk, save upon necessity, and seem never to conceive their animals can be tired or overladen. The wretched quadruped, on home being reached, is not released and permitted to rest. It has to support the tray while the family wash the stock, display the viands, and get their morning meal; after which it is started with a kick and a blow, and an exclamation of, "Come up, lazy! why, what ails ye, this marning?"

Animals have generally less ability to endure fatigue than have the human race; but if the donkey has to work before man's daily round commences, so also do its toils increase after the period of mortal labor has been fulfilled. My readers must recollect to have frequently beheld the coster's tray, now emptied of the green stock of the morning, but occupied by several shouting fellows, and drawn past the windows by a little donkey. The street purveyor of vegetables often travels far to dispose of his wares. But the green stuff distributed, he considers his labors for the day to be ended. He then has time to appreciate his own sensations. He flings his body full length upon the tray, and, with the good nature which belongs to his class, does not refuse a ride to any wayfarer so long as the vehicle can accommodate another passenger. All, then, fully impressed with the popular credulities concerning the donkey, commence shouting and thumping, while the animal, which has been upon its legs before the light began, is forced to travel homeward at a pace which is compelled to be faster in proportion as it may be distant from its lodging.

In the country, the houses being more separated, the animal is deprived of the frequent stoppages and the lighter draught of the towns. The pull is heavier, and the distances are longer; but still the donkey must progress until the master has earned a certain sum, without which he rarely turns the creature's head toward his home. If the proprietors of asses have few faiths, they are all thoroughly imbued with one belief, which is, that the animal in their keeping cannot possibly feel exhaustion. Their credulity does not stay here. They are impressed with a conviction that no creature of the donkey tribe has any sort of feeling. The quadruped, they know, can bear an unusual amount of beating with the thickest possible bludgeon, and simply requires only the coarsest of refuse for sustenance. Moreover, such conviction leaves the proprietor his own convenience to consider, when imposing burdens on "the beast within his gate."

The last article of belief makes the man select the weakest portion of his dumb servant's spine for a seat, when he is inclined to play the jockey. The reader, to whose notice diagrams of the equine spine have been submitted, knows that the loins alone are unsupported by other bones. The absence of that which renders this region the weakest division of the vertebræ, also makes this portion of the quadruped's back the most yielding and elastic. Here the fashion of vulgarity fixes the rider's seat when he strides the ass. The veterinary student will remember that few of the lumbar bones in the carcasses he dissected, when at college, were in their integrity. The author has encountered two, three, and even four bones of the six which compose the part locked together by osseous deposit.

Such a form of union proves the animal to have suffered inflammation. The injury must have been endured and the agony must have run its course; for an osseous junction is positive evidence that all the stages of inflammation have been survived. Few persons, when they behold the young donkey stagger under the weight of its six-foot rider, care to think of this; nay, the writer has beheld really worthy gentlemen stand and enjoy the scene of activity presented at evening time by a rural gipsy's encampment. The women were laughing, the men were shouting, while the more jovial of the gang were racing on the common. Those poor donkeys, which already had been goaded to the performance of no ordinary day's toil, were carrying terrific loads, and beaten till they galloped, despite the deep-seated anguish with which they were afflicted.

CHAPTER II.

PHYSIC, THE MODE OF ADMINISTERING IT, AND MINOR OPERATIONS

Let the reader ask any gentleman of his acquaintance, "Whether man is not morally answerable for the welfare of those animals which are gathered beneath his roof?" The individual thus appealed to will most probably lean back in his easy chair, and, with a look of amiable surprise, may reply "Certainly! certainly! Assuredly, my dear sir, I regard myself as fully responsible! Every horse in my stable costs me one hundred pounds, or very nearly, a year. The poor animals ought to be well looked after for that money! Clerks—many young city men—receive only fifty pounds annually—from respectable houses too. Therefore, my horses ought to be especially well cared for!"

But to drive this matter home, allow the author, with all humility, to inquire if it be in the power of money to discharge the smallest or the slightest moral bond? Is there no difference between paying and doing? May there not be certain duties which are equally stringent upon the very rich and the very poor? Can the wealthy compound for such obligations, and are the needy, only, to be judged for the non-fulfillment of these responsibilities?

It is among the worst features of modern society that, while it boasts of several worthy gentlemen who can draw largely upon their bankers, there are in its ranks so very few who would willingly submit to the smallest personal exertion for the fulfillment of that which they confess to be a moral duty. Would these most agreeable and amiable individuals occasionally lounge toward the stable, the cost of its maintenance might be decreased, and, nevertheless, the creatures for whose welfare the owner is confessedly responsible be better treated at the diminished outlay.

When a dumb slave fails in the service of some affluent proprietor, all that might be done is not accomplished when an order is hastily given "to call in" a veterinary surgeon. It is not sufficient that baskets of drugs are delivered and paid for; that physicking and bleeding are practiced and remunerated; that a "horse doctor" is constant in his attendance, or that a building, by its odor, attests to the activity of his measures. No. Man is formed capable of investigation, and is blessed with a power of locomotion. A man is bound to go, to see, to hear patiently, and to judge conscientiously, of that which is done to the lives intrusted to his responsibility. Had this duty been discharged, many processes, still sanctioned by custom, might have fallen into disuse; some habits, now indulged, might have been discarded; while a few objectionable measures might have been altogether forbidden as useless formalities and needless cruelties.

Horse Balls—particular forms of veterinary medicine—are generally sent to stables by the dozen. Physic is thus placed at the pleasure or the caprice of ignorance to administer. The author has seen a large chest full of such abominations—looking very pretty, and made up all of one size, each labeled, and bearing some distinctive title—directed to an English nobleman resident in the country. Such a supply, the writer was informed, is dispatched to "my lord's" address twice in each year, and is always used by the grooms, and by the stated period, in accordance with the accompanying directions.

The only safeguard attending such implements of destruction was that the majority were harmless, either from the worthless nature of the drugs composing them, or from the change which took place between the agents being compounded and at the time of their being employed. Many, no doubt, were thrown away; but that fact excuses neither the professional man who sent them, the honorable person who ordered them, or the ignorant servants by whom they were accepted. Each was impressed with a belief that such things were potent. It is astonishing how much of this world's sin is gilt over by its credulity. All concerned regarded these things as mysterious projectiles, strong enough to regulate the eccentricities of health and powerful enough to vanquish the dangers of disease.

One form of ball, however, is neither innocuous nor safe—it is the aloetic. Aloes is the common purgative of the stable. So general was the use of the drug, and so unquestioning appears to have, formerly, been the confidence lavished upon its operation, that this medicine always took the precedence in every sickness, and, ultimately, by popular consent, engrossed to itself the significant term of "physic." "Has this horse had physic?"—"Prepare this horse for physic"—when spoken in the stable, signify, has such an animal had aloes? or imply an order that another quadruped is to be prepared for a dose of aloes. The groom can only imagine that to be worthy of the title "physic," which is capable of producing visible effects; and, certainly, when judged by the stable-man's standard, aloes merits the distinction bestowed upon its drastic results.

Other things will move the bowels of the horse, and will empty its intestines much more gently, and with altogether more safety; but the stable cannot, therefore, afford to part with its favorite representative of the many forms of medicine. Bran mashes, four of these being given daily, it is well known, will relax the animal's system; but the groom employs these agents merely as *preparatory* to the favorite dose of aloes; and, though repeated mashes will induce purgation in the equine patient, the groom is never satisfied unless that result be aggravated by a dose of aloes.

The horse's body does not quickly respond to opening medicine; but the action, once elicited, is not invariably easy to command. The animal's life is frequently a prey to a potent purgative. The veterinarian knows that the different creatures vary much in their capability of swallowing amounts of aloes; that the dose which will not move one quadruped may destroy the inhabitant of the next stall. One creature will imbibe two ounces of the drug without marked effect; another will be shaken by the action of less than half an ounce of the preparation Nevertheless, the stable-man always craves for aloes, and always experiences an odd delight when watching for its hydragogue operation.

The farmers in Norfolk are strongly tainted with the superstition of the London mews. They also crave for aloes, and the youthful veterinary surgeon frequently yields to the demand. Young practitioners delight in strong doses. Accordingly, a full dose of aloes is sent to the Norfolk farmer, and by him rammed down the throat of some unfortunate teamster. The next time the novice encounters his customer, the man of the diploma is greeted with "Hey, doctor! doctor! what beautiful physic that were you sent for Slyboots! Oh! how it did work the poor thing, to be sure! If anything could have saved the beast, that must have done! But the time were up, and he died of a powerful inflammation. Thanke, thanke, doctor! Let's have your bill!"

This is the more lamentable when we consider that in nine cases out of ten, or rather in twenty-nine out of thirty, the administration of aloes is unnecessary. In the great majority of cases, its place could be advantageously supplied by bran mashes, which are readily made according to the following receipt: Put a peck of bran into a perfectly clean stable-pail. One person should stir the bran as briskly as possible, while another person, with speed, empties a sufficiency of boiling water into the pail to render the contents a pultaceous mass. The vessel is then covered up, and when it has become cool, the pudding is thrown into the manger.

However, one horse shall devour bran mashes with avidity, another will not touch them. This will not partake of the potion unless it be partially warm; another will not eat until it is perfectly cold; while most will partake of the mess if it be flavored by the admixture of a little salt or a few crushed oats.

So it is, also, with water. Certain horses, when feeding upon bran mashes, refuse all drink; others enjoy frequent draughts of cold fluid; while a third set seem to crave warm water; and a fourth will neither imbibe freely nor entirely abstain, being wholly indifferent as to the temperature of the liquid. Thus the order, which is inserted in most books, to give to the horse, after the animal has swallowed a dose of aloes, copious draughts of warm water, is frequently rendered futile; for, as the proverb teaches, "one man may lead the horse to the pond, but forty men cannot make the quadruped drink."

Bran mashes, however, will act without the aid of repeated doses of warm fluid. Of themselves they do not debilitate, though from the length and size of the horse's intestines, purgation cannot be long maintained without inducing serious exhaustion; and it is never safe to work the animal while any looseness is observable. A tendency to inflammation is often announced by repeated and liquid discharges; therefore, never let the horse be taken out while the bowels are in a state of excitement, for exercise may increase that action to one of positive disease. Bran mashes, however, are the safest and the gentlest of laxatives. Any condition may be induced, according to the number and frequency of the potions. In general, they act mildly, without inducing that bodily discomfort and that constitutional weakness which throws the animal out of condition and renders rest an absolute necessity for recovery. Altogether, these mixtures are the best and the safest laxative of the stable; but even these should never be administered to the horse without the special direction of the proprietor.

On the other hand, aloes can, in no form, be administered to some horses. Very many cannot receive a full dose of the drug. Several can only with safety swallow the medicine when highly spiced or in solution. While a few are all but insensible to the action of the agent. Alarming spasms often follow the exhibition of a moderate quantity of aloes, which always renders the quadruped sickly ere the effects are visible. The drug, in most instances, lies dormant twenty-four hours; during which period the appetite is lost, the spirits oppressed, the coat dull, and the entire system evidently shaken. It is not esteemed prudent to work the patient till several days' rest have been allowed for its restoration.

It used once to be the custom to trot the animal which was sickening under a dose of aloes; but experience has shown the danger of the habit. The horse is now left in the stable, has an extra rug thrown upon the back, while a pail of warm water is in most instances placed in the manger. Where safe, it is obviously unnecessary to ride the quadruped which is sickening under aloes; since the loss of appetite shews the medicine has affected the system, and the natural effects of the physic may, therefore, be anticipated.

Very many animals, when suffering from chronic debility, may be slaughtered by a moderate dose of aloes, while many never sufficiently recover from purgation to do a day's work after the medicine has ceased to operate. Of all the preparations the veterinarian has at his command, the writer does not know one which exerts so decided an effect upon the constitution; nor does the veterinary pharmacopœia contain an agent which could be more advantageously dispensed with. During the years the author was in active practice, he does not remember to have ever given a dose of aloes that the symptoms did not afterward cause him to regrêt the administration.

There is another fact rendering the aloetic ball an unsafe agent to be intrusted to the keeping of a groom. These things, as commonly compounded, become, in a short time, as hard as stones. The author has handled many which might be broken, but which could not be indented. Such bodies are not in a fit condition to be thrust down a horse's throat. All unyielding substances are liable to stick in the gullet, and to provoke choking—the digestive passages of the horse not contemplating the deglutition of other than moist and soft pellets of thoroughly masticated food. Aloes was, at one time, in spite of the objections urged, very popular in the stable; for that consequence, the late Professor Coleman was mainly answerable. They are at present chiefly employed in accordance with the dictates of routine, and usually take precedence of other forms of medicine.

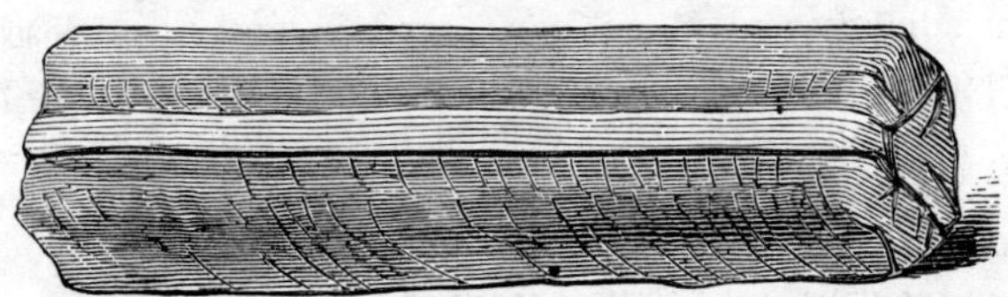

A BALL, AS SUCH THINGS ARE SENT FROM THE VETERINARY PHARMACY.

A horse ball represents some substance in powder mixed into a mass with some moist ingredient, such as soft soap, treacle, palm oil, etc. The compounds, when united, are usually rolled into sticks about three-quarters of an inch in diameter. These sticks are subsequently cut into lengths of two and a half or four inches in extent, according to the amount required for a dose; each piece is weighed, is dusted with some non-adhesive powder, is securely wrapped in paper, is labeled, and is packed away for use or sent out to such stables as delight in strange property.

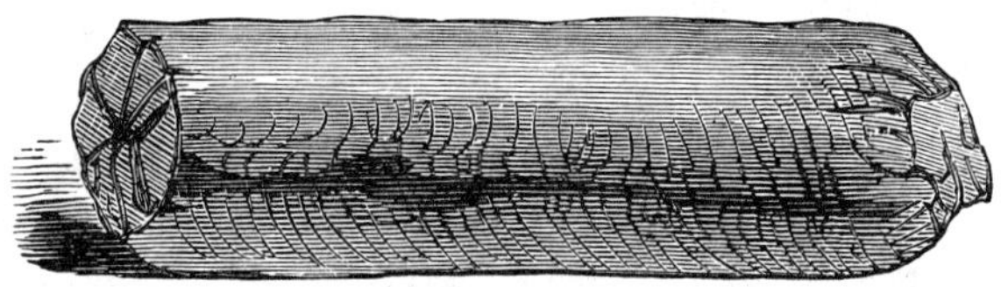

A BALL, OF THE FORM WHICH IT IS GENERALLY MADE TO ASSUME WHEN GIVEN.

Previous to a ball being delivered it is customary, with the generality of practitioners, to pinch the sharp edge of the forward extremity until that part of the substance becomes rounded. The intention, when doing this, is so to modify the shape as to facilitate the passage of the body down the gullet. Where the medicine is soft, as all newly-compounded drugs must necessarily be, the muscular contractility of the horse's swallow would render such trouble useless; but, as the ball must be rather pulpy which can be thus moulded by the fingers, it would be no more than a prudent regulation should every proprietor insist on this custom always being complied with. Whether the present practice in any degree is beneficial to the animal, the author is very dubious; at all events, the horse were very fortunate if the sharp edges of the forward extremity were the only danger it encountered when swallowing the physic which is supposed to be curative in its effect.

Several potent caustics rank among the most common of horse physics. Those agents are of great power; as bichloride of mercury, arsenic, nitrate of silver, sulphate of copper, etc. These burning compounds are frequently administered in substance, and in enormous doses. Even where the quantity prescribed is not objectionable, the form in which the caustic is generally given is calculated to be highly injurious. In the first place, the use of such things in the veterinary pharmacy is too common an occurrence for the compounder to bestow much care upon the accuracy of the weight—a scruple more or less being commonly esteemed of no importance. Next, small thought is bestowed upon the necessity of incorporating such fiery components with more mild ingredients before the mass is forced down the sensitive throat of a living creature. A ball made of linseed meal and treacle is quickly snatched from one of the drawers of the surgery; the powerful agent is speedily reduced to powder; the placebo is torn from its envelope; a slit is cut down its center; from the mortar the potent material is emptied into the cavity thus formed for its reception; and the whole, after having been rewrapped in fresh paper, is esteemed to be ready for delivery.

When such an article has been swallowed by the creature, in whose welfare no living being seems to take a genuine interest, the paper or outward investment is speedily removed by the action of the stomach. Then, the retaining cover being destroyed, the burning mass falls out upon the fine, moist, and velvet coat lining the viscus; this fact may very probably explain why stomachic diseases are so general with the majority of old favorites. As such substances are caustics when applied to the external flesh, it is only reasonable to infer that no tissue within the body could long withstand the burning properties of such potent destroyers. It is true that certain inhumanities, miscalled experiments, have been practiced upon living horses. Enormous quantities of the most destructive compounds have been poured down the living throats of submissive quadrupeds. Some animals long survived such disgusting brutality; but others have succumbed at the very commencement of the trial. Veterinary therapeutics, however, take no notice of such as yielded to the smaller dose. The men who conducted these cruelties delight to dwell upon the fact that a certain horse actually took so much of such a poison, and, *apparently*, suffered no ill effects from imbibition of the deadly potion.

A COMPOUND BALL, AS PREPARED IN TOO MANY VETERINARY PHARMACIES.

However, supposing such an experiment were made on human beings. Let a certain number of cripples be procured from the workhouses; aged creatures whose span of existence was almost run, and on whose countenances years of suffering had impressed the lines of prolonged misery. Let such poor mortals be deprived of speech, and let all the signs of suffering in them be disregarded. Then force these wretched beings to swallow large quantities of the various poisons. Would all perish simultaneously? By no means. Affliction often acts as a defense to those whom it envelops. Men in different stages of distress have endured strange things, as during every hour the record of calamity makes known.

The poor animals which served for the subjects of the so-called veterinary experiments were procured from the knackers; they were in the last stages of disease, and the poison, which would kill healthy horses, acting upon frames exhausted by every possible accumulation of agony, probably may have stimulated the exhaustion of excessive debility.

That which would destroy an ordinary life, acting upon an existence sinking to its last sleep, may, to the blindness of mortal recognitions, appear to work without sensible result, or may seem to recall the fleeting spirit back to earth. At all events, no sound deduction can be drawn, as to the action of any medicinal substances upon the healthy body, from the apparent influence exerted by such agents upon decrepitude and upon senility.

The so-called experiments, which are here alluded to only to reprobate them as horrible cruelties, very probably have induced the carelessness that prevails throughout veterinary practice as to the use of caustic bodies among its customary medicines. Such salts should, on no account, be exhibited in substance, if, indeed, their supposititious virtues should recommend them at all to the prescriber. During the years which the author was in practice he scrupulously abjured all these abominations, and the results which were obtained by gentler agents were such as did no discredit to the adoption of milder measures.

Humanity should prevail consistently throughout all acts forced upon the life which Providence has intrusted to our mercy. If the recognition of this duty, as an actuating motive, be a weakness, in its adoption is carried its own defense. If charity does no good, it cannot possibly work harm to the dumb life upon which its offices are expended; whereas, when administering balls to horses, the cruelty often indulged causes many of these gentle animals to acquire those habits of resistance which are at first no more than the wild efforts of conscious helplessness aiming at self-defense. Such timid creatures, influenced by fear, will instinctively rear, kick, and vigorously attack whoever may approach them.

He who will have the patience and the courage to encounter what is in stable language denominated "a savage horse," may do so with every confidence. Let him approach the quadruped alone, when the groom is absent and silence reigns around. Nothing must be done quickly. When the horse moves, the man must remain stationary. Every symptom of alarm must be assuaged by kind looks and gentle words. When the horse is convinced that no injury is designed—and it is astonishing how quickly a generous spirit will comprehend the intentions of benevolence—in proportion as ferocity was previously displayed will gratitude gush forth and submit the huge body to man's pleasure.

If, however, the person has neither time nor inclination to undertake such a trial, then, with an animal having a tendency to become excited, he must adopt one of those mechanical restraints known as **balling-irons.** These things are not altogether safe for their employer, while they are decidedly not beneficial in their operation upon the quadruped. A balling-iron is simply a piece of metal, so shaped that when thrust violently between the creature's jaws it forcibly holds the mouth open. Therefore, it will certainly prevent biting; but an irritable or a fearful horse can rear up and strike with its forefeet. Such an animal is not entirely subdued when the iron is adjusted. Moreover, these instruments occasion pain, and the horse, instructed by repeated agony, soon grows very cunning, and equally resolute in its efforts to oppose the insertion of the dreaded instrument which causes its suffering.

The man using a balling-iron has, therefore, to guard himself from blows rapidly dealt with the forehoofs of a desperate animal.

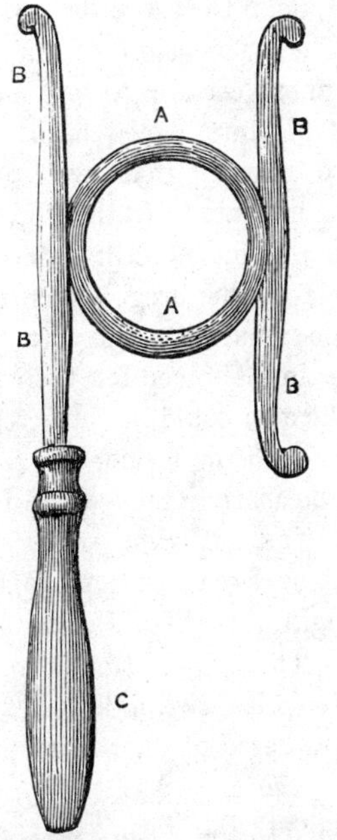

THE COMMONEST FORM OF BALLING-IRON.

A A. The ring of iron which, being forced into the animal's mouth, keeps the jaws asunder.
B B, B B. That portion of the metal which steadies the ring by remaining against the jaws.
C. The handle

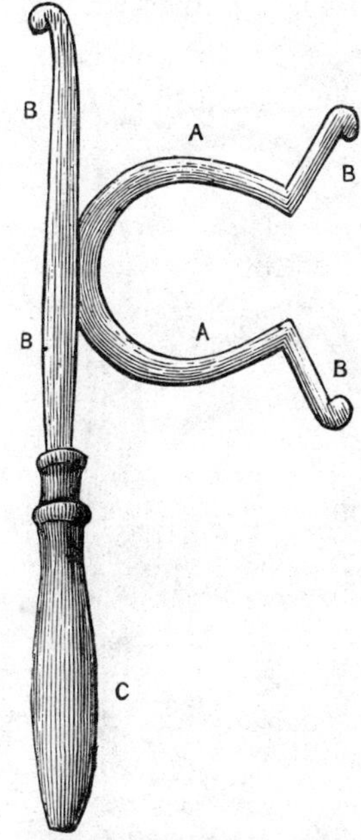

THE IMPROVED FORM OF THE COMMON BALLING IRON, WHICH AFFORDS A PROBABILITY OF ESCAPE FOR THE OPERATOR'S ARM.

A A. The part forced into the mouth.
B B, B B. The parts which remain against the jaws. C. The handle.

He has also to be ready at the slightest intimation of an intention to rear, so that he may withdraw his arm on the instant, otherwise the operator is dragged upward with the elevated crest, and, hanging by the inserted member, he is very lucky if a broken limb does not reward his tardiness. The use of the balling-iron, consequently, is not free from danger; and in practice it will be found safer to subdue by kindness than to partially conquer by the employment of mechanical restraints.

The most common form of balling-iron is constructed according to the model indicated in the preceding illustration. The circular piece of metal is inserted into the mouth of the animal. A straight bar is attached to either side of the metallic ring, the design of these last being to steady the instrument after it has been forced into its proper position. Through the circle the operator's arm is thrust, and the iron ring affords security so far as it disables the jaws from closing upon the member. But, though safe in one direction, such a protection also creates its particular peril; for, should the horse rear, the arm, being surrounded by a metallic rim, could not be withdrawn with the speed requisite to insure the operator's safety. The suspension of the man's body is almost certain to provoke the fracture of his imprisoned limb; consequently, to remedy that evil, the improvement indicated by the right-hand illustration was introduced.

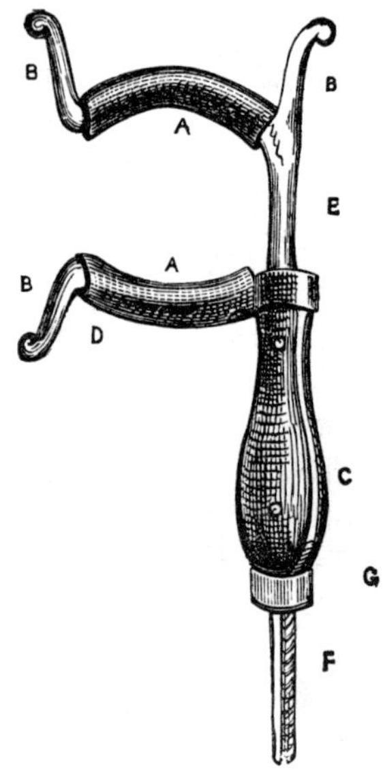

A NEW BALLING-IRON, INVENTED BY PROFESSOR VARNELL, OF THE ROYAL VETERINARY COLLEGE, LONDON.

A A. India-rubber tubing, to protect the mouth from the harshness of the metal bars.
B B B. Side pieces to keep the iron in its situation.
C. The handle.
D. The lower bar, attached to the handle.
E. The side piece, which can be raised or depressed.
F. The screw, at the extremity of the side piece.
G. The nut which, fastened to the handle, acts upon the screw and fixes its position.

The circle in the foregoing is left free on one side; thus, the inexpert have a little more time allowed for their movements. The arm could be retracted with greater ease, and the former danger was, in a great measure, removed. Still, this new shape was not wholly satisfactory. The form was fixed: horses are not all of one height, one breadth, or of one capacity. There are small creatures designated ponies; while horses are not rarely encountered of enormous proportions. As the iron has no power of being adapted, the form that should prove not large enough for one may be altogether disproportioned to another quadruped.

The weight of metal necessarily employed to assure the requisite strength, also rendered it inconvenient for a veterinary surgeon to carry more than one of these bulky articles; and though small was the amount of ingenuity which had hitherto been lavished on the improvement of the thing, for years it continued of the last character. Mr. Varnell, assistant professor at the Royal Veterinary College, however, appears to have entirely removed all former objections, and to have invented a balling-iron which seems to possess all the qualities that such an instrument is capable of exhibiting. The restraining bars of this last amendment are formed of polished steel, and are covered with a stout piece of India-rubber tubing, thus in some measure protecting the mouth of the creature from injury by what hitherto was the exposed metal. The lower bar, moreover, is attached to the handle, and the handle can be readily raised or depressed by turning the nut situated at its base. It can, therefore, be quickly adapted to any possible capacity of jaw.

THE USUAL MANNER OF GIVING A BALL.

Such a form of immunity is, however, seldom sought, save by the very inexperienced in the veterinary practice. A few years of active employment enables any person to discard this defense. A sufficient security is in all ordinary cases afforded by the horse's tongue, which, when a ball is about to be administered, is grasped by the left hand, and withdrawn to the right side of the mouth. The hand thus employed is fixed, being lightly pressed against the inferior margin of the lower jaw; for, when retained in such a position, the tongue is pressed upon the foremost of the huge molar teeth. Of course, the animal, thus held, cannot approximate its jaws so as seriously to harm the operator without biting its own flesh; by that circumstance is safety supposed to be rendered certain. But should violence be exerted, animal fear is apt to be superior to bodily pain; the tongue and arm may be simultaneously bitten through. The practiced veterinary surgeon, however, takes advantage of the first emotion of surprise which the creature experiences at the liberties taken with, and the indignities offered to, its person. Having the ball ready in the right hand, he, standing on the left side, quickly introduces the bolus into the wondering quadruped's mouth.

The medicine is lodged at the back portion of the tongue, whence, as the horse does not expectorate, the creature has no ability of expelling it, save only by coughing. During the spasm, which accompanies this act, the soft palate is raised and the ball is carried outward with the volume of violently-expired breath. Some horses acquire a habit of thus returning all forms of physic, and will cough up a ball twenty times. Such a circumstance illustrates the necessity of distracting the attention of the quadruped the instant the hand is retracted; for in the confusion of the moment the most inveterate "dodger" may be surprised into swallowing any abhorrent morsel.

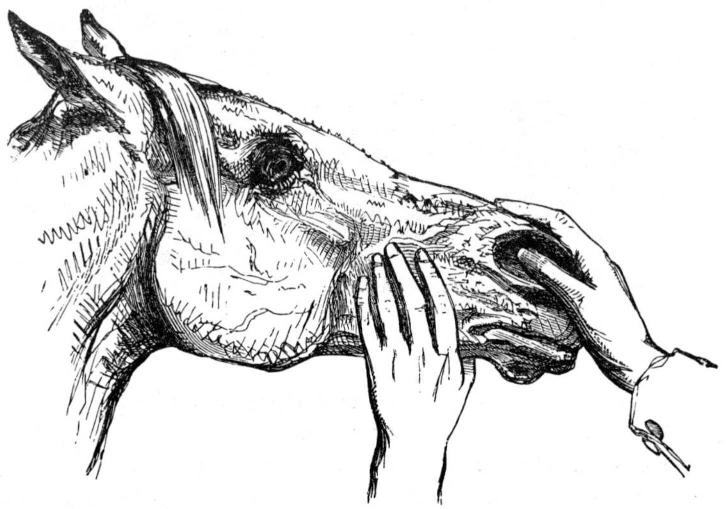

THE CUSTOMARY MODE OF DISTRACTING THE HORSE'S ATTENTION, AFTER IT HAS RECEIVED A BALL.

The hand, during the delivery of the ball, being rapidly thrust into the mouth, is frequently cut by the sharp edges of the molar teeth. No knowledge, which has hitherto been attained by veterinary science, can point out the animal possessed of grinders of this dangerous description, and the only protection as yet suggested is to cover the hand with a glove. But a glove cannot be washed and dried so readily as the hand;

it, moreover, is highly objectionable to introduce the saliva of one animal into the mouth of another, as disease may be thus conveyed from horse to horse also, it being impossible to provide a new glove with every fresh patient, the protection is not universally adopted.

The medicine being delivered, the hand is quickly withdrawn, and the jaws of the animal are clapped together. The nose is then rubbed somewhat roughly, for—the upper lip being the organ of prehension, as well as the seat of feeling, in the horse—this part is excited with the design of preventing the quadruped from dwelling too intently on the unpleasant nature of the substance which has just been forced into its mouth.

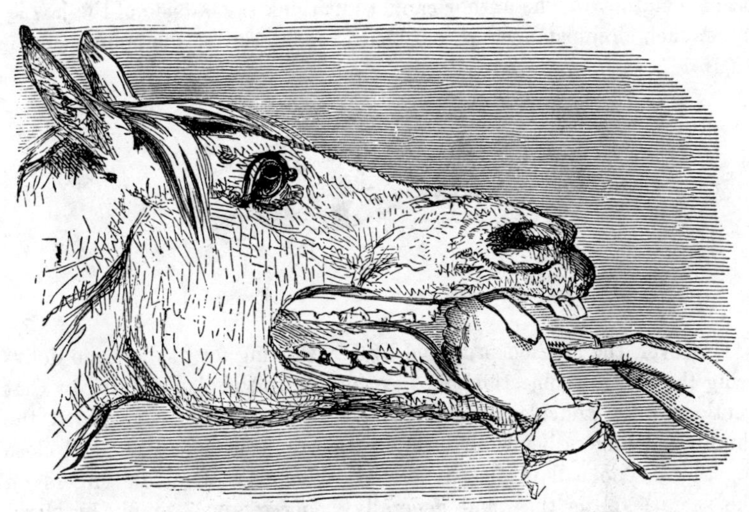

A BALL BEING ADMINISTERED ACCORDING TO MR. GOWING'S DIRECTION.

Mr. Gowing, the excellent veterinary surgeon, of Camden Town, has, with his usual ingenuity, endeavored to remove those objections to which the previous manner of delivering a ball is obviously liable. This gentleman grasps the tongue rather higher up than is customary; and, having done so, does not retract the member, but fixes the hand upon the gums which cover the upper margin of the lower jaw. The point of the tongue protrudes between the thumb and fingers, and it is then plain that the animal cannot close the mouth without biting upon its own flesh.

Yet candor obliges the author to state that he does not view this method of grasping the tongue as an improvement on the old practice. The tongue, not being drawn out of the mouth, is not so decidedly fixed upon the molar teeth; while the hand appears to be placed in a somewhat dangerous position. For if, under excitement, the horse can become so oblivious as actually to bite through its own flesh, how would the hand of the operator fare when the closing of the jaws should lacerate the lingual body? The only advantage which can attend upon Mr. Gowing's proposed plan must result from the smaller outrage it offers, thus leaving the amiable disposition of the animal the better chance of controlling its emotions.

It is, therefore, demonstrated the tongue can afford the operator no decided protection; the question, consequently, resolves itself into which of the methods affords the hand the greatest immunity, should the animal become alarmed. The author cannot but think the outside of the jaw is, under such circumstances preferable to the interior of the mouth.

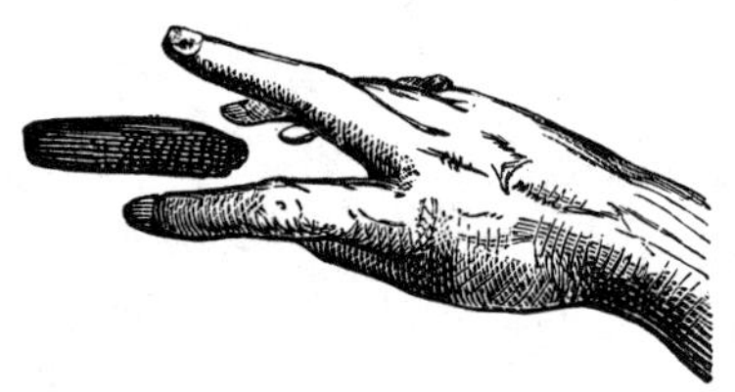

MR. GOWING'S EXCELLENT MANNER OF DELIVERING A BALL.

However, the method proposed by Mr. Gowing for holding and delivering the ball is unobjectionable. According to the plan adopted by that gentleman, the knuckles are not elevated; but the hand is extended, the thumb and fingers being all brought upon one level and all held close together. The ball is placed between the fore and middle fingers, on the same level as the hand generally, being retained simply by slight lateral pressure. In this position it is introduced, and evidently demands less space for its entrance than was required according to the former system. When the ball has been advanced to the desired situation, a separation of the fingers allows the morsel to drop into its place.

Some stress, however, is laid upon the manner of clasping the head after the ball has been lodged. Mr. Gowing claps-to the jaws and evidently contemplates holding them in apposition. This is a mistake; for the muscles of the horse are not to be controlled by the utmost power of the strongest human being. The old custom, which applied friction on the most sensitive portion of the horse's body, the writer esteems as better calculated to distract the attention of the quadruped.

The delivery of a horse ball is, however, rendered difficult in proportion to the number of persons who surround the animal, and to the noise made on the occasion. For the above reason, all the pupils at public schools have to learn this portion of their profession under heavy difficulties. The fuss which accompanies this simple operation in such institutions alarms the horse. It is turned round in its stall; the twitch is put upon the upper lip; a futile attempt is made to hold the jaws apart; while the nervousness of the young student who is about to perform,—all are likely to exercise an evil influence upon a sensitive and a timid creature.

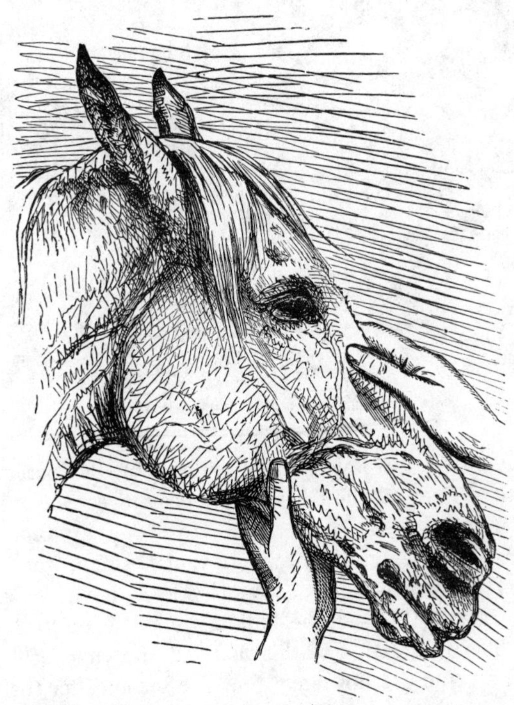

MR. GOWING'S METHOD OF GRASPING THE JAWS AFTER THE DELIVERY OF A BALL.

Veterinary surgeons, however, soon learn to give a ball with greater speed and with less ceremony. They go alone up to the head, and play for a time with the quadruped's face. Confidence being thus established, the practitioner gently withdraws the creature's tongue. This being accomplished, of course the jaws are sundered; when, without any sign of flurry, the hand is introduced into the cavity and the medicine properly lodged. After such a manner, the practiced veterinarian gives many balls in the course of the day, and is hardly ever known to fail. Indeed, were the practitioner, when going his rounds, to wait till four or five assistants could be collected ere he administered the requisite medicine, the duties of the day could never be discharged.

THE QUIET METHOD OF GIVING A BALL.

The physic being introduced into the mouth, the person who has undertaken to deliver it should on no account esteem his business finished, and thereon leave the stable. He should proceed to the left side of the horse and watch the neck. In that position, when the animal swallows, any substance can be seen to travel down the gullet; this proof having been witnessed, the building may be quitted with a safe conscience. The illustration of this fact was drawn on the wood correctly; but the artist did not make proper allowance for the transfer of his sketch by the engraver. The last process has made that which was originally on the left side of the neck appear as on the right side of the body.

Drinks or **draughts** are not in favor with the majority of veterinary surgeons. Most practitioners urge, in justification of their dislike to such a form of medicine, that solutions are attended with danger—being apt, when administered, to pass into the trachea, and thus to flow upon the lungs. Admitting this objection, it does not decide the question: for the advocates of solid physic can possess small experience if they are to be told that balls have proved injurious by also entering the forbidden channel. Likewise, that when the popular form of physic has grown hard, much harm has been occasioned by the mass becoming impacted within the gullet. Evil can, therefore, be caused by physic in either form, if given without the necessary caution; and the balance of fact can incline the judgment to neither one side nor the other.

A BALL PASSING DOWN THE HORSE'S GULLET.

But it is curious to read of serious dislike being entertained against drinks, and at the same time know that several practitioners are accustomed to administer this kind of medicine after a particular method, which evinces a desire to illustrate the very circumstance which constitutes the objection to every solid. Many country veterinarians are accustomed to pour all the liquids which they exhibit down the nostril of the animal. Now, the nostrils terminate immediately over the larynx —the direct channel is from one chamber into the other cavity—thus, any fluid administered after so unnatural a method will probably find its way on to the lungs.

Such an abuse of nature's designs being largely practiced upon a powerful quadruped, is proof of the perfect submission with which the creature has accepted its appointed master. Such an absolute negation of self, deserved considerate recognition from the reasoning and superior being. Veterinary medicines are too generally composed of pungent and of caustic materials, while the nostrils are lined with a highly sensitive and delicately moist mucous membrane. It was created to come in contact with the air, to which the nostrils in the horse afford the only legitimate passage. The notion of disregarding the mouth and selecting so tender a channel, down which to pour acrid and burning solutions, appears to be such a refinement upon ordinary barbarity as must puzzle the reader to discover a motive to excuse.

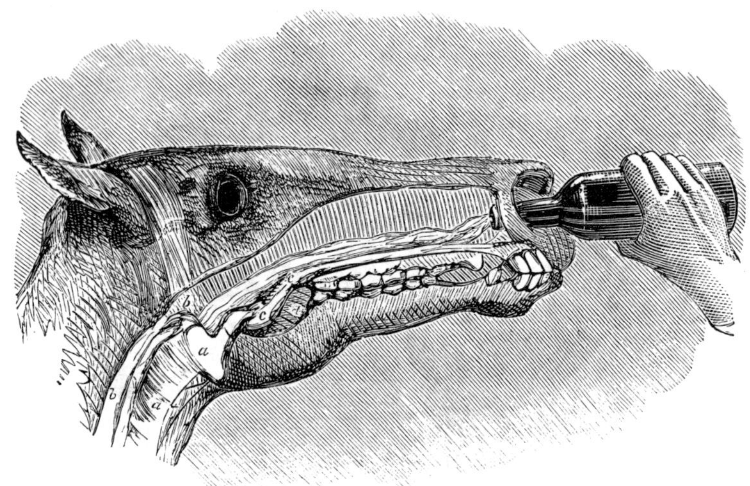

THE NATURAL CONSEQUENCE WHICH IS TO BE EXPECTED WHENEVER THE FILTHY CUSTOM OF POURING DRINKS INTO THE NASAL CHAMBER OF A HORSE IS ADOPTED.

a a. The windpipe. *b b.* The gullet. *c c.* The soft palate. *d.* The tongue.

The fact appears the more monstrous when we consider the practice is adopted by the veterinary surgeon, and that it is exhibited upon the sick horse whose welfare he is especially bound to conserve. The irritation consequent upon so abhorrent an abuse cannot but be most prejudicial to that quietude which is, upon every form of existence, healing in its effect. The motive which prompts so outrageous a proceeding is the love of display, acting upon an ignorant or unscrupulous individual; joined to this, is the knowledge that medicine can be administered with greater speed than when delivered according to the natural method. The horse has no power to check the course of any liquid emptied into the nostril of the elevated head; whereas the animal will frequently occupy a considerable time before a fluid, delivered by the mouth, is swallowed By one canal, the will is powerless; by the other channel, volition is operative. To save his time, as well as to excite surprise, are the only motives which can prompt a careless man to tamper with that welfare it is his duty to tenderly protect.

To render this subject the more intelligible to the reader, the natural process which enables the horse to imbibe liquids shall here be detailed. The mouth of this animal is peculiar for having at its backward extremity a fleshy screen, which hangs pendulous from the bony roof. This soft palate explains why the quadruped, under ordinary circumstances, breathes only through the nose; and why, when it vomits, the regurgitated matter is ejected by the nostrils. That specialty is of service, however, during the act of imbibition. The posterior entrance to the nasal chamber being open and the head in a pendulous position, were there no special provision to the contrary, the water, after having passed the mouth, would, from the mere force of gravity, have

FIG. 1.

DIAGRAM, (FIG. 1,) EXPLANATORY OF THE COMPOUND ACT OF DRINKING IN THE HORSE.

a a. The water drawn into the mouth and forced into the fauces by the compression of the forward part of the tongue and the enlargement of the backward portion of the organ.
b b. The fluid passing down the œsophagus or gullet.
c. The larynx, lowered to admit the passage of the liquid.
d d. The tongue, dilated at one place and contracted at another.
c. The soft palate, floated upward and effectually closing the nasal passages.

a tendency to return by the nostrils. This actually occurs whenever cold, strangles, influenza, sore throat, etc. interferes with the activity of the health of these parts now under consideration. Disease renders the organ sensitive, and tenderness makes the animal exert its volition to prevent the employment of the inflamed structure. In consequence of this cause, the nasal chambers are imperfectly closed, and a great portion of the fluid imbibed by the mouth flows forth again through the nostrils. Such a tendency to gravitate is, during health, effectually prevented by the soft palate. Before any substance can pass from the mouth toward the throat, that appendage must be raised, and its rising closes the posterior entrance to the nasal chambers.

The tongue is the primary agent employed when the animal slakes its thirst. The backward portion of the organ is contracted, and the forward part compressed by muscular volition, (*d d*, fig. 1.) A vacuum would thereby be created, were not the water propelled by atmospheric

Fig. 2.

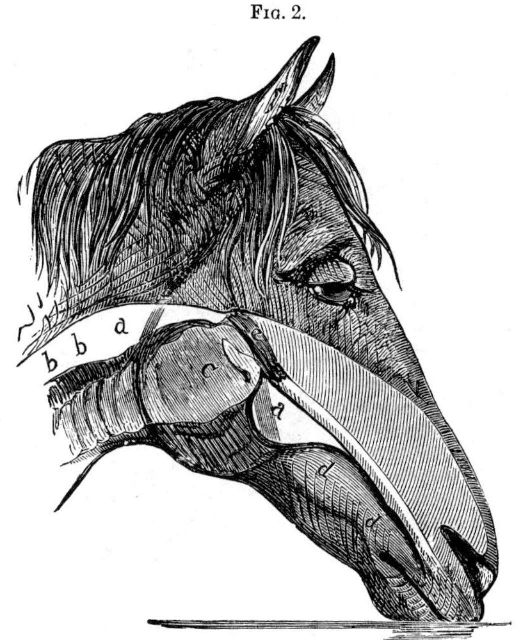

DIAGRAM, (FIG. 2,) EXPLANATORY OF THE COMPOUND ACT OF DRINKING.

a a. The water driven backward by the forward dilatation of the tongue and the upward movement of the larynx.
b b. The full current forced down the gullet.
c. The larynx propelled against the soft palate.
d d. The tongue, dilated anteriorly and compressed posteriorly.
e. The soft palate.

pressure into the void thus formed, (*a*, fig. 1.) The posterior of the tongue is then relaxed, while the anterior division of the organ is pressed against the roof of the mouth, (*d d*, fig. 2.) The fluid is thereby driven to the backward part of the cavity, (*a*, fig. 2.) The tongue, during the act, continues to alternate the states of contraction and relaxation, each motion of the lingual agent serving to pump the water into the fauces, (*a*, fig. 1.) But, before that can be accomplished, the soft palate must be elevated. The soft palate (*e*, fig. 2) then closes the nostrils, (*e*, fig. 1;) and also in its course to take this position sets in motion the cartilages of the larynx. The last cover over and effectually protecting the windpipe, (*c*, fig. 1,) the fluid is forced onward by the contraction of the tongue, passes into a secure chamber, the roof and floor of which are but of temporary formation, (*a*, fig. 1.) Here it remains only during the inactivity of the larynx. The upward motion of the latter body (*c*, fig. 2) propels the fluid into the pharynx, whence involuntary contractility sends it into the gullet, the muscular action of which tube conveys it onward to the stomach, (*a b b*, fig. 2.)

From the foregoing explanation, the reader is in a position to judge whether the nasal chamber is a fit passage for acrimonious mixtures, since he now understands the evident pains the *All-wise* has bestowed to prevent the temperate fluid, of which the animal customarily partakes, from intruding upon the elaborate, delicate, and highly sensitive membrane that lines the air-passages. All veterinary students are not educated men, neither are all attentive to their studies while at college; but it should require an extraordinary amount of ignorance and conceit to thus grossly misconceive the *intentions* which are so plainly impressed upon the body of the quadruped.

The author, however, doubts if those objections generally advanced to drinks are in any degree derived from the results of actual experience. Balls can be manufactured by the score, and then stored away for subsequent use. Drinks would decompose if thus mixed and kept ready in the surgery. Drinks must be separately compounded, as required. Balls occupy little space, and being solid can be safely carried or forwarded to any distance. Drinks being contained in bottles, are less convenient for transport, and the vessels are liable to fracture. Balls, moreover, are to be quickly thrust down an animal's throat; require no assistance for their administration; and being wrapped in paper are not exposed to inquisitive discussion as to their ingredients. Drinks being inclosed in glass, protected only by a cork, are open to investigation, and likely to provoke remarks which are not always soothing to the pride of a pretender; liquids likewise necessitate more time should be devoted to their exhibition, and generally require the assistance which is not invariably at hand to aid the veterinary surgeon.

The above reasons and objections are not without influence upon practitioners, whose earnings are greatly dependent upon the speed of their movements; who generally give the medicines to those animals they treat, and habitually carry with them, ready compounded, the drugs which they administer. Drinks, moreover, demand several bulky articles for their proper administration, and are apt to soil the person who delivers them. Balls, as a rule, call for no other apparatus than the hand. Moreover, it causes delay at starting, if there are twenty or thirty drinks to be previously mixed, bottled, labeled, incased in paper and so packed as to be in no peril of breakage; whereas any number of balls can be almost instantaneously transferred from the drawer in the surgery into the gig at the door.

The usual mode of giving a drink is, moreover, a complex business. A twitch is mostly kept in regularly appointed stables, and the string or loop is fixed over the animal's upper jaw, prior to other measures being proceeded with. The groom then grasps the stick and takes his place by the shoulder of the horse. At a previously arranged signal, he raises the pole; the string, paining the gums under which it is fixed, causes the head of the quadruped to be elevated. Supposing the horn having the larger mouth to be employed, the drink is then emptied into the hollow of this rude appliance until the liquid nearly fills the interior. The fluid is next carried upward, two fingers of the operator's left hand being fastened on to the gums, so as to further expand the jaws and enable the veterinary surgeon to steady his body while straining to administer the medicine. The large end is pushed into the quadruped's mouth, and, by a sudden movement of the wrist, the contents of the horn are meant to be splashed upon the animal's tongue.

THE COMMON FORM OF THE HORN EMPLOYED TO ADMINISTER DRINKS.

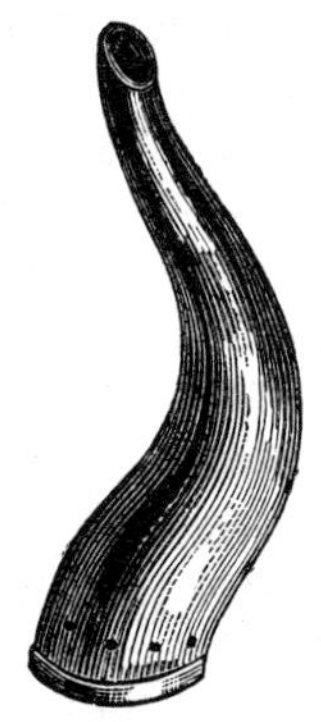
AN IMPROVED FORM OF HORN.

This, which is the more common method of administering a drink, is open to several objections. The horn, being of a limited capacity, can hold but a small quantity; and the lengthened time required for frequent replenishing, necessitates that the animal should be long held in an attitude of unnatural constraint. In the next place, the fluid is, by the action of the wrist, rather rudely thrown, than gently emptied, into the mouth, much of the medicine is generally lost, and no little of it, guided by the inserted fingers of the operator, is apt to find its way down the sleeve of his left arm.

To remedy these obvious defects, the tip of the horn was sawn off; while a piece of wood supplied a bottom to the larger extremity. A rude bottle was thus formed that would hold a larger amount of fluid. and from which the medicine could flow more gradually. The smaller opening afforded greater facilities for inserting that end between the horse's extended jaws, and was less likely to pain, when introduced into the animal's mouth. Still, drinks usually consisted of much more than the horn of an ox would contain, and as the smaller opening demanded greater care, when the article was being replenished, little time was saved by the last improvement.

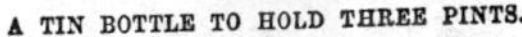

A TIN BOTTLE TO HOLD THREE PINTS.

THE MANNER OF USING THE TIN BOTTLE.

A large tin bottle was next employed. It is of dimensions sufficiently capacious to require no replenishing; this was an advantage in one direc tion, an objection in the other; for in proportion to size it became inconvenient to transport. It rather aggravated than ameliorated the fault urged against drinks, because of their bulk. The mode of its employment is made plain in the right-hand illustration, where a loop of string is depicted as hung upon the prong of a pitchfork, and is made to do duty for a twitch—such a substitute being far from unusual, even in well-appointed stables.

Should the operator, having much fluid at command, fill the mouth too full, or the animal cough during the time of its administration, the administrator is saturated with the medicine. Any irritation of the larynx is invariably productive of this effect; the result of which a reader will the better understand, after the relative situation of those who are engaged in delivering a drench is fully comprehended.

The misfortunes which the delivery of drinks almost necessarily involve, will very readily account for any amount of dislike to the fluid form of medicine, more especially when it is stated that veterinary surgeons are somewhat slow in adopting new ideas, but seem, with the fervor and tenacity ignorance displays toward a favorite superstition, to love and cling to the practices in which they have been educated.

GENERAL METHOD OF ADMINISTERING A DRINK TO A HORSE.

Else, it must have occurred to some member of a large profession that to violently oppose the instincts of an animal was hardly commendable in people who professed an observance and a worship of nature's teaching. Most animals, however, and the horse among the number, lower the mouth during the act of drinking. The veterinary surgeon, when proceeding in his professional capacity, employs a twitch, with which the head is to be violently upheld while a fluid is being deglutated.

To illustrate the consequence of such conduct, the reader will pardon the author if he state the results of such opposite proceedings upon a dog in his possession. A saucer of milk being placed upon the floor, the head is lowered and the liquid lapped, without the act being characterized by any unusual circumstance. But should the vessel be held on the ordinary level of the mouth, the draught is certain to be interrupted by repeated fits of coughing. Now, the danger that exists of the horse coughing and spasmodically drawing the fluid upon the lungs, constitutes the strongest argument urged against the administration of drinks; but such an objection sounds oddly if he who listens to it is aware that, during the administration of fluids, the horse's mouth is fixed according to the manner which will certainly provoke the obnoxious act in another quadruped.

GIVING A DRINK, ACCORDING TO THE QUIET METHOD.

All this is very sad and may readily be corrected. Let men endeavor to rightfully interpret the disposition of the horse. The creature is a most pleasant study; it is so timid, so loving and so confiding, that it immediately responds to the kindness which is intelligible to its understanding. Should it hang back, the fault rather lies with its limited comprehension than with the promptings of its inclination. Let the person who intends to deliver a drink fearlessly approach the animal: allow the huge nostrils to smell their new acquaintance, and not till the process is concluded, proceed to such trivial familiarities as may establish perfect trustfulness between the man and his dependent. So soon as the steed's confidence is gained, the animal is all submission to the pleasure of its superior. Then let the practitioner uncork the bottle, and, putting the left hand gently under the quadruped's jaw, empty with the other the contents, gradually, through the interspace which divides the incisors from the molar teeth.

But when adopting the above plan, the operator must be alone. No noisy or officious assistant must be near at hand to excite alarm or to create distrust. No pain must be inflicted; no angry words should be employed; no violent or hasty action ought to be used to frighten native susceptibility. All must be quiet. Should the animal be slow to swallow a nauseous draught, the creature must not be scolded for a natural dislike; but it should be encouraged by kind and cheerful accents, spoken as softly as though the words were addressed to a sick child. So alive is the equine heart to the seductiveness of benevolence, so unsuspecting is the full confidence of its species, and so happy is its spirit made by the praises of its superior, that rather than not deserve his commendation it will gulp down the most distasteful solution.

Blistering.—It is not praiseworthy to the human race that the animal given to man, with a mind thus impressible and yearning for kindness, should be treated with severity, and regarded as a brute, to be beaten and to be subdued. Such, however, is the case, and upon the poor body of this amiable life all kinds of cruelties are practiced. There is no barbarity more common than to blister the legs of the quadruped. Only of late years has the blistering application been somewhat reduced in strength; but it is still far more potent than is necessary. Our fathers, however, added all kinds of fiery and irritating drugs to Spanish fly, and never used to filter the extract; whereby particles got into the sores and cracks induced by the blister, and it was common for large pieces of skin to be removed by the sloughing process. A blemish was thus created.

Horses have perished under the agony attendant upon the blistering of all four feet. It is, however, still a recognized custom for horse doctors to score a leg or sometimes two legs with the red-hot iron, and over the lines thus created on a living frame to apply a liquid blister. To fully appreciate the abhorrent barbarity or the inutility of such a custom, the reader must recognize that animals suffer awfully from the wounds occasioned by fire, and understand that the sores are newly made, when the irritating liquid is placed upon the tender parts. A blister necessitates that the oil which contains the extract of the fly should be thoroughly rubbed in. Therefore the horse, when blistered, after having been fired, has to endure the friction of a rough hand, applied with all the coarse energy of an uneducated man, made upon a member smarting under the agony produced by the agent of which the creature has an instinctive dread.

Blisters, as at present used, are far too powerful. Were they diluted with three times their bulk of bland oil, or of solution of soap, they would be equally effective and far less dangerous. But, unfortunately, there is a prejudice among the partially educated, to which class nearly all veterinary surgeons belong, in favor of potency in their applications. Such persons seem to reckon the benefit to be produced according to the strength of the agent employed. By what other reason is it possible to explain the foolish perversity which still clings to the abuse of the heated iron? By what other motive can we account for the prejudice which tempts the use of the fearful blistering oil, as now commonly exhibited?

The parts of the horse most generally blistered are the legs, and the explanation commonly given to excuse the folly is a desire "to freshen the old animal on the pins," or "to brighten up the manner of going." The legs are parts of the living frame, and one part can hardly fail without the general system sympathizing. The author was once as tired as the horse commonly may be supposed to be; but, on that occasion, his feet were restored long before his body recovered from its exhaustion. Such a personal testimony seems to witness that fatigue affects the system generally. Indeed, the legs may be the means of progression; but it is the life which puts them in action, and it is the nerves which transmit energy to the muscles; none less ignorant than the generality of veterinary surgeons and the lower order of horse proprietors, would have conceived the possibility of restoring animation to a debilitated system by torturing the parts in which the symptoms of decay are most prominently testified.

Moreover, there is a maxim, first made known by John Hunter, and subsequently recognized by the profession of which he was the ornament. This maxim declares that "two great inflammations cannot exist in the same body at the same time." Upon the truth of this discovery, the practice of counter-irritation is based. Then to fire and to blister simultaneously may increase the torture of the poor existence thus barbarously treated; but, according to the doctrine largely accepted by the medical profession of this country, the double process accomplishes nothing surgical or curative, since the blister must destroy the action of the fire; and the man who is greedy to obtain the benefits of both operations, secures the advantages of neither measure.

To blister, however, is a very antique custom; so, also, is the application of fire, which was first performed upon the human body. Old medicine does not bear a very good character, and only exemplifies the much which suffering can endure, or the little which cruelty can accomplish. So far as horses are concerned, little would be sacrificed were the entire list of vesicatories lost to the knowledge of mankind. The blister is, according to present veterinary practice, employed more often to gratify the passing whim of some wayward proprietor than with any medical intention or with the remotest regard for the quadruped. A man, while lounging through the stable of an evening, a prey to lassitude and the victim of idle thoughts, but without the slightest pretense to medical knowledge, may conceive he will have the entire stable blistered "right through," and few veterinary surgeons will presume to expostulate with so wild a notion.

The compliance of the professional attendant is, however, in strict keeping with opinions implied by the expressions commonly employed by "horsemen." Thus, it is very general to hear these persons speak of—"a good horse with battered legs"—"a beautiful animal, but with legs that have done their work"—"an excellent frame, but not having a leg to stand upon," etc. Such phrases are sheer nonsense! But they serve to countenance the equine superstition which regards the legs as distinct from the body. The stable-man cannot conceive a want of liveliness in the motions to be one of the indications of failing health. Yet this symptom pervades all nature. It is exhibited by beasts, by birds, by fishes, and by insects; nay, the very vegetables, when disease attacks them, no longer spread their branches to the breeze, but droop their heads and incline their bodies earthward.

To propagate such opinions, however, must destroy much of the power so dearly loved by the vulgar horse owner, and abolish much of the pleasure such a person experiences when surveying his long rows of miserable dependents! These men are always corrupt! It is astonishing how unfitted human frailty is to possess absolute authority in any shape! The men who live and think in stables are never so happy as when exercising their despotic power. The next illustration is an example of this fact. An omnibus proprietor has entered to speak with a veterinary surgeon, who is witnessing the man's orders fulfilled on the fore-legs of a wretched stud. Let the reader contemplate this engraving, and he will soon perceive the animals stand in need of something far less costly than any mixture which can proceed from the cheapest pharmacy.

It will be remarked that the creatures represented are separated by "bales," or long poles, suspended by chains from the ceiling. This kind of arrangement permits more horses to be packed into a limited apartment, and is, therefore, adopted whenever the expense of lodging becomes a primary consideration. It will also have occurred to the spectator that the roof is depicted as very low, and the gangway or free thoroughfare behind the animals is exhibited as exceedingly narrow.

Now, creatures imprisoned in such a building are actually perishing of starvation! The food, the water, and the medical attendance may each of its kind be unexceptionable; but the animals housed in such a locality soon droop from positive inanition. To breathe, is the primary necessity of existence. There is no living thing that can thrive where air is excluded. The quadrupeds represented below have to pass twenty-two out of every twenty-four hours in a locality barely lofty enough for each to stand upright in. Let the reader, knowing the duration of captivity, conjecture how long it will be ere the huge lungs of a horse have inhaled and contaminated the limited amount of atmosphere which the place can contain, even were such an abode contemplated as the dwelling of a single subject.

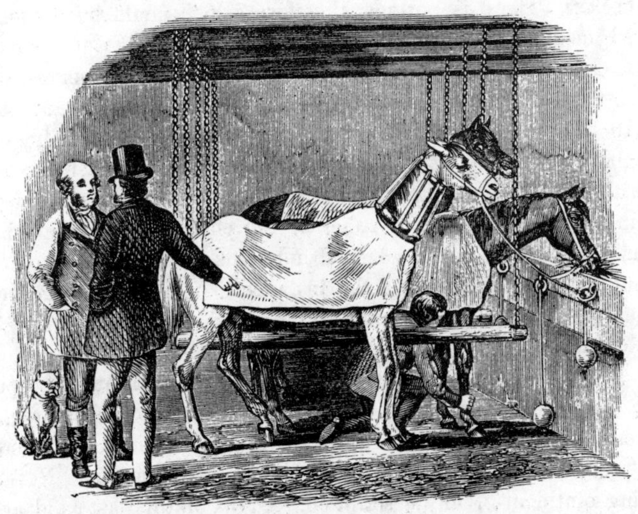

BLISTERING A STABLEFUL OF OMNIBUS HORSES.

It is true, such sheds are seldom air tight. Were all draughts excluded, the prisoners would speedily be released from their captivity; but the wind holes, though large enough to prolong misery, are too small to render such places the abodes of health. The wretched inmates cannot be tortured into a show of activity. When will the legislature, in its wisdom, notice these hot-beds of contagion? When will it empower the police officer to enter any stable and authorize him to destroy the animals therein, hopelessly diseased and purposely concealed? Who can, viewing the stables where the hardest worked of the equine race are stowed away, wonder that glanders is rarely absent from such nurseries for contamination?

Horses have thus been housed, and have been physicked, fired, and blistered, for ages. The folly of such practices is continued even to the present hour. However, let the gentleman who keeps his stable filled take warning from the errors of his inferiors; and when the groom informs him that "Blossom" is getting stale upon her legs, refuse to have the creature tortured. A blister incapacitates a horse for six weeks. The cessation of toil for such a period may do good; but let the man who pretends to judge in this matter grant the holiday which the measures, if adopted, would occupy, and employ the time in looking jealously around his premises to ascertain wherefore his dumb servant flags!

Let no man blister a horse's legs. There is no motor agent situated in or near to those parts. The shin, foot, and pastern are almost without muscles. There is nothing, therefore, which could be freshened or rendered more brisk. But these parts are susceptible of the acutest agony. They are largely supplied with purely sensitive nerves. Consequently, let all gentlemen discharge the veterinary surgeon who proposes to blister the legs of their horses. He does so merely to gain time: the professional man is totally unworthy of confidence who can play with his employers' ignorance and tamper with his patients' sensations, merely from reasons of policy or the chance of pecuniary benefit to himself! The author has beheld hundreds of blisters applied to the legs, but he cannot remember the instance in which such applications were productive of the slightest good.

Blisters are seldom required, and are only beneficial as counter-irritants. Equine medicines are generally too coarse, and much too powerful. Some practitioners mingle euphorbium, corrosive sublimate, aqua fortis, etc. with the blistering agent, to increase its potency. Therefore, never procure the oil of cantharides from a veterinarian. Never use blistering ointment of any description. Stuffs of this last kind are, for the most part, made of the refuse flies, exhausted by having been used to form the oil of cantharides. Buy the oil of some respectable chemist. Add to this four times its bulk of olive oil; should it not blister after it has been once used, it may be rubbed in a second or a third time. Counter-irritation is certain to be thus secured, and vesication is only a sign which pleases the uneducated eye rather than benefits the animal.

Never employ any oil that is not perfectly clear. It should be filtered after it is made, and the slightest opacity is proof that some impurity is present. This direction is imperative; for, though the ingredients which compose the oil are not expensive, there is scarcely an article in the pharmacopœia more liable to adulteration. Let, therefore, the liquid seem as transparent as that which is represented in the accompanying illustration.

A BOTTLE CONTAINING OIL OF CANTHARIDES.

It is a common custom with most veterinarians to purge the horse before they blister its legs. The intention is to remove any lurking irritability out of the animal's system; but such irritability will most probably be provoked by their coarse and potent blistering agents; therefore, a purgative, by increasing the debility, is only likely to render the quadruped more sensitive to outward impressions. A nice "freshener" is embodied, to the eye of reason, in a drastic purgative, followed by an active irritant applied to a most sensitive part of the body!

Whenever a blister is adopted, rather too little than too much oil should be used. Enough to permeate the hair and reach the skin is imperative; but the action rather depends on the amount of friction which accompanies the agent than on the quantity of the vesicatory that may be employed. The friction should be regulated by the condition of the surface on which the oil has to act, and all adjacent tender places, as the points of flexion in joints, parts where the skin is thin or is thrown into crevices, should be previously covered with a layer of simple cerate, after the method exemplified in the left-hand illustration on the next page, wherein the back of the pastern is exhibited as thus protected.

After the part has been rubbed for ten minutes in summer, and a quarter of an hour during winter, all oil may be wiped off the hair. Its presence there can do no good; but as oil becomes more liquid with the continuance of warmth, the heat of the body may cause the blistering agent to run on to parts which it is not desirable to subject to its action.

After the horse has been blistered, it is customary to tie up the head and put around the animal's neck a kind of rude apparatus denominated, but wherefore the author cannot tell, "a cradle." This last instrument is designed to prevent the creature from gnawing the blistered surface. No such act will, however, be indulged where the agent employed is proportioned to the sensitiveness of the quadruped; but it is the agony produced by the effect of undue stimulation which generates the madness that induces the wretched creature to use its formidable teeth in tearing its own flesh.

THE BACK OF THE PASTERN AND THE HEEL PROTECTED BY BEING COATED WITH A THICK LAYER OF SIMPLE CERATE

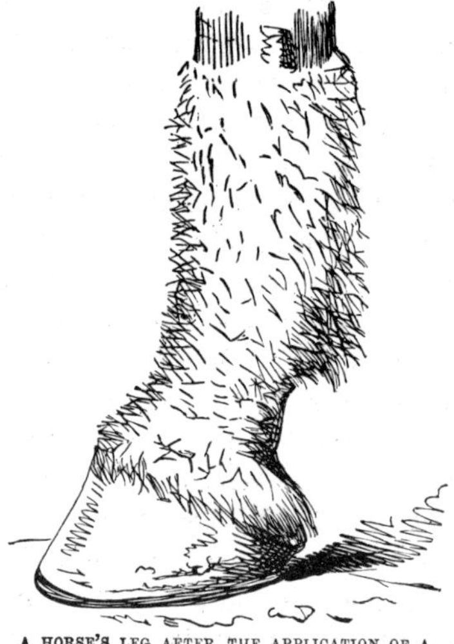

A HORSE'S LEG AFTER THE APPLICATION OF A BLISTER.

About three days after the application of the blister, the surface will have become dry and incrusted with a solid exudation. It is well, at this period, to soften the part with some emollient liquid, and one can hardly be found better suited to this purpose than that known as **lead liniment.** It is made by mingling together one part of Goulard's lotion

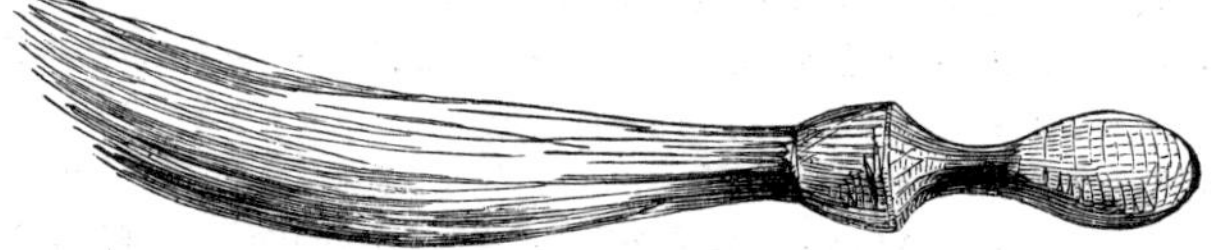

A BRUSH FOR APPLYING LEAD LINIMENT TO THE LEG OF A HORSE WHICH HAS RECENTLY BEEN BLISTERED.

and two parts of olive oil, whereby is formed a thick creamy compound. The oil soothes the harshness of the exudation, while the lead serves to mitigate any pain which may reside in the part. This mixture, being well shaken, is applied to the surface by means of what cooks call "a paste brush."

The liniment usually causes the "crusts" to fall off; but the hair generally comes off at the same time, testifying the severe irritation to which the skin has been subjected.

The most pliant medical individual—the pedantic man who always acknowledges everything emanating from the schools to be correct—would, the author imagines, be puzzled to discover any necessary connection between the processes of **balling, blistering, firing,** and **bleeding**; yet somehow the four operations are associated in veterinary practice. A ball reduces the bodily activity; a bleeding lowers the action of vitality; irritants are thought to stimulate organs to which they are applied, but to lessen the general tonicity. An animal subjected to the first action appears fitted to dispense with the second; while the last two seem somewhat similar to the first. But there is no accounting for incongruities when men, deserting reason, consent to adopt routine as a guide in the treatment of so capricious a development as disease.

Bleeding.—To lose blood was once deemed a healthful custom by the human race. Then, horses were regularly depleted every rise and fall. An old practitioner can remember the period when, on a Sunday morning, he beheld long sheds full of agricultural quadrupeds waiting to be bled. The fleam used to be struck into the first horse; then the entire row were, in succession, similarly treated. The operator afterward returned, and, pinning up the wound which had been made in the neck of the first animal, again moved down the line, pinning as he went. No account was taken of the amount lost by each patient, nor was any pains thought needful to control the current that flowed upon the ground; but the creatures did not all suffer an equal depletion. The fleam was soon struck; to pin up, however, took a comparatively long time for its performance. The first horse of the group, therefore, lost but little blood; while the last of the line bled for a considerable period before its turn to be attended to arrived.

The foregoing anecdote will show how nice our fathers were in their operations; but it is sad when we reflect that all this carnage was a sacrifice made to a mistaken idea. Human medicine has abandoned the antiquated custom. Veterinary physic, however, is not quite so versatile; still many quiet spots in the country may be found where old physic is in force, both with the employers and the practitioner. Dogs, even in the metropolis, are sometimes bled; and there still exist persons who esteem the use of the lancet upon these animals to be a laudatory accomplishment. Cats were, formerly, operated upon; and the author knows an aged lady whose medical practice was confined to depleting grimalkins. There exist, even at the present enlightened period, few of the equine species which do not bear several scars, each testifying to a separate operation. Raise the jugular vein in the neck of any animal, by simply stopping the downward current that flows through the vessel; it is ten to one but numerous circular prominences will bulge forth, to denote the medical activity which has been lavished on the quadruped.

No matter what may be the age, the condition, or the occupation of the horse, certain practitioners always discover that the mute drudge requires depletion; thus, an unscrupulous man may at most times earn a ready shilling by performing an easy operation. Every kind of animal is liable to be so treated or so abused; and there are very few stables throughout this kingdom in which the sight of the fleam, blood stick, and can do not create the groom's delight. The strangest fact is, that most rural proprietors love to see the purple life drained from the necks of their possessions; and bitter are the reproaches usually lavished on the veterinarian should a horse perish of any disease without the fatal termination having been hastened by the favorite measure. Indeed so fully are several country practitioners aware of this probability, that it is customary with them, when alone, to strike the vein and to pin up the orifice immediately. The necessary sign can then be adduced, should death end the case; and a professional reputation be thereby saved from the assaults of aggravated stupidity.

RAISING THE JUGULAR VEIN.

To show the necessity of venesection in most forms of disease, the author must be pardoned if he intrudes upon the reader a portion of his own experience. Some years ago a medical man, then residing in West bourne Terrace, kept a well-stocked stable. The family going out of town during the autumn, some of the animals, much against the author's opinion, were allowed a few weeks' "run at grass."

When the horses were taken up, none were found to have been benefited; but one was discovered to be much worse for its period of liberty. It was very weak, and its constitution evidently was shaken, for nothing seemed capable of invigorating it. If put into harness and driven merely round to the street door, the body was sure to be white with perspiration, and the poor quadruped exhibited signs of exhaustion. If permitted to remain in the stable, the creature would generally be found with the head depressed, the corn untouched, the breathing audible, and the body leaning for support against the trevise.

The animal was in this state when the family again left London for a few weeks; the horse was taken with them by railroad. Before they quitted town, the author found occasion to speak with the proprietor. The writer said that, during the sojourn of the family in the country, it was probable the urgency of the symptoms would necessitate the calling in of a local veterinary surgeon; therefore the proprietor was warned that the ailing quadruped was on no account to be bled; for to deplete a life in so exhausted a condition was positive slaughter.

As the author had conjectured, so events literally happened. The symptoms suddenly became alarming. The attendance of the nearest veterinarian was requested. To him the warning given to the proprietor was repeated. The gentleman replied that the author had not seen the animal in its then serious state, or he could not have tendered such advice. Medical etiquette forbade positive injunctions. The operation was performed, and the family returned to town leaving a carcass behind them!

It is very seldom that the system of a horse, when doing full work, can endure depletion. The labor is exhausting, and the toil is sufficiently severe to employ it all had the animal twice its normal energy. Many observant stable-men are of opinion that, nurture as they may, the provender consumed cannot be equal to the work. There are, however, too many persons who study to underfeed, and who nevertheless are morally convinced that every quadruped in their keeping not only possesses a sufficiency of vigor, but can part with a gallon or two of blood, twice in every year, with positive advantage.

Here are two opposite convictions; and the cost of horse flesh to each party, could we inspect the private accounts, would certainly best settle the dispute. But as men mostly object to laying open their books to public investigation, we must, therefore, endeavor to decide this point by drawing inferences, after having submitted the lives of most quadrupeds to review. None, except the wealthy, keep horses, save for use. The feelings of men are seldom gratified by feeding idle animals. Two horses very commonly have to perform extra duty, while the master is looking about him and in no haste to purchase a third laborer. Rarely do we find three animals are kept where the owner has full employment only for two of his slaves.

The horse, therefore, is generally worked to the limits of its strength. That there may be no doubt upon this matter, the person who has to judge of its capabilities is he who has an interest in the amount of an animal's exertions. The fact is, however, proved by the wonder excited when a quadruped is recorded to have reached the natural period of its existence. The great majority of horses in this country perish of exhaustion before their maturity has been attained. The sad reality, that of the numbers reared in England the great majority of humanity's humble, obedient, and willing slaves are goaded to early graves, before all their second teeth are up, and before the consolidation of their bones fits them to endure the strain of fatigue, too fearfully establishes the fate which beauty and submission receives at the hands of avarice.

Man is a hard task-master! He was so when the pyramids were raised; he is so still in the Southern States of America. There is something wrong in the creature who can thus abuse all that serve him. Had the horse twenty times its present strength, it would still be below the point of human requirement. It is a very painful occupation to look into a London street, and, having an understanding which can interpret equine significances, to observe the lame, the deformed, the starved, the overloaded, and the weary animals staggering along the thoroughfare, but to perceive none without the goad, to enforce exertion, flourished by its side. Yet the creatures thus used, unconscious of a holiday and worked through sickness or through suffering, are thought by some persons to possess such a redundancy of health that they can support or be benefited by the life's blood being drained, at stated periods, out of their wretched bodies!

Nevertheless it is possible a timely depletion may, upon certain occasions, save life. Neither the present reader nor the writer may witness so rare an occurrence; yet because of the possibility, every horseman should be equal to such an emergency. For the performance of so trivial an operation certain tools are imperatively necessary. The first among these is a **blood can** or a tin pail, which is generally divided, by indented lines, into eight equal sections. The receptacle being made to contain two gallons, each compartment, when filled, indicates a quart to have been withdrawn. Wretched horses

A BLOOD CAN, WHICH IS MARKED TO INDICATE WHEN A QUART OF FLUID HAS BEEN EXTRACTED.

have been drained to a greater extent even than two gallons; but should the reader possess a blood can, it is hoped that it will be indeed an extreme case in which he would behold the vessel once filled.

One or two quarts should be the limits of an ordinary venesection; but even that quantity may be of much more service, when aiding the circulation, than when withdrawn and permitted to coagulate apart from the body. Many practitioners, however, deplete without either excuse or justification. Having opened a vessel, they will allow the stream to flow until the poor horse staggers. Some are proud not to possess a blood can; but they hold up the stable pail to catch the vital current, and are quite content that the most ample drain of the system, conducted under their supervision, cannot be otherwise than restorative.

The next instrument requisite is a **fleam.** This article is much preferable to the lancet, though there exists a species of foppery among veterinary surgeons which tempts them to employ human implements.

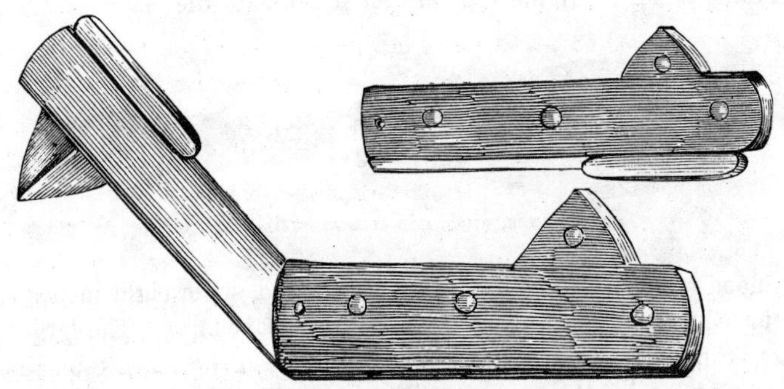

FLEAMS, OF THE NEWEST FORM, OPEN AND SHUT.

For that reason they flourish a lancet as the more scientific indicator. A lancet is, certainly, necessary to puncture the eye vein, which is visible upon the cheek of the horse; but as regards a vessel which is as large as a cart rope, for such is the dimensions of the animal's jugular, this last cannot demand the exhibition of vast scientific attainment to pierce it, or admit of the display of nice manipulation in him who operates on such a structure. For this reason the old-fashioned fleam is very much to be preferred. Assuredly it does not appear so pretty as the lancet; but it always cuts with certainty and leaves a limited orifice; whereas the more genteel blade has inflicted awkward gashes upon living flesh when the creature proved restless under its infliction.

The instrument with which the veterinarian extracts blood has been represented having the blade bared and having it closed. It is readily admitted not to be of an inviting aspect; but it is not in reality quite so barbarous as it appears to the beholder. The point which projects from one side of the blade marks the extent of its cutting surface, and indicates the size of that puncture which the fleam can leave behind. It is more safe than the lancet, which, though of a more innocent aspect, has inflicted wounds of awful dimensions. For the last reason, the employment of the lancet by veterinary surgeons is not to be commended.

Above the cutting point of the fleam, and upon the opposite side of the blade, is seen what is intended to represent a bulging piece of metal. That indicates the place which the operator occasionally strikes with the side of his hand; its intention is to afford a blunt surface for delivery of the blow. It is advantageous to possess a fleam of the above form, because, under rare circumstances, the possibility for which it provides may be encountered; but for general use a blood stick is more instantaneous, and is more certain in its result; wherefore it is to be preferred to the human hand, as giving the smarter impetus to the blade.

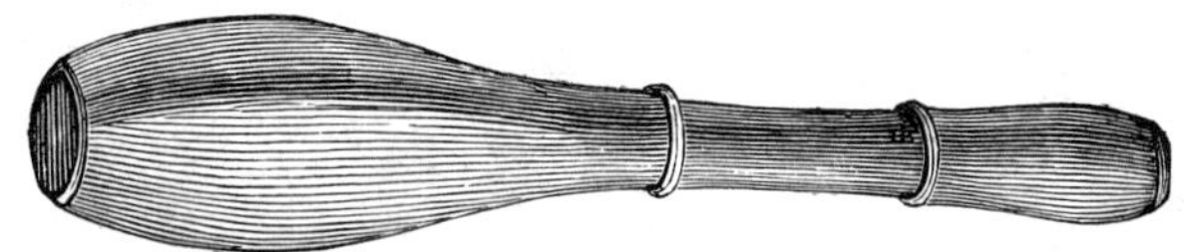

A BLOOD STICK, WHICH IS LOADED AT THE LARGER END.

A **blood stick** is merely a hard piece of wood, six or eight inches long, and turned in a lathe till it has assumed the above form. The larger end is then hollowed; the cavity is loaded with lead. Such a tool, though very diminutive, can be made to deal a heavy blow, and it is quite powerful enough to send the point of the fleam through the skin and thin layer of muscular fiber which externally cover the jugular vein.

However, before any attempt is made to bleed the horse, the animal's eyes should be bandaged. This should invariably be done before the fleam or blood stick are produced; as some quadrupeds show their intelligence by dreading the operation which most veterinary surgeons regard with complacency. Many persons doubt whether beasts are gifted with imagination; but it is not rare to encounter a steed which will stagger at the sight of a fleam, and when the blood stick and can are produced, will give every indication of approaching syncope. Consequently, if the reader is determined to have his horse depleted, let the eyes be disabled before any instrument is produced, more especially before the stick is attempted to be employed. Most animals, from natural timidity, shrink if they can discern when the blow is about to be delivered, and the point of the fleam is thereby frequently displaced.

The sight should first be obscured; then the vessel raised; afterward the fleam arranged upon the huge pipe thus brought into view; when a sudden blow being dealt with the blood stick will cause the current to spurt forth. Should any accident prevent the first attempt from being successful, the operator should not strike twice in the same place. Repeated blows upon the same spot are likely to bruise the part, or to cause a ragged wound; neither of which circumstances are favorable to the healing process. Leave the slight incision to nature, for it very rarely requires any treatment, and choosing a fresh mark, repeat the process with better success.

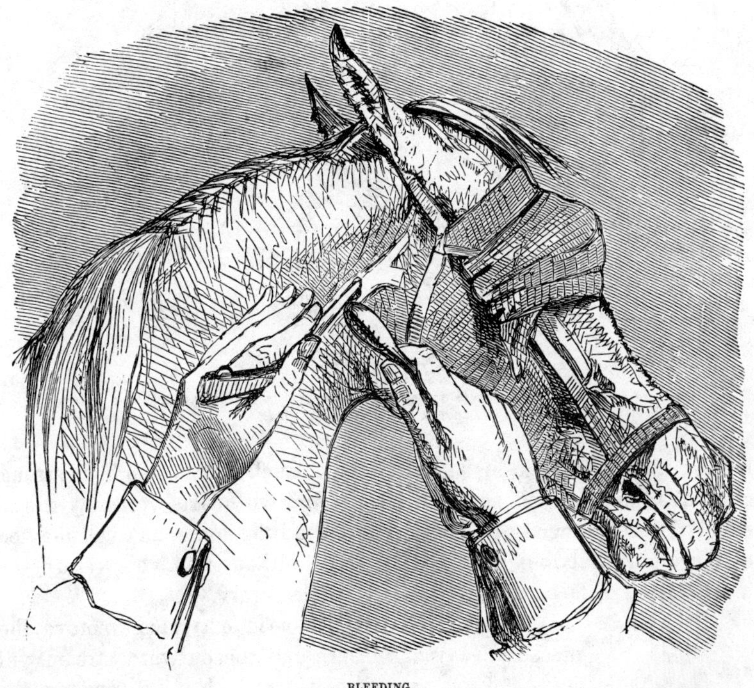

BLEEDING.

Blood being obtained by the operator, the groom approaches bearing the blood can. This the man presses against the horse's neck, thereby impeding the downward stream within the vessel and causing the vital current to gush forth.

Whatever may be the urgency of the business which may demand your presence elsewhere, never quit at this stage of the proceeding. However experienced or meritorious the servant may be, always remain until the operation is concluded. These poor men invariably possess opinions of their own that are stronger because of the ignorance upon which such notions repose. The groom may have seen a gallon, or even two gal-

PRESSING THE BLOOD CAN AGAINST THE NECK, TO ARREST THE DOWNWARD CURRENT, AND TO CAUSE THE BLOOD TO FLOW FORTH.

lons extracted, when in his last situation. Such people delight in strong measures; and he will sneer at the one or two quarts you may desire should be withdrawn. Be absent only for a brief space, and you may be certain your directions have been violated, although on your return the most solemn of faces should protest to the contrary.

TWISTED SUTURE.

When the quantity has been extracted, remove the pressure below the orifice and the outward stream will cease. Then proceed to pin up. Having rendered the point of a pin somewhat angular, by cutting off the tip, the wire will pierce the integument the more readily. Drive it through each side of the wound, and, being in this situation, twist, after the fashion of a figure of ∞, some tow or thread, or a hair pulled from the horse's tail, round its either extremity. Subsequently remove so much of the pin as may protrude, and the orifice will be closed by what surgeons denominate a **twisted suture.**

When performing this, a few precautions are imperative. In the first instance, the surfaces should not be brought immediately together. The wound should be left open until the lips become sticky, as when in that condition they unite the more readily. Next, when closing the orifice, all hairs should be removed, which is sometimes difficult should the integument have been torn asunder with a blunt fleam. The skin then is twisted and forced from its integrity; but if a sharp or proper instrument has been used, the presence of hair is never annoying; indeed it seldom requires attention.

The sides of the incision should be adjusted with all nicety, because, subsequently to bleeding, healing by the first intention, or by the speediest natural process, is desirable. Hairs, when present, prevent that union from being perfected. They irritate the part and act as minute setons, which provoke suppuration. The advent of the last action is always to be feared after a vein has been opened. The pus gravitates into the vessel and the blood becomes vitiated. The consequences frequently are fatal, and are always much to be lamented.

A HORSE, AFTER BEING BLED, HAS THE HEAD TIED TO THE MANGER FOR TWENTY-FOUR HOURS.

When the wound has been properly secured, all has not been accomplished. The rack and manger must be cleared. Food or drink must be withheld for twenty-four hours. The halter must be fastened up to the bars of the hay rack; for the animal which has just been rendered faint by having its blood extracted must, for the tedious space of one entire day and night, neither feed, allay its thirst, nor repose its tottering limbs. Some certain benefit, substantiated by very potent proofs, are necessary to justify the measure which must be followed by such deprivation; for if lack of nutriment and want of rest can generate debility, what must be the effect of enforced abstinence, when ensuing upon a sickening depletion?

CHAPTER III.

SHOEING—ITS ORIGIN, ITS USES, AND ITS VARIETIES.

Shoeing a horse is understood to signify fastening a piece of iron to the horn which envelops the foot of the animal. Such an operation, at first glance, appears to be so simple an affair as to admit of few remarks; but there is no subject associated with veterinary science on which more research has been expended, about which more bitter discussion has been indulged, or with regard to which proprietors and practitioners are more at variance. Certainly no matter can possibly be more intimately connected with the sufferings and the comforts of the equine race.

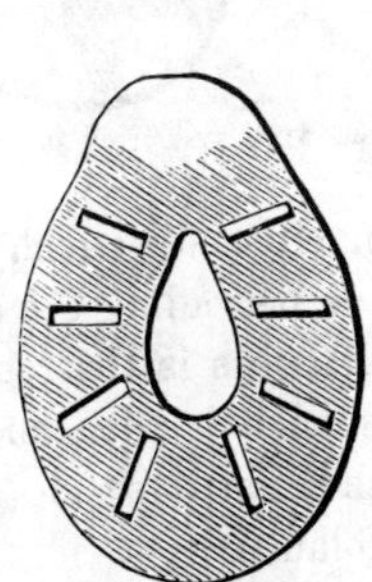

EARLY ARABIAN SHOE.

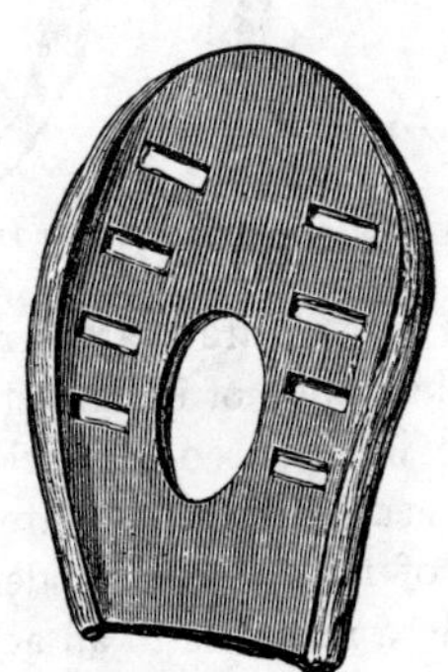

ARABIAN SHOE OF A MODERN DATE.

The custom of fixing iron to the hoof of the quadruped would seem, at the present moment, to be all but universal. This habit was probably derived from the East. In portions of the Desert of Arabia a primitive looking shoe is still employed, which, like most things in that region, has possibly remained unaltered during the passage of centuries. Such articles retain the impress of a by-gone era, being merely pieces of sheet-iron stamped, not forged, according to a particular pattern. The reader may be puzzled to form an accurate notion of such things; therefore illustrations, representing present and ancient shoes, are appended. Both partake of the same general characteristics, but, among a people so widely scattered as "the children of the Desert," doubtless numerous variations, as regards particulars, might be selected.

The preceding look like things produced during the childhood of civilization; but to assure the reader that at one period horse shoes resembling the foregoing were almost universal, below is subjoined sketches of those adopted, even at a recent date, by the Moorish, the Persian, and the Portuguese nations. These people are widely distributed; but they all are characterized by the tenacity with which each has clung to the habits of its ancestors. The shape pervading the examples brought forward is too eccentric, the generic likeness is too remarkable, and the peculiarities of feature impressed on each is too conspicuous, to permit of their united evidence being pushed on one side with any commonplace reference to an accidental resemblance.

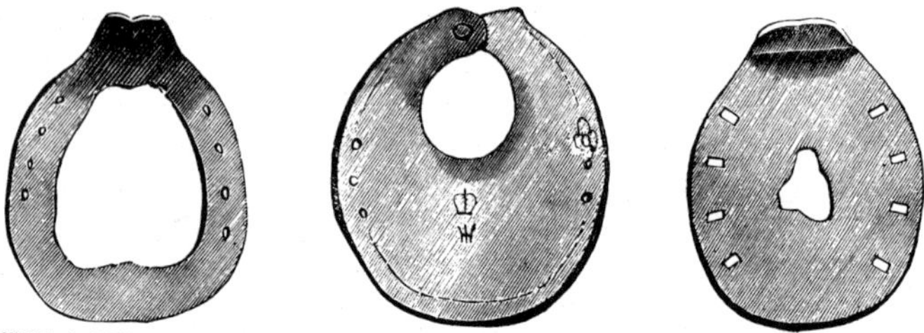

A MOORISH, A PERSIAN, AND A PORTUGUESE SHOE. COPIED FROM GOODWIN'S SYSTEM OF SHOEING HORSES.

Succeeding the former engravings is appended an authentic sketch of the old English horse shoe which was in common use at the commencement of the last century. When compared with the plate of the Arab, which doubtless was the original, it assuredly exhibits signs of intention. The calkin, intended to prevent slipping, we here see, as likewise in the foregoing examples, is by no means a modern invention. The position of the nail holes has been materially altered: they have been moved from the center, and have been made to range around the outer margin and to pierce the solid horn of the toe, which previously was scrupulously spared. The fastenings, likewise, have increased in number, having grown from eight to fourteen. The central opening has been enlarged; but the thickness of the iron and the general figure, however, demonstrate the source whence the original was derived.

OLD ENGLISH SHOE. COPIED FROM CLARK'S WORK ON SHOEING.

Thin plates of iron were once nailed as shoes to the hoofs throughout

Great Britain. The breadth was not, perhaps, considered a decided disadvantage, when roads were few and much marshy soil had to be crossed in a day's journey. But if this peculiar form enabled a steed to walk more securely on a soft surface, the suction, inseparable from such land, must also have exposed the animal to the frequent loss of the appendage. When regarding these unavoidable results, we can perceive the reasons which have dictated all the subsequent alterations. The central opening had been enlarged, in the expectation of thereby counteracting the sucking effects attending the movements over a marshy country; while the nails had been increased in number, in the expectation of thus gaining additional security. The fastenings had likewise been ranged round the rim, so that these might be driven directly through the hardest part of, and have longer hold upon, the most resistant portion of the horn.

Such plates were at one time, no doubt, in general use throughout Great Britain; and illustrating whence they were derived, there may be adduced a well-known fact. The race-horse is of almost pure Eastern blood. The trainer's stable is a very conservative locality, into which changes slowly enter, and where names are retained long after their applicability has ceased. A thorough-bred is spoken of to this day as running in "plates;" although the contest is decided in shoes resembling those worn by other animals, only of lighter make and of the highest possible finish.

The aspect of the old English shoe evidently suggests a resort to the hammer; it also indicates that the introduction of regular roads had began to compel the employment of a closer and harder species of metal than heretofore had been esteemed necessary. No modern Nimrod dare, however, essay to career across the best-drained portion of country on a horse shod with such a shoe as that last represented. Before a second field were entered he would anticipate a steed with bare feet. No cabman, however reckless, would take a quadruped on to the rank shod in such a fashion. Were an article of this form brought out now, no one who knew anything of such matters would patronize the novelty. Nevertheless, though it be deficient in all present requirements, it displays certain features, which have been preserved by the smith and handed down from father to son until the supposed improvements have reached the existing generation.

The arrangement of the nails near to the outer edge, and the fixing of them into the hard outer wall of the crust, are methods still followed. though experience has demonstrated that such numerous bodies, driven almost perpendicularly into a thin and a brittle substance, were better calculated to break the hoof than likely to hold on that which it was their single office to retain. The modern smith, moreover, does not generally puncture the toe of the foot; but the situations of the nail holes and the direction of the nails within such a part must have been originally regarded as a vast improvement upon the prevailing customs.

That which was formerly an innovation is, however, now the custom. No other mode of driving the nails is at present in general practice; though the modern veterinary surgeon recognizes all the evils which attend the habit, yet these evils he contentedly classes as diseases, instead of seeing in them the natural consequences of a faulty system.

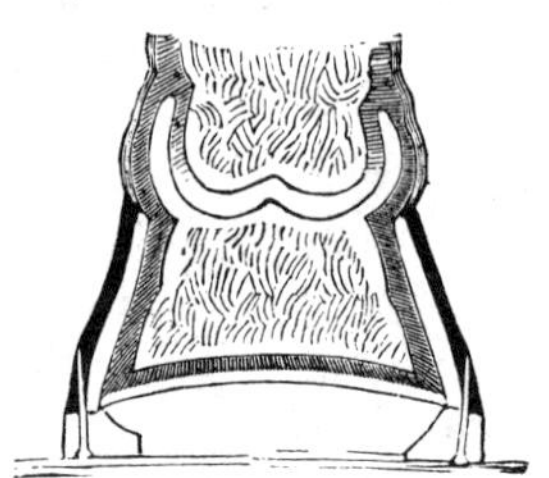

THE PRESENT METHOD OF FASTENING THE ENGLISH HORSE SHOE ON TO THE HORSE'S FOOT.

In the sandy Desert of Arabia, where a flat and perfectly dry country rendered suction impossible, any degree of tension, however feeble, might serve to keep the horse's shoe in its situation. On such a soil, eight lateral fastenings—each no stronger than a stout wire—might afford all needful security. The size of the holes assures us of the bulk of the nail heads, the projection of which, probably, served to give security to the tread, as well as to retain the metal; being inserted at one end and driven with the hammer to the other extremity of the opening, they might be an ample provision for such a purpose, when the desert permitted no vast amount of wear, and the nature of the animal assured lightness of motion.

The English reader may feel disposed to sneer at the Asiatic manner of fastening the shoe upon the horse's hoof; but he will do well to inquire, "whether the modern method of attaining the same object is altogether free from objection?" To enable him to do this, it is necessary that the composition of the outer wall of the equine hoof should be explained.

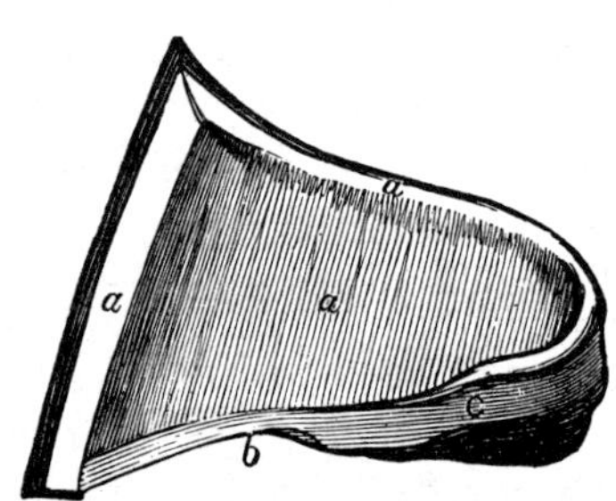

DIAGRAM, ILLUSTRATIVE OF THE DIFFERENT KINDS OF HORN COMPOSING THE HORSE'S HOOF.

a a. The wall. The outer dark portion is called the crust of the wall, and the light-colored, soft, inner horn is thrown into the laminæ, or thin leaves, whereby it gains extent of attachment to its secreting membrane.
b. The light-colored and yielding horn of the sole.
c. The tinted but elastic horn of the frog.

The **wall** of the foot is so much horn as can be seen when the hoof rests upon the ground, and when it is viewed either immediately from the front or directly from the sides. This wall is supplied from two sources. The coronet, or the prominence to be seen immediately above the hoof, secretes the outer layer of horn, which is the darkest, is very much the hardest, and is the most brittle of all the constituents of the hoof The laminæ, or the highly-sensitive covering of the internal foot, secrete the inward layer of horn, which is soft, tough, and devoid of color.

These two opposite and distinct secretions are, by nature, joined together, forming one body. Now, the intimate union of opposite properties endues the substance, thus compounded, with the characteristics of both. The hard, outward horn was needed to protect the foot against those stones and rocks over which the animal was intended to journey. The internal, white horn, being fastened upon this substance, acted as a corrective to its harsh nature, preventing it from breaking, from splitting, and from chipping, which it else must have done under the weight it was destined to sustain, and when fulfilling the purposes to which the horse's foot was designed to be subjected.

Pathology has indirectly recognized the intention of this junction, by acknowledging that condition to be a state of disease, wherein the two

FALSE QUARTER, OR A DEFICIENCY OF THE OUTER WALL.

(E ONLY POSSIBLE RELIEF FOR FALSE QUARTER.

SECTION OF A HORSE'S FOOT AFFECTED WITH SEEDY TOE.

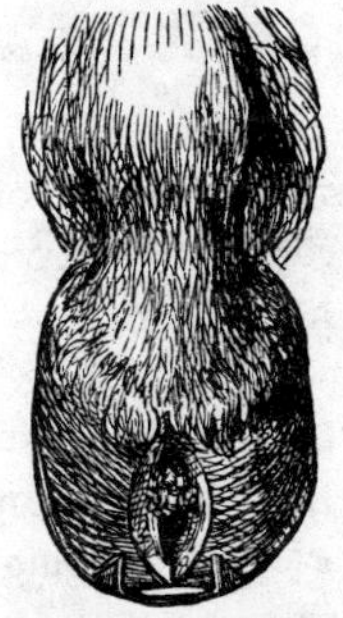

A FOOT WITH SANDCRACK.

kinds of horn are separated. Such a division is known as a seedy toe and as false quarter; and the foot is recognized as weakened when such a want of union is discovered. The outer, dark-colored horn becomes more brittle; the white, internal horn grows more soft for the want of that junction by means of which each communicated its attributes to the other. So also when the two descriptions of horn, although united, cease to influence one another, pathology acknowledges this condition as a morbid alteration, known as a changed state of hoof. Thus, when a sandcrack is visible, or the wall divides from the ground surface to the coronet, the foot's incasement is recognized as unhealthy; but in the forge, the application of such facts is, by most smiths, utterly ignored.

The untutored Arab, however, takes advantage of the united properties of the horn. In warm countries the horse's hoof grows strong and thick. The uninstructed Asiatic allows the wall to descend half an inch below the sole, and right through the entire of this portion of projecting hoof he drives the nails which secure the shoe. Proceeding thus, he does not injure the foot by the insertion of foreign bodies through its more brittle substance, while he secures the united resistance and tough qualities of the complex covering of the foot.

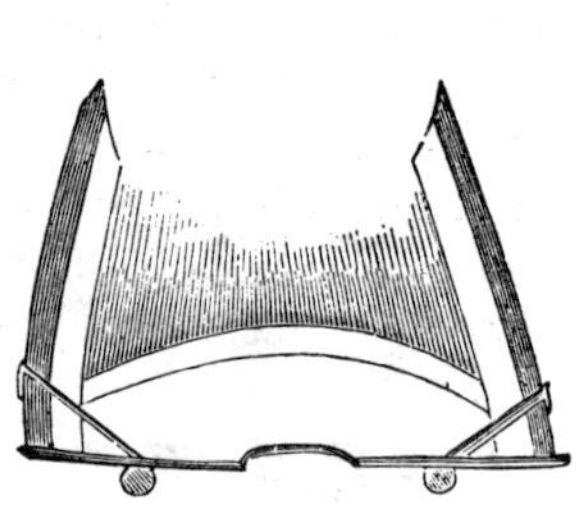

THE MODE OF FASTENING THE ARABIAN SHOE TO THE HOOF OF THE HORSE.

FRACTURED CONDITION OF THE HORN, CONSEQUENT UPON DRIVING NAILS THROUGH THE BRITTLE OUTER CRUST OF THE WALL.

The English smith, on the contrary, by ranging the holes for the fas tenings round the edge of the shoe, drives the nails only into the harder kind of horn, and transfixes the crust for a considerable distance. The English shoeing nail is meant to pierce only the black or outward substance of the wall. This may, seemingly, afford the better hold; but it also offers the more dangerous dependence. There is, likewise, the peril to be braved of pricking the sensitive foot, should the nail turn a little to one side—an accident which not unfrequently happens. There is, moreover, another danger, namely, that which the forge calls driving a nail "too fine;" that is, forcing it near the white horn rather than sending it directly through the center of the narrow dark crust. There remains to be enumerated a third peril. Horses, with thin walls, present difficulties to the shoeing smith. He is afraid of either pricking the foot or driving the nail "too fine;" should the last accident ensue, the nail will, upon the animal being worked, bulge inward, will provoke acute lameness, often causing pus to be generated. To avoid these evils, he points his nails outward; and, by so doing, not unseldom induces the harsh outer crust to crack, to split up, or to chip off. To such an extent does this sometimes happen, that the smith is occasionally puzzled to find the place where a nail will hold.

It is a common thing to hear veterinary surgeons, throughout the length and breadth of the land, attribute to the operation of shoeing all the evils by which the hoof is affected. They generally assert that a colt invariably has an open, healthy foot, until it is shod; but, from the day upon which the animal enters the forge, the horn begins to be irregularly secreted, and the hoof to grow misshapen; while horsemen have a well-known saying, that "one horse could wear out four pair of feet."

Every rider knows how vexatious it is for a horse to fling a shoe. Every horseman appreciates the consequence of walking his steed, even one mile, along the common road, to gain the nearest forge, where the loss may be made good. Such an accident were an impossibility, if the nails were firm. There is always danger, as they are at present fixed, of these fastenings breaking away from the substance of the hoof; yet no one has hitherto ventured to question the existing method of shoeing prevalent throughout Europe.

But the worst evil which results from a shoe becoming partially released, is neither the inconvenience it occasions the rider, nor fracture, often produced, on the hoof of the animal. Some portion of the horn first yields. This mishap throws greater stress upon the remaining fastenings. The shoe becomes loose. The majority of the nails give way, but one may continue firm. This is the greatest peril. The shoe is fastened as by a pivot, and with every step swings from side to side. The released nails stick upward—the earth or roadway, as well as the clinches, preventing these from leaving their places. When the foot is in the air, the shoe hangs pendulous. When the foot is placed upon the ground, it may be impaled upon the nails that protrude upward. Many steps are seldom taken without such a result. The shoe gets under the foot. The blunt and jagged points are, by the huge weight of the quadruped, forced through the soft sole or frog at the bottom of the hoof; a dangerous wound is inflicted, the uneven metal being often driven for some distance into the body of the coffin-bone.

THE SHOE PARTIALLY BREAKS FROM THE INSECURE FASTENINGS, AND ONE OF THE NAILS, STICKING UP, PIERCES THE SOLE OF THE FOOT.

Against the Arabian method of driving the nails, it may be advanced that if the equine hoof is permitted to grow, the elongation of the horn at the toe and its non-removal by the knife would occasion this portion of the foot to protrude, and ultimately curl upward like a Turkish slipper—such being the result of long-continued neglect, as is exemplified in the feet of too many donkeys.

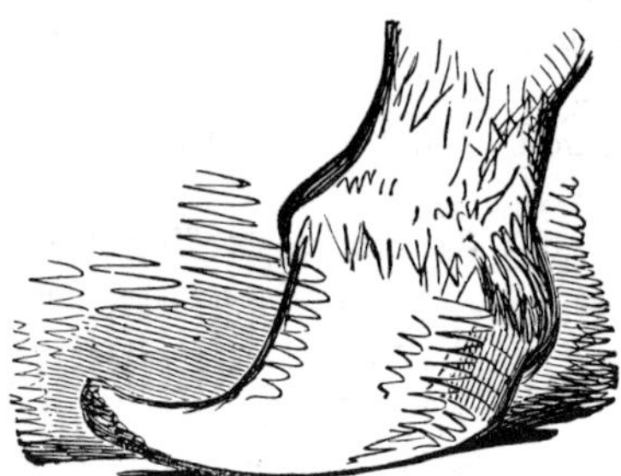
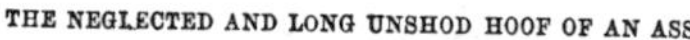
THE NEGLECTED AND LONG UNSHOD HOOF OF AN ASS.

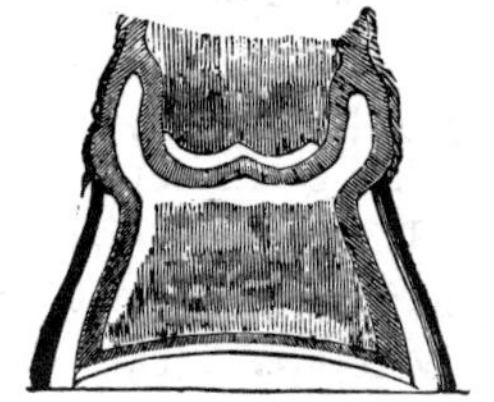
ENGLISH MODE OF PARING THE HORSE'S HOOF.

It is not proposed to subject the horse's foot to anything like the usage to which the hoof of the ass is habitually exposed. All the writer contemplates is moderating the smith's employment of the drawing-knife and of the rasp, enforcing some caution in the application of the red-hot iron, when burning a seat for the shoe. Why need the wall be always cut away till it is level with the horny sole? Why bring this last portion of the pedal covering, which is naturally soft and yielding, on a line with that part of the crust which is imbued with a power of resistance? Nay, the harder wall is protected by the shoe on which it rests; while the softer sole is brought near to the ground, being left exposed to an injury, which the lesion known as bruise of the sole proves not unfrequently to happen.

The sole, being exposed thus close to the earth, is the fruitful source of several "accidents." The soft horn of this region being brought so low, is rendered constantly wet. The consequence is a harshness of texture, perfectly opposed to the evident intent of nature. This harshness is one of the most common sources of corns. The edge of the sole rests upon the web of the shoe—the descent of the coffin-bone, being unable to play upon a yielding sole, squeezes the flesh between the inferior surface of the bone and the upper surface of the shoe. This is acknowledged as the principal source of corns. Stones and other rubbish often become impacted between the horny sole and the shoe. In this situation, the foreign substances are retained so firmly and provoke such acute lameness that it is common for all stable-men to keep by them, as well as it is general for most horsemen to carry, a curved tool denominated "a picker." Such annoyances, with many others, might be easily avoided, could the English smith only be prevailed upon not to pare the sole so thin that blood bedews its surface, and then to make the level of the diminished part the point whereto the crust is to be lowered.

Another probable consequence, attending the customary cutting away of the horse's sole, has not been sufficiently considered.

The shape of this part, its yielding character, and its position immediately under the coffin-bone, all should be accepted as proofs that it is of service in supporting the weight of the body. It proves nothing to assert that if the sole is removed, the pedal bone will not fall down. The burden may repose upon the numerous laminæ and upon the bulging rim of the coronet, as well as drag upon the lateral cartilages. Here is sufficient material to uphold even a greater load; but can such a force be arbitrarily imposed by human authority without provoking nature's resentment? The parts here named are the very regions which are the common seats of foot disease. Ossified cartilages—irregular secretion of coronary horn and laminitis, in the acute or in the chronic form—are very common to stables; so also is navicular disease, which the trimming of the frog is also likely to induce. Horse proprietors, therefore, would do well to reflect upon the above possibility, when their property is again submitted to the unchecked abuses of the forge.

Humanity is not pleaded in this case. Human interest alone is urged in favor of the plan proposed. Every horse owner knows how common it is for the animal to return tender-footed from the forge. Every person can appreciate the unpleasant sensation experienced when a nail has been pared to the quick.

Immediate lameness, or violent exhibition of acute disease, is required to convince some people that dumb animals feel anything; but a peculiarity displayed in the manner of placing the foot on the earth is, to the author's mind, sufficient proof of some painful sensation. In two or three days, the newly-exposed horn may resume its protective function, and the mode of progressing, by such a time, is generally restored to its accustomed soundness. But such is not invariably the case, and, when it does happen, the seeds of future disaster may, nevertheless, have been sown. Indeed, so conscious are dealers of the injury done to the horse's foot by the rasp and the drawing-knife, that, as a rule, they avoid having their new stock reshod while these animals remain in their possession.

To rectify the foregoing evils, the author would humbly propose that half an inch of crust should be allowed to protrude below a sole of moderate thickness. That all idea of breadth of shoe affording the slightest protection be at once abolished; because the broad web has been proved, by the general employment of the picker, rather to afford harbor to hurtful particles than to protect the sole from injury. That the shoe be made only just wide enough to afford bearing to the wall of the hoof, and to allow sufficient room for the nail holes to pierce the substance of the iron. The crust was designed to sustain the weight of the animal's body, and the most ignorant smith would not think of permitting the entire burden to bear upon the sole. A space large enough to give room for the nails and to provide an ample rest for the wall of the hoof is all that can be of use; and, being so, all additional width only renders the shoe of an unnecessary weight.

The use of the sole is well known to be distinct from directly supporting any portion of the body; but it may be of all service in upholding occasional weight. That other parts receive the primary burden, is illustrated in the forge every day—it being an ordinary custom with the smith to pare the sole of the foot till it yields readily to pressure from the man's thumb, or until blood oozes through every pore of the structure. A further proof of this is the custom of removing a portion of sole when the animal chances to be bled from the foot; also, by the veterinary surgeon, without hesitation or fear of consequence, taking away large pieces of the horn whenever the sole happens to be bruised and under-run. The function of the sole is to endue the tread with spring and elasticity; that it may perform its proper office, the removal of it from all possibility of hinderance to its freedom of motion becomes a necessity. This requirement is best complied with by allowing the part to remain so high as anticipates all possibility of its coming in contact with either the web of the shoe or the ground.

Nature makes nothing in vain; or, in other words, every part which she creates has its destined uses. To recognize such a maxim, and then to employ a smith to destroy the horny sole which nature provided, is to acknowledge wisdom, but to follow ignorance. At all events, putting every appeal to higher principles of action on one side, let mere cunning or let worldly prudence decide the point. The present method has been tried, and has lamentably failed; consequently it is proved an annoyance which countenances any feasible change.

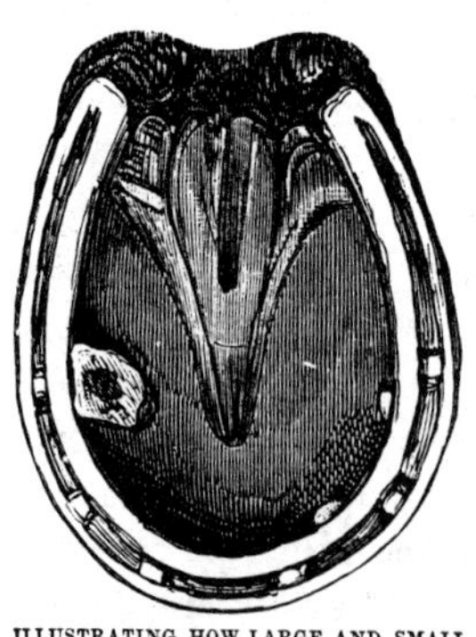

ILLUSTRATING HOW LARGE AND SMALL STONES BECOME IMPACTED BETWEEN THE SOLE AND THE WEB OF THE SHOE.

But those who are prejudiced in favor of the usual proceedings may exclaim against the annihilation of the web, and talk about the need of protecting the sole. The old English shoe (in which the web was so broad the horse's foot rested on a flat metallic surface) did not defend the sole, else the web would not have been sacrificed. But what kind of protection does the present form actually afford? Why, its only use really appears to be that of affording a place of lodgment for gravel and for pebbles, or of a medium for the generation of corns.

Were half an inch of crust allowed to remain, the web and all its dangers might be abolished. The weight would thereby be lightened, while the tenacity of wet clay would be deprived of any leverage on which to act. Two primary requisites toward a good hunting shoe would then be obtained. The nail openings also being brought close to the inner margin, and the fastenings being driven in a direction slanting outward, a hold would be taken of both species of horn which unites to form the wall of the foot; and the nails, being firmly clinched upon a tough body in lieu of a brittle substance, would be retained with greater certainty. The weight of metal required for such a shoe would be decreased, thereby materially lessening the labor of the horse; while if the nails pierced the toe of the crust, a firmer hold would be obtained, and the quarters would be left free instead of being fettered, as is unavoidable so long as the present system of nailing is continued. Corns, bruise of the sole, brittle hoof, etc. would be avoided, and the dangers of the forge no longer perpetuated. Lastly, the comfort of the animal being more tenderly considered, the motions of the quadruped would be so much the easier, and the more pleasant—man's real interest being best consulted by strict attention to the happiness of all the lives which serve him, as every form of existence succumbs to protracted suffering.

The reader, however, may have experienced the deception which commonly attends every novelty in horse shoes. Therefore he may think, when the author proposes a return to an old, a barbarous, and an exploded form of fastening on the horse's shoe, he simply aims at trying an experiment with the living property of other people. The writer does not propose to contend against suspicions; but he produces the plan which he advocates, and contrasts it with the ordinary method of nailing; when, having placed the evidence before his judges, he leaves them to decide on the merits of the adverse modes, as regards their likelihood to perform the offices of retaining a ring of iron with safety and with advantage upon the foot of a horse.

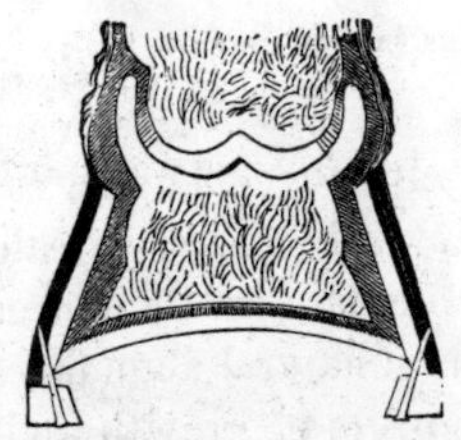

THE AUTHOR'S PROPOSED MODE OF NAILING.

According to the above plan, the hold would be much firmer; it would embrace the two kinds of horn which nature ordained should unite to form the wall of the hoof. The nail would pierce those tough and resistant substances which were designed in their unity to support the animal's body, instead of being driven perpendicularly into the more brittle covering of the foot, thereby dividing the fibers and frequently injuring the hoof, by causing large flakes to chip off its protecting envelope.

The present practice of the forge chiefly consists in removing as much horn as possible: as if the covering of the foot were not a natural growth, sent for a healthful purpose; or it was the sprouting of disease, which it became imperative should be excised. The shoe is dragged off, and afterward the punch, the pliers, and the drawing-knife are employed.

The author does not object to the legitimate use of the last-named instrument; but to its abuse he dissents. As the shoe alone rests upon the earth, of course the hoof lacks needful attrition. Therefore, were no cutting resorted to, the horn would be prolonged, and the shoe ultimately afford no protection to the foot, being carried forward by the growth of the toe. It is not unusual to see the iron, which originally was nailed to and encircled the hoof, borne onward by the continued development of the horny secretion, in consequence of neglect having allowed the shoe to remain on the foot for months.

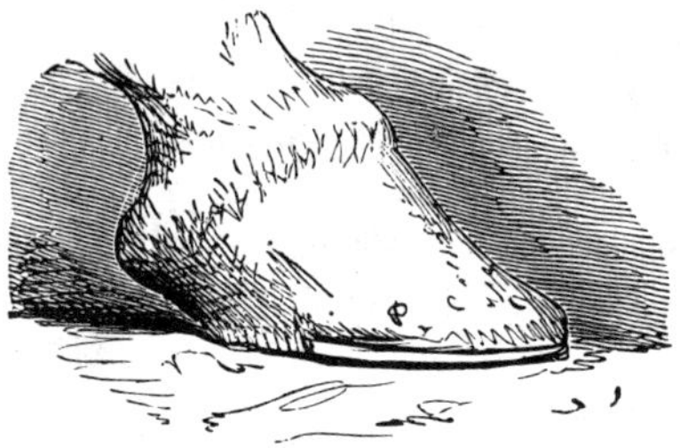

THE SHOE, WHEN SUFFERED TO REMAIN UPON THE FOOT FOR TOO LONG A PERIOD, IS CARRIED FORWARD BY THE GROWTH OF HORN, AND LEAVES THE HEELS UNPROTECTED.

It is well known to physiologists, that the constant removal of any natural growth is calculated to result in one of three effects: it may stimulate production, causing the willfully-excised material to be secreted in unnatural abundance; or, on the other hand, it may interfere with the powers of growth and occasion the material to be withheld altogether; else the operation may cause the product to be secreted in a diminished quantity. These conditions of hoof are those which the English smith most often complains of, little suspecting that he may innocently have aggravated the very evil over which he so loudly laments. Weak, shelly feet are generally attributed to the colt having been bred upon marshy soil. This accepted reason may answer its purpose; but it does not explain why, upon the horse being taken into work, or being carried a long distance from the place of its birth, the deficiency should become more conspicuous, and the weakness grow more annoying with each successive shoeing. Thick, stubborn hoofs are too common to need much comment; but this effect is generally attributed to the lateral nailing, which confines the expansion of the quarters. Does not this excuse suggest the wisdom of carrying the fastenings to the toe, where the greater thickness of the horn would afford better hold to the nails, while at the same time the amount of substance would forbid all idea of motion?

SPECIMENS OF A LOW AND OF A HIGH HEEL.

In reply to the above suggestion, it may be answered that English smiths like to spare the toe of the horse's foot. All the strain of draught is thrown upon this part, which must be dug forcibly into the earth whenever the load is heavy or is difficult to draw. In fast-trotting animals, the toe receives the impetus of the blow when the foot descends upon the ground; therefore, it is urged, the smith has found out by experience that no nail should weaken this portion of the hoof. The answer appears to be final, but, on consideration, it will be found of small value. Mr. Woodger, one of the best veterinary surgeons in London, informs the writer he prefers to drive nails through the toe of the horse's foot.

In the first place, the different methods of fastening on the shoe have to be properly considered. The author proposes a simple puncture through all the substance, which, as the opening made is filled with metal, can hardly produce weakness in the structure. The smith drives the nail perpendicularly, not through the wall of the hoof, but into its outward investing envelope, or into a material particularly harsh and resentful of interference—thus separating the fibers of the horn, destroying its integrity, and, of course, weakening its capability of sustaining violence.

But, bearing in mind the foregoing reply, supposed to be urged in defense of the established custom, let it now be asked, does the English smith really respect the part, about the integrity of which he appears to be so anxious? How does he act, when he fits upon the foot of a horse a shoe having a clip at the toe? Does he, then, scrupulously respect the most forward portion of the hoof? No! He actually employs his drawing-knife to cut away the horn, thus forming a bed or seat within which the clip can lie ensconced. Nor is this all; he turns up the heels of the shoe afterward, thus forming a calkin, and actually throwing the bearing of the hoof on that portion of the foot which he has just denuded of its natural protection.

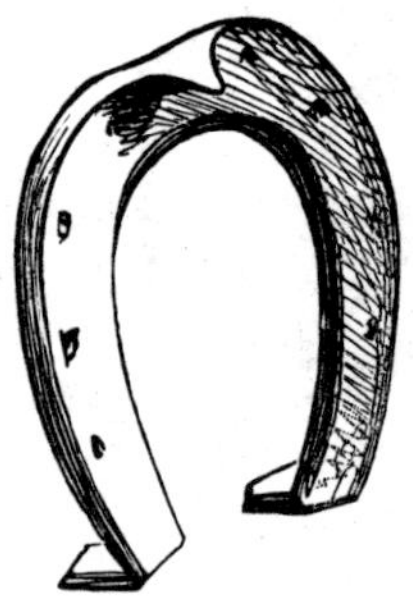

A SHOE WITH A CLIP AT THE TOE.

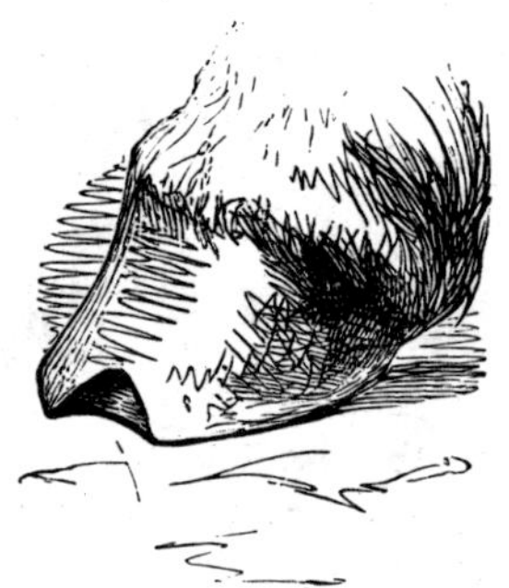

THE INCISION WHICH PREPARES THE FOOT TO RECEIVE THE CLIP.

Against all objections embodying the cruelty of this mode of proceeding, it may be responded that the horn is not endowed with sensation; that it can be cut or burned without awakening the slightest feeling; and, therefore, the introduction of the present remark is entirely out of place. While listening to such talk, it might be inferred those processes which a few people speak of as exciting no feeling, were positively the sources of pleasure to the animal. But if shoeing is to the horse so perfectly painless an operation, what makes many of these quadrupeds dread its infliction, and refuse to enter the forge? Is it excess of happiness that occasions several of these creatures to resist the office of the smith, and provokes a few actually to struggle so violently to escape his attentions as to sacrifice their existences? Is it any form of ecstasy that renders most animals fidgety while being shod, or is it the restlessness of perfect bliss which induces nearly all to move about as though they were anxious to escape?

The horse is naturally docile and obedient. To serve man is its destiny, to obey its master is its delight. To please the human savage, it deforms a beautiful frame before it is matured; and, under the impulse of fear, submits to usage which destroys the value of its life. In such a creature, which is denied the use of words, actions must be reasonably construed, if we desire to interpret its emotions. The acquiescence of ages has viewed contortion as the evidence of agony; and universal opinion has regarded nervous movements as being indicative of fear or of suffering.

The smith, to quiet timidity, may strike "the brute" with his heavy hammer, or with his scarcely lighter pincers. But no severity can deprive flesh of its inherent privilege to writhe, when tortured. Fearful injuries have resulted from the smith's impatience. Every blow, however, does not lead to an inquiry; though any animal, having a most retentive memory, may on the next occasion shy as it approaches the door of the forge; or it may ever after, with that strange perversity for which thoughtless proprietors are at a loss to account, prove resistful at the approach of the shoeing smith. Nevertheless, though the pantomime of terror should be a language universally comprehended, few of those most accustomed to horses can see anything in the nervous spasms of the animal but the exhibition of a vice which needs to be resisted! Such people will imagine they deserve to be commended when, by the exertion of their utmost force, they have overpowered the mute timidity which was endeavoring to appeal to the sympathy of its heartless superiors.

Calkins to the shoes of the horse, as at present made, are positive abominations. The shoe, in the first instance, is forged too long for the foot, when, the extra length of iron being bent downward, a calkin is established. Below, the author presents a sketch, made from memory, of the highest calkin he ever remembers to have looked upon. It was encountered in the country, soon after the breaking up of a severe frost; and, probably, it was intended to counteract the wear of metal which invariably accompanies a frozen condition of the highways. It would, however, with a change of weather, fail in its intent; for the principal wear is then endured by the toe of the shoe, and the heel comparatively escapes friction. All such things operate according to their height. They fling the entire bearing forward, where, without any such aid, it must strongly press. Although contraction of the tendons is mostly confined to cart horses, (and this constrained position of the foot must favor such an affection,) nevertheless the smith

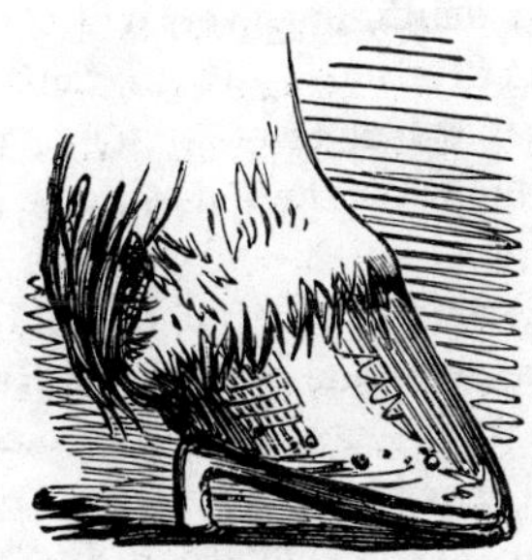
A HIGH CALKIN.

may receive it as an unjust accusation when he is told that high calkins are to blame for the spread of such a state of disease.

The author, probably, has said enough about the evils attendant on the present system of shoeing; and, although the subject is far from exhausted, he yields to the reader's desire of learning what the writer would substitute in the place of that which causes the numerous evils he has denounced. The reformer's office is but half performed when the bad is exposed. The most difficult part remains to be discharged—that of conceiving and of declaring the good which shall fill the void left by the necessary destruction of the evil.

The author is conscious that, after having condemned so much, he has placed himself under an obligation to adduce that which he believes to be grounded on right principles. When doing this, the mighty question of expense is entirely ignored. It is his office to make known the remedy; he has no concern with the cost of its application. Gentlemen, however, though exacting the utmost service from the horse, generally begrudge the price of the iron which must be ground down while the patient quadruped is laboring for its task-master's benefit. With too many proprietors the cheapest is the best form of shoe. The temptation of saving a few pence frequently sways the judgment in favor of some particular article. The welfare and the life of earth's most beautiful ornament is, by too many human beings, reduced to a money consideration. So thoroughly is this fact appreciated that, when a new shoe is submitted to the notice of the forge, its chances of success are always judged by the charge for which it can be manufactured, apart from the merits of the invention.

There is, however, a custom general in the forge which has been discarded by other trades. The linen-draper tickets up the goods in which he deals; and, be the customer rich or poor, the price is known to both. The smith, however, will charge the tradesman three shillings and sixpence, or four shillings, the set, for a horse's shoes; while the person of independent property, or in the upper sphere of life, he makes pay five shillings for the self-same article. This rule can be based on no principle of fair dealing, and it needs only to be exposed to be immediately overthrown. Yet, even up to the present time, so exploded and so antiquated a rule of trade prevails in the forge, where the addition of an extra sixpence is unjustly made to turn the scale of merit.

However, the author has here nothing to do with such considerations. His duty is confined to freely stating his conscientious convictions, and to acknowledging the reader as the appointed judge of the soundness or unsoundness of his conclusions. Impressed with such a belief, the following form of shoe is submitted to the public. It is, by the writer, designated "a slipper shoe;" and the appearance of such a protection, when fixed upon the foot of a heavy horse, is presented below.

The principal peculiarity in this shoe is the long strip of metal which rises above the upper surface and conceals about three-quarters of an inch of the toe. This is not an enlarged kind of clip, but a hollow receptacle, which projects above the shoe and covers part of the hoof. The use will be best understood when stated that it confers the name—the slipper shoe. The toe is sheltered within the shallow cavity, and its purpose is to afford the stay which the clip imperfectly provides at the expense of the horn's destruction. When the fore portion of the foot is being dug into the earth, this provision, while it allows the hoof to be employed in its integrity, will prevent all the stress being transferred to the nails, and thus hinder the clinches being loosened.

THE FOOT OF A HEAVY ANIMAL, WITH THE SLIPPER SHOE FIXED ON IT.

This shoe has no web. It consists of a piece of iron the breadth of which is merely sufficient to afford a secure lodgment for the crust. The thing possesses true calkins, but their existence does not interfere with the level of the upper surface on which the foot rests. The shoe is forged of one thickness from toe to heel; and a portion of metal under each quarter being removed, leaves the calkin, which thus only serves to maintain the evenness of the bearing. A slipper shoe, adapted for a lighter kind of animal than was supposed in the above illustration, and not fixed on the foot, is presented on the next page.

It may possibly be urged that in thus forming the calkin, the author has weakened the strength of the quarters. Nature has, however, set the example, by weakening the horn at the quarters; nevertheless, by so doing she has not destroyed the strength of the hoof. The quarters of an old shoe, when removed after six weeks' hard wear, invariably are not sensibly diminished in substance, showing that the lessened amount of horn communicates small friction to the metal. Besides, the toe is supported upon massive iron, while the heels are upheld by blocks of the same metal. A law of mechanics instructs us that if the extremities of any powerful substance are adequately sustained, the body which bridges over the space may be without support. The heels being raised to an equal height with the toe, the metal left at the quarters, as it is removed from attrition, is imagined to be fully equal to the necessities of its position.

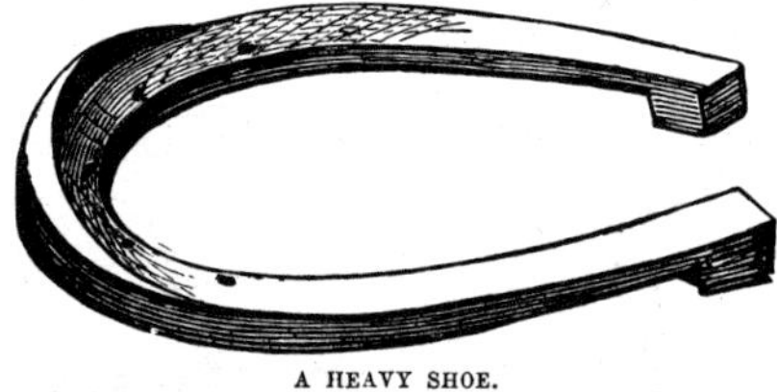

A HEAVY SHOE.

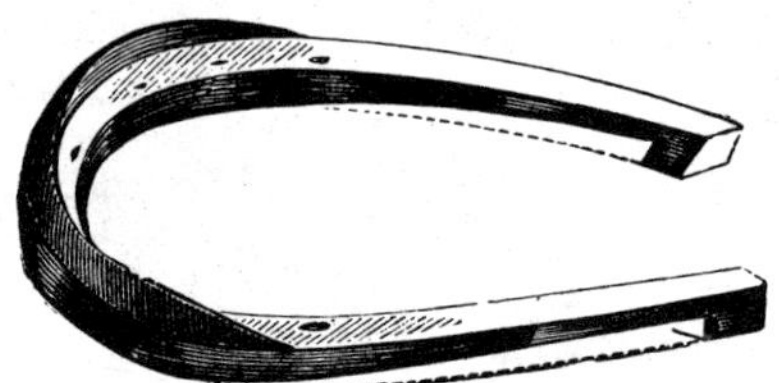

A LIGHT SHOE.—SHOWING THE MANNER IN WHICH CALKINS MAY BE FORMED, WITHOUT ANY INCREASE OF WEIGHT.

The diagram exhibits the Slipper Shoe, as suited for different breeds of animals; also shows the sameness in both kinds of manufacture.

Most existing shoes are **fullered,** or have a hollow space, narrow but long, near to the outer margin. Into this empty void or groove the heads of the nails are received; but as the substance in front is ground down by wear, of course the duration of the shoe must be shortened in proportion to the depth of the fullering. That the reader may fully comprehend the signification of a fullered shoe, on the following page is a copy, made from Mr. Goodwin's excellent work on Shoeing, which the author can recommend as the fullest, the most explicit, and altogether the best book on this topic which was ever written in the English language.

By inspecting the next illustration, which represents the ground surface, the reader will perceive an indented void near to the outer margin.

Behind this indentation or fullered cavity the iron gradually slopes away so that the substance which is exposed to wear, and on which the horse must travel, consists of the narrow strip that extends round the outward edge of the shoe.

A SHOE, WITH THE NAILS COUNTERSUNK.
(Ground surface.)

A FULLERED SHOE.
(Ground surface.)

The author's proposed shoe contemplates iron of an equal thickness at every point which is usually exposed to wear. The nails are driven into

DIAGRAMS, SHOWING THE DIFFERENCE BETWEEN FULLERING AND COUNTERSINKING, FOR RECEIVING THE NAIL HEAD OF A HORSE'S SHOE.

Fullering, or a free indentation round the shoe. This space is indicated by the dark portion of the diagram, and within which the heads of the nails repose.

Countersinking, or only removing so much metal as may be filled up by the heads of the nails which are to retain the shoe upon the horse's foot.

holes made to fit close around the heads of those fastenings, so that the shoe being fixed, no loss of substance is to be detected; for the nail heads fill the spaces which were countersunk for their admission.

The nails pierce the toe of the proposed new shoe. This part is selected, because this portion of hoof is covered with the thicker horn; therefore is indicated as the region where all stress should bear. The author is aware that, among smiths, there is a strong objection to driving nails in the center of the wall. Yet it seems to the writer that a more violent outrage is inflicted by actually removing a portion of its substance, so as to make an abiding place for a clip, than by piercing obliquely the strongest part of the hoof, subsequent to the toe having grown below the true foot.

The thickness of wall there offers several advantages, when considering the retention of nails. The solidity of the secretion is a proof that this portion of the hoof is not endowed with motion. Consequently, when fastening a piece of iron to it, we are not fearful of interfering with the exercise of a healthful function. Such would be the case if the nails were to fix the quarters, where the joint thinness, moisture, and elasticity of the horn afford the best evidence nature meant should reside expansion and contraction.

When the contents of the foot are compressed by the superimposed weight of the animal, or when the hoof is resting upon the ground, the quarters yield to the downward pressure, and they accordingly expand. When the burden is removed by the hoof being raised, the quarters again fly back to their original situations. The sides, therefore, being in constant motion, are entirely unsuited for the purposes to which the smith compels them. No wonder the clinches are loosened, or the shoes come off, when the nails are driven into parts hardly ever at rest; this action is important to the circulation, for the contraction still allows the arterial blood free ingress, while the expansion permits the full return of the venous current.

Therefore, because the thickness of horn denies the possibility of movement; because the amount of inorganic secretion likewise presents a reasonable hope of not injuring other and more delicate structures; and because the toe affords those numerous properties which, for the retention of the fastenings are rendered imperative, the nails, in opposition to the usage of ages and the experience of thousands, are fixed within the anterior of the hoof—seven or five being there employed to fix the shoe.

There is another quality appertaining to the proposed shoe which may be briefly touched upon. The thing is equally applicable to the field or to the road. For hunting purposes, it is superior to any modern shoe. It possesses no unnecessary surface, being absolutely without web, and is lighter for the absence of so useless a provision. It is also fixed more firmly upon the foot, being the better able to withstand the drag, always present, when riding in winter over stiff clays. Moreover, it does not fetter the quarters of the hoof or necessitate vast removal of the sole; consequently it leaves the pliable horn to aid the spring, thereby allowing the horse the full exercise of its natural power.

This reference to one kind of sport, naturally calls to mind another form of amusement in which the horse is a principal performer. Thorough-breds, before they start for the race, are shod in very light, but in equally thin shoes, of which the appended example may convey some idea. Now, thinness and lightness, where metal is concerned, are attainable only by the sacrifice of strength. The sad accidents which have occurred through using the present racing plates, and by these being broken, bent, or twisted, during the violence of the contention, ought to provoke their abolition.

Such accidents are, however, fortunately more rare than the substance of the shoe might lead most readers to suppose. Nevertheless, a greater injury is consummated by affixing a fetter, which prevents the elasticity of the quarters aiding the exertions of the animal, while, from its dimension, it can afford but little protection to the foot. How much the speed of the racer must be dependent upon that elasticity with which the quarters are endowed, may be judged of by any person who has ever visited a race-course and beheld the horses trot previous to the start. Who can have failed to notice the play of fetlock by which "the blood action" is characterized? Now, nature never forms one part an exception to the

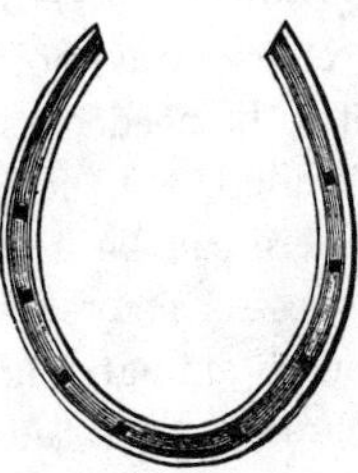

AN OLD AND A MODERN RACING PLATE.

whole. She delights in harmony; consequently the spring which resides in the fetlock is positive evidence of the elasticity which belongs to the unfettered foot. But the bounding property, which the frog, sole, and quarters would naturally provide, the trainer counteracts, in order to impose a dangerous article, which is not a horse shoe, nor even a respectable substitute for one.

It is so formed, however, as to exercise the worst functions of the regular shoe. It is a fetter upon the foot, and firmly impales the quarters, thereby seriously crippling the animal and impeding the natural power. If any part of a thorough-bred's foot required metallic protection, it could only be the toe; for this part alone is employed during the horse's quickest pace. The other portions of the hoof touch the ground, when aiding the spring; but these are never used with that amount of energy which necessitates anything approaching artificial defense. Now, the plate and its nails check expansion; these also oppose that force of rebound residing in the hoof and in its various structures. The best horse must feel the bondage

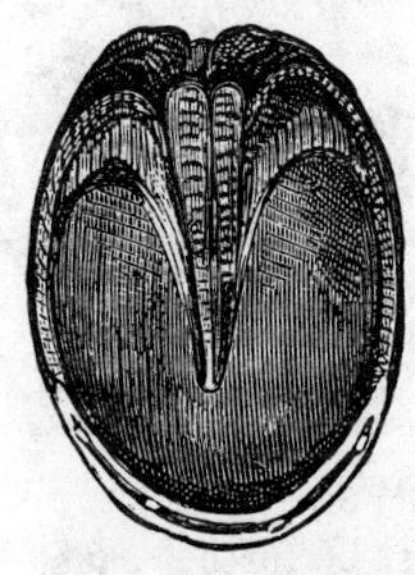

A TIP OR HALF SHOE NAILED ONLY TO THE TOE, AND LEAVING BOTH THE QUARTERS FREE.

most The spring or rebound is to it of most value. But that function is destroyed. Many a fine animal has, doubtless, been condemned for having "no go in him," which, could it have exerted all its natural power, would have been declared winner of every race for which it was ever entered.

The late William Percivall, the respected author of Hippo-pathology, many years ago informed the author that he had long ridden a young horse about town with no greater protection to its forefeet than tips could afford. He showed the hoofs of the animal to the writer, and more open or better examples of the healthy horse's feet need not be desired. Why could not tips be employed by racers, instead of the present ridiculous pretense at a shoe? If any greater protection is imperative, or is thought to be needed, the shoe proposed by the author would give all security, while it left the pedal structures free to exercise their important uses. There can be no doubt as to the safety of tips; in which, if Mr. Percivall could for years take his quadruped through the streets of London, another animal might, surely, scamper over the well-kept turf of a race-course, where the heels merely touch the earth during the intervals of leaps, and then only for an instant.

Were tips more generally employed, this form of shoe would be more highly valued. They are, however, now thought only to be of service when the animal is, "for a season," thrown up; but there can be no reason why the racer—trained, exercised, and worked always on choice turf—should ever be crippled by any more regular form of shoe. Most horsemen, however, like the warriors of old, place their great dependence on the accumulation of iron. The nearest approach they ever make toward a tip, and then only when guarded by a veterinary surgeon's advice, is a three-quarter shoe. The tip is a protection to be worn only during the run at grass, and to be discarded so soon as the stable is entered. Is not the racer always at grass, since the rail or the van generally carries it over the roads? How often do the feet of the thorough-bred fail, though there must be further cause than the work they have undergone? But no one is silly enough to suspect the shoeing can be at fault!

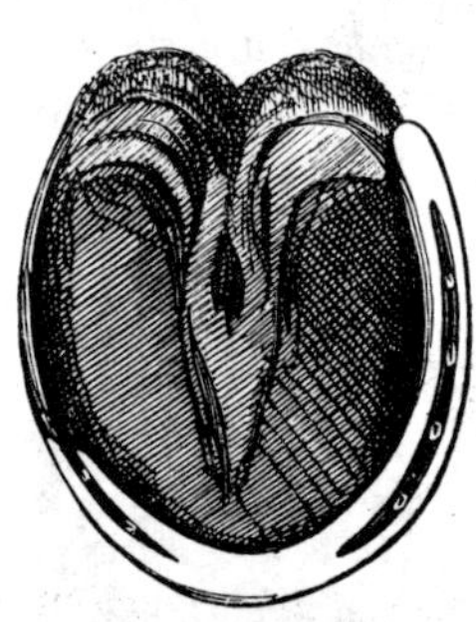

A THREE-QUARTER SHOE, WHICH ONLY LEAVES ONE-QUARTER UNFETTERED.

The three-quarter shoe is but an enlarged kind of tip. Most horsemen appreciate the unilateral nailing, which was revived some years ago by that excellent veterinary surgeon, Mr. Turner, of Regent Street. They can understand the advantages of leaving one-quarter without nails so long as the unfettered part be covered by a regular shoe. They comprehend that by omitting the nails on one side of the hoof, that side is left free to exercise its natural property of expansion. Therefore they perceive that the unilateral mode of shoeing is a partial remedy for contraction.

Though always worked on grass, and ever lightly shod, no animal is so troubled with mule hoofs as is the racer; yet no quadruped is so entirely under the inspection of man. The mode of shoeing must be at fault. That cannot be right the results from which are purely evil. The consequences experienced from the custom of fettering that portion of the foot on which the pleasure of motion and the extent of the rebound both depend, argue strongly in favor of tips, not only as training, but more especially as running shoes. Men with fleshy feet, having no protection from leather, fearlessly tread the race-course; yet the owners of blood stock seem afraid of trusting their animals to perform an act not equally bold—although nature sends the horse into the world with ready-made and stout-made shoes. There can be no just reason why the steed which never quits the turf need be hampered even with a unilateral shoe, were the horn only carefully, and not ruthlessly, cut away.

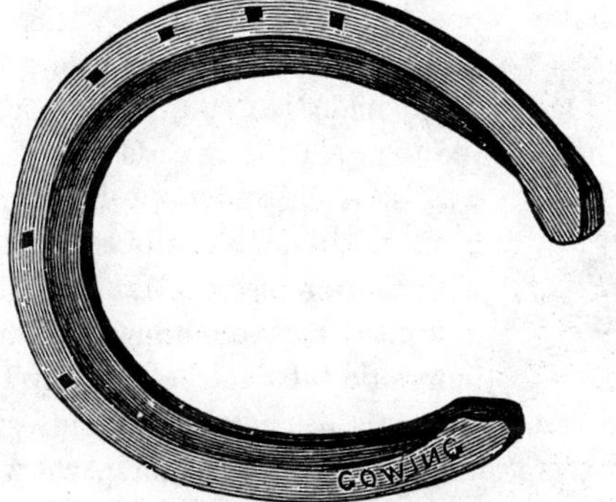

A SEATED AND A UNILATERAL SHOE.

A seated shoe implies a regular shoe, which has only so much upper surface left as will admit of the crust resting upon it. The remainder of the web slants away, till the posterior or inner margin becomes a comparatively fine edge. Such a make of shoe may lessen the weight, but it can afford no protection; while it offers a snug lodging for stones or grit, and presents an extended surface for the huntsman's dreaded heavy clay to act upon. Yet, for the sake of its prettiness, the seated shoe is all but universally adopted. No other form is so largely patronized by what should be the informed class of society.

Mr Bracy Clark once brought forward a jointed shoe, which was intended to admit of expansion; and was offered to the public as a radical cure for all the evils to which the foot of the horse was liable. The joint was placed at the toe, the shoe being forged in two halves, which were united by means of a rivet. The thing was wrong in principle. The toe, which nature intended should be fixed, was obliged to move, before the heels could expand; then, parts could not yield in different degrees, but all must move at once, according to the motion of the iron. It was soon discovered to be terribly injurious, when brought into use. The battering speedily fixed the central rivet, and afterward wore away the joint, leaving the two halves disunited. A thing which turns out defective, both in principle and in practice, merits that neglect into which the jointed shoe has now fallen.

MR. BRACY CLARK'S JOINTED SHOE.

Another mechanical ameliorator was termed the screw shoe. This had two rivets—one on either side of the toe, operating on two movable quarter pieces. The sides, therefore, were capable of all motion, and, being nailed to the quarters, were, by turning the screw, to be forced outward. The screw was situated under the frog, and was retained in its position by a stout bar of iron connected with the toe piece. Man, however, cannot treat any portion of an organic frame as it were an inorganic substance. He may tear flesh, but he cannot stretch or strain living tissues according to his pleasure. Moreover, all outward secretions are regulated by the parts which they cover and inclose. Thus, supposing a lad born with a diminutive head, the cranium cannot be enlarged by any degree of force; but educate the boy, exercise the intellect of the youth, and, with the greater development of the brain, the bones of the head will sensibly expand. So it must be with the heels of the horse's feet. These parts may become rigid and wired in by the fixing power exercised by the nails of the shoe. But remove the nails, allow the hoof that motion which is needful to its health, and its internal structures may recover their lost functions; a gradual restoration to the normal shape may be the consequence of strength regained by the internal organs.

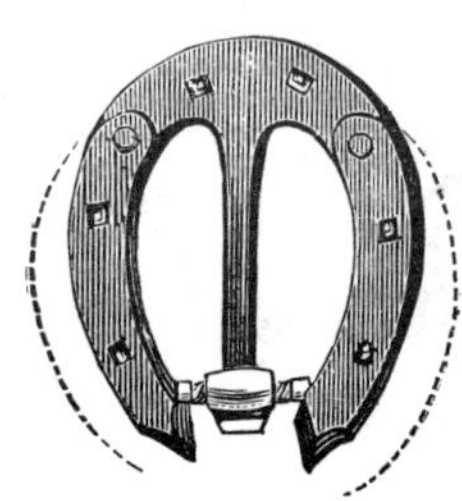

A SCREW SHOE.

The veterinary mind was, however, slow to recognize so plain a rule.

Like all nature's laws, the truth necessitated not that show of mastery in which the ignorant especially delight. The famous screw shoe is everywhere admitted to have been a decided failure; nevertheless, the pride of poor humanity could not relinquish the hope of compelling life, through the power, to direct mechanical force. Screws and rivets had proved alike hurtful, but there still remained other artifices, which were as yet untried. The frog-pressure shoe was one of these, which ultimately lamed many horses, without having benefited a single one. The wedge-heeled shoe is, however, occasionally encountered, even at the present day. It consists of a shoe, imperfectly seated upon its upper surface, and which has the heels much thicker or higher than the toe. The iron, at the inside heel, is beaten into an angular form, the apex of the angle looking toward the foot. The intention is, that the heel, resting upon a slanting surface, should slide downward and outward, thus being forced gradually to expand. The shoe may be said, up to a particular point, to answer the inventor's expectations. The hoof certainly does slide downward and outward; only, when this is accomplished, the wall has been torn from its attachments, while the apex of the wedge, coming into contact with the soft sole, has actually forced its way through the horn covering the last-named part, thereby lamentably laming the poor horse. Could the teaching of principle have been interpreted, so sad a result might have been understood without positively experimenting with breathing life.

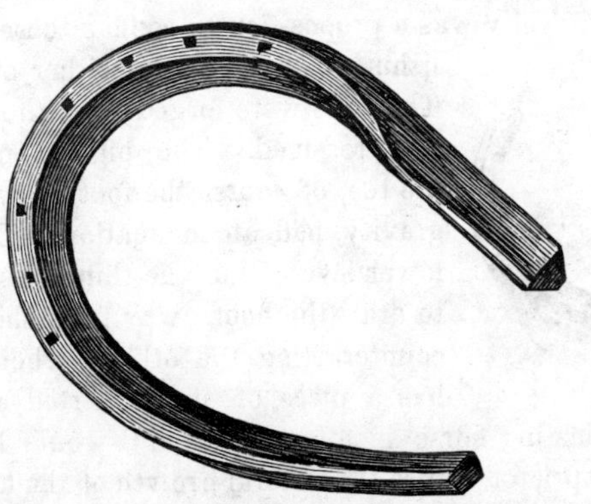

A WEDGE-HEELED SHOE.

But pride has no brains, and a very limited degree of feeling. A modification of the above shoe is still to be met in the London shops. The nail holes are principally at the toe, one only being inserted at the most forward part of each quarter. The author's proposed plan of fastening the shoe is, therefore, no positive novelty; since the smith, before now, has impaled the toe of the foot. A return to perfect freedom, however, could alone cure the evils caused by unnatural restraint. The wedge heel pointed the toe toward the earth; injured the bars and the sole; often causing large portions of the coffin-bone to exfoliate. Seeing the plan did not answer, the next inventor lowered the heels and raised the forward part, this thing being named a "thin-heeled shoe." However, one extreme could not heal the wounds provoked by another; and the position of the hoof, which the pavement of the stalls enforces while the horse is in the stable, the thin-heeled shoe perpetuated whenever the animal was taken abroad. Ceaseless discomfort can advantage no form of existence.

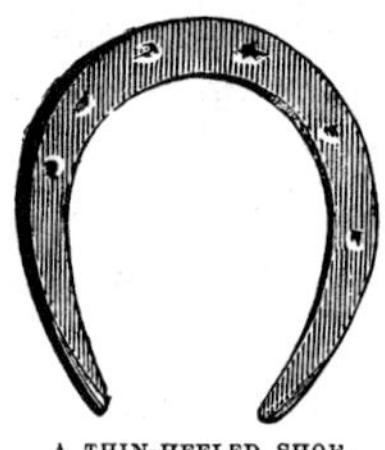

A THIN-HEELED SHOE.

The last shoe, moreover, besides being thin at the heels, also displayed a mild desire to retain the feature of the wedge. This was done without the inventor suspecting that, when he fixed the quarters of the hoof at a high altitude, and invited the heels to slide down an inclined plane, he was only laying a trap for loosening the clinches; since, the quarters and the heels being continuous, one cannot move without the other being displaced.

All men having, theoretically, insisted on the necessity of permitted freedom of motion to the quarters, in order to secure the health of the foot, the next novelty was a proposition to confine those parts, by establishing a large clip at either side of the shoe. The clips were forged; but the thin heels were also retained. The highest portion being at the toe, of course the foot, obeying the laws of gravity, had an inclination to drag toward the lower level—thus the thin heels had a tendency to draw the hoof away from the clips, one part counteracting the other. Then, the clip shoe has a piece of steel inserted at the toe; but could an everlasting horse shoe be produced, it would bring but small gain to the proprietor; since the natural growth of the horn necessitates that the metal should be removed, that new nails should be inserted, and that the foot should be pared out every third week. However, the steel toe and the thin heels were incompatible with each other; since the thin heels took the bearing from that part which the steel presupposes to be alone liable to attrition.

A CLIP SHOE.

It would, however, be vain to review all the shoes which have come before the public. A certain rim of iron has been pinched up, flattened out, squeezed in, twisted about, has been lengthened and has been shortened, subjected to every species of treatment but the right; and each trivial alteration has been patented to the public as a final and a wonderful improvement. After all the many changes, at the present time a modification of the shoe originally introduced by Clark, of Edinburgh, is in general use, or, if such an assertion requires any qualification, the hospital shoes, or shoes suited for particular forms of disease, are the principal exceptions.

The generality of grooms will undertake the relief of those injuries occasioned during motion, or which are produced by one leg being hit by the opposite foot.

Of **cutting** there are two descriptions. One is spoken of as "brushing," and this kind occurs near to the pastern joint. The other is called "speedy-cut," and it takes place immediately below the knee. Both are equally annoying; but the last is the most dangerous. "Speedy-cut" will destroy the rider's security in his horse; for a blow on the seat of injury may bring the animal suddenly to earth. Both affections are likely to occasion exostosis; for the repeated injury may so irritate the bone as shall cause it to enlarge or tumefy. Thus, the renewal of the accident produces a result which must increase the probability of its recurrence.

Almost all weakly, long-legged, and narrow-chested horses cut. Creatures with cow hocks are said to be exposed to this calamity. Many young horses strike in going; but they lose the habit as age matures the strength. Nearly all animals, when exhausted, will "brush," and often very severely. Lately, a ring of India-rubber has been employed as a protection against this annoyance; but it is a mere fantasy, and one not at all calculated to realize any practical expectation. Confirmed disappointment engenders a feeling allied to desperation; but when nostrums fail, advice should then be sought from more lofty counselors.

The speedy-cut has already been alluded to in the Illustrated Horse Doctor; but in that volume no mention was made of what is ordinarily implied by "brushing," which is confined principally to the hind extremities. It is astonishing how great may be the annoyance which a matter apparently so trivial will occasion; and it is a legitimate source of surprise how deep the wound can be, or how lasting the blemish, produced by slight blows, frequently becomes. The groom may exhaust his stock of remedies, and the master may expend some money and much patience, watching for a cure which is never effected.

Let the defeated proprietor then apply to some practical veterinary surgeon, who will inform him of the real cause of the injury which has already been intimated. Some horses will only cut during the latter portion of a long journey, or when thoroughly exhausted. Other quadrupeds are afflicted with a chronic description of weakness, and such animals may cut with the first step. These creatures require less work or entire rest, with a course of tonics, both in food and medicine.

However, make and shape certainly have some control over this affection. The horse which exhibits a wide chest, and stands with the feet not too close together, very rarely speedy-cuts. The animal which possesses well-made haunches with prominent hips and swelling thighs, that appear full, round, and fleshy, especially when such a creature places the fetlocks under the hocks, must be driven very far and pushed very hard before the pace shall become injurious.

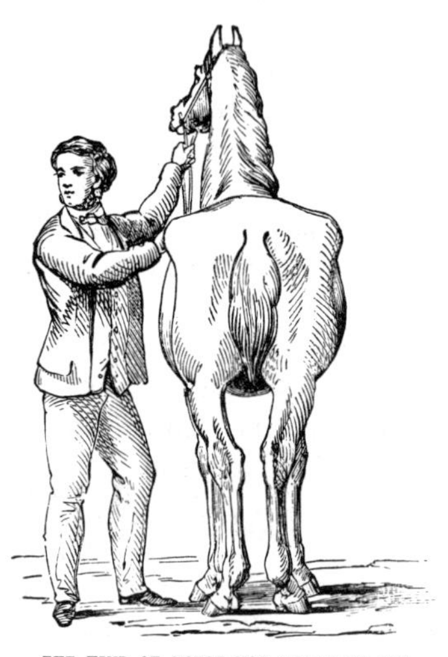
THE KIND OF HORSE NOT LIKELY TO CUT.

Several repeated remedies have been sold for the relief of this defect. Saddlers keep in stock pieces of leather, or small flaps with straps appended, which last, being buckled round the leg, hang pendulous, covering the wound. Such applications, however, rarely are satisfactory. The horse, during the motion of the feet, repeatedly kicks the leather,

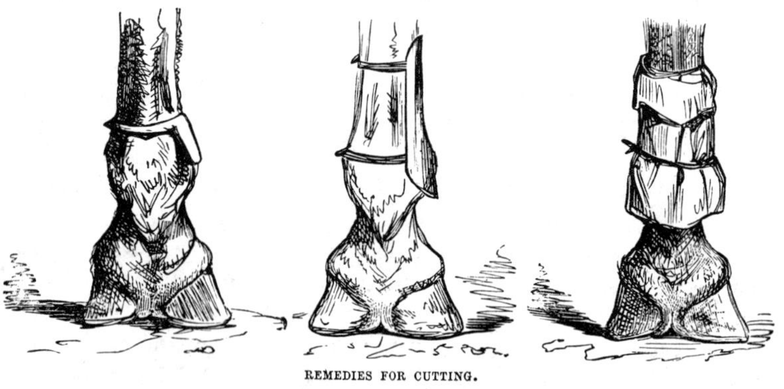
REMEDIES FOR CUTTING.

and the frequent blows generally remove it from its original situation; thus, long before the journey has ended, the remedy hangs over some sound part of the leg, and the sore is bleeding from renewed injury.

A better plan is to procure a piece of cloth which matches the color of the animal, and to fold this round the leg, ultimately tying it at the top and the bottom. Such a contrivance cannot be displaced, and is less likely to attract attention than the leathern flap recently alluded to. However, it must be tightly wrapped round the shin or it will bag and appear unsightly, as it is represented in the previous illustration. Still, such a resort affords but a partial protection, cloth being unable to stay the entire consequences of a blow; nor can it be regarded as exercising a curative influence.

That which appears better is a leathern boot, of the color of the skin, or made of prepared horse skin, having the hair on, and laced upon the member. Over the seat of injury a concave piece of stout leather is let into the covering, and the hollow thus formed, which acts as a protection, can also receive a portion of lint saturated in the lotion, prepared by adding one grain of chloride of zinc to an ounce of water. Thus, while the sore is spared a renewal of the cause, curative treatment is not stayed.

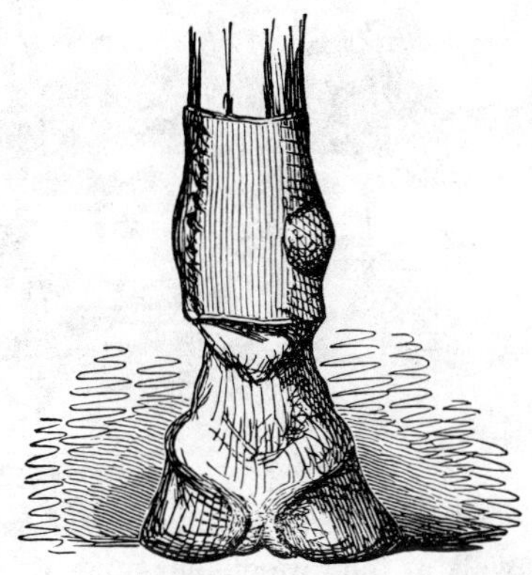

A LEATHERN BOOT.

The chloride of zinc lotion is the only remedy which an ordinary case of cutting would require; but aggravated instances of this annoyance will also be benefited by rest and a course of restoratives to amend the constitutional debility. Other matters consist in a warm lodging, an ample bed, prepared food, walking exercise, a loose box, and, above all things, no work. Should the animal be changing its coat, which is generally a period of weakness, throw it up till the operation is completed; give extra nourishment and one ounce of liquor arsenicalis, each day, to assist nature. Never turn out to grass; for numerous are the examples of flagging quadrupeds which, after the supposed invigoration of a month's "run," have been taken up in a condition which disabled them for labor ever afterward.

Such an animal should enjoy the very best of softened food—beans in excess—and should be retained at the homestead. It should be handled, not ridden, to exercise, of which it can hardly have too much, provided the motion does not excite perspiration or cause evident fatigue, neither of which states is desirable. Should the horse sweat in the stable, remove all clothing, open the door, and pour over the body several pails of the coldest water—having a helper ready to dry the saturated coat with all speed; then, putting on a bridle, send the animal out for one hour's brisk walking exercise. Order the man who holds the rein to

THE RIGHT AND THE WRONG WAY OF WALKING A GENTLEMAN'S HORSE.

walk at the rate of four miles an hour. An active quadruped can travel much faster, so there can be no excuse, beyond the indulgence of his individual laziness, for the servant creeping along, while the animal hangs the head as though it had some intention of laying down.

Much injury is done every year by the indolent manner in which idle lads "walk horses." The urchins who infest the streets of London display nimbleness while they run by the side of an equestrian, shouting out occasionally, "Hold your honor's horse?" No sooner, however, have they received orders to walk the quadruped about, than all their activity departs; they creep along at a pace which only just renders it impossible to charge them with standing positively stationary. The horse may be warm, and the master may desire to prevent the body from chilling while he is detained by business. A ready affirmative testifies that the command to move briskly has been comprehended; but who ever beheld one of these youthful idlers, when in possession of a job, stirring even at the pace of a lady's ordinary walk?

However, to return to the subject which at present is more especially under the reader's consideration. *Cutting* is often combined with clicking or forging, for both words signify the same act, implying the noise made by striking the toe or quarter of the hind shoe against the metal nailed to the forefoot. This sound is not generally considered pleasant by those who hear it; because, besides being of a monotonous character, it announces something to be the matter—either that the horse is not exactly in proper working condition, or that the journey has been a trifle too long for the strength of the animal, while the repeated blows endanger the retention of a fore shoe.

SHOE, DESIGNED WITH THE INTENTION OF ERADICATING CUTTING, AND OF RENDERING CLICKING AN IMPOSSIBILITY.

The smith generally is consulted to cure this defect. He, however, who regards the cause, will perceive that the eradication of the evil more concerns the stable than the forge. The man of the anvil, nevertheless, will put on a novel kind of shoe which, with all the confidence of ignorance, he shall assert must stay the annoyance. The remedy totally fails, and the horse is led to another forge. The new blacksmith picks up the foot, and, of course, is cunning enough to profit by what he there perceives. A different shoe is tried and pronounced an absolute remedy. Still, this disappoints; the quadruped seeks some other shoemaker. The next bit of iron leads to no new result. The clicking and the cutting only get worse during these numerous trials; till the proprietor becomes alarmed, and the horse is thrown up to undergo regular curative treatment.

The rest thus obtained often effects that which no change of shoe could accomplish. The smiths, however, are only to be blamed for pretending to perform impossibilities. The best veterinary surgeons in the kingdom having no better appliances, could have labored to no better result; the fact being that the kind of shoe which shall answer in all such cases, does not and cannot exist. That article has the best chance which is adopted when the owner deems it necessary to lighten the work of his exhausted servant. Thus, it is a matter of uncertainty which shoe will succeed. The first smith may, or perhaps the last will, prove the very clever tradesman in his employers' estimation.

The next engraving is a type of the shoe commonly employed for the alleviation of this unpleasantness. The number of altered shapes and adapted peculiarities is infinite; but one pervading model is readily detected through all such modifications. There are, however, several shoes claimed as inventions by different smiths, and each is warranted to cure the most aggravated case of cutting or of clicking on the first application. The author has known many of these to fail; while the ordinary shoe often answers admirably, so the horse be "up" to his work, and not pushed too far or too hard.

The fact being, that flesh and blood, if overtasked, will flag, and no mechanical contrivance can anticipate the natural consequences of such exhaustion. Clicking and cutting are not local ailments; therefore, though they may be mitigated, they cannot be eradicated by any local application. They doubtless are both produced by the irregular movement of the feet; but the motion of the extremities is regulated by the condition of the body. If the reader is ever on a journey, and the horse he is guiding chances to click, the bearing-rein should be let down—if the driver sit behind harness disgraced by such an instrument of folly. Should that not succeed, accept the warning: pull up at the next tavern, and have the quadruped taken from the shafts, rubbed down and rested.

SHOE, MEANT TO PREVENT CLICKING.

After a couple of hours spent by the traveler in the coffee-room, the journey may be resumed, though, of course, a longer stay will rather benefit than injure the steed; yet, in either case, the subsequent pace should be a little slackened; and if, on reaching home, the work is slightly lightened, the noise may never after startle the "ear of propriety."

These remedies should always anticipate the setting in of winter; because wet roads necessitate heavier shoes, by which a severer blow can be inflicted. Nevertheless, the majority of horse owners are extremely careless about the necessities of the seasons. The winters, in this climate, are more generally characterized by their severity than remarkable for their mildness; yet the frost appears always to take horse proprietors by surprise. Gentlemen, to be sure, during this season allow their dumb servants to remain within the stable; but quadrupeds which have to work for their own and their masters' sustenance, creatures which have to labor long and to labor hard, slaves which toil before the sun has risen and never cease till darkness has long set in, are never prepared for the season which in England seems a certainty.

A horse shoe is, however, not a perishable commodity, nor does its store necessitate any sacrifice. Supposing it were forged in the summer, and because of death or change, it should not suit in the winter, the smith, at such a period, would gladly accept its return. Many forges are comparatively idle during the warmer months, and any amount of winter shoes would be most thankfully manufactured. Then no one will employ the men; but scarcely does a severe frost or the snow set in, than people throng into the forge, all clamorous to have their horses' shoes suited to the weather. They crowd the building; they even stop the roadway. The inside is full of men and horses—horses and men cluster deep about the entrance. The smiths have to work fast, and often hang over the fires for three nights and three days, without looking on a bed. Beer is abundant; but nature cannot labor continuously on any amount of stimulant, and the men ultimately sink, exhausted, to sleep soundly on a heap of old rusty horse shoes, while many voices are shouting and many anvils are ringing around them.

THE BLACKSMITH'S FORGE AT THE COMMENCEMENT OF A HARD FROST.

Such scenes might be prevented and the work much better done, would owners lay in a stock of shoes, properly frosted, against the coming winter. The labor executed during the leisure portion of the year would not be hastily performed by overtaxed workmen; the only extra charge such a provision would necessitate is the interest on the slight cost of the articles supplied: though very often even such an increase of expense would be avoided, since it is by no means uncommon for the smith's account to remain longer than six months before it is liquidated; while the confusion, loss of time, and those accidents which often occur, would be banished.

Frosting or roughing, as it is termed, is generally performed in a coarse and careless manner, because of that excessive press of business amid which it is executed. In the first place, the shoe is hurriedly torn from the hoof, without the nails being properly unclinched, or any trouble being taken about the process. Should the proprietor expostulate, he only elicits an uncivil reply; for the journeyman is vexed with boisterous solicitations from a crowd of impatient customers, and irritable from inordinate fatigue. The shoe is then heated; after which the free extremities are turned downward with the hammer, and the ends are hastily beaten into a rude, sharp edge. In some particular cases, the toe is likewise favored by having a clip forged; but occasionally the toe is turned downward, forming a third and a front calkin. The article is thus rendered too short for the foot, and, with all shape destroyed, is nailed on to the hoof from which it was recently removed; and the animal is led from the forge wearing shoes supposed to be properly "frosted."

THE SHOE OF THE HORSE AS FREQUENTLY FROSTED.

The rudeness of the above process has long been appreciated by the more reflective portion of the public. To rectify it, various innovations have been proposed. The meditated improvements, however, have all sank into disuse, because of the attendant expense or of the necessitated exertion. A common man thinks it no trouble to remain through the night in the blacksmith's forge, waiting for his turn, at an expensive, a ruinous, and an inefficient operation,—because other people do the same. But when his turn arrives, perhaps a new set of shoes is spoiled; for the ordinary "roughing" is generally of no service after the third day, the sharp calkins being by that time ground blunt.

The huge weight of the animal grinds the edges off the iron, especially upon London stones, so that in three days they are no better than ordinary calkins, and cease to enable the quadruped to progress on ice. The constant removal and renewal of the shoe—the horn each time having to be repierced by fresh nails—seriously injures the hoof, so that frequently animals are forced to remain idle because there remains no more horn on which to fix a fastening. Those horses which escape such a fate, nevertheless carry the scars which commemorate the period of frost for months afterward; for there is no horseman, who has the most trivial experience in such matters, but will bitterly complain of the damage done to the quadruped's feet, when it is forced to work through the winter season.

Some person, many years ago, proposed to use nails with large steel sharp-pointed heads, during the prevalence of frost. This plan was tried, and signally failed. The constant renewal of the nails was found ruinous to the hoof; for the strongest of the projecting heads was unable to resist the grinding action of a horse's foot longer than twenty-four hours. Then, many of the heads broke off while being driven, and not a few were fixed in a damaged condition, owing to the blows received from the heavy hammer of the smith.

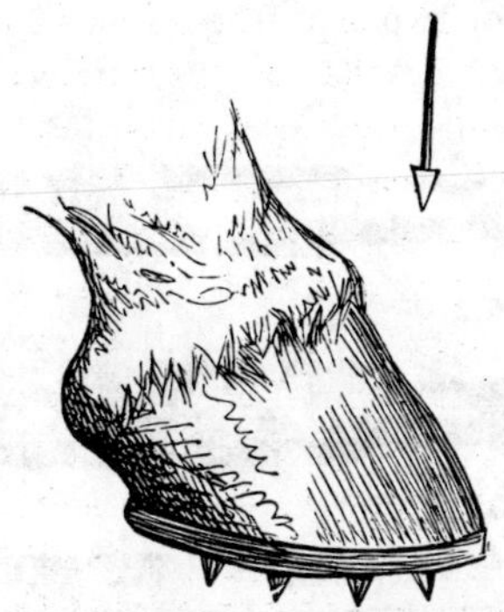

A SHOE, INTENDED TO ENABLE A HORSE TO WORK IN FROST, WHICH IS FIXED ON TO THE FOOT WITH SHARP HEADED AND PROJECTING NAILS.

A SHOE, WITH POINTS, WHICH SCREW ON AND OFF, DESIGNED TO FIT A HORSE FOR WORK DURING FROSTY WEATHER.

Mr. White, however, proposed a plan concerning the utility of which Mr. Lupton, a living and a most intelligent writer, bears favorable evidence. Large holes, containing the thread of a female screw, are made through the heels of the winter shoes, and several steel points, manufactured with a male screw, adapted to the dimensions of the holes just mentioned. Whenever frost coats the roads with ice, all that is requisite a boy might perform. The hole in the shoe has to be cleared out, and afterward, with an instrument known as "a spanner," one of the points, before alluded to, is screwed into the opening. When these points are worn down, they are easily renewed; thus the terrors of the frost are overcome without exposing the horse for hours to the chilly air, or yourself submitting to the incivilities of the forge.

On the above subject, the following is extracted from the excellent weekly newspaper *The Field*, and is here quoted because of the information it affords, and because of the lucid manner in which it explains the measures necessary to be pursued.

"About this time last season we inserted in *The Field* an account of the plan of frosting horse shoes, recommended more than fifty years ago by Mr. White, veterinary surgeon, of Exeter. Since then, nearly one thousand sets of the sharp cogs used for this purpose have been sold by the engineer to whom we intrusted the task of making them; and the plan appears to give unqualified satisfaction. At the suggestion of several correspondents who have not seen our former article, we are induced to repeat the notice, with the addition of an engraving representing the tools necessary; these being a drill of the required size, which every smith possesses, and with which a hole is drilled in the heel of each shoe, and, if needed, in the toe also. These holes are then converted into female screws by means of two taps, (figs. 1 and 2,) one

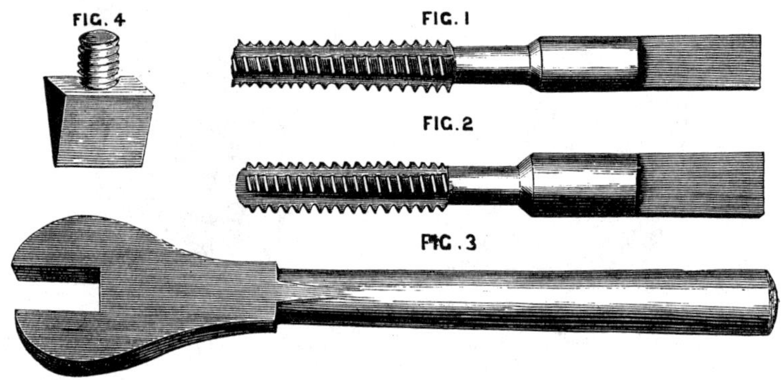

being slightly smaller than the other, so as to make a perfect female screw by using first the smaller one and then the larger. Besides these, a spanner (fig. 3) is required to fix on the cog firmly; and the cogs themselves (fig. 4) should be made by a competent smith. These may all be obtained of S. Morris, 50 Rathbone Place, Oxford Street, London, the price of the tools being six shillings, and of the cogs, three shillings per dozen. With this outlay, any shoeing smith can fit a set of shoes by drilling the heels, (and the toes, if the roads are very slippery, but for ordinary work the cogs in the heels are quite sufficient,) tapping them with the taps furnished to him, after which they are nailed on; and the horse so shod can in five minutes be roughed by his groom, by screwing a cog in each hole, with the aid of the spanner. It often happens that the roads become frozen after a horse leaves home; but if the groom has the spanner and cogs in his pocket, he is independent of the smith, and neither the delay caused by 'roughing,' nor the danger from its omission, is incurred. A specimen shoe, properly fitted, may be seen at the office of *The Field*."—*December* 20, 1861.

The plan is excellent, but it requires a little forethought and a slight expenditure of ready cash. The tools for the tapping, or making the female screw holes, and for the points, Mr. Lupton obtains from Birmingham; the former at a cost of five shillings—the last for one penny or three half pence each. Tapping a set of shoes is by the smith charged fourpence; and for so small an outlay the gentleman just named escapes the unpleasantness and the annoyance which are inseparable from the old method of "roughing" horses during frosty weather.

A FOOT PROPERLY SHOD, AND A FOOT WHICH HAS BEEN CRUELLY RASPED, TO MAKE THE HOOF SUIT A SHOE THAT WAS TOO SMALL FOR IT.

The author believes he has now touched upon all the *necessary* heads connected with the subject he is at present considering; still this article cannot be closed without apprising the reader of a practice not unusual in some forges, but never indulged in by the respectable tradesman. This is, paring and rasping the horse's foot till it be small enough to fit the shoe, rather than kindle a fire and forge a new set which shall suit the feet of the animal. It may to some readers seem like a jest, to write seriously about the horse's shoes being too tight; but it is, indeed, no joke to the quadruped which has to move in such articles. The walk is strange, as though the poor creature were trying to progress, but could obtain no bearing for its tread. The legs are all abroad, and the hoofs no sooner touch the ground than they are snatched up again. The head is carried high, and the countenance denotes suffering. It is months before the horn is restored to its normal condition. The animal must, during this period, remain idle in the stable; and, that the reader may be enabled to recognize the foot, under such circumstances, the last illustration was introduced.

It is trusted that whoever may possess an animal which is thus treated, will, in the first instance, secure the evidence as to fact from three or four of the principal veterinary surgeons; then enforce, with its utmost rigor, the law against the individual who has knowingly been guilty of this most heartless attempt at a positive fraud.

The horse is so entirely given into the hands of man, and is so submissive to his treatment, that the active supervision of its master is doubly necessary for its protection. While the present mode of nailing is continued, every proprietor willfully exposes his quadruped to danger who sends the creature to be shod. Any journeyman may, therefore, be pardoned if, occasionally, the foot be pricked; but the pains and the labor required to adjust a hoof to a shoe of small dimensions are absolute proof of evil design, and are irrefutable testimony which should forbid the remotest thought of leniency toward the offender.

CHAPTER IV.

THE TEETH—THEIR NATURAL GROWTH, AND THE ABUSES TO WHICH THEY ARE LIABLE.

"No legs, no horse," is, with a particular class, a very familiar phrase. This assertion, becoming a maxim, has apparently directed attention in a special manner to the lower extremities. All purchasers are particular about the legs and feet of an animal; but the teeth are merely glanced at, to ascertain the age. Such a custom is evidently wrong; since it would be as true of the organs of mastication as it is concerning those of locomotion should the horsemen also say, "No teeth, no horse." For the creature that is valuable only on account of its labor, cannot be equal to its toil if it do not consume a fitting quantity of sustenance. Though the majority combine, as it were, to pass the teeth over without notice when inspecting the horse, nevertheless many owners seem to appreciate the value of these organs to the welfare of the quadruped, it being not uncommon to hear horse proprietors complain, "the beast cannot eat sufficient for the demand which is daily made upon its capabilities."

The animal was sent on this earth provided with every apparatus necessary to crop, to comminute, and to digest the green verdure of the earth. Man has seized on and domesticated the body, which is exquisitely adapted only for special purposes. He works it while in its infancy, or forces it to labor until the sight is lost and the limbs are crippled. To fit the creature for his uses, he changes the character of its food. Artificially-prepared oats and hay, with various condiments, are used to stimulate the spirit. No one inquires whether such a diet is the fitting support of the animal. But when the energy lags, beans, beer, etc. are resorted to as restoratives for exhaustion. The quadruped, thus treated, men have agreed shall be aged by the eighth year; but the author has seen very old horses which had not attained the fifth birthday. Opinion seems to be based upon the circumstance that, by the time recognized as "aged" in the equine species, the indications of the teeth do no more than tempt a guess. The cessation of dental growth, however, does not announce maturity to be consummated; but man appeals to the teeth as corroborative of his judgment, without asking himself whether those parts have been doomed to unnatural wear, and therefore may not have assumed an unnatural aspect.

The author has not lately seen a specimen of **bishoped teeth**. In Ireland, such sights obtrude themselves at every horse fair. The majority of horses are, in that country, sold cheap, most of the purchasers being clothed in rags. It is a sad feature in the practices of imposition, that it is always violently rampant where there is the least certainty of reward.

To fully explain in what bishoping consists, it is necessary to inform the reader that on the nipping or cutting surfaces of the young horse's front teeth there mostly are dark indentations or deep hollows. Below is presented an enlarged engraving of this portion of a tooth, taken from the head of that which was a three-year old colt. The dark spot in the middle of the diagram represents the situation of the hollow into which the food naturally falls, rendering the interior of the cavity of a deep color approaching to blackness. Bishoping supposes the cavity always to be present; invariably to be of one form, and in every instance to sink to the like depth, which suppositions are contrary to fact; but even were such rules observed by nature, there are still means by which the cheat may be detected. Immediately around the dark-colored space is developed a fine line of enamel, which is always white. The rogues can counterfeit the black mark, but they cannot imitate the crystalline white bordering which surrounds the opening. The presence or absence of this is of more importance, therefore, than the existence of a black indentation. Again, those who tamper with the teeth cannot change the shape of the surface on which they work. The young tooth is wide from side to side, and narrow from the front to the backward margin. He who ventures where bishoped horses are to be found, should familiarize his eye with the shape of the youthful organ.

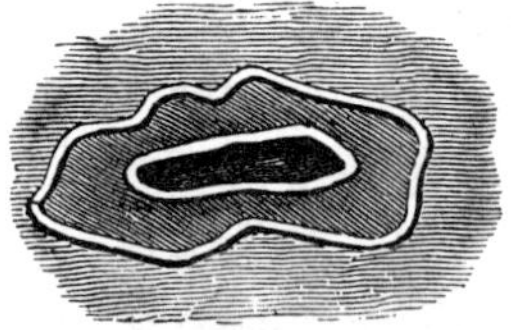

THREE YEARS OLD.

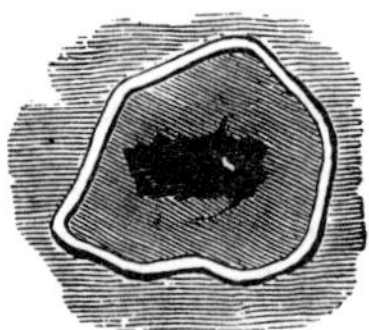

TWELVE YEARS OLD.

An enlarged view of the difference in form and in aspect which separates the table of a twelve-year old bishoped nipper from the same part in the three year old colt.

In contrast with the natural tooth, the reader is also presented with an exaggerated sketch taken from an organ which had been tampered with, and which was extracted from the head of an animal that had at least attained its twelfth year. The natural size has been considerably enlarged, as the author thereby hoped to render the contrast the more obvious. This last member, it will be remarked, has parted with its juvenile width, or is now characterized by depth and angularity. The central cavity, it will also be observed, bears small resemblance to the natural depression which it is meant to imitate. The color, moreover, is quite black, and of an even tint throughout, while the presence of the girding line of enamel cannot be detected.

The difference, however, is more striking, when two full rows of teeth are placed in contrast one with the other, after the manner in which they are displayed in the next engraving. In the young mouth, the incisors are arranged in a gracefully curved line; the posterior margins of the organ present little peculiarity. In the aged teeth, the prominent center of these has retracted, while all idea of grace in the order of their disposal has departed. Each member in the old jaw evinces an inclination to become equally prominent, and the posterior borders evince an obvious angularity.

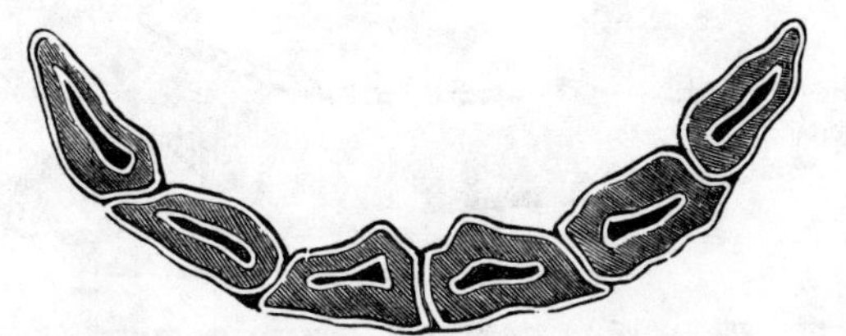

DIAGRAM, SHOWING THE TABLES OF A NATURAL ROW OF FIVE-YEAR OLD TEETH.

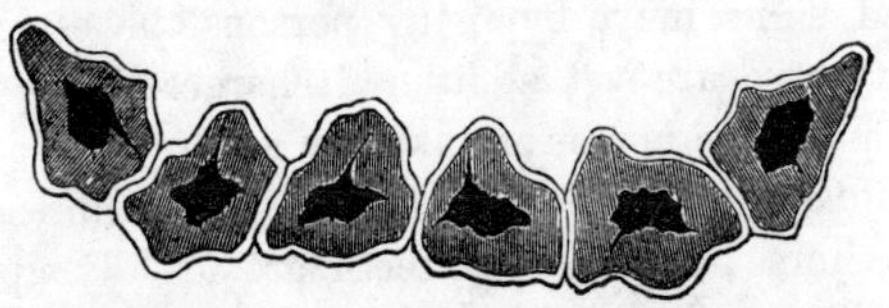

THE TABLES OF THE BISHOPED TEETH WHICH BELONG TO AN ANIMAL SIXTEEN YEARS OLD.

Then, if the marks in each are examined, the central cavities in the bishoped have jagged edges; while from these indentations arise certain eccentric lines, which invariably run toward the circumference. Such lines evidently were not made with any design. They were caused either by the inaptness of the operator, the coarseness of the tool with which he worked, or they were provoked by the natural struggles of the animal that was subjected to a merciless operation. The marks, moreover, are of a deep-black color; while the lines are remarkable for sometimes being of a lighter hue than the surface on which they repose.

There are, however, other signs which faithfully denote the age of the quadruped. The permanent incisors, when first cut, are almost perpendicular; but as years accumulate, these organs assume a more horizontal direction. The tushes also, when they first appear in the mouth, point forward. These members, after a time, become straight; but as age progresses, they ultimately lean decidedly outward and at length incline backward. Besides these well-marked indications, from the disposition of the front nippers to arrange themselves in a line, only two can be seen in old quadrupeds when the mouth is viewed from the side; while the membrane covering the gums altogether loses its fleshy hue, becoming evidently thick, yellow, loose and baggy.

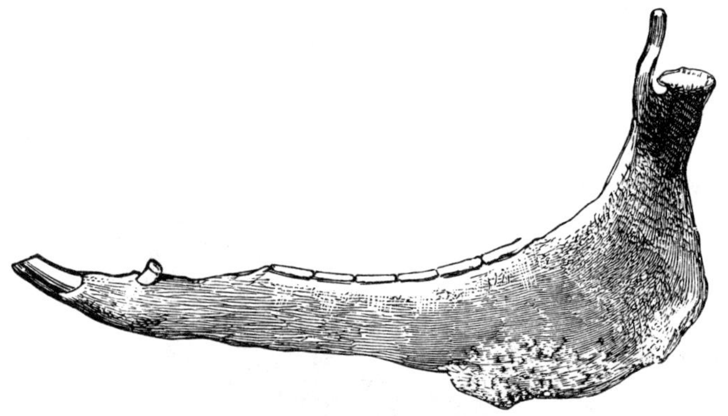

THE JAW OF A HORSE WHICH WAS THIRTY YEARS OF AGE.

Such marked signs may, by many persons, be esteemed sufficient protection; but there are yet additional characteristics with which all who venture to purchase horses of unknown sellers should be acquainted. The general indications of senility are strongly impressed both upon man and upon horse; though the teeth are usually appealed to, the appearance of the mouth should not be absolutely and solely regarded. A white horse is rarely young, any more than a white-haired man is, as a rule, in the possession of youth. Then, as the juvenile period ceases, absorption begins to operate. Deposit no longer takes place; but with senility a rapid wasting ensues; both bones and flesh suffer under this new action.

The branches of the colt's lower jaw are wide apart, and in the cavity thus formed the tongue reposes. This space is called the "channel." The lower margins, also, of the inferior maxillæ are in the colt full, round, and prominent. When age is present, the edges retract, the channel narrows, while the lower margins of the bones appear to the fingers of the examiner, accustomed to handle young horses, to be positively sharp.

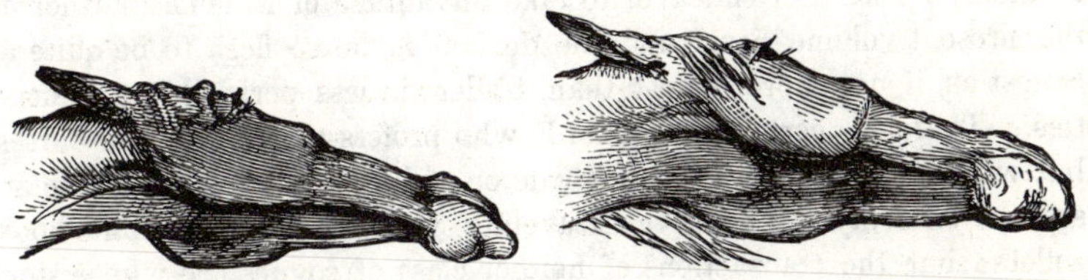

A YOUNG HORSE. AN OLD HORSE.
Comparative difference in the channels or in the spaces between the branches of the lower jaws.

When a person having a horse to sell talks boastfully of all "the marks" being present in the mouth, avoid him as a suspicious individual. Honest men know, or at least all honest men should by this time be aware, that there is no dependence to be placed in these so-called "marks;" therefore they do not strive to direct attention toward fallacious indications.

SHOWING THE HORSE'S TEETH.

By simply parting the lips of the animal, a judge can see everything which he cares to behold. The kind of teeth present are easily recognized; or when such signs declare the animal to be aged, the position of the teeth, the condition of the bones, and the general aspect enable him to guess as to a probability. Therefore, when a gentleman requests to see the mouth, the horse dealer, unless specially commanded to do so, no longer endeavors to tug the jaws asunder, a proceeding which, when conducted hastily, is apt to provoke resistance; but the groom is ordered to merely separate the lips, a measure to which most animals will complacently submit.

Should the person to whom the teeth are exhibited, by an evident lack of recognition declare his ignorance of their announcement, the honest dealer may slyly quiz his patron's want of knowledge; but assuredly he will not endeavor to take advantage of it. The author of the present volume has found the dealers in horse flesh to be quite as honest as, if not more honest than, traders in less perishable commodities. There are certain blackguards who profess to be dealers in horses, but who have no fixed place of abode or of business. So also there are scamps who style themselves traveling jewelers and itinerant booksellers; but the transactions of neither class of rogues (he whose stock in trade consists of a whip, or they whose most valuable possession is the mahogany box or the specimen number which is carried from house to house) can be taken as evidence against the more respectable members of the calling to which all will assume to belong. A gentleman, ignorant of any acquaintance with jockey-ship, can walk with perfect safety into the yard of any respectable dealer; look at the animals which are for sale, and walk out again, without encountering any undue solicitation to purchase. How many shops are there in London, in which a person, equally uninformed, could perform the like manœuvre?

When this is written, it is not meant to imply that a horse dealer keeps all his stock open to public inspection. On the contrary, in most respectable yards there are certain snuggeries which conceal the more choice articles. The pick of these are not even open to every purchaser who can pay the price. No! Horse and picture dealers are alike in one characteristic trait: each has a pride in the article he sells. The first individual will allow his dinner to grow cold, while he remains gloating over the points and beauties of some fresh acquisition. "How it would look carrying Her Majesty!" The image amuses his fancy! "What a spanker to hold a first place in the Beaufort hunt!" He warms with the idea! "What a charger it would make for Cambridge at a Hyde Park Review!" He is in ecstasies at the thought! He cannot possibly decide what so much perfection is fit for. He can never consent to treat such loveliness as a mere chattel,—a thing to be sold and then to be enveloped in obscurity. The animal must not be parted with to any unknown individual! The feeling common to his order forbids him to exhibit the object of his pride to general inspection. But he might dispose of it, even at a sacrifice, were he convinced it would occupy such a position as he esteems it is fitted to adorn. He then could point to the animal and vaunt that it came from his yard. Honor, fame, and profit must accrue to him who could refer to such exalted dealings;—therefore there is a strong sense of self lurking under that which at first glance appears to be mere Quixotic denial of self.

At the same time, if all respectable dealers are above positive imposition, it is not every dealer who will prevent a self-conceited novice from imposing upon himself. Such a person, acting upon his own judgment, may be allowed to purchase the worst screw which some yard contains, at the money that should procure a first-rate animal. Even then, the dealer has an escape, which every form of worldly honesty will not provide. The quadruped, if not approved of, can be exchanged within the fortnight following the transaction. To be sure, such exchanges generally advantage only one party: but a tradesman must live; he cannot be expected to waste hours showing his stock and chattering with fools for no business purpose!

However, to protect the reader from every chance of imposition, so far as the age of the horse may be concerned, let him attentively accompany the author through the following pages; let him also particularly notice the engravings with which the text is illustrated.

A foal at birth has three molars or grinding teeth, just through the gums, upon both sides of the upper and of the lower jaws. The little animal, however, generally displays no incisors or front teeth; but the gums are inflamed and evidently upon the eve of bursting. The molars or grinders are, as yet, unflattened or have not been rendered smooth by attrition. The lower jaw, moreover, when the inferior margin is felt, appears to be very thick, blunt, and round.

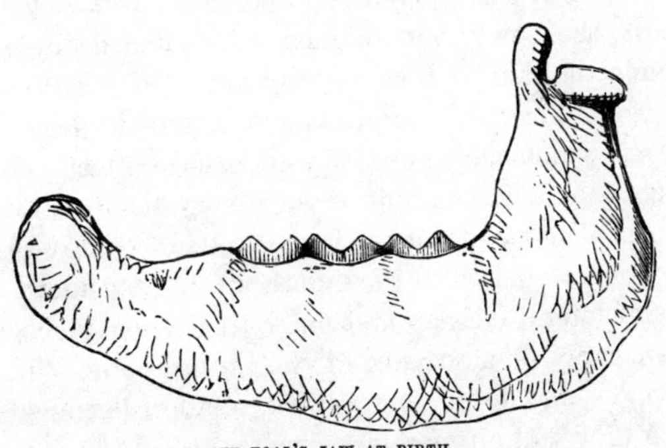

THE FOAL'S JAW AT BIRTH.

A fortnight has rarely elapsed before the membrane ruptures, and two pairs of front, very white teeth begin to appear in the mouth. At first, these new members look disproportionately large to their tiny abiding-place; and when contrasted with the reddened gums at their base, they have that pretty, pearly aspect which is the common characteristic of the milk teeth in most animals. They must occasion pain to the foal at this period: the appearance of the little mouth affords sufficient evidence of that fact; but it is astonishing how meekly these beautiful creatures will submit to our examinations of their teeth,—as though they came into the world possessed of all confidence in man's intentions and with every dependence upon his sympathy. Some of the diminutive strangers seem even to derive pleasure from their irritable gums being inspected. They behave almost as though they recognized their future master and felt flattered by his notice. Alas! that brutality should ever repel the trustfulness of nature, and that experience should instruct most of our mute fellow-beings to regard mankind as enemies

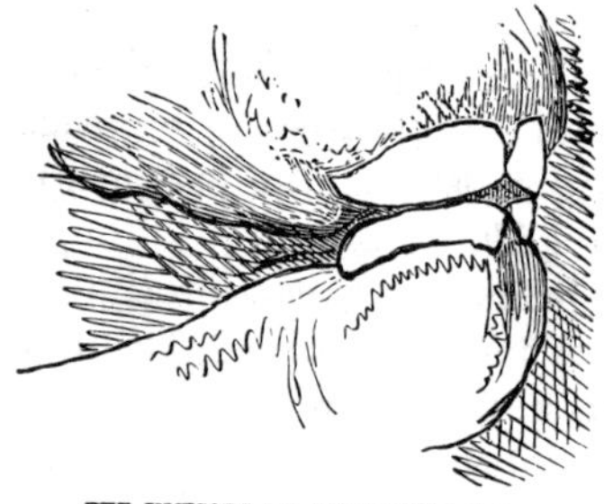
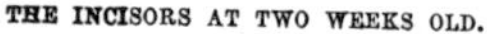
THE INCISORS AT TWO WEEKS OLD.

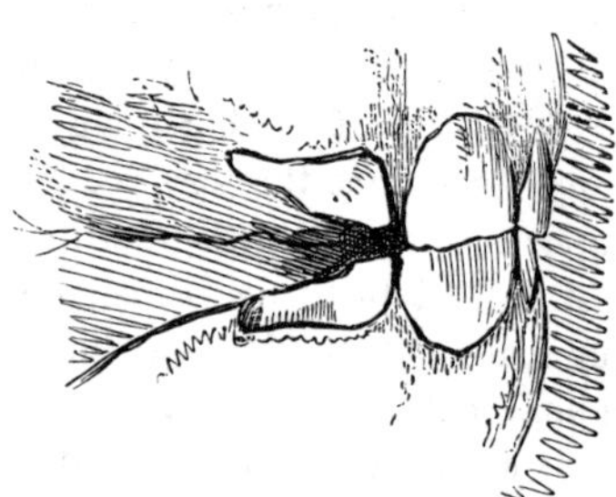
THE INCISORS AT SIX WEEKS OLD.

It is not until another month has passed, or until the foal is six weeks old, that more teeth appear. By that time, much of the swelling present on the gums of the newly-born animal has softened down, though all trace of it cannot be said to have entirely departed. The membrane, as time progresses, will have to resign much of its scarlet hue. In the brief period, however, which has elapsed since the former teeth were gazed at, the growth has been such that the sense of very disproportionate size no longer remains. The two front teeth are now fully up, and these appear almost of proportions suited to the mouth which they adorn. But when the two pairs of lateral incisors first make their appearance, it is in such a shape as can imply no assurance of their future form. They resemble the corner nippers, and do not suggest the smallest likeness to the lateral incisors which they will ultimately become.

The foal, during the first six weeks of its existence, does not learn to appreciate, at its just value, that which poets have termed "the milk of human kindness." A little shyness, however, exhibited about this period shows that doubt has partially shaken the confidence with which the appointed master was formerly welcomed. But the little being is still docile; it does not altogether avoid mankind. It will yet accept their caresses, permit patiently their mercenary inspections, acting as though its mild disposition, the natural inheritance of its tribe, derived actual pleasure and amusement by submitting to the will of him whom it must shortly recognize as an earthly tyrant.

Why should not the primary lessons of domestication be now gently commenced, when the spirit requires not to be subdued and the temper needs not to be conquered? Is there not unnecessary cruelty in the plan which is commonly adopted? The young life is allowed to roam at large till the time arrives when man conceives the colt ought to be "*broken in.*" There is no gradual instruction; no endeavor to coax or to soothe by a display of gentleness. Obedience is remorselessly wrenched out of the being. Harshness naturally engenders resistance; but increased severity is employed, till the willing creature is literally conquered and its spirit "broken." This is done to an animal which is born anxious to please its superior. Let the reader ponder over this custom, and then reflect upon the retentive memory of the subjected race. They must remember—they have no ability to forget. Consider the custom, and also regard the nature upon which that custom operates; then say whether the breeder goes the proper way to develop that sweetness of temper and that gentleness of disposition which increase the value of equine property.

But, to return to the subject of the present paper. There is now a long pause before more teeth appear in the mouth. The little one, in the mean time, lives chiefly upon suction, and runs, during the period of perfect happiness, free by its mother's side. Upon the completion of the first month, seldom earlier, it may be observed to lower the head and nip the young blades of the shooting grass. From the third month, however, the habit becomes more frequent, until, by the advent of the sixth month, the grinders will be worn quite flat; or, having lost their pointed and jagged prominences, will, by the wear of constant mastication, have been reduced to the state which is suited to their function.

THE FRONT TEETH AT NINE MONTHS OLD.

The corner incisors come into the mouth about the ninth month, the four pair of nippers, which have been already traced, being at this time fully developed. Above is a view of the foal's teeth, as these are exhibited at the period named. The reader will remark that the corner incisors, which are depicted as through the gums, do not yet meet, though these organs point toward each other; neither has the membrane of the mouth at this time entirely lost the deepened hue of infancy.

From this date, however, the gums gradually become pale, till, by the completion of the first year, the membrane has nearly assumed that complexion which will endure throughout the earlier period of existence All the incisors are, by the first birthday, well up. The masticatory agent, although consolidated, has not, when the quadruped is one year old, entirely lost the roundness and bluntness of its inferior margin, for which the jaw at birth was peculiarly remarkable.

This fullness of the bone is caused by all the grinding teeth which are in the mouth when the foal first sees the light being of a temporary character; the enlargement is consequent upon the jaw, therefore, having to contain and to mature the long permanent grinders which, within the substance of the bone, are growing beneath the temporary molars. To contain and to allow the large uncut teeth to become developed, before appearing above the gums, causes the small jaw of a diminutive foal to be disproportionately thick, especially when this part is compared with the same structure in an aged horse; but the mind is reconciled to its apparent clumsiness when apprised of the uses to which the organ is subservient.

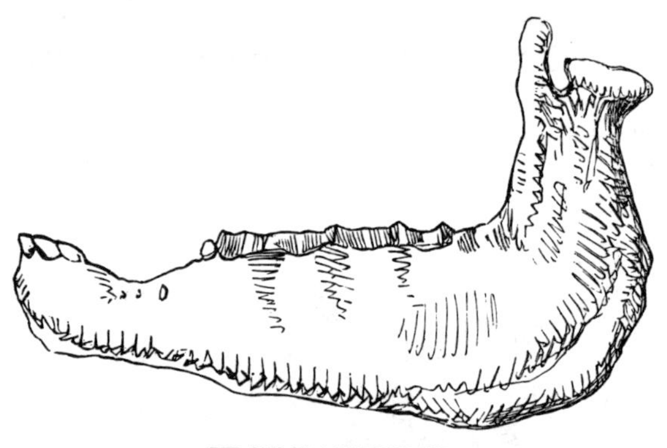

THE JAW OF A ONE-YEAR OLD.

At one year old, the first permanent tooth appears in the head. This is the fourth molar, or that which is represented as the most backward grinder in the appended engraving. The reader will not fail to remark the greater length which the jaw-bone presents at one year old. The additional extent also in the opposite direction cannot otherwise than be observed. This increase of size was necessitated to cover the increasing size of the recent molar; also, to afford room for the partial development of two other grinders, which, as age progresses, will appear behind that which is now the last tooth.

About this time, frequently at birth, little nodules of bone, without fangs, merely attached to the gums, appear in front of each row of grinders. These are vulgarly denominated "Wolves' Teeth," and were once held to be of vast importance. At present, however, they are recognized as the simple representatives of those organs which in other animals (as in man) render the teeth a continuous or unbroken curve. They are, by experience, found to be harmless. It is idle to remove these organs, especially as they generally disappear with the shedding of those members facing which they are located.

Although by this period the foal has lost the furzy tail, nevertheless it has not assumed the aspect of the horse. Its face and its back want length; its trunk needs bulk; its legs are much too long; and no one in his senses should, for an instant, imagine it could be a full-grown specimen of its race. Indeed, the author would not mention such a possibility, did he not know a single instance where an error of this nature was actually perpetrated with a creature of the equine order. A cockney gentleman took up his residence, a few years ago, in one of the channel islands, and wishing to procure some safe animal for the amusement of his children, the simple Londoner actually purchased and worked a little donkey, barely one year old, in his ignorance mistaking the animal for an ass which had attained its maturity. That no reader of the present volume may commit so cruel a blunder, the portrait of a horse, as it appears at the first year of its age, is presented below.

ABOUT ONE YEAR OLD.

The changes in the teeth, after the first year of life has been attained, are characterized by the longer periods which divide them. Nature appears, as it were, resting to draw breath for a mightier effort than she has hitherto undertaken. Months have, heretofore, separated the advent of single pairs; but, from this date, these appearances are to be reckoned by numbers and by years. The foal, to the point of its present necessities, has been provided for. It has teeth sufficient to support and to maintain its growth.

Nature has now to render perfect the body, before the teeth. Accordingly, between the first and the second year the alteration in the general aspect is very marked. All the helplessness and pretty ungainliness of infancy disappears by the expiration of the time mentioned. The animal's frame then suggests something of those beautiful proportions which it is soon to display. Its body, however, still needs maturing; and no one, less wanting in common sense than a racing man, would think of subjecting the youthful and tender form to the hardest of all actual work.

ABOUT TWO YEARS OLD.

The very aspect of the creature should denote it to be unsuited for such performances. It must, to foreigners, read as strange intelligence, that the *nobility*, who patronize the English course, applaud the contests between two-year olds; while the *bumpkins*, who breed horses for the general market, allow the quadruped to enter the third year before the colt is given over to the breaker. Alas, for the hardihood or want of sensibility displayed by the most exalted, when prompted by the greed of gambling!

Nothing in the above sketch is more striking than the contrast presented by the character of the head, when compared with the image which immediately preceded the last illustration. The face has perceptibly lengthened; for by this time a second permanent molar, making five grinders on both sides of the upper and of the lower jaws, has broken through the fleshy covering of the gums. Preparation is also being made for the advent of the sixth grinder, and for changes in those milk molars which were in the mouth when the animal was born. At the same time, additional width is imperative to allow the permanent incisors to appear when the proper season arrives for these last organs to displace their temporary representatives.

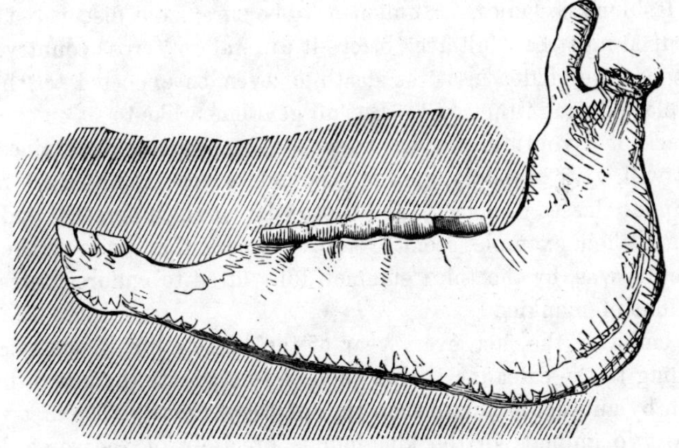

JAW AT TWO YEARS OLD.

Should the front teeth of a two-year old mouth be examined, there will be perceived a want of that fixedness which, one year before, was

THE INCISOR TEETH AT TWO YEARS OLD.

the characteristic of these organs. The central nippers appear to have done their duty, or, at all events, suggest something approaching to maturity has, during their brief existences, been attained. It will hardly provoke regret—certainly it cannot excite wonder—should these once beautiful ornaments of the foal's mouth be displaced. Indeed, the aspect of jaws in the two-year old plainly intimate approaching alteration, which in a few months will become apparent.

Three years old is the period when the greater number of colts are brought to market. About this age most animals begin to perform work. Omnibus horses are purchased when only thus far advanced in life. The army also buys its remounts when no further matured. Carriages are drawn by young horses which, when they become three years old, are resigned to the bit, the bearing-rein, and the exactions of London's fashionable ladies. Huntsmen, to be sure, have discovered that a quadruped must be "full five" before it can gallop "cross country," take fences, and be ridden in at the death, or even be expected to "hold" a good place during "the run." But all gentlemen like to sit on the yielding back of a youthful steed; though, to be properly maintained, such a seat will, very probably, cost fifty pounds a year, if not more money. The upper classes of society, and those who sacrifice personal judgment to mimic their example, seem to act as though they were assured that equine life was, by the third summer, fully fitted to endure the severest extortions of mankind!

To embitter the fact, every year of the horse's life is not calculated according to the calendar. Man chooses to estimate the age of his possession by another standard than that of the seasons. The first year of hardly two animals in the kingdom is precisely of the same length. Horses are, by the Jockey Club, permitted to have only two birthdays. Thus, all blood foals must first see the light on the first of January; or, should one presume to peep at the world upon the thirty-first of December, the decision, which admits of no appeal, will esteem the intruder one year old when the second day of its existence commences. Then all animals, not thorough-bred, must forbear to look upon creation until the first of May comes round; or, if they dare to mistake the time, even by an hour, they are absolutely pronounced one year old, before the little beings can fairly stand up and look about them.

Such regulations may be very convenient for the purposes of the Jockey Club; but nature has not yet given in her submission to human institutions. Medical men know that ladies cannot always calculate to the minute; therefore mares, which have not yet learned arithmetic, should not be held so very strict to their reckonings. Moreover, when men will pay to sit upon the back of a three-year old, it is of all importance to the spine, which has to endure the burden, whether the nominal birthday represents the actual time or merely implies the animal is two years and half an hour of positive age. However, the teeth most obstinately ignore the sage code of the Jockey Club; but the laws of that controlling body disdain to notice any variation; for the creature which has lost but one nipper, and the quadruped which has four permanent incisors fully up, are both esteemed to have been dropped at the same hour, though an animal suffering the first-named change, speaking truthfully, may be only rising three.

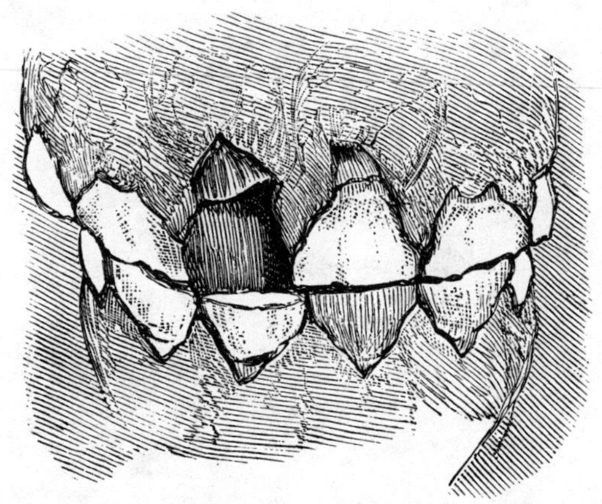

THE INCISORS DENOTE THREE YEARS OLD.

At the same time, the confirmed mouth, with the nippers thoroughly consolidated, and gums not showing a tinge of redness, can be esteemed of no greater age: both are three years old; for both must have been born on the first of January or on the first of May,—they had no business to appear at any other time. If they were presumptuous rebels against the just authority and recognized dignity of the Jockey Club, then they are beyond the pale of all consideration, and must bear the consequences of their temerity. The differences exhibited by their mouths are, therefore, held to be of no account.

The age at this period ought to be absolutely ascertained; for most horses, when three years old, undergo the greatest exertion. At this period, the animal generally has to suffer the instruction of a rude and an ignorant—frequently of a brutal and a savage—man, who is justly denominated "*a breaker*." Then, should the "broken" be thought worthy of a saddle, it is given up to the gentle mercies of a rough rider, and has to be tortured till it is gotten well together, and has thoroughly learned its paces. In short, its gentle spirit has to be subdued, or fear has to master timidity. How little does man know about that life he has been accustomed to coerce! The pride of this world prefers the compulsory drudgery of a spirit-broken slave, to the happy service of a willing friend. The horse is sent upon earth, prepared to serve and eager to share the happiness of its lord; but it is not understood; it meets with no sympathy; it is treated as a wild and ravenous beast, whose subjugation must be enforced and whose obedience must be compelled.

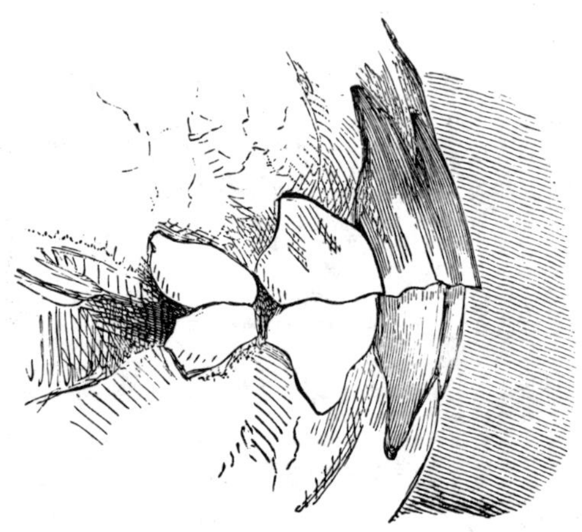

THE INCISORS DENOTE NO MORE THAN THREE YEARS OLD.

The bit is put into its mouth when the third year has been attained. It is driven from the field and from the cool grass; at a period of change and of debility it is expected to display the greatest animation, or to learn strange things from him who teaches only with the lash or with the goad. When its gums are inflamed; when the system is excited; when the strength is absorbed by an almost simultaneous appearance of twelve teeth, it is led from the plain and made, with its bleeding jaws, to masticate sharp oats and fibrous hay. At this age, when fever prevails in its blood, and the growth of its frame naturally weakens the muscles, it is expected to have leisure to master new teachings, animation to show off strange acquirements, and stamina to endure the weight of the tyrant on its back.

From this date, it is the inhabitant of a close, a fetid, and a heated stable. It may languish for a cool draught of pure air; but its head is haltered to the manger, and there it must remain, to inhale the tainted atmosphere of its abode. The fire natural to its condition may rage; but it must not slake the thirst which consumes it till the groom brings a pail, only to permit so many gulps or "go downs" to be imbibed. Nay, if the poor captive should shift its feet, turn its head, or change its attitude, in the restlessness of fever, it offends its custodian, who, lounging upon the locker, watches to maintain order, and can punish, should any horse sin against a groom's notion of propriety. Within the stable, of an afternoon, all is silent! The man is uneasy, because of an inward consciousness that he is not discharging a humane office. The animals are fidgety under unnatural restraint. The very air of the place is oppressive. Nothing appears at ease, save the cat, and this creature dozes and purs with enjoyment. But for the poor colt there is no sympathy. For should the cutting of many teeth inflame the gums and destroy the appetite, an iron is made red hot and violently forced into the mouth, under pretense of burning away the groom's favorite disease—"the lampas!" which is purely an imaginary disorder.

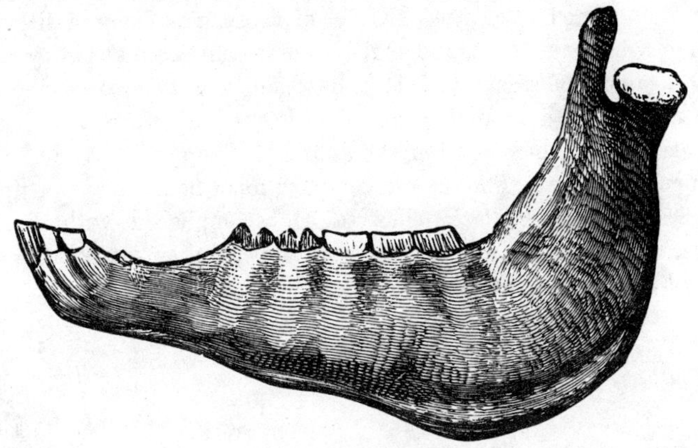

JAW OF A THREE-YEAR OLD.

It has been described that a three-year colt cuts twelve teeth. The above engraving represents half the lower jaw of an animal which had seen three summers. In it the reader will readily recognize those organs which are of recent appearance, by their darker color, by their larger size, or by their differing in shape from the other members. These new teeth are a central incisor and the first two grinders. The horse has two jaws and two sides to each jaw; therefore the same number being present within each side of both jaws, the teeth already alluded to appear during the third year. However, even the quantity named rather understates than overrates the fact, for frequently the tushes are cut during this period; should such be the case, the colt acquires no less than sixteen teeth in twelve months. We know what the young beings of our own species suffer when the gums are ruptured and the bones absorbed by the organs of mastication; the danger then encountered leads to a belief that the great agony endured is increased by a rapid growth of the body simultaneously weakening the system. The teeth are only a part of the living organism; therefore, as when a part moves we may conclude the whole system is in motion, the advent of sixteen huge teeth, alone, might reasonably unfit the quadruped for commencing its education, or for undergoing the severest portion of its labors. But how do the customs of humanity appear, when illumined by a consideration of the sufferings which nature is imposing at the time the colt is tasked to its greatest exertions?

Some *very low* classes of horse proprietors will, however, make the work of the three-year old colt as light as possible. The vulgar generally regard the frame at this age as not perfectly matured, and they treat the strength as not equal to full labor. A nice practical comment is thus published upon the behavior of those gentlemen of title and of fortune, who train, start, and make animals run races at two years old! Few members of existing society, however, will accord any indulgence to a colt during its fourth year. Yet if the quadruped once possessed any claim upon consideration, the animal at this period has positive title to our forbearance. For the second effort must be more exhausting than the first; since the latter has to be accomplished with diminished power. Thus the four-year old has to perfect as many teeth as are known to protrude into the mouth of the three-year old.

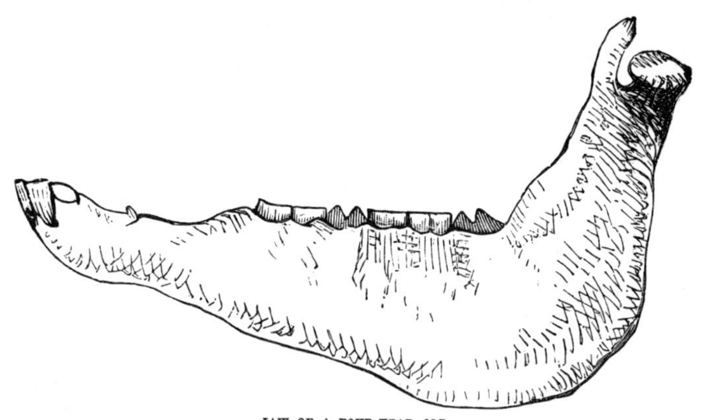

JAW OF A FOUR-YEAR OLD.

The tushes in this view, however, must be disregarded. The precise time of appearance is uncertain with these analogues of the canine teeth in man, or of the tusks in the porcine race. They may come up at the third—they often are delayed to the fourth year; sometimes these teeth never pierce the membrane of the gums, it being very far from uncommon to see horses' mouths of seven years in which the tushes are absent.

By the completion of the fourth year, the colt has certainly gained twelve teeth; that is, by this time there should exist, on each side of both jaws, one new lateral incisor and two fresh molars, being the third and the sixth in position. The appearance of the mouth now announces the approach of maturity; but the inferior margin of the lower bone still feels more full and rounded than is altogether consistent with the perfect consolidation of an osseous structure. We cannot take cognizance of the swollen and enlarged condition of the jaw, without being assured that some important process is going forward within its interior. It is among the firmest physiological truths, that nature is a strict economist and never does anything without intention; that every enlargement or every depression — however insignificant it may appear to human eyes—is a permanent provision for some appointed purpose, and has its allotted use in the animal system. Accordingly, it is discovered the sign we just remarked upon indicates the process of dentition is not finished by the termination of the fourth year. There are more teeth to be cut, as well as the fangs of those already in the mouth to be made perfect. This must be a laborious effort. Nature always toils slowly in proportion to the density of her work; when we regard the compact structure of a horse's tooth, we may conjecture the quantity of blood, the amount of inflammation, and the intensity of suffering which are necessary for its perfection.

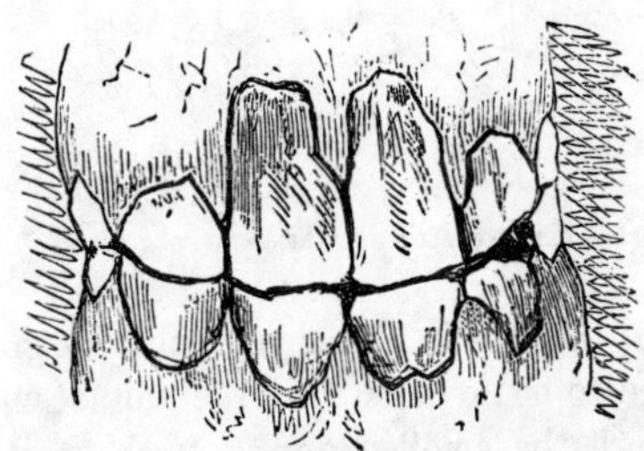

ONE LOWER LATERAL INCISOR BEING THROUGH THE GUM DECLARES A FOUR-YEAR OLD.

Still a gentleman may purchase a colt with one lower lateral incisor barely through the gum. Nevertheless, such a condition of mouth must be accepted as announcing the animal to be four years old. That fact is not to be disputed, for have not the Jockey Club proclaimed it? Being four years old, most people view the colt as needing no indulgence. The creature, at this age, is generally urged to the extent of its power. Would mortal intellect think on that which it beholds, and endeavor to understand the evidence which is presented to its sight, how much that is now carelessly passed by unnoticed would be read as a plea for forbearance, and how much misery might be banished from that abode which the idle complacently term "a vale of tears"! The gums newly lacerated or the jaws bleeding do not indicate that conformation of parts or announce that established strength which could endure extreme exhaustion. Such signs rather suggest pain, and declare that life is suffering the penalty of existence. They ought to kindle the sympathy of him who likewise is born to sorrow, and crave the commiseration of one whose sad inheritance it is to draw breath at the risk of misery. Would any man expect his child—whether girl or boy—when only acquiring the permanent front teeth, to be equal to the toil which a task-master should allot to fully-developed strength in its prime or in the maturity of its power? The horse is not a speaking creature. It has no voice to plead or to complain. But what right has the lord of earth, being blessed with ability to control his acts and with reason to comprehend the signs of nature, to enforce that fate upon the dumb slave in his possession from which he would esteem it a duty to shelter his own offspring?

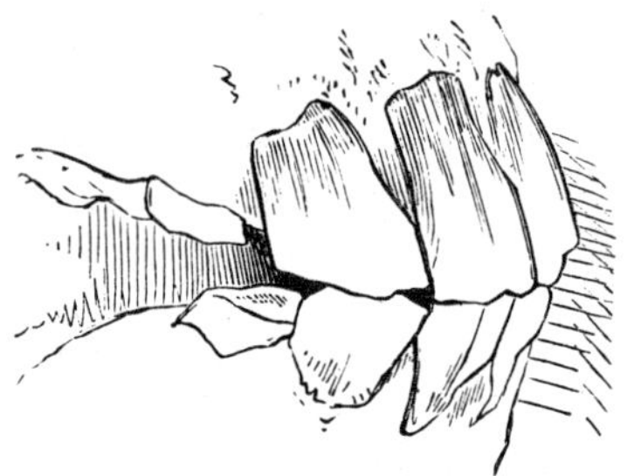

THESE TEETH EQUALLY DECLARE ONLY FOUR YEARS OLD.

The colt with four incisors in either jaw, all fully grown and worn flat with use, is esteemed to be no older than the animal with only one lateral nipper barely through the swollen gum. Both creatures, according to man's reckoning, are of one age. Neither can, says the Jockey Club, be an hour in advance of the other. Yet the colt with four pairs of permanent incisors in the mouth has not paid the penalty which nature exacts from early life. There are still the corner milk nippers to be shed; yet, while the provision necessary for that labor is taking place within the body, or while nature is preparing her mute offspring for the coming struggle, man considers the poor quadruped as fully developed and as enjoying the prime of its existence.

The teeth may be scarcely visible in the mouth, nevertheless such a sign announces the fifth year to be attained. Man, who estimates a horse's life according to the laws of the Jockey Club, and ignores nature's mode of declaring the duration of existence by signs and attributes; man, who in his impatience refuses to reckon age by those functions which the body has perfected or which it has to mature—man seizes upon the imperfect being, as a creature fitted for the accomplishment of any kind of labor. There are, at five, no more bothering teeth to cut. All are through the bone, and the mouth will soon be sound. The animal must be in its prime, and the longest day or the hardest run should not beat it to a stand-still. Therefore, show off your horsemanship. Mount, trot, prance, gallop, and leap, as you please. Everybody says the horse at this time is in its prime. Tear on to plowed fields.

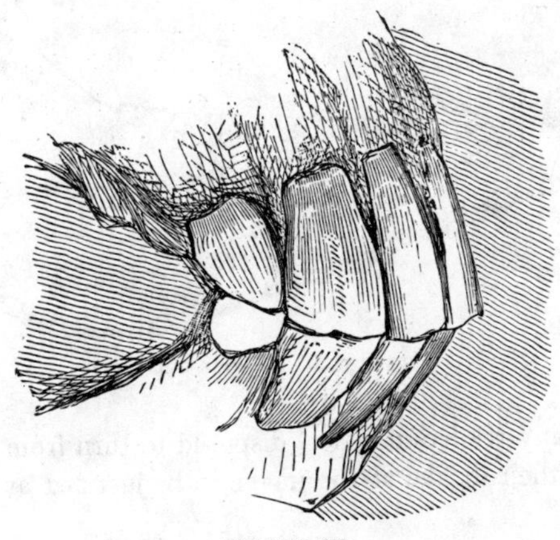

FIVE-YEAR OLD.

One upper corner permanent incisor has been cut. The lower corner milk incisor is still retained.

Whip the brute over the widest ditch. Dig your spurs into the flanks and take the stiffest hedge. The laboring beast may breathe a little hard or possibly may reel: but, so the quadruped does the performance, and is scarcely alive after it is accomplished—the owner can hail his five-year old as a seasoned horse!

Were the writer to pursue this line of observation from year to year, the features becoming more minute as time progresses, the investigation might ultimately grow wearisome. As age increases, so do the bones contract, till absorption at length commences: or at thirty years all the appearances of strength, which were conspicuous, will have entirely vanished in the domesticated quadruped that has been subjected to hot stables and hard food. The jaw no longer seems endowed with greater bulk than is needed for the discharge of its function. It has become comparatively thin, and where it once was wide, it is now narrowed

Then, the grinding surfaces of the molars are no longer even or straight. Comminution of an artificially-prepared diet, continued for a number of years, seems to have worn the organs of mastication into a shallow and eccentric curve; or, as pressure persevered with upon any living substance promotes absorption, probably the constant grinding of hardened food has caused parts of the once even surface to be removed.

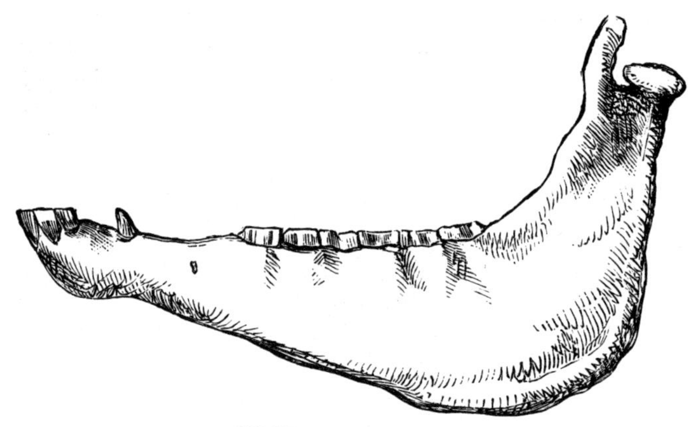

THE JAW OF A FIVE-YEAR OLD.

However, many readers may feel disposed to turn from the next illustration, feeling their dislike of the image to be justified by denominating

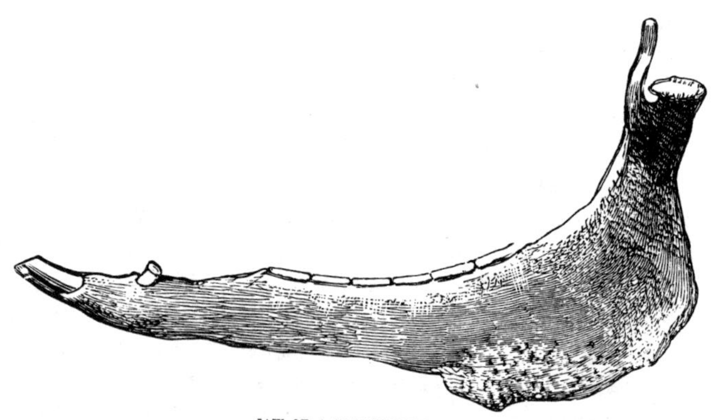

JAW OF A THIRTY-YEAR OLD.

it an extreme instance. As such it is adduced, and no wrong is, therefore, done by so regarding it. It was inserted simply as bearing conspicuous evidence of that fact which it was the desire to establish. Few, very few English horses live to reach the thirtieth year; but to show that those signs which were remarkable in the last engraving commence at an earlier period, below is the jaw of a twelve-year old horse, in which the presence of all the indications that at the thirtieth year seem exaggerated, may be clearly discerned in their commencement.

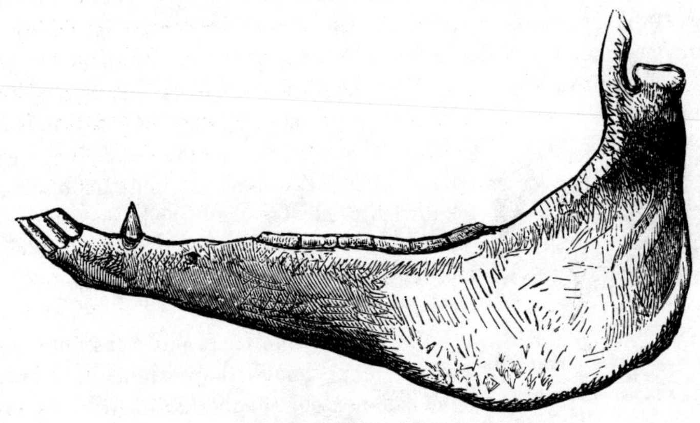

JAW OF A TWELVE-YEAR OLD.

The author must now explain the phenomena to which he has directed the reader's attention. The molar teeth are not all of the like size, nor of one form. The organs occupying the upper jaw are nearly, not quite, double the width of those which are located in the lower jaw. The inferior molars are the grinding agents, or the active organs of mastication. The superior teeth are simply the passive tables upon which, or against which, the food undergoes comminution. The slab is always the lowest of the two in human mills; but nature has more to provide for than the mere pulverization of certain substances. With mastication, actually commences a very compound process. With the act of chewing, digestion begins; it was ordained that more than any mechanical invention can accomplish should be imperative to the due performance of this function. The benevolence of the All-wise instituted that while his creatures were promoting the healthy exercise of the appropriative necessity, they should likewise excite their enjoyment. Therefore when pulp is masticated, the pressure of the teeth expels the juices, which fall directly upon the seat of taste. When a harder substance has to be comminuted, the bulk is first shattered into fragments; the particles, descending upon either side of the teeth, have to be gathered up and placed again between the masticatory organs. The movements of the tongue and jaw excite the salivary glands; the broken substance becomes mingled with the secretion of the last-named bodies. Saliva extracts the savor from the food; and the tongue also brings these in contact with the seat of taste, while discharging its office of collecting the broken pieces.

The reader being now fully informed as to facts, may have patience sufficient to peruse an explanation of the principles on which the foregoing statements are founded. Such a mode of proceeding may, to certain methodical writers, seem to be transposing the proper arrangement. The author does not undertake to defend his actions on the score of their propriety; but he feels that he is addressing human beings in whom a desire to know is the best possible foundation on which knowledge can be established; consequently, principles become less repulsive when communicated after incidents have kindled curiosity.

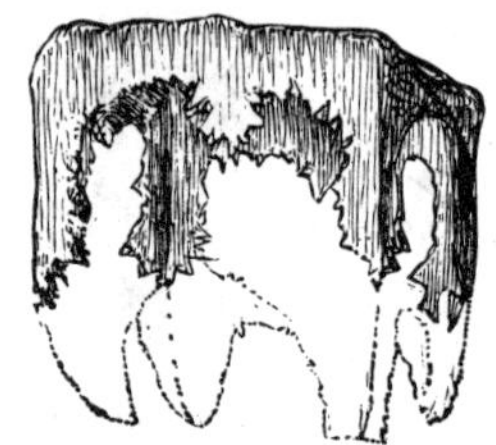

THE CONDITION IN WHICH THE TABLE OF A TEMPORARY MOLAR IS CAST FROM THE MOUTH OF A HORSE.

The dotted lines merely indicate the extent of the tooth previous to absorption.

The primary molars cannot boast the length of the fang, though they exhibit very nearly the same extent of superficial surface as characterizes the succeeding teeth. They have rather shallow roots, which are not composed of those consolidated materials that are present in their immediate successors. When the original molar is shed, the temporary tooth is not expelled entire from its position, but the pressure of the growing organ (which comes into the mouth exactly where the milk grinder stood) causes the root to be absorbed, till nothing but a superficial shell has to be ejected.

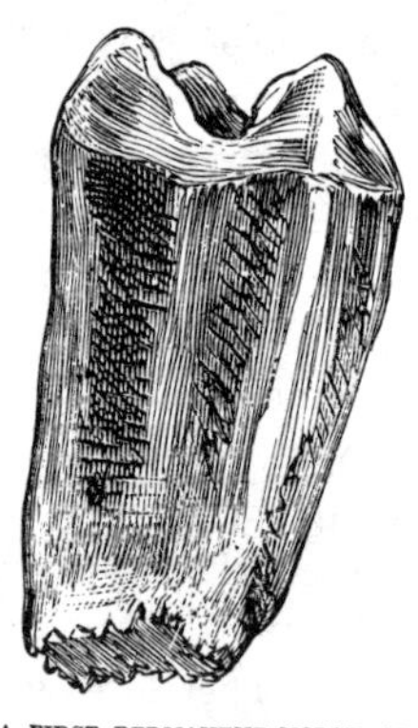

A FIRST PERMANENT MOLAR, AS IT APPEARED IN THE MOUTH, UNCOVERED.

This tooth occupied the fourth situation in the jaw; therefore the root would require to be considerably extended by subsequent growth.

The horse, in its natural state, exists on fibrous grasses; it therefore becomes essential the animal should retain the power of masticating such substances. Nature never withholds what is necessary to the well-being of her creatures. The mode in which the Common Parent provides for the preservation of this ability in the horse is perfectly distinct from any provision that He makes for most earthly creatures. The temporary remains of a molar tooth are not shed till another organ is in the mouth at hand to permanently supply its place. But the permanent tooth does not appear ready flattened and prepared to discharge its office. It is cut with certain angular prominences upon its masticating surface, which must render the animal disinclined to employ it on the instant of its development. This disinclination allows a pause, during which the various structures can be consolidated, and at the end of such brief space the prominences have become blunted, while the organ, being firmly planted, is then ready for mastication. Is it not surprising how a plain statement of facts can reasonably account for that disinclination to feed which, to the groom's mind, announces a state of disease that shall necessitate the employment of burning iron to eradicate what the man styles "Lampas!"

There remains, however, to account for that width and depth of jaw by which the head of the youthful horse is distinguished. The reader is requested to attentively inspect the last illustration. The size and length of fang cannot fail to awaken his surprise. Nevertheless, if this part be regarded it will be seen depicted as of a ragged, incomplete, and apparently of a hollow condition. So, when the tooth has displaced the temporary molar, and has taken its station within the mouth, it has still to grow. The protruded portion may be consolidated; but the unfinished extremity is denominated the cavity of the pulp. That pulp consists of a fine bladder, on which ramify numerous blood-vessels; but the interior of which contains simply a clear fluid. This is the secreting membrane of the tooth. Out of this watery bag the wonderful chemistry of nature can extract the most condensed material that resides within the strong body of a horse.

SECTION OF A MOLAR TOOTH.

Another feature of the above tooth, because it balks expectation, can hardly fail to attract notice. The dark hue of the outward covering, being abhorrent to human notions of youth or of purity, is generally attributed to dirt. The tooth of the horse is, however, composed of three substances: a tough and fibrous material, called crusta petrosa; a thin layer of crystalline deposit, named enamel; and a kind of compact bone, spoken of as dentine. They occur according to the order in which they are named. The bone exhibits a yellow tinge, and is present in the greatest quantity, for it forms the inner bulk of the tooth. The crusta petrosa is a comparatively thick external envelope, being about five times the substance of the enamel, to which it is an outward protection. The components are thrown into various convolutions; but the order alluded to is always preserved. The bone or dentine is invariably the internal substance; it needs to occupy such a position, as within it the sensation resides. The crusta petrosa and the enamel may be tampered with without perception being aroused; but the dentine is capable of communicating the acutest agony; and it is upon the dentine that rogues operate, when they "bishop" an old horse.

To convince the reader that nature has not needlessly sacrificed the whiteness of the horse's tooth, the author will dilate fully upon the many services afforded by the dark-colored crusta petrosa. To render the explanation more intelligible, reference will be here made to a common tool seen every day in the hands of an ordinary mechanic. The bricklayer's trowel appears to be nothing more than a thick layer of metal; but it is hourly put to uses for which iron would be too soft, and steel would be too brittle. Therefore, the blade is composed of a thin layer of steel, inclosed within two comparatively thick layers of iron. By the combination of opposite qualities, perfect utility is produced; and this trowel, it seems hard to believe, was not suggested by that arrangement which is conspicuous in the horse's tooth.

The enamel, hard, brittle, and readily fractured, but presenting a fine or a cutting edge, is developed as a thin layer, convoluted upon the sides of the dentine, and securely covered by crusta petrosa. That the incisive substance may fulfill its office, may sever or comminute the tough and fibrous herbs upon which the equine race subsist, it is inclosed between two elastic bodies, the whole being held together by the vessels which pass from the exterior to the interior of the organ, though these vessels do no more than travel through the enamel without nourishing or supporting it; the latter structure being of a crystalline nature, or strictly inorganic, therefore not fitted to appropriate nutriment.

The crusta petrosa is, however, of further use than has been already stated. The horse's grinders are generally supposed to be gifted with a power of growth whereby they are enabled to repair that perpetual loss of substance to which their employment must subject them. The teeth, certainly, are not perfected when the crowns first appear in the mouth; so far the opinion is capable of being upheld. But when once completed, the dentine is not endowed with any innate ability to renew its loss of substance. The wear consequent upon continual use is provided for by the length of fang which characterizes the permanent molar of the quadruped. As the surface gradually decreases, so are the lower parts of the teeth, by the contraction of the jaw-bones, forced into the mouth, while the outward investing substance—the crusta petrosa—being gifted with a limited power of increase, is enabled thereby to firmly retain the protruded fang in its new position; although the contraction of the bones, which is always going forward as age advances, does not necessitate the power of growth should in early life be largely exhibited.

With almost every form of being, as years accumulate, the ability to masticate becomes enfeebled. It is with the horse as it is with other animals. The thin coating of enamel does not extend to the ultimate root of the fang, so that in advanced age the power of the molars is almost destroyed by the absence of the cutting agent upon the grinding surface. The chief component, moreover, or the dentine, diminishes in quantity as in solidity; the last portions of the molar, therefore, could not fill the socket, only for that ability to increase with which the crusta petrosa is gifted. Upon the extreme roots of the grinders, taken from the jaws of very old horses, this substance is always found in great abundance. In illustration of this fact, a sketch made from the tooth of an aged quadruped is here inserted; the body has been sawn asunder, to exhibit the proportions and the substances that entered into its composition. The reader will remark certain dark lines upon the dentine. These indicate the places where existed the cavity of the pulp, which once served to nourish the organ; but it is lost as vitality lessens with the advance of senility. Does not the reader, as he inspects the engraving, perceive the wickedness and the folly of placing harsh and dried food before a creature which nature, in age, deprives of ability to comminute such a form of sustenance?

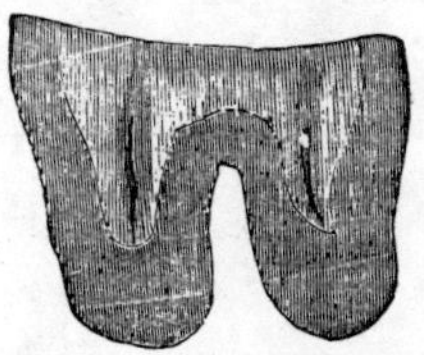

SECTION OF AN AGED MOLAR TOOTH.

The permanent incisors are not cut after the same manner as the molars. The nippers being merely employed to bite the grass, a wide vacancy does not necessarily incapacitate the other portions of the excising apparatus. A blade can cut, even though a large notch exist upon its edge. Whereas the points which are developed upon the upper surfaces of the newly cut molars must render the grinders entirely useless; although the short period of enforced abstinence, which announces the appearance of a fresh double tooth, may be nature's own medicine to quiet a feverish system, burning with morbid excitement.

The front milk teeth have fangs when they appear in the mouth; but no fang exists when the primary members are shed. The root of the temporary organ, when perfect, however, resembles that of the permanent incisor. It is only sufficient to fit the member for its purposes. In the same canal as was occupied by the milk tooth, the permanent incisor generally appears. Much suffering must attend the absorption of bone; yet, during the time the huge permanent nipper is forcing its way through the narrow channel, which held firmly the diminutive milk tooth, and while the smaller fang is by pressure being also absorbed, the colt receives no consideration at the hands of the groom or of its master. Both are equally ignorant of the necessity for kindness; but each regards any indication of pain as one of those visitations of disease to which young horses are said to be peculiarly liable.

When the foal has shed the front milk teeth, the entire of the serviceable or visible portion of these members is displaced. They are endowed with no power to supply any diminution of their substance, neither are they capable of renewal; whereas the long permanent incisor may be viewed as all tooth, and possessing no fang; for as the upper portion wears, so does the lower part protrude or supply its place. The two teeth, however, present a strong contrast when considered as

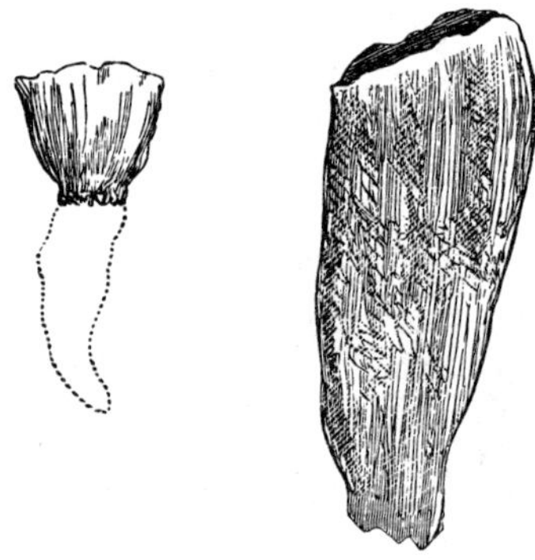

A MILK AND A PERMANENT INCISOR TOOTH.

organs, both occupying one cavity, and both united to fulfill the like uses in the same animal. The illustration last displayed represented a permanent and a temporary incisor; the uneven mark dividing the milk tooth indicates the appearance of the organ after the absorption of the fang causes it to be cast from the mouth, while the dotted line shows the shape and the extent of the fang previous to its absorption by pressure.

The amount of root natural to the permanent incisors enables those organs, as years increase, to alter their arrangement, length, and direction, without being displaced. In youth, the united front teeth compose a curve, or almost a semicircle. In age, the same members incline toward a straight, or at best form an irregular line. In the colt, the teeth are flat, smooth, and filbert shaped; but in the old animal, they are decidedly long and angular. When the permanent teeth first appear, they are nearly perpendicular; but when they have been a long time exposed, they protrude almost in the horizontal direction. Looking, from the side, at a young mouth, the spectator can behold half the nippers;

but when inspecting the old teeth from the same point of view, two onlv will be visible, though the full number shall be present in the mouth. In

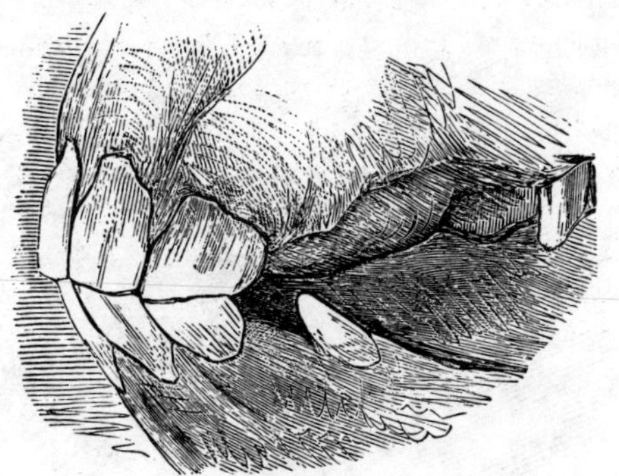

SIX YEARS OLD.

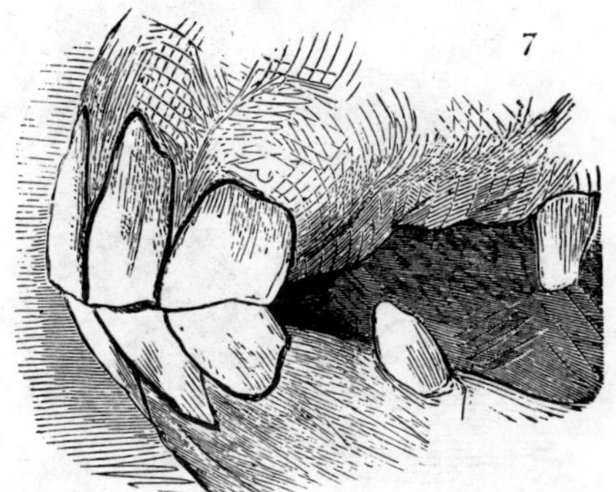

SEVEN YEARS OLD.

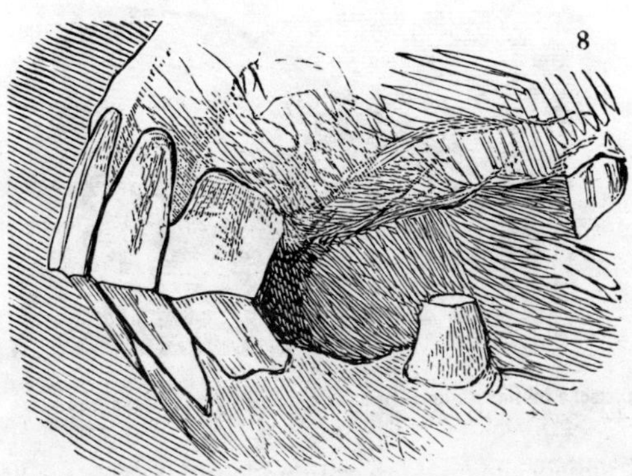

EIGHT YEARS OLD.

THE INCISORS OF HORSES OF DIFFERENT PERIODS OF AGE AFTER THE FIFTH YEAR.

the aged quadruped, moreover, the narrowing of the incisors allows the spaces between the organs to be vacant. Within these spaces the food

TWELVE YEARS OLD.

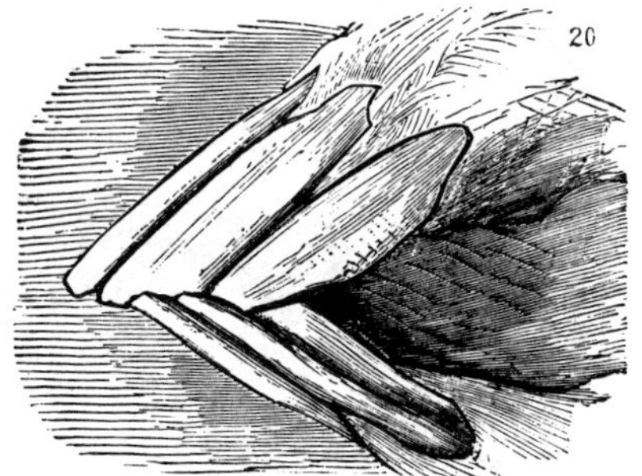

TWENTY YEARS OLD.

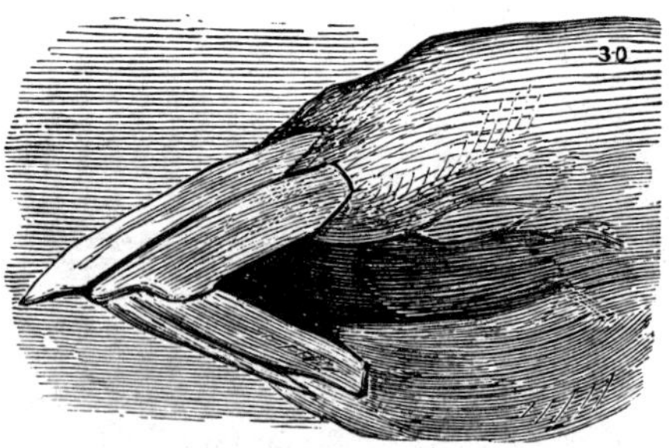

THIRTY YEARS OLD.

THE INCISORS OF HORSES OF DIFFERENT PERIODS OF AGE AFTER THE FIFTH YEAR.

accumulates, which, being there retained and becoming black, looks as though the creature had been chewing tobacco. Such signs are too fixed to be disguised. The accumulation of blackened food, it is true, may be taken away; but its removal will leave the interspaces, if possible, still more conspicuous. So also the long teeth may be shortened; but they will not be elevated to the perpendicular, or changed to a filbert form, or restored to the semicircular arrangement.

The tushes likewise may be regarded. These teeth are sometimes absent in mares, and in animals of the female sex are seldom developed of the size which they commonly exhibit in the male. When first cut, the tush is spear shaped, having well-defined grooves running down its margins. As age advances, all pretension to this form is lost. The tooth either becomes very flat upon its crown or it may be rendered level with the gum; else it grows very long, looking more like a coarse spike than the organ it really is. Also, when it originally appears in the young mouth, the tush ranges evenly with the parts from which it grows, and points forward. As senility is attained, the member is directed outward; with extreme old age, it faces backward. The contraction of the jaw causes the tongue to protrude from the free spaces between the teeth, while the consequent shallowness of the canal formed by the branches of the bone occasions the saliva to dribble forth when the lips are parted.

The indications of extreme age are always present, and though during a period of senility the teeth cannot be literally construed, nevertheless it should be impossible to look upon the "venerable steed" as an animal in its colthood.

No man can accurately interpret the signs of the teeth after the fifth year. A guess, more or less correct, can be hazarded; but nothing like confident judgment can be pronounced subsequent to the period just named. Cases will frequently occur, which shall set our best endeavors to be correct at defiance. But for such instances it is not difficult to account. The Jockey Club may order as it pleases about birthdays; but children and foals will, nevertheless, obtrude upon the world all the year round. Such downright absurdity, as a pretense at controlling the operations of nature, was never perhaps equaled, save by the burlesque monarch depicted by Mr. Planchè, who, because he is hungry, *wills* that it *be* one o'clock, when the sun declares the time to be only twelve. It might be more convenient, certainly, if foals could agree all to put in appearances at a particular date; but until such an arrangement has been entered into by the parties principally concerned, it is idle presumption for any set of men to issue ordinances which, never being observed, render "confusion worse confounded."

The difference between the times of birth in various animals, it is true, may cause different aspects in the teeth, and even induce men, in obedience to the rules of the Jockey Club, to call a colt four, which truth and the teeth declare to be only three. Horses may therefore be readily reckoned older than they really are: but there is a general belief that rogues in Yorkshire can make the teeth say five, when the actual age is only four; or, in other words, can so successfully tamper with the mouth as to induce the teeth to belie the actual age. Ignorant people have a blind faith in the power of those who chance to be more knowing than themselves; but the author can only regard the general belief in "Yorkshire fives," as illustrating the total unacquaintance of the public with all that concerns equine economy.

An elderly lady once laid claim to a dog which she beheld led about the streets for sale. The possessor disputed her title, and the pair were by the police introduced to a magistrate. Both gave a different name as that belonging to the animal. The dog came to either appellation. When put down on the floor of the court, it went to man or lady with equal indifference. It was a puzzling case. At length, the bench was illumined by a bright idea. "Hand me the dog," cried his worship, who quickly placed it out of sight. Then, addressing the female supplicant, he said, "I beg your pardon. All you have said about signs and marks may be perfectly correct; but such things, possibly, in two animals, may be the same. The creature evidently does not appear to recognize its mistress; for, though it comes to your call, yet it will leave you when spoken to from an opposite direction. I beg your pardon, madam, we have settled, apparently, all points but one. Pray excuse me! But was your animal a gentleman or a lady?" "Oh! sir!" replied the distressed female, "mine was a lady dog." "Then I am afraid I must give the case against your ownership, for this dog is decidedly a gentleman." With that, he returned the animal to the man. "Stop, sir! Stay! Oh! pause! Consider, sir, those dog stealers can play such tricks," sobbed forth the disconsolate female.

So particular people appear to credit Yorkshire horse dealers with an ability to perform "such tricks." No doubt they have every wish; but the author questions whether they have yet attained the power to compel nature at their bidding. All they are said to do, as pulling out the milk teeth, firing and blistering the gums, are like the arts which were formerly used to raise the evil one; and, in the writer's opinion, about as likely to be attended with success. Cruelty is more calculated to retard than to promote development. However, if the mouth exhibit the signs proper to a five-year old, the animal may with safety be purchased, as being of that age. Should it be younger than five, the owner is the gainer; since the teeth do no more than indicate the development of the body, and an early maturity is the best evidence that the quadruped, during the previous years, has been tenderly nurtured.

Certain readers may feel opposed to the illustrations which have been inserted into this division of the present volume. It may be justly ad vanced that, in the earlier portion of the present treatise, the author asserted horses could live until the animal had reached its sixtieth year. However, recently he adduced the mouth of a quadruped which endured but half that period; yet this specimen exhibited features indicative of immediate decay.

Such an accusation would be well grounded; it could not be denied. The sixty-year old of which the writer spoke was not feeding in the stable. The creature whose teeth are delineated to represent the appearances displayed at the thirtieth year was not in the field, but tied up in a stall. The one quadruped was consuming its natural food, the other had to masticate those artificially-prepared substances which man finds it most convenient to place before the dumb captive.

The engravings inserted to illustrate the aspect of the mouth, during the thirtieth year, may therefore be regarded as exemplifying the evils which result from the present mode of feeding. Hay and oats, as now given in dry and hard conditions, are the most expensive articles of sustenance which could be found. Much of the hay passes through the system only partially digested. In what condition the oats are voided, the sparrows of the roadway and the chickens on the dung hill equally attest. Under the present system at least half the diet is ejected from the body unappropriated. Much more would be lost, but for the capacious and convoluted intestines of the equine race. Within these, the provender swallowed is long retained, and during the entire period of its retention it is exposed to the digestive action which its components are beautifully formed to resist.

Aloes, a most drastic purgative, is the one in common use with stablemen. It takes four and twenty hours before its operation is witnessed; for an entire day it lies dormant within the body, notwithstanding the aids of warm water, bran mashes, and occasional exercise are resorted to, so as to quicken its laxative effects. The animal, during this period, is obviously ill, and the medicine may be heard causing a "rumbling noise" within the bowels. But if a drastic purgative is four and twenty hours traveling along the digestive track, what period will be occupied by those dry materials which must have positively a constipating effect? However, the latter kind of diet is not all acted upon when cast forth; that portion which is ejected in an unchanged condition represents so much cash which has been expended to no purpose.

Of course, the mastication of artificially-prepared food wears the teeth, and also taxes the powers of nature far more than would the natural diet. By the operation of both causes, the horse's life is rendered much shorter than it would be were the animal kept after a natural fashion. The diminished period of existence we will mildly estimate at one-half the natural duration; therefore, under the existing mode of stable management, every gentleman pays twice as much for an animal as under a better system need be given. Nay, the extravagance does not end here; for the unnatural nourishment first generates weakness, and weakness is the beginning of disease. There is, therefore, to be added to the account—annoyance, loss of service, and the veterinary surgeon's charges. To crown all, the proprietor cannot obtain the full exertion from the animal; the body being only partially supported even during the seasons of imperfect health. The incompletely digested food has also to be considered. Altogether, as the author has no desire to make out a case, suppose the latter influences reduce the value of the remaining portion of life one-half, and we arrive at the conclusion that the horse proprietor literally squanders fifteen shillings out of every pound he pays for his horse; and he is thus extravagant, simply because, to consult the convenience of his groom, he will persist in feeding the animal upon a most unnatural and injurious kind of diet.

This subject will, however, be fully considered in the next chapter, where "food" is separately regarded. The author must only here state that he is not advocating a return to grass, although grass may suggest an idea as to the proper kind of nutriment without itself being the thing desired. It is certainly true that horses look round for their food, and the stable is always in commotion when the hour arrives for its distribution. This fact, however, establishes nothing. Horses are fidgety equally during the period of watering. Horses, in other countries, are uneasy when the stable companions are being fed; yet in all countries they do not live as in England. In the extreme northern parts of the world, they eat dried fish; in the Crimea, they gnawed one another's tails; in Arabia, they feast upon barley and chopped straw; in India, rudely cut grass, which has frequently parted with its moisture as well as shed its seed, and a dark grain termed "gram," is their support. In Germany, they enjoy black bread. In Ireland, they delight in raw potatoes. In various parts of England, they enjoy different sorts of nourishment. In some countries, boiled substances are the favorite dish. In others, cut roots are swallowed with avidity; while there is a growing custom of administering those various seasonings, all of which bear the general designation of "patent food." In short, the stabled horse can apparently be brought to consume anything; but of all the known varieties of diet, the author must regard that which is harsh, dried, and artificially prepared, as the most convenient—but the most injurious and unnatural

Its consequences are, perhaps, best exhibited by the thirst which it will generate. The horse is not, naturally, a large drinker; but if the internal portions of the body have to supply moisture, in order that these parts may extract the nutriment from dry food, the water must be replaced from an outward source. Horses have been known to be ill from excessive thirst. Mr. William Percivall, the late respected author on veterinary subjects, has recorded a case of this description. Nevertheless, copious draughts of cold water are frequently attended with danger; only, does it not exhibit a refinement upon cruelty—firstly, to imprison an animal, and fasten it to one spot; secondly, to give only such provender as must generate a craving for fluid; thirdly, to withhold the liquid which our folly has created a desire to imbibe?

The stable diet, moreover, throws the incisors out of use. These teeth, in the domesticated animal, are employed only to grasp a little hay and to pull it from the rack. They are of no further service. One of their popular names, "nippers," is in general a misnomer, for they are permitted to nip nothing; much less are they allowed to exercise their incisive faculty. Therefore, being thrown out of use, the members have no function to control their natural growth. They continue to protrude as age advances, till, by the thirtieth year, or by the time the quadruped has attained half the period of its natural existence, the front teeth have become long spikes, and are actual deformities within the mouth they were designed to adorn.

So palpable a sign is, however, not understood. To be sure, the present treatment of the horse slaughters the majority of its fellows before dentition is perfected. Few gentlemen, therefore, may have looked upon an aged quadruped; for prevailing fashion declares the creature, whose strength and youth have been devoted to man's pleasure, should be sold so soon as the advent of age is apparent. The chances, consequently, are, that the present chapter will be "news" to the greater number of readers. It may record facts which will be perused with wonder, and it may adduce circumstances which will be read with surprise.

Though up to the present moment these things may not have been properly regarded, from the present time there can be no excuse for continuing existing customs. Why should the teeth of the horse alone be subjected to abuse? The dog lives off biscuits and cooked flesh; the cat enjoys the scraps from the family table. Why should the horse, of all strictly domesticated creatures, be doomed to consume raw food? It would be cheaper to prepare all sustenance for digestion, since, in that form, less would communicate more nourishment; and if the matter is to be decided as a money question, there can be no doubt as to the side on which pecuniary interest would range.

CHAPTER V.

FOOD—THE FITTEST TIME FOR FEEDING, AND THE KIND OF FOOD WHICH THE HORSE NATURALLY CONSUMES.

THE folly of perversity or the madness of abuse can imagine no possible wrong that the human race have not inflicted upon the creature to which civilization owes its heaviest obligations. The horse, which more than shares in mortal toil, is forced to work before its bones are matured. When strained and deformed by the severity of labor, it is sworn at and lashed because its body shares, with all things on this earth, the perishableness which is inseparable from mortal existence. It is created to enjoy the freest breezes of the plain; but, by the superior power which has domesticated, the type of activity is doomed to stand, throughout life, within the narrow confines of a stall. It is the emblem of timidity; yet it is driven into every species of peril. Nature endowed it with fleetness, and formed it to delight in action; but mankind expect it to exhibit health during years of inactivity, and think its limbs should not become stiff from incessant lack of motion.

Its food grows abundantly on the surface of earth; every fresh mouthful necessitates an additional step; for the animal, when free, walks as it eats, and lowers the head, to collect its sustenance from the ground. Mankind imprisons the poor life; the hay is placed level with the ears, and the corn is given even with the chest of the animal. Nay, the very groom, when he permits water to be imbibed, raises the pail, resting its edge upon his knee. Nature enabled the horse to feed by night,—when the air is cool; when all is quiet; when the grass is moist, and when the flies are not abroad: then the emblem of concord pastures in peacefulness. The stabled horse is allowed to eat only by day. Though intended to be watchful, horse masters insist the wakeful quadruped should accept twelve hours of repose; and they lock the stable door, that its imaginary slumbers may be undisturbed.

The sufferer wears clothes only while under shelter. During summer it always retains its coat; but, as frost and snow approach, the covering which nature sent to conserve the body's warmth human wisdom either clips or singes away, dooming the native of a sunny clime to shiver in the blast of a northern winter. Man knows that heat benefits his slave; yet the horse only feels it as the product of impurity; so that, either it must suffer from the lowness of temperature, or it must languish from the inhalation of a tainted atmosphere.

The summit of wrong, however, seems to be attained, when we consider the food which the companion of man is condemned to consume within the walls of its dungeon. The corn is gathered after it has become ripe, or after all moisture has ceased to circulate within the grain; and even then it must be hardened and further dried by age before it is cast into the manger. The juicy herbage of the field—the soft verdure of the earth—is the natural support of the creature. Nevertheless, man presents grass to his captive only after the wind and the sun have expelled moisture from the stems; and after fermentation in the stack often has parched the blades till these crumble beneath the touch.

When time has accomplished the hardening which human perversity regards as most essential toward maintaining the health of a horse; when both corn and hay have been transformed into stubborn and unyielding substances; at the age when the first will rattle harshly on being shaken in the sieve, and the last grate audibly when moved by the fork,—then, only then, is either placed before the quadruped. Such provision the prisoner must consume or starve. Hunger is the hardest of all task-masters. The dumb being cannot tell of the agony occasioned by man's forcing its organ's of mastication to uses which will wear down the hardest and coarsest of stones; it cannot portray the torment of thirst, begotten by the long pulverization of matter rendered tough and dry by artificial processes; it cannot describe the agony produced by the grating of such nutriment upon the tender membrane of the stomach; nor can it announce those cruel diseases which afflict the sufferer,—each being engendered by mistaken treatment, against which the afflicted is powerless to appeal.

That which the mouth was designed to prepare, the stomach was intended to appropriate. Moist food is most enjoyed by the horse, and moisture is likewise imperative for the completion of digestion. Upon the accomplishment of this process health and life are dependent. There is no part of the frame which is endowed with an independent existence. By that which the root absorbs, the remotest twig is nourished. The feet or the limbs may fail; man may term such a failure a misfortune, or speak of it as an accident; but the weakness of the body is the primary necessity of almost all such occurrences. The trunk must bend before the vigor of inflammation can be displayed; and health must have departed before the presence of disease is possible.

"Nonsense! folly! downright stupidity!" some sporting reader may exclaim. "Look at all men, when in training. Do not they, during such time, live upon *dry food?*" Certainly not. Not upon food "*dry*" in the same sense as is implied by the sound hay and seasoned oats of the stable. Bread, seen upon any human table, whether as loaf or biscuit, is a moist substance, when compared with either of the articles on which horses subsist. But what shall be said about the contents of the rack or the manger, when compared with the under-done rump steak of which man, when in training, so frequently partakes?

Nor is the subject fairly reviewed, when the form of food is alone considered. The horse does not graze without selection. Certain herbs are scrupulously avoided; others are eagerly sought for. The animal does not eat straight before it; but the head moves to either side, each mouthful being carefully collected with the lips before the juicy tops of the plants are operated upon by the teeth. The horse feeds only off the growing ends of the grasses. The varying herbage may be supposed to present numerous savors to the keen scent of the pasturer; and a fresh flavor may be relished with each new mouthful. Nature has evidently scattered variety, where the dull sense of man can perceive only sameness; and, to the temperate palate of a horse, the verdure of the fields may afford a delicious and an ever-varying banquet.

The instinct which enables the animal to make a selection among numberless growing plants, fades and is lost when moisture has departed with the color, and the perfume natural to the herbage has been changed by art. The animal perceptions may be puzzled; for art can defeat instinct. Some quadrupeds, as if much perplexed, will pick the hay, eating little, but spoiling more than is consumed. Others appear to distaste the preparation, and these refuse it altogether. Few inhabitants of the stable will accept all that may be placed before them, though the rejection may depend more upon the fastidiousness begotten by captivity, than be generated by positive dislike. Few animals exhibit either choice or discretion in the selection of certain portions of prepared fodder. The rejection of particular parts seems to be guided only by fancy or caprice. That which in the green state would be abhorred, when "cut and dried" may by preference be devoured.

We can reasonably conclude that the impulses of instinct, being natural instructors, convey wise admonitions. Many people are so credulous as to believe that the Creator is all-wise, and that nothing formed by the will of Omnipotence is without a special purpose. It is man who converts grass into hay; thus rendering nugatory that discrimination which was bestowed as a protection upon the lower life.

Some persons may feel disposed to assert that all power to injure is also lost, when the natural odor of prepared herbage has been changed; they may argue that what was injurious, with the scent has also lost the characteristic capability to harm. Does chemistry uphold such a conclusion? The dried and powdered herbs of the Pharmacopœia point to an opposite inference. Experience and experiment warrant a con trary judgment. The yew-tree is an active poison to the horse. Gardeners annually clip the compact hedges of yew, which too frequently surround and shelter country lawns. The twigs often fall into fields where horses are pastured. While the cuttings remain green, the animals recognize the poisonous nature and refuse to partake of the fallen leaves. But let exposure dry the refuse, and the grasses of the meadow are deserted, to devour that which was previously avoided. The poison, however, has not evaporated with moisture. The odor, by which danger was recognized, alone has been lost; but the deadly nature seems to be more concentrated: or the issue may be rendered speedier by the lessened bulk of the dried vegetable, and the greater amount of it which therefore can be swallowed.

Apply the above illustration, and, guided by its teaching, say how far man is justified in presenting the wholesale gathering of a field to a hungry horse. It is true, we know of no injury being produced by hay. But we know that the stable, as at present managed, is far from a healthful abode. We are certain, instinct was not created without a purpose; and we have seen that the vegetable, which is avoided when fresh, is not rendered powerless by its moisture being expelled. Therefore, guided by such monitors, we can do no wrong by endeavoring to render hay a wholesome food. None of the grasses are positively poisonous; but the animal prefers those which have a crisp and clean appearance. Soft or woolly provender is never relished. It were an easy labor for a youth to select the good from the bad; while doing this, the boy might be instructed to reject all and everything which was not the fitting kind of grass. The cost of such a process would be very trifling, and the welfare of the animal might soon repay all extra outlay.

However, few, very few people know how to tell a good from a bad sample of hay. Vast quantities of that which no proprietor should oblige his imprisoned slaves to consume, are daily sold; some persons even prefer particular kinds of produce; while others, urged by parsimony, will purchase only damaged hay. There should be, however, in this substance little room for the exercise of choice or of discretion. The characteristics of good hay are very marked, and such only should be purchased by the careful horse owner.

It is the intention of the author to offer some remarks upon this simple but excessively important topic. The comments will be accompanied with tinted wood engravings, which will help the judgment, though these cannot inform the reader on every particular. Therefore, he must kindly assist the writer, as few things are more difficult to describe than taste or smell; since these senses are always under the control of individual predilection.

LAD SORTING HAY.

Upland Hay should look clean. Every fiber should appear distinct. The color should be bright and should convey an idea of newness. No dust ought to be present; neither should the sample, however much it may have been disturbed, lose its prominent features. The constituents will all point pretty much in one direction. Of course this order is not so absolute as to appear like arrangement, but the confusion which generally marks the fibers of the after-meath is never present in a fair sample of well-carried "Upland hay." The scent is commonly very pleasant—not so strong as, but in other respects little different from, the perfume of new-mown hay: to most people its odor is highly agreeable. Weeds should not be abundant; but the presence of foreign growths is clearly indicated by their darker hue, by the browner tint, and the fuller form. The stems should not have shed the seeds, though grasses vary so much in the period of their ripening that it is vain to expect some will not have broken this rule. When a portion is placed within the mouth and is masticated, it rather communicates a mild and pleasant flavor than yields a strong or pungent taste. In short, cleanness and delicacy are the prominent characteristics of "Upland hay;" which some growers imagine is scarcely injured by long keeping. New hay is certainly objectionable. But the year's growth is wholesome feed by November; and, in the author's judgment, it is best when it first comes into use.

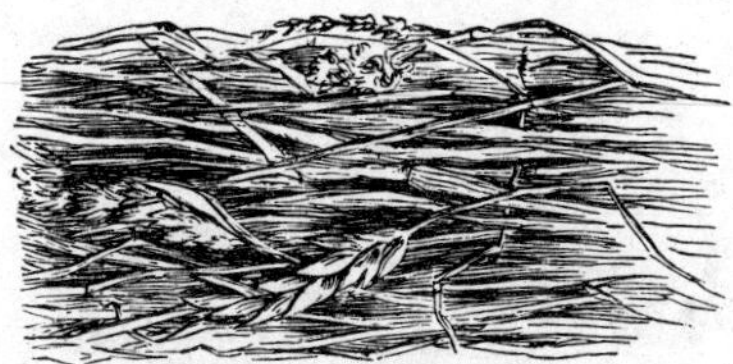

THE CHARACTER AND THE COLOR OF UPLAND HAY.

Lowland Hay.—This kind of preserved grass lacks the bright color, being more tawny than the preceding; indeed, the absence of the green tint is conspicuous, and can hardly fail to be remarked. The arrangement of the fibers is not so well preserved, neither is the crispness or the newness of aspect, for which "Upland hay" is notable, to be remarked in the "Lowland truss." The flowering heads to the stems are all but absent. When felt, it communicates a sense of softness. If rattled, no brisk sound is elicited. It has a stronger and a more pungent perfume.

THE CHARACTER AND THE COLOR OF LOWLAND HAY.

The odor is very far from being so delicate; neither is the taste characterized by any pleasantness of flavor. When placed between the teeth, mastication communicates a sense of softness and toughness: the taste is coarse, almost disagreeable: at first it is vapid, though after a short space a certain amount of pungency is developed. The woolly texture; the want of boldness in the component parts; their comparative smallness; with the washed-out aspect of the whole, and the confusion of the mass, should prevent a novice even from accepting "Lowland" for "Upland hay."

Rowen or After-meath presents a greater confusion than even "Lowland hay." The softness is more conspicuous; flowering heads are only occasionally met with; the stems are few in number, are small in point of size, and form no prominent feature of the whole. This species of fodder lacks perfume altogether; but, as regards color, it may have a slight greenish tint clinging faintly to it. Still, by its want of the brisk or the healthy aspect, and by its darker hue, it is at once recognized for the thing it is,—an unseasonable produce, reaped late in the year, and

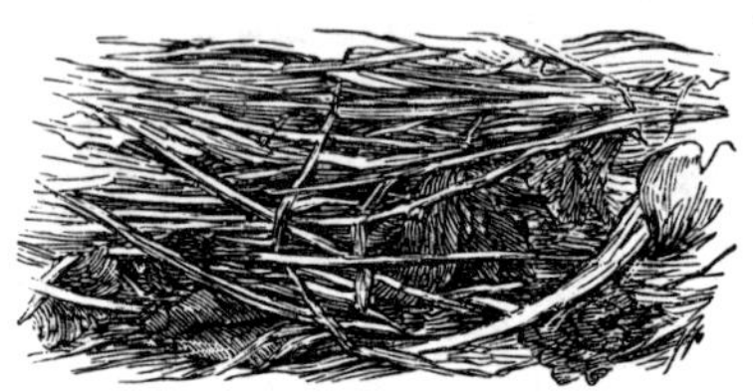

A VERY FAIR SAMPLE OF ROWEN OR OF AFTER-MEATH.

got up long after the freshness of spring had departed. To the mouth it imparts a strong and slightly bitter taste. The odor is not objectionable, although it does not approach to a perfume. Horses which have been accustomed to the better sort, refuse Rowen, or only accept it after actual hunger has been experienced.

Clover Hay is universally mixed with grass and weeds. A good sample of this produce, a novice might easily reject as being too foul a specimen for his approval, and the hay of the second crop (which is not generally remarkable in that particular) be selected in preference. The stems also appear to bear a large proportion to the whole, when compared

A SPECIMEN OF THE FIRST CROP OF CLOVER HAY

with the flowers and the leaves. The fact of the stalks being rarely viewed in the clover field may render this feature the more conspicuous. But the stems are hollow, and consequently lose little bulk when dried. The flowers and leaves, on the contrary, are juicy; and no insignificant portion of their substance is, apparently, lost during evaporation. In the first cut of clover, however, the stems, though numerous, are comparatively fine, and the leaves, though dark, have no tinge of blackness. The flowers are abundant, and faded, of course; but they still retain indications of their original color. Though compressed, they nevertheless suggest what has once been their figure. In taste, a marked resemblance is recognized between the slight flavor of the hay and the strong aroma of the growing plant.

The Second Crop of Clover is distinguished by the grasses and weeds of the first cut being all but absent. The stems are larger, firmer, and bear a greater proportion to the whole. The flowers are not so numerous, and are more dingy in appearance, as well as apparently less carefully

THE SECOND CROP OR AFTER-MEATH OF CLOVER.

preserved. Mastication also enables to be recognized a coarser and a stronger flavor than characterizes good hay of the spring's harvest. The leaves approach near to a black tint. When a truss of the first and one of the second crop of clover are placed together, the last appears remarkable for depth of color.

Heated or **Mow-burnt Hay** is that which has been subjected to such uncontrolled fermentation as shall scorch the substance, and, if not

A VERY EXCELLENT SAMPLE OF HEATED HAY.

checked, would ultimately fire the stack. A certain amount of fermentation is needful for the development of sound hay, but should the necessary action be suffered to proceed too far, "heated or mow-burnt hay" is the result. Most horses will eat this kind of fodder with appetite when it is first presented; but after the novelty of the diet has subsided, there are few animals which do not apparently loathe such produce. The illustration by no means represents the worst specimen which the author has encountered, but it is of that medium character which best conveys a just idea of a general subject. From this sample, however, certain leaves could be chosen that are perfectly black, and which, when attempted to be rolled between the fingers, would crumble into powder. Such a peculiarity, together with the darkened hue, affords the easiest means of recognizing this provender, which, although some silly people by preference employ in their stables, is very far from being a wholesome food for horses. Burnt vegetable matter produces potash; therefore there can be no cause to reject, as a groundless prejudice, the assertion that much "mow-burnt hay" will occasion diabetes. It has a powerful odor, resembling the mixed smell which pervades a public hay market; but the taste has little to distinguish it, being somewhat vapid.

Weather-beaten Hay is equally devoid of smell or of taste. It has a ragged, a confused, and a broken aspect. The hue is deepened; but the color greatly depends upon the period of its exposure, the soil on which it has lain, the amount of wet to which it has been subjected, and the condition in which it has been "got up." So delicate a produce as carefully prepared hay, of course cannot be long exposed to the effects of wind and rain without its more choice qualities being deteriorated, while to the extent of its deterioration, of course the farmer can oppose no check. Therefore a fair general specimen, exhibiting the common characteristics of the majority of samples, is submitted to the reader; but it cannot be expected that a single illustration should embody the multiform aspects which are generated by diverse and powerful influences acting upon a perishable substance.

WEATHER-BEATEN HAY.

Musty Hay is readily recognized by its strong and peculiar smell, resembling the refuse which has been employed to stuff articles of cheap furniture. This it likewise calls to mind by its rumpled and confused appearance. It should never be offered to any animal as a substitute even for better food.

"Upland Hay," as will be seen by the foregoing remarks, is a fair general fodder for the horse. To it, however, a portion of clover hay should be added; but this last is best given in the form of chaff. Ready-cut chaff should never be purchased, because most persons have extraordinary notions as to the ingredients suited for such a form of provender Hay, which the animal refuses to touch when placed in the rack, is often salted and cut into chaff. Thus seasoned, and in such a shape being mixed with corn, it may be eaten. The horse is imposed upon by the salt and the oats which were mingled with the trash; but the sane proprietor has only to calmly inquire of himself—whether that savor which disguises the taste can also change an unwholesome substance into a wholesome nutriment?

It is likewise a prevailing custom to cut straws of different kinds and to throw the rubbish into the chaff bin. Such a practice is spoken of as among the improvements of modern horse-feeding. The quadruped may consume this species of refuse, but it is, in the author's judgment, not a matter for doubt whether such articles merely distend the stomach or whether they can nourish the body. People who advocate cheapness may be favorable to the use of straw; but these persons should not deceive themselves, far less ought they to impose upon others, by asserting so exhausted a material can possibly prove a supporting constituent of diet.

Within the stem of the ripened wheat plant no sap circulates. All the strength of the growth has gone to the seed. Were not the sapless stalk cut and preserved by man, it would shortly topple over, and, by decay, be mingled with the soil. It is well understood that grass, after it has shed its seed, is unsuited for making a nutritious hay. Grain-yielding plants are only cultivated grasses; and the art which has enlarged the seed and lengthened the stem cannot pretend also to have mastered the laws of nature by having endowed a refuse material with nutritious properties. Persons who desire to have straw mingled with the manger food of the horse, should take some pains to procure articles rightfully prepared. The plants should be mown while green; be properly treated, stacked, and husbanded with more than the care usually bestowed on ordinary stems. The same rule should be observed with regard to bean stalks, or whatever else is to be severed into lengths, and is to be esteemed a fitting food for the horse.

Thus prepared, the wheat stem might prove worthy the repute which is at present bestowed upon its exhausted representative. When harvested after this plan, the stalk would retain all that virtue which, at a later season, is expended upon the seed. It would nourish as well as distend. Indeed, the popular custom of giving horses that for food which adds to the bulk of provender, but does not support the system, cannot be too strongly reprobated; yet such a practice is followed in the great majority of existing stables. The animals, to satisfy the cravings of appetite, are compelled to devour more than their diminutive stomachs should contain. Over-gorging is likewise promoted by the habit of subjecting all kinds of horses to prolonged and unnatural periods of abstinence. The consequences of such customs are exemplified in the attenuated stomachs of most old subjects. Often this viscus, upon the muscular and secretive actions of which the health and the strength are dependent, when taken from the body of an animal which has long been subjected to the abuses practiced in the modern stables, is of so stretched a nature as to be semi-transparent, and sometimes as thin as brown paper.

When a horse returns home, after a long fast, it is most unwise to place the famished life before a heaped manger. First attend to its immediate requirements. These satisfied, and the harness removed, a pail of gruel should be offered to the animal. The writer knows it is said by many grooms that their horses will not drink gruel; the author likewise is aware that most servants dislike the bother attendant on its preparation, while few understand the manner in which it should be prepared. The general plan is to stir a little oatmeal into any pail containing hot water, and to offer the mess, under the name of gruel, to the palate which long abstinence may have rendered fastidious. The horse only displays its intelligence when it rejects the potion thus rudely concocted.

No stable is complete unless its furniture embraces a two-gallon pot, and a pail which is kept sacred to cleanly purposes. Then, with regard to oatmeal; this substance, as commonly sold by corn-chandlers, and some bakers, is positively rank. It is naturally sweeter even than other meals; but, by long keeping, it contracts a pungent and a most unpleasant taste. To be good, it should be fresh; and the coarser it is, the finer is the gruel which it yields.

There are few places in London where the oatmeal which is purchased can be depended upon. The writer, however, has for several months enjoyed, every morning and night, a mess of most excellent porridge, made from coarse Scotch or "round" meal procured of Mr. C. Rayment, corn-chandler, Queen's Buildings, Knightsbridge. It is so sweet and pleasant that the diet requires no "Kitchener," or accompanying condiment, to recommend it. The preparation is eaten without flavoring; and it seems to possess medicinal properties, as under its use the writer has lost that yellowness of skin which formerly denoted the liver to be deranged, while he is rapidly regaining health, and has entirely discarded the employment of drugs.

One quart of Mr. C. Rayment's Scotch oatmeal should be thrown into the two-gallon pot, which is to be gradually filled with boiling water, a little cold being first used, merely to divide the grains. The saucepan is then placed on the fire, and its contents are to be briskly stirred until the liquid has *boiled* for ten minutes. After this, it may be put where it will only just simmer; and, in one hour, the gruel will be ready, or in shorter time, should the fire be fierce. The liquid is then poured through a sieve, or should the steed be excessively exhausted, the gruel may be mixed with one quart of sound ale and with half a pound of sugar. The solid part is mingled, while hot, with an equal quantity of bran, and this mixture, having been closely covered, is placed in the manger half an hour after the gruel has been imbibed.

Some horses, however, purge when brought home after a long fast. Such animals are generally of a loose and weakly constitution. For creatures of this description the bran would prove injurious, and an additional pint of meal had better be boiled in a quart of water, which, when mixed with the solid from which the gruel has been strained, will constitute a moist and highly nutritious diet for a delicate horse. The author has, for experiment, tried this form of food upon several quadrupeds, which he was assured abhorred everything like mash or gruel; but only in one instance was the preparation not eagerly consumed. In the exceptional case it was not entirely rejected, being partly eaten; but the writer suspects the apparently dainty quadruped had been previously supplied with a more than usual quantity of oats, as the behavior rather testified to want of appetite than denoted any positive dislike of the nourishment which was before the animal.

Besides hay, corn is commonly used in this country as a food for horses. The corn of the English stable is almost confined to oats. In foreign lands various substances are employed. General, however, as the adoption of oats may be in this kingdom, few, very few persons, beyond the limits of the corn market, have any distinct notion concerning this kind of grain. With the vast majority an oat is an oat, and all oats are of one kind. In exceptional cases, gentlemen are partial to oats of some particular hue. Certain persons will purchase only a black oat; another class prefer a full golden tint, to distinguish the kind they favor; while a few admire a whiteness of husk. Such differences, however, do not affect the grain; the colors are limited to the chaff—the kernels of all are of one tint.

The kernel, or the mealy substance of oats, differs in each variety of corn. One sample shall be thick in the husk, and possessed of a superabundance of beard; but the body of such corn will be narrow, also of contrasting sizes and of various colors.

The inferior specimens are commonly mixed with other seeds, with pieces of stick and portions of straw, as well as sometimes adulterated by the presence of other grain. These oats may impart a saltish flavor to the taste; likewise they may have a faint, smoky, or fusty odor. Such corn seldom weighs more than twenty-two pounds to the bushel.

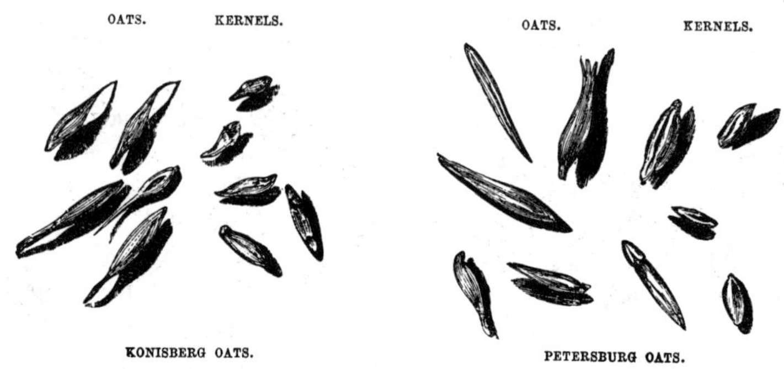

KONISBERG OATS. PETERSBURG OATS.

Another sample, of a different country, will rattle briskly as it is poured from the bulk into the palm. Such has a clean aspect and almost a metallic luster. It is full or plump, being positively beardless, and exhibits no more husk than is needed to surround the kernel of such grain. When attentively scrutinized, perhaps no specimen of oats will be found to be all of one size; but no very striking inequalities will catch the attention, when the better sort are viewed. These are entirely tasteless; and do not even suggest the possibility of a scent appertaining to them. Corn of this quality is too valuable not to be carefully harvested; consequently the hardest pressure of the thumb nail leaves no indentation; while the kernel rather chips than tears asunder, when compressed between the teeth.

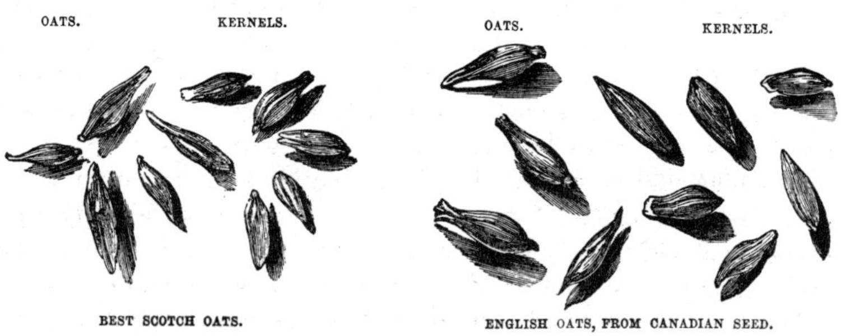

BEST SCOTCH OATS. ENGLISH OATS, FROM CANADIAN SEED.

The absence of beard, however, is not an invariable sign of excellence: if the weight per bushel be heavy, this feature should not be too strongly insisted upon. Some good corn is distinguished by a greater length of husk than is requisite simply to surround the kernel; but such atones for this peculiarity by the bulk of the grain. It is true that a sample of this kind seldom attains to the highest weight, and the purchaser loses somewhat by an excess of chaff.

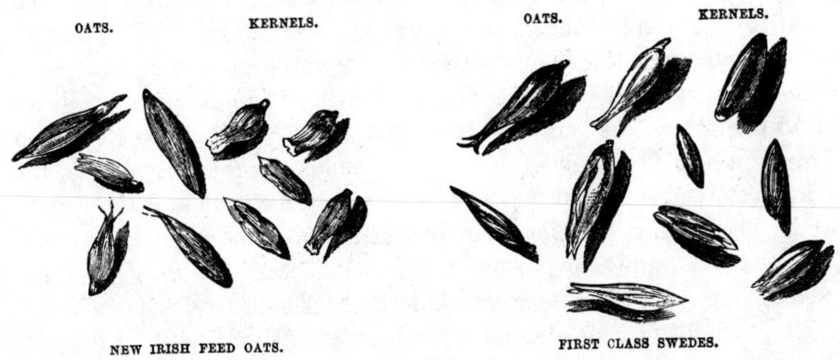

NEW IRISH FEED OATS. FIRST CLASS SWEDES.

Yet in England, which country on the continent is esteemed to be a land of horses, very few stables are supplied with other grain than that of an inferior description. The better kind is bought by the miller and the trainer of racers or hunters. The inferiority of most corn, however, seems not to disturb domestic tranquillity. The majority of proprietors open an account with some neighboring chandler, and the groom is empowered to fetch the provender, which the horses are supposed to consume. Dealers in grain do not enjoy unsullied reputations. It is a custom with grooms to exact ten or five per cent. on all the master's bills which refer to the stable. The gentleman, therefore, always purchases his fodder very dearly, where such an arrangement exists.

Oats should never be bought by measurement, but should invariably be purchased by weight. A prime sample will weigh forty-eight pounds to the bushel; whereas the author has heard of, although he does not pretend to have seen, oats so very light that the same bulk was only equivalent to sixteen pounds. However, a grain which is professed merely to reach twenty-two pounds is to be met with in every market.

The difference of weight should be more than accompanied by an equivalent diminution of price: because a prime oat of forty-eight pounds will yield thirty-six pounds of pure grain, after the chaff has been removed. A fair oat gives half its weight of kernel; but an excellent sample will afford three-quarters of its entire weight in prime nutritious substance; whereas a poor specimen will produce no more than eight pounds of clean corn to the bushel measure!

Consequently, supposing a choice sample to sell for thirty-six shillings, the inferior article can be worth only eight shillings the quarter; for no man can esteem the husk as a food suitable for any living creature, nor would any person purchase such utter refuse, even at the fraction of a penny per pound. Cheapness, in such particulars, is therefore very far from the truest economy.

Most chandlers do not keep the better specimens of oats. With the majority, thirty-six pounds is about the prime standard. As a proof of the correctness of the above assertion, the author, a few months ago, visited a friend, and being grieved to see that the best price was paid for an inferior oat, he purposed to call on all the neighboring dealers in corn, inquiring for grain of only forty pounds weight. Even this the writer was unable to obtain—all naming thirty-six pounds as the gravity of the highest article which they had in stock. The gentleman, therefore, who determines to procure only the choicest corn, must purchase of some large and respectable retail dealer. Should any chandler assert the impossibility of his obtaining the heavier kind of grain, let the gentleman at once seek some tradesman who has dealings at the Corn Exchange, where any quantity of any species of grain can at all times be secured, without further trouble than usually attends upon business transactions.

HEAVY AND LIGHT OATS AS EACH LIES IN THE MEASURE.

The animal is doubly defrauded where poor corn is served out by measure. The grain, in the first place, contains less nourishment; in the next place, the solid bulk is not the same; because the husks not only occupy more space, for, by acting as props to one another, frequently clear cavities are formed. Therefore, were the light and the heavy corns, required to fill a given measure, to be counted, probably no vast difference would be discovered in their number. The reader must, however, himself determine how far it is possible for a horse to be cheated, without the master suffering from the fraud in its effect.

Further injury is inflicted by permitting the quadruped to consume only an inferior corn. Whoever will carefully examine the drawings of oats given in the present division of the book, can hardly fail to remark that the denuded kernels appear of a size disproportioned to that represented as the dimensions of the perfect grain. The microscope makes plain the source of this apparent disparity. The epidermis or the covering of the kernel is coated with numerous fine hairs, which are too small to be perceptible to the unaided vision. These hairs are closely compressed when surrounded by the natural envelope; but when released from the husk, the hairs expand, and thus occasion the naked eye to behold something far too large for the case from which it has recently been released.

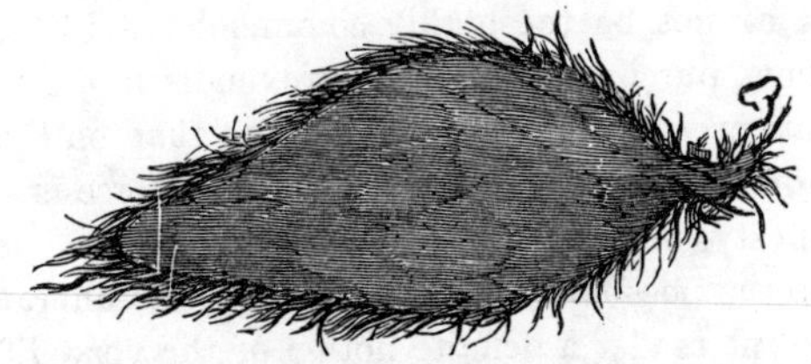

A MAGNIFIED ENGLISH OAT.

In the inferior sorts, the hairs are rather longer, and likewise more numerous, than in the better kind of corn; while, of course, the covering, according to the smallness of the grain, becomes serious, when regarded as a proportionate weight of the whole. These diminutive hairs are perfectly indigestible and entirely indestructible when taken into the stomach. The peristaltic action releases them from the surface of the kernel; being set free, they are frequently felted together by the moisture and rolling motion of the stomach. However small the hairs may be separately, nevertheless by their union they form masses of immense size, provoking such serious impactment as often leads to a terrible and

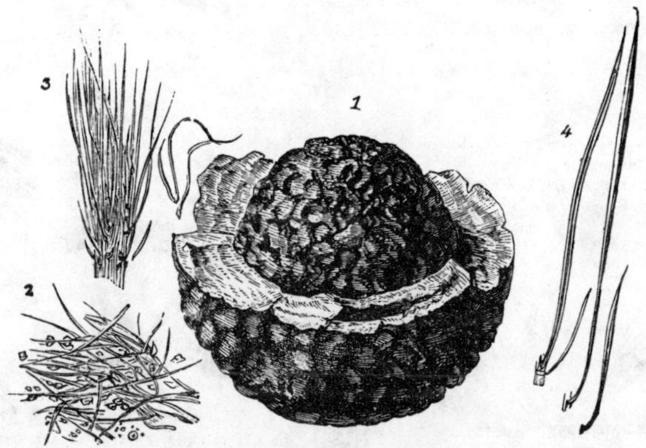

ILLUSTRATIONS OF THE OAT HAIR CALCULUS. COPIED FROM THE INTERESTING WORK ON CONCRETIONS, BY PROFESSOR MORTON.

1. A section of an Oat Hair Calculus. 2. Magnified hairs, mixed with crystals of the phosphates. 3. Hairs, further magnified. 4. Hairs, so enlarged as to display their bulbous insertions and curved forms

a fatal issue. A further reason, therefore, exists for employing good grain in the possibility of such accumulations, the true nature of which was first pointed out by Professor Morton, and by that learned gentleman these concretions were appropriately designated **Oat Hair Calculi.**

It has long been known that digestion is promoted by crushing the corn before placing it in the manger. This custom, as a part of the proper process, cannot be too highly commended. But careless horse owners sometimes purchase the stable provender in a crushed state, or send to have this process performed elsewhere than on their own premises. Such habits are strongly objected to; the horse is surrounded by so much dishonesty, that a prudent man is not justified in trusting the animal's food to the possibility of exchange or of adulteration.

To convey to the reader a definite notion of the very different characters impressed upon various samples of oats, the following illustrations of a few of those which were kindly supplied by a wholesale firm, transacting business at the Corn Exchange, are here presented.

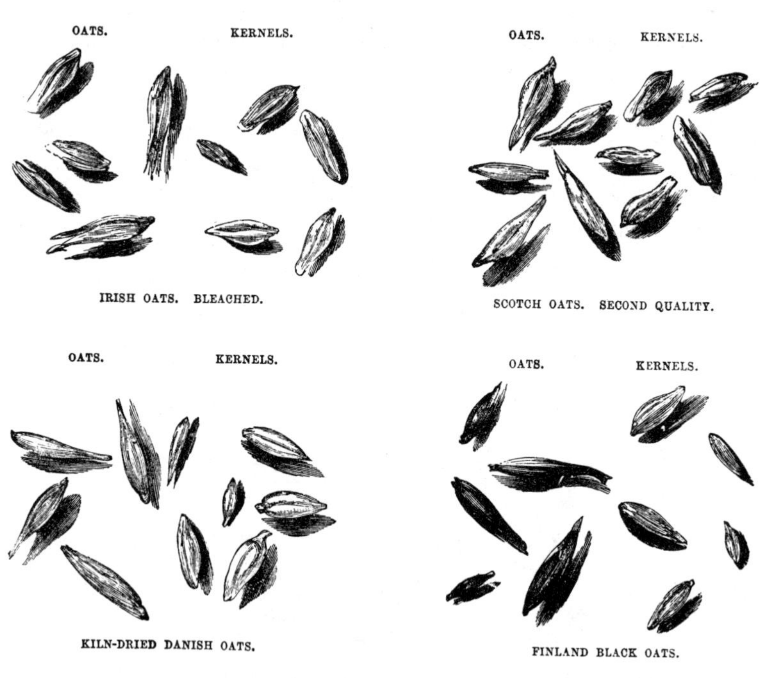

IRISH OATS. BLEACHED.

SCOTCH OATS. SECOND QUALITY.

KILN-DRIED DANISH OATS.

FINLAND BLACK OATS.

A horse owner should invariably have all corn crushed and chaff cut on his premises. The necessary machines are well known, and will soon repay their cost. New grain will not break or crush, but will rather leave the mill flattened or bruised. Corn of this description is easily told by its being soft and yielding; also by its retaining the mark made by the pressure of the thumb nail. Should that test not be perfectly satisfactory, a convincing proof is soon obtained by placing the suspected grain between the teeth. A sound oat should be dry and hard: it should almost chip asunder, and not be torn or broken into pieces by compression. In the autumn months, great care is needed to procure sound corn; the non-professional purchaser is, perhaps, best protected, when he deals for such an article with responsible trades-people, who, in their business, have a character to sacrifice.

OATS. KERNELS.

ENGLISH FEED.

It is a custom to expel the moisture from new grain by drying it in a kiln. It is thereby, in some degree, improved; but it cannot be said to be rendered as wholesome as sound corn, hardened by the natural process. Moreover, oats badly harvested or damaged by wet are frequently placed in the kiln, where they are exposed to the sulphur, in order to change or amend their color. The husks, however, at the conclusion of the process, are seldom all of one tint. If closely examined, indications of the original defect may be discovered on some grains, while others will be of an unnatural whiteness. Kiln-dried oats sometimes betray a shriveled aspect on that part which is near to the beard, such puckering being occasioned by the sudden expulsion of much dampness from the interior. The best test, however, is the rapid rubbing of the sample between the palms of the heated hands; when, should sulphur have been employed, its peculiar odor will be developed.

The author has been thus careful in describing the signs which declare the presence of sulphur, because that mineral, although much employed by ordinary farriers, can occasion the most terrible belly-ache, gripes, fret, or spasms. This affection is one of the most fearful to which the horse is subject, and is the more to be dreaded, as it too often leads to other complications. Perhaps a greater number of animals annually perish through causes resulting from spasms, than die under any other equine ailment.

Healthy corn, having been bruised, is not even then properly prepared for the equine digestion. The stomach of the horse is a delicate membraneous sac, which is easily perforated or ruptured. It has no provision suited to digest hard corn, neither are the teeth of the animal fitted to masticate so resistant a substance. Unlike the similar organs in man, the equine tooth is destined to wear by attrition, and anything calculated to hasten that process equally diminished the existence of the animal. The inappropriateness of the stable and its food must be the reason why English horses are so lamentably short lived. The quadruped was, according to the briefest calculation, designed to exist for forty years; but the majority in this country cease to breathe before they attain the sixth birthday. How much money is thereby sacrificed! How much barbarity is by this lamentable mortality proved to exist! What a terrible amount of unmerited abuse must be yearly perpetrated! What a lack of appreciation of the Creator's goodness is exemplified by the cruelty which thus shortens the duration of His choicest gift to the human race!

Prior to the grain being placed before the horse, it should be softened. Where a building is heated by steam, the accomplishment of this would always be at command. Let each feed of corn and every portion of hay, whether cut into chaff or not, be cooked by being exposed to the action of the vapor for a couple of hours. Moisture, in the form of steam, is

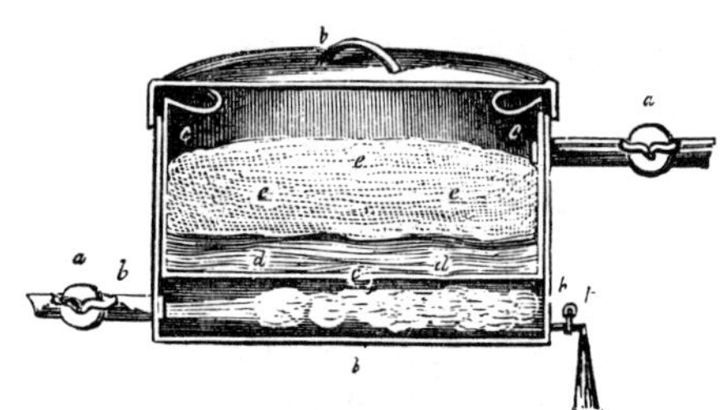

APPARATUS FOR PREPARING HORSES' FOOD.

a a. Pipes, having stop-cocks to regulate the steam and to allow it to circulate when the boiler is not employed.
b b, b b. An iron pot, having a close-fitting lid, but pierced to admit the steam pipes.
c c. A shifting interior case, made with a perforated bottom.
d d. A layer of straw or of hay to prevent the crushed grain clogging the openings.
e e e. The broken corn undergoing the process of being prepared.
f. A small tap to drain off the condensed fluid.

known to be very penetrating; and the ingredients of the manger, when thus prepared, are always more relished than in the raw condition, while the liquid which drains from the provender will prove a highly grateful and a most nutritious beverage to the tired quadruped.

Hard substances taken into the stomach of a horse are well known to derange the animal's system—a fact which has long been proved to the horse-copers and other rogues who live by imposition. A pound of shot will, for a time, conceal the peculiar breathing characteristic of broken wind, though this temporary escape from an outward symptom of disease is often followed by disastrous consequences. Hard grain, if fired from a rifle, would prove no contemptible missile; much of it is bolted by the quadruped before which it is cast, and consequently passes out of the body undigested. The actions of sparrows and the luxuriant green crops which often adorn the tops of dunghills are both evidences of the waste attending the ordinary mode of feeding.

General, all but universal, as the employment of oats may be in this kingdom, very few of Her Britannic Majesty's subjects have the remotest idea of the use which this corn subserves in the animal economy. Drivers will stop, when proceeding upon long journeys, and order their nags large feeds of oats, to enable them to complete the distance, or, in other words, to aid the muscular power. Corn, however, is now ascertained to generate only fat, which rather detracts from than favors the development of motor energy. It certainly sounds strangely, after the expenditure of millions of money, after ages of experience, and after the training of horses was thought to have been fostered into a science, to hear it broadly asserted that the purpose and end attained by the administration of England's favorite feed for horses is totally mistaken! Such, however, is the unvarnished truth; the gallops or the sweats that frequently injure animals while in training are no more than the efforts of ignorance to remove those consequences which its own acts have occasioned. They are attempts to get rid of the fat, which the employment of much corn has naturally produced.

Besides oats, however, beans are used in the best stables; but there is much dispute as to the quantity which a horse can advantageously consume. The English field bean should always be hardened by age

ENGLISH BEANS—A GOOD SAMPLE.

before it is suited for the manger; even then, it should be prepared; for a substance which, when rattled in a measure, emits a sound like to that produced by so many pebbles striking one against the other, can hardly be in a condition proper for comminution between most sensitive and highly-organized members. They should be crushed and subjected to the action of steam, which will, in a couple of hours, remove the objectionable quality without reducing them to a watery mass.

Horse beans, as grown in England, however, are very coarse and astringent substances. No wonder if the large employment of such produce is found to act upon the bowels; surprise should be expressed if so

ENGLISH BEANS—A BAD SAMPLE.

harsh a food could be consumed without inducing constipation. The Egyptian bean, nevertheless, is free from such objectionable properties,

EGYPTIAN BEANS—A GOOD SAMPLE.

being mild and sweet. The author thinks a larger quantity of this crushed and moistened seed might be with benefit presented to the animal. As at present imported, however, it is very imperfectly harvested Most samples exhibit the shriveled and the discolored skin, which de-

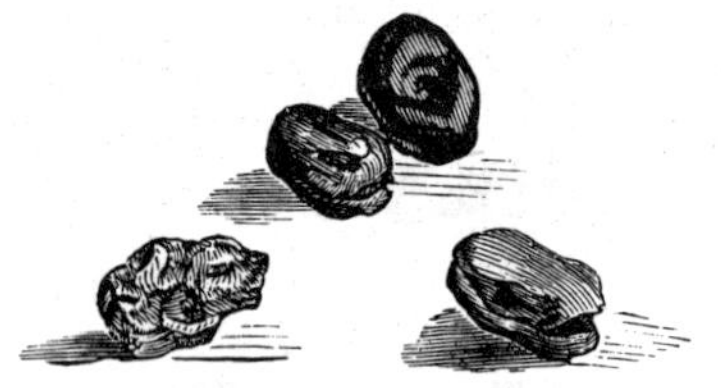

EGYPTIAN BEANS—A BAD SAMPLE.

notes the sickle was resorted to before the plant was matured—an error perfectly inexcusable in a climate which is for nine months of the year free from rain.

Might not some sound Egyptian beans be procured; from these could not a milder and better species of bean be raised in this country? The field pea is open to the same condemnation; but field peas are not generally employed in stables. Those used for horses are small and white, of foreign growth, and quite unobjectionable. Tares are given only to farm teams; but if this plant possesses only a tithe part of those virtues for which it is accredited, its employment might be advantageously extended. Why should hay be made only of grass which, though admirable sustenance for the bovine tribe, evidently is not equally suited to the equine species? The dropsy of the abdomen and legs it induces in nags, together with the foulness of coat which it engenders, are perhaps the best evidence of the injury that attends the long employment of green grass, or even of hay, as a solitary sustenance.

Might not beans, peas, and other leguminous substances be sown broadcast, and mown when in flower? Hay thus produced would be of all value in the stable, because grass, like corn, whether exhibited green or dry, simply induces fat; whereas leguminous plants all favor the development of muscular fiber or support the strength of the body. Such hay might be charged a little higher; but then its feeding value and its worth as a promoter of condition would far more than recompense any extra money at which it might be charged.

It may be asked why, if hay produces fat, are the horses of the poor so lamentably lean, since such quadrupeds receive little else than hay to sustain them? The reasons are numerous. The hay such horses obtain is not often of a good quality; and it is to be feared the stuff is not, frequently, presented in sufficient quantity to promote obesity. Besides, this substance leaves the muscular power unrefreshed. The frame being exhausted by a life passed in exertion, the body's weakness effectually counteracts all tendency to fatten.

A MAGNIFIED MUSTY OAT.

Beans are not known to be much exposed to deterioration; but oats are liable to an affection of the epidermis or of the skin, which causes them to be covered with little granules of a dark color, which the microscope discovers to be fungoid growths resembling a species of very minute toadstools. Corn, when in this condition, is readily recognized by a very powerful musty smell; and the grain, of course, is not adapted to nourish any animal. Musty provender is supposed to engender worms and other unpleasantnesses; but the author is disposed to attribute the production of the parasites to a want of resistance in the system, which may be inherited, or spring from a sickly state of the body, or which may be produced by the consumption of unwholesome diet.

Another advantage which is attendant on the employment of heat and moisture is that, by its operation, the unwholesome nature of food, if not absolutely corrected, is greatly ameliorated. The horse proprietor is thus, in some measure, protected from those accidents to which every stable is liable where a stud-groom does not preside over the establishment, or where the owner is not remarkable for activity. The benefit resulting from heat may, in a certain measure, be secured where no steaming apparatus exists; but then two stout closely-shutting boxes of galvanized iron and a scoop, together with a large kettle, are required.

MACERATING BOX AND SCOOP.

The food is placed in one of the receptacles; then so much boiling water should be poured upon it as experience has ascertained will be entirely absorbed. This done, the lid is closed, and the confined steam will partially cook the provender. The need for two boxes is to allow the hay, chaff, or grain to remain for a longer period subjected to the moisture, so that these substances may be thoroughly softened. This, however, is a more troublesome method, and the mode does not equal, in its results, the employment of steam where the vapor can be commanded; but, whichever practice is adopted, the following regulations should always be observed when the horses are fed.

The mangers intended for the reception of softened provender must be of a peculiar construction. The feeding compartment should possess a lid, which may be let down when the manger is removed. This last should always be taken out of the stable after it has been emptied; the interior should, at each removal, be thoroughly cleansed. The form of the receptacle should, in some measure, resemble a large pudding dish, and should offer no sharp angles, where the moist provender may accumulate and turn unpleasantly acid. A broad rim should surround the hollow, into which rim should be let two movable handles, the use of which is to expedite the manger being carried from place to place. The substance ought to consist of galvanized iron, but the interior may advantageously be coated with enamel.

IRON DISH OR MOVABLE MANGER FOR HORSES' FOOD.

Such an article, when placed in the wooden frame adapted to receive it, would be supported by its rim and kept by its own weight in the proper situation. When taken thence, it ought to be carried to the

GIVING OUT THE MACERATED FOOD.

pump and cleansed, after which it is lodged in the provender house. When feeding time comes round, two helpers or stable-boys wheel two barrows to the door of the building and there wait. The head groom, attended by two others, enters the room, and with the scoop serves out the provender, each groom by turns holding a manger to be filled.

As the basins are loaded, these are arranged on the barrows; when the macerating box has been emptied, the grooms and helpers proceed upon their rounds. As each barrow stops before a door, the man who wheels it goes to the outside of the building, and, pulling a string, thereby raises the lid of the manger. He next proceeds to the entrance, and, having undone the fastenings, stands ready to admit the groom on his approach. This being done, the lower half is closed, and only opened again to allow of the groom's egress.

CARRYING THE FOOD ROUND TO THE STABLES.

Where a horse, of a known restless or ravenous habit, is confined, an external slide affords the means of supplying food. The manger, in such a box, should be replaced after it has been cleansed; for, as it is then empty, the food cannot be lost in consequence of the impatient hunger or of the nervousness of the animal. When the feeding hour comes round, the lid of the receptacle having been raised by pulling at the string, the shutter is lifted up and the provender shot through the open space. The steamed oats and chaff are not absolutely wet. The condition is rather less sticky than the same bulk of brewers' grains. The substance, therefore, would readily fall down into the manger; but, as this mode necessitates that the incline be constantly scraped and cleaned, it is not, because extra trouble is enforced by it, recommended for general adoption.

Thus, without that excitement, delay, and ill humor which too frequently distinguishes feeding time in large establishments, each horse may be speedily supplied. All needed is a little drilling by the head groom, so each man may understand his office: that when fulfilling it, no one may obstruct the path of his fellow. The steaming or maceration of food may, by certain readers, be imagined to have originated in a desire to write *pretty* about horses. The author denies such a motive. Besides, the plan has no pretense to originality. It has for many years been practiced: but not in *high-class* stables. The writer, however, had an inducement, in truth, to recommend its general adoption, and, therefore, to some portion of the implied charge he may plead "guilty."

All horse owners bitterly complain of the expense involved in the support of an animal. Nor is this surprising, when it is considered that one-half of its provender passes through the body of the animal undigested, being no more than so much material literally wasted; while a great portion of the remainder, though dearly purchased, is absolutely without nutriment. As a matter of economy, nothing should be placed in the manger which is not fit to be appropriated, or is not proper to nourish the strength. Such is the purpose of food: that is not food which does not feed, although, like the clay balls of the American Indian, it may be swallowed under the promptings of appetite; for when received into the stomach, like the substance alluded to, it probably will engender disorder.

Improper articles, therefore, presented as food, are in a double sense extravagant. In the first place, they do not sustain the life; in the second place, they entail the expense and loss of service which are inseparable from disease. Whether with horse or with man, everything offered as food should do more than merely appease the appetite Unless it also uphold the vigor, devouring it is to waste the substance; and whatever adapts provender to the requirements of the digestion, cannot in reason be esteemed either extravagant or unnecessary. Of course, prepared food entails trouble. It cannot be forked into a rack or tossed into a manger speedily and without soil to the garments. There are plenty of reasons why grooms should cling to "hard meat;" and why this class of servants should object to prepared fodder.

Grooms, however, as generally treated, are most exceptionable domestics. Other servants are occupied throughout the day. The stable attendant turns the key upon the day's duties at six o'clock in the evening. He is the most wasteful and costly of all the servants in or about the house. He wastes even that which Heaven has supplied in the greatest abundance. He wastes the air; since, to obtain warmth, he will not permit the horse to breathe other than atmosphere contaminated by the creature's excretions. He wastes the quadruped's strength; since he works it out of season, and is pleased to view the limbs, when not in action, "cribbed and confined" within the narrow limits of a stall. He upholds every abuse. He is opposed to every improvement. The sum which a fashionable groom costs his master is not to be estimated by the money paid to the individual as wages.

Hay, oats, and beans constitute the horse's daily sustenance. These articles are quickly measured out, and do not soil the hand which apportions them. No doubt the groom will resist any change in so convenient a diet; but the subject, as it at present stands, concerns the liking of no person. It simply involves a moral duty. Nature has sent food in abundance and in variety. Is man justified, when he opposes nature's obvious intention? When he first imprisons a life, and then dooms it to subsist for the period of its being on a monotony of provender, does he act rightly or wisely? What motive can be urged strong enough to warrant the pigmy in placing his insignificance between the creature and the liberality of the Creator?

Horses are not confined to England. Elsewhere the quadrupeds thrive on other food than hay, oats, and beans. The Arab, which stands first among the tribe, and is by some writers recognized as the original of the species, thrives on barley and on chopped straw. The American breed rarely taste oats, being fed on Indian-corn; as, likewise, are many animals inhabiting the south of Germany. Damaged wheat is eaten by agricultural teams all over the world. Rye is given as a supporting diet, when long journeys are traveled in Russia. In India, the cavalry charger exists chiefly on a grain called "gram." In Ireland, the general feed is raw potatoes. In Iceland, dried fish is employed as provender; while during the needy period of the Crimean campaign, the English horses devoured the tails of their stable associates.

England, however, can supply or can import all the articles enumerated. Why, therefore, are oats preferred as the fittest food for horses? The kernel of this grain is covered by a solid coat of chaff. That chaff adds to the weight of the corn, and is charged to the purchaser as so much nutritious matter. It is not supporting; but it occupies space when first taken into the stomach. That space allows the dried kernels to swell without occasioning inconvenience to the animal; for the same moisture which enlarges the oat, also softens the husk, and allows it to be compressed with little absolute force.

As dry food, given separately, oats no doubt are the most wholesome provender for horses. Barley, rye, or wheat, if dry, would require a proportion of chaff to be mixed with those grains, so as to render either of them safe. Few things are more common in agricultural districts, than for animals to be injured by eating the latter kind of food. Quadrupeds often break loose, and gorge upon wheat; when the cereal, swelling after it has been swallowed, not unseldom ruptures the stomach and destroys the life. All dried grain should be moistened before it is placed in the manger. When properly soaked, barley, wheat, or rye are more wholesome than oats. Mingled with chaff, they are quite as beneficial, even when administered in the dried state. They are, moreover, when regarded in the view of weight for weight of nutriment, far cheaper than the vast majority of England's favorite provender.

Might not the ship biscuit, which is now used only as a food for dogs, be profitably employed in the stable? It contains no husk. Its surface is not surrounded by dangerous hairs. It is all nutriment; and, being slightly moistened by the action of steam, would doubtless be consumed with avidity, after the first distaste, natural to timidity, had been overcome. This species of provender would be cheaper than the raw, hard, and unprepared grain, which might with advantage be superseded by crushed biscuit mingled with a proportion of chaff.

The action of heat is well known to change the nature of corn, while fermentation converts the starch of the raw seed into sugar. Might not a coarse kind of bread be made for the stable? This is no whim of the author's imagination. Such a plan is common throughout Germany, where it is not unusual to see a carter feeding himself and steed off the same loaf. The groom might possibly resist such an innovation upon his rights and leisure; but a better order of dependents could be found, to whom the extra labor would merely prove a pastime.

Besides bread and biscuits, there are various roots which might prove very acceptable to a vegetable eater. The digestion of all such articles is promoted by the substances being cooked before they are presented. The fire extracts much of the water with which they all abound; heat also, in some measure, arrests the tendency to ferment. Why should such simple and natural food be denied to the creature which nature has sent upon this earth with an appetite fitted to consume it? There is ample room for choice in the list which has been indicated; so far as experiment has hitherto tested the value of such articles of food for horses, results have been obtained which seem to say the change might be generally adopted without danger.

A sameness of diet is known to derange the human stomach. Under such a system, the palate loses its relish, while a loathing is excited which destroys appetite. How often do grooms complain of certain animals being bad feeders! May not such disinclination for sustenance be no more than the disgust engendered by a constant absence of variety? Is there any large stable in the kingdom where one or more quadrupeds are not equally notorious for being ravenous feeders? The disinclination for the necessary sustenance and the morbid desire for an excess of nutriment are alike symptoms of deranged digestion. Some horses will devour large quantities of earth,—stones, *worms*, and all. Other animals will, if not muzzled, consume the litter of their stalls, no matter how tainted or filthy it may be. Strange tastes and unnatural likings are not unfrequently displayed by the inhabitants of the stable, among which, the instances cited are only the most common, all such whims being declarative of a diseased stomach.

The stable, its management, its formation, and its food, do further injury than merely to derange the digestion. Such may be its primary effect; but the stomach is to the animal as the root is to the plant. Through it all the nourishment is absorbed. By its healthful operation, the trunk, limbs, and strength are maintained. The rootlets cannot be diseased without the remotest twigs drooping and withering. So the deranged digestion induced by the modern stable leads to those fearful results which render life valueless; and which would terminate the existence, were the event not anticipated by the office of the knacker. Cribbing, weaving, quidding, surfeit, inflamed thorax, bowel complaints, broken wind, glanders, diseases of the legs and of the feet, with the majority of those injuries which are complacently recognized as accidents, may all be directly traced to that domestication which assumes a right to dictate how a life shall exist; the atmosphere it shall breathe; the space it shall occupy; and the substances it shall eat. Heaven, when this earth was first inhabited, did not create beings without investing them with rights, which man cannot abrogate at his convenience or set aside at his pleasure.

Of late years a class of traders has sprung up who profess to sell "patent foods," or nostrums, which are to be cast into the manger with the corn. The economy and the marvelous effects of these secret preparations are loudly trumpeted; and from the numbers who now deal in such articles, these persons evidently find many customers. The mixtures consist of certain seeds and spices, which, in consequence of a relish being given to the monotony of manger diet, are eagerly devoured. They may even stimulate a false appetite; but, after a time, this effect will cease, and a loathing greater than the previous excitement will succeed. It is not, therefore, with surprise that the author hears of people, once very enthusiastic admirers of such additions, having, after some experience, relinquished these foreign aids to provender

After all, "patent foods" contain matter which is as old as the hills. Grooms and coachmen have, for a longer period than is to be reached by the memory of man, had a confiding faith in certain charms, or nostrums. Such innocent people have long held secrets for working wonders—either by improving the coat, promoting condition, or creating spirit, etc. These mysteries were made up either as balls or powders. So general was this practice that certain veterinary surgeons kept particular articles solely to meet the demands of such customers. These ingredients, which were always retailed to ignorant people, late in the evening and with much secrecy, are, in very many cases, even to particulars, the same as are now the advertised "Blessings to Horse Owners." There is, however, this difference: such things are, at present, purchased by the proprietor, whereas they formerly were secretly procured by the servant. The master esteems it commendable in him to administer such stuffs to his animals; whereas, a few years ago, the retainer was assuredly dismissed from his situation, if not punished, who was detected mixing any substance with the provender of his horses.

With regard to quantity in the matter of diet. All animals are not of one size, neither have all horses the same capacity of stomach. It is usual to measure out so much corn as the allowance proper for a horse, and to toss the quantity into the manger, without paying any attention to the desires of the creature. Such a custom may be extremely convenient; but it is very wasteful. Horses differ quite as much as men do in their appetites. By the common practice, one animal receives more than it requires, while another gets less than satisfies its cravings. Some slight notice of the body's necessities should be insisted upon in those who pretend to comprehend the quadruped; and a master should instruct the servant that a creature endowed with life cannot be justly regarded as a manufacturing machine.

Then, as to the times of feeding. The horse is essentially a creature of the night. Man may shake up the straw and lock the stable door; but he does not, therefore, put the quadruped to sleep. Long hours of watchfulness are apt to generate habits of mischief, as well as lead to many indulgences which are no more than the results of want of employment, or the absence of amusement. The solitary confinement, now popular in prisons, in workhouses, and in some schools, is evidently wrong in principle; more especially wrong is it, when practiced upon children, as loneliness, acting upon immaturity of intelligence, invariably leads to an evil desire, which is, in penal prisons, spoken of as "breaking out."

The horse has to pass twelve hours of weary time awake, without food and without supervision. Why should not one feed, at least, be given late at night? The present custom, of allowing the stable-man his time after six o'clock, is not beneficial to the servant; nor is it advantageous to a master. It merely encourages habits which are expensive. Expensive habits are not commendable or innoxious, where the weekly income is reckoned by shillings. A little more of wholesome employment would greatly improve the stable-retainer. The man is now corrupt; but those who suffer by his vices, expose him to that temptation which subverts the uprightness of his inclinations. After six, is a better hour for equine exercise than during the heat of the afternoon. Subsequent to the setting of the summer's sun, during the cool, moist time of twilight, the quadruped would delight in being abroad; but, during the hours when nature formed her creature to roam, man, for a servant's convenience, imprisons his slave; and, having perverted every intent or purpose of its existence, complains aloud because the laws of Creation are not made subservient to his perversity!

Could society be rendered a trifle more sympathetic and a little less conceited, horses would largely benefit by such a change in the dispositions of their masters. But this cannot be with present thoughts and existing institutions. The modern age essentially delights in *knowing;* it rather sneers at, than cultivates, *feeling.* England abounds in schools, and is thickly strewn with colleges. Education is much lauded; but the education at present given neglects the higher and the better part of the pupil's mind. Everywhere knowledge is inculcated; nowhere is feeling cultivated. Nay, in the majority of existing educational establishments, the sensations are blunted and the emotions suppressed. Yet to elevate the feelings of its followers, is the purpose and the object of Christianity. Reverends and Dignitaries preside over places where, under pretense of being properly trained, youths are unchristianized. Most young men quit their tutors with the knowledge quickened; but where is the being who began life with the heart improved, or with the moral sense to guide him through the many obligations he was newly called to discharge, upon his becoming a member of this world's society? The horse especially suffers under the consequences which result from the present evil tendency of the community.

To talk of the feelings, the instincts, and the inclinations of the quadruped, is to earn a character for maudlin affectation. The populace in the public highways hourly stare at or carelessly pass spectacles which, were the general mind really educated to understand what is before it, should awaken the keenest commiseration; but which are now viewed as sights that enliven the prospect. Whence is derived such hardness of heart? Whence springs such general and such a deep-rooted insen sibility? No man seems capable of interposing a voice of expostulation, when the streets display living and feeling flesh creeping toward its early grave; when he beholds the animal driven slowly to death: when he looks upon an animated being, so worn and so dejected that it is the last office of humanity to summon the knacker to end a hopeless misery. The existence of a Society, with two constables, poorly counterbalances a national display of spurs and of whips. The foremost humanitarian, so the skin be whole, can afford to gaze upon a lean and spiritless horse, tired beyond man's most exaggerated conception of fatigue, slowly creeping before some over-burdened cart, while the driver, whip in hand, adds his weight to the disproportionate load. Misery in front, brutality behind, and hard-heartedness around; while a fellow-inhabitant of earth totters onward to its death!

Yet, how universal is the lamentation about "the instability of the horse's health," and "the uncertainty of equine life!" Knowing what stables are, and having learned the air, the food, and the exercise allowed to maintain a horse's existence, is there any just occasion for appealing to sympathy, because a life, maltreated in every essential, generally droops before the fate which abuse provoked? Forced into early toil; never seen abroad without the goad by its side; worked to the point of convenience, and nourished according to the dictates of economy,—is it wonderful that the majority of horses perish before their youth is matured? Is it not rather a justifiable reason for surprise that a country should boast of its morality, should exalt its civilization, should vaunt its Christian feeling—and, nevertheless, that its inhabitants should tacitly combine to practice the grossest inhumanity upon the meekest type of earthly sensibility?

CHAPTER VI

THE EVILS WHICH ARE OCCASIONED BY MODERN STABLES.

THOSE gentlemen who have deeply studied such subjects, assert that man is incapable of originating a single idea. Certainly an intelligent being would not have been required to originate anything if, when intending to confine an active animal, he had been expected to credit the joyous creature with the common attributes of life. It could have evinced no excessive servility if, before the building was raised for such a purpose, nature and her requirements had been, in some slight measure, considered.

It obviously is folly for mortal pride to contend against those ordinizations which govern the universe. However, in the case of exercising power over the horse, centuries of defeat and ages of loss seem incapable of causing mankind to relinquish a hopeless struggle. The strife has been going forward almost from the commencement of time; nevertheless, human beings, though always beaten, press onward to perpetuate the contest. They scorn to retreat, and will suffer rather than own a victor; they will not, to make an advantageous peace, desert a silly custom or discard an ancient usage. They can sustain punishment; they can endure chastisement; but, like land crabs, when once upon the march, they cannot deviate from the line which they have adopted. They can abuse the master, but they cannot listen to the instructor. "Nature," men exclaim in chorus, "is very stubborn." "Horse property," respond another gang of culpables, "is particularly hazardous!"

All this noise, however, might at any moment be avoided, would the human race only stoop to employ a little reflection. Would man not fight quite so obstinately, but merely think over the cause of combat, he might possibly be a gainer in happiness as well as in pocket. Could he only condescend to admit the horse is a living creature, he would take a step toward his recognition of the truth, because a fact would have been acknowledged. This being granted, then let mortals, in their collective capacity, decide in what the lowest proof of life—mere animal existence—does prominently consist.

It does not require any vast expenditure of thought to discover that life is action; "to be," is synonymous with "to do;" therefore it is a sheer necessity of existence that an animated being must be doing something. Such is the primary consequence of existence. Thus, to breathe and to move, imply one act; since, if the lungs cease to dilate, respiration immediately terminates, and, with it, animation comes to an end Yet it remained for mortal perversity to rebuke the first principle of established philosophy, when stables were built in which a breathing animal was to be treated as it were an inanimate chattel.

Nature, like a kind mother, is to this day endeavoring to teach her wayward children a plain truth, which they may hourly behold enforced by visible examples. The willful brood appears to be in no hurry to learn. Man still treats the horse as though he honored the quadruped by enslaving it, and ennobled a life by conferring upon the animal the title of his servant. He acts as though, by such conduct, sufficient reason was exhibited why he should oblige the creature to resign its instincts and relinquish its desires.

The equine race, when in a wild state, are gregarious, or congregate in herds. Man captures such a quadruped and places it in a stable, built to enforce the extreme of solitary confinement. The plain is the natural abode of the herd; on their speed depends both their pleasure and their safety. Man ties the domesticated horse to a manger, and pays a groom to enforce absolute stagnation upon innate activity. The "panting steed" is the most timid of living beings. Man insists the charger is possessed of extraordinary courage; he declares it delights in the tumult of battle; and he esteems it a glorious achievement to brutally coerce the timorous sensibility. The mild-eyed horse is, perhaps, the most simple of all the breathing beauties which adorn a wondrous world. Man declares all of the gentle breed have dangerous propensities, and are most inherently vicious.

Before subjugation, the creature fed off the surface of the earth. Man builds a house specially designed for the captive, in which the corn is placed on a level with the chest, and the hay is stationed as high up as the head. The animal is gifted with affections; it longs to gratify their promptings; it yearns for something upon which its abundant love may gush forth,—a fellow-prisoner—a goat—a dog—a cat—a fowl; no matter what, so it be some living object on which may be lavished that excess of tenderness which, confined to its own breast, renders being miserable Man esteems it his primary duty to clear the stable of all possible companionship; but the creature which would rejoice, were it only permitted to worship its enslaver, he rarely approaches without a loud voice, a harsh word, or a harsher blow announcing his presence to the captive

The inhabitant of such a prison, a domesticated horse miserably drags through a shortened life, under human *protection.* The nearest approach it can make to freedom is its period of exhausting labor. It always rejoices to quit its confinement; but, enfeebled by imprisonment, and subservient to man's exactions, it ever gladly returns to the place of its sorrow. In proportion as its limbs are finely made and its actions are graceful is it prized. It is never esteemed for its instincts or credited with intelligence. It lives in so limited a space that, in comparison with the dimensions of its abode, a man in a sentry-box dwells in a mansion; or a lion in a cage roams over a domain. A reasonable and an intelligent being commands his horse should be fastened to such a spot, and supposes that a living organism is to endure the confinement which does not permit the body to turn round; that animated functions are to exist where most ordinary exercises are rendered impossible: nevertheless, he anticipates the creature will appear bounding with health in answer to his requirements.

To be sure, the prisoner, although its head be fastened, (a restraint not imposed upon the most savage of carnivorous beasts,) is permitted now to bear upon one leg, and then to change it for the other. It may perhaps lie down or stand up, without provoking chastisement Neither head nor tail are forbid a *proper* degree of motion. But at this point all indulgence is exhausted. It is tied to a rope two yards in length; but it may not go even to the extent of its tether; neither may it move close up to the manger; both acts are equally unpardonable: a *properly* behaved animal should stand quietly in the center of its compartment, and always remain there when not lying down.

It is beaten if its head be raised just to peep over the paling, to exchange a rub of the nose and to give, as well as accept, a warm stream of fragrant breath to and from its nearest fellow-misery. It must taste the full flavor of its captivity: no trivial act may distract attention from the horror of its position. It must lie down where it stands; and stand where it laid down. It must not display the grace and ease of motion with which it has been endowed; nor must it indulge the kindly feelings Providence has gifted it with. To exert the faculties which the ALL-WISE has planted in a beautiful body, man regards as evidence of its vicious disposition; though it has yet to be demonstrated that nature ever bestows any quality without an intention that the gift should be actively employed.

The feelings of the master are more than sympathized in by the groom. A servant's pride always induces him to exaggerate both the virtues and the vices of his employer. What in the superior is a mere anticipation, which gratifies when it becomes realized, in the bosom of the dependent swells to a positive demand, compliance with which it is noble, at every hazard, to insist upon. The man, therefore, permits the cat to purr; but among the horses he is resolved to enforce the extreme of quietude.

The menial does not inquire whether an exquisite adaptation of sight, so as to inspect the minutest particle and to view the most distant object; whether a sensibility of hearing, to which movements are audible, when to the duller perceptions of the proprietor no sound vibrates on the air; whether a keenness of scent which can appreciate qualities in substances that to human sense are devoid of odor; or whether that fleetness of motion, which the Creator permitted as a protection, the ease of which machinery, when urged over common roads, has failed to rival,—the servant does not inquire whether such attributes were given by nature only to be fastened by the head, or to be confined within a space in which absolute stagnation must ultimately induce bodily incapacity. For nature's intentions the groom cares nothing. "He has his doty to discharge and he will do it! Master wishes the osses to be kept quiet on a arternoon; and he's the chap as will see the guv'nor is not disappointed!"

Such a doom can alone be varied by the hours of labor and the periods of feeding. To the animal thus surrounded, recreation is impossible, and its lodging is so small that bodily ease is unattainable. Yet the horse is kept for the use of its limbs; those who have observed the quadruped canter round the field into which it has been newly loosed, know that enjoyment is not incompatible with its existence. No pleasure, however, can be permitted within the stable. There, the slightest rustle or the gentlest indication of motion is jealously noted. Most equestrians like their quadrupeds to be still after feeding; because perfect quietude is supposed to promote digestion and to encourage thrift among the horses. The groom loves silence, because, to his mind, it is so nice and so respectable. Besides, when no sound disturbs the monotony of the building, the groom can luxuriate in the sense of absolute idleness—a feeling which most servants recognize and enjoy. If any sound interferes with the afternoon's luxury, a harsh and taunting shout rebukes the inconsiderate disturber. "Now! Then! There! What ails you?"

The dreaded accents of the tyrant's voice may, for a space, banish the oppression of captivity. The animals, under the influence of newly awakened terror, may be enabled to shrink into absolute silence; but, as the fear fades, the full reality of their position cannot otherwise than be felt in all its horrors. Fed upon stimulating food, how their spirits must languish, and how poignantly the aching limbs must suggest those pleasures there is no prospect of the prisoners ever again enjoying! Every little incident is seized upon with an eagerness which attests the prevalence of utter despair. Should a visitor enter the building, every head is raised and every eye is turned toward the welcome intruder.

A STRANGER HAS ENTERED THE STABLE.

The universal bustle which follows his appearance bespeaks how the lucky arrival has allowed the limbs to be stretched and the positions to be altered. For a moment or two, the straw is in audible commotion, while the sinkers, or blocks fastening the collar reins, may knock against the mangers, and the noise elicits no angry remonstrance.

But as joy hailed his appearance, so does the dullness deepen on the stranger's departure. From that moment, any relaxation becomes a fault. All pastime is unlawful; the most innocent amusement must be practiced silently and in secret. Certain animals, however, try to get through the long hours of enforced idleness by quietly nibbling at the topmost rail of the manger. Large portions of tough wood are often removed after this fashion; and to him who can rightly interpret signs, a thick post bitten away, fiber by fiber, will present melancholy evidence of that longing for employment which could induce so great a waste of perseverance; for animals are naturally great economists of labor.

NIBBLING THE WOOD-WORK.

Other prisoners will endeavor to cheat the time by licking their mangers, apparently in the hope that some stray grain of corn may have escaped previous attention. The soft tongue of the horse, passed over the hardened surface of the wood, occasions no noise. Often a few grains will have lodged in the corners; then the effort to displace these affords a long game. Others, from want of something to do, or from finding impure air and inactivity do not, in accordance with the general doctrine, promote equine digestion, learn "to crib;" a few, from the operation of the like causes, become perfect as "wind suckers." All "speed the weary hours" as they best can; and many heads are turned round to discover if it be feeding time again; not that they are hungry, but eating is an occupation, and they sadly wish for some employment.

Certain quadrupeds, under these circumstances, adopt a habit, which is the more remarkable because hours of tedium have generated the like indulgence in human beings. Mortals, when compelled to remain stationary, and forced to preserve silence, often strive to kill time by rocking to and fro, or by "see-sawing" their bodies. Such a pitiable excuse for amusement is very common among the little people whose undeveloped limbs are perched on high forms, and in whose hands are fixed very uninteresting primers, from which the infant mind wanders into vacuity during the hours of imprisonment which occur in those abominations termed "Preparatory Schools." The horse, also, when forbidden the pleasures in which nature formed it to delight, will move its head methodically from one side of its stall to the other, and will continue thus engaged for hours together.

So exciting a pastime, most sane people might deem to be harmless enough. It interferes with nobody; if it can amuse the solitude of the creature, it should certainly excite no person besides. But in the arbitrary notions of rectitude entertained within the stable, such a very simple custom is punished as a positive "vice." A horse which "see-saws" is said "to weave," and "weaving" is, by grooms, esteemed highly culpable. What the poor animal is "weaving," no one can point out; but, supposing an idle time to be so creditably employed, "weaving," though not a highly remunerative occupation, nevertheless does not usually entail penal severity upon the offender. But grooms act upon their own convictions, and disregard the general morals of mankind. When a monotonous sound, however gentle, but long continued and regularly repeated, falls upon the ear of watchful ignorance, the awful fact that one of the imprisoned is endeavoring to cheat its misery, causes the lash to be grasped; the smart of a well-directed thong cuts short the melancholy recreation, to inform the captive that its keeper is determined the fullest flavor and the most distant relish of the situation shall be silently appreciated.

The imagination cannot picture a harder fate! Man, under such a doom, would be relieved by insanity. The horse has few pleasures; but nature makes all life suffer acutely when forced to continue inactive. The creature cannot seek occupation in what young ladies term accomplishments. It has no power to consume its existence in silent study. Like all animal vitality, its delight is to do, and that is the very thing which the groom insists it shall not perform. It can taste no other kind of pleasure. All created beings have some sphere of enjoyment. Activity constitutes that of the equine race; but to prevent an innocent creature knowing the only happy sensation of which its nature is capable, the animal is placed in a compartment; tied up to a manger; while, behind, there sits a man who is specially engaged to chastise the smallest infraction of the prevailing silence of the prison-house.

It remained for human perversity to conceive a life without a pastime, and vexatiously to impose this terrible fate upon the creature whose existence is devoted to man's service. When in the field, the horse is never idle. The only amusement of the simple animal lies in its perpetual occupation. What a despairing sorrow must therefore afflict such an existence, when dragging through its time under the fostering care of the enslaver! Yet how proudly do some intellectual beings boast of their stables and of the ceaseless attention lavished on their studs! What is it this assiduity realizes to the creature on which it is expended? Stagnation to the active, and solitude to the gregarious. Movement draws down punishment, as it were a fault. Any attempt to while away the tedious hours is esteemed "a vice;" sensation must be checked, and feeling, man insists, shall be suppressed. But who, among the millions of intellectual masters, sufficiently understands the quadruped over which they all usurp authority, to regard the huge bulk of that endurance as the embodiment of the acutest form of every possible earthly misery?

To ascertain how far the foregoing remarks are founded upon reason, let it be supposed that man and horse were to change places, though the two animals, not being alike on the score of comprehension, no trial could be exactly equitable. Restlessness of spirit is the invariable attendant upon weakness of intellect. The advantage must, therefore, preponderate upon that side where intelligence might lose a sense of self in the excitement of thought, or where reflection could be amused by passing observation. But, granting all advantages to the human being, be it imagined that, for a single week, man inhabited a stall; shut in from all society; standing on one spot by day, and lying there by night; having the same food and the water brought to him at regular intervals; being obliged to make his meals without turning round; but, all the while, with his nose fastened close to a blank, white wall. After one single week of such probation, what does the reader conjecture would be the report delivered by the groom, who sat behind with the whip, ready to enforce silence? In what respect, does imagination picture, would be the distinction between man and horse?

Stable propriety conceives that the dumb inhabitant of such a building is fitly occupied when gazing upon the whitened interior of its prison. It is barely possible that stable-men may think this a most engrossing amusement; but there evidently exist horses which are so naturally perverse as to imagine that sight was, by an all-wise Creator, bestowed for a more active purpose than to merely look at vacancy when at home, and to be blinded by blinkers when abroad. These are, generally, the new-comers. Colts, not thoroughly broken in, or quite inured to the customs of civilized equine existence, are such wayward creatures! In their inexperience, they are too impatient; the first taste of captivity is apt to generate in them a desire to look around, or to gaze on the fellow-beings about them.

Inspired by a feeling of dissatisfaction with the boards which human care has placed on either side of their compartment, these youngsters are likely to gratify the promptings of the moment, by rearing up and by lodging the forefeet within the manger. Their heads are thus raised above the limit of their partitions. Where the corn is commonly thrown, the front hoofs now repose; and, as a consequence, the view instantly becomes more extended. The scene is novel; the exalted quadruped can exchange glances with its companions. The prospect is pleasing, and the sensation it awakens is decidedly gratifying. But, unhappy creature! While its eyes drink in delight, it cannot perceive the angered visage of the groom; nor can it even think of his existence, till the smart of a well-placed lash recalls the sufferer back to the hopelessness of that solitude, under submission to which it can alone hope to escape from positive torture.

This grave offense, like too many human failings, is engendered by idleness. The offending animal was without occupation. Its spirit was sick with inactivity. Therefore, in despair, it indulged that forbidden gratification which most men in their own persons do not view as meriting severe corporal punishment, or find to be a very stimulative amusement, when, to kill time on a rainy day, they glance out of the windows of their apartments. The equine sin was, however, of no greater magnitude; if it could, with strict justice, be said to attain to such lofty dimensions. The culpability, nevertheless, lay in an animal acting as though it had a right to use its own life for its selfish enjoyment. A horse obviously is the property of its master. The title to such property is absolute The creature, consequently, has no right to act on its own authority; and to do this, regardless of the peril incurred, is positively contemplative dishonesty, which merited the heaviest possible visitation!

A HORSE WITH THE FORELEGS IN THE MANGER.

The altitude assumed, certainly, was not altogether safe. Mangers are built to merely uphold grain and chaff. Carpenters, in their collective capacity, are a knowing set, and are notorious for manufacturing articles of a strength merely proportioned to their uses. A heavy weight resting on fragile boards might have broken or have displaced some of them. In such a case, the animal having fallen through the opening, probably would, in its fright, have fractured a limb. The inside of its manger, assuredly, did not offer a secure foundation for a steed to stand upon; but, when tracing causes, we are bound to inquire, who or what provoked the act? The chastisement, it is true, has, according to this world's custom, been inflicted upon the weaker and the more simple; but consummation of such an act cannot establish the justice of the usage.

The circumstances of the case presuppose something condemnatory on the part of the horse, the contemplation of whose conduct could excite such indignation in the groom. This fact is further supported by that surprise which mingled with the anger of the man. Even his habitual lassitude was conquered, through the energy aroused by the spectacle of such enormity! His bile boiled; his voice grew indistinct with passion; would excitement have permitted clearness of speech, oaths might have been overheard; the cat was thrown aside without the smallest show of ceremony; the servant leaped to his feet; with evident determination he seized the whip and essayed to punish the offense.

Discarding inferential evidence, and looking at the case for positive testimony, it may be well, before we engage in such an inquiry, to determine whether the horse has done wrongly, and whether the servant has acted rightly—the conduct of each being temperately reviewed. The quadruped, standing in the manger, and being naturally a timid creature, the sight of a whip and the smart of its application might cause the terrified life to perform several very energetic and eccentric movements. If the animal's fault laid in its mounting on so frail a platform, that, certainly, was a reason which should not have excited the groom to chastisement during the perilous position. Fear often banishes caution, and the exhibition ground of the contention, then, being specially limited, any alarm was calculated to provoke the danger which it was the office, and doubtless the intention, of the groom to dispel. During the struggles caused by sudden fright, hair is often removed and sores established. A horse, surprised by terror, has engendered fearful blemishes; troublesome wounds have been produced, and prominences of bone have been fractured by the wild efforts of timidity, when excited by horror. The horse had no business to stand in the manger; but, being a non-reasoning animal, we may overlook that transgression. The man, however, being an intellectual agent, did very wrong in flogging the steed while the quadruped retained its perilous position.

To beat a horse, admits of justification by appealing to custom; but to flog a horse when tied to a manger and confined to a stall, is certainly gratifying the human passion at the risk of injury to that property which every owner is supposed to possess in the perfect condition of his animal. Now man, being blessed with power to think, violated his duty when he indulged his own instincts at the hazard of harm to his employer, or when he chastised the colt for braving the possibility of injury; since, by so doing, he was guilty of defying the probability of damage, and therefore stands convicted of a worse fault than that for which he punished his charge.

Let us now endeavor to ascertain the real extent of that misdeed the contemplation of which provoked an amount of anger sufficient to banish prudence from among the virtues of a reasonable being. The colt is, in the first place, located and fastened within the stable. The fact certifies to no choice having been exercised on the part of the culprit; therefore it is blameless, so far as being inside a building might imply an error. It was fastened within a defined and an arbitrarily limited department. The animal, however, did not plan the edifice, erect the partitions, or halter its own head to one of the mangers; consequently, so far it must be esteemed guiltless. But the creature, being there, leaped into a receptacle intended for food, and placed before it, thus obtaining a power of seeing around it.

The last act argues discontent, and discontent has never been ranged with amiable qualities. Still, it is not commendable to be contented, when we possess ability to improve our situation. Eyes certainly are natural gifts; their presence supposes a divine permission that sight should be exercised, since the wish to use them is an innate impulse. Man himself often endures much inconvenience and pays large sums, simply to gratify his eyes with the momentary spectacle of some gorgeous procession. The act, which has never been accused as a crime in the lords of the creation, should not, therefore, be esteemed unpardonable when exemplified by an animal which is occupying an inappropriate position.

Next, let us ask, what excuse can be urged to extenuate a deed which has already been shown to be less than a fault, and to be far removed from the category of crime? The horse is formed by nature with a love of action. In a modern stable it is tied by the head, while the stall partitions are of sufficient height to isolate its misery. The poor quadruped may have stood where it stands for several consecutive hours. The manger is fixed directly before it; the receptacle has been empty some time; the thing is clearly not wanted now to hold food: yet, there the open box remains. The head is tied to it; the animal cannot escape from looking on and into it; till speculation, which concern the possible intention implied by the fixature of the article, takes absolute possession of the equine mind.

At last a bright idea descends; the manger is thought to be placed where it is, as an easy step for the animal's feet to rest upon. The wood-work is situated at a convenient distance from the ground. Man could not have supposed the horse wanted victuals lifted to its mouth, when every field exhibits one of the tribe lowering its head to gather herbage from the earth? Such a notion is ridiculous! The corn must be cast into the manger, simply because the thing is ready to receive it; but its real purpose has only been recently discovered. A slight but pleasing effort raises the forefeet on to the imaginary platform. The creature is delighted with its elevated position, for the view from it is agreeably extended. Assuredly, to discover a new use for an old article, merits esteem; and blame, if any blame be called for, should light on him who has imprudently placed temptation before an idle spirit, believing animal nature to be too passive for any temptation to affect it. Man, therefore, was disappointed by the quadruped proving more intelligent than he bargained for. The exhibition of intelligence should form no excuse for chastisement, though disappointment is too apt to expend its rage in blows.

There remains, however, to decide whether the act on the horse's part, not being a fault, may be justly esteemed to be a virtue. A dull, phlegmatic beast had slept away the time "between the feedings;" had been content, so no exertion had been demanded. All men abhor what, in stable phraseology, is termed "a slug." It certainly is meritorious to seize every opportunity of displaying that sort of temper which our superiors desire should be presented. All horse owners love a gay, lively, spirited nag. Leaping into the manger was a proof of animation. The act may have violated stable propriety; but the simple nature of the quadruped could not comprehend those regulations which man is incapable of communicating to the equine understanding; therefore the rules of the place were nothing to the captive. The culpability should rest upon him who planned a building with fixtures capable of being readily perverted. Leaping into the manger was certainly commendable, so far as it testified to intelligence, intrepidity, and liveliness. The blame must reside with him who doomed a gregarious creature to solitary existence, and fixed before the prisoner a feeding trough, certainly at an inviting altitude.

There is another supposed "vice" which animals doomed to lengthened and solitary confinement occasionally exemplify. Some gentlemen own several horses. Those parties possess ranges of stables, and every stall is occupied. When a person has a stud at his command, he is apt to conceive a dislike for riding. Days, and even weeks, may pass without the saddle or the carriage being ordered for the master's gratification. During such a period, the grooms are supposed to give the animals a healthful amount of exercise.

But when superiors neglect their duty, inferiors will probably follow the example. A powerful propensity to imitate is one of the human peculiarities; the truth of this observation is far more vigorously illustrated in the stable than in the mansion. Much time may have gone by since some of the horses sniffed the breeze or looked upon the face of heaven; let the period be still further extended, and the grooms will not complain. The quadrupeds may continue idle, and gorge until their livers burst with disease; but their custodians can never tire of too little employment. When an establishment is thus managed, the grooms do not generally rise till the hour for morning exercise has passed; if a stray thought of the captives should trouble their consciences, the qualm is always quieted with, "Oh! let the poor devils enjoy a long rest."

Breach of one obligation, like the falling of a first brick, is seldom a solitary mishap. The stable attendant, not being kept strictly to his work, grows to regard his own likings more than to consider his master's orders. These people are always pleased with the exhibition of fat. The proprietor may talk about condition; but the servant knows his master's favorite hunter should carry a "*little*" fat. It looks so gentlemanly to see a horse that is well fed. Every groom has a rare, secret nostrum which will load any animal with fat in a week. He will spend his perquisites to purchase this mysterious powder, a spoonful of which, given in a mash, at night, acts like a charm. At the same time, he serves out the oats and beans pretty generously. He fills the rack, heaps the manger, gives a dose of his secret mixture, and then, slapping the horse under the flank, exclaims, "There, old boy! I think you may enjoy yourself now!"

We are told an alderman was once solicited for halfpence by a crossing-sweeper, because the man was "so hungry." The city magnate paused, looked at his petitioner, and, with feeling, exclaimed, "Lucky dog! I wish I was also hungry." The horse, wanting exercise, stares at the provender, but has no appetite. The food piled up before it is,

A HORSE WASTING THE HAY.

to the animal, no other than "matter out of place." Desire is needed to give value to such abundance; and a non-reasoning being cannot be expected to prize that which it does not require. It cannot eat, but it lacks amusement. The hay is before it. In sheer idleness, a few stalks are pulled from the rack. Of these, one may be leisurely masticated; but the remainder, after having been twisted about by the lips, are allowed to fall upon the litter. The sport is followed up until the rack is emptied, and the creature is a little happier, under a conviction that it has escaped from absolute stagnation.

Yet, when we consider the heap of "prime upland" which has been spoiled, the subject cannot be allowed to pass without one word of inquiry. Who or what is to blame, when so much fodder is wasted? No animal will prize food after its cravings are appeased. Fowls, having eaten, trample the superabundant barley under foot; dogs will sleep beside, or bury, a half-gnawed bone; nay, man himself, subsequent to a good dinner, nauseates the greasy smell from the kitchen, and abhors the sight of a reeking joint; school-boys form bread seals out of their breakfast superfluity; and domesticated gentlemen, located at the bottom of the table, have, when dinner was finished, been frequently known to amuse their fingers by making crumbs upon the cloth. Then the act of wasting victuals, after satiety has been achieved, being, with various beings, all but universal, the deed cannot be urged as a heavy accusation against a simple animal.

Yet the scattered hay having been observed by the master, the groom then severely punishes the wasteful quadruped. In that case, however, it is the master's observation, which the animal could not possibly prevent, that drew down its chastisement; the blows can establish no fault on the part of the horse. Its stomach being crammed, the creature could eat no more. The hay, however, was converted to some use. It was made to lighten the heavy hours of captivity. Such a purpose may not have fulfilled the proprietor's intention; but it was the only service the captive could put it to. The sin, if there be any sin, certainly must remain with him who piled up provender before an animal which was without an appetite. Waste was indulged when fodder was thus misappropriated; and the horse endured punishment from the hand of the individual who, had strict justice been administered, should have received the lashes on his own person.

Simple natures, when entirely disengaged, generally make their own employment, and that employment, being intended for a passing amusement, commonly consists of what thrifty people designate "mischief." The knowledge that displeasure will follow upon discovery, may spice the proceeding which otherwise might want interest. At all events, so it is with children; and it may be thus with animals. When a heaped manger is before a satiated quadruped, the impossibility of feeding makes the creature meditate upon the uses to which the grain can possibly be applied. None can be discovered. The head of the captive is tied, and the manger is fixed. At length, in carelessness of spirit, a mouthful is taken from the heap. The portion cannot be swallowed, so the lips are moveo and, as they part, the corn falls over them upon the ground This may not be a very exciting recreation; but the prisoner is restless with repletion. It cannot sleep; and the grain passing over the lips, in which equine feeling concentrates, produces a slight and a novel sensation.

WASTING CORN.

Can any man seriously pronounce that an animal, standing in enforced solitude and compulsory idleness, is to blame for such conduct? Boys, during their school days, when wanting appetite, or having unnecessary food before them, will not they, in satiety, play with needless abundance? Are men to demand that prudence from an animal which we should certainly not anticipate in the young of our own species? Yet the child enjoys a certain amount of confidence; and its misdoing is, therefore, aggravated by a certain abuse of trust. The horse is confined between boards, and enjoys not the smallest personal liberty. The severity of captivity argues that no reliance reposes upon the captive's discretion. All responsibility is lost, when all freedom of action is denied. Yet the poor prisoner is cruelly beaten for playing with food, although the true fault rested upon him who was too idle to give the exercise which would have generated appetite; and was too lazy to proportion the animal's sustenance to the requirements of its situation.

Moreover, if we had listened to the man's speech, as he entered the servants' hall, we should have heard a boast, that the horse had been *given* a good supper. Now, when a thing is given, all right of ownership passes away with the transfer. The groom, obviously, lost every remnant of title to its possession when he presented the corn to the animal as a free gift; and the beating which he administered to the quadruped was, therefore, an act of wanton severity. The horse had as great a right as the late Duke of Newcastle, to do as it pleased with its own. The flogging could be no more than the gratification of an evil passion—out of which motive is generated the most serious crimes; and consequently, it was anything but a commendable action in the groom who needlessly chastised a quadruped.

Within the same stable is lodged young master's favorite mare. It is a beautiful creature: not so slight as to be weedy, but made to carry weight with ease, with speed, and with action. The young master on this occasion has traveled to London by rail, and the entire day has been passed by the mare within the walls of its abode. The fellow quadrupeds have had their exercise; but the groom dislikes this horse. It will not remain by itself, while the pipe is enjoyed with a pint of "early purl;" the man's pride revolts against drinking his morning's stomachic in the street. Besides, the animal, when first taken into the open air, will perform a variety of caperings. Young master likes such nonsense: but more than once it has thrown the groom. The mare is, therefore, abhorred with all the malice of a little mind. Yet the creature is all grace and animation; it is only pleasantly excited, when its master gets into the saddle. Can horses possibly possess aristocratic predilections, and can the quadrupeds tell whether hirelings or proprietors are seated on their backs?

The mare is no favorite in the stable. Its feeling of vitality is too powerful to admit of that perfect quietude which the monarch of the locker loves should pervade his dominion. It is always making some noise. Moving about; looking around; nibbling the wood-work; soiling its coat or rumpling its hair. A most perverse brute to look after! It can't be alone and continue quiet! It will not suppress its spirit: hang its head and appear to fall asleep like the other wretches.

Such an animal, weary of captivity, has pawed its bed, till not a single straw remains within the reach of the forefeet. The manger has been repeatedly licked, till the possibility of a stray oat no longer stimulates further endeavor. The quadruped has strained its neck and elevated its head, till it is quite tired of staring around at nothing. It lacks amusement, and is half inclined to provoke a beating rather than endure the weight of silence and the horror of that monotony which pervades its abode. In this state of restlessness, the vision alights upon the collar-rope. It essays to catch hold of it. The cord, however, being fastened near to the halter, of course it moves with every motion of the head. The feat is not, therefore, so easy as to lack excitement. The prisoner becomes quite elated. A new pastime has at last been discovered!

At first the rope is seized between the lips. The tether, however, often escapes from such a hold: the teeth, therefore, are ultimately employed. The texture of the firmest cord is easily compressed by the muscular power of the horse's jaw! The substance is not unpleasant to bite; nor is the taste of hemp altogether disagreeable. The teeth, consequently, do not relinquish their grip with the termination of the game. The thing is, from mere vacuity, bitten with different degrees of force. Fiber after fiber yields, till, without any design or the slightest intention, the substance is divided. The creature is then released; but it does not at first comprehend that its bond is destroyed. At length, the welcome truth is recognized, and, bounding with delight, the released captive scampers about the gangway, peering into forbidden places, and reveling in its temporary freedom!

GNAWING THE COLLAR-ROPE.

The amazement of the groom is excited at the spectacle of a horse enjoying liberty! No thought is wasted upon the intelligence which was able to achieve so great a blessing. All animals, within the building, are credited only with evil qualities; nothing praiseworthy is looked for or expected to be displayed by them. The only virtue a horse is esteemed capable of exhibiting is brutish submission. The groom, seeing the creature roving about, exclaims in anger, "That wicket beast, agin! It is up to every 'vice!'"

Another and a stouter rope is procured. The fastening is renewed, and made more strong than it was before. But what has been accomplished once, will be repeated. It may be some days before limited intelligence can recall the precise manner in which its accidental pleasure was secured; but, after an interval, the audacious animal is again in possession of unlawful license. Such occasions subsequently occur more quickly. Till, at length, the groom, puzzled and aggravated by the ingenuity of his charge, substitutes a thick chain for that which had hitherto been represented by a hempen tether.

Iron is not so pleasant to the teeth, neither will it yield so readily to force as did the hemp. The chain is, consequently, an effectual check to some animals. Others, however, are not thus readily subdued. The recollection of forbidden sweets, once tasted and longingly remembered, stimulates their faculties. The teeth soon instruct the understanding that iron cannot be bitten. Is there no other way of breaking the fetter? All living things, when desirous of freedom, pull violently against the bond which restrains them. The quadruped adopts the general artifice. The chain stretches. It perceptibly yields. Then, all the strength and weight are brought to bear: the fetter breaks. Only, the door is locked for the night, when this second offense is consummated; and the horse is the next morning discovered by its groom, careering about the gangway or sharing the stall of a companion.

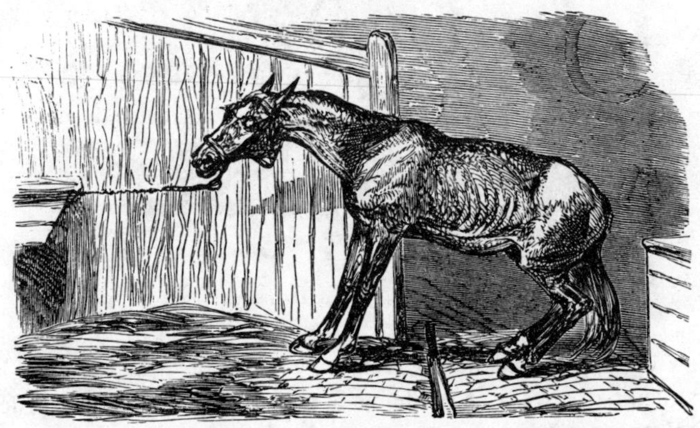

BREAKING LOOSE.

That which one chain is powerless to retain may, nevertheless, be confined by double fetters. The groom, accordingly, has a second ring fixed upon the manger rail. A stout leathern strap is then buckled round the upper portion of a horse's neck. To that additional and heavier chain, passing through the second ring, an extra sinker is fastened. The head of the animal has, by this plan, to endure a double, or more than a double, weight. A constant drag, therefore, does not improve the carriage of the crest; but it may serve to remind the quadruped of its recent successful plan of escape, while it certainly cannot otherwise than stimulate the desire for liberty.

The struggles which, in the first instance, were so effective, being now proved powerless, the groom would joyously chuckle over his contrivance, only perseverance in the horse is causing its neck-strap to interfere with the personal appearance of the animal. Constant friction and perpetual strain have made an unsightly notch in the mane, while the neck-strap has generated a circular mark totally devoid of hair. The mane is nature's embellishment, and neither horse nor lady looks more pleasing, when their flowing tresses have been partially destroyed.

This is very vexing. Yet, when bad begins, worse generally remains behind. Animals which have adopted an idea seem incapable of relinquishing the notion. The creature having once broken its tether resorts to its former plan of operations; it pulls and pulls, only the bonds not yielding to the same force as before, the horse, following the groom's principle, increases the strength requisite to overpower the difficulty.

THE EFFECT OF THE COLLAR-STRAP.

A man being defeated in his first essay, probably would resign himself to sullen despair. But the horse is possessed of a different order of mind. Man can conceive a futurity; animals have a knowledge only of the past. All the tales told of animal instincts are capable of explanation by reference to their experience. Chastisement or chiding must be often repeated before brute intelligence can connect the infliction of pain with the commission of certain acts. But, the two being associated, the teaching is generally retained, and, apparently, remains as fresh in the memory upon the day of death as it was upon the first acknowledgment of the lesson. The horse is, however, expected only to obey certain signs, and submit to certain restraints. Its intellect remains, therefore, in a great measure uncultivated. What has been once must be again, embraces the range of its understanding.

The additional chain, consequently, makes no alteration in the behavior of the horse. Present failure only excites to increased exertion. The entire weight and the utmost strength are brought to bear upon the fastenings. The simple quadruped, incapable of calculating the probable results of the sudden absence of resistance, plies with greater energy, till the chains snap, and the huge body, instantaneously released, shoots violently backward. Bones have been broken. Lameness is the general result; but lucky, indeed, is the creature which can rise after such a misfortune, and merely display several huge portions of its skin abraded.

The reader is here invited to examine the facts which have resulted in this serious damage to living property. To bind the strong is not necessarily to subdue the strong. To fetter the creature in whose welfare man has an interest, is evidently a defiance of probabilities,

THE CHAINS HAVE BEEN SUNDERED.

though it may not have been intended so to operate when the bonds were secured. The majority of horses can be stayed by a simple show of authority. We see a boy hold an animal from which the strong man has newly dismounted. So also would many a human culprit be secure in the old-fashioned prisons. Jails, however, are not erected with any regard for the passiveness of their inhabitants; but such edifices are built of a strength which may defy the efforts of the resolute, and are planned with an intent to counteract the ingenuity of the most cunning. Not so with stables. These edifices are erected to confine a creature possessing ten times the strength of any human being. The partitions, however, are of wood, and the bonds usually of rope. Those who are most fluent about the "vices" of the equine race evidently never thought upon the possibility of the animal conceiving a wish to escape; for so very unequal are most stables to their contemplated uses, that the author has known a horse, in the delirium of agony, kick into ruins the building which, during health, had for years served to confine its huge capability of destruction.

The stable, however, is essentially a prison; and so long as it retains that character, it should be of sufficient strength to resist the wildest efforts of the captives. Not being thus, it reflects disgrace on those who put it to uses for which the building is unsuited. The animal, being in bondage, loses all responsibility. Its safe custody is the duty of its self-constituted keepers. It has no trust reposed in it; and, obviously, can violate no faith. It is held in durance by the right of the strong; and if in the struggle which ensues it can prove the strongest, clearly the right which imprisoned it is upturned.

In another point of view, the decision must be favorable to the animal Nature has gifted the horse with faculties, and blessed it with instincts. Foremost among these faculties is, a facility of varied motion, displayed in particular yearnings; as a fondness for fresh air, green fields, and a desire to roam abroad, unfettered, in the company of its kind. Man violently seizes the quadruped; without caring for the innate promptings of nature, he forces his slave to live, severed from all its longings and away from all it loves. Which is the horse to obey? Is it to deny the charter planted by its *Maker* within its bosom? Or is it any crime to rebel against the will which will shorten its life, withhold its pleasures, and cripple its body,—studying nothing but the pigmy's personal gain and heartless advantage?

Then, when the reader turns to the consideration of the custodian's conduct. Had the circumstances deprived him of all choice, and limited his means of restraining to a doubling of the customary bonds? It is folly for the weak to engage in a muscular contest with the powerful. It is madness for the feeble to place dependence on straws, when the design is to bind a giant In both respects the groom was in fault. Had he only thought for an instant, reason would have suggested that plan by which the resistance of the horse might have been subdued, and his master's property might have continued uninjured.

The animal's struggles expressed merely a dislike to the rope attached to the head. Two fastenings were not calculated to remove the abhorrence which a single bond excited. Had the horse been led from the stall and placed in the solitary chamber of a loose box, the change had quieted its spirit. At so small an expense might all the subsequent damage have been avoided. But a loose box does not acknowledge the pride of man, to use all the life with which this world abounds according to his convenience. It was for pride's sake that mortality waged the battle; and in loss did pride undergo defeat.

Endeavor to explain the reason why a valuable horse has been damaged, to any professed groom, and try to make him understand how the miscalled accident might have been avoided;—the man, while you are speaking, will put on that look of dogged indifference which informs you the fellow has closed his comprehension against every argument. When you cease talking, the servant stares you in the face, and replies, "He wants no gentl'man to teach him his doty;" and, by so saying, announces a determination to persevere in that course of conduct which has induced such lamentable consequences. There are men in this world who only employ their reason to perpetuate their ignorance. It is one thing to teach; but it is more difficult to find a pupil willing to be instructed

In many genteel families, stables are esteemed as places in which lumber may be stored; while grooms are regarded as odd men, always ready to be engaged upon any passing necessity. The stable attendant is seldom upon the locker; and the one animal, kept for fashionable purposes, is commonly left much to its own society. The creature, thus housed, does not generally get its meals with regularity. Many hours are made longer, endeavoring to discover the pastime which shall lighten the tedium of its confinement. A melancholy game with such quadrupeds consists in an endeavor to hit the collar-rope with the hoof of the fore extremity.

This recreation, to the reader doubtless appears easy; but to the horse it presents difficulties sufficiently numerous to keep up excitement. The rope is a small object; it is situated high up; it occupies a central situation. The sinker to which it is attached keeps it always straight, and prevents it from being lowered. The cord, moreover, being fastened to the head of the quadruped, moves with every motion of the body; the neck cannot be held stationary when the limb is raised to any unusual height. The game may endure for months, without the animal being so unfortunate as to succeed. At length the hoof hits the mark and becomes fixed. The horse instinctively pulls against any restraint. The tether is thereby rendered tense, and the pain of the situation becomes extreme. At last, by a violent effort, the foot passes over the bond, and the poor captive is fixed, until the groom enters the building and removes the sinker.

A FORELEG OVER THE COLLAR-ROPE.

The lightest consequence must be, the hair abraded from the back of the limb, the skin lacerated, and the muscles of the neck sprained by the efforts to escape from constriction. Lameness, of some duration, is the usual result. Inquire the cause of mishap, and the groom will petulantly inform you "it were occasioned by the pranks of that fidgety beast, which is always up to some mischief." Perhaps you object to this explanation, replying, "'Mischief' is not a fitting term, since it supposes intentional annoyance to another; whereas the horse has injured no one but itself." The man stares with surprise, and rejoins, "Ar'nt it, though! But it has injured me! When shall I ever hear the last of it?" Truly, the stable mind must quit the scene of its present labors, before it will submit to be enlightened. It is now so protected by a wall of selfishness, ignorance, and prejudice, that it is open to no assault.

This misfortune is, however, gravely reckoned one of the "vices" of the stable. It is seldom repeated; but a single instance is sufficient to confer the "vicious" character. Poor animal! When even mishaps are regarded as the planned results of its deliberate wickedness. Having so many virtues, yet not credited with a single good quality! Wholly and entirely misunderstood! Else, who in this accident would not perceive intelligence striving to invent some solitary pastime, which might while away the flagging hours? Else, who would not recognize that this evil arose out of the foolish custom of tying up an active creature to a manger? Else, who could fail to discern that a loose box would have rendered such an injury a positive impossibility?

The author is aware that were horses fitly housed and properly treated, the expense of maintaining these creatures must be increased. But against all additional cost there are benefits to be balanced. The animal would live more than thrice as long; it would, for so much greater period, be fit for its master's service. The accidents occasioned by modern stables would be abolished; the sickness and the disease, produced by inappropriate food, by rigid confinement and impure air, would cease to exist. With change of building, there should also be a thorough change in the stable attendant. The present race of knowing deformities are too full of tricks to be worthy a gentleman's trust. The groom should be forbidden ever to mount an animal, save in obedience to his superior's special command. Now the men ride at their pleasure; as a consequence, they very rarely walk. The quadruped is supposed to be only one person's property; but the poor drudge has to serve "two masters."

Under the present system, the horse is relinquished to the pleasure of the servant. The man's report constitutes the all of a proprietor's knowledge. The mansion, therefore, reflects the ignorance and the prejudice of the stable. The persons occupying the buildings should change places. Most masters ride slowly, merely exercising the nags. Most grooms love speed, and in reality wear out the lives which credulity thinks sacred to another's service. Yet, though surrounded by abuse, ill treated and often robbed of its food, the creature has no voice with which to accuse or to complain. There is no one who even cares for its welfare. It is credited with every "vice" and supposed to delight in malice. It is imprisoned, beaten, libeled, and nevertheless gentlemen are often encountered who pride themselves upon the care and the money which are lavished upon their stables.

When all that concerns mankind—the formation of their houses, their kind of food, their dress and manners, their laws and customs—have, with the progress of the period, thoroughly changed; even to such an extent has this alteration been accomplished that it has been often said, were our ancestors resuscitated, they would not recognize the land of their birth; it becomes very painful for the mind to perceive that the habits and usages which formerly surrounded the horse remain to this day all but unaltered. It is a proof of the indifference which encircles the stable, when the buildings erected to receive horses at the Royal Veterinary College, and which date from the last century, are, at the present moment, regarded as models of perfection. Man cares only for himself: of his property in the life which he imprisons, he evidently takes no heed. He pays dearly for his carelessness; and "the beast within his gate" shares none of those blessings which Providence has allowed the human race to enjoy, although religion should teach him that the mere mention of such a possession by Deity, ought to enforce a duty upon humanity!

Another so-named "vice" of the horse is frequently the occasion of more serious results than any of the before-mentioned accidents. No person has hitherto explained why the skin should be more irritable by night than during the daytime. Such, however, is the case with horses, as it is with men. A quadruped in the morning is often found disfigured by the hair being removed from comparatively large surfaces. Itchiness has provoked the animal to rub itself against any prominence, or to scratch its body with the toe of its iron shoe; this indulgence has caused the blemish.

Itching and scratching are numbered among the worst "vices" of the stable. Such faults, however, are only discovered in their effects; the groom never estimates, when flogging an animal for this wickedness, how far the abhorred sin may have been produced by stimulating diet, by want of exercise, and by impure atmosphere. No! He clothes up the body of the animal; shuts every window; stops every cranny; and locks the stable door for the night. The last meal being consumed, and the quadrupeds not being inclined for sleep, they one and all begin to itch. Legs are nibbled; necks are rubbed; and tails are lashed. At length one is sensible of an irritation behind the ear. The head is turned toward the side; the body is curved to the full extent; and the hind leg brought forward. Then, the groom not being present, the toe of the hind shoe can touch the part, and the horse luxuriates in a hearty titillation.

When the head was turned toward the quarters, however, the collar-rope, being attached to the halter, was also stretched in that direction. The hind foot having performed its office, a desire is felt to return it to the natural position. The attempt is made; but this is found to be impracticable. The creature strains against the opposing force, but its struggles only render its comfortless attitude the more fixed. The truth is, that while devoted to the act which allays cuticular irritability, the pastern has slipped over the collar-rope. Such a mishap not only fixes the leg, but fastens the head. With the neck bent and one leg disabled, the animal cannot exert half its power; neither can simplicity comprehend the source of its unnatural constraint. Long continuance of the position becomes painful; alarm seizes upon timidity; the struggles grow desperate; and the poor quadruped, at length, is cast with terrible violence upon the straw which had been shaken down for its repose.

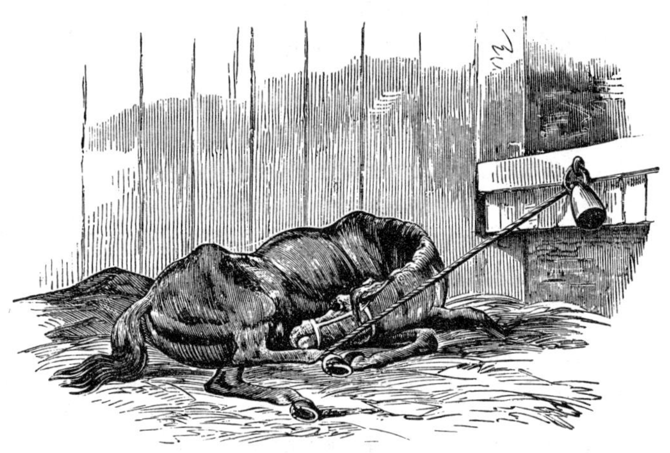

CAST IN THE COLLAR-ROPE.

The animal is lucky which should be overthrown in a limited space and escape serious misfortune. It can hardly encounter such an accident and rise from the ground uninjured. The slightest consequences are contused wounds or fractures of small osseous prominences. The worst result, however, usually follows the body being forcibly contorted throughout an entire night. Bones have been dislocated, or a limb has been so sprained as never to have recovered its functions. Necks have never afterward been restored to their pristine grace of motion; and, in short, a valuable servant has, by such a misfortune, been so "wrenched from its propriety," as to be rendered utterly useless. Nevertheless, the groom will persevere in hailing the fate of an animal which has been cast in the collar-rope as a just punishment induced by the sufferer's inveterate "vice."

Carters are open to complaint, because their horses are "cast in the halter," even to a greater degree than those of town grooms. In agricultural districts, it is a common practice to turn the teams out to graze during the night, and to take them from the field to work in the morning. Some animals, however, prove troublesome to catch, preferring the cool grass and partial liberty to exhausting toil upon an arid roadway. To facilitate the capture of such quadrupeds, many carters, when freeing the creature, will not remove the halter, but suffer it to remain, because this affords a ready hold for the person who fetches in the horses on the following day. The result is easily anticipated. The ear itches. The foot, scratching the part, gets entangled, and that which was a valuable horse on the previous night, is found, in the dawning light, to be a disabled cripple, or a worthless carcass.

The sane mind will, however, behold in this misfortune only a startling proof of the folly which ties the head to a manger, and leaves the animal at the hazard of a fearful accident. Such events have been common ever since the race was first domesticated; yet, to this day, the custom is practiced. Where one quadruped enjoys a loose box, ten thousand are confined to the manger. Neither loss nor the spectacle of the misery produced by his folly seems able to instruct man where the life of another is delivered over to his keeping. As, in America, the master coerces and lashes his slave, so, in England, do proprietors starve, torture, and slay the animals which all pretend to love. The devotion of a life cannot even purchase those necessaries which are needful for the preservation of health. Though the strength and the service are contingent upon the maintenance of bodily vigor, man, with the capriciousness of tyranny, is neglectful of that upon the continuance of which the value of his possession entirely depends.

It may be urged that the size of the horse's body necessarily limits the dimensions of its abiding-place. This is a strange reason; but it is one commonly used among architects. We, however, do not apply the principle to our own race. Because the Horse Guards are tall men, we do not insist they should sleep in infants' *cots*, or wear the clothes of children. Giants are not forced to inhabit the houses fit only for dwarfs. Neither do we carry out the maxim with other creatures. Large rabbits boys put into large hutches. Were smaller horses desired, ponies, even no higher than full-sized dogs, are not scarce. But greater weight and strength enable the quadrupeds to perform larger services. Does it not seem like meanness to select size for our own purposes, yet, where the creature is concerned, to make size a motive for stinting the necessities? The horse is useful to man in proportion to its magnitude; and the poor slave, therefore, ought not to feel the bulk to be its misfortune!

The author cannot here report the grooms' opinions upon such a topic, though, doubtless, these persons would be the advocates of misrule. There is no class, however, which suffers more than stable-men, from the present custom of confining horses. On cold, wintry nights, when snow is on the ground, these persons, who generally live above the stable, are often awakened from their first sleep, forced to leap from warm beds, and, thinly clad, to hurry down stairs to quiet the horses. The entire stable are lashing out at the same moment. Each hoof seems to be leveled at the stall post, which all violently strike; hence the disturbance.

But what occasions horses to kick by night? That question is perhaps best answered by another. What occasions children to cry by night? Both wake suddenly, and each finds darkness or solitude and silence around it. The horse is a timid creature, and it is of a limited intelligence. Children are not generally conspicuous for courage, and, in them, the reason is undeveloped. Infants are born with a natural sense of helplessness; hence they are the easy victims of alarm, and when frightened, they scream aloud. Horses are brought into the world with an instinctive dependence on the propulsion of the heels, and when frightened, they kick. Children have startled up from fearful dreams, and have screamed themselves into fits. Animals also dream; horses having awakened suddenly, have used their heels as a defense, and have been found lying dead upon the ruins of a battered wall in the morning!

The feet, when cast out, hit the stall post. The blackness of night prevails throughout the place; or fear being kindled, the vision is abused. No eye can pierce utter darkness, and terror lends shape or form to every obstacle which the hoof encounters. The dread which sleep has generated, the awakened perception seems to confirm. The animal lashes out with redoubled violence. The noise made by the act soon arouses its companions. Nothing is so sympathetic as horror. Armies have been actuated by panics. Why, therefore, should animals escape from such senseless emotions? When thousands of men have scampered away from no existing peril, cannot the reader understand that many animals may be impelled by a feeling of fear, when no dangei is present?

This is sooner admitted, when it is perceived that the fancy is active in proportion as the intellect is weak: the groom, not having a very powerful understanding, nor having yet slept off the potions and fumes of the previous evening, curses those "vicious varmints," as he shiveringly opens the stable door. No sooner, however, does the candle illumine, or his presence destroy the loneliness of the place, than fearful eyes cast backward glances, and seeing nothing, all instantly becomes silent. Our engraving of the above incident represents every horse in action; though, frequently, the more slothful will remain passive, notwithstanding the tumult which prevails around them.

KICKING IN THE NIGHT.

This is the effect invariably produced, as soon as the quadrupeds have sufficiently mastered their terror to regain their natural perceptions. Sometimes, however, a minute may elapse before consciousness is perfectly restored. That is the period of danger. Many silly fellows, impatient of their thin clothing, pierced by the frosty air, will approach the animals, during the interval, without remembering that though his voice may produce its usual effect, his costume is altogether a disguise. The man not being recognized, his strange figure may renew the general alarm: when the gangway, having on both sides the hind feet of terrified horses projected into it, becomes anything but a safe promenade.

Now, what produced this excitement of the stable? It was not the dream of one animal which caused it. That may have commenced the tumult, but it was not of itself necessary to the perpetuation of the uproar. The hoof of one quadruped striking the stall post also was distinct from the subsequent noise, which started into existence only with the spread of alarm. Then was generated the terror; for the feeling must have preceded the act, which announced itself by violence. It was the darkness or the silent solitude of the night which allowed full play to the fancy, and conjured up those shadows that drove the horses into temporary madness.

Had not the heads been fastened, the animals, by moving about, could in some measure have tested the reality of their fears. But, fastened to one spot, the fact of having no ability to escape augmented that alarm which the darkness of the stable and the oppression of silence caused and subsequently confirmed. A loose box and a little light would have rendered this noise an impossibility! The horse's eye can see perfectly in that dusk which to the feebler vision of man might represent an approach to positive blackness. There are few horsemen who, when riding by night, have not had reason to be grateful to the keen perception of their four-footed servants. There are, however, fewer horsemen who are aware whence the animal derives this faculty of distinguishing objects in all but perfect darkness.

Cats, owls, and other creatures are popularly reported to see in the dark. The discernment of every form of vision is disabled by *perfect* darkness; but the eyes of such animals are so constructed as to collect and reflect upon the optic nerve any remaining ray of light. The horse has an eye endowed with a similar faculty. Most people must have observed that horses assemble under the trees, and apparently sleep during the daytime. Who, however, ever beheld one of the equine race resting during the night? When summer prevails, night is the feeding time of these quadrupeds. When the flies are no longer abroad, but the dewy grass is cool and crisp to the bite,—when the absence of glare soothes the sight is the period of equine enjoyment and the season of equine watchfulness. Does not the reader acknowledge intention in such circumstances? The carnivora, all of which delight in the flesh of the steed, prowl by night, and abound in those regions of which the horse was originally a native. For the conservation of the tribe, therefore, these creatures were formed very fleet, very enduring, but no less quick to detect the approach of an enemy, being as restless by night as the beasts which esteem the horse's carcass a favorite repast.

The steed, therefore, does not require a chandelier to be fully illumined and to be suspended in the middle of the gangway. An ordinary night light would enable the animal to see perfectly over a large building; and the expense, when divided among numerous individuals, would for each be too small for any English coin to represent. No light, however, could prevent some quadruped occasionally waking up, and in the fright of imperfect consciousness flinging out both its heels. Such accidents no forethought could anticipate. But a slight flame, only sufficient to dispel absolute darkness, would mitigate if not quite abolish those panics during which every foot in the stable is employed to create the greatest attainable noise.

There is another so-called "vice," which is more directly brought home to the groom than any of the previous mishaps. Probably the statement may, to the reader, appear impossible, which asserts that the servant can impose upon the master so many of his own faults as proofs of "mischief" on the part of an innocent quadruped which it is the menial's duty to look after. This cheat the fellow is enabled to practice chiefly because he is supposed to be incapable of explaining or of distorting those circumstances which he reports. Thus mishaps are called according to their final effects; and no notice is ever given to the causes which led to such results. A horse is said to have "leapt into the manger;" "to have broken loose;" "to have gnawed the collar-rope;" "to have got one leg over the collar-rope;" "to have cast itself in the collar-rope," etc.

Were inquiries instituted, the truth, no doubt, would be speedily discovered, and long ago a remedy would have been apportioned. No domestic, however, enjoys so much of the master's implicit confidence as he who governs the stable. Persons, moreover, of the class respectable are far more swayed by their servants than might be pleasant for the gentlemen to acknowledge. Under this feeling, a vast amount of abuse lies concealed, for the weakness is by no means responded to by respect from the inferior. The "respectable" is always asserting his dignity, and afterward compounding for hastily-spoken words. The groom neither forgets nor forgives these verbal injuries, although his mind is amply stored with maxims against upstarts, to protect his vanity from any wholesome teaching which the admonitions might convey.

Gentlemen, when detained late abroad, generally ride home fast; partly, from a consciousness that it is long past their usual hour of "retiring for the night," and partly, because they know the groom is "waiting up" for their return. When the stable is reached, the coat of the horse may be wet with perspiration; or a badly-made saddle may have disturbed the smoothness of the hair; or the night may prove rainy, and the animal be brought home drenched to the skin. There are other causes; but be they what they may, the master walks off to bed, while the servant, noting the example, extracts from it no additional humor to discharge his duty. The man is, likewise, cross and sleepy. He turns the horse into the stall without attempting to dress it. He places oats and hay before the quadruped, and says, "If gentl'men will remain out till all 'ours o' the night, they may sit up and dress their oss 'emselves; for it is rather too much to expect any se'vant, after a 'ard day's work, to keep out of his bed and do it for 'em." Accordingly, the man hurries to his room, and soon sleeps soundly.

The quadruped, when the satisfaction of hunger allows the personal feelings to be appreciated, becomes aware that the partial dryness of the coat has produced much irritability of the skin. The animal, therefore, throws itself down, and commences to enjoy the luxury of a roll among the straw. Darkness disables the vision; but, were the light at its greatest power, the horse, in its state of torture, would probably notice nothing about it, for domestication destroys the natural instincts of all animals, making man the custodian of the cares as well as the bodies of the captives. The paving of the stall, also, being highest near to the manger, the inclination of the floor, together with the writhing of the body, occasions the quadruped to insensibly slide backward, until the tension of the collar-rope forbids its further progress.

This check induces the wish to rise; an attempt is made to bring the legs under the body for that object. But as this movement is endeavored to be accomplished, the hinder shins strike violently against some hard substance. The effort is renewed again and again; till the animal, deprived of sight and prevented from supplying the loss of one sense by the exercise of another, ultimately becomes alarmed, and the struggle commences, during which the hind legs are certain to be bruised, abraded, or other evils are sure to be inflicted upon the organs of propulsion. Nor is this all the peril in which the creature is now placed. Noise awakens the natural timidity of the companions; and should other horses be startled by the violent drumming on the partitions, probably they will become the victims of alarm. The sight of the animals is likewise useless in the utter darkness; and horses, when frightened, usually "hang back," or try to escape from the ropes which fasten the heads to the several mangers.

Under such an impulse, the obtruding legs stand a good chance of being broken; and the animal then must remain in its misery till master has approved the employment of a pistol Should nothing beyond bruise and abrasion be present, the groom himself undertakes the immediate relief. Another man is procured, and the knot below the sinker being untied, the head is released from the manger. But it is not usual for quadrupeds, after such a misfortune, to rise immediately. However, the servant always hopes for the best, so he and his assistant jointly pull at the tail till the legs are free from impediment, and then leave the wounded creature for master's wonder and inspection.

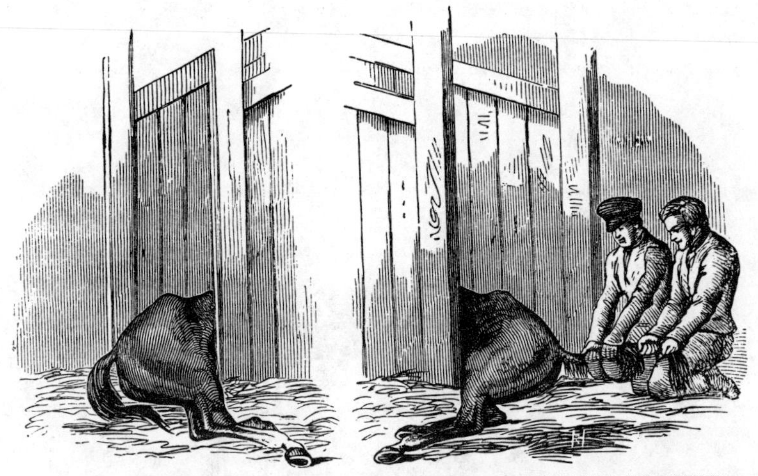

A HORSE CAST BY ROLLING IN THE MANGER. A HORSE BEING RELEASED FROM THE PREVIOUS SITUATION.

The remedies applied to all injuries (excepting fractures) which occur in the stable are equally simple, and few in number. These consist of a lotion, composed of two ounces of tincture of arnica, which is put into a pint bottle, to be subsequently filled up with water. This is used till all symptoms of bruise or swelling have disappeared, after which another lotion is to replace the first. This last is formed by adding one grain of chloride of zinc to every ounce of water, or one scruple to each measured pint of fluid. These lotions are to be applied frequently, not directly to the injury itself, but a sponge, saturated with each liquid, is to be squeezed dry above the sore, the moisture being allowed to trickle over the wound.

The strongest testimony, however, against stables, as such buildings are at present erected, is perhaps borne by the animals which inhabit those places. The horse is a delicate test, which man would do well to attentively observe when he is desirous of ascertaining the healthfulness of any locality. Naturally it is all animation and gayety of spirit. But, however much these qualities may be esteemed, such equine recommendations will soon fade before the joint influence of impure air and close confinement, although you may groom and feed at discretion. The natural period of life is diminished one-half, while much more than half of the remaining years is rendered useless by age, prematurely brought on by inappropriate treatment.

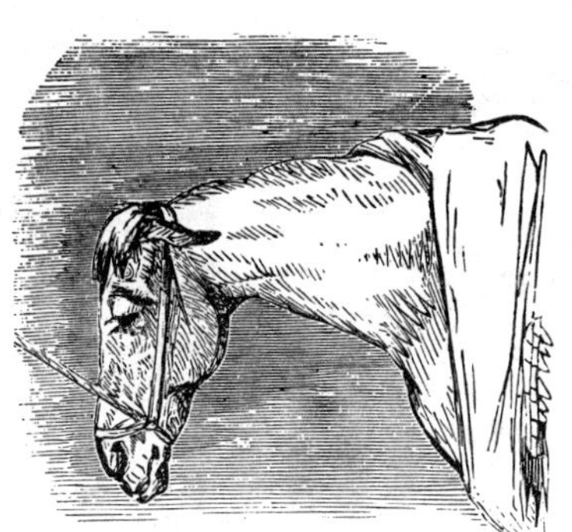

THE EXPRESSION OF COUNTENANCE INDUCED BY LONG STAGNATION IN THE STALL OF A WELL-PROVIDED STABLE.

CHAPTER VII.

THE FAULTS INSEPARABLE FROM MOST PRESENT ERECTIONS WHICH ARE USED AS STABLES.

No gentleman regards his country-seat as finished until to it ample stabling is appended. The mansion is the first thing looked to. All its rooms must be noble; all its offices must be convenient. The pleasure-grounds must be magnificent; the kitchen-garden should be much larger than is absolutely necessary. Nothing must interrupt the view from the drawing-room windows. A park, or its imitation, must terminate the lawn. No wood must be sacrificed. Everything must imply more wealth than the owner's purse actually contains. As to stables, of course they must be most excellent; only, being situated in the back-ground, no great expense need be lavished on such out-buildings; any waste spot will serve for their erection. A small space, judiciously employed, can be made to house a great number of horses.

The architect, being informed of the wishes of his employer, unhesitatingly asserts that four feet, or four feet six, or, in extreme cases, five feet, are considered ample width for stalls. The proprietor agrees to grant the last-named space for the abiding-place by day of a living horse, and the spot on which rest must be enjoyed during night by the same huge quadruped. Many a human pigmy sleeps on a more ample couch, which, moreover, is situated in a spacious chamber. Such is the distinction drawn between master and slave; although, when rightly considered, life is but life, and the larger animal has the greater necessity for more abundant air!

This decided, the gentleman rubs his hands, and, warmed by the contemplation of his own liberality, applauds "the nice arrangements," which he has sanctioned "regardless of expense." But the carriage-house, he is positive, shall be built quite large enough. He cannot forget that those rascals grazed his last new vehicle on the very day it came home from Long Acre. The accident happened while putting it into a narrow building. No! Let what will be cramped, the carriage-house must be spacious.

Thus, men take much care of that species of property which, being damaged, can be repaired for money; but they treat with neglect, and thrust into unwholesome corners, that life which, when injured, not all the wealth accumulated upon this globe could restore to soundness. With the inanimate, there is nothing to remove the full force of blame, which man must accept as his fault alone. The deterioration of such articles, when it occurs, cannot be laid to the charge of any other living being. This renders man more careful of such things. With life, there is always something which can be made to take the weight of culpability from the master's shoulders. The horse was obstinate; it had a bad temper; it possessed a vile mouth; it bolted; it refused; it shied; it reared; it jibbed; it kicked, or, in some way, it resolved not to do its duty. The dumb creature can make no answer to the accusation; and human nature is readily convinced of its impartiality when its errors have been mainly cast upon another life.

The builder is, of course, governed by the architect; the architect is anxious to exhibit plans which shall elicit the approval of the proprietor. So, in the end, those arrangements, upon which the well-being and the health of many lives must depend, rest upon the caprice of an elderly gentleman, who now, for the first time in his life, may give serious thought to such a subject. However, this is the rule, whether a house is intended for a family residence or is erected as a speculation: the stables almost invariably occupy the space which is left after every other want is satisfied.

When picturing one, the author designs to portray most modern stables: very few of which are erected after maturer considerations than the imaginary elderly gentleman has bestowed upon his contemplated "out-houses." Proverbially, according to this world's usages, the submissive are the abused; it would indeed be difficult to discover a more perfect type of absolute submission than is exemplified in the powerful body of a domesticated horse. Are we, therefore, to conclude that in this attribute lies the reason why it is the most ill-treated, the worst-nourished, and the meanest-lodged of the many inhabitants upon this earth?

However, that the writer may not be accused of drawing on his fancy, or of representing as actualities things which have no existence in fact, he will, where reference is necessary, quote from the pages of a work on "Stable Economy," written by Professor Stewart, of Glasgow. This book, when a pupil at the Royal Veterinary College of London, was purchased by the author, he being induced to procure it by the high character which it bore among the members of his profession. Therefore it is selected as an authority upon the subject of which it treats;

and when quoting it, the present writer will, so far as may be prudent, forbear to adduce his personal opinions.

Concerning doors, permitting egress from and allowing entrance into stables, Professor Stewart directs that these should be made "eight or eight and a half feet high and five feet wide." The dimensions here laid down are evidently regarded as large or of model amplitude; for, subsequently, we are informed "accidents often happen from having doors too low and too narrow." Aware, therefore, of the necessity for space, the Professor must have imagined he had allowed room sufficient to anticipate those accidents which he was contemplating, when the passage was indited. The reader may, therefore, reasonably conjecture that, when proposing the above measurement, the Professor not only thought he had permitted every requisite freedom, but that he had even provided large marginal capacity for extraordinary occasions.

Certainly, when compared with the vast majority of existing doorways, the proposed entrance may be viewed as exceeding the utmost limit of boundless liberality. The next sentence encountered in the book already referred to, apprises the reader that "three feet six inches is the usual width of a stable doorway; a few are four feet." Consequently, the author of "Stable Economy," warming as he contemplates the munificence of his conception, adds, "no care is necessary, when taking a horse through a space five feet wide and eight feet six inches high!"

Nevertheless, though the difference between the height and bulk of man and horse is altogether in favor of the animal, there are many doors admitting people to human habitations, which considerably exceed the dimensions laid down by a kindly disposed and an amiable writer, as the utmost space necessary for man and horse, simultaneously, to pass through. Within the domiciles of the lesser creature, it is by no means a rarity to discover entrances of a much greater height than Professor Stewart allows his imaginary model stable to possess.

Many gentlemen love to own tall horses. Persons having such a taste will not look at an animal unless it stands sixteen hands high; or unless it will measure five feet four inches from the top margin of the withers to the ground. The foregoing measurement, however, does not allow for the head and neck, which, though not reckoned in the general estimate of equine altitude, still cannot be left behind when the horse quits the stable. Some animals exceed sixteen hands: such quadrupeds, if they carried high crests, would have to lower their ears when passing under one of those beams which the learned Professor evidently intended to be so lofty as should release the groom from every care, and free him from all responsibility.

It is by no means unusual to encounter a man who stands more than six feet in his stockings. Such persons, when seated, measure at least three feet from the crown of the head to the cushion of the chair. One yard, therefore, added to the height of the horse makes more than eight feet; or, allowing for saddle, hair of rider, etc., approaches unpleasantly close to the highest point of that space which was to release a groom from every care.

Some persons prefer to mount in the stable. Many horses will only, while there, allow a rider to quietly cross their backs. Most gentlemen have their hats on before the feet are placed in the stirrups. But supposing a tall man to get upon a high horse, the covering to his head must be extremely shallow if it is to receive no damage when passing through the doorway which, the reader has Professor Stewart's assurance, is so lofty as to dispense with every care!

To ride out of the stable is very far from an eccentric habit. A model door should, therefore, contemplate the passage of any ordinary sized horse, with any rider of average proportions seated upon its back. The tallest man probable, as well as the smallest possible, should be equally accommodated by its dimensions. A model door ought to provide for every customary purpose. When considering such a structure, it is not sufficient that its size is proportioned to the majority of purposes, but it should be fit for all, save only very extraordinary uses.

The width customary with such entrances—"three feet six inches"—must not be passed over unnoticed, if only to convince the reader of the entire inadequacy of such a space. The author, however, could readily point to many stable doors of even narrower capacity than is implied in the foregoing limitation; but having bound himself not to adduce his own experience, he gladly accepts Professor Stewart's testimony concerning those things which are to be reviewed in this place.

When a horse is led, not ridden, out of the stable, the groom commonly proceeds according to the following method: The man grasps a rein, and, walking by the side of the animal, servant and slave pass the threshold together. The three feet six inches of clear space has to permit the passage of two bodies at the same moment; therefore, dividing the allotted width, and giving half to each, allows one foot nine inches as the share of either. A groom, however, when in full livery, and within his own dominion, is an important personage. He permits no familiarity from his inferiors; he expects only proper behavior from the horse, while he is beneath the shadow of his realm. That groom must be devoid of all self-esteem, and unworthy of his post, who could allow the cleanliness of his costume to be soiled or the polish of his boots to be sullied!

A person of ordinary stature, and in average health, will measure across the shoulders, from seventeen to twenty inches. An animal of moderate size can barely squeeze through a clear gap of twenty-two inches width. Then, taking the man at the lowest standard, and adding seventeen to twenty-two inches, we obtain thirty-nine inches, as the smallest amount of room which servant and quadruped could manage to pass through. Such a close measurement, however, supposes the two living beings to touch one another, as well as to graze the sides of the passage. Against such gross usage, the innate dignity of cockade, leathers, and riding coat would alike protest!

Three feet six inches, however, allow exactly one inch to divide the door posts from the man and from the horse; while an inch also remains to separate the dignity of the domestic from the simplicity which it is conducting. The margin is not very ample; and both creatures must march with uncommon steadiness for neither of the animals to touch the posts, or to rub against the other.

Five feet, certainly, afford more ample quarters. Through such a frame both man and horse, supposing each to be quietly disposed, may pass with ease. Even so vast a limit, however, will not allow the groom to dispense with every care. An animal may, reasonably, be delighted when it sniffs the fresh air; and it may be permitted to perform a few pranks, as it quits positive stagnation to make the nearest approach to freedom which its enslaved condition can sanction. School-boys do not observe any severity of order, when they cast aside their tasks to throng into the play-ground. Yet the youths are confined to study only for a comparatively short period. But what must be the feelings of the steed, when leaving the heated stable and the narrow stall, where it has probably been imprisoned for twenty-two consecutive hours?

"DOWN IN THE HIP;" OR A HORSE WITH THE BONE OF ONE HIP FRACTURED.

Who among us, if he had the power, would check the graceful prancings and elegant curvetings, by which a simple nature announces its sense of happiness? To human feeling, an idea of having to carry another's weight, in the direction and at the pace the rider pleases to command; to have a sharp bit pulled against the tender angles of the lips; to be flogged with a heavy whip, or goaded with sharp spurs,—conjures up an image calculated to awaken no special delight. But long imprisonment may induce that eagerness to breathe the air of heaven, which may possibly render the prospect of labor, beyond the confines of its jail, welcome to the captive.

Quadrupeds have been injured while passing through the widest of modern entrances. The pleasure of escaping from the tedium and from the faintness of actual stagnation generates a joy which banishes the sense of prudence. All feeling and every caution appear to be engulfed in the exultation of the moment. The horse dances as it walks; the tail is gayly whisked; the neck is arched; the mane is shaken and the body is twisted, by those numberless undulations which have often excited the admiration of enthusiastic spectators. If, during one of these expressive movements, the trunk should be inflected more than the seven inches which the five feet allow, or the animal, influenced by the impetuosity of excitement, should come in contact with the door post, the consequence may be fearful. The possibility of check, certainly, does not enter the thought of the joyous creature. The blow is proportioned to the heedlessness which induced it. A bone can be fractured on such an occasion; nor is it an unusual accident. Most horses which are beheld with one "hip down," have had the deformity produced by striking against the post of the stable door.

"Down in the hip," is a groom's phrase, and merely signifies that one of the prominences of the haunch-bone, or, employing anatomical language, that one of the inferior spinous processes of the ileum, has been broken off. This osseous projection is of great importance to the value of the quadruped; it gives origin to numerous muscles, but more particularly to the powerful extensors of the hind limb. That ease, grace, and rapidity with which the member should be moved are by this misfortune destroyed, and the animal is thereby unfitted for the more highly esteemed half of its future services. By the accident it loses caste, and moves downward in the scale of equine employments.

This terrible affliction to the life principally concerned may also be occasioned in another manner. Grooms, when leading a horse from the stable, commonly walk by the side of the animal. Such persons are usually fully dressed to attend their masters, when called upon to perform this duty. Thus arrayed, the vanity of these men is extreme. Their importance almost exacts homage from the quadruped upon which it is their office to attend. Should the creature in its joy, when passing through the doorway, touch the coat of the domestic, such familiarity elicits the utmost indignation. Pride frowns at the pollution of its vestments. A loud word, a kick or a blow, instantly resents the insult. The animal, in terror, skips about to avoid further punishment. The door post is struck; the haunch is fractured, or the pain is inflicted which renders the creature, with its retentive memory, ever after fearful when passing through an entrance.

BOLTING THROUGH THE STABLE DOOR.

The ordinary life of a domesticated horse is so monotonous that recollection of events cannot otherwise than be retained. The animal subsequent to such a calamity, even though no bone should be fractured, cannot gaze upon a door with calmness. In future, alarm is exhibited whenever an entrance has to be approached. It cannot enter or quit its abiding-place without displaying those symptoms of terror which to the groom are the representatives only of inveterate "vice." The most violent or the blandest of tones cannot restore placidity to the brain which is troubled by fearful recollections. It is useless to coax, to threaten, or to punish: the animal has no ability to assume its former quietude when passing through the terrible opening. But it strives to brace up its nerves for the performance of the necessary act. All its resolution is summoned, till, maddened by excitement, it wildly dashes through the entrance, dragging after it the boy to whose custody the more dangerous quadrupeds are usually intrusted by the prudent sagacity of stable-men.

Terror, once generated in the equine brain, is never removed, until years of misery have ruined the health and destroyed the spirit of the horse; rendering it a mere suffering machine, careless of the present and hopeless for the future. The weight of affliction which nearly all of the unhappy race have to sustain, as age increases, changes the temper and the bearing of the creature. Its prostrated existence seems almost to have become indifferent to human malice. Mankind would, certainly, not be the less happy could they be induced to trust in the goodness which their Heavenly Father has placed around them; would they discard those doubts and abandon that defiance which implies a belief only in the *existence* of evil.

With regard to the subject on which recent comments have been based, horsemen should order their servants never to walk through a doorway by the side of the quadruped, which general belief supposes to be led through such openings.

A boy should not be employed in such an office. Prior to leaving the building, the groom should place himself directly in front of his charge. A short hold of either rein should then be taken in each hand. When there located, he can with ease and certainty guide the head of the horse. The motions of the head regulate the movements of the body, and having the controlling power entirely at his command, the servant should commence to back slowly out of the stable. However, there is one objection to the proposed method, which is the rightful mode of proceeding. In the majority of London stables there is but one man, who acts as groom, as coachman, and occasionally as pad groom, or the servant who rides after his employer. This personage being in front of the creature's nose, should the horse sneeze, cough, or clear its nostrils, any ejected matter must alight upon the highly-decorated garments of the man. The self-love of the individual fears such a mishap to the luster of his afternoon's costume; when the interests of the proprietor are opposed to the vanity of ignorance, no spirit of prophecy is needed to pronounce on which side victory will be declared! These accidents may be greatly mitigated by the hat being laid aside, as from all else the soil may be removed, and leave no stain behind.

Supposing this obvious recommendation to be adopted, should any symptom of alarm or any disposition to display restiveness chance to be exhibited, progress must be immediately stopped; nor ought it to be again resumed, until the animal has thoroughly recovered its composure. No matter how long a period may be required to restore tranquillity, the groom should, contentedly, continue stationary till every sign of timidity is banished or dispelled. In such a manner, servant and quadruped should leave the building: nor ought the man to quit his post before the doorway has been more than cleared.

LEADING A HORSE THROUGH THE STABLE DOORWAY.

It must certainly be read with a sensation of surprise that, since a stable was first erected, horses have been constantly injured by passing through narrow doorways. It will assuredly excite wonder that, after centuries of experience, enforced by serious loss, the easy, safe, and natural remedy for such miscalled "accidents" needs to be gravely pointed out, or to be promulgated as it were a novel suggestion. The mind of the master has, however, been otherwise engaged; the horse has never been regarded as a living creature, having certain attributes and rights, with which all keepers of the quadrupeds must comply. It is rather viewed as "something" absolutely *given* to mankind, concerning which the human being has, therefore, merely to consult his will and his pleasure. Consequently, when regulations are formed for the government of the equine race, these are never framed as though there were the habits, the instincts, and the wants of an existence to be considered.

The assumed evil disposition of the most placid of beings has been wrongfully abused as the cause of every injury. The possibility of so groundless a reason being advanced to cover that carelessness which provoked punishment, is by no means complimentary to the wisdom of mankind. The care needful for the safe guidance of a timid animal is denied; the trifling outlay which would secure the immunity of the creature is selfishly withheld. Nevertheless, how frequent and how poignant is the lamentation, which complains that horse flesh is a "very hazardous species of property!" Yet, when investigated, what does the cry import, more than that a beautiful living body is not sent upon earth superior to man's power of abuse?

Nature endowed the horse with every faculty needed to enjoy the freest existence on the most extended plane. It was created the graceful embodiment of the wildest liberty! The classic mind rightfully recognized its attributes; for by it, as Pegasus, the boldest flight of a poet's fancy was significantly allegorized. The ancient intellect, in its freshness, beheld in the steed the fitting representative of that which prisons should not confine, neither should chains fetter. Yet, formerly, the full truthfulness of the image was but partially demonstrated. Years of after-experience have shown the animal can thrive in opposite regions; it can live on almost every variety of sustenance; it propagates its race under the extremes of too much care and of absolute neglect; the creature which man sorrows over as so very delicate has the strength of a giant, the docility of a dog, and a constitution which is well characterized by a proverbial expression, "strong as a horse!"

The boasted civilization of the present age has degraded the animal into a living type of stagnant misery! It was gifted by its Creator with a speed which defied pursuit; with a sight which could endure the sun's fiercest ray, or could penetrate the darkness of the night; and it was gifted with the recognition which is telescopic in its range of inquiry. It was sent upon this earth with an ample nostril, and a sense of smell capable of appreciating the varied odors of an Eastern plain. How has human perversity distorted the intentions of Beneficence! Now it is locked into an outhouse, where either total darkness prevails, or the eye is fastened close to a whitened surface. It is tied to a manger, while the floor on which it stands so slants as must banish ease from the feet, and the partitions which confine the body prevent rest from change of position. If the place is cold, the creature's home is possessed of no means to counteract the effect. If it should be warm, it is contaminated by the fermentation of filth; the air is loaded with gas, which must pain the nerves, occasion the eyes to smart, disgust the fine sense of smell, and destroy the health by preventing perfect oxygenation of the blood

Misery, solitude, and confinement will generate disease in a man. Wherefore should an animal be esteemed superior to such influences? Impure air, sameness of food, and being tied to a manger, inducing feeble bodily health, gradually undermine the powerful equine constitution. Other evils, of a local nature, result from causes which might easily be removed, were man, in his wisdom, only convinced such influences ought to be destroyed. The forelegs of the stabled horse are always the first to yield. Yet the prisoner may endure severe lameness in these members, and, nevertheless, the body be so slightly sympathetic with the affliction as actually to lay on fat. It is different with the hinder limbs! Should one of these last be injured, the entire frame languishes. The quadruped then evidently pines in torture, and its flesh sensibly wastes.

Very different is the manner in which various physiologists account for this peculiarity. Some appeal to the greater proximity of the anterior extremities to the heart, or to the center of circulation. That, perhaps, is the generally received doctrine; but as the free circulation of the blood is essential to the healthy functions of the nerves, it is difficult to comprehend why nearness to the heart should deprive a nerve of its ability to communicate sensation. The head is supposed to be rendered conspicuously sensitive, because of the great proportionate quantity of blood which circulates in that region. The pretended rule, therefore, will not bear the test of general application; it must be discarded as an assertion boldly put forward to cover ignorance.

The forefeet of the horse are those portions of the frame which have to endure the utmost limits of mortal perversity. The flooring of the stall invariably inclines from the manger to the gangway. The hind hoofs may, should the animal hang back the full length of its collar-rope, rest in the open drain with the toes downward; or the hind hoofs may, in some cases, stand upon the gangway, the width of which the gutter defines. The front limbs, however, can scarcely change their position. The hoofs must rest upon the slanting bricks, which incline the anterior of the foot in the upward direction. The forelegs must sustain, and continue subject to the unnatural stress of their enforced position. This silly and arbitrary arrangement in some measure accounts for the fact that the front limbs of the horse are the first parts of the body to fail, for these parts never, in the stable, are capable of rest, nor can they be sensible to ease.

It has, of late years, become the general practice to bleed the horse from the sole of the forefoot. When such a custom is adopted, the first portion of blood extracted is, commonly, cold as spring-water, or from thirty to forty degrees below the standard recognized as "blood heat." Now, a certain warmth is imperative to the existence of vitality, which is arrested so soon as the natural heat of the body is sensibly diminished. The functions are stayed when any region has parted with its caloric. Dentists take advantage of this fact when, after having employed the chilling process, they extract a tooth without pain. Cold, therefore, which can destroy sensation in the human jaw, likewise renders the foot of the horse insensible to agony.

But why is the foreleg subject to a degree of cold which does not also affect the hind extremity of the animal? Because the stable permits the hind limbs to enjoy the greater freedom of action. These may be in perpetual motion; for the posterior members are situated at the boundary of a circle, of which the ring of the manger represents the center or fixed point. Has the reader ever beheld a column of soldiers move in obedience to the officer's command, to "Wheel?" The man at one end of the line can hardly run quickly enough, while he who is placed at the opposite extremity is troubled to be sufficiently slow in his movements. Now, the hind legs of the horse represent the man who has to scamper, and are sensibly exerted whenever the quadruped "comes over;" the anterior extremities are types of the soldier who scarcely moves, for very seldom are these members necessitated to change their position. Their stable office is to uphold the body, and to remain fixed while the toes are inclined upward! Were the motion permitted to both extremities equalized, the fore limbs would naturally be the warmest, since the great distance from the heart and the greater angularity of form must render circulation of caloric within the quarters much more tardy.

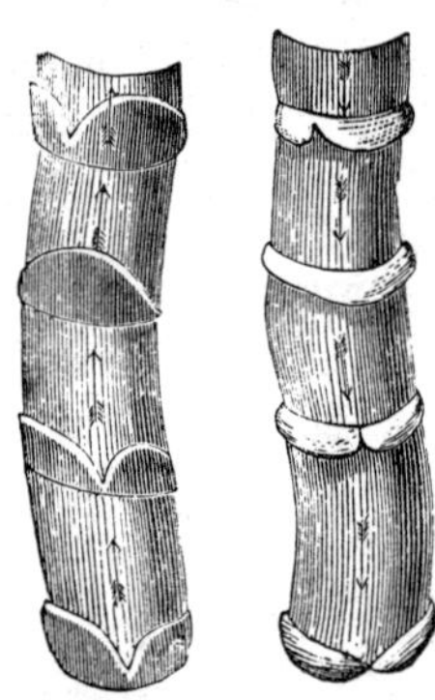

VALVES OF THE VEINS IN THE LEG.

1. The valves of the vein laid against the side of the vessel by the upward current of the blood.

2. The valves projected from the sides of the vessel by the attempted retrogression of the vital stream.

But why do not other parts become as cold as the fore limbs, when all belong to the same body, and all derive their heat from one common medium, or from the same circulation? The veins in the legs have valves. Then, if these vessels are so provided, and the distribution of warmth is one of the purposes of the circulation, why do not the valves favor the return of blood from the foot, and thus generate heat within the member? When answering the foregoing inquiries, the reader's patience is entreated, since the reply, to be intelligible, cannot also be concise.

Anatomy affords the best explanation of the peculiarity. On removing the horny case from the hoof of a dead horse, a secretive membrane is exposed; this membrane constantly renews the horn. Beneath the secreting surface, a complex mesh-work of large veins is discovered. which, by their size, inform us they serve as receptacles or sinuses quite as much as vessels. These veins have no valves, though such are commonly present in other tubes of the same class. The absence of this provision is, in them, remarkable, because the blood has to move against gravity; valves are a means instituted to favor the current under circumstances of this nature. Valves are composed of duplicatures of the lining membrane of veins: when the venous current flows toward the heart, these valves, by the impetus of the stream, are forced upward, and remain close against the sides of the vessels; but, should the slightest retrogression of the current be endangered, the backward motion of the blood carries the numerous valves outward or downward, and effectually locks the interior of the veins.

The anatomy of the foot, however, proves the horse unsuited to confinement. The animal was created to dwell upon the plain. The foot, for its health, requires perpetual motion. When free, or before man subjected it to his convenience, every bite the creature took necessitated a fresh step. The mesh-work of veins was large, the vessels freely communicated with each other, and were devoid of valves, that the blood might readily flow into, while it might as readily be expelled from, the tubes; and because, in the habits of her creature, nature had established a force which rendered the development of valves unnecessary. The horse, as it progressed, alternately lifted the foot from the earth and rested it upon the ground. When the hoof was raised, the blood rushed into and filled the mesh-work of veins. When the foot was again placed upon the soil, the superimposed weight squeezed the vessels, between the bones and the horn, thus pumping out the blood, or forcing it toward the heart.

Blood which has become cold has lost the first of its living properties. Blood deprived of heat cannot support health, or supply secretion. Hence the feet of stabled horses—notwithstanding the care of science, the numorous applications, and the endless variety of shoes, all of which are designed to benefit the hoofs—generally become diseased. The quadruped of the agriculturist, although it be neglected and badly shod, yet, because of its slow or constant work, and habitual freedom in the field, usually exhibits feet which are sound and open. The donkey, though much abused and shamefully treated, rarely inhabits a stable, and more seldom enters a stall. Its feet become misshapen; but the curse of the gentleman's steed, foot lameness, and especially navicular disease, are all but unknown among this tribe of the equine race.

The foregoing statement also affords an explanation why the most valuable or the stabled horse is so frequently afflicted with contracted hoof, with brittle hoof, with an unhealthy secretion of horn, and with the various other ailments which may be classed under the diseases of the foot. It likewise supplies the most clear reason for the beginning of that disorder which has been denominated "the curse of good horse flesh"—Naviculartbritis, or ulceration of the navicular bone. Bone is slow to take on morbid action, and ulceration is the accompaniment of low vitality. When the circulation is retarded, the animal powers are enfeebled. Ulceration, affecting a lowly organized structure, is that which a pathologist would anticipate as the consequence of prolonged inaction. It is impossible to say what evils the continuance of such a condition may not induce; but sand-crack, seedy-toe, and various painful affections can be clearly traced to have thus originated.

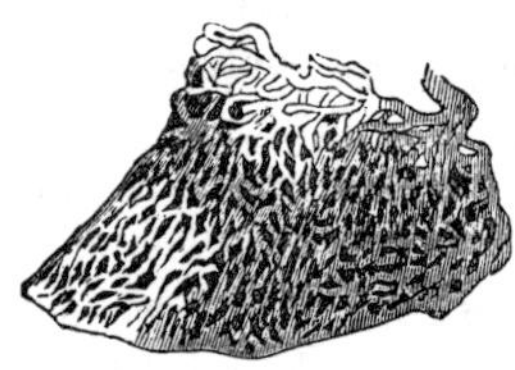

THE VEINS OF THE HORSE'S FOOT.
The mesh-work of veins, without valves, which are situated immediately under the secretive membrane of the hoof.

The effect of the stable, also, accounts for the farmer riding his nag for many years, while few gentlemen approve of a horse for saddle purposes after it has passed the sixth summer, notwithstanding their animals are better groomed and more carefully fed. In the country, farmers' quadrupeds are generally turned into the field, and have to walk for their living. Grass is a poor food; but the constant exercise keeps the creatures in sounder health than can be maintained by better sustenance combined with perpetual confinement.

An absolute necessity for the constant movement of the feet is to be deduced from the arrangement of the vessels. The arterial blood falls almost perpendicularly down the fore limb, while the venous blood has likewise to ascend against gravity. This arrangement rendered imperative some propelling force to return the effete fluid; hence the necessity for the perpetual employment of the squeezing or pumping action of the hoof. The habits of the animal to graze only from choice portions of the herbage occasion a vast distance to be traversed; but such leisurely sauntering was, by nature, kindly intended to keep sound that portion of the frame on the integrity of which the safety, the welfare, and the pleasure of her creation was dependent.

"Certainly," the reader may exclaim; "but if the warmth of the body is dependent upon arterial blood, the coldness of a part cannot be accounted for by stating the facility afforded for the oxygenating current reaching that which is chilled." Very true. But before any substance can fall down, the space through which it has to pass in its descent must be made clear. The quickness with which the arterial blood reaches the foot is, consequently, regulated by the speed with which the venous current is expelled. The hoof of the stabled horse is constantly congested, or the effete blood accumulates within the horn; because motion, in the venous stream, is impossible. The current hardly stirs, and the fluid, by stagnation, becomes cold. Did the possibility of action allow the pumping force fair play, then the forefoot would, doubtless, be as warm as other parts of the animal's system.

Anatomy demonstrates these facts; but the habits of the quadruped have never been attentively noted. Had the instinctive promptings of its desires been studied with a wish to profit by such instruction, stables had been erected for some better purpose than to closely confine an active animal, and to illustrate the earliest principles of surface drainage. As it is, a building has been raised totally inadequate to its pretended uses, and one in the arrangement of which the convenience of man has alone been consulted. In such a place, a horse has, for ages, been im-

HORSES, WHEN FREE TO CHOOSE, ALWAYS STAND WITH THE FOREHOOFS ON A LOWER LEVEL THAN THAT OCCUPIED BY THE HIND FEET.

prisoned. It is true, the captive did not thrive. Yet this consequence was rather excused than inquired into. Humanity has endured loss, disappointment, and vexation; but pride found it more agreeable to accuse the works of Heaven with the results of its own culpability than to suspect the adequacy of its own institutions. Nature has, in vain, labored to instruct the waywardness of conceit. Mankind could endure all evils before it could afford to question the perfectibility of mortal invention.

Horses, when disposed to remain stationary, always select ground where the forefeet can occupy a position lower than the hind legs. In stables, this inclination is reversed, the hinder limbs invariably resting on an inferior level to what the forefeet range upon. The motive upon which the dictates of nature are outraged is the facility which a floor slanting in the backward direction affords for surface moisture to flow into the open gutter that runs along the extreme margin of the gangway. Science, evidently, has not been consulted in an arrangement which sacrifices the health and the comfort of an inhabitant of the stall to obtain so obvious, gross, and poor an advantage. Stables, evidently, were built only to please the fancy, and propitiate the prejudices of ignorant proprietors. No thought was bestowed upon the quadrupeds such edifices pretended to accommodate. The consequence is seen in the discomfort, torture, and the speedy decline of lives which are forced to dwell within one of these notorious charnel-houses.

WHEN CONFINED TO THE STALL, HORSES GENERALLY STAND WITH THE HIND FEET UPON A LOWER LEVEL THAN THE FOREHOOFS OCCUPY.

Knowing the object desired, the reader will naturally expect to be informed whether dryness is secured by the present arrangement. When answering this inquiry, the author must describe the general plan according to which the floors of most stables are laid down. The pavement of the stalls is composed of small, hard bricks, known as "Dutch Clinkers." Bricks, however nicely they may be placed, cannot form an absolutely smooth or even surface. They must present spaces in which fluid will be retained; and, being porous, bricks cannot prevent effluvia from rising through their substances, or cannot hinder liquid from percolating into the soil on which they rest. The urine acquires acrimony as it corrupts beneath the pavement, which makes a renewal of the flooring of a stall an efficient reason for ordering the inhabitants of a large building to be removed, since the pavement will have to be disturbed.

To demonstrate that the urine of the horse undergoes a speedy change when exposed to the action of the atmosphere: the fresh fluid will produce no change in litmus paper; but after a few minutes' exposure, the liquid changes the blue dye to a red color, having, in the brief interval, become acid, and in that condition it yields strong fumes of ammoniacal gas. It is the presence of this gas that chiefly occasions that peculiar pungency which is characteristic of the stable.

To promote such an alteration, and to procure from the excretion the greatest possible amount of noxious effluvia, the liquid is made to gently flow over an open, a rough, an uneven, and a slanting surface; thus subjecting the greatest possible quantity to the direct action of the atmosphere. Should not the whole change be thereby accomplished, the fluid slowly drains into an open gutter, which slopes so gradually that its contents frequently refuse to move. Had the architect who originally laid down the plan of a modern stable designed to make the interior poisonous, it would have been difficult, having no more active agent at command, for him to have conceived means better calculated to fulfill his object.

The groom, to warm the place, stops up every crevice through which the vapor could escape, or pure air could find admission. Many stablemen, also, exclude the light, under a groundless notion that horses thrive best when in the dark. Darkness does not necessarily lead to sleep—it simply disables one of the senses; thereby animal life is deprived of a harmless enjoyment, while at the same time the exclusion of light causes the eye to shrink from the glare of day; while the continuance of the evil is likely to induce blindness. Hours of weariness, passed in a confined space, and within a tainted atmosphere, are strange means when employed to promote extraordinary thrift. More especially, when we consider that the inclination of the floor forbids rest to the feet, while the exclusion of light incapacitates all visual recreation.

Horses, not having a knowledge of chemistry, cannot, of themselves, purify the air; but certain animals, instructed by their instincts, do all in their power to counteract the evils which the slanting nature of the flooring has a tendency to produce. Such steeds lean first upon one foot and then upon the other; thus the entire weight bears alternately upon either hoof, while each is in turn released from all pressure. If not checked, quadrupeds will often continue thus employed for hours. The creatures know nothing concerning the structures of their own bodies; but the most learned physiologist could not have invented any plan better calculated to supply the pumping action which accompanies the walk, and promotes a healthy circulation, thus securing soundness to the hoof.

Indeed, human intelligence would appear to be incapable of appreciating the benefit which must result from the simple artifice of an inferior being. The animal which is detected when endeavoring to correct the evils of mortal perversity, is always severely punished. The indulgence is, by the pure mind of the groom, recognized as a wicked "vice," and is stigmatized under the term of "weaving." The highly intelligent

WEAVING.

horse is fiercely lashed for laboring to prevent the consequences of man's stupidity, and for striving to improve its master's property, while solacing its confinement, by an act as harmless as it is innocent.

A creature standing on a slanting floor, with the head pointing to the most elevated part of the incline, occupies the same relative situation which the body would possess, were the quadruped journeying up the side of a hill. By the sloping nature of the ground, the weight of the frame is partially removed from the insensitive bones; and to such an extent as the osseous structures are relieved, is the burden thrown upon the flexor tendons, or upon the back sinews. It is imperative for the health of bone that it should endure almost continuous pressure. On the other hand, tendon or sinew feels no pain from occasional tension; but pressure, if long sustained, produces the acutest agony. When one structure is denied to fulfill the uses for which it was created, and another structure is condemned to discharge services for which it never was designed, the first soon degenerates, from not having sufficient employment, while the second speedily becomes disorganized, from the necessity to perform too much labor.

Bone, tendon, and cellular tissue almost compose the shin and the foot of the animal. Horsemen know how difficult it is to make and keep the legs of a stabled quadruped hard and fine. It is, however, folly to rub and to bandage while inactivity is permitted to generate congestion. No application can possibly destroy the effect while that cause is allowed to be in operation. Nor can the foot secrete sound horn while the exercise which is imperative for health is withheld. No shoe can give that which is dependent upon motion. There are many more pieces of iron curved, hollowed, raised, and indented, than the author has cared to enumerate. All, however, have failed to restore health to the hoof. Some, by enforcing a change of position, may, for a time, appear to mitigate the evil; but none can, in the long run, cure the disorder under which the horn evidently suffers.

Anointing the hoof, or using various stoppings, are equally fruitless. Both leg and foot, after a day of hard labor, only return to the stable to undergo more excessive, because more continuous, fatigue. The sloping pavement renders ease an impossibility. The exhaustion cannot be banished from limbs forced to occupy such ground. Longer rest but induces additional enervation.

The inquiry suggested by the above remarks is, whether a horse does not return with eagerness to its stable? Is it natural for a creature to exhibit eagerness when it enters the abode of its agony? In answer to the foregoing, it may be advanced that all grades of inferior life which exist under the care of man are in so unnatural a condition as allows no inference to be drawn from apparently voluntary actions. Birds were intended to cleave the air. No one can believe but the goldfinch must be more happy when bathing its wings in light, and freely sailing on the atmosphere, than when the gay spirit is cramped within one of those small cages in which certain people delight to confine the joyous heart.

Yet, let the bird be captured and immured within such a space. After some time, it will require perseverance to drive the feathered captive from the prison which must make stiff the wings and cause the breast to sorrow. The act, however, will be difficult; when accomplished, unless the wire door be closed, the shelter of its inadequate abode will be speedily sought again. Do birds, therefore, love to be caught, and to be caged?

Should the above instance not be perfectly satisfactory, another is ready to illustrate the subject. Everybody has heard of the French noble, who had grown old, gray, and feeble while in durance. The gentleman, when released from the Bastile, shed tears, entreating to be restored to his cell. Are we, therefore, to infer that the French love imprisonment? Each case may, perhaps, be interpreted to exemplify the power of habit. One year of sheer animal life will stand against a long term of human existence. A horse lives in the facts which surround it. It exists in the present, and has no imagination to embitter the hardness of its fate. Man is always escaping from the circumstances which engirt him; he is always fancying something brighter than his present lot, or is straining toward the future; he may be said to exist most in anticipation. Give humanity no prospect to dwell upon, deny it all hope to contemplate, the soul sinks into utter dejection; and a palace or a jail are alike regarded with indifference.

The horse was, by nature, formed to be the companion and the servant of man. The original of the breed, which in animals intended for the wild state it is difficult to destroy, is, with the equine race, unknown. It is, in heart, in body, and in soul, the obedient servant and willing helpmate of the human race. It does not submit to its doom; its lot is accepted as a foregone decision; it has abandoned every thought of liberty, and has embraced its fate. But is it worthy of the intelligence to which the creature has devoted its existence, to convert such perfect and entire abnegation of self into a reason for perpetuating those tortures that were invented by barbarity, and are, it is hoped, only continued through ignorance? The reader needs no prompting to afford the fitting answer.

This question is not affected by the love or hatred of the animal for the stable. The only point which really remains to be decided is, does the stable, as at present built, represent the most healthful and the most pleasant abode which man's imagination can picture for his tired and submissive companion? If it be possible to suppose a better home for the quadruped, then it becomes the moral duty of man to raise such a structure. All pretenses about the sacrifice of existing property and the regards for pecuniary outlay are of no weight when urged against a rightful obligation. Man is blessed with reason, and is constituted, in this world, the only judge of his own actions. So high a privilege should bind him to be even more than just in his decisions!

To return. The reader will observe that, in the sketch No. 1, the bones rest one upon the other. That arrangement ensues when the

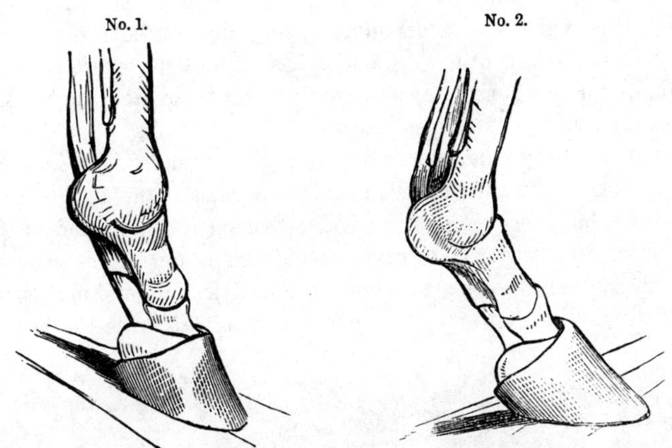

THE STRESS ENDURED BY THE DIFFERENT STRUCTURES WHICH COMPOSE THE LEG OF THE HORSE IS DEPENDENT UPON THE POSITION OF THE FOOT.

animal descends an incline. There can exist no man but must have enjoyed the ease which is imparted by walking down a slope. Every person must also be acquainted with the fatigue consequent upon ascending an acclivity. The effect is generally explained by stating that, in one case progression is favored by, while in the other it is made in opposition to, gravitation. Such a cause, certainly, is in operation; but the different structures on which the strain reposes, when moving in opposite directions, to the author's mind supply a better illustration of the fact.

Do not muscles, and does not tendon participate in the burden which is upheld by bone? Assuredly they do; but in various degrees. No limb can move unless some muscle contracts. Every muscle in the body arises from bone, and is inserted into bone by the interposition of ligamentous fiber. Before a member can be elevated or depressed, some muscle must drag from some bone, that it may move some other bone more distantly situated. Then, tendon cannot escape strain, since in no possible attitude is every portion of the frame in absolute rest. Motor muscles, however, generally exist in pairs. They are spoken of as elevators and as depressors, or as flexors and as extensors. Their uses are opposite, but not opposed. When one set works, the other is inactive.

The bones in the sketch, indicated by No. 2, evidently press against the backward tendons. Such a position, if long maintained, leads to fatigue, and ultimately induces pain. Man cannot enjoy rest under such a condition of parts; though both tendon and muscle are benefited by brief tension, continuous strain soon exhausts either structure. The reader must have beheld two travelers meet upon a mountain's side. One shall be descending from the heights, the other is ascending from the valley. But while the men converse, they do not hold their relative positions one to the other. Each, without thought or reflection, exchanges it for the horizontal situation; while their dialogue lasts, both present their sides to the spectator.

This is precisely what many horses learn to do. Much indignation is always excited in the groom's bosom because an animal, prompted by its instinct, has discovered a method of easing its limbs and of saving the master's property from injury. Standing for hours upon an acclivity, however gradual, throws stress upon the back sinews, and must pain the tired limbs. To counteract that effect, the animal turns the head from

STANDING ACROSS THE STALL.

the manger, and stands across the flooring of the stall, after the same plan as actuated the two travelers when they paused upon the mountain side. But the conduct which in man draws forth no remark, when exhibited by the horse is abominated by a virtuous groom as the declaration of inveterate "vice."

Pitiable vice! It is melancholy to behold a man cruelly punish an animal for a reasonable act. But heavy castigation does every horse receive that is guilty of exercising the instinct with which Heaven has endowed it. The groom, being excited to resentment, grasps a stick and deals well-aimed blows, while his voice shouts forth harsh words, which pain and terrify the patient creature, whose only faults were too much sense and too great feeling.

When a horse is terrified, danger is likely to ensue in exact proportion to the smallness of that space which can be commanded for the display of its alarm. The timidity being excessive, of course the contortions of the body are equally demonstrative. The animal dashes about, regardless of its own safety, and heedless of those around it. It sees nothing; it can remember nothing, save only that some horrid torture is imminent. Its struggles are wild efforts to escape. In the momentary panic, it may break, or it may damage anything. It may kill any person who shall stand in its way, or, in the furore of its agony, it may, through misadventure, do serious mischief to its own body.

Such consequences are always to be expected when a horse is beaten within the stable while the head is fastened to the manger. By the latter circumstance, the probability of an injury is increased. Harm, however, to his employer's property, danger to his own person, and peril to the safety of his charge, the groom despises, or willingly hazards, rather than allow an odious "vice" to escape correction! No severity, however, can teach a quadruped not to seek the ease which it has discovered the means of realizing. When the groom is absent, or during the night, the act of "wickedness" is always renewed, although, in the presence of its attendant, the indulgence may be suppressed.

Slanting pavements likewise instruct horses in the practice of other habits which the groom, in his peculiar sphere of mental elevation, cannot otherwise than recognize as "vices." As such, he punishes their exhibition without mercy. Some public-house companion may visit the stable-man while he is dozing through the afternoon upon the locker. Most servants notoriously have no choice between stubborn duty and the relaxation of "pipe and pot." The groom is always the ready victim of temptation, and upon the slightest persuasion quits the stable for the parlor "over the road." Some sad and patient animal may have been silently watching, longing for the man's absence, during a considerable period; no sooner does the creature hear the door slam, than it begins to take small steps backward. The horse thus feels its way till the sudden fall in the pavement announces that the posterior hoofs have reached the gutter, within the hollow of which the toes are immediately depressed.

Such an attitude being attained, all stress upon the flexor tendons is removed from the backward legs. The bones, while the toes can be depressed, sustain the weight of the haunches. Partial ease is thereby secured, and with the new sensation, a numbing torpor creeps over the animal. Its feelings are soothed by present pleasure, and the senses, thrown off their guard, grow dead to all outward impressions. The victim of former ages, when taken from the rack, must still have endured agony; but the lull occasioned by the cessation of acute torture threw the sufferer into a lethargy, which is reported to have resembled the luxury of sleep. So is it with the horse. The forefeet are still undergoing torment; but, under partial relief, the animal seems to doze, or becomes unconscious to the facts around it.

THE HIND FEET ARE EASED IN THE GUTTER.

The horse is tranquilly luxuriating, and cozily reveling in the moments of forbidden ease, when the groom quietly returns to the stable. His eyes rest upon that "abominable wicious creatur, agin brakin o' the law!" The animal has actually dared to indulge in so much ease as instinct can discover among the cruel invention of centuries by which its body is surrounded. The quadruped excites the more anger by seeming to enjoy its wickedness! The groom is infuriated by the contemplation of such depravity! Beer and tobacco stimulate his indignation. He creeps slyly toward the whip, and commences to lash the culprit.

Some persons may be inclined to suppose the being who has so recently deserted his post, ought to look indulgently on what he conceives to be the fault of another and of an inferior animal. But the vile always are the pitiless; for charity is the foundation of all goodness. The lash is plied with energy—the groom, between every blow, lamenting "that he can't step away for a few moments, 'thout the plaguey brute being at its old tricks agin." The thong curls round the quivering and perspiring body. But severity in these cases is useless. The animal has discovered a partial solace for its misery; it cannot choose but indulge its pleasurable knowledge at the very next opportunity.

The stabled horse, however, has not only to stand upon a slanting pavement through the day; it must throughout the night lie upon a similar incline, rendered slippery by a covering of dry and polished straw. Did the reader ever attempt to repose upon a bed slightly out of the horizontal? The body cannot rest on such a couch. The sensation communicated is, an incessant fear of slipping off. The sleeper is constantly wakened up, with a vivid impression that he is falling, or has fallen, on to the floor. The night is passed in discomfort. But what is the excitability of a human being, when compared with the excessive fear which haunts the most timid of all created lives?

Man, when in a bed of the above description, naturally grows restless; the bed-clothes are disturbed, and the body laid in an opposite direction. All will not allay anxiety; at last the would-be sleeper is obliged to remain contented with occasionally nudging himself higher on to the pillow. Like man is the horse in many things, even as though the animal studied and mimicked its master. Yet the inflation of pride hails the resemblance as an insult, and regards animals as things created for use, and doomed to be subservient to the caprice of mortal pleasure.

Precisely as man would behave, did he chance to get upon a slanting bed, the animal conducts itself, only with such difference as the circumstances enforce. The human being reclines his head upon a pillow. But the horse sinks the head while it slumbers. Man, therefore, nearly touches the board situated at the topmost part of his resting-place. Three feet, or even a larger space, may divide the quadruped from the stable wall which forms the extremity of its couch. The floor on which the creature lies is strewn with straw. That condition, however, rather aggravates the inclination of the resting-place, for dried and glossy stems of a circular figure accelerate more than they retard the backward gravitation of the body.

The creature therefore—unable to reason, acting under the impression that its body is continually sliding backward—endeavors to recover its original position by nudging itself repeatedly forward. The horse has neither light to see, hands to feel, nor sense to measure the distance. Imagination is the only dependence which it can boast of. The advances become energetic in proportion as the supposition which provokes them is annoying. The annoyance is regulated by the irritability of the quadruped. Some stable inhabitants grow more morbidly nervous; with these, the advances are proportionably frequent; so that the head of the captive, guided by the collar-rope, is speedily brought into violent contact with the further end wall of its compartment.

Not comprehending the meaning of the blow, but suffering from pain and fright, the animal attempts to rise. The commencement of this movement always is the elevation of the head, which, after being raised, is strained backward. This action is a necessity of its existence; and, dreaming of no danger, the quadruped essays to fulfill the natural law. The head, however, which has struck the wall of the stable, must at the time he immediately under the manger. Imagining no impediment, the animal exalts its crest with that impetuosity which characterizes all the motions of the horse. It strikes against the manger, and a heavy concussion sends the member into its original abiding-place.

The stricken creature cannot comprehend the reason of those blows it has received. But it is often chastised for nothing, so beating is to it almost a matter of course. It crouches in terror for some moments, no doubt hoping its tormentor may move onward. Then, as the strained senses can detect no sound, it ventures once more to raise its head. The result is the same as it was before. The horse, after repeated efforts, becomes alarmed. Mad with fear, and wild with desperation, it now exerts its utmost strength. The contention may continue until the groom enters the stable in the morning, when, bruised and panting, its head swollen and bleeding, its strength exhausted and almost its life expended, the wretched animal is discovered prostrated upon the pavement.

This consequence of confining an animal in darkness is the serious, and probably the permanent, deterioration of property. At the best, the services are lost for many days. In any case, time must be allowed for the necessary recovery. Few, very few people have the generosity to recognize, and even fewer still are educated to perceive, that a life has been for many hours breathing in agony and that the existence may hereafter, notwithstanding all the present state of art can accomplish, probably drag its wretchedness about the world in a crippled condition

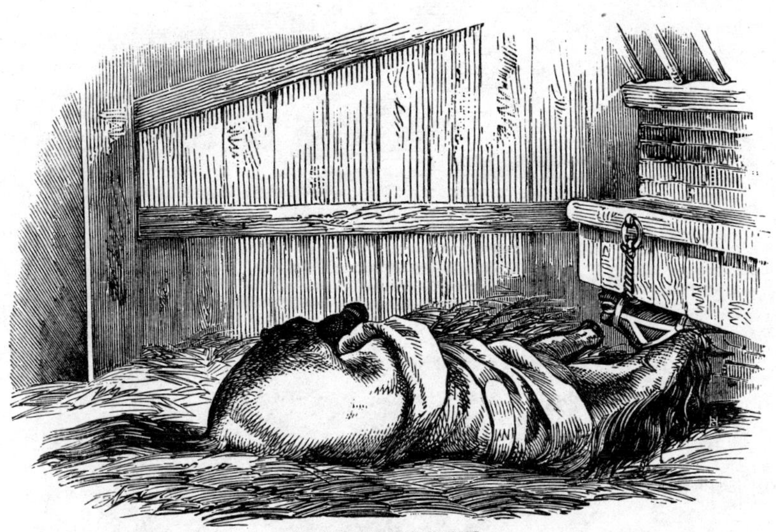

CAST UNDER THE MANGER.

No person living possibly will, when inspecting the maimed and disabled horse, reflect upon the fate which dooms the animal to years of sorrow, laboring through the lowest species of earthly trial; no one will heave a sigh that such a fate overtook a placid, gentle, and obedient creature, which was dangerously and cruelly confined during the time of serving a being who was bound to study the necessities and administer to the happiness of the life over which he had assumed absolute authority.

Other evils also spring from obliging the horse to sleep on a surface which is not level. The head of the animal being fastened to the manger, it has no choice but to couch where it stands, or to remain erect and endeavor to sleep in that position. There are quadrupeds which adopt and which maintain the last alternative: their bodies never repose on earth, until their injuries and their wrong are engulfed in the common doom.

It is not every animal, however, which can hold to such a resolution, in spite of the aches and agonies by which it must be enforced. Certain creatures, feeling their bodies glide backward, rather facilitate than endeavor to counteract the motion—hoping to soon rest upon the gangway, which experience has taught them terminates the stall. Others sleep so soundly as to be unconscious of the movement; while a third class, having attained philosophy through a life of misfortune, pay but little regard to the circumstances around them. In all instances the frame descends the slope, till the quarters pass the gutter and repose upon the gangway.

A HORSE STANDING WHILE IT SLEEPS.

Yet, before the body can move such a distance from the manger, the neck and the collar-rope must both be strained. However, finding its body, at length, to be comfortably located, the animal meditates composing itself to sleep, which is not to be done while the neck is outstretched and the chain is raised far above its natural position. To accomplish this, the muzzle must be considerably lowered and the neck be retracted; but, before either can be done, the collar-rope must be loosened. It is obviously impossible to change the attitude while that fastening remains in a state of tension: the position in which the horse invariably sleeps cannot, therefore, be assumed.

In this dilemma, the intelligent quadruped determines to rise and to return to the manger. But a natural law has ordained that before the horse gets up from the ground, the head shall be thrown backward; thus lightening the weight upon the fore quarters, which parts are always first raised. The straightening of the front limbs is thereby facilitated. But this movement cannot now be put in practice because of the rope which retains the neck outstretched. Struggles are useless;

the position is fixed, and the creature is powerless to alter it. The limbs are free, but these can only be used to kick and to aggravate the pain of the situation. The animal is a prisoner, and so it must remain, vainly contending with its doom, and exhausting its energies in fruitless efforts to escape.

Assuredly, he should have possessed an enlarged capacity for evil who first conceived the notion of making a living creature, which was conspicuous for its strength, its activity, and its timidity, exist in a niche; to have its head tied up by day and by night; and subsequently doomed it to rest upon a floor which sloped in a painful and an unnatural direction. No surer means could have been invented of shortening the life, of deforming the body, or of injuring the limbs of the creature in whose prosperity man conceived he had "a property." Arms of all kinds, and of every description, the quadruped might have been safely trusted with;

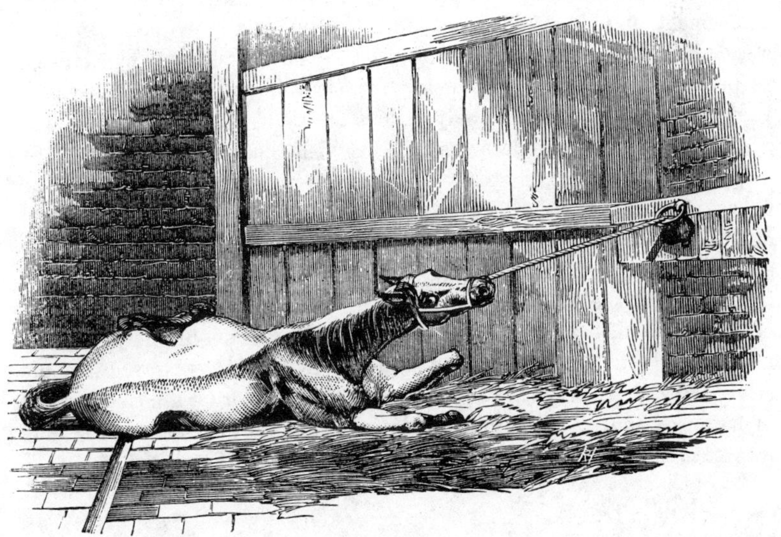

LYING ON THE GANGWAY.

but to require of activity, that it should be fettered and forego all motion; to demand of timidity, that it should be bound or imprisoned, and not display sensibility; to ask, that strength should endure and not attempt to struggle, was surely expecting too much from an inhabitant of a world in which fear, as the natural instructor of organized beings, is universally prevalent.

The horse, thus located, was only presented with the ready means of doing injury to itself. It was provided with the only weapons which nature had empowered it to employ. A more unwholesome, a more unnatural, or a more dangerous abode for any of the equine race than the stall of a modern stable, it would be impossible for the utmost stretch of the most excited malignity to imagine. Still, daily accidents, which must have occurred for centuries, seem to be incapable of instructing mankind, where the welfare of another and of an inferior being is concerned!

Animals have been lamed; have lost the power of vision; have bred terrible disorders, and have been found stretched in death upon the straw bed, in consequence of the folly which has persisted in building modern stables. Such accidents must, as a necessity, continue so long as these edifices are erected. They are totally unsuited for the creature which they torture, cripple, and confine. Yet, because such abominations are sanctioned by custom and approved by ignorance, it is far more than probable that the author's exposure of their unfitness will be read with amusement, and admitted to be just; but the scourge which is recommended by its existence and patronized for its convenience will still be perpetuated. It may continue to disgrace this country for more than another century, although the judicious outlay of a few shillings would greatly amend even modern stables. Banish the stalls, and divide the interior into loose boxes. Lower the mangers and the hay racks to the floor. Soften the food before presenting it to the quadruped; and abolish the loft, now placed over where the animals repose. Allow the entire space, from the ground to the roof, for the huge lungs to breathe in. Improve the drainage. Warm the building by means of a slow combustion and by water pipes. To effect all this should not cost very much; and, as his reward, man would gain the longer service of his slave, together with an inward approval, springing from a consciousness of having done his duty toward the meekness which Beneficence has intrusted to his keeping.

CHAPTER VIII.

THE SO-CALLED "INCAPACITATING VICES," WHICH ARE THE RESULTS OF INJURY OR OF DISEASE.

THE word "vice," when applied to the horse, represents any quality which may annoy the prejudices of the groom, or may prove displeasing to the expectations of the master. It is purely ridiculous to suppose the animal can possibly be "vicious." The simple nature of the quadruped is gifted with no power to distinguish good from evil. It lacks the imagination to conceive those acts which man esteems to be heroic or to be grand. Were the creature able to embody ideas, the race would possess the ability to combine; anything approaching to the present patient docility would then be exchanged for open rebellion against the earthly tyrant.

Human intelligence, however, seems to derive a strange pleasure from regarding the obedient and most forgiving horse as a "vicious," a savage, and a most relentless "brute." There seems to exist some happiness in the exhibition of those cruelties which such notions alone can justify. It is true that such unseemly contests do not invariably terminate in favor of him who always originates the strife. The master, who could by mildness have retained his power, by resorting to blows occasionally becomes worsted; but the horse, although it should prove victorious, always has to grieve over its triumph. The prowess of the quadruped draws down the heaviest punishment of other members of the race, an individual of which the animal has defeated.

A great many "accidents" would be avoided, and, probably, the amount of happiness permitted to mortals would not be materially lessened, could the populace be instructed to think a horse was endowed with senses, was gifted with feelings, and was able, in some degree, to appreciate motives. Such powers are enjoyed by all the higher grades of animal life. In asserting this, there is not the most distant desire to confound the living creature with the intellectual being. Reason believes in and can contemplate a futurity. The human eye takes easiest cognizance of forward objects. The vision of the horse does not behold objects directly in front of its head, but glances backward, without necessarily turning the face. Man can imagine events ere they are embodied facts. An animal's ideas are strictly limited by its individual experiences. By these, its mind is moulded and its conduct is shaped. It has no power to forget. The past, with it, is the present. To suffer once, is to endure a constant dread of suffering again. To be pained, is always to fear a repetition of the agony. What has been, *is*, so long as memory shall last; for the quadruped can conceive no future on which to fix its thoughts, or in the contemplation of which to escape from the misery that begirts its existence.

Would those persons who have no interest in any contrary opinion, adopt the above view of the subject, how very much of danger and of unpleasantness might the good people escape! It is not unusual to behold an elderly gentleman, of the highest respectability, flog most unmercifully, in the public street, some inoffensive steed, until a reddened face announces temper to be lost. Foot passengers look on the spectacle; but no one, even in thought, condemns the needless severity. Hospital surgeons, however, can testify to something more permanent than temper being occasionally sacrificed through these unseemly contests. In such cases, man has provoked his fate. Reason, in vain, shows a broad and pleasant path, where dwells security. Passion blinds humanity, pride justifies passion, and the refuge is unheeded!

Will the reader kindly grant the author patience while the present subject is pursued a little further? To prove the horse cannot, in any accepted meaning of the word, possibly be "vicious," it is only necessary to comprehend that vice of every form, whether it be lewdness, drunkenness, gluttony, or malice, always, in some gratification, seeks for a personal reward. It is no more than the concentration of selfishness. It always presupposes an intention. The difference between crime and insanity lies only in the idea of some recompense to be secured by the commission of a particular act and in sin without a motive. When the horse was created without ability to comprehend a future, the power to be "vicious" was, with the possibility of a contemplated motive, withheld. The creature, being unable to anticipate consequences, lacks incentive; therefore it can display no "vice," though it may exhibit insanity. The animal, however, may not always please its master; it is the "vice" of authority to call trivial offenses by harsher names than the actions in fairness should receive; but no man has, hitherto, stigmatized the horse, which he deems "vicious," as insane.

Having premised thus much, the author will attempt to explain some of the worst forms of equine "vice."

"Rick of the back" and "chink of the back" are terms which represent some indefinite injury to the spine of a horse. The quadruped is essentially a beast of burden. The load is commonly supported on the back. It is so, entirely, when the creature is used for saddle purposes; and, in the heavier species of draught, the balance always inclines toward the back of the "wheeler," while the spines of some coarse horses are sadly tried when they are obliged to trot back with a heavy springless cart, after the load has been delivered.

It is the general custom of this country to place young cart-horses between the chains, or, in other words, to employ such animals only in the capacity of leaders. The practice is equally wise and humane. The draught is not easier as the propelling force is situated distant from the load, but the pull then is entirely upon the collar, and no weight is allowed to rest upon the immatured and yielding spine of a youthful body. These benefits, however, are all rendered nugatory by the conduct of most carters. Such men are, generally, of Herculean proportions, and are conspicuous for no lightness of person.

The cart, dray, or wagon leaves the office with the driver in his proper place, walking beside the horses. Here he continues until the load is delivered; but, on the return journey, he is apt to experience fatigue. He does not reflect how far his individual sensations are likely to be shared by the animals which have been drawing some heavy burden during the time he has been simply walking at their sides. No! Seeking his own ease, he casts his body upon the back of the most forward, and, therefore, upon the youngest horse of the team. His seat is the loins, or directly upon the weakest portion of the vertebral chain. There he rides, squatting with his legs dangling upon one side. No doubt, the situation is pleasant; but where all is conjecture, the reader must decide how far the repetition of such an act may account for rick of the back being common among the heavier kind of horses.

It was otherwise with the old fly wagons of a former day. The driver of those vehicles used to have fastened behind his load a stout pony. When fatigued, the man would mount the supernumerary animal, and, riding beside his horses, would rest his own legs while he continued to guide his team; an act which the London carter is, by his position, disqualified for performing. While the driver rests, the "luck which attends on ignorance" must take care of the vehicle.

The spine of the horse, in a natural state, is characterized by a highly elastic property. As every form of mechanism is exposed to injury in proportion as it approaches to perfection, man should not feel surprised if the delicately-organized back of the animal is not exactly equal to all the usages unto which civilization has compelled it to submit. Indeed, when we feel how unscrupulous the human being can become, if urged onward by the pursuit of gain or prompted by a sense of personal indulgence, it will hardly provoke wonder that the creature doomed to be the helpmate of the avaricious, should occasionally suffer in their service.

Rick or chink of the back is among the most common and the least understood of equine affections. Its symptoms are confounded — one and the same name being employed to indicate every stage of the disorder, thus confusing inquiry. Those effects which result from organic change are regarded as the promptings of that "viciousness of spirit" with which it has pleased mankind to credit the horse. The liberality of mortal imagination is extreme, especially where causes have to be assumed. Grant man the right to conjecture, and there is no mystery in nature for which he cannot account. Thus, the sharp pangs of agony which induced the contortions of a dumb creature were conjectured to be the gratification of an innately "vicious disposition." This pretended explanation has remained unquestioned for ages, abusing the intellect of mankind and hardening the hearts of those whom it was thought to enlighten. No doubt many very worthy people will feel much inclined to quarrel with the book which presumes to question the interpretation that generations have approved and time has sanctified.

However, to expose the manner in which the personation of meekness has been abused by the arrogance of ignorance—certain animals are supposed to indulge a morbid habit, or "vicious" propensity, which is, by the lower orders, spoken of as "kidney dropping." Creatures thus viciously disposed are generally aged, and are devoted either to heavy draught or to harness purposes. They are sometimes met in those stables where horses are let out by the "hour, day, or job." One thus afflicted will be drawing a gig along some pleasant country road when "the vice" shall be suddenly displayed. The attacks may appear in rapid succession, when they render the life worthless; or they may only come on at distant intervals, being separated by long periods of apparent soundness. No jockey, however knowing he may be in his vocation, or however boastful he may be about "my 'sperience 'mong 'orses," can, by any visible sign, announce the day or foretell the hour when a particular quadruped will be afflicted with an attack of "kidney dropping."

The horse shall be harnessed to some light vehicle, within which may be seated some tradesman, by whose side smiles the eldest daughter of a numerous family. The animal is not overloaded, and seems to be journeying pleasantly at its own pace. He who holds the reins is delighted; while she who sits beside him ever and anon leans forward to pat the croup of "the dear pet." The sun is shining; the birds are singing; the trees are bright with new foliage; and the country smells most pleasantly fresh; when, suddenly, the gig is brought sharply up, and "the wicked beast" is discovered squatting upon its haunches like a dog.

A "KIDNEY DROPPER."

This is an unnatural position with the horse. It is perfectly true, animals are made to assume it in the circle of most amphitheaters; but if the reader remembers, he also beheld men, in the same place, put their arms and legs in positions which were quite as unnatural to humanity in general as sitting on their haunches possibly could be to the community of the equine race. What, therefore, may have been exhibited at a circus signifies nothing, when regarded in its fitness for universal application; in all other spheres, sitting on the haunches, when exemplified by the horse, must be accepted as proof of bodily derangement.

If the attitude of the animal be observed, the hind limbs will be seen to have fallen in such positions as suggest no notion of comfort or of design. They may cross one another, or they may be sprawled out on either side of the body; they are never arranged with that grace and care which indicate the attitude to have been deliberately assumed. Moreover, should the skin be pricked with the point of a pin, no sign of sensibility is usually elicited from the hind quarters. Strike the prostrated members, and no evidence of pain follows the blow. The posterior portions of the body, obviously, are dead to this world and to its malice.

However, do not fuss about the horse; allow the sufferer to remain undisturbed where it has fallen. Have patience with the distress which no cruelty can quicken. Loosen the harness; remove the shafts; procure some water, and permit sensibility to allay its parching thirst. After a short space, the quadruped may get up of its own accord. No time has been lost; but disease has not been aggravated by needless torture. When the creature rises, the fit has passed; but the author doubts if the recovery can then be pronounced complete. He would, certainly, brave "an accident" who should essay to drive a horse but recently recovered from an attack of "kidney dropping," though this hazard may be frequently incurred with apparent impunity.

Allow the injured quadruped to remain in the stable, undisturbed for the night. The following morning will be time enough for its examination; for the disease under which the horse languishes is of a nature that cannot be affected by the lapse of a few hours.

The next day, having selected a piece of clear ground, cover the spot thickly with straw, and have the horse led on to it. The services of a veterinary surgeon are not imperative. The proprietor may himself conduct the investigation: or, should he feel distrustful of his own ability, any person possessed of the necessary amount of confidence may undertake the active duty. All idle spectators should be first requested to retire. Then the investigator takes his position as close to the quadruped as possible. He runs the forefinger and thumb gently over the superior spinous processes of the vertebral chain, or down the center of

TEST FOR RICK OF THE BACK.

the back. This action is repeated several times, additional force being brought to bear with each succeeding trial, until the whole strength of the operator is exerted. While he is doing this, the person who undertakes the investigation fixes his attention on the head of the horse. If, upon pressure being made on any particular spot, the ears are laid upon the neck, or the crest is suddenly elevated, the fact must be mentally noted. The trial should be renewed, and if the like symptoms be elicited. the conclusion naturally is, that the seat of injury lies immediately under or very near to the place indicated.

This point being ascertained, the operator puts a hand on either side of the tender part, and casts his full weight suddenly upon the spine. Such a proceeding, to be demonstrative, must be rapid and energetic. Horses, under the sudden pang thus produced, have shrieked in agony. Generally, animals crouch under the torture, and burst forth into copious perspirations. The author knows of no instance where a desire to employ the teeth has been exhibited, although there is no predicating in what manner a creature may behave under the powerful wrench of actual torment. He, however, who undertakes such an inquiry, must be prepared for every eccentricity; and, while regretting the necessity which obliges agony to be inflicted on a gentle and a timid creature, he should also be far above those coarse and brutal punishments which are too frequently indulged to check the writhings of the potent suffering.

The affair is thus decided. The spine has been injured, and the spinal cord which it sheathes is also involved in the lesion. Horses in such a condition are commonly, with that utter want of morality which in every species of horse transactions appears equally to sway all degrees of the human mind,—such animals are commonly cast upon the market, or publicly disposed of by auction. The cause of sale is willfully concealed: the purchaser is designedly imposed on, and his life is knowingly endangered. Persons of every class, from most noblemen to the ordinary tradesman, engage in this form of arrant cheatery. They swindle their sense of rectitude by giving no warranty at the time of sale; but the law presumes that everything sold contemplates a fitness for certain purposes; whereas a horse liable to an instantaneous loss of power in its limbs is dangerous in any employment. Yet so flimsy an excuse seems to justify the reputedly *honorable* man extracting, possibly, the last penny from the pocket of or imposing upon some struggling and needy individual.

The animal, being sold, is soon found to be worthless; it speedily becomes the property of the lower class of horse-copers, to whom that which they call a "kidney dropper" is a real prize. The quadruped is soid "cheap" to people of worldly respectability; but it is seldom retained long by its new owners. It is rebought, for little more than its real value, by its former proprietors, to be once more palmed off on some aspiring equestrian. After such a manner—selling in the dearest market and buying in the cheapest, a maxim of very questionable morality—a large profit has been realized by a carcass which was actually worthless.

The author, never having dissected the spine of a "kidney dropper," cannot positively say in what condition of parts the disease resides. A knowledge of anatomy, however, aided by a comprehension of the symptoms, demonstrates the vertebral chain is the seat of injury; while the want of motion which affects the hinder limbs indicates the spinal marrow to be suddenly pressed upon. Subsequent recovery likewise proves the injury to the nervous center is of no more serious a character; while the perfect restoration of the animal's power shows that the pressure is either caused by displacement, or by such a partial fracture as rest will enable nature to surmount. This explanation, deduced from observation, and based upon inferences drawn from the study of effects, will to most persons appear so probable as to be perfectly satisfactory. Still, there do exist minds whose faith in an antiquated name it is hardly possible for any argument to destroy; the generality of readers, therefore, must grant the author patience, while he, most probably in vain, attempts to disabuse such persons of their strange belief.

The term "kidney dropping" is an ignorant combination of words to which no absolute meaning can be attached. The kidneys are no more than the renal glands. The horse which falls exhibits no sign of urinary disease. These organs are usually healthy; of that fact the writer has positive information. The kidneys, moreover, are not *specially* endowed with motor nerves; no physiologist has hitherto asserted that these glands are in any way concerned in the movements of the body. The renal organs have, by the French, been unwarrantably removed, without the general sensation or the body's motion being affected. When the horse drops, not only is motion gone from the hind limbs, but sensibility is lost. The quarters have dropped, not in accordance with the will of the creature, but because the posterior division of the body was released from the control of the sensorium, or was suddenly cut off from the influence of volition.

The spinal marrow regulates the motions of the limbs, being subject only to the dictation of the brain. Volition and motion are in these organs associated, but not absolutely united. They both are capable of separate existence, though the mechanical derangement which destroys the one usually puts an end to the other. Nevertheless, they can exist apart. Convulsion exhibits motion, as independent of the will; while painful paralysis displays sensibility increased, although power of movement has been lost. In "kidney dropping," consciousness is retained;

but motion and sensibility have departed from one-half of the trunk. This result indicates the nervous current to be partially checked, and points to the great medium of transmission as the seat of injury.

There is, however, another form of chink in the back, where the spinal marrow is in no vast degree involved, and in which the animal exhibiting the affection is not generally devoted to harness purposes. The horse is commonly showy in appearance, and is usually disposed of exclusively for saddle uses. But the existence of a disease is not denoted by any outward sign; therefore its presence is sneered at as a positive impossibility. Quadrupeds, thus disordered, are, by the generality of horsemen, condemned as "irreclaimably vicious."

One of the bones of the spine has been rendered loose in consequence of the ligaments being overstrained; the animal has been abused in some manner. The ligaments, when in this condition, are acutely painful; though no visual disorder may be observable to the post-mortem examiner, nevertheless the slightest weakness in such a structure may, during life, occasion the severest agony. The bone is not fractured; but one of the vertebræ, through the leverage of its superior spinous process, may have been wrenched slightly to one side. This may not affect the appearance of the quadruped; neither may it elicit signs of pain when the weight is evenly seated upon the back; therefore, only during the act of mounting, the drag then being entirely to one side, it occasions the most poignant anguish.

The horse, being dumb, of course cannot explain its sensations; nor can it appeal to the forbearance of its master. Its ailments are entirely subjected to the merciful consideration of man. The animal's actions, therefore, are always liable to be misconstrued; the promptings of torture are frequently confounded with the exhibitions of the worst forms of "vice." Thus, a creature with the ligaments of the back strained is always condemned as an inveterate kicker; because the drag, produced by the weight of the rider resting on one stirrup, occasions so sharp an agony as alarms the quadruped, and naturally excites a determination to repel some imaginary enemy. The creature, consequently, commences to "lash out" with its utmost energy. This violence is repeated so often as the owner has occasion to remount. The action is always sudden, and not to be inferred from the previous aspect or behavior of the nag. It is, therefore, attended with the greater danger, not only to the proprietor, but also to those who may be collected about the horse.

A good illustration of the above facts occurred a few years back, in front of certain spacious "rooms," then much frequented by "the fashionable world." A cavalry officer, recently returned from India, went to hear a morning concert at the place just alluded to. There he met some old friends, who had changed their residence since he had left the country, being then located at Richmond. The party had ridden to London; the military gentleman was pressed to return, and to spend a pleasant day at the suburban villa. A servant was dispatched to hire a horse; the man soon returned with a rather small, but very showy, black nag.

NEVER MOUNT A STRANGE HORSE IN A CROWDED LOCALITY.

The officer thought, before the concert was ended, he would retire and form the acquaintance of an animal he was shortly to ride for several miles. It was well he did so; for no sooner was his foot placed in the stirrup, than what previously appeared to be a remarkably steady quadruped began to "lash out." The action was continued, creating terrible confusion among the crowd which thronged the street, and ultimately throwing the would-be rider. The military gentleman was probably more hurt in feelings than in person by the incident; although the latter circumstance formed an excuse for not journeying to Richmond, and the occurrence, on the following morning, was circulated throughout London as a newspaper paragraph, bearing a heading of "SERIOUS ACCIDENT TO A CAVALRY OFFICER."

Violent, however, as may be the resistance provoked while the foot is in the stirrup, the seat of the saddle is no sooner attained than composure is restored. When the rider is once fairly on the back, the steed assumes its natural timidity, its docility, and its obedience. It is then transformed into all the most fastidious proprietor could desire. That circumstance has induced some horsemen who were more thoughtful than the generality of the race, to change the habit usual in this country. Such persons have tried the effect of mounting upon the wrong side; this has usually, for a certain time, been attended with perfect success; but the custom, after a space, has seemed to involve the sound ligaments, when the kicking has been renewed with more than double vehemence. A horse which kicks in the way described, should always be transferred to harness work, when no vast weight being upon the back, the quadruped generally behaves admirably.

Rick or chink in the back is, however, the common property of creatures of heavy draught, and, with such a description of horse, the consequences are usually more marked and much more severe. The reader will readily imagine that a "kidney dropper," falling suddenly while pulling a weighty load, can hardly escape "accident." Therefore, quadrupeds of the coarser breed, and thus afflicted, rapidly come into the possession of those who do not scruple to trade with misery; and, as this form of disease enables the sufferer to appear with a blooming coat, as well as with a carcass carrying a quantity of fat, the copers often reap a rich harvest by their unscrupulous dishonesty.

A common cause of these accidents is the thoughtlessness or the greediness of horse proprietors. It has become almost a custom, with needy masters, to send out one-horse carts upon two wheels with long reins attached to the harness. The motive which induces such silly behavior is obvious enough. The tradesman imagines that by the animal being hurried back after the load is delivered, time can be saved. He does not consider that the limbs, which have been strained dragging some fearful weight to a particular spot, may, before another task of magnitude is imposed, possibly require the comparatively easy walk back to recover the full use of their functions. He probably, and it is hoped actually, has never reflected that perpetual fatigue soon exhausts, and ultimately disables, animal energy.

The cart horse, moreover, being forced to quicken its pace, is urged beyond the habits and the uses for which man has bred the creature. It is compelled to execute a duty for the performance of which its bodily formation renders it totally unsuited. The poor animal that is called upon to fulfill opposite uses, generally endures the shorter period: because of the excessive labor it is obliged to undergo. The custom, therefore, accords with the saying, which illustrates waste and extravagance, by supposing a candle to be lighted at both ends. The wretched horse is now a cart horse, loaded to the extent of its ability; next, it is expected to display the activity of a gig horse, although it is harnessed to what badly represents the lighter vehicle; while, the long day of continued toil being ended, the slave is required to trot briskly homeward with a crowded load of human laborers.

The dismissed cart is generally well burdened, after the hour for striking work has arrived. The men usually leave off their toil as the first stroke of the clock is heard; but no such relaxation is permitted to the creature which, of the many over-worked bodies, has toiled the hardest and needs rest the most. The quietude of London suburbs is regularly broken with the thud! thud! thud! produced by the heavy shafts pulling down the chain, which has been jolted upward by the ungainly trot of the tired slave. The sound declares the force which falls every few moments upon the same part of a living spine. The falling of a single drop of water, long continued, on the same place, can occasion direst agony. The Inquisition illustrated that fact. But the cart is heavier than many drops of water. Any one who has beheld a spectacle of this description, can have hardly failed to observe the faintness, mingled with suffering, which propels the load. The driver commonly stands up near to the front; he jags the reins and loudly cracks the long whip, that fright may quicken the movement of those limbs which tire seems to glue to the stones over which they pass.

THE COMMON CAUSES OF RICK OF THE BACK IN HEAVY HORSES.

Rick or chink in the back is, generally, generated by that want of sympathy shown by the community of proprietors in regard to their property in horse flesh. It would be a legitimate cause for wonder, were horses not a hazardous investment, when breathing and living frames are subjected to the united effects of ignorance and of prejudice

Upon the earliest indication being perceived of the spine having been badly injured, the horse should be instantly thrown up for at least six months. The animal ought not to have a layer of pitch, rosin, etc. smeared thickly over the back, and be turned out to take its chance upon a green diet. But it should be placed in a roomy, loose box: it should have the hair cut off close over the seat of injury, and the place should be constantly moistened by means of cloths dipped in a lotion, composed of tincture of arnica, two ounces, and water, one pint. This remedy, with softened food of the most supporting kind, should constitute the treatment for the first month of recovery.

At the end of that period, we may assume that inflammation has been subdued; thereupon the measures adopted may be changed. Some compound soap liniment should be rubbed on the surface every morning. Should the application blister the skin, the liniment must be withheld for a time; but so soon as friction can be quietly endured, the stimulant must be renewed. All this while, the quadruped should be well fed; but medicine should be strictly withheld, grass and bran mashes being solely employed to regulate the bowels if their action be sluggish.

When morbid sensibility no longer exists in the spine, and moderate pressure with the fingers can be borne upon the back, the liniment may be discontinued; but the restoration is to finish with the repeated use of liquid blisters. One side of the spine, near to the seat of injury, is first to be acted upon; when the action of the vesicatory appears to be subsiding, the other half of the back should be attacked. This plan must be pursued till the fifth month has expired, the horse being sustained upon the best and most nutritive food. After this period has elapsed, a handful of ground oak bark should be mingled with each allowance of provender. The animal, during all this time, never being flurried, or allowed to leave its ample stable.

Upon recovery, the quadruped ought never to be employed for that same kind of service in which the injury was received. No weight should, subsequently, be placed upon the back; for the spine which has been once injured, can never, by human art, be restored to its pristine soundness. However greatly the animal may have been prized, even as a hunter, it is safer and much more profitable to doom the steed to the collar, in which last employment old hunters particularly delight in exhibiting their highly-prized excellences of action. Many a horse that appears in the London streets running before some brougham, and which, by the gayety of its spirit, excites the admiration of the foot passengers, will, after death, be found to have one or more bones of the spine joined by osseous deposit, proving that the back, during life, must have suffered serious injury.

Horse owners, however, should be very careful, not knowingly to risk cnink or rick of the back; for such an "accident," according to its intensity, may reduce the animal of fabulous price to an article which shall literally be almost valueless. It brings down the steed which excited universal envy, to the cripple which no honest man would sell, and which no prudent man would keep. The mischief once established, too often sets science at defiance, for the rick, when bad, is terribly apt to terminate in fearful fracture of the spine.

THE PATENT TRACE-SHAFT.

The above illustration is copied from the heading to a bill which announces a patented invention, which is manufactured by Messrs. Gibson & Co., of Coventry Street. The novelty consists in the shafts being so made as to render the employment of traces unnecessary when the animal is driven in single harness. The weight of the vehicle, or so much of it as usually rests upon the back, is dependent entirely from the collar. For horses troubled with any of those "vices" which indicate the spine to be affected, this kind of harness affords, at all events, the most rational hope of working such creatures without provoking the annoying and the dangerous symptom.

When it is remembered that all animals which have been worn out under the saddle, old hacks and hunters, are doomed to end their lives in the more ignoble duties of propulsion, it is not surprising to find many of the quadrupeds, sold for double or single harness, are affected with those complaints which indicate the back to be disordered. The worst exhibitions are confined to gig horses. Few carriage or brougham horses are thus disabled; that fact almost proves the author's inference, as well as demonstrates the utility of that novelty which was in the last illustration introduced to the notice of the reader

As heavy quadrupeds are likely to be similarly diseased, the carter should be informed of the fact, and cautioned against ever riding on the backs of his teamsters. So also with lighter animals, the groom should be forbidden to mount the horses which are very liable to this misfortune. The shafts of a cart are of course calculated to aggravate this malady; but such a horse may perform easy or reasonable labor between the chains for a long succession of years; only, when the pull is severe, the driver should go to the head of the disordered teamster, to prevent any undue strain upon the back, or it would be certainly better if, during the period of exertion, the chains were unhooked.

It is strange, when the importance of the spine to the utility of the animal is considered, and when the well-known fact is regarded that the lowest class of copers make a species of property out of horses suffering from rick of the back, that this particular region receives no special attention during a quadruped's soundness being subjected to the test of an ordinary veterinary examination! The creature's head, tail, eyes, teeth, shoulders, haunches, limbs, feet, etc. would all be scrupulously investigated; but the back, on the soundness of which the utility of the body must depend, would probably be only honored with a passing notice.

Animals, however, which are ricked in the back, are generally sold through one of those Horse Auction Marts that abound in the metropolis. Such places offer great facilities to dishonest practices, and afford much encouragement to the class of copers. These persons never care to possess a sound horse. They have always some bargain ready to be imposed upon a novice; and the ignorant in horse flesh are ever eager to snap at any supposed "awful sacrifice." The uninitiated is a frequenter of auctions. Being there, he walks down the gangways, staring at the equine chattels; going dangerously near to their heels, but not venturing up to the head of any quadruped. It is not long that this person is permitted to stroll unattended in such a sphere. His notice is soon directed to "one of the right sort." The groom is ordered to bring the animal into the yard, and show "its action" to the gentleman.

While the groom is putting on the bridle and removing the cloth, the uninitiated accompanies his new companion into the yard. The coming of the animal is soon announced by the cracking of numerous whips. The poor creature is hurried and flurried about the little space outside the stables, or it is made to prance and caper along the public street. The intention is not to exhibit the natural pace, for no person possibly could judge of a horse when the animal is thus circumstanced. Fear will conceal the presence of disease, and the symptoms of alarm are, in the quadruped, readily mistaken for the evidences of spirit

The novice should shun such society; and the gentleman deserves small pity who ventures into such a locality. Let the person who desires to possess a horse, and who can afford to pay for the luxury he covets, enter the premises of some respectable dealer. Let him be prepared to exchange a fair sum for a sound and serviceable animal. Let him never walk into the yard, and wait the appearance of the quadruped; but rather let the would-be purchaser remain near the stall, and observe attentively the groom while the man is putting on the bridle. Some creatures are alarmed when a hand approaches the head—an indication, either that the sight is imperfect, that severe punishment has been inflicted, or that the brain may be diseased. This symptom also warrants other suspicions; and it is never suggestive of health or of good treatment. The precautions taken by the man, when going toward the head, will also be characteristic, and may inform the spectator of very much concerning the educated temper and disposition of the nag he contemplates acquiring.

BACKING ON TO THE GANGWAY.

Such things, however, being noted, the stranger must still retain his situation. Some horses, though not absolutely "ricked," are nevertheless stiff in the back. Such quadrupeds are unpleasant to the rider, and are unable to turn in the stall; but whenever their removal becomes imperative, they are backed out on to the gangway, and then turned toward the door. A stiffened spine can be no recommendation. but it may fairly be accepted as evidence that the animal has either been overweighted or has, in its time, done some hard work. It is invariably detrimental to the value; for, the vertebræ being the base of the anatomical body, their healthy condition is of the greatest possible importance toward even an approach to soundness.

It is highly improbable that an animal with a decided rick of the back should find admission into the stables of any respectable dealer; but there are numerous places, termed Commission Stables, which a novice unacquainted with names and localities may, from outward appearances, easily mistake for premises of the purest character. Should the imaginary personage, whose conduct the author has supposed to be the subject of remark, have entered such a stable, much art will be employed to persuade him to leave the building. If the gentleman should be firm, and refuse to retire, possibly the proprietor may be seized with a sudden fancy to show another horse; but any trick of this nature will be readily detected, and the fresh animal, though subsequently led into the yard, should never be looked at.

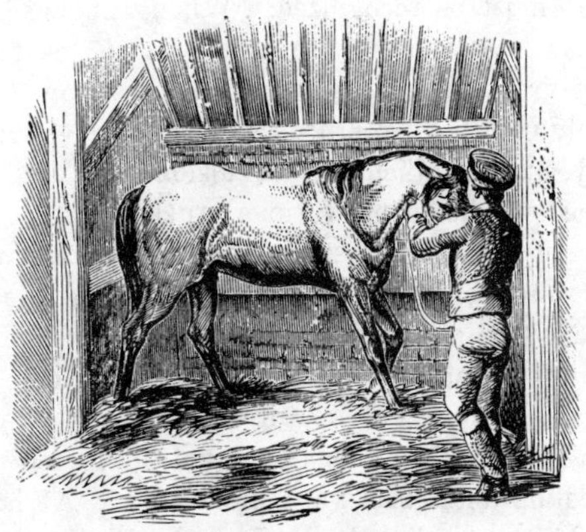

TURNING IN THE STALL.

A horse cannot turn in the stall without twisting the back. Some animals, however, can turn quickly in one direction, whereas an attempt to flex the body the contrary way will produce the acutest anguish. Therefore, when the groom bids the horse come round, the gentleman should observe the mode in which the act is accomplished. Should the quadruped's head be turned from the door, such a fact may be regarded as suspicious; for grooms always prefer the shortest roads, and trivial matters, where horses are concerned, often lead to important discoveries.

The diseases of the horse are not yet thoroughly understood. Mankind have acquired a habit of accepting words, without insisting that the ideas such terms represent shall be strictly defined. No word is more common in the mouths of horsemen than "jibbing." It, however, does not specially imply one act; for there are many kinds of behavior which are designated as "jibbing." Thus, a horse which is unable to start, is called "a jibber." A quadruped which, in the middle of a journey, shall be suddenly impelled to move in a backward direction, is said to "jib." The animal which, upon hearing the command to proceed, will commence throwing up its head, and, spite of chastisement, shall bear in the opposite direction, is also supposed to have learned the "vice" of "jibbing."

"Jibbing" of every kind appears to be no "vice," but a nervous disorder,—a sort of equine epilepsy. A word, spoken sharply, can summon the attack, which generally deprives the animal of all power of motion, or forces it to move in a direction the opposite of the road on which it wishes to proceed. The movements are independent of the will; and if any person will attentively inspect the countenance of the horse, when in the act of "jibbing," the author imagines the real character of the supposed "vice" must be recognized. When "jibbing" is exhibited, a spasmodic fit has possession of the frame. It is useless to flog or to inflict other tortures. The attack will last a certain time, and then, perhaps, suddenly vanish. No brutality can shorten its duration, though cruelty, possibly, may lengthen the convulsion.

On such occasions, however, various cruelties are commonly perpetrated; but severity has then lost its power to quicken timidity. The lash has ceased to influence; while the human voice, though sent forth in volume and exerted in the bitterest execration, no longer is invested with the attributes of authority. The body is acted upon by a power higher than mortal sway. The creature is then carried by disease above this world's malice. The whip or the signal to proceed may elicit only a staggering motion, or a backward movement. At last the spell is broken. The ability to guide the limbs suddenly is regained: but the brain is congested and the senses confused. The creature, upon the first partial recovery, may exhibit a desire to bolt—may, for an uncertain period, be all but unconscious. Sometimes it will recover its powers suddenly, almost as though its previous condition had been assumed. On other occasions it may, under some impulse, tear onward, regardless of the road, as though it sought to fly the scene of its late suffering, or endeavor to lose the agony of convulsion in the rapidity of motion.

The probability that such an act may conclude the fit of jibbing, instructs us in the folly of adding the irritation of man's cruelty to the pain necessarily accompanying acute disease. Severity can only lend violence to the impulse which is almost certain to succeed the attack.

It may endanger the life of the driver, but it cannot shorten the duration of the fit. Every kind of brutality has been speculated in without effect. Such treatment, most probably, has prolonged insensibility; for noise, confusion, or agony is not likely to be sedative to the nervous system which a word has morbidly excited. Yet such practices are generally adopted. Nay, the author has heard of a professional man who, residing near London, possessed a fine animal which was thus afflicted.

A POPULAR CURE FOR THE IMAGINARY VICE OF "JIBBING."

This person actually had some straw kindled under his quadruped's body, and, to quicken what he called "an obstinate vice," partially roasted the breathing flesh of his living property! So monstrous an artifice was successful on the first occasion; but, upon repetition, it ceased to operate. Such a custom is not unusual among the uneducated boors of distant villages; but the writer had hoped that no vexation could have induced an individual, possessing the most distant claim upon the name of gentleman, to adopt so inhuman and useless a resort.

The horse is a gentle creature; it has no courage; it can display no resolution. Its impulses always incline it to flee from danger. It is made up of alarms, and a child's puny hand may guide its huge strength. But the history of the animal supplies too many instances where the perversity of mankind has mistaken the prompting of disease for the display of malice. It is disgraceful to the boasted civilization of the present age that, while knowledge has much benefited every sphere of human legislation, the errors, the practices, and the brutalities of the last century should be in full operation,—where the scant necessities of the most gentle, the most submissive, and the most valuable of man's earthly helpmates are concerned.

Jibbing is most common among harness horses, the faces of which are disguised and partially concealed by the blinkers. Were the countenance exposed, its expression could hardly be misinterpreted by any person who cared to observe its indications. But nothing can obscure the comprehension of mankind like prejudice. This weapon has been frequently employed against the life of human beings; but animals, to this hour, are tortured by its operation. Could the countenance of a horse, when in the act of jibbing, be calmly contemplated, all belief in "voluntary vice" would be at once dispelled. The eye is strained inward; the teeth are firmly set; the nostrils are dilated; the breathing is spasmodic; and the muscles are rigid.

THE COUNTENANCE OF A HORSE DURING A FIT OF JIBBING.

There is, however, one symptom which, although expressive of terror, agony, or faintness, all horsemen are agreed in regarding as the declaration of a "vicious intention." Such an indication is the backward position of the ears, or the laying of those organs upon the animal's neck. The forward carriage, or the "pricking" of those members is recognized as expressive of delight, of gayety, or of attention. What, then, should the backward position truthfully signify? What ought sense to imply, from the falling of a part the upright bearing of which is interpreted to be the sign of liveliness? Yet, how many tender-hearted gentlemen, abused by the prejudices they inherited, will, when they observe the ears laid back, unhesitatingly cause the lash to sting the body which, probably, was far from contemplating mischief!

When an animal is thus afflicted, never pursue the course which is usually adopted. All noise should be prevented; no flurry near to or about the creature should be permitted. Do not use the whip or jag the reins: relinquish both. Order those within the vehicle immediately to dismount. Undo the bearing rein: loosen the harness. If possible, remove the quadruped from the shafts. Go to the head: speak soothingly; pat and caress the agitated frame. Procure some cold water; soak a thick cloth in the liquid, and lay it over the brain and upon the eyes. Sponge out the mouth and nostril; then empty the vessel, by dashing the remaining fluid into the animal's face. When the incapacitating stage is subsiding, have ready two powerful men, who, placed at the head, shall prevent the disposition to bolt from being indulged. This done, return the horse to the stable. Never hazard riding behind a creature which has recently been afflicted with "equine epilepsy."

Such an animal is best put out of its misery at once, as the attempted remedy occupies too much time, is too expensive, and is far too uncertain in its result, to be prudently adopted. However, should the horse be young, it may be kept on prepared food for eighteen months—not turned out to grass; but stabled, properly exercised, and fed on the best, in the hope that nature will, with maturity, banish the disease. Such persons, however, as will drive a jibber, which merely exhibits a tardiness at starting, should be particular never to have the coat singed or clipped; for cold, acting upon the large surface of exposed integument, is very likely to provoke an attack. The horse, when brought to the door, should be briskly walked, and the journey, when commenced, should never start off at a tearing pace; but should begin most gently, and very gradually become more speedy. Such treatment, with carefully prepared food, plenty of old beans, bran mashes for laxatives, and an occasional tonic, is the best means the author knows of to render the quadruped ultimately useful.

The power of kindness is, perhaps, shown most strongly in the case of the horse thus affected. The love of the creature for the individual who is fond of it, is not well or truly characterized when spoken of as affection: it is something more than such a general term can represent: it amounts to positive devotion. Even when the fit is strongest, and all ordinary sounds are lost to the animal's sense, the voice of the person who has been constantly kind will evidently be responded to. His caresses will soothe at a moment when the most potent pangs would be powerless: his presence will restrain the wildness which naturally ensues upon the first dawn of reviving consciousness. Whereas he who is habitually a careless or a harsh master, in whose hand whip and reins are equally instruments of torture, may, only by his appearance, induce the attack; and his foot upon the vehicle is likely to generate the agitation which shall assuredly bring on the disease.

But the man who would win the love of his steed, and is fond of the animal, should be a frequent visitor to its abode. That simple or negative quality which consists in the absence of actual cruelty, will answer no end. The human being, thus distinguished, only elicits the passive indifference by which his treatment is characterized. It is feeling, which even in animals, responds to feeling. The horse and the dog love those who like to take pains with them, or submit to trouble for their sakes. The two animals are alike in this respect. How fond the dog, which may for years have slept before the fire and grown enormously fat upon the plentiful meals supplied by an indulgent but an indifferent master,—how attached the animal speedily becomes to any person who, though a stranger, will devote some time to the teaching of little canine tricks! So also with the horse; the best way, indeed the only way, to win the entire love of this creature, is to expend some labor in brightening its intelligence.

To return to the matter at present especially under consideration. The jibbing which is confined to a delay at starting may be annoying, but it is seldom dangerous. The animal which merely moves backward, when commanded to proceed, may vex the driver, but the malady, being known, its consequences can, in a great measure, be guarded against. There is, however, one form of this disease which renders any animal very far from a safe possession. It is, where the horse will suddenly stand still in the middle of a journey, and commence backing. The more inopportune the place for such an exhibition, the more likely is the visitation to be brought on. A crowded thoroughfare or a dangerous road,—any incident calculated to excite or to alarm the steed, will assuredly produce a display of the worst symptoms.

A medical gentleman, of whose acquaintance the author is justifiably proud,—and whose practice laid upon the western coast,—one evening, after a hard day's work, which had tired all his horses and fairly knocked up their master, was, before his boots were pulled off, apprised that a wealthy lady, and resident eighteen miles distant from his pharmacy, required his immediate attendance. There was no choice but to obey such a summons. The gentleman's own horses he could not think of compelling over such a distance. Therefore the place was scoured, and at last an individual was discovered who was willing to lend, for a consideration, "the very best horse in the whole country." The doctor was soon mounted, and progressing to his destination, at the rate of twelve miles an hour. The distance had nearly been accomplished, when the road ran close to the sea. It was in fact no more than a broad ledge cut in the side of a precipitous cliff. This spot being reached, and the heart of the rider made glad at the prospect of soon accomplishing his journey, the steed suddenly came to a stand. It first trembled all over. The gentleman endeavored to soothe the creature, which he perceived was suffering, but which he concluded was alarmed. He was thus engaged, when the nag commenced to back toward the sea. Whip and spur were tried to no purpose. The impulse could not be checked or altered; and the writer's friend, perceiving his danger, had barely time to throw himself out of the saddle, when the horse toppled over the cliff, and was discovered a mangled mass on the following morning.

JIBBING.

The various aspects which disease can assume, of course are multiform, and unfortunately these, when exhibited by the horse, are all exposed to the arbitrary conclusions of prejudice. Men of education appear, in all that concerns the stable, to passively resign their intellects into the hands of the groom, and to be swayed by the hardihood of assertion, or to be ruled by the conjectures of selfishness. Thus the declarations of morbid sensibility are accepted and spoken of as the antics of the "rankest vice." "Jibbing" has been punished as the instigation of malice; the chastisement has been inflicted without mercy, and has continued for many ages; but cruelty has not been able to check the exhibition of disease. The symptom is to this hour as general as it was in previous centuries. It still delays the vehicle, after the driver is ready to start: it often propels the wheels in a contrary direction to that the coachmen desire they should travel: it commonly stays the wayfarer, when eager to conclude his journey. At the door of the mansion, in the public street and on the high road, the signs of the malady are frequently to be witnessed.

So it is with the indications of various disorders. The horses of the existing race of proprietors are, for a life, doomed to subsist on the same substances: four or five times a day, dried grass, oats, and a few beans are placed before them: some have chopped straw, and, in exceptional cases, prepared food; but that being only allowed for the last meal on Saturday night, does not interfere with the monotony of diet. Now, a sameness in the articles consumed, as medical men now recognize, disorders the digestion; but when aided by a want of exercise, a total absence of amusement, and an impure residence, perhaps no better means could be invented to derange the tenderest radicles of being. The sympathy which exists between the stomach and the skin is now so universally understood that it will generate no surprise if the creature, thus housed, imprisoned, and sustained, should be occasionally troubled with an obstinate cutaneous affection.

Stabled horses often are the victims of an acutely sensitive condition of the integument. Yet the possible existence of such a state is never admitted by the groom, because the affection is unaccompanied by any outward sign. There is no tenderness displayed when the hand is laid upon the body. The coat looks bloomingly. The scurf is not developed in increased quantity. The hair does not prove loose or fall off. There is nothing visible for ignorance to perceive. The animal feeds well, and seems in the highest possible condition. The groom cannot, therefore, believe in the presence of disease. Nevertheless, the quadruped may acutely suffer, especially during the spring and autumn. It may even, by the irritation, be provoked to gnaw large patches from the sensitive covering of the body; but the more common form of the disease urges the poor horse to destroy the heavy rug in which stable attendants are fond of wrapping their charges, before quitting them for the night.

What precise form the irritation assumes, it is impossible to ascertain; but no sooner is the quadruped clothed up, than it begins to fidget. Its legs are in almost perpetual motion, and the body repeatedly leans with violence against the trevise. The creature is evidently uneasy, and the animal's eye watches the groom until that individual, having finished his work, retires to the consolation of the adjacent public house.

No sooner is the animal certain of being alone, than it commences to tear off the hateful clothing. Large portions are seized between the teeth, and these are rent off with an energy which borders upon madness. Nor is the mental fever, which actuates the horse, to be pacified, so long as a vestige of the hated envelope remains to be removed. The passion seems to be very engrossing while it exists; for, during the period, anybody may enter the building, and even approach the irritated quadruped, without his presence being observed. But, the feat being ended, the creature looks around, seems to recover its recognitions, nibbles different portions of its coat, licks the coolest parts of its manger, being evidently thirsty, and ultimately lies down, apparently well satisfied with its recent performance.

TEARING THE CLOTHING.

The recognized remedy for such a condition does not regard the morbid state out of which the destruction arises; but it consists in placing upon the back of the horse a garment which shall pain the lips, tongue, palate and gums when it is grasped by the teeth. Cloths of such a description are manufactured of coarse horse-hair, and are commonly kept by most harness-makers, so general is their adoption. After such a fashion, the biting impulse may be sometimes checked; but there are quadrupeds which seem to be goaded to still greater violence by the device. Other animals, though the cloth of hair acts as a preventive, become restless, and evidently pine under the remedy: their appetite fails: their spirit vanishes, and their flesh wastes: nay, the author has known the introduction of the favorite cure to be followed by an internal and a fatal form of disease.

Why should all inhabitants of the stable be subjected to a sameness of treatment? Why should all horses be expected to consume the same food; to eat the like quantities of provender; to drink a particular amount of water, and to be clothed in uniform, when left for the night? It may please the eye of the groom to behold the animals all wrapped up and bedded down to match, as he quits the stable for the night; yet, where life is concerned, something stronger should regulate arrangements than the gratification of a servant's prejudice.

To propitiate the inclinations or the whims of a retainer, constituted no part of the motive which caused the stables to be erected. Such places are professedly built *for* horses, and the animals, therefore, should be primarily regarded. Yet, wherefore oblige a quadruped to be covered up with a rug, when the creature, by a nightly destruction of the wrapper, asserts the envelope to be objectionable? Why compel an unwilling steed to endure that which is not requisite on the score of decency; which cannot be adopted on any plea of appearance; and which, in the most emphatic manner, is declared not pleasant to the life on whose body it is suspended?

It is impossible to comprehend that the groom possesses any excess of modesty which can be offended at the notion of a horse sleeping naked in the stall; and if the absence of covering is agreeable to the party which is principally concerned, it seems odd a reasonable being should insist that a contrary practice shall be adopted. Still, persist these individuals certainly do; and even carry their persistence to other particulars. The skins of the equine race are as various in degrees of sensibility as can be those of human beings. There do exist many men who, for pleasure, first soak their bodies in warm baths, and subsequently polish the cuticle with the hardest possible of flesh brushes. Others would only be gratified were they daily rubbed down with brick bats. On the contrary, there exist individuals on whom a ruck in the finest linen will inflict a discomfort which, in its intensity, almost amounts to an agony.

AN EXCITED HORSE'S MOUTH.

So there are horse possessing hides to which may be applied with impunity the sharpest and coarsest of curry-combs. But there also live many animals having skins to which the oldest and bluntest of those antiquated scratchers will occasion a sensation the acuteness of which is testified to by the violence of resistance with which the morning's dressing shall be accompanied. Yet, rather than obey the hint so energetically conveyed, or discard the employment of anything with which use has familiarized them, the least venturesome of grooms will brave daily danger. In vain does the irritated quadruped writhe, frisk, stamp, kick, snap and bite, under the infliction; the servant has been taught that a curry-comb is an instrument to be applied to the skins of horses. The head will be tied up—the leg-strap employed; nay, the hobbles and the twitch will be applied, before the lesson he has learned to regard in his youth shall be discarded. Such tools of the lowest routine are the ignorant in everything which does not involve their personal gratifications.

The consequence is, that because the animal, while being dressed, cannot forbear biting at all objects which are near to it, the incisor teeth rapidly lose the cutting edges, and become rounded. Such a shape of the nippers used to be viewed as indicative of *crib biting;* but the fallacy of this notion having been exposed, the idea is generally abandoned. Nevertheless, an animal having rounded front teeth would fare badly at an equine banquet where the provender had to *be cropped* from the earth. It is, therefore, only prudent to prevent the creature from spoiling its mouth. To accomplish this, remove the curry-comb; for, should it be allowed to remain in the stable, the chances are very strongly against the groom's favorite tool being discarded. Have the skin dressed

A HORSE, HAVING A SENSITIVE SKIN, IS DRESSED BETWEEN THE PILLAR-REINS.

with a penetrating brush; or, should that prove too sharp, order it to be groomed very gently with the wisp and water brush. Animals possessed of extremely sensitive skins generally carry very fine coats: therefore they can well afford to dispense with very much labor from their stable attendant.

19

The snapping may, from long indulgence, have become confirmed as a habit. In that case, nevertheless, ameliorate the dressing; but, before the groom undertakes the cleansing of the skin, the quadrupeds should be fixed by two strong pillar-reins, each of which is of sufficient length to reach, from opposite sides, to the middle of the dressing stall. The head, thus bridled, is comparatively fixed, and is, of course, fastened away from any substance which might be seized by the teeth. However, the skin is sometimes, when thus tender, loaded with a scurf which no curry-comb, however long it may be applied, will do aught but increase. In this case, always change the provender, and particularly see the food is properly prepared ere it is presented. Give, daily, one ounce of liquor arsenicalis, in a pint of cold water; and every morning damp the skin, *not the hair*, with a mixture composed of animal glycerin, one part; rose-water, two parts.

For an animal that destroyed its rugs, the first measure is, to refuse all further supply of such articles. Then attend to the food, after the method already advised; next anoint the body with glycerin and rose-water, subsequently employing a hay wisp regularly night and morning. Place the animal in a cool, loose box, and, if possible, leave both window and half the door open. When night arrives, permit the quadruped, at its pleasure, to move in or out of the stable—allowing a piece of rather closely bitten meadow land for exercise, when the sun is down and the flies are at rest. Take the animal in before insects begin to throng, which they seldom do till the sun has gained full power. By way of medicine, daily give one ounce of liquor arsenicalis, in a pint of cold water, together with one quart of good (not publican's) beer. Keep the bowels regular with bran mashes or with green meat. There can be no necessity why all labor should be relinquished: the work, however, ought not to be excessive, or the pace too exhausting; for any extraordinary exertion is apt to lead to excoriations which are, in their turn, disposed to end in large and obstinate sores, when the skin is in an irritable condition.

Every part of the horse is of importance to the owner: the teeth are not secondary to the feet; the legs are of no less value than the lungs; and the skin cannot be esteemed more lightly than the eyes. Indeed, every rider ought to make himself acquainted with the appearances natural to the healthy eye of the horse; for a shying steed will effectually destroy the pleasure of an entire day. The horseman should notice the eyes of every animal he intends to mount. As a precaution, such a measure is imperative; for, being forewarned, he may be prepared to encounter the danger into which defective vision is almost certain to lead the rider. For the method of proceeding, when examining the eyes of a horse, the reader is referred to the "Illustrated Horse Doctor," (pp. 49 and 56,) wherein the proper plan is amply detailed.

The reason for recommending what the reader may regard as a troublesome acquisition and a strange knowledge for a gentleman to bore over, is, because those livery stable-keepers who let horses out to strangers, can hardly be expected to maintain a very valuable stud for such purposes. It is not asserted that these tradesmen knowingly send out very defective animals; but they could not, perhaps, in the way of business, warrant, as decidedly sound, any inhabitant of their stables. The eyes are the parts which generally fail. Exposed to a tainted atmosphere and fixed close to a whitened wall, when at home; wearing blinkers unpleasantly near to the organs, when abroad; while, at other times, they carry a saddle, having the eye exposed to the full glare of the sun,—it is not a subject for wonder that bodies so sensitively endowed and delicately organized should become diseased.

Added to the natural results of such causes is the treatment experienced from brutal and ignorant fellows, whom a few shillings have invested with a whip. Such persons are fond of slashing the horse over the head, and may thus produce partial opacity of the cornea. (See "Illustrated Horse Doctor," p. 46.) The effect of imperfect vision is to create alarm in a highly imaginative but an excessively timid animal. Shying is the consequence, and this act is as various in its developments as its causes may be numerous. Probably this will be best explained by relating a circumstance which, a few years ago, occurred to a friend of the author's.

A young gentleman, native of Ireland, complained one street was so like another, that though he should live a thousand years in London, he should still see nothing of the town. He wished to view the suburbs to ascertain the situation of the metropolis; with this purpose in view, he, one afternoon, hired a horse at a West End livery stables, and trotted upon the Uxbridge Road. Everything went pleasantly till steed and rider had reached Ealing Common, when, there being nothing in view, the gentleman gave the quadruped its head, and allowed it to proceed at its own pace. The pair, however, had only gone a short distance, when, from some motive not recognizable to human perception, the creature was seized with a violent fit of "swerving;" or, in other words, it suddenly left the road, and, moving sideways, began describing a rather wide semicircle upon the common, which was, at the place, fortunately smooth and level.

But Ealing Common appears to be a favorite spot with laundresses, who there hang out their wet linen. The rider was dragged under one of the lines, loaded with damp clothes, while his horse pushed against an elderly washerwoman, and, spite of her screams and resistance, propelled her a considerable space. The gentleman, almost thrown by the unexpected motion of his nag, and half smothered by the wet garments, which clung about his head, was wholly at a loss to comprehend the cause of the female screams, rendered yet more discordant by the shrill cries of her terrified grandson.

SWERVING.

When, however, he understood everything, a donation calmed the agitation of the female, while, hastening to a roadside inn, he found a man who was willing to take the horse back to the livery stables. The rider returned by another conveyance, and he has never since trusted himself outside an unknown animal.

Swerving, however, is no more than a mild form of shying, when compared with the numerous evils which result from defects of the visual organs. Every possible variety of eccentric gait is not to be imagined, much less is it to be described. One consequence of this peculiarity, perhaps the worst shape it can assume, is bolting or running away

When a horse is thus impelled, it is, as was insisted upon in the "Illustrated Horse Doctor," useless to tug at the reins or to slash with the whip. Such acts may aggravate the peril, but they cannot check the movement, which originates in a dread that lifts its victim above all earthly restraints. The brain is then excited and confused; the pain, which the body shall fail to recognize, nevertheless may prove an additional stimulant to the wildness that approaches near to positive despair.

The quadruped is not to blame. It has been guilty of no fault. Its behavior may displease its present master; but the horse has no ability to struggle with a fear which was generated by disease. The alarm was the offspring of a cause beyond the aid of medicine and removed from the help of surgery. Such an animal, however, should not be left entirely to its fate; for "running away" is apt to become more frequent upon repetition. The eyes, thus afflicted, should be covered when the quadruped is taken abroad; for it is safer to sit behind a creature which is sightless, than one which is possessed only of a dangerous or of an imperfect vision.

Then, to explain the motives for that forbearance and to render clear the prudence of that gentleness which the reader has been recommended to practice. Let it be inquired, can pain be esteemed a corrective of terror? It was an apprehension of suffering which created the alarm. To render such a dread a reality, does not appear to be the readiest method of dispelling the feeling which has been generated by the imaginary possibility of agony being encountered. The quickest plan by which any particular sensation can be destroyed, certainly is to excite another emotion that is the opposite of the one we are desirous should be dispelled. Then awaken an assurance of security, and, of course, alarm is annihilated. It may not be a popular or an heroic line of treatment which the author has presumed to propose; but, assuredly, the safest way to destroy a fear is to kindle an emotion which shall be antagonistic to that it is desirable to remove.

Such conduct, however, would be directly opposite to what is at present generally exemplified by the majority of mankind. A horse bolts, or it runs away, and the act is hastily concluded to originate in a "vicious propensity" which the animal delights in indulging. The creature is spoken of as a "bolter." The topmost speed and the blindest flight is, by equestrians, regarded as the gratification of a malicious spirit, and, thus considered, only elicits a firm resolution to subdue its exhibition at every hazard. The reins are sawn and the whip is plied, until agony has driven terror to madness, and some awful disaster puts a termination to the unsightly proceeding.

The following is intended to be an accurate representation of an incident which the author witnessed, some years ago, in the neighborhood of Holloway. In the issue, however, no person was injured; even the horse escaped unharmed. It would have been difficult to say which of the principal actors was the most frightened. Probably the alarm of each was as great as it was possible to be; but the breakage of the shafts, the rupture of the traces, and the snapping of the reins mainly secured the immunity of all. No one, having seen the aspect borne by the event at one time, could have foretold how it was to terminate; assuredly the fortunate result was not facilitated by the gentleness or the self-possession of the driver. That person did his best, no doubt without the intention of whipping up a catastrophe: he acted according to the recognized rules; but it was owing to the reflection such a scene gave rise to that the author was led to recognize the folly of that behavior which is generally displayed under the like alarming circumstances.

RUNNING AWAY.

Before concluding the present chapter, the reader is earnestly counseled to discard the many foolish tales he may have heard about the horse being naturally a "vicious animal." What reward is reaped from the indulgence of the creature's imaginary designs? Death, injury, or disfigurement! Such consequences might ensue upon the promptings of insanity; but no one, however, has supposed that madness instigated the conduct which man recognizes as "vice" in the horse. There is, in the world's opinions, a wide distinction separating the mad horse from the "vicious brute." The attributed "vice" is certainly not recognized as madness, although it may be accompanied by the temporary absence of consciousness. The vicious acts display too great a similarity throughout the entire equine race, distributed over the world, to be reconciled with the presence of recognition; while they are too regular in their development and far too heedless in their execution to accord with the promptings of any wicked disposition which would be dependent upon individual inclination.

Then, the sameness which pervades the entire group of supposed "equine vices," cannot be reasonably accounted for in accordance with the popular belief. In the human being, each example of a vicious disposition is conspicuous for adopting an independent and an eccentric course of action, though it occasionally practices imitation. Can animals instruct or mimic one another? Have horses, only, the power to communicate "vice" to their companions? Can they, only, teach self-mutilation, and learn suicide? That is not to be credited. But will the reader, viewing them as inferior beings, consider the conduct of all as regulated by the impulses of instinct, generated by sudden emotion? Then, sameness is by no means extraordinary. Eating is in man an instinctive act. The modes of preparing food are various, and the methods of its division are as dissimilar in different nations,—for these actions are shaped by conviction or by reason; but the manner in which the instinctive portion of the act is performed, the way in which the sustenance is masticated and is swallowed, though in some degree influenced by refinement, is mainly similar in all regions, and in every race of human beings.

To run away from danger is an instinct in a horse. The animal does not fly from battle, only because man has deceived it into a faith that there is no danger where gunpowder is consumed. Terror renders the animal blind and unconscious. It has no more power to check the last effect than it has ability to contend against the first consequence. Pain induces a natural desire to escape from the cause of suffering. Its wish may be gratified at the sacrifice of property; but property is an artificial institution, of which most animals have hitherto refused recognition. Sameness of cause generally induces like results. Idleness leads to mischief; satiety promotes waste; terror generates alarm; and itching provokes scratching. These acts in the animal may be imprudently indulged; but the horse, having no conception of a future, of course cannot nicely calculate probabilities. Thus, if we run through the list of the so-called "vices," each will admit of a very easy and of a remarkably ready solution.

Let no man, therefore, speak of a "vicious horse." Let no reasonable being so far forget himself as to attribute design as a motive to the creature which nature has endowed only with instinct. Needless torture, though inflicted on a brute, rebounds to strike humanity. But mankind have not yet so emerged from barbarism as to have entirely lost all relish for those prejudices which justify cruelty. The written history of the world is the sad record of a long struggle midst blood and suffering. Only of late years have men dared to relax the laws, and only recently have they sought to lessen crime, by educating the debased to perceive the beauty of goodness. Might not a similar spirit, applied to horses, diminish the number and lessen the fatality of equestrian accidents? At all events, such a suggestion deserves a trial. It should be experimented with, if not for its novelty, because it proposes the adoption of behavior which must gratify the better feelings of the master, and because it holds forth a reasonable prospect of decreasing some of the more serious evils by which human life is, at the present moment, too frequently endangered.

Before joining in the cry against equine vice, always investigate the act which is adduced to justify the prejudice. Do this quietly. Look fairly at the surrounding circumstances, and think how these might possibly act upon a timid and a non-reasoning creature. Find out the cause, if possible; because, by so doing, you will best serve your own interest. Knowing the cause, it is probable you may eradicate the effect. But, before this is undertaken, the party must be prepared to exercise his utmost patience; for animals are slow to learn, and have to conquer their terrors before they can exemplify the easiest of lessons. Only, once taught, they are retentive scholars; and, by the pride they evince in their acquirements, reward their instructor.

To stimulate the proprietor unto that course of conduct which is recommended above, it surely must be sufficient to remind him that the opposite method has been long as it has been most perseveringly tried. Severity, however, although enthusiastically exemplified, notoriously has only imperiled man, without in any way amending the habits of the animal. Therefore the reader is asked, if it is reasonable to continue the proceeding which, having been largely tested, has induced nothing but misfortune?

CHAPTER IX.

STABLES AS THEY SHOULD BE.

When considering this subject, the writer is freed from all restraints. He has to describe things which exist only in his own imagination; not to depict any object which has been embodied as a reality, or which has been fancied by another individual. The author, however, will endeavor to picture such an edifice as in some of its modifications any one, keeping a horse, should possess ability to erect.

To some persons the following description may appear so grand as to border on the ridiculous. Compared with existing buildings, the author's proposal, no doubt, must seem to be of unnecessary dimensions. But a question of this nature is decided, not by what it seems but by that which it actually is. Is any provision hereafter made, that health does not demand? If the place is large, so are the animals which are to be harbored within its walls. What is unnecessary, or where is the article which is useless? As to the accommodation being too ample, what would a Saxon king of Britain say, could he be resuscitated and made to behold the palaces which her present Majesty possesses? Nay, what would a workman who had existed during the reign of "glorious old Harry" exclaim, could he contemplate the accommodations which surround his descendants of the modern time?

Stables, as they now exist, are tainted with all the evils of antiquity. Improvement has changed the homes of the people, and has even amended the prison of the caged songster; but it has entirely skipped over the jail of the horse. The place and the people about it smack of a time when corruption was the rule and filthiness was a fashion. The question therefore to be considered is, not what stables are, but what they should be. What the animal requires to maintain it in its beauty, in its health, and in its usefulness, is that which we now wish to ascertain. All the world has witnessed how much the quadruped can endure, when the master cares not for its comfort, is careless about its health, and does not study the requirements of its nature.

Bricks and mortar, however expensive such articles may be, are about the most economical purchases which the horse owner can invest his cash in. It is folly to pay large sums for thew and muscle, when the place in which such properties are to be lodged will destroy the health and undermine the strength that are imperative to their preservation. One or two deaths in a prime stud may cost more dearly than would the largest of the proposed buildings.

The money which shall be expended upon the improved stable must not be viewed as cash sunk in an unremunerative object, but as a sum invested in that which will immediately yield an exorbitant interest. It will decrease the veterinary surgeon's bill; it will conserve the health and prolong the usefulness of the horse; it will put the animal in better heart, and will enable the proprietor to dispense with those repeated purchases which now occasion the horse owner to stare at every fresh steed he chances to meet, and to inquire "if it be for sale?"

When we wish to raise any erection, we should, before we begin to plan, thoroughly comprehend the purposes which the new edifice is to serve. A stable is not the home of a horse, in the same sense that a house is the home of a human being. The animal has not one room for day and another for night. It cannot retire; it must remain in its compartment; and it becomes the author's duty to point out what is imperative to render the limited space a healthful abode.

In the first place, everything like a stall must be abolished—the uses of such abominations being supplied by loose boxes. Each box is to be eighteen feet square; of these there are to be six, ranged in pairs; three upon either side of the interior. Every box shall be rendered dry and sweet by six deep gutters, three on either side; and all emptying into a central branch drain, which discharges its contents into a main drain, running through the length of the entire building.

The gutters commence eighteen inches from the side divisions of the boxes; the first is situated three feet from the external wall. Six feet divides the first from the second gutter; the same space separates the second from the third gutter, which is removed only three feet from the central partition.

The flooring or pavement between the gutters is arranged in gentle undulations, like the walks in a gentleman's garden. It is raised three inches higher in the center of each division than where its borders terminate in the gutter. The two pieces of pavement at either end of the box begin at the elevation of three inches, and sink to the level of the lowest surface as they approach the gutter. Thus every portion of the pavement will incline one in twelve, a fall of fully sufficient magnitude to allow of the speedy disappearance of fluid, which is always ejected with force and in quantity. The gutters all terminate in "stink traps," which give admission into the branch drains; these last, as well as the main drain, consisting of circular earthen pipes.

The undulations of the pavement not only facilitate the speedy removal of fluid, and thus tend to keep in a state of purity the atmosphere

MODES OF STANDING AFFORDED BY AN UNDULATED PAVEMENT.

within the building, but the surface presents every variety of standing ground to the choice of the quadruped. The animal, by this arrangement, can select an upward slope, a downward incline, or a level plane whereon to rest the feet; an ability of appropriation which intelligence will not be slow to comprehend or tardy to appreciate.

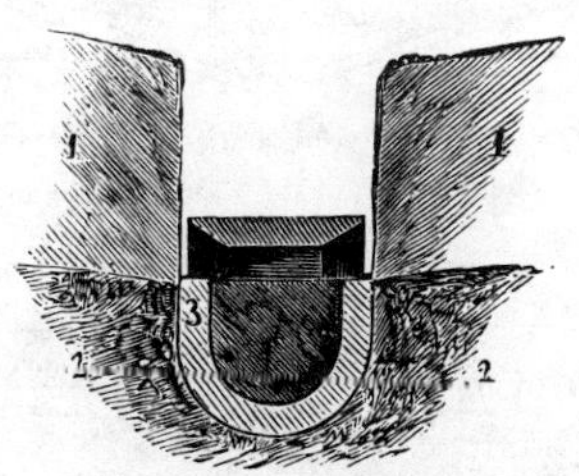

DIAGRAMATIC SECTION OF A SUPERFICIAL GUTTER, SEVERAL OF WHICH KEEP DRY THE LOOSE BOXES.

1 1. The Dutch clinkers.
2 2. The prepared ground on which the gutters and the pavement repose.
3. The semicircular earthenware gutter along which the fluid flows, covered by the loose iron grating.

Each gutter should be two inches wide and two inches deep. They ought to commence at the depth of a Dutch clinker from the surface, and be covered by a perforated loose iron grating, the holes in which are a quarter of an inch wide, one inch long, and the last distance asunder. Thus should the horse, when down, lie over one of these gutters, the body cannot then repose on a good conductor of heat.

The gratings are not flat, but incline on every side toward the openings. This pattern was selected, because the author has beheld flat bars eaten into by the acridity of the fluid, and retaining liquid that yielded an abominable stench. Neither are these coverings fixed into their situ-

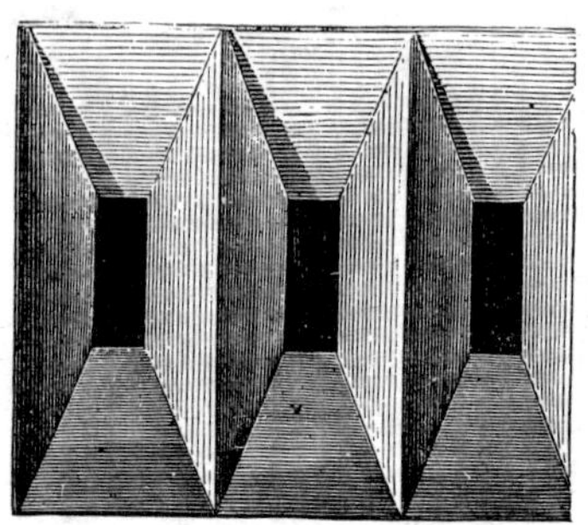

PATTERN OF THE LOOSE IRON GRATING WHICH COVERS THE GUTTERS.

ations. They are merely laid upon the sides of the earthen gutters, which are three inches wide at the openings; the iron can afford to dispense with other fastening than its own weight supplies. Should the channel which the grating guards ever become clogged, then the easy lift of the metal-work will allow the gutter to be cleansed.

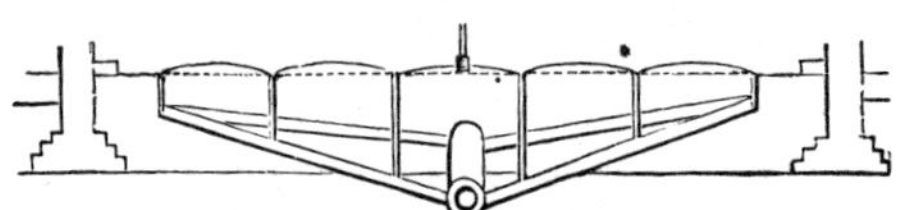

CROSS SECTION OF THE DRAINS IN LOOSE BOXES.

Supposed to be seen on the line D E, in the plan of drains to be shortly introduced.

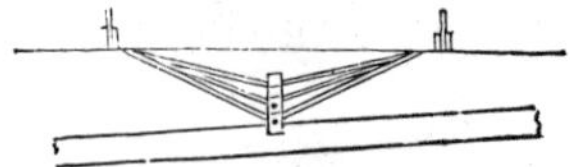

LONGITUDINAL SECTION OF THE DRAINS IN LOOSE BOXES.

Supposed to be viewed on the line E F, which is marked on the plan of drains.

The openings, which are ample to permit the escape of all liquid, are purposely made small, because rats and other vermin too frequently enter stables by the drains. It is by no means unusual for such pests, where they are numerous, to attack and gnaw the hoofs of living animals. The horn is without sensation; therefore it can be gradually removed without the horse being at all inconvenienced; but, assuredly, the proprietor will be vexed at a destruction which necessitates the quadruped should be idle until nature has repaired the loss of substance

The branch drains, which commence at twenty inches from the surface, can be only entered through a stink trap; that article also opposes an obstacle to the free passage of vermin. All these branches terminate in the main drain, which, where the tube begins, is situated thirty-four inches within the soil, and, as it proceeds, has a fall of about one foot in fifteen feet.

Neither the pipes, the gutter, nor the clinkers are placed within or rest upon unprepared soil. Such may be the usual plan after which most stables are now built; for the drainage of these places does not generally extend beneath the surface. The pavement of the contemplated stable, however, is to be raised two feet above the level of the ground on which it is erected. For the entire space which the structure will occupy, the soil is, in the first instance, to be removed to the depth of one foot. After the foundations have been properly laid, the walls are then to be raised till they are built up two feet above the natural level of the surrounding surface.

A layer of large flints or of coarse brick rubbish is then to be thrown in; this layer is to be two feet six inches in thickness. Within this, the main and the branch drains are to be arranged, though the principal drain will also have, toward its termination, to be sunk into the earth. The remaining six inches is to be filled in with coarse sand; upon this the gutters are to commence.

DIAGRAM, EXPLANATORY OF THE MANNER IN WHICH THE GROUND OF THE STABLE IS FORMED.

The gutters are two inches deep. They all originate at five inches from the upper surface of the clinkers. The shallowest has a fall of fifteen inches, but others have a much greater inclination, as all empty into the branch drains which communicate with the main drain. This last, sinking deeper as it proceeds, quits the building at a depth of six feet six inches from the exterior of the sand within the walls of the stable.

The contemplated structure will be thus thrice drained. First, there will be the deep tubular main and branch drains; next, there is the sand and brick rubbish; while, lastly, there is the surface drainage effected by the grated gutters. So much pains have been consciously bestowed upon the dryness of the building, because nothing will, in the end, prove more detrimental to the horse than confinement in a damp abode. Not only does perfect drainage conserve the health of the equine inhabitants.

but it likewise tends to preserve the bricks, the mortar, and the expensive fittings that should adorn every stable.

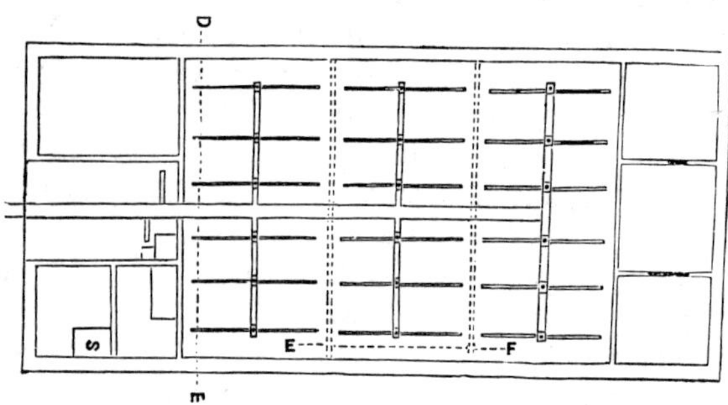

PLAN OF DRAINS.

S indicates the position of a trap door, which leads to the coal-cellar under the gig-house.
The dotted line, connecting the two letters D E, represents the situation of the supposed section of drains, previously introduced.
The dotted line, indicated by the letters E F, points to the supposed situation of the cross section of drains, which has likewise been exhibited.

According to the supposed view, which forms the frontispiece to the present volume, there is a free but covered space, twelve feet wide, extending all round the building. The soil of this free space, covered ride or ambulatory, should also have been removed, and subsequently have been filled up, after the plan already described, as necessary for the interior of the stables. It need not, however, be paved with clinkers, as sand forms a better ground for a horse to exercise upon than can possibly be made with the hardest of known bricks.

The roof, having sheltered the ride, terminates immediately over a metal gutter. This gutter communicates with five pipes upon the western and upon the eastern sides, with two pipes upon the southern, and with three upon the northern aspects of the building.

The roofing of the ambulatory is upheld by thirty-one posts, each twelve feet high, and the same distance apart. Between every two of these posts, on all sides of the stable save the front, are placed smaller uprights, which reach only to six feet. By these smaller posts are supported one end of three movable bales on either side, the opposite extremities of the bales resting against the larger posts; each bale being six feet long, and reaching from the small uprights to the main supports The first bale is one foot from the ground; while the others are at equal distances, and so placed as to leave four inches of clear pole to project above the highest rail.

The pipes leading from the metallic gutter are fastened to the pillars and empty into a drain, which encircles the building and receives the water from the roof; it also conveys away that which is used in washing the carriages, or for general purposes. This is carried to any convenient pond, while the liquid manure of the stable is, by the tubular pipes, conveyed into a tank situated at least twenty yards from the principal building.

Drainage of the entire roof is thus assured, and the dryness of the ambulatory in all weathers is rendered a certainty. No large stable can approximate to its requirements, in which a covered ride is not provided. It is, however, by no means uncommon to behold grooms trotting the animals on which they are seated, and which the servant is supposed to be taking out for the morning exercise; but if a horse is to be mounted and put to its paces by the man as well as by the master, it necessarily follows that the quadruped must perform double duty, or endure excessive wear.

Many grooms habitually do more than merely ride. These men are, generally, excited when in the saddle, and removed from all chance of supervision. Some of these individuals delight in antics. Most stable attendants love to display the spirit of the quadrupeds they wait upon; and all of lively dispositions, when their companions in service are looking on, naturally strive to convert duty into a pleasure. The horse is his own for the time, the animal being then entirely subject to the servant's authority, and he being far away from all that might control his actions.

An anecdote will, perhaps, best illustrate the above observations. A medical gentleman, established in the north of England, possessed a handsome bay gelding, for which he had recently given a heavy price. Soon after the groom professed to have brought the quadruped into working condition, the doctor began to use the animal for his afternoon exercise. He was fond of a particular road; but he could not persuade his horse to pass a certain low, roadside tavern. At the door of this place the quadruped would always stand still. Punishment was of no further use than to make the animal, much to its master's disgust, leave the door and bolt into the yard.

There was nothing, then, to be done but to turn the creature's head homeward. No sooner did the quadruped's face point in this direction, than the steed began to exhibit a speed which seemed to say the doctor was riding on affair of life or death. The gelding, in consequence of the disgust which its strange proceedings had awakened, was shortly afterward sold at "an awful sacrifice;" nor does the medical gentleman, to this hour, comprehend the reason of his dumb servant's eccentric behavior.

The public house was famous as the resort of grooms. Here, "early purl" was prepared in perfection; while, at later hours, nothing could excel either the "neat liquors" or the "dog's nose" which the tavern provided. The horse was accustomed to stand before the door; or, during those days when the doctor might walk abroad, the animal was concealed within the yard. Intelligence had learned its lesson, and its owner, being a timid rider, wanted the resolution necessary to force his slave to receive and to obey a new instruction.

The foregoing anecdote should also enforce the wisdom of masters making some further acquaintance with their living property than simply to know it for its uses. There are, however, a numerous class to whom anecdotes are not illustrations, but nothing more than amusing stories, easily invented and readily embellished. With these people, nevertheless, seeing is believing. The writer, accordingly, with all humility, invites his readers to peep down some of the many dealers' yards, which they must pass during a morning's walk through the streets of London.

One side of such a place is always thickly littered with straw, and securely roofed in. Slowly riding up and down this covered way may be beheld a mounted groom, who is leading another horse. Now, horse dealers are not deficient in knowingness, and many of them have, during former years, been in service themselves. Therefore, most of the class are well acquainted with the secrets of domestics; and they never trust a steed to be exercised where some of the family may not overlook the groom. "Oh, yes, they do!" the reader may exclaim; "for I have often remarked 'breaks' being driven through the highways of the metropolis." Perfectly true! Such articles are to be met with in the middle or the after-part of the day, propelled by high-actioned and well-matched horses. A little inspection will show the reins are in the possession of no ordinary groom. The master or the foreman guides the quadrupeds which are then being shown to the public, and are not simply raw purchases receiving exercise.

Dealers always exercise the horses at home; the windows of the house invariably face the ride. Every London inhabitant may not be able to command a covered way opposite his drawing-room windows; but he may prevent his servant from playing tricks with his animals, by ordering the man, when out exercising the creatures, to pass the family residence at stated periods. By such an arrangement, some of those strange accidents, which occasionally spoil the proprietor's breakfast, and which are ever reported to him as having been done by the horse in the night, might be prevented. While the owner, by claiming a right of supervision, would also instruct his servant that the quadrupeds the servant is engaged to attend upon are not absolutely given up to his pleasure.

The proprietor will, however, gain much by never permitting his animals to be exercised off the premises. This can only be done in the country, or where an ambulatory surrounds the stable. Under a sheltering roof all weathers are immaterial; the owner can easily ascertain whether his commands are shirked or fulfilled. A sick or a lame horse can be led about upon such a spot; for the soil, consisting of sand, and being always kept properly watered, is cool and soft to the feet, as well as free from dust; while a machine called a "tell-tale" will in some measure announce the time which the quadruped may be kept walking; it will also bear testimony as to the rate at which the man travels.

A PEEP INTO A DEALER'S YARD.

These things, when supervision is impossible, are now left entirely to the groom; whereas a "tell-tale," fixed at any part of the building, will render the rate of exercise cognizable to an absent master.

Exercise should never, save in illness, be given at a less pace than four miles an hour; the horses, while it is administered, should always be clothed more lightly than when standing still within the stable. It is fashionable for a groom to exercise a horse in full body-clothes: such a custom seems like tempting cough and cold, to which the quadruped, in this climate, is too much disposed. It must feel the change when its owner rides forth upon its unclothed body, and must suffer severely, should the master not return to the stable till the sun is down. Any active man should with perfect ease walk four miles in an hour; but such a rate is quick enough to oblige the animal to proceed at a gentle trot, which should not provoke perspiration, but will be sufficient exertion to promote a healthy glow of the skin.

Each groom, when on the ambulatory, should walk between two horses, holding a rein in either hand. Should one of the animals show signs of excitement, he is to leave the quiet one behind to the care of any person who may be at hand, and to run once or twice round the building with the spirited steed. Such a manœuvre is all that is necessary to quiet those creatures which, on first quitting the boxes, may skip or prance about.

When returned to the stable, the horse does not enter solitary confinement. Its loose box is eighteen feet square, and is inclosed by a fence seven feet high. Only four feet of this partition is composed of close inch and a half boarding. At that height, a stout rail, having its edges rounded, is fixed upon the topmost edge of the wood-work. From this rail spring round iron bars, placed three inches asunder, and having the higher extremity inserted into another rail, which is also rounded.

Since the author, many years ago, first thought of an open trevise, he is happy to see the idea has been generally adopted. Too many of the parties who embrace the notion, however, make it secondary to ornamentation, and compel the simple intention to assume the shape of scroll work or of an elaborated pattern. The object is to permit the prisoners to see and to communicate one with another. Both of these purposes are better attained by a straight iron bar than by a fanciful decoration, which last, moreover, must be further objectionable on the score of expense.

All needful security would be well assured by an inclosure which, unlike the common trevise, would allow the quadruped to see its companions, and to exchange those recognitions which must lighten the tedium of captivity. Nor can the writer comprehend why such simple pleasures should be denied to these gentle creatures, which most men imprison more closely than carnivorous ferocities are commonly confined. The prevention of certain deadly diseases might apply to the stables of an inn; but such occurrences have no right to be regarded as probabilities when a gentleman's establishment has to be considered.

The bars forming the upper portion of the divisions are not so close nor so bulky but the interspaces will allow the horses, after the Australian mode of cementing friendships, "to rub noses," or to exchange large draughts of fragrant breath with their fellow captives. Such innocent familiarities will often lead to lasting friendships, from the establishment

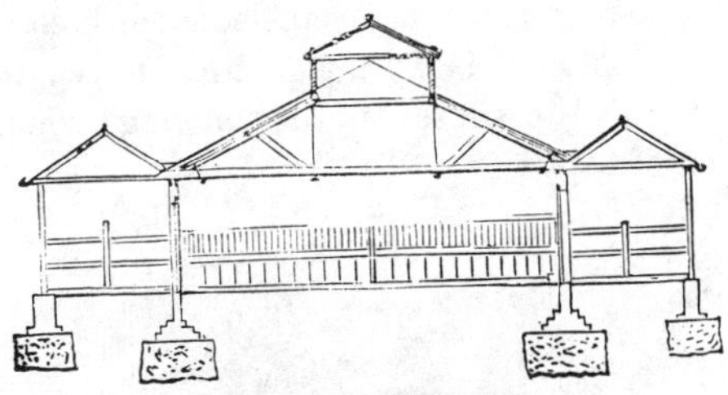

SECTION OF THE LOOSE BOXES.
Supposed to be taken where the dotted line A B is situated upon the ground plan.

of which the proprietor will reap an advantage. Quadrupeds perform much more gayly when harnessed with a companion that they love; and should the owner be, at any time, pressed for room, one or two additional spare boxes can always be commanded by allowing equine friends to enjoy the same compartment.

There is, however, running throughout society, a strange prejudice against permitting any communication between the inhabitants of the stable. Such a dislike cannot be justified by appealing to nature, as horses, when free to exercise a choice, always congregate in herds. Neither is it warranted by universal custom. In cavalry stables, the quadrupeds are merely separated by bales, or by poles suspended at either extremity by chains, and hanging between the animals. The habit also does not gain any support from consistency of conduct; since the gentleman who shall shudder at the possibility of any communion in his stable, will, nevertheless, allow numerous equine creatures to assemble together, and leave them without check, when he turns his stud into the field to be "freshened up" by a "run at grass."

The boxes have each a distinct entrance. The doors are fixed in the wall, and open upon the ambulatory. Each entrance is nine feet high and six feet six inches wide, all sharp edges and projecting iron-work, as hinges, latches, locks, etc., being strictly forbidden. Such things often injure animals while in the act of passing through these openings, and should never be permitted to project in any well-managed establishment.

The folding doors are divided into two parts, though not absolutely in the center, since the lower portion extends only four feet from the ground. The upper part can be thrown wide, without releasing the quadruped. The ventilation is thereby rendered far purer, while the captive is indulged with a more animated view than the walls of the interior can afford. The quadrupeds will protrude their heads through such spaces, and remain in that position for successive hours, looking the pictures of mild contentment, and contemplating liberty, which a generous nature appears to have relinquished almost without regret. A simple creature may here in shade enjoy the summer breeze, as it blows aside the forelock; for if man is, by his position, forced to confine the steed, he is not compelled to aggravate the sufferings which necessarily attend the condition of captivity.

A HORSE LOOKING THROUGH THE HALF-OPENED STABLE DOOR.

The doorway, being of those dimensions which have been already described, should afford all necessary security, especially when the groom adopts the proper method of conducting an animal through the ample space.

No possible accident should impress the memory of the captive with the notion that doors and anguish are associated one with the other. The habit of the animal, being accustomed to advance the head through the upper space, would, moreover, be of some service in dispelling all idea of pain, should the impression have been received prior to the horse coming into the possession of its present owner. The sight also of the man, to whom the affectionate creature may be attached, would, moreover, attract the notice and inspire the confidence of timidity.

CONDUCTING THE HORSE THROUGH AN ORDINARY STABLE DOOR.

The lower division of the door should, on fine nights, after dusk, be opened, that the prisoner may stretch its limbs and bathe its hoof in the evening dew. So the grass is kept sufficiently short, not to afford more than a nibble, no harm, but much good, will arise from sanctioning so innocent a luxury as a stroll in the free air. The eye of the horse fits the creature to roam by night; and man should, by this time, have suffered enough to cause a doubt as to the wisdom of crossing nature in her many wonderful provisions for the welfare of her children.

Such a suggestion may startle the prejudices which are inherent in the proprietors of most training stables. These places are, however, chiefly situated on the open downs, where ground is cheap, and the herbage scarcely affords a bite for the close-feeding sheep. Half an acre of such land could, without much expense, be attached to each box. On to this the flock might be turned by day; but so much liberty could be afforded the equine captive during the night. The racer being reared for speed, it is surely wrong to cramp its limbs by too stringent a confinement!

Something also is attained, beneficial to other parties than the quadrupeds, by having the doors of the boxes to open on the ambulatory. The necessity for mounting many animals within the stables would thereby be avoided; while the groom, upon rainy days, need not exert a dangerous haste, for fear of wetting his best livery. Hurry is never a safe emotion, when exhibited within the stable. The inhabitants, when they behold their attendant looking vexed, see him move quickly, and hear him speak loudly, from such signs infer danger; or timidity flushes with a certainty of his displeasure. It is the fault of the present race of stable-men, that they regard the horse as a senseless thing; whereas the dumb are always the observant, and, generally, are very sympathetic. They draw conclusions from scenes and acts which it may be beyond their stretch of reason to accurately comprehend. Being liable to misconstrue, the less they see of exciting spectacles the better.

Within the loose box there is no rack for hay, to strain the horses' necks, and shake seeds into their eyes, which must be open to direct the teeth. The ordinary manger is also absent. The horse does not sit to eat, nor can it lift the food to the mouth; but naturally it lowers the head to its gratification, and thus has no need to be accommodated with exalted fixtures. As it can with ease feed off the ground, why should man, in the nineteenth century, persist in forcing the animal, which he domesticates, to forego the habits which nature has engrafted on existence?

No rope fastens an animal directly under the opening to a dirty hayloft. No puffs of cold wind, therefore, can blow upon the quadruped through such an aperture, which is not a loss, for horses are very susceptible to colds, which modern stables are ingeniously arranged to encourage. Like all life, when hotly and impurely inclosed, the steeds become morbidly delicate: the pampered daughters of the wealthy cannot, possibly, be more vulnerable to evil influences than are those equine slaves, whose service demands a body vigorous with health, strong and able to encounter all the seasons in their vicissitudes.

There are, within the building, three small compartments, placed against the outer wall of each box, and resting upon the ground. Two are situated on one side of the entrance, the third stands by itself in the opposite corner. All project eighteen inches from the wall, and two are eighteen inches high. One compartment is used for water, and is raised two feet, being, as regards length, of the same dimensions. One is intended to hold prepared food—this is three feet long; while that meant to receive the occasional allowance of grass extends one foot beyond the last dimension. The bottoms of the food receptacles are both raised six inches from the level of the stable; an arrangement which hopes to anticipate any strain upon the muscles of the neck, should the animal be more than usually compact in its developments.

Certain horse proprietors are loud in their commendations of cut food, which they assert can be eaten quickly, and, therefore, allows so much longer a period for resting the body. Stable condiments also are advertised as fattening and appetizing adjuncts. To both propositions the author must object. The body's rest depends not upon the quickness with which the contents of the manger can be swallowed, but upon the ease with which they can be digested, after sustenance has entered the stomach. The last function is not facilitated by the provender being bolted; nor does it at all depend on the shortness of the period in which a certain quantity of victuals can be put out of sight. As to those stimulants which are supposed to increase the appetite and to favor the accumulation of fat, carters having, for ages, been condemned because they resorted to such nostrums, it is difficult to understand the reason why these things are patronized, when openly compounded, puffed, and sold by advertising tradesmen.

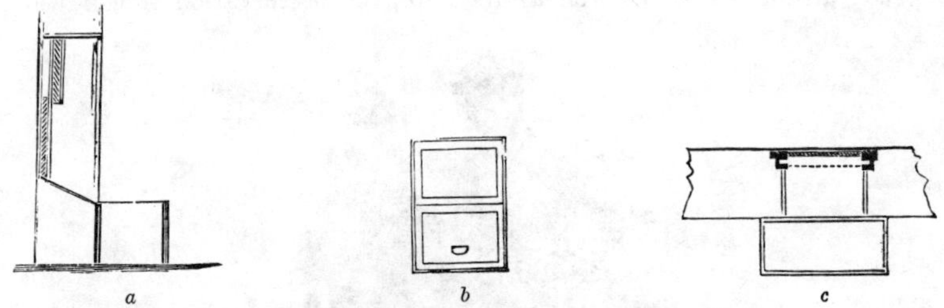

SECTIONS OF THE SHOOT LEADING TO THE FEEDING TROUGH.

a. The movable or sliding shutter, which, by a slanting surface made within the substance of the wall, leads to the corn trough that is situated on the ground.

b. The sliding shutter let into the wall, the lower compartment of which alone admits of an upward motion.

c. The corn trough and slanting surface, guarded by the shutter, as seen from above.

The capacity for rest, moreover, depends upon the constitutional necessities of the body which is to enjoy it. The horse is a creature of activity. It sleeps lightly, and is fitted to eat its food as it walks. The quadruped requires little rest. To force those conditions, necessary for the repose of weary existence, upon wakeful life, such as silence, solitude, and darkness, is merely to increase the severity of that imprisonment which every English animal is born to undergo. It is torture, and betrays only the ignorance of those by whom such cruelty is practiced.

The receptacle for the prepared food can, by means of a sliding aperture inserted into the wall, be filled from without: thus the necessity for a groom entering the compartment of a restless or ravenous quadruped, whenever the animal is fed, may be avoided. Contention between the man and a voracious horse can be, by this arrangement, rendered an impossibility; and it is a great point in the conduct of a stable to keep the attendants in good humor. Ignorant servants, when enraged, are too much disposed to vent their bad temper upon any inferior over which they may be invested with authority.

ONE OF THE BOXES IN WHICH THE FOOD IS PLACED, THE BETTER TO SHOOT IT INTO THE CORN TROUGH.

Moreover, a great deal of the excitement generally displayed by particular animals, where every prisoner can witness the distribution of the food to the rest, is, by the above plan, entirely abolished; and every observant stable attendant well knows how greatly quietude favors a speedy attainment of, as well as tends to, the preservation of condition.

A GROOM SHOOTING FOOD IN THE TROUGH, WHILE STANDING OUTSIDE THE STABLE.

By means of the box and the sliding shutter, the food may be served to all almost as rapidly as a man can walk. The provender is first divided into portions, and these are put into open boxes, which are placed upon a barrow. One of these boxes the man empties through each shoot, and then, having washed out the utensil at the pump under the covered way, returns it to the provender-house. This last plan, however, entails some trouble; therefore only in exceptional cases should it be adopted.

As to the supply of liquid, some arrangement is also needed: the bottom of the water trough is level with the surrounding pavement. The supply pipe is commanded by a tap, and all the receptacles can be simultaneously filled by means of the tube that rises above the superior margin of the trough. Below the earth is a conduit, which conveys away the superabundant liquid. Into this tube or drain two smaller pipes empty, both of which arise from the interior of the receptacle. The smallest pipe reaches almost to the topmost edge of the compartment, and is simply intended to prevent the possibility of an overflow. The other and the larger tube is inserted into the bottom of the trough, and the removal of a plug, which commands the entrance, permits the contents of the trough to flow through this pipe into the larger conduit below, which empties its contents into the main tubular drain. By turning on the supply, which is derived from a cistern to be hereafter mentioned, and by also opening the waste pipes, all the troughs can at any time be quickly cleansed.

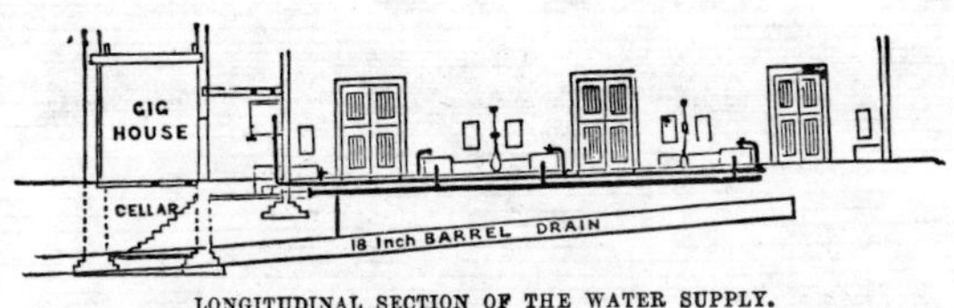

LONGITUDINAL SECTION OF THE WATER SUPPLY.

The cistern is situated in the boiler-house, and is elevated several feet above the level of the stable. The boiler-house adjoins the boxes, and from the raised cistern springs the supply pipe, which is carried under ground through the stables. Water, however, will always rise to its own level; this property convinces us that the troughs will be speedily filled whenever the taps are turned. The taps by which the flow is commanded are both placed in the first box, and by this arrangement the animal can receive fresh water four times daily, without fluid being carried to the horse. The contents of the customary pails are too frequently spilt by careless grooms. The horse naturally thrives best in a dry abode. Besides, the drink, as in nature, is always before the creature; for if presented only at stated periods, the draught may be offered when desire does not require liquids; or it may be withheld when thirst is so powerful as to engender a disinclination for solid nourishment

Moreover, servants are not always attentive to their monotonous duties; and the animal, in consequence, may be denied a necessary supply of fluid.

The water troughs are, moreover, recommended by further reasons. Horses are blest with acute senses; and everybody must have observed the animal blow upon, or rather smell, fluid before it partakes of the refreshment which it needs. The stable pails generally stand about; such things are exceedingly handy; and we need not be surprised if they are occasionally used for other than for cleanly purposes. The troughs, being fixed, are secured to one service; the pipes emptying into the receptacles prevent the purity of the supply from being tampered with. The above advantages are also associated with the ascertained fact that the horse, with water constantly before it, drinks less than the animal to which the pail is brought only after hours of enforced abstinence have generated a raging thirst.

The roof of the proposed stable should be of the ordinary description, or should slope from a central ridge toward the outer walls. The central compartment is eighteen feet from the walls; it is twenty-two feet from the level of the interior; and its margins rest upon walls which are raised twelve feet high.

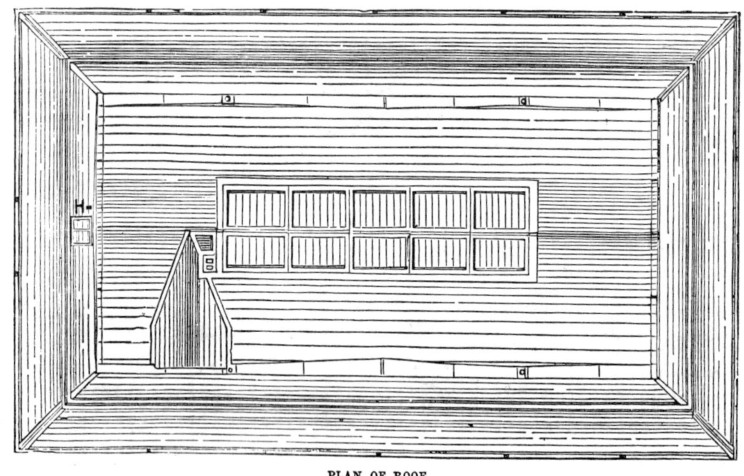

PLAN OF ROOF.

H. A trap door in the roof of the ambulatory, which leads to the entrance of the loft above the sheltered ground.

A plan of the contemplated roof is presented to the notice of the reader, who will perceive it consists of two parts. The larger portion is gabled at each extremity, and has a span of thirty-six feet. The smaller, or surrounding division, merely protects the covered ride or ambulatory. Where the two inclines meet, are hollows, which are technically spoken of as "valleys." The water within these valleys is conveyed away by means of four large pipes, two on either side, which are let into the outer wall; while the rain, which flows down the outer incline of the smaller division, drains into a metallic gutter, whence it is carried away by fifteen smaller pipes.

Over the center of the larger division of the roof is placed a ventilator. It commences twenty-one feet from the northern extremity of the building, and it extends, on either side, six feet from the center. It is thirty feet long, and its sides are four feet high. The sides are composed of four-feet louvre boards, which, being set in working frames, can, by means of lines which reach to the ground, be opened or closed as the increased temperature calls for air or the cold demands protection.

The ventilator is roofed with six-ounce glass, which is of more than a sufficient stoutness to resist any tempest that occurs in this climate. The central ridge of the ventilator rises twenty-eight feet from the pavement; and it is laterally supported by the boarded sides which have already been described. The roof of this part of the edifice also serves the purposes of windows, admitting light to the interior.

Should any person feel disposed to complain of the probable cost likely to attend this last provision, let such person remember that the first oulay, in this particular, is likely to be the last. The material is, moreover, cheaper than it formerly was; while its elevation removes it from all reasonable chance of breakage. The rain will wash the outer portion, while the position of the interior surface will prevent the accumulation of much soil; consequently the glass will be spared all those accidents which too frequently disturb the peace of housekeepers during the cleansing of ordinary windows.

The glass is designedly placed upon the roof, as when stable windows occupy the usual situations, they are generally suffered to be in so foul a condition as almost to counteract the purpose of their institution. Some of the panes are commonly broken; and where the glass is absent, its place is rudely supplied by rags or by paper, while the window-ledge is crowded with those articles which it is desired should be ready to the hand, or which it is wished to store snugly away.

When a stable is without windows, the dark house encourages a lazy servant. The architect's neglect also teaches the man a want of regard for that cleanliness which is essential to the well-being of the horse. With sucn a place, the absence of care soon becomes an unavoidable necessity, which the cunning of ignorance will not be slow to perceive, and to act upon, as being a justification of idleness. Nothing either in or about the stable should be sanctioned which would not accord with the cleanliness of a home or with the sweetness of a dairy. No dust should be suffered to accumulate in holes or on beams; while the animals are taking their early exercise, the flooring ought to be thoroughly washed down every morning, and the wood-work should be scrubbed once every week.

A stable, to be the abode of health, cannot command too much air, nor can it possibly admit too much light. The interior, however, should not be whitewashed in accordance with the general fashion. This glaring absence of color may, at first, look excessively clean, but it also exposes the smallest neglect of purity, which cannot always be present where animals are lodged. The cheapness of the wash may be its recommendation with those who are very studious of economy; but, in the end, it proves a dear substitute for a better covering, as a white surface causes that strain upon the optic nerve which renders blindness a common malady among the inhabitants of snowy regions.

Let the roof and walls be colored with a green which is made by mixing blue and yellow together. The light will, by the green tint, be partially absorbed, while the eye of the captive will be soothed by gazing upon the hue which constitutes the livery of nature. The pigment should not be purchased, for though the color which may be bought will be probably brighter than any made at home, excessive brightness is, in the present case, no advantage, and the more brilliant compound is dangerous, because it may consist of arsenic combined with copper. Or should a brighter color be very much desired, such can now be obtained, which is uncontaminated with any preparation of arsenic: though, probably, at a greater expense than that which is easily made by mixing together damp blue and powdered yellow ocher with size and water.

The roof is slated; but as this species of covering is always very hot in summer and equally cold in winter, the temperature of the interior will, in some measure, be less liable to such variations if the spaces between the joists are filled with solid plaster. Over the last material laths are nailed; and the surface is then to be thinly ceiled. The laths should, however, be of a stouter kind than those which are generally employed; the reason of their introduction is to anticipate the possibility of heavy lumps of plaster falling, and either injuring or frightening the horses.

The reader will now accompany the author to the back of the imaginary stable, which faces the north, and is divided from the last loose box by a stout wall.

The northern extremity is of the same width as the other parts of the building; it extends twelve feet beyond the last loose box. Its interior is divided into three rooms, each twelve feet square, and all separated by brick walls. Entrance to these apartments is gained through three doors, the upper parts of which, being glazed, will also serve the purposes of windows.

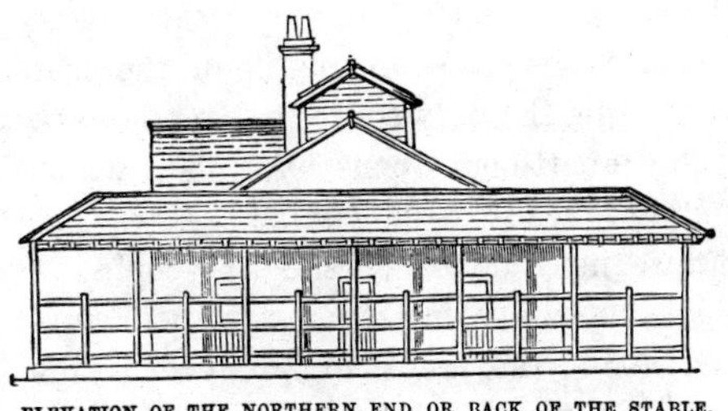

ELEVATION OF THE NORTHERN END, OR BACK OF THE STABLE.

The center division is sacred to the harness: it is kept warm by means which will be hereafter described. The trappings of the horse are too perishable and too costly to be housed within the stable. Damp, dust, and ammoniacal fumes are all injurious to this expensive article. Damp cannot but be present in the abode of animal life; the breath, insensible perspiration, evaporation from the water-troughs, washing of the pavement, hoofs, etc. are the common sources of the supply. The dust is occasioned by the spreading of the litter, the movement of the grooms and of the animals, as well as by many causes of motion, which can never occur without sending the finer particles of decaying matter flying from the various substances which are strewn about. Ammoniacal fumes are also generated by the decomposition of the equine excretions; however carefully the interior may be drained, or however pure the atmosphere may seem to human sense, this gas must more or less exist in every stable. Such taints, besides damaging the substances, also necessitate extra cleansing; though moderate attention is preservative in its nature, anything approaching to excessive labor not only destroys the fresh aspect of the harness, but is provocative of its speedy annihilation.

Within the harness-room all the clothes (after being dried and aired) are to be placed, and in this apartment every piece of harness (subsequent to being cleansed) should be stored; it is there hung upon appropriate fixtures and kept ready for instant use, being protected by thick curtains, which are made to fall over and to cover the several pieces.

On the left of the spectator, looking toward the building, is another room, which acts the part of a hay-loft. Within twelve feet square is stored all the provender and the litter immediately required for the horses. The space may appear somewhat limited for the supply of six horses; but enough for present use can be housed, and grooms are not rendered careful by the contemplation of anything like a superabundance. It is the filthy custom, now prevalent, to keep the food of a cleanly animal in a loft immediately above the stalls in which the horses are confined. Thus the store-house is commonly located in the situation which is the most directly exposed to the volatile or the heated emanations of the stable. Nor is this the only source of contamination. The groom's living and sleeping apartment opens by a door, which is not generally shut, and immediately leads to the equine pantry.

The author dare not further pursue this topic. The fancy of the reader, guided by the above facts, can readily picture everything that could be written about the fitness of provender thus housed, for promoting the health of a creature remarkable for the niceness of its habits, the acuteness of its senses, and the delicacy of its tastes. It may be forced to consume, and may, at length, morbidly "grow fond of that it feeds upon;" but such food cannot otherwise than undermine the health which sustenance should promote.

On the opposite side to the harness-room is another compartment, which is used as a tool-house. There are various items employed about a stable which commonly litter the space inhabited by the horses,—such as brooms, mops, forks, pails, combs, brushes, leathers, bandages, etc. Everything occasionally used, or daily employed, either on the animals or for the vehicles, is deposited in the tool-house. For such articles as come under the denomination of lumber, and are not of any present or probable utility, another place is provided, which will be shortly alluded to.

By thus allotting a store for everything, and encouraging habits of regularity, a considerable sum is saved, while the comfort of the grooms is provided for by every article being, at all times, to be readily found. By ordering all appliances to be carried back when no longer in use, nothing is left about the stable to litter the place, or be damaged by the animals.

Stable implements, in the hands of an irate groom, have proved terrible weapons of offense. A horse has been stabbed with a fork; a blow given with the edge of a pail has inflicted a fearful gash. The formation of the cranium in most existing stable attendants should suggest the prudence of not allowing temptation to be too convenient to such individuals when they become excited.

Having inspected the northern extremity, the reader will now be kind enough to move, in imagination, to the front of the erection. Before this can be seen, the sides and northern end of the ambulatory, or cov ered ride, will have been observed; in the front view, the intermediate posts and rails, which elsewhere define the path, are absent. The floor of the ambulatory being raised on all sides two feet above the surface, from the level of the front there extends, for twenty feet, a sloping pavement, which gradually reaches the surrounding ground. This arrangement is fully illustrated in the frontispiece to the present volume.

ELEVATION OF THE SOUTHERN END, OR FRONT OF THE STABLE.

The stable, notwithstanding the last provision, is not supposed to be placed on a marsh, within a hollow, or even upon a decided level; but, when a choice is possible, it should be located upon the brow of a hill. It is there favorably situated for the dryness of the interior as well as for the action of the drains.

Having defined the position of the building, the author will now consider the last engraving, which was an imaginary front view of the suppositious building. This portion of the erection stands before the loose boxes, and, like the back, is also divided into three compartments. It is separated from the stables by a stout wall, consequently there is to the interior no entrance by this direction.

The corner space to the left of the spectator, who is supposed to stand in front of the edifice, consists of one room, which is plastered, ceiled, and boarded—the dimensions being by breadth twelve, by depth eighteen feet. The entrance is guarded by a pair of well-made and closely-fitting folding doors. The interior is meant to serve as a double coach-house. The place is made as comfortable and is kept as free from drafts as its uses will permit.

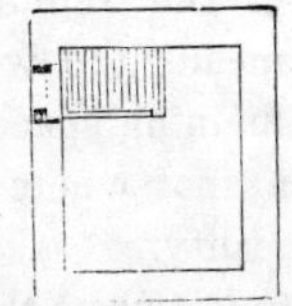

PLAN OF THE COAL-CELLAR, WHICH IS IMMEDIATELY UNDER THE GIG-HOUSE.

At the opposite corner exists a similar but smaller apartment. It possesses doors like the first; also, it is similarly provided with such things as ceiling, plaster, and boards, which are not customarily to be seen in these places. The room is as wide as the coach-house, but reaches back only ten feet; it is meant to serve as a gig-house. Beneath the flooring is the coal-cellar, and which is gained by a trap door cut in the floor of the present apartment. Close to this trap an entrance is pierced in the parting wall; and upon the last door being opened, as well as the trap being raised, a direct descent is formed, leading immediately to the cellar.

Between the gig and the coach house there must exist a clear space, eighteen feet deep, twelve feet wide, and of the last extent in height, when measured from its roof to the pavement, which is level with the ambulatory. The covering to this ground being flat and less lofty than the slates of the building, is proof that a clear space must exist above it. The place itself, however, contains nothing that can tempt cupidity. It is evidently a sheltered ground, where the carriage may be got ready, the harness may be cleaned, or any job be executed which might soil other portions of the interior. Such a spot is handy for many purposes, and serves as a loitering chamber for those idle gossips who delight in hanging about large stables.

Against the wall of this last locality, and near to its right-hand corner, is a projecting block of brick-work, which measures three feet by two and a half feet. It is evidently neither useful nor ornamental; therefore the reader rightly conjectures it merely indicates the presence of a chimney. Close to the chimney, but nearer to the entrance, is fixed a pump. From a plug, ready to be inserted into the muzzle, and from a pipe running some feet up the wall, which it ultimately pierces, evidently the pump is occasionally used to force water into a hidden receptacle situated above the surrounding level. In the left-hand corner of this clear space is built a convenience for the stable servants, which should be kept as clean as any other part of the edifice.

Looking once more at the front of the stable, we perceive there is a clock above the sheltered ground, while immediately under the clock something resembling the top of a door can be discerned. The roof of the ambulatory has also a trap let into it, which must be situated directly beneath this door. The trap being raised, and the door opened, by means of a ladder, which should hang upon the outer side of the ambulatory, admittance is gained into the clock-loft: by this means the works of the time-piece can be regulated; while the remaining space affords ample accommodation for storing, and also offers a spot where are housed those articles which are of no immediate utility.

Between the gig-house and one of the first loose boxes there is a space of eight feet by twelve feet. This forms a room which has two entrances: one is by a door pierced through the wall of the gig-house; the other is by a door, the upper part of which is glazed, and which opens from the ambulatory. Leading to the floor of the apartment are placed before each door two steps, the pavement of this room being two feet lower than any other level in the building. The ceiling, however, is ten feet removed from the floor.

In the farthest corner, raised against the northern wall of the compartment, is situated a self-acting and slow-consuming boiler. The fire faces toward the door, and the chimney has already been alluded to as built out on to the covered ground. Commencing in the farther corner, at the opposite extremity to that occupied by the door leading to the gig-house, is a staircase, which obviously conducts to an upper apartment.

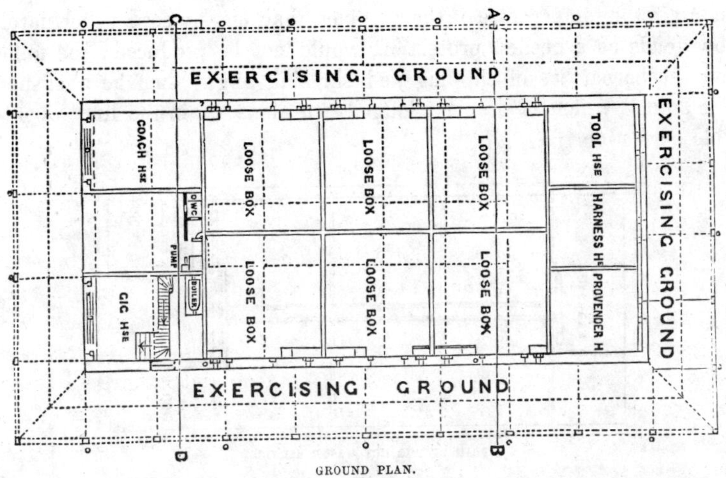

GROUND PLAN.

The oblong space above the loose boxes, which is indicated by dotted lines, denotes the size of the central ventilator.

Above the boiler, and removed but one foot from the ceiling, is a cistern, which occupies the entire length of the wall, or extends for twelve feet: it is four feet high and three feet wide. The situation of the cistern explains the use of the forcing pipe, which leads upward from the pump and supplies the cistern as has been noticed. From this reservoir the boiler is replenished, and the water troughs are kept perpetually filled. The pipe leading to the stable quits the cistern at eighteen inches from the bottom; consequently the horses will want fluid, while the cistern holds a supply sufficient to last some time when only used to fill the boiler. This arrangement involves a necessary artifice. Pumping is hard work, and grooms are not famed for a love of mechanical labor; but these men are always clamorous at any stint within their dominions. They will grumble loudly if the horses lack water, and persecute their fellow, whose turn it may be to pump, until the defect is remedied; whereas the boiler might become red hot, and an explosion threaten to demolish the building, without one of these people being moved by the likelihood of such a catastrophe.

From the boiler proceed pipes which travel into the loose boxes, into the harness-room, into the coach-house, and into the gig-house. Within these tubes circulates warm water, the fluid being returned again to the boiler when its caloric has been diffused through the interior. Few persons imagine how important warmth is to the welfare of the horse. Cold immediately roughens the coat, and if not speedily counteracted, stiffens the limbs or depresses the spirit. Were gentlemen willing to maintain the temperature of their stables, that lengthy coat, which nature now sends as a needed protection, would not be produced: the follies and the barbarities of clipping and singeing might then be abolished The animal which is properly lodged can alone attain the limit of possible perfection.

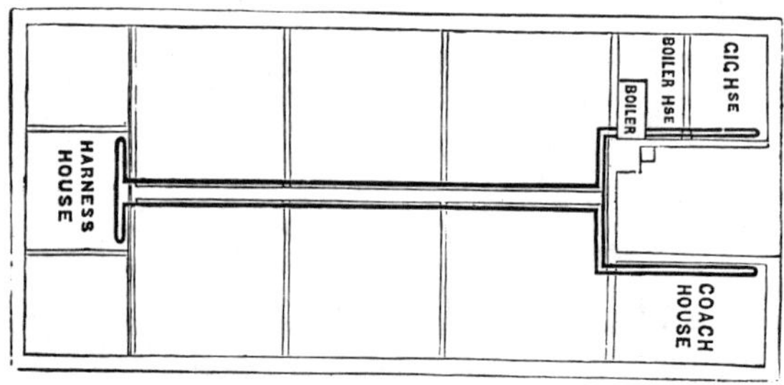

PLAN OF THE HOT WATER SERVICE.

Impure heat generates damp: the moisture derived from such a source, being finely divided, is far more penetrating, far more destructive, and altogether more noxious, than a similar amount of water could prove. It destroys clothing, encourages moths, dims plated and painted ornaments, rusts steel, soils varnish, rots wood and leather,—in short, there is nothing within the stable but suffers more or less; while in the animal, colds, coughs, and influenzas are but the intimations of its presence, the full effects being shown by the breaking forth of farcy and of glanders. Better be without horse and stable, than to be possessed of both, and be forced to lodge the quadruped where cold and damp prevail.

Few gentlemen care about, or probably no gentleman has ever seriously thought about, the coach-house being aired. Yet persons tenderly brought up, nursed in luxury, and frequently in delicate health, have the carriage kept near to a close stable, or housed in a building sadly exposed to the moist atmosphere of this northern climate. The vehicle is pulled out of such a place, is hastily made to wear an outward smartness, and is then whisked to the front door of the mansion. Ladies, habited in the thinnest of evening dresses, leave their warm apartments and subject their exposed beauties to the chilling effects which must necessarily be present in vehicles so carelessly sheltered. Here, after the bustle of preparation, they remain inactive for some period. They are set down at a fashionable hotel, and return thence in the same conveyance. The next day they naturally complain of a cold, supposed to have been caught *at* the party of last night!

People when seated within a carriage, the windows being up, may esteem themselves protected from the night air; but they would be safer walking through frost or rain than traveling inactive within such a receptacle. Consumption is far more prevalent among carriage folk than it is common among races which are supposed to exist in spheres liable to all the ills of life. Poverty has to encounter many perils, and is obliged to endure many privations; but it is not exposed to those snares which the ignorance of wealth has invented for its own destruction.

Perhaps, in this country, of many classes, the richer are most troubled with colds, with coughs, and with diseases of the air-passages. Good living, no labor, and careful nursing may enable them to linger on to a good old age; but comparatively few know the blessings of a vigorous being after the fiftieth year has passed. Warm rooms, a study of the weather, and ample envelopes prolong the life; but such things cannot restore the health. Gout, paralysis, epilepsy, with numerous brain disorders, are not common in agricultural districts, where carriages are scarce. Bronchitis and laryngitis are almost the property of the wealthy. Yet many men have paid pleasing compliments to the aristocracy concerning their longevity; but no one has hitherto traced the cause which bows the youthful scion to an early grave, and makes a valetudinarian of the noble who should be still enjoying a vigorous middle life. Invention has been racked to keep the feet warm when within the vehicle; but it seems not to have occurred to those numerous parties whose office it is to minister to the luxuries of the rich, that the interior of a carriage might be benefited by a secure lodging, or by its being thoroughly aired. Such conveyances, for hours, during the most rainy nights, crowd about the doors of fashionable mansions, the woolen lining or the cotton covering of the interior imbibing the malaria which resides in the heavy midnight atmosphere of most large towns. Women, in the tenderest dawn of approaching maturity, and flushed with the pleasure of the dance, enter these seemingly-sheltered receptacles, where, lulled by the motion, they soon fall asleep. Activity is changed for instantaneous stagnation; the bustle of amusement for the stillness of repose; the heated room for the cold interior of a damp carriage; and, during the drive home, every pore of the body being open, need we feel surprised should the seeds of any lurking evil be kindled into activity?

It is better to be without a carriage than to command one of the ordinary description; one that is seldom employed, or that is kept in a moist shed. All which comfort requires might be attained, were damp excluded from the coach-house, and were this portion of the building warmed with the same means as keeps up the temperature of the stable. To prove how readily and how cheaply this might be accomplished, the warm water pipes which enter the boxes and the harness-room also penetrate the coach-houses—all being supplied by a furnace which is denominated "slow-consuming."

These boilers are of modern invention, and do not require constant attendance. They occupy comparatively little space; and as they burn coke, of course they are maintained in operation at small expense. An advertisement informs the author they can always be seen in operation at No. 155 Cheapside, being denominated "Riddle's Slow Combustion Boilers." They are merely proposed to the reader as the most recent improvement of which the author is apprised.

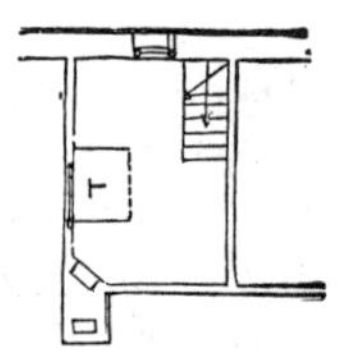

PLAN OF THE WATCHER'S-ROOM.

T indicates the position of the trap, which allows of entrance to the interior of the cistern.

Having enlarged upon the advantages to be secured by the existence of a boiler, the reader must next accompany the author up the stairs which lead from the boiler-house to the room above. Close to the northern wall, near to the center of its space, is seen an ample trap door. Recollection assures us it is situated immediately over the cistern; its evident use is to permit the reservoir to be

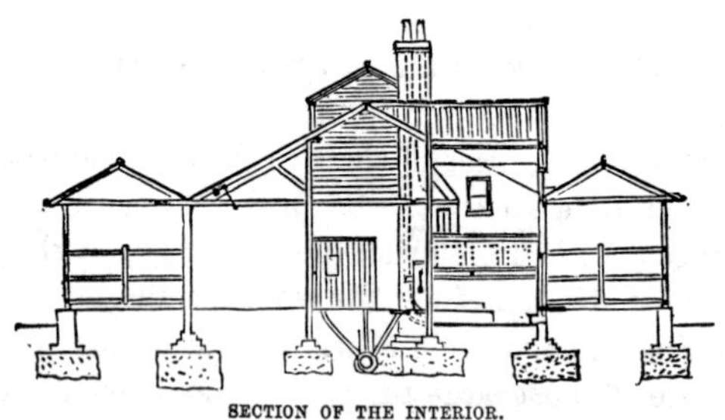

SECTION OF THE INTERIOR.

Supposed to be drawn where the letters C D point to a line which runs across the ground plan.

cleansed of the deposit which most kinds of water will soon leave behind. Additional room is secured for this small apartment by the insertion of a large dormer, or garret window, which allows the ceiling to be even with the highest rafter of the roof. There is also another and a smaller window, that enables the person looking through it to command a perfect view of the stable.

Connected with this apartment is a bell, which sounds in an adjacent cottage, where the grooms reside. Should assistance be required, the bell, being gently touched once, intimates that the help of one groom is necessary. A violent ring indicates the need of all haste. Two sounds announce that two grooms are wanted. Thus the number of men is always told by the number of sounds; and the occasion for quickness is suggested by the violence with which the wire is moved. A number of loud sounds, rapidly succeeding one another, is a signal to come immediately, and to bring such extra assistance as can be readily procured.

Another advantage is secured by a man being awake, and upon the premises. The present necessity for cramming the entire quantity of food down the animal by a particular hour is thereby avoided. The natural habits of the horse can be attended to, the animal not being left twelve long hours alone and without employment. The five feeds might be better distributed if given at six in the morning, twelve in the day, five in the afternoon, ten at night, and two o'clock on the following morning. If this plan of feeding were tried and the fodder properly prepared before being placed in the manger, the animal would enjoy its provision more, and fewer complaints would be heard about the fastidious appetite of a creature whose natural propensities are, by present customs, openly violated.

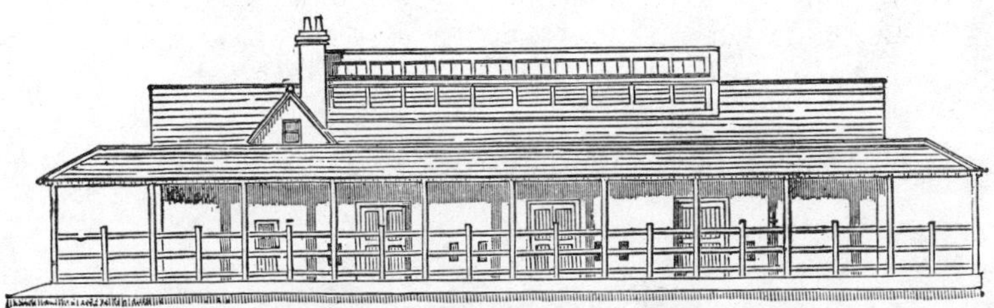

THE ELEVATION OF THE EASTERN SIDE OF THE CONTEMPLATED STABLE.

The night watcher of a stable has more serious duties to perform than most people associate with a comfortable, although a humble room. The groom, having finished the day's work, ascends to the apartment, and remains there until his fellows return on the following morning, or unless some business occasions him to quit it. There are light, fire, table, chair, couch, and rugs provided. The man is not forbidden to sleep; but while he rests, the window which overlooks the stable should remain open, so that any noise within the boxes may disturb his repose. The watcher is expected to wear his clothes through the night, so that should an accident, at any time, require his aid, he may always be prepared to afford assistance; or should any horse be returned, after the other grooms have left for the night, he may be ready to receive, to dress, and to feed the animal.

The architectural designs which embellish this part were drawn by the author's brother, Mr. Julius Mayhew, who, under the inventor's direction, will be happy to employ his talent in erecting the supposed stable for any gentleman intending to follow out the plans which have been exhibited.

CHAPTER X.

GROOMS—THEIR PREJUDICES, THEIR INJURIES, AND THEIR DUTIES.

GROOMS, if generally the most loose of servants, are, by the middle classes, morally subjected to the worst treatment of all the domestics. In the larger number of the purely "*genteel*" families, they occupy an intermediate and an uncertain position. Few of them live in the house; but all of this order have household duties to perform. Very many have to clean the family boots; to rub up the mahogany; to polish the plate; to wait at table; and to fill those multifarious offices which every woman is certain no female ought to discharge "while there is a great hulking fellow on the establishment."

The author does not altogether dissent from the somewhat coarse conviction just recorded. Where a single conveyance and one horse are kept, folly alone could pretend that these can, or should, occupy the entire services of a male retainer. It is far from unreasonable to impose other duties upon the man: only the horse and the stable should be allowed to have the foremost claim upon the groom's attention. Whereas, at the present time, the animal is made secondary by the authority of the mistress; its attendant is too often so crippled with multifarious employments that it is at chance times only an opportunity is found to discharge the obligations of the domestic's nominal office.

In suburban villas, where only one man is kept, the groom often is expected, over and above the foregoing list of duties, to keep a garden in order. To be sure, the vast majority of genteel grooms understand quite as much about horticulture as they really comprehend concerning horses. If asked for their qualifications with respect to the latter, they assume a look half insolent and half indignant before answering, "They have lived 'mong osses all their lifes." The author was born in a house, and he has lived among houses till his hair is white, and age has more than began to tell upon his activity; but he does not, therefore, esteem himself qualified to comprehend all about those structures.

Still the suburban groom can dig in manure; can dibble holes into soft ground, and can drop seeds therein; can stick peas, and can top beans;

can tie up flowers, and can gather in fruit; so, to the height of his mistress's requirements, he is better than a person of loftier qualifications. If any garden produce should thrive, it is hailed as the evidence of Thomas's ability; should aught totally fail, the loss is attributed to the influence of the season. Thus credited for the good and shielded from the bad, it is scarcely cause for wonder should Thomas increase in fame, or soon grow to regard himself as perfection in the gardening capacity.

To recompense for the extra toil of servitude, the country groom takes his place at the kitchen table, and is thereby saved from many temptations to which the London outdoor domestic is necessarily exposed. He can occupy a chair before the kitchen fire when the day and the day's work has ended. In such places there is never any lack of conversation, while the conduct of master, of missus, and of the family is open to criticism. But the town groom knows nothing of such enjoyments; he may leave his horse, during the day, for the performance of domestic duties, but, after dark, it is essential to his master's peace of mind that the man should be thought located in the stable.

Within the last-named place he has a solitary room allotted him, which lies immediately under the slates and directly over the coach-house. If he has a family, his wife and children have to share the one small apartment, within which has to be performed the sleeping, the cooking, the eating, and the washing of the home clothes, to which, very frequently, is added the soiled linen of some patronizing neighbor. Within such a spacious residence, devoted to so many and to such opposite uses, a human being is expected to live and to thrive; to be healthy and to regard the place as his haven of domestic felicity.

Scientific investigation, however, has demonstrated that a London mews affords the most unwholesome abiding-place which is to be found within the limits of the metropolis. With only slates above to ward off the summer's parching heat, or to keep out the winter's biting frost; with the huge lungs below constantly vitiating the atmosphere of the place, it is no reason for surprise if the woman soon becomes a quarrelsome hag; if the children grow "fractious" imps; while the man learns to shun his home, and to practice arts which are needed to supply his extravagances elsewhere.

Undermine the bodily health, and assuredly the moral principle has a tendency to give way. Squalor is not friendly to the maintenance of probity. This fact is illustrated by nations as well as exemplified among individuals. The most necessitous are, as a tribe, always the most dishonest; but healthy poverty does not always indicate the keenest craving. The millionaire may be more greedy than the pauper. Yet when want arises from a loss of health, the desires generally increase as the powers of enjoyment diminish. The sicklier the neighborhood, the more criminal are its inhabitants. Among a people emaciated by disease, the exemplification of virtue is an exception, as witness the fearful sins which invariably accompany the visitation of devastating epidemics.

When in town, the one groom's duties necessitate he should be up before the family have opened their eyes; his functions are nearly discharged when master's dinner table has been cleared. The morning he is supposed to occupy by attending to the horse. The evening he is imagined to pass in the bosom of his family, or, if single, in solitude; but always in his home over the stable. Before his employer's breakfast, and subsequently to the "Guv'nor's" evening repast, the man is, by an amiable fiction, conjectured to be laudably engaged; although, at such times, a sickly being and a disordered mind is freed from the restraint of authority.

The homes of too many London stable-men are such abodes as no life should reside in. The place may be crowded with the elements of happiness: in it may exist wife and children; but to it can be attached none of those characteristics which should hallow domesticity. A noxious vapor at all times prevails; this undermines the health, and gradually saps the soul's integrity. The impurity of the atmosphere induces a languor which almost compels a resort to stimulants. The man's evenings are his leisure hours; but what choice is there to him between the blazing fire, with the cheerful society of the tap-room, and the inadequacy of accommodation or the "fractiousness" of debility, that are the chief attractions of the room which is over the stable?

A genteel groom's wages range from one pound one to one pound ten shillings per week, together with outside clothes and an unwholesome lodging. The better class give the higher sum; but the vast majority of London grooms do not receive much more than the first amount. How, then, on so small a wage, can the men afford to visit so frequently the bar round the corner? In the first place, job masters, or men who let out carriage horses, retain persons whose duty it is to call round at the stable and see how the creatures are progressing. These men spend large sums in "treating" grooms; where an animal of a known delicate constitution is placed, their calls are proportionately numerous, and their "tips" are uniformly liberal.

A tradesman cannot look into a stable without inviting the presiding ruler of the place to take a "parting cup." There is no class of masculine servants who levy "black mail" so universally and so unmercifully as they of the London mews. The groom, therefore, does not pay for half of the much he swallows; and to liquidate his disbursements, he collects an ample revenue. Five per cent., over and above the perpetual "treats" and gratuities, is the general tax on all the bills which his master pays.

Of the oats, many grooms claim a partner's share. On the services, all exert the larger right. Nay, even fashion, perverse and capricious to other people, seems to pander to the wishes of the stable. The animal delights in a flowing mane and tail, which not only beautify the creature, but serve to guide the motions, to fan the body, and to flap away the insects. The groom, however, regards the long horse hair as his property, and, to aid his views, there exists an instrument the use of which is to extract the equine adornment without exciting suspicion. Few gentlemen's horses appear with the mane or the tail in a natural condition, and genteel prejudice sneers at the profusion on which tribute has not been levied. Thus, while the quadruped lives, it breathes to enrich him who is engaged to tend the animal.

Nothing can enter the door on which an acknowledgment is not demanded, while nothing can leave the premises which is not regarded as the groom's lawful perquisite. The first maxim commences with the newly-purchased animal; the last terminated with the carcass which was drawn out of the stable.

For the servant's shortcoming, however, the master is to blame. It is neither morally right nor socially just to debase a man by exposing him, for the sake of convenience, to the certainty of enervation, while you place him in a situation of trust and of authority. Perhaps few of human kind are fitted to uprightly support the double responsibility; but, certainly, he commits a sin who invests another with such powers and then turns poor frailty into an exhausting atmosphere, removed from the possibility of supervision, and exposed to those temptations, while the employer's act has deprived his menial of the energy requisite for successful resistance.

The groom, for the convenience of the master, is forced to stand where man is not fit to be placed. He is despotic over the lives which cannot complain; he is the occupant of a home which is incompatible with health; he has property at his command, which it is impossible to check; with much idle time, he is surrounded by the examples and by the temptations of vice. His wages, however, are barely sufficient for the most rigid economy. The money he receives is certainly not fitted to satisfy the demands of the smallest extravagance. What justification can be urged in behalf of that educated gentleman who bribes an uneducated dependent to occupy so corruptive a position?

From the disinclination of employers to adequately discharge their duties, assuredly spring the many vices which beset the majority of London stables. In the country, where things are managed with less of systematic formality, and where the groom lives with the servants of the family, the same corruptions do not prevail. Tradesmen, away from the metropolis, give Christmas-boxes; they likewise occasionally "treat" and "tip," but the custom has not degenerated into a tax, neither is the ruler of the stable paid five per cent. on the master's bills, nor is the man thus bribed to promote that extravagance which is detrimental to the interest he has engaged himself to serve.

These things cannot be amended with the present race of grooms. They are corrupt beyond all hope of reformation. With new material, a new system must be established. The servant should be accommodated with a wholesome home. Such might be cheaply built, but it ought not to be crowded into a corner of the horse's dwelling. It should be distinct from the stables, and ought to possess two windows, from which the horses might be overlooked. One should open from the sitting-room, the other from the sleeping-chamber. The wages at present paid may be ample for one man's food, but no money can satisfy the unhealthy gnawing generated by a contaminated domicile. To permit a human being to marry, when his earnings will not support a family; then to thrust wife and children into one small room, the air of which is vitiated, naturally leads to the want of integrity, which, properly regarded, is in its effects no more than the consequences of injustice rebounding to strike the wrong-doer.

Against the proposal to erect distinct apartments will certainly be urged the expense which must be necessitated by such a measure. But when the year's accounts are settled, it might be found less costly to liquidate all needful charges than to feed the continual drain which the present custom creates. However, the wealthy have no right to urge their parsimony when the health of an inferior should be the sole consideration; but it ought to be recognized as a religious obligation to sacrifice personal gratifications rather than to purchase our pleasures by the corruption of those whom Providence has permitted to exist as our dependents. The police, who are empowered to enforce the observance of certain decencies in the lodging-houses of the poor, should also be authorized to watch, that the regulations necessary to the conservancy of health and life are not violated to propitiate the parsimony of the wealthy.

The last word of the foregoing sentence is employed to denote that species of possession which should appertain to all of those who, according to the well-known definition of the witness on Thurtell's trial, merit the term of "*respectable.*" To those establishments in which only one servant (generally without the assistance even of a stable-boy) is retained the following remarks are chiefly directed. Where numerous domestics are retained, over whom a stud groom or even a coachman presides, no specific rules are required to be laid down.

The larger stables are, for the most part, variously but admirably ordered. These sin only inasmuch as he who governs shares the ignorance which pervades all modern society. But the animal suffers from other causes in the simply genteel establishment. Two grooms can better attend even to six horses than one man can do all which a single quadruped requires. For instance: how can any domestic lead the creature to exercise, and, while he is thus employed, also freshen up the stable during the period of his absence?

Every groom should be allowed a lad, for the above reason. Where only one animal is kept, few metropolitan stables are fit abodes for either man or horse. These are both retained for the labor each can perform; but, to exert this labor, a healthy residence is in both cases of equal importance. To show the reformation which in the great majority of London stables is imperative, the next engraving is introduced; and it is seriously recommended to the consideration of the public, not as a luxury or as an appendage to affluence, but as an alteration which would be favorable to absolute economy.

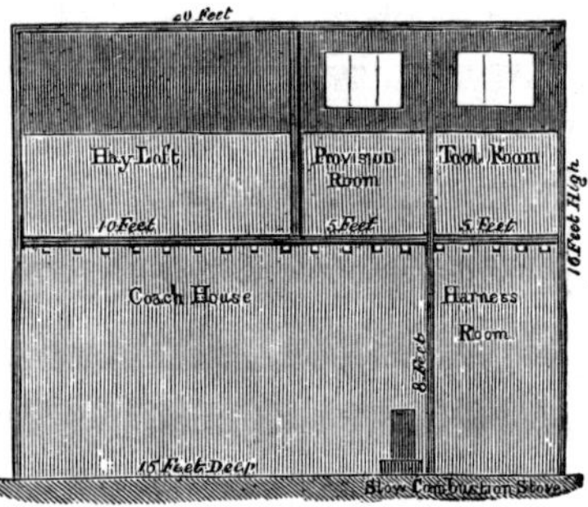

A MODERN STABLE, AS IT MAY BE ADAPTED AND IMPROVED.

The above plan supposes the entire space occupied by a London stable to be appropriated to its legitimate purpose. Within the building no "groom's room" is crowded. The interior of the horse's apartment extends "clear up" to the roof. Such a height may, when contrasted with existing places of a like description, appear enormous; but before that opinion can be established, those purposes to which the house is devoted have to be considered.

A stable into which four inconvenient stalls were crowded may be converted into a receptacle for three small loose boxes, each measuring six feet eight inches broad by sixteen feet deep. The divisions are similar to those alluded to in the previous chapter; but the first two boxes must be passed through before the third can be reached. There is no gangway, and the door opens into the first compartment, through one box being the only passage to the others. This is inconvenient; for it necessitates that when a quadruped has to be taken out, all the horses between it and the entrance should be previously haltered and fastened up to the farthest side, or to where the manger was originally erected.

The hay-loft, instead of being directly over the horses, is separated from the animals by a stout wall. This arrangement obliges that the provender should be fetched as it is wanted; but it also provides that the food shall not be contaminated before it is offered to the quadrupeds. The vehicle is likewise removed from the possibility of soil; and the coach-house contains a stove, of the kind called "slow-consuming." Connected with this fire is a boiler, from which hot water pipes diverge. Above the coach-house, the space is divided into hay-loft, etc.

The annual cost of a coach-house and stable in the best parts of London is thirty pounds. A house of the proposed dimensions, where the rent is highest, would necessitate an annual outlay of fifteen pounds extra. Such an amount might be easily saved from the present expenditure, while the horses would be better lodged, and last the longer; the carriage would be better housed, and not require renovation so frequently; the food would be kept sweeter, and not be as often wasted as eaten; the servant would possess a healthy home; while the master could not but gain, by the better strength and amended feelings of his dependents.

But before such changes can be witnessed, gentlemen must have released their minds from the fetters of fashionable custom. The prevailing folly, which insists that every groom shall be a stunted affectation, is a stain upon the boasted enlightenment of the present period. It is true, a light weight is essential in a jockey; but men of station should be above aping those necessities which the trainer laments being obliged to obey.

To ride, is the last qualification required in most grooms, and it is one which few of the existing deformities can properly perform. The horses, when exercised, should not be mounted, but should be led; and height is an advantage when this is being performed. The animals are likewise more readily dressed by a tall man; for many a quadruped is rendered restive by the mingled fuss and spite vented on their charges by the modern diminutives.

There is, however, one groom, whose weight should not much exceed eleven stone. This is the pad groom, whose peculiar duty it is to ride after his master or mistress, when either indulge in equestrian exercise. The man, being a personal servant, should be active and attentive. When on the road, he should follow his employer at such a distance as will prevent him from overhearing conversation, and will render it impossible for the horse he is riding to challenge or to excite the animal on which his superior is mounted. At the same time, he should be sufficiently close to observe the slightest action of his employer; and, so soon as his master shall stop, he ought to appear on the off side, ready to hold the rein while the gentleman dismounts.

The nag is, however, at the present time more the property of the servant than of the proprietor. It is more ridden by other persons than by its nominal master. The groom rides to exercise; the smith rides from the forge. When a message is sent, the servant never walks; if a parcel has to be fetched or left, the man always carries it upon another's back than his own. In short, the steed has to work whenever the hired domestic is employed beyond the walls of the mansion.

Now, to work the master's horses is no part of his duties who is engaged to attend upon the inhabitants of his master's stables. It may be more pleasant to ride; but which, does he imagine, would prove most advantageous to the animals? To him whose province it is to "look after" the quadrupeds, their welfare ought to be more studied than his personal convenience. There is an accepted maxim about "serving two masters;" but this is that which all horses have to do; and very often the tyrant of the mews is far more exacting than the ruler of the mansion. People, before they complain of the expense attendant upon keeping a small stud, should ponder over the foregoing facts; for where two duties have to be simultaneously discharged, we may anticipate that health will occasionally fail, and "accidents" will frequently occur.

Gentlemen are not safe, if they mount horses which have not received the morning's exercise. Grooms are seldom to be absolutely depended on for the invariable discharge of early duties. Hence arise the majority of those terrible misfortunes which condemn wide circles to adopt sad-colored garments. When the master is thrown, the servant's neglect is too frequently the cause of the supposed "accident." Therefore, where saddles are much employed, the stable attendant should never be free from all supervision during the performance of his essential duties.

After long confinement within a tainted atmosphere, the pure air seems to intoxicate the inhabitants of the stable. People, subsequent to severe sickness, generally suffer when first leaving the house. But a human chamber is kept ventilated, and the patient commonly sits near an open window before venturing abroad. The equine apartment is always foul, and during the night it generally reeks with impurity. The food and the drink of the animal are simple in the extreme. Its limbs, while in the stall, are motionless. No wonder, therefore, if sudden action and the inhalation of untainted atmosphere act in a strange manner upon a sensitive and delicately-organized body. The creature's senses are not to be measured by human perceptions; neither are its acts to be accounted for by appealing to the conduct of its master. We must reason temperately, and accept the mute behavior as strongest evidence. Then, all horsemen must have remarked the excited caperings which signalize the first release of the horse from its unwholesome abode. During such a time the saddle cannot be a desirable seat; neither can we assert how soon the quadruped is free from its excitement, nor what circumstances may induce a renewal of the extraordinary exhibition.

The next thing to be desired is, that those persons who do not employ a stud groom should find some one to represent this important functionary. Where groom and coachman are kept, it is easy to invest the coachman with authority; for the servant is always a severe task-master to his fellow. When groom and coachman are united, the proprietor should pay more than visits of ceremony, at regular periods, to his stables.

Grooms, however, dislike to be overlooked. They constantly assert a stable is "no place for a gentleman;" and aping outward respect, they manage to render this opinion influential. When the proprietor appears in the stable, all work ceases. The groom stiffens with the most rigid propriety. Under a pretense of duty, he dogs his employer's steps. He answers in monosyllables, and in a low voice. The face grows unpleasant in the blankness of its expression. He will not talk; he will not work; he will only watch his master, with an air partly of offense, partly of mystery. The gentleman soon grows uncomfortable; and there is small cause for surprise should the proprietor, having been thus treated, be in no hurry to repeat the visit.

The stable is then relinquished entirely to the servant. There, the man fears no eye observing his actions; and he knows there is no tongue to report his behavior. Before an uneducated individual is thus left in unchecked authority, it were well to think if his surroundings are of a character which neither passion nor malice could convert into instruments of danger.

The attention should be seriously given to the banishment of steel from every tool employed about the horses. Those who are not in the secrets of such matters cannot imagine how many injuries, which are reported and accepted as "accidents," are really wounds willfully inflicted during moments of irritation.

An instant's reflection will, however, convince the least credulous reader of the feasibility of the above assertion. Stable-men usually pass their evenings at an adjacent public house. After a night's endeavor to sleep in a foul atmosphere, their duties oblige them to be early risers. They enter the stable, having their stomach upset; with their temper consequently unhinged, and in no mood to attend upon the wants of an unsympathetic animal. At such moments the iron tools must be employed, and the lightest of these things can inflict the most terrible injuries. The stable fork is commonly spoken of as a dangerous weapon. The man may be removing the bed with this implement, when he mutters, "kim ovare." The horse does not hear or does not understand the command. The order is shouted out in the topmost key of an angry voice. Fear incapacitates the quadruped for obedience. The arm is raised before the creature has recovered; and a blow from a pitchfork will leave a fearful mark behind.

"KIM OVARE."

To avoid such "accidents," banish the use of metal from within the stable. All requisite implements can be made of horn or of hard wood.

To scrape the perspiration off the body of a horse, a slip of whalebone will leave nothing to be desired; to toss up or to carry away thirty-six pounds of loose straw, tough wood may answer as well as iron. The curry-comb will scrape enough, if composed of horn; although, save in exceptional cases, and under veterinary advice, such an implement of torture is better abolished, for it generates the scurf which its constant use is thought to remove. The man can work longer and accomplish more with a hair cloth, a brush, and a whisk. Should the skin appear dry or scurfy, forbear to irritate it with the curry-comb. Moisten it the night before with the following preparation; on the ensuing morning dress the animal with the utmost gentleness.

Preparation for a scurfy skin.

Animal glycerin	One part.
Rose-water	Two parts.

Mix.

A small teacupful of the above should be sufficient to moisten the entire body of a horse; for the skin, not the hair, requires merely to be lightly damped with a small bit of sponge. To execute this properly occupies considerable time; it cannot be quickly performed. But if this is done occasionally, the integument will continue soft; for the effect of glycerin, as a wash for the skin, cannot possibly be too much confided in. Should the smell of the animal glycerin prove offensive, the property may be overcome by adding to the mixture a sufficiency of any cheap essential oil. To harness horses, however, animal glycerin is not so powerful as to necessitate any corrective.

A further benefit will be secured by the banishment of the curry-comb. Those noisy and unseemly contests, which are provoked every morning, will no longer startle a quiet neighborhood. The shouts of "stand still," and the blows with which these orders were accompanied, will cease to be heard; for the writhing which elicited both will terminate when the curry-comb has been abolished. Grooms, by the gentler behavior of their charges, may be tutored to abandon those very emphatic expletives that sound oddly when addressed to the animal, which is the most patient and the most obedient of all creation. Mild words commonly accompany gentle actions; under better regulations, man and horse may learn ultimately to cherish for each other those emotions natural to two living beings that are thrown so much into each other's society.

Tying the horse's head high up to a wall—putting on the necklace—using the muzzle, or employing the arm-strap—are but artifices which enable a groom to employ a needless instrument with unnecessary se verity. Animals with tender hides suffer so acutely under this affliction, that lamentable consequences have been caused by that desperation which the torture has induced. It is better to adopt gentler means, when these are more certain and more effectual than any restraints can possibly be rendered, while the curry-comb is retained.

Having so far changed the habits of the stable as to prevent the groom from riding on all occasions—having brought the man to believe that, where strength is not required, articles made of wood or of horn are as useful as tools manufactured out of iron—having convinced him of the folly exemplified by the employment of such very energetic language to an animal,—there yet remains something more to be accomplished. Small respect is evinced by sullen demeanor. The man, having acknowledged the entrance of his master, should proceed with his ordinary work, until the voice of his employer calls his attention from it, or desires his presence elsewhere. This the domestic ought to comprehend and to acknowledge before he is required to exemplify it by his actions. The servant must be also taught to remove pails, cloths, or instruments from the stable the instant such articles are no longer employed. Thus those unsightly objects, as stopping-box, dirty rags, soiled bottles, forks, brooms, sticks, etc., which now usually litter such places, would be totally banished into obscurity.

These things should never be suffered to remain after they are no longer needed. Grooms often acquire a habit of striking their charges; this practice is likely to be encouraged by the means of chastisement being always ready to the hand. Insist that the interior be kept invariably clear; that all tools are brought into the stable as required, and are carried thence when no longer employed. Jars, bottles, etc. should never be allowed to accumulate, under a pretense that such refuse may prove useful on some future occasion, or may hereafter be sold as a legitimate perquisite. Forbid the insertion of nails or hooks into the walls; for such projections have occasioned fearful rents in a horse's body; and so have the sharp edges formed by the building, whether these are of brick, of wood, or of iron: all should be very carefully rounded, for this last precaution being unheeded has induced lamentable injuries.

In a properly-regulated stable, water should be abundant, and ought to be freely employed. Grooms dislike this. At present, even books are written which, as an innovation upon confirmed habits, seriously propose that the flooring of stalls should be washed once a week. The author recommends that the loose boxes should be thoroughly flooded every morning, and that, while this is done, they also should be well scrubbed with a stiff birch broom. The pavement ought to look clean, and the stable should be perfectly free from any taint. Many ignorant or idle persons assert dirt to be preservative of health; but if the reader will experiment with a little cleanliness, he may afterward be trusted to decide upon the merit of the opposite extreme. While the grooms are walking the horses the stable-boys can cleanse the boxes, and these places being warmed during winter, there is no peril to be anticipated from excess of moisture, though inconvenience may be experienced in consequence of its deficiency.

The stable thus regulated is not only a safer, but it is a more healthful abode for horses. Another advantage is gained by keeping the building perfectly vacant—no excuse is then ever ready to justify the intrusion of idlers. When groom and horses reside under one roof, such an order cannot be insisted upon; but when each has a distinct home, the man's visitors evidently have no business within the master's offices. Vulgar people are apt to become excited by the presence of numbers, and to illustrate their dexterity upon the quadrupeds, which cannot comprehend that action to be intended for play, when their part in the amusement generally calls on the creatures to endure. Moreover, grooms are fond of dogs; some of their pets are remarkable for ferocity. Nor does the educated savagery of the canine species form the only objection to their presence; these animals have a tendency to exhibit a fearful disease, to inoculation from which the horse is very susceptible.

Cleanliness, quietude, and regularity should prevail in every stable. Where one horse alone is kept, the groom should be placed over a lad; for a stable cannot be well managed by one pair of hands. The door of the building should be unlocked punctually at six o'clock. The horse should be inspected, to see that no mishap has occurred during the night; after which the animal, at present, receives the earliest feed of corn, mixed with two pounds of clover hay cut into chaff, the whole having been steamed or macerated. While this is being consumed, the night clothes should be removed; the unsoiled straw divided from the soiled bedding; the clothes should be spread out to become perfectly dry; the exposed body of the animal should be again thoroughly inspected; stopping (when used) taken from the feet; the water renewed; the feet looked to; the clinches of the nails, which fasten on the shoes, should be felt; the unsoiled bed heaped into one corner of the box; the day clothes put on; and those things generally attended to which are required to give the place a smart appearance.

Seven o'clock.—The day clothes are either allowed to remain, are changed for lighter sheets, or are entirely removed, according to the weather: the horse is bridled, and the animal is led forth to one hour's exercise; the helper or the stable-boy throws every outlet open; puts the bedding out to dry, if requisite; washes the pavement; sluices the drains; cleans the manger; allows a full stream of water to flow through the troughs; getting the building sweet and ready by the expiration of the hour.

This morning exercise is, in London, often neglected; but it should always be strictly insisted on. Perhaps it were better, were the animals at once conducted from the place in which they slept and led through the air upon the first opening of the doors: after which they could return to sweetened apartments, with bodies refreshed and appetites stimulated by the morning breeze. Moreover, it is better to divide the exercise and the work by as long a period as possible; and the food must be more nutritive and wholesome when eaten in a clean apartment, than when devoured in a chamber reeking with the fumes of twelve hours' imprisonment. No fear need be felt concerning the delay, as the exercise is no more to the horse than is the early walk before breakfast, in which so many gentlemen indulge with advantage to their constitutions. During winter, however, the morning exercise is often delayed; and then is seldom given. The only legitimate excuse for the absence of such a necessity to health, is the presence of a severe frost. Otherwise, winter and summer, the early walk should never be neglected.

Eight o'clock.—The horse is brought in, and, being stripped, the grooming commences before the body cools. This is performed outside in very warm weather, but within the stable when the day is either cold or wet. Hair cloth, dandy and water-brush; hay wisp, sponge and comb, are only employed in this operation. The hair cloth is used, save in cases of absolute necessity, instead of a curry-comb: the other things are employed after the manner in which grooms are accustomed to use them.

The groom should always cleanse the body in the line of the hair. To ruffle this, causes annoyance to the animal, and interferes with the beauty of its appearance. The daily renovation ought to commence with the head. On this part more time and patience should be lavished than is usually bestowed. The groom is not perfect in his duty until his office affords pleasure to the creature on which he operates. The ears are smoothed and made glossy with the hand. Then the fore quarters are dressed; afterward the animal is turned round, and the other parts are attended to: but one agent is always fully used before the next is introduced. The openings having been sponged and the long hair combed, the toilet is then finished. This being done, the groom sees about his harness, etc., till nine o'clock.

To ascertain whether an animal has been properly groomed, inspect the roots of the mane. Should scurf appear, set the servant to remove it. Also finger the body, which should communicate no thick and greasy soil to the hand. Grooms will assert it is impossible to prevent these effects; but if their labor cannot clear the coat, they must be either very ignorant or very idle. It is useless to dispute with an inferior. Tell him you insist upon your desires being accomplished, and you will only retain the man who *can* effect it.

Nine o'clock.—The horse receives another feed, consisting of two and a half pounds of soaked peas or of soaked tares, one quart of soaked and crushed barley, with three pounds of clover hay cut into chaff, and also steeped: all soil is removed from the boxes; the groom then returns to finish his harness. Every piece is unbuckled and cleaned separately, and all metal articles polished, after the leather has been overlooked and renovated.

Ten o'clock.—The man goes to the house for the day's orders: these obtained, he returns to the stable; he finishes the harness and he cleans the carriage. The cushions should be removed and daily aired: in hot weather, in the sun; in wet or during cold seasons, at the fire. This is done before the vehicle itself is attended to.

Twelve o'clock.—The horse has another feed, composed of half a gallon of crushed and macerated oats, with two pounds of properly-prepared pea or bean chaff.

Two o'clock.—The horse, when not required by the master or mistress, is led out for two hours' exercise. When its services are needed, the eyes, nostrils, etc. are sponged over; the mane and tail combed out; the coat is dried and smoothed; the exterior of the hoofs slightly glycerined; the feet and shoes specially noticed; then the saddle or harness is put on, and the animal is walked, not hurried, round to the front door. If the quadruped's services are not required, the last directions are unheeded.

Four or five o'clock.—When the horse returns, either from abroad or from exercise, the bed should have been littered down, and the body should be slightly dressed; the night clothes should be ready; the animal is fed with four pounds of Egyptian beans, soaked and mingled with half a peck of upland hay chaff. When the horse is out late, the groom and the stable-boy should be up to receive it. Further instructions will, hereafter, be given concerning the treatment of the animal's possible condition when it is brought home at unseasonable hours.

At dusk.—A small light is ignited, and placed in a lantern.

At ten o'clock.—The horse receives the last meal, which consists of the same ingredients as the twelve o'clock feed.

In the foregoing directions, only those things have been mentioned which require to be executed with regularity. Many small acts are, of course, not named. These are done between the more important duties. But, as a general division of the labor, a good groom should always make the horse the primary consideration. Thus, the fore part of the day is entirely spent upon the quadruped, upon the harness, and upon the vehicle; while the afternoon (where such an arrangement be possible) is devoted to the employer or to the stable, and to those small matters which always demand attention.

A better division of the feeding is, to withhold the nine o'clock portion, and to give it at two o'clock in the early morning; for as the horse delights in comparative darkness, and is by nature formed to be hungry and active after sunset, man certainly would gain by following the plan which best accords with the animal's instinct. Thus horses, being observed when in the field, will invariably be seen either resting or sleeping during the hot hours of the afternoon. The cool of the evening, consequently, would be a better time for enforcing exercise than the period when, according to existing customs, it is generally administered. In private establishments, however, many of the latter proposals would be attended with inconvenience; but the author can imagine no household in which the ten o'clock feed and the evening exercise might not be undertaken, and, in several public companies, everything here suggested could be accomplished. The morning's exercise should likewise be given before the day becomes hot or the light is fully confirmed. Then the quadruped is braced by the spirit of the hour, not rendered miserable by the heat and annoyed by the stings of innumerable insects.

The only peculiarity in the above regulations consists in the length of time over which the feeding and the exercising are distributed. The ordinary day of most stables lasts only eleven or twelve hours. The author makes the period to extend over sixteen hours. His reasons for so doing are twofold: in the first place, the horse is by nature formed to enjoy the night much more than it is made capable of roaming during the day; in the second place, the author never dissected the carcass of an aged animal without finding the capacity of the stomach morbidly enlarged, and the walls of the viscus rendered dangerously thin by repeated distention. The manner in which the small digestive bag of the quadruped must be overloaded, by the usual plan of cramming five full meals into twelve hours, accounts for the latter characteristic, and also explains why indigestion should rank among the most fearful and the commonest malady which attends upon domestication.

The curry-comb is abolished; but the generality of grooms also require to be cautioned concerning the use of the wisp and the brush. The first article is generally brought down upon the sides with a succession of heavy blows. Now, beating is not cleaning; neither is one act necessary to the proper performance of the other. The brush is often applied so quickly and sharply as to cause the animal to shrink. The groom would not admire being himself dressed according to such a method. The hair cloth should be used to remove impurities; the brush is employed to expel loose particles, and to smooth any hair which the previous process may have disturbed or roughened; the wisp is intended to polish the coat. Any violence over and above that requisite to fulfill such intentions, is needless cruelty, and should, when detected, be immediately checked.

The more important portion of a groom's duty, however, concerns the treatment necessary for a wet, a tired, a dirty, or a heated horse. Most servants are successful in dressing an animal when the stable is entered in the morning, but few comprehend how to groom a steed in any of the conditions which have just been named; and, of that number, fewer still care to stay out of their beds to cleanse the soiled coats of the creatures intrusted to their custody.

Clipping and singeing are processes which all stable-men greatly admire. However, before the grounds of their admiration are criticised, it may be as well to reason a little upon what appears to be a growing custom. British horses are deprived of the thick, warm covering which nature bestows only in the winter. It certainly does sound somewhat paradoxical, when it is stated that the English allow their quadrupeds to run about in full costume during the summer's heat, but take off every protection as wet, snow, and frost approach. Certainly, if extra covering is requisite at any period, man, by great-coats, cloaks, mantles, overshoes, respirators, boas and comforters, has declared that Christmas is the time for additional warm clothing. But the groom protests it is impossible to keep a wintry equine garment dry; he says that when the creature has been made comfortable the previous evening, the coat is often found to be quite wet on the following morning.

Still, in some very cold climates, it is not unusual to wet the garments, for the purpose of confining the animal heat, or of preventing cuticular evaporation; therefore, the moisture of the skin may be ordained with a benevolent design. But granting all the groom can object to wintry perspirations, the body which perspires is confined in a stable, and an impure atmosphere can occasion a faintness which shall provoke a copious cuticular emission. At all events, man has, in his treatment of the horse, made such egregious blunders that he ought to be careful how he presumes, in future, to differ from the ordinances of nature.

To illustrate the effects produced by a thick, wet covering, and by a tnin, wet envelope, let the author narrate the result of a very simple experiment, which the reader may without much trouble institute for himself. Obtain two bottles. Wrap one closely in several layers of calico; around the other fix only a single, tightly-fitting covering of the same fabric. Saturate the cloths of both bottles with water; also fill the interior of each with the same liquid. Renew the moisture to the two coverings as either becomes dry. After twelve hours, test the temperatures of the contents poured from either bottle. That from the thickly-covered (which may remain wet) vessel will be unchanged, or warmer for its confinement; that contained within the thinly-protected inclosure (which possibly shall be quite dry) will be cold, very cold—so cold, that in warm climates water is thus rendered a refreshing draught. Nay, the hotter the medium to which the bottles have been exposed, the colder will be the temperature of the thinly-coated liquid.

Now, the stable is always a heated medium. The animal with a thick coat is represented by the vessel with a thick incasement, the contents of which are not chilled by the moisture which saturates its envelope. The clipped steed is represented by the bottle thinly enfolded, the liquid within which became cold. But, it may be urged, the clipped horse is never moist. Then perspiration must be checked, and fever must be present; for, during health, the pores of the skin are never inactive. Where the coat is removed, superficial perspiration, accompanied with constant evaporation, must always be taking place. Where the hair is thick, moisture naturally accumulates; because the covering prevents superficial evaporation, and thereby checks the operating cause of internal frigidity.

For the reasons explained by the above experiment, horses which have been clipped or singed are thereby rendered more susceptible to many terrible disorders. Any internal organ may be acutely attacked; because the perspiration has, by exposure of the skin, been thrown back upon the system. Numerous hunters (which animals are always clipped) fail, at the beginning of the season, from this cause. Nor can the author comprehend the purpose served by the prevailing custom, excepting the propitiation of a servant's humor. It is said, the animal moves so much more nimbly after the long coat has been removed. This may be the fact, though the author has hitherto seen no such marked change follow the operation as will allow him to deliberately corroborate the general assertion.

Moreover, let the servant, when he notices the animals for the first time in the morning, observe the breathing of the quadrupeds. The building has been closely shut for the entire night, and the impure atmosphere will necessarily excite the respiration. Now, it may not be exactly in accordance with the groom's notions, but scientific men have long known the skin and the lungs to be joined in one and the same function. Then, what right has ignorance to expect one to be idle when the other is oppressed?

Perspiration only implies cuticular activity. It is a healthy action; the emission of the horse is only an effort of nature to cast off those impurities which man obliges his prisoner to inhale. The clipped animal must also perspire if it also inhabit the building, and remain free from disease. The skin must equally exhale, as a law of its existence; but the hair being short, and the surface of the body exposed, the heated medium in which the creature stands may cause the moisture to evaporate as rapidly as it is emitted. Still, all this will not satisfy the stableman. It is not only the wetness of the coat which he dreads, but it is the presence of dirt that he abominates. Long hair attracts and protects mud, which, however, is easily removed from any substance, after it has been allowed to yield up its component moisture.

Viewing the insensible perspiration as an established fact, the prevailing customs are not unattended with danger. The advent of the summer's covering is delayed, and the system seems to suffer greatly during the subsequent period of changing the coat. The pace flags; the spirits fail; and the quadruped becomes more susceptible to disease, at a time of year when equine disorders are commonly more general and more virulent.

Yet, it may be urged, that in the winter season the roads are far dirtier, and the long coat is so much more retentive and more difficult to cleanse. Here again the argument returns to the groom, and to his distaste for his avocation. It is true, a long-haired heel should not be made clean after the usual fashion. The man should not take the horse outside into the night air, and should not tie its head to the stable walls. He should not dash a pail or two of cold water over the soiled and heated members; and should not lead the horse back to its stall, retiring to bed with a comfortable conviction that he has done his duty.

To fling about water necessitates little trouble, therefore it is a favorite practice with all stable attendants. Whether it meets with equal favor from the life whose heels have to sustain the deluge, no one has, hitherto, been weak enough to inquire. That nature intentionally clothed the horse's heels with long hair, to keep lowly-organized parts warm and free from dust, is a fact neither thought of nor cared about. The man specially retained to look after the quadrupeds cuts away the provision which was instituted by the Source of all mercy; then applies cold water to the organs which Wisdom saw reason to shelter, leaving the members to chill and chap, while he retires to his repose.

The animal, with its dripping heels, is hastily fastened in a stall. The clipped legs of a horse are admirably adapted to exemplify the effects of evaporation That portion of the body where the circulation is most feeble has to endure the effects of the process which can generate cold, even during the extremity of the summer's heat. Cracked heels, grease, etc. (see "Illustrated Horse Doctor") are the immediate results; and the master who makes the welfare of his steed subservient to the idle prejudices of his groom, is fitly punished in the lengthened period of his animal's compulsory idleness, appropriately finished by the payment of a long bill to the veterinary surgeon.

THE USUAL METHOD OF CLEANSING A HORSE'S HEELS.

The author seriously proposes that all horses' legs should be permitted to retain the adornments which were sent by the bounty of nature for the comfort of her creatures. The clipped or singed horse is a deformity: the color is unnatural: the coat is dull and stubborn, looking most unlike that polished surface which is native to the beautiful quadruped. Moreover, those who live in a temperate climate should be content to forego certain elegances which are natural to warmer regions: or, if they will have tropical loveliness, they should encourage it by those means which enable oranges to ripen in England, and not descend to meannesses which may expose their desires, but can deceive no one,—not even the most ignorant in horse flesh.

Supposing a horse to be brought home with unclipped but with soiled heels; with the lower part of the abdomen covered by dirt, and the coat drenched with rain:—the animal is led into the stable; the bridle and saddle are removed; the body is first quickly scraped; then it is rubbed over with a few dry wisps; afterward it is lightly hooded and covered with an ample sheet. The master, who has hastily taken off his boots and changed so much of his clothing as was wet, now returns, bringing a quart of warm beer in a pudding dish, and he remains to see the quadruped drain the draught.

GIVING A HORSE A QUART OF MALT LIQUOR.

Horses soon learn to drink and to enjoy malt liquor. Were such stimulants equally at their command, certainly the animal would excel its superiors in habits of intoxication. The majority of quadrupeds may, with the first few draughts, require a little coaxing; but the primary disinclination overcome, the craving for such an indulgence seems to be immoderate. An occasional stimulant is, however, very useful in the stable. It revives exhaustion, and restores vigor to the circulation. The timely administration of a quart of fermented liquor to a jaded steed nas often prevented those evils which usually attend upon bodily prostration.

The drink being swallowed, the sheet is taken off, and the body made thoroughly dry with wisps and cloths. The lad again employs the scraper: the man with a cloth dries the eyes, channel between the thighs, chest and abdomen, always performing his duties with gentleness, and discarding the cloth for a hay wisp, where the hair is thick, or wherever the water appears to have lodged. While this is doing, the proprietor should comb out the tail, the forelock, and the mane; he should also discharge those many little offices which are not laborious, but which add greatly to the comfort of a tired animal. Other portions of this matter will be treated of in another part of the present article,—such portions being, the food proper subsequent to fatigue, and the right method of cleaning the heels. However, it may be necessary to observe in this place that before the quadruped is left for the night, the sheet should be removed, and the usual night rug put on to the body.

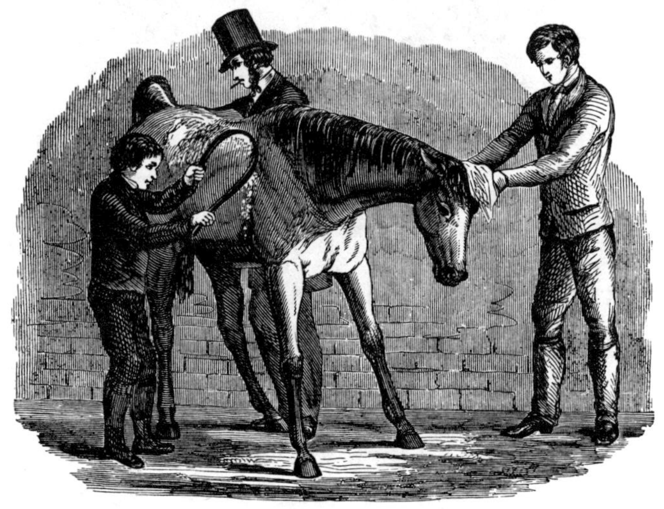

CLEANSING AN EXHAUSTED HORSE.

When a horse is brought in, covered with perspiration, it is led at once into the stable; master, man, and boy should join in its purification. The lad takes the scraper, and, beginning at the quarters, hastily presses out the excess of moisture; while the groom procures a pail of cold and a pail of warm water. All being ready, the master not having left the stable, the lad brings forth a dish of diluted soap, (half a pound of soap whisked about till it has dissolved in one quart of water,) and, dipping his right hand in this preparation, he smears it all over the body. So fast as the youth rubs the soap into the hair, the groom washes it off, by pouring warm water over the place. The warm water carries away the soap, and with it are also removed all the impurities natural to the soiled condition of the skin.

After the groom comes the master, who pours upon the body, already washed with warm fluid, a stream of cold water from the rose of a watering-pot. The intention of the process may be thus explained. The dissolved soap and the warm water are simply used to cleanse the body; having done this, the cold water is applied merely to close the pores of the skin, and to invigorate the system which exertion had debilitated.

CLEANSING AND COOLING A TIRED HORSE.

This accomplished, all hands present, after the manner already directed, should set to work: scraping, rubbing, combing, and using their utmost endeavors to dry the animal as quickly as possible. The horse is then lightly hooded and clothed. Where there exists a covered way, the animal should be run up and down the protected road six or seven times; then returned to the stable. Should there be no ambulatory connected with the premises, the friction ought to be continued longer than otherwise, so that the surface of the skin may be gently warmed, and the circulation slightly quickened, that being all the little amount of motion which was ordered could accomplish.

With regard to the legs and feet of the animal, these parts are so much exposed that to them the same danger does not attend the presence of damp as is commonly dreaded in the human subject. The water with which the body has been drenched will naturally flow down the legs, and remove from them no inconsiderable quantity of soil. All, however, having been performed as directed, the groom takes up each hoof and cleans it thoroughly out with a picker and a hard brush. Then he goes upon his knees; with several straw wisps, he removes so much dirt and moisture as will yield to friction. This done, he brushes over the outer wall of the horn with glycerin, and rolls bandages round the legs.

DRYING THE HEELS.

In the above illustration, the size of the horse cloth cannot otherwise than have appeared strange to the reader. But things as large, if not of a greater magnitude, should be in every stable—not for general use, but for special occasions. The ordinary rug merely covers the spine, not doing so much toward keeping warm the carcass of a horse as would be effected by a Guernsey jacket upon the body of a man. Yet, who would think of employing the last article as a sole envelope for a cold and fatigued traveler? This, however, is all modern custom sanctions for the comfort of a tired and exhausted steed! The folly of so inadequate a provision is apparent, and the necessity of the innovation suggested by the last engraving must be obvious to all who will condescend to think seriously on the subject.

While the legs are being attended to, the supper may also be before the horse. The meal, however, should not be of the full quantity or of a heavy nature. The stomach sympathizes with the general exhaustion of the body; the digestion is too much weakened to appropriate its ordinary nutriment. For a steed whose feeding capabilities are not hearty, a little bread and salt, offered from the hand of its human favorite, will frequently be eaten. Half of a half quartern loaf, lightly seasoned, commonly will be gratefully accepted, if given in the manner directed. Often, however, the craving is limited to liquids, all solid provender being refused.

The animal should not be annoyed by any well-intentioned coaxing to eat, when nature commands it to abstain. The inclination of the quadruped should, at this time, always be respected; for a tired steed stands upon the borders of inflammation, and in proportion to the value of the quadruped invariably is the danger of an attack. Hard-worked horses often want the stamina which enables nature to resist the effects of exhaustion. The bread, if not accepted, should be immediately withdrawn, and a pail of well and smoothly made gruel, with which the meal was to have concluded, be alone presented. All other food should be removed, and the animal left, supperless, to its repose.

GET UP!

If the gruel is rejected, take it away; place it in a cool situation, and it may be swallowed with avidity on the following morning. If allowed to remain, the animal will breathe upon it, and grow to distaste the nourishment. Suffer the horse to take the rest which a disinclination to feed will have informed you is nature's primary requirement. Only, order the groom once or twice to peep at the nag through the window which overlooks the stable. Should the creature have laid down, the man may retire to his bed, convinced that all his well; but should the animal, upon the second inspection, be beheld standing up, no time must be lost. The servant ought to dress himself, to apprise his master, and to descend to the stable; for this attitude, being long maintained, is among the earliest and surest indications that disease has commenced.

A good feeder may simply require an allowance of bruised beans and corn, to be well boiled in a sufficiency of water, and, before being presented as two meals, quite cold. No hay, but a little bran or chaff should accompany the mess, as the desire is to nourish the system without overloading the stomach. Should, however, this potion be refused, it is soon converted into gruel, by stirring to it a sufficiency of water and placing it on the fire; afterward by pouring the liquid through a strainer, the husks are readily separated. It is but seldom that full feeders are thus far exhausted. A voracious appetite is commonly united to so much slothfulness of body as saves the horse from the aggravated effects of absolute muscular and nervous prostration.

On the following morning—supposing no mishap to have occurred—when the time arrives to groom the horse, the bandages should be taken off, and, as each wrapper is removed, the leg ought to be dressed. Firstly, the member should be well rubbed with several wisps of straw. The more apparent dirt being removed, the part should be further cleansed by application of the hand. After this the hair should be combed; then again ruffled with the hand—these processes being terminated by a thorough application of the dry water brush. This operation should be repeated upon each leg, no hurry being indulged in the performance of this operation; but water should not be applied to the heels, without the special leave of the proprietor having been obtained. The case should be very marked before such permission is accorded; for wet to the heel is the cause of numerous troublesome affections.

Most grooms are convinced of the propriety of walking the horse up and down when the creature has returned, and perspiration has moistened the winter's coat. The author has, elsewhere, illustrated the folly of this practice. The body soon chills, upon a change of action; notwithstanding a most conscientious individual might swear the legs have never ceased moving. It is better to have the horse at once brought into the stable; to cleanse the skin with liquid soap and warm water; and to close the open pores by the application of cold fluid; then, with vigorous friction, using straw wisps, to cause a reaction in the circulation. Only, where the author's last recommendation is adopted, the friction must not cease until the skin glows, which it usually will in a remarkably short period.

THE GROOM, ON HIS KNEES, TAKING OFF THE BANDAGES AND RUBBING THE DIRT OUT OF THE HORSE'S LEGS

All grooms are much disposed to treat the foot of the horse as a mysterious organ, which none but a person reared in a stable possibly can comprehend. This is the result of impudence and ignorance, working for the exaltation of selfishness. The foot is not generally understood, because people, in their folly, will insist on regarding a very simple member as an uncommon and a complicated structure. The horn being porous, insensible perspiration should escape through its minute openings. To prove this, let the gentleman accompany his nag to the farrier's, the next time the animal is shod. When the sole is pared, let a wineglass be held over the part, and the surface of the vessel will speedily be bedewed with the exuding moisture.

Now, grooms understand nothing, and care less about the perspiratory property of the horn. They cannot understand how the stoppage of perspiration may induce serious sickness. Therefore, most of the secret nostrums employed to embellish and to keep healthy the horn of the horse's foot contain tallow, wax, lamp-black, and various solids, which must clog the pores of the hoof, and, by arresting one of its functions, provoke disease. The best application to adorn this part is a little of the glycerin mixture, directions for preparing which have already been given. This moistens and renders pliable the hoof, which, be it black or white, will present a polished surface, without the pores being clogged up by the tenacious property of its substance.

It is a general custom to contract with the groom, that he shall supply the horse with cloths, brushes, etc. The sum usually given is four or five pounds, over and above the yearly wages. This custom is attended with two evils and with one advantage. The evils are,—should the man quit his situation, he commonly leaves an empty stable behind him; or the master has to buy a second time those things which his money has already purchased. The other objection being,—that grooms are likely to procure less than is essential, when the fewer articles they can make shift with puts so much money into their pockets; thereby the horse is either imperfectly attended to, or the vehicle (where the groom has to look after one) suffers from the want of proper appliances. The solitary advantage which attends this kind of arrangement being,—that it enables the proprietor to estimate, with greater accuracy, the cost of his establishment.

London stables are all faulty. Such places are much too small. A stable which is professed to contain four stalls, should be divided into two loose boxes; or it might, if the stalls are of the kind which is denominated "roomy," be converted into three small compartments. Therefore, every gentleman hiring a building for this purpose, should rent one which, in London, is generally esteemed larger than he is supposed to require. The alterations are quickly made; and the proprietor may be certain that his outlay will bear a most liberal interest. Where valuable horses are concerned, rent is not a weighty consideration.

The stable being taken and altered, order the groom to watch the eating capacities of your horses. If he report that each feeds alike, or that all clear their mangers, either investigate the matter yourself, or have the animals observed by somebody on whose report you can better depend. It is seldom that three quadrupeds meet, having precisely equal capacities in any particular. The author has, seemingly, ordered one general quantity for all horses; but those who serve out the provender should apportion the amount by the results of experience.

There is one quality for which most London grooms are remarkable; nevertheless this conspicuous characteristic appears to have, hitherto, escaped observation. They all display a strange union of extreme innocence and the height of knowingness. They profess to understand everything which concerns the horse. In every essential of the many circumstances which surround all animals, they will not quietly permit their knowledge to be questioned. But with regard to that particular sphere which it is their duty to be acquainted with, they ape an innocence which, in its excess of wonder, amounts to the possible extent ol impudence.

The groom prides himself on the power of being "*close;*" but he exhibits this attainment chiefly to his master, and principally at his employer's cost. Let anything be broken in the stable, and it only excites the groom's surprise. He knows nothing about it. If a horse is seriously injured, the man who looks after the animal hails the event as an "accident:" is perplexed by its occurrence, and never has the remotest idea how it could have happened. Should anything be missing, the servant recognizes its absence with astonishment, and remembers to have recently seen it; but cannot imagine where or how it has departed!

On the other hand, his knowledge masters impossibilities. He can make any lame horse go sound; he can induce prime condition in less than a week; he can cure glanders; he can render the most savage horse as tame as a lap-dog; he knows how to plan a stable; how to make harness look well and last long; understands carriages; and, in short, is a perfect proficient in everybody's business, though he never knew anything that immediately concerns his own immediate department.

The reader will have drawn the inference from the above fact that a groom is never to be believed. The author laments he cannot gainsay such a conclusion. The master will only be misled by following his servant's teaching. Domestics of all descriptions are to be employed; theirs is no office of instruction. Yet grooms deal largely in advice, and always have an opinion ready to be advanced. The gentleman will gain who can afford to discard such pretensions. Keep the stable-man entirely to his duties. Never allow him to exceed these. Never permit him to quit his legitimate sphere; for, in any other province, he is the very dearest assistant that money could possibly procure.

In conclusion, never permit the London groom, save at certain unemployed and stated periods, to engage in household duties.

He speedily grows to be worthless in both occupations, when his labor equally concerns the home and the stable. The horse is the excuse, when any domestic order is not fulfilled; the house is his justification, whenever complaint is made that the quadruped, the vehicle, or the harness exhibits evidences of neglect. This is one of the reasons why so many disgraceful single horse "turn outs" may be beheld journeying through the streets of London. Sights which are melancholy to contemplate, and disgraceful for any gentleman to acknowledge.

In a previous chapter the author has described what a stable ought to be; but he anticipates it will be a long time before the public shall consent to adopt the writer's notions. Most persons will not soon amend or speedily change the conveniences attending the present form of stables. However, when renting a building divided into stalls, anybody may command one loose box. This is readily made by placing two bales across the gangway, reaching from the farthest trevise, each bale resting against the wall of the building. Such an extemporaneous makeshift has been found very useful in cases of severe injury or of sudden disease.

THE MANNER IN WHICH THE LAST STALL OF A STABLE MAY BE READILY CONVERTED INTO A LOOSE BOX.

CHAPTER XI.

HORSE DEALERS—WHO THEY ARE, THEIR MODE OF DEALING, THEIR PROFITS, THEIR MORALITY, AND THEIR SECRETS.

"All horse dealers are rogues!" Such is a common belief, which too many persons are willing to indorse. The term "horse dealer," however, embraces individuals of very adverse and of entirely different pursuits, each seeking business in opposite spheres; one rarely meeting the other; but all trading with the animal, though with a very dissimilar description of horse. Horse "copers" and horse "chaunters" assuredly buy and sell horses. So far they are entitled to be called "horse dealers;" but all such characters are unscrupulous rogues. Most liverymen, and the various people who live in a mews, or write "job master" after their names, delight in "a deal," when they can contemplate a speedy and a safe profit. Carters, cab proprietors, farmers, and the heads of all commission stables either buy or sell—or do both occasionally—horses. There is hardly a gentleman in Britain who, if buying or selling an animal could constitute a dealer in horses, might not wear the title. The genius which presides over an auction mart has always a desire to knock down, to himself, any very cheap lot; while the majority of blacklegs and of men about town can, generally, inform an inquiring friend of "the very spiciest thing," which will "be given away for the merest trifle."

Of all these cheats, for all are ready to become such upon opportunity, the bad one, perhaps the least suspected, is no other than gentlemen who, over a glass of wine, will reluctantly part with a "screw" for fifty times the value of its carcass. The worst specimen of unmitigated imposition, having any pretense to fair bargaining, which the author can call to mind, was thus palmed off upon an unsuspecting friend. The gentlemen looked fierce and talked loud when expostulated with, having strong motives for not hearkening to reason. There are always one or two very pleasant fellows of this stamp, riding after every pack of hounds. They usually are careful equestrians, very saving of their steeds, excepting when near to some youthful member of the hunt; then the rein is slackened and the spur quietly applied. But of all the impostors who practice with horses, the rankest and the most indefensible is the scamp who advertises "the property of a gentleman deceased." Such a "dodge," judging by the numbers who adopt it, must prove a paying pursuit. Yet this form of roguery has been so frequently exposed, and is apparently so thoroughly known, it becomes difficult to imagine the spell by which its daily victims are fascinated.

A PEEP INTO A DEALER'S YARD.

The horse dealers of whom the present chapter pretends to treat belong to none of these parties. They shun the mews, and each possesses a private yard, with his name painted above it. These places are always scrupulously clean. The entrances are ever adorned with a sprinkling of fresh sand. Facing the gateway is a covered ride, invariably deeply littered with clean straw. On one side of this ride is a spotless wall, opposite to which there exists a paved space or broad roadway. On the farther edge of this paved space stands a sort of cottage, looking as smart as new paint or whitewash can render it, and adorned with all kinds of cockney rusticity. Here resides the master,—a person favored with a goodly presence, and, when waiting for customers, always clothed in spotless apparel, generally of a sporting character.

This tradesman does not pretend to sell cheap horses. Most ignorant people, however, hunger after bargains, and out of such desires the numerous dishonest traders make their market. A really cheap horse is not to be honestly purchased in London. Those who wish for such an article, should follow the example of the regular dealer; they should travel among the northern breeders, or they should visit the far-off fairs, where such people congregate. If to do this involves too much trouble, or necessitates too great an expense, then they should be content to pay those persons who, in the way of business, encounter both the fatigue and the cost.

THE NIGHT BEFORE THE HORSE FAIR.

The London visitor to a Yorkshire farm or to a country fair must not, however, expect that any cash will enable him to pick "the field." Liberal as may be his offers, there is an influence which can take precedence of money. On the farm and at the fair, the London dealers are expected, and generally have the earliest information when anything very choice is for sale. Their advent is anticipated at the several inns which they frequent; their arrivals are bruited about, long before dealing is supposed to have commenced. All breeders are anxious to sell to these notorieties. Private views are proffered and accepted; sales or exchanges are made, and business may be very brisk, days prior to the fair beginning. In short, too many gentlemen visit the gathering for amusement. The farmer cannot by outward signs distinguish such from the would-be purchaser; whereas the dealer always means buying. This constitutes the purpose of his visit. His time and money are wasted, if he travels far and makes no purchase. The certainty about his intentions, as well as the prospect of securing a future customer, insures him the first offer from all who have colts for sale.

The legitimate horse dealers are, as a body, most honorable and highly respectable men. They are not all profoundly educated, though there are among them exceptions even in this respect; but in their business with mankind, no class is more undervalued; no class is more exposed to annoyance; and no class can display a finer sense of probity. There is, perhaps, only one failing that could be justly maintained against the entire body: that one may not be denied, although it is easily excused. They are habitual liars! In the way of trade, no horse dealer can speak the truth concerning any animal he may possess. All such creatures are without fault, trick, or blemish! The whole stud are spotless pictures! Each and every one must be perfect!

It cannot be imagined that honest people delight in needless lies. The violation of a moral obligation can afford no gratification to an honorable mind; but when a large body of men exemplify any one particular failing, it may be reasonably concluded that the pressure of society has induced the deficiency which we, who are removed from the crowd, must not too severely stigmatize. The public well know that a faultless horse—one perfect in form and pace—which can do everything and can carry anything—a creature without a "vice," and free from blemish—is a species of sphinx, which the oldest equestrian has never looked upon. Yet no one ever enters a dealer's yard, except he be hunting after this impossible perfection. Were the willing customer met with candor; were the tradesman to show his stock, and truthfully to catalogue the defects of each,—who, to reward veracity, would purchase the confessedly faulty articles? No one! Therefore the public force the dealer in horses to abjure truth, when they unite and they insist he shall possess creatures which in this world are known to be positively unattainable!

Society is clearly answerable for the dealer's misstatements, since men will only visit him on certain terms, which declare he shall lie to live, or he may tell the truth and starve. His customers tacitly unite to entangle the man in a web of falsehoods; while not one of these persons even the most credulous, believes a syllable of the needless assertions t which they listen. No one accepted a horse as sound, because the dealer protested it was, "as a roach." A warranty would be taken, although the oath of the seller should attest to perfectibility of the animal. A species of fiction is, consequently, employed by the class as a business requisite; but the habits of trade are not transplanted into the transactions of private life. The author has known tradespeople among horse dealers whose characters were as estimable and whose private words were as trustworthy as those of any gentleman whose friendship he has the honor to enjoy.

All callings have certain prides or weaknesses in which the community at large cannot be expected to sympathize. Horse dealers are not exceptions to this rule. The first qualification for the calling is the recognition of a good horse,—no matter where or under what circumstances it may be seen. With the recognition must also exist a power of correctly fixing the selling price or the marketable value. Complex calculation must also be instantly solved. The quadruped may be lean : then must be estimated the time and the money requisite to promote the selling condition. The animal may be worn out with unsuitable employment: then must be reckoned the sum which will train it to a more fitting use. The creature may be a colt, raw, and at a distance from the dealer's home: quick as thought, however, must be ascertained the probable cost of breaking and of conditioning, with the hazard, etc. attendant upon a long journey. These things must be summed up at a glance; and, while the brain is engaged, the countenance must not betray the matter of cogitation.

An ability to do this is the attainment which enables a stout person to stand the center of a group,—drinking, laughing, and chatting; nevertheless keeping his mind so steady and his eye so clear to business as will justify him in purchasing young stock which has only been once led past him. All horse dealers, however, are not thus gifted: very many live to repent the hasty judgments on which their money has been staked; but the ideal, to which all aspire and which not a few certainly embody, is fairly stated in the above qualifications necessary for the successful pursuit of the trade.

Not the easiest portion of the business is to form a just estimate of the taste of the customers; so that when a horse is shown, the purchaser may ideally behold some patron upon the animal's back; for a dealer rarely likes to buy without he can discern his way to the end of the transaction. "Ah! just Sir William's stamp!" "Lady Louisa would give her heart rather than miss that, after having seen it!" Or, "The very cut for Lord Harry's hunt!" These, and similar mental ejaculations, are at once acted upon. The tastes and foibles of various customers are always estimated. It is astonishing how seldom comparatively coarse and uneducated judgments err, though all such calculations may not invariably succeed. The failures, together with cheap purchases, however, constitute the ordinary stock-in-trade of most yards.

The foregoing qualifications are imperative in first-rate purchasers; but other accomplishments are also requisite in the perfect dealer. His manner must be so brusque as to provoke laughter; nevertheless so apparently simple as not to alarm the most timid customer. This suggests a nice medium; but it is astonishing how tenderly some unrefined intellects will embody it. The stout person who, as you enter the gateway,

THE MAN, GRACED WITH THE SWEETEST MANNERS, WHO SELLS THE HORSES.

salutes you with a not altogether ungraceful lift of the hat, and rings the bell as he approaches to learn your wishes, may be barely able to read or to write. In a particular line of diplomacy, however, he is a model worthy study; for, smiling as his face may be—bland as his manners are—or studied as his dress appears—still, he is reckoning you up in his own mind; and all the time you are quizzing him, he is cunningly endeavoring to fathom your intentions and to form a correct estimate of your character.

Certain members of the trade possess in an extraordinary degree a power to comprehend the unacknowledged purpose of those individuals whom they encounter. Without such an accomplishment, no man is fitted to take charge of the yard; as, unless he be thus qualified, the horses might be trotted up and down when quiet was needed to rest the bodies or to lay on flesh.

Gentlemen who do not exactly know their own minds, very rarely become purchasers; but these uncertainties are seldom tired of seeing the dealer's stock run out before them. Were not such individuals to be recognized, the grooms might be vexed, the master might be fatigued, and the animals might be plagued,—only to extort a verbal promise "to look in some other day." Whereas popular prejudice insists that on the dealer's premises all should be smiles—men and horses must appear overflowing with life—gay and happy; as though the place sheltered no anxiety, and none within it knew a care.

The regular horse dealer rather avoids than encourages customers who are called "flats." He does not object to inexperience, when it will rely upon his generosity, and confide itself to the more practical judgment of the tradesman. Such a person, under the dealer's guidance, perhaps would be safer than he would be in the hands of most fashionable friends. But there is always an absence of welcome when a young gentleman lounges into the yard, who wants something and never buys anything until he has been thoroughly taken in.

When an individual presents himself to the attendant of the ride, it is necessary the standing of the new customer should be ascertained before any quadruped is submitted to his notice. Curious mistakes are sometimes made; but it is now understood that such a matter must be decided prior to the commencement of any business. This arrangement saves time, and also secures other advantages; for, obviously, nothing could be gained by showing "a park hack" to a city merchant; neither would much satisfaction be expressed were the animal suited to drag a spring cart submitted to the notice of some titled turfite. The time would be wasted, during which a cob worth five hundred pounds was paraded before a person whose ideas were limited to something under forty guineas; and the quiet nag, qualified to carry age with safety, would not be even inspected by a youngster who was impatient to be mounted upon his first "May bird."

The phrase last employed—"May bird"—may not be intelligible to all readers. Therefore the equestrian must pardon the author, if he here interrupts the course of the present description to explain its meaning. A "May bird" implies a young animal of no great height, with some showy points, but with no constitution to stand work. These quadrupeds are kept, during the spring season, in the stables of most London dealers; and they are shown to young gentlemen as handsome saddle horses. The majority, however, soon succumb to work; many yield as the warm weather increases; and few endure even to a second season.

A MAY BIRD.

To establish a connection requires that each customer should be better suited even than pleased. Both are, of course, desirable; but a person well suited generally becomes well pleased; whereas the individual whose pleasure is alone consulted, not being suited, is certain to grow ultimately dissatisfied. Horse dealing, therefore, is attended with considerable anxiety; yet the members of the calling generally grow fat upon such a diet. Few, when of middle age, retain a figure fitted for the saddle, although nearly all have been good and fearless horsemen during youth. The pursuit, however, is not one of laziness; but often obliges the endurance of great bodily and mental fatigue.

All dealers travel much. They always attend those large horse fairs which are held in the north of England. Their business compels them to make periodical journeys among the distant breeders of stock. When walking over the breeder's farm, they often interrupt conversation to bid for some foal; and may, off-hand, purchase the animal which shall please their fancy. Business always seems the last subject which occupies the dealer's thoughts; nevertheless, he is invariably alive to the opportunities of trade. Some of the calling will buy unbroken or very young colts, though such speculations are rather exceptional with the general body. All, however, will make a conditional bargain for the "likely thing." Such transactions are arranged in few words; and though no writings may be drawn up, these understandings are usually observed by both parties to the contract.

At the successive horse fairs, a dealer generally occupies the same station. His back may rest against some rail; and here, surrounded by an eager group, he appears the most gay of the party. Various young horses are brought and run before him; for, at the accustomed spot, the little man is always anticipated. Some horses he buys; others he rejects. Respectable dealers usually accept their purchases upon no better security than their personal judgment. They ask for no written warranty; a verbal assurance that "all is right," is with them sufficient. Though should any palpable defect or injury, which has undergone treatment, be subsequently discovered, of course the bargain is void.

But low or sharp tradesmen are very particular about written warranties; consequently they cannot command the choice of the market. Breeders know perfectly well the dishonest uses to which a written warranty can be converted. A horse may be sold; but it is not always got rid of when a written warranty accompanies the sale. It may be taken to London. Months afterward, the breeder may receive a letter which shall contain a veterinary surgeon's certificate of unsoundness, stating that lameness or "the seeds of disease" must have existed at the time of purchase. This letter generally concludes with a demand that the purchase money may be returned, all expenses be paid, and the animal be fetched away; or, if these conditions are not convenient, the late purchaser will consent to retain the horse, supposing twenty pounds of the sum formerly received are forwarded to the address of "your humble servant."

Now, to dispatch a man to town, to bring an animal many miles, to risk the chances of the journey, to return a sum of money which was probably spent as soon as received, and lastly, to pay for several months of keep,—are bad conditions. The farmer may be morally convinced that the report is unfounded; but he has three choices before him: either to risk an action at law, to expend a considerable sum, or to be swindled out of a comparatively small amount. Any person can see which of such terms must be the easiest to a needy man; and the last is generally accepted. Thus, by a dishonest practice, the unscrupulous dealer obtains a colt cheap; especially should the subsequent sale prove a fortunate transaction.

The honest dealer purchases the young animal when fresh from the breaker's hands, before a day's work has been performed, and has the quadruped led or conveyed to London. If the journey is accomplished by the road—the stages, of necessity, being short—the expense and hazard are, of course, equal to the time occupied on the way. The railroad is a cheaper mode of transport; but it is attended with a certain risk, which is peculiarly its own. Some young horses will perish from the fright engendered by the journey; others are made seriously ill by the novelty of the situation; while many knock themselves about, and arrive at the journey's termination seriously blemished.

Several respectable dealers would prefer to have their stock rather killed outright, than behold it seriously blemished. In one case, the loss is by no means certain; in the other instance, the pecuniary sacrifice is small, when compared with the annoyance and the trouble consequent on the treatment of acute suffering. Besides, all dealers dislike to have an ailing quadruped on their premises, which they are desirous should be known only as the abode of happiness and of health. For such reasons, not a few of the fraternity, when any animal may be diseased or blemished, invariably dispose of it for whatever it will fetch, rather than incur the chances of recovery, or open their gates for the admittance of damaged stock.

A business so conducted—requiring a considerable outlay, necessitating heavy risks and attended with frequent losses—must be recommended by certain profits. The costs of every dealer's establishment are very serious. Animals—especially very young animals—make no immediate return. The charge has not terminated when the colts are stabled in the place of trade. The creatures are then raw and wild. They have to be gradually brought into selling condition, and have to be fattened till unfit for work. They also have to be groomed until their coats shine "like satin." Such are the obligations of the London market; and though all animals in this state are dangerously near to disease, yet whoever, inhabiting the metropolis, should attempt to dispose of horse property in a more sound condition, will, in the certainty of loss, be heavily rebuked for his temerity.

Moreover, when fresh from the country, young stock have to be accustomed to the bustle and noise inseparable from the streets of London. They have to become familiar with the difference of handling, voice, and manner, which distinguishes Yorkshire from Middlesex. The dealer, therefore, has some further employment, after his purchases are all safe in his stables. He has to rise early, before respectability is awake to watch his doings, in order to break in his fresh acquisitions. None but perfectly-trained horses are suffered to go out into the thronged thoroughfares. An animal is often secreted for months before it is permitted to "show abroad," and it is then expected, like a beauty at Almack's, "to ravish the eyes of all beholders." Lastly, the dealer in horses has to endure those checks and disappointments which attend upon every known speculation with life.

Then, if not sold, the quadrupeds nevertheless must be fed. Thus several, before they meet a purchaser, "*have eaten their own heads off twice over;*" or, in the language of ordinary life, have for provender cost more than their selling value. No reflective man can, therefore, anticipate a London dealer is to dispose of his stock-in-trade at what is implied by "reasonable prices." Some animals may fetch double or treble the purchase money; but the majority do little beyond paying their expenses. Nevertheless, as the dealer makes the selection, his judgment may be taunted, should he not choose horses that shall prove remunerative.

We shall, however, best judge of the enormous profits attending this pursuit by considering results, as exemplified in the wealth of individuals. Perhaps for every man who succeeds in the business, three persons attempt it and become bankrupts. The fourth man may do a large trade; and, spite of the fickleness of fashion or the accidents of the London season, may maintain a position for several years. But how seldom is society startled by hearing of a deceased horse dealer having left behind him any vast sum of money to "his heirs and assigns!" On the other hand, the author knows of many instances where reputed thriving dealers have refused to rear their children to their own calling. Such acts do not denote horse dealing to be a highly lucrative speculation. Judging from long experience, the author would not point to the dealers of London, as a body, remarkable for the possession of any considerable amount of property.

Carriage horses no London tradesman professes to keep. Thus one source of profit is relinquished; but should a pair of extraordinary beauties be encountered, when "on the travel," these will be secured; because the dealer knows there is always a market for such commodities. The treaty for the transfer of these rarities may even have been concluded before the prizes reached the marketable age; for, as a rule, extraordinary quadrupeds are seldom brought into the common market. It is an ambition with the trade to point to a pair of showy bays in Her Majesty's stables, or before the vehicle of an exclusive nobleman, and to boast "those horses came from his yard." Of such scarce opportunities every dealer will joyfully avail himself; but there are many cogent reasons which prevent him from constantly keeping his stables supplied with the ordinary kind of carriage quadrupeds.

In the first place, the horses known as Cleveland bays are costly to purchase and expensive to keep. These creatures soon lose condition, and almost as rapidly yield to disease. Then, their sale is mostly confined to the London season. If not disposed of during their third year, age does not increase their value. Moreover, there are parties styled "large job masters" who, almost exclusively, trade in this kind of animal. These persons all keep extensive studs, some of the body being said to possess more than a thousand horses of this particular description. Such animals are let out by the year, for amounts varying from fifty to one hundred and fifty pounds; the latter sum, however, mostly includes a contract to supply the stables also with food.

Should a quadruped, while thus engaged, be taken ill, the owner receives back the invalid, and fills its place with a healthy substitute. If an animal is not approved of, it can always be exchanged. Thus, for a fixed sum, a carriage is nearly certain to be well horsed; which, when equine episootics prevail, cannot be assured, where even more than the necessary pair are maintained. The gentleman is consequently spared the fruitless trouble of searching for, and the great expense of purchasing, those horses which fashion points to as, *par excellence*, alone fitted to run before a stylish equipage. The person, however, who lets out the animals does not always provide the food; very rarely does he pay the cost incurred for shoeing, for lodging, or for attendance; though, for a proper consideration, he will contract to provide everything,—even the carriage in which his patrons shall ride.

The owner of the carriage generally has to find shoes, stables, and servants, the jobbing being limited to the horses or to their sustenance. Job masters are generally much more wealthy than dealers, notwithstanding the feeble character of the Cleveland bays, and the notorious want of care bestowed by most persons who hire other people's property. Such a business evidently requires some tact and a large capital, to be successfully pursued. It is imperative the job master should stand especially well with the servants of his patrons. Such a necessity implies a perpetual drain upon the pocket, as the menial's good-will, if desired, must be purchased. Then, there is a large body of retainers to keep and to trust. The employment of these persons is to loiter about the different mews; to treat the servants; to coax information concerning masters' habits and missuses' exactions.

Such particulars are essential, that the jobber may know where to place his animals. Young horses would be battered to pieces in the service of a lady who likes to be driven fast, pulled up sharp, or who stays "out late o' nights." An elderly person, who never ventures abroad after dark, and is averse to speed, has the carriage sometimes beautifully horsed; because such stables are regarded as nurseries, al though, more than occasionally, they are used to coax a sick animal back to health. Here the jobber's understanding with the coachman comes into play. The driver makes repeated complaints of a certain horse. "It nearly overturned them to-day." "The servant is certain an accident must happen." "He must really leave a kind employer, if that horse is to be kept." The job master at length is sent for; of course he is deeply pained; but, to oblige Lady Everard, he most reluctantly consents to receive back a vigorous young horse, and agrees to supply its place with a debilitated cripple, which has but recently left a loose box in some veterinary establishment.

One hundred and fifty pounds may appear to be a heavy sum to pay annually for the use of a single pair of horses; but the agreement is not strictly of this nature. The job master contracts to keep a carriage horsed for one year, and to feed the animals while so engaged. To do this properly will, on some years, require the services of four or five horses. The job master also agrees to take back all sick quadrupeds, and to pay for all necessary treatment, as well as to put up with every kind of unavoidable accident. In London, moreover, all Cleveland bays are expected to possess high action. Such a form of stepping soon disables the feet; while the bearing-rein speedily renders the animals "roarers."

These evils are, generally, confirmed before the advent of the sixth birthday; thus, few of the quadrupeds live to be discarded,—in proof of which, Cleveland bays are not to be generally seen upon the cab rank: very rarely is this favorite of fashion to be encountered performing any of the lower grades of equine service.

With these creatures the London dealer does not habitually meddle; neither does he pretend to regularly trade with racing stock, although it is not unusual to meet in his stables some thorough-bred which was at its birth entered for the Derby. These bloods, however, are always "weeds;" or, in plain language, they are quadrupeds which have been rejected by the trainer as worthless. Their bodies are short, and lack substance; their chests are narrow; while their long legs are deficient in bone and in tendon. Their quarters are mean, and their withers low. One or two of this kind stand in the stalls of most dealers. They are pretty and graceful, being agile and light; but, when shown to a customer, they usually stand upon slightly rising ground, which may "*accidentally*" give to them an extra half hand of height; for such specimens of horse flesh are all of stunted growth.

Hunters are not, as a rule, to be bought in London; nor does the term, in strictness, imply any particular breed. Animals in a condition for the chase must generally be sought in the neighborhood of the various "meets." Nevertheless, many a stout horse, which would make an admirable hunter, is to be often bought of a London dealer. The handsome nag, the showy brougham horse, the spanking trotter, the pretty May bird, etc.—in short, all such quadrupeds as ladies admire, and as gentlemen love to exhibit during "the season," may be met with in every regularly-appointed yard.

A WEED.

When before a dealer, if the gentleman is no judge of a horse, or has no confidence in his own opinion, he should not attempt to be thought wise on such subjects. The salesman may not stare at the purchaser; indeed, the trader may appear impressed with an overwhelming idea of the customer's importance, as he humbly asks a question and submissively waits a reply. But, long before the first animal has been run out, he will accurately have taken the measurement of his patron. The man will know the limits of his visitor's equestrian attainments as perfectly as though they had been companions from the hour of birth.

Never demand a warranty. Such things are only temptations to take proceedings. They may influence a jury; but the plaintiff, frequently, only recovers a loss. The verdict is often unjustly given against a dealer whom a gentleman drags into court; but private or extra costs generally consume more than the money which marks the difference between a legally sound and a tolerably serviceable quadruped. All dealers are not, in attorney's phraseology, "worth powder and shot."

Rumors about law may render the tradesman's creditors pressing; while the certainty of loss may induce a man to be somewhat careless in his expenditure. Should failure anticipate the trial, the plaintiff will have to pay his own expenses; for, under such circumstances, a verdict is simply so many recorded words, awarding nothing!

Nor is the seller always to blame. All dealers are not positive judges of soundness. Moreover, soundness is often variable. An animal may be sound in the morning, unsound at noon, and sound again at night. Life is fixed to no one condition. A man may be well when he rises, he may distraught before mid-day, and nevertheless may be quite hearty at eve. Horses are subject to temporary influences, like those which affect their masters. But society will regard horses and saucepans only as articles of use. A wide difference divides the animate from the inanimate; but, notwithstanding the advance of education, mankind have yet to observe in their behavior those broad distinctions which nature has instituted throughout creation.

"ANY GENTLEMAN AS REALLY WANTED A SOUND AND SERVICEABLE BROUGHAM HORSE, I——"
"WELL! YOU MAY SEND HIM TO FIELD'S—AND GET HIM EXAMINED."

It is the safer and the better plan for a gentleman not to bother about soundness. To keep his ideas fixed upon the horses only to discover whether these are equal to his desires. He sees a horse run up and down the ride; observes its manner of going; notes its make, shape, and height; remarks its color; ascertains the price, and roughly estimates its qualities. But he had better not finger the animal, or attempt to investigate matters which concern more than his personal approval. Having seen these things, when the dealer begins to talk, he had better turn upon his heel, and do no more than order the quadruped to be taken to the veterinary surgeon who may be honored with his confidence.

The horse dealer generally feels his opportunity has opened when the gentleman meddles with matters which he does not fully comprehend; and very few gentlemen are qualified to act as veterinary surgeons. By adhering to the above plan, the purchaser is the more likely to please himself by his selection, and is certainly less likely to be imposed upon. The attention is steadily fixed upon the individual points of recommendation, and the mind refuses to enter upon scientific questions concerning which the non-professional man cannot be instructed.

The examination being passed, before the money is paid the quadruped is either saddled or harnessed, and is tried by the contemplating purchaser. When mounted upon or when sitting behind a strange horse, no person should indulge any attempt at display. The object being to ascertain the acquirements of the steed, the rider should allow free scope to its humors, and should encourage its confidence. Employ neither whip nor spur. Reject such articles, if they are offered. A good animal will necessitate no coercion; but severity may, possibly, disguise either good or bad qualities. Should chastisement be imperative, refuse to administer it; but reject a sluggish animal. Allow the reins to be almost loose: let the creature go its own pace, and take its own road: watch every movement, however, and carry the bridle hand ready to check or to support, should either become necessary.

A lively and desirable nag should answer to the voice. Often the intention will be comprehended, when no sound is uttered. There is a speedy and mysterious freemasonry soon established between an intelligent nag and a proficient equestrian. This, it is desirable, should be developed. When the rider or driver is seated, he should reject all further service from the groom. Permit the horse to walk, trot, canter, gallop or bolt out of the yard: should it go quietly, watch its head and ears as it passes through the gateway. Many young quadrupeds will be alarmed during such a passage; some will evince their feeling by very demonstrative behavior. Therefore, allow no man to hold the rein, and, under a pretense of attention to the gentleman, give confidence to the nag, now controlled by a strange master.

Should the first trial not answer expectation, the treatv ought not therefore to be abruptly broken off. Many a promising and a valuable horse is thus cast upon the dealer's hands, the estimable qualities of which a little patience would have made apparent. But a good horse may require to be educated, before it will carry a certain master as he desires; this reason forms an almost unsurmountable objection to any conclusion being just, which is based upon a solitary trial. Most dealers, if they know the animal should suit, will grant a fortnight's further acquaintance, before the bargain is concluded. The terms generally are, that if the sale is broken off, then the gentleman pays for the services he has engrossed: should the treaty be ratified, then the purchase money covers all demands, the purchaser paying only for the provender consumed during his period of hesitation.

In every horse transaction, treat the tradesman with consideration. Many gentlemen, when speaking to a dealer, assume a familiarity which is an impertinent, and not unseldom proves to be an expensive, affectation. Others adopt a superciliousness which is very offensive and rather dangerous; for, while the customer is supporting a foreign behavior, the dealer may be humoring the whim, and covertly flattering, though watching his opportunity for revenge. Above all things never lose your temper, or by your language violate the rules of decency; as, by so doing, you descend to a level where you are certain to be mastered. These cautions must be observed during personal intercourse. With respect to the rest. Avoid lawyers. This is the more easily done, if the few directions here laid down are rigidly adopted.

Dealers are, generally, very accommodating in their trade transactions. They will do anything, excepting return money; a condition with which most of them are not able to comply. They will take back an animal which does not suit. They will allow the dissatisfied gentleman to walk through their stables, and to choose another horse, on the terms that the choosing party pays the difference of price between the nag which has been sent back and the steed which is afterward preferred. To be sure, such exchanges are apt to prove costly, and, generally, are prosecuted very much to the dealer's advantage. Therefore, a gentleman has reason for suppressing his discontent; and may do well to endure, a little longer, the quadruped which originally pleased him, and which may turn out an estimable acquaintance after the first qualms of early proprietorship have subsided.

If dealers have an aversion, it is to be bothered by the visit of a "greenhorn," who does not know exactly what he wants. Consequently everybody, before entering the premises, should ascertain his desires. He must not request "to see an animal fit to run in a gig, but which can carry saddle occasionally." He should not inquire for "a nag which he or his sister can ride." He must ask to behold a horse fit only for one purpose. If to be ridden, the weight of the rider should be stated, and the age of the equestrian is likewise desirable, as well as the habits—that is, whether the gentleman is old or is young, is used to the saddle, or is about to take horse exercise for the first time, under medical advice. These things are necessary, that the dealer may judge of the strength, the spirit, and the temper which will answer a purchaser's expectation.

So also when a brougham horse is wanted, the weight of the vehicle should be given. If a harness horse is sought, it ought to be named, with the kind of conveyance the animal is required to pull. If a carriage needs a quadruped, other than a Cleveland bay, every particular should be detailed, the dealer being also asked to step round and to look at the creature which it is desired to match. Nothing is better calculated to win a dealer's respect than to have such points ready; for, though these may give some trouble to the novice, they occur as matters of course to the practiced proprietor. Moreover, such particulars save much vexation, and prevent the horses being needlessly disturbed—an occurrence which invariably annoys the best-tempered of tradesmen.

When you enter a yard, never request to see "the horses." Such a demand is a lamentable confession. Ask to speak with the proprietor or with the salesman. State what you wish to obtain. Be precise, even to particulars; and inquire if there is such an animal among the stock. The reply most probably will be negative. Then ask if the person you are addressing knows of such a creature, and could procure you an inspection. Very likely an appointment for some future day will be embodied in the reply given to the last interrogatory. Then you must retire immediately, and patiently wait the promised opportunity.

Never be in a hurry, or exhibit any impatience, in the yard of a dealer. Take everything coolly, and act as though it were far from your desire to look at horses or to walk through stables. Greenhorns are always greedy concerning such particulars. Consult the master; rather confide in his judgment and trust to his activity, than display any forwardness to encounter personal responsibility and to undergo bodily fatigue. Horses are numerous, and dealers are always eager to effect a sale; therefore be quiet and rather reserved, being conscious that, to procure the animal which shall exactly suit in every particular, cannot be a very ready, a very easy, or a very speedy affair.

When buying, always, in regard to strength, purchase a horse rather above than in any degree below the purpose you have in view; or, in other words, obtain an animal apparently too strong, in preference to a little too weak or just strong enough, for the work it is wanted to perform. Do this, because strength denotes value when labor has to be executed; and most men are cruel judges, where the exertions of another's life are concerned.

Always enter a dealer's yard prepared to pay for that which you seek, for, in horses, the cheap is, to the general public, the worthless. Bone and muscle, united to spirit and activity, will always bring their value, and are the cheaper, because they will endure longer than a dozen of those lanky and misshapen substitutes which are disgracefully over-weighted in the majority of genteel broughams which traverse the streets of London.

However, pay what he may, no unknown individual, walking into a dealer's yard, should expect to have the positive choice of *all* the trader's stock. Anything *very* good is never offered to a stranger, who can boast of no better recommendation than his banker's account. In country meetings, at fairs, and at public sales, the highest bidder has a better chance, though at these places the market is commonly forestalled; but the dealer knows by experience how difficult it is to procure a prime piece of horse flesh. When he gets such a treasure into his hands, the feelings of his class will not allow him to throw away his good fortune. A fair equivalent or a heavy price can be everywhere obtained; but the one chance of years—the beauty which is rarely seen and scarcely to be purchased—is always regarded as something out of the sphere of regular business. The dealer hoards such a treasure, and hopes to behold it where, for a number of years, it will remain an honor to his judgment, and a living proof that its late master has dealings with the most exalted of England's aristocracy!

In this country, a good horse will always fetch its value, and that price includes something more than money. This is the reason why plain Mr. Smith, who is known to pay the highest prices, never can exhibit a vehicle so well horsed as are Her Majesty's carriages. The gentleman's animals even do not shine forth, when compared with those possessed by some fashionable but notoriously poor scion of nobility. The feelings of the dealers are opposed to Mr. Smith's ambition; notwithstanding treble his money were expended, he could not be gratified by commanding the excellence which his superiors may purchase *tolerably* cheap.

There is, however, in London too much eagerness to possess a well-furnished stable, for a really fine animal ever to be cast upon the open market. The tradesman, when he sees a prime quadruped, buys it always with a mental determination as to the person best qualified to be the future proprietor. The differences between the sums paid will not, therefore, fully account for the noble creatures which inhabit the stables of my lord, and the respectable lot which consume moneyed Mr. Smith's corn.

The existence of such an influence will no doubt be denied by most established dealers, as it will assuredly be abjured by all the outside members of the fraternity. The struggling tradesman is, however, not likely to be tempted by such a possession. A Yorkshire breeder watches his stock from the day of birth. No sooner does the practiced eye notice the promise of extraordinary worth, than the most liberal of London purchasers is invited to travel northward and to consider its probable value. Any trade connected with horses must therefore be of a speculative character; and a fine foal is sometimes partly paid for before the first year has been attained. A kind of deposit is made, to secure the offer of the animal when fit for the market—the money being lost should the purchase not be completed, but the sum being deducted from the price should the dealer agree to perfect the transaction. Thus the principal traders incur great risks, and in return secure a legitimate power of selection, prior to the opening of the public market.

UNCLOTHING THE BEAUTY.

When a promising colt approaches the period of publicity, the greatest possible care is devoted to its developments and to its education. It is not exposed to the common gaze. No Eastern slave merchant regards with greater jealousy the flower of his female flock than does the London dealer survey what he believes will, in his sphere, prove "the prize of the season." The door of its stable is constantly locked. All its requirements are profusely supplied. It is never taken abroad, save when fully clothed and closely hooded. Only before the earliest hour of business or after the gates have been shut upon the bustle of the day does the dealer feast his eyes upon the bare perfections of his treasured possession. The ceremony of unveiling is then slowly performed, and every particular is minutely examined, lest unforeseen accident should have interfered with the realization of equine loveliness.

The pursuits of the dealer, therefore, are not without excitement, are not devoid of care, nor free from trouble. His stock-in-trade is very perishable, and is peculiarly exposed to deterioration. But most of these people seem to fatten on anxieties. They generally are a heavy, a happy-looking, and a corpulent race; but, like all people who engage in a business which admits of no standard of excellence but success, the established dealer in horses has an overwhelming notion of his own abilities. This is the weak point in his general character. Science is ridiculed, and the results of experience are despised, when either are opposed to the personal opinion of *the yard.* Consequently, few of the calling consult a veterinary surgeon. In the mysteries of disease and in the properties of medicine they acknowledge no superior; for the owner, commonly, is the possessor of secret nostrums which he esteems to be of marvelous efficacy.

After the gates have excluded the confusion of the street, the dealer usually walks through his stables, attended by his head groom. Then frequently such orders as the following are issued: "Jim! Get a cordial; this young thing is scouring!" "Jim! Let Bartley's bay have a warm mash, and shake an alterative into it." "Jim! Mind me to-morrow, that Clement's chestnut wants blooding—the legs are filling." "A pinch of diuretic would do no harm here. Jim! Break me half a one from the locker!" "Jim! Somehow, this brown youngster don't mend kindly. It must be some flying humors;—prepare him for physic." "As for Blossom, I'm tired of seeing her. She has eaten her head twice over! Well! well! Jim. Well, give her a condition ball; and perhaps some greenhorn may fancy her to-morrow."

To dabble with danger is the last madness of conceit. Persons thus imprudent will not bear to be carelessly approached or slightingly addressed. Such an infirmity is soon provoked to impertinence. The reader, therefore, will be only rendered more safe, who observes every recognized form of courtesy when treating with the dealer. This is best done by avoiding that silly familiarity which must be insulting to the sensible man, but which the knave likes, because it affords opportunities for his practices. Let the gentleman keep his proper station, and the dealer, without being offended, will observe his. But, before the yard is entered, above all things it is imperative to ascertain what is desired, as neither civility nor compliance will be elicited by a general request for "a horse." When the animals are being shown, let the contemplating purchaser be silent. He must not allow any false notion of his equestrian knowledge to betray him into a discussion or expose him to designing compliments. Keep the head cool and the attention clear. Do not finger the animal. Decline all invitations to feel the condition of its legs. Undervalue your own accomplishments, by professing not to comprehend such things; and leave the premises with the understanding that the horse is to pass the examination of some veterinary surgeon of repute.

The dealer will not submit the quadruped of known unsoundness to such a test; because, in case of rejection, the property is not only deteriorated, but the owner has to pay for the process which casts a taint upon his stables: whereas, should the examination be passed, the purchaser takes the nag and pays for the certificate which assures him of its value. These things being done, before the bargain is concluded always specify for a trial, which can alone inform the future master of matters most essential to his personal pleasure, but which no veterinary inspection could discover. It is prudent to attend to these particulars; and it is folly to imagine a warranty can shelter the person who knowingly disregards the security which these alone can afford.

The customer is thus fenced in or protected on *all* sides. The conduct of the dealer should declare the personal opinion of the man who is best acquainted with the animal. The professional judgment, being deliberately pronounced and duly certified, guards the points where a gentleman's knowledge may be deficient; while the trial permits the individual to ascertain such traits as mouth, temper, habits, step, spirit and mode of going. After such qualities are approved, the horse may be safely accepted; and no warranty can be necessary, if the above directions are observed.

CHAPTER XII.

POINTS—THEIR RELATIVE IMPORTANCE, AND WHERE TO LOOK FOR THEIR DEVELOPMENT.

A GENTLEMAN, when designing to purchase a horse, should think about the matter, and should determine, in his own mind, the kind of animal he desires to obtain. The want of such definite knowledge is the great deficiency with the majority of would-be buyers, and is the chief cause of those annoyances which, ultimately, tempt too many well-disposed persons into dishonest company.

Having settled the minutest particulars to his own satisfaction, the gentleman should never seek to secure a cheap article. Knowing as may be the general public, horse dealers are quite up to the mark of popular cunning. Goodness in horse flesh is money's worth at any market; and every horse dealer in London is fully sensible to the merit as well as to the value of all creatures in his yard. Therefore, the gentleman will best court civility and honesty by being prepared to give a fair price for that excellence which he is desirous of securing.

The above maxim must be attended to, because a feeling person, when he buys a horse, will be sensible he is taking a new member into his family. No right-minded man can ever treat life as it were an inanimate article;—to be accepted at his will and to be discarded at his pleasure. A lasting bond should, through ownership, be formed between mute submission and honored authority; for man, having the right of choice, tacitly undertakes to shelter and to protect, as a return for willing service rendered. Such is the implied or natural agreement: its obligations ought to enforce that gentleness which should guard the inferior.

To fit the reader for exercising a right of selection in a dealer's yard, is the intention of the author. The gentleman who peruses this page must, therefore, pardon an impertinence if, in the following descriptions, he is treated as one entirely ignorant of horse flesh. When all must be addressed, it is clearly impossible to make allowance for degrees of learning The most ignorant must be made to understand, and the best informed must generously overlook those discursions which, disregarding personal attainments, appeal to the condition of the uninitiated. To be intelligible, it will be necessary the author should point out the importance of certain structures, and explain the uses which appertain to particular organs or parts of the animal economy.

The skeleton is the framework of the trunk and of the limbs. The vertebræ are the base, toward which all the other bones concentrate, or from which all the other osseous parts originate. Therefore, to start from the commencement, we see at one end of the back-bone the skull is situated; while at the other extremity the tail is pendent. The arrangement exactly accords with the system observed in every well-regulated vessel. The sailor who is appointed to look out, stands forward; while

THE SPECIAL USE OF THE HEAD, MANE, AND TAIL, WHEN EMPLOYED TOGETHER.

the individual who steers is always stationed at the poop. The tail, in the quadruped, principally directs the course. Hence we perceive the folly of those people who, to gratify a whim, excise or mutilate the motor integrity of so important a part: thus sacrificing positive safety to a false notion of improved appearance.

The animal, gazing in the direction which it desires to proceed upon, inclines the body toward that point; while the tail, being likewise moved in an opposite course, sways the trunk into the proper track. The flowing hair, operated upon by the wind, gently favors the inclination. By understanding this, the reader will comprehend the reason why a short tail is rarely compatible with perfect safety. The appendage, which mankind regard as chiefly of service to switch away the flies, therefore has a higher and far more important function assigned to it.

The want of alacrity in avoiding danger is justly esteemed a great defect; but what right had man to complain of his dumb companion's tardiness, when, to gratify a caprice or to conform with the fashion, he deprived his servant of the agent by which all sudden motions were regulated? Happily, however, the barbarous custom which once prevailed is now generally discarded; although docking is even at the present moment occasionally practiced, under a notion of improving deficient quarters, while thinning the tail and mane are commonly adopted

Nevertheless, the reader of any experience can hardly have failed to remark that, since the practice of mutilation has become less general, those fearful horse accidents which during the old coaching days were of almost hourly occurrence, have not so frequently shocked the sensibilities of society.

Such a circumstance cannot be accounted for by the smaller number of animals at present retained for private use. It is well ascertained that railways, which it was originally supposed would prove detrimental to the breed of horses, have had a decidedly opposite tendency, the animals being about twice as numerous as they were during any previous period. Thus, with more universal distribution, greater security has been attained; and we perceive, in general operation, only the one cause to which present security can be assigned. Masters are not much more prudent now than they were formerly; while fast coaches were not the sole causes of the catastrophes of our fathers' days; neither did such vehicles start at every hour nor travel upon every road.

The turning or guiding power having been pointed out, the attention must next be directed to the region where all strength centers, and from which all ability for motion proceeds.

THE BACK OF THE HORSE, AS SEEN FROM ABOVE.

When the reader has been riding in any vehicle and looking down upon the spine of the horse, he can hardly have failed to remark that the widest portion of the body was the prominence of the hip-bones. The posterior parts, or those behind the projections, are not continuous of size; but they nevertheless are far more bulky and altogether more fleshy than any of the forward surfaces of the body. Flesh is only another term for muscle; consequently where flesh is most conspicuous, strength most resides. The muscles of the hind limbs spring from a large bone, variously named in common parlance as the haunch-bone or the pelvic-bone. It is also spoken of by anatomists as the os innominata. This large bone joins the spine at the hips, and thus lends support to the posterior region. But the vertebræ, immediately before the hips, are aided by no such accessory. The loins stand alone, or are placed entirely without support. This part of the body merely consists of certain bones, over which and under which run thick layers or solid masses of muscular fiber.

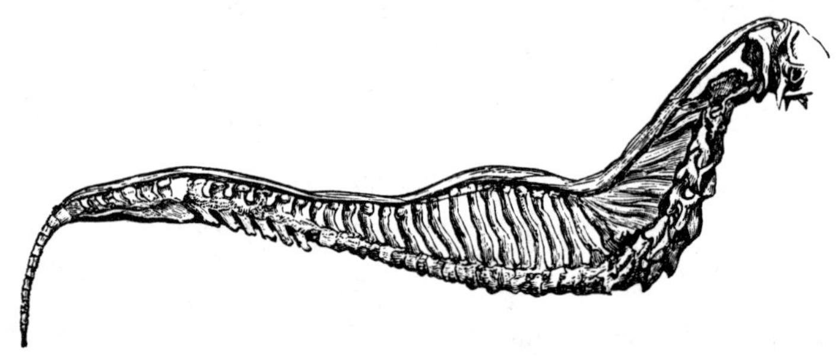

THE BACK-BONE OF THE HORSE.

A thorough comprehension of the osseous weakness apparent in the skeleton of the loins must convince the reader of the absolute necessity which exists for some compensating agency, so as to fit the back for its burden. The loins therefore should be bulky or muscular. They cannot be too large; but may easily be the reverse. Small loins or weakly loins admit of no compensation. The author does not remember an instance where such a formation was not associated with mean quarters; whereas he does not recollect a case where size, in this region, was not evidence of general strength and of remarkable vigor. The position of the part is peculiar. It is intermediate and lies between the haunches, which are the propelling powers, and the thorax, which region is formed to endure, to support, or to uphold what the back carries. All intermediate structures demand strength; because such a position exposes the part to the full impulse of adjacent force, its office being simply to transmit that impetus which it directly receives. Accordingly, the development of the loins, both in man and in horse, may be cited as the best proof of the vital power which resides within the frame.

The loins, to evidence the transmitting office peculiar to this region, receive and convey onward the propelling force of the quarters. So, when the body is suddenly checked, the loins have to master the first energy of the onward impetus, or have to endure the full violence of the sudden arrestation of the forward motion in both the animal and its burden. In the brief but dangerous feats of leaping, galloping, etc., the position of the region and the duties involved by it are so obvious, that the author cannot presume to dilate upon what appears to be self-evident.

Muscular loins are imperative in racers and in hunters. They should also characterize all saddle horses; for it is impossible the rider should be safely carried unless the back be strong. The animal designed for light harness purposes can, perhaps, best dispense with such an essential, although even in that case the deficiency is very far from a recommendation; for weak loins are usually associated with a narrow chest, a lanky frame, and a total lack of every property which characterizes endurance.

In fact, every purchaser should first glance at this part; for here reside those proofs which the scientific mind and the practical judgment unite in esteeming. No matter what quality may be desired: be it strength or appearance, be it speed or endurance, breadth of loins is always important. Lumbar development is essential in all cases. In short, there is no property for the possession of which the quadruped can be valued that is not, more or less, and generally much more than in any degree less, dependent upon this portion of the frame for its exhibition.

A HOLLOW-BACKED HORSE.

The back-bone of the horse—lumbar bones and all—is often remarkable for very opposite developments which pervade its entire length. These are sinking down or curving inward, and rising up or arching outward. When the line declines more than usual, the form is denominated a "hollow back" or "a saddle back," and is generally supposed to be indicative of dorsal debility. Animals of such a formation, however, commonly are possessed of high crests, of full loins, as well as lofty haunches, and they generally exhibit very proud action.

The late William Percivall, Esq., in his valuable work upon the action of the horse, alludes to a creature which displayed this peculiar formation, and nevertheless was an excellent hunter. Many readers will remember that the once fashionable Lord Petersham used to drive a quadruped of this description about London. His lordship's cabriolet could never stop, but a crowd of admirers immediately gathered about it. Animals thus shaped, notwithstanding the opinions of horsemen, are always highly regarded by the populace, and always afford a very elastic seat for the rider. Judging from inquiry, and guided by the reports of experience, the author—although such a make does not warrant an idea of any excessive strength—yet inclines to think that the decision which condemns it as symptomatic of extraordinary debility, needs further confirmation before it should be universally accepted.

Animals with hollow backs are usually conspicuous, even among the equine race, for many estimable qualities. They are generally very docile, and uncommonly good tempered. Putting the undue sinking of the spine out of the question, they display numerous excellent points; and, even admitting all that may be said about weakness, they exhibit such prominent good qualities as in many occupations may be justly esteemed more than an equivalent for their bodily deficiency,—especially when employed to carry a lady's saddle.

The very reverse of all that has been recorded above usually characterizes the "roach back." The author has hitherto found creatures thus made, distinguished for the absence of that power with which prejudice is inclined to invest them. Such animals are to be seen feeding upon the commons about Essex, being the pictures of checked development and the representatives of heartless neglect. The offsprings of aged dams or colts that have been forced to submit to early labor, every feature testifies to the abuse which they have undergone. Quadrupeds equally misshapen and equally neglected may frequently be seen dragging agricultural carts through the streets of London.

Such deformities are usually vicious and spiteful. They are capable of little exertion, and offer a seat of torture to the individual who is so unfortunate as to be mounted upon a roach back. Some years ago, the author chanced to dissect the body of a quadruped of this description. Death had not affected the upward protrusion of the spine, which retained its peculiar curve. The loins were very poor, and several of the lumbar bones were joined together by abnormal osseous deposit. The quarters were mean, the belly large, the withers low. the neck ewe-shaped, the head big, and the legs long. In short, such horses are equally misshapen and mischievous. Any gentleman had better endure fatigue than accept such a creature for the companion of his journey.

A ROACH-BACKED HORSE.

My respected friend, Mr. Waller, informs me that he once had a "roach-backed" or a "hog-backed" mare which was remarkable for an ungainly aspect. But it had very large loins and an excellent barrel. It could draw a loaded gig fifty miles in one day, and, at the journey's end, go direct to the manger. Here malformation was compensated by the existence of other qualities; but the above example was not benefited by the "hog back," which must have interfered with its natural powers. The same gentleman bears testimony to an excellent hunter, of the above conformation, having likewise fallen under his observance. The animal, to be sure, used to "buck jump" its fences; or, in other words, it used to spring suddenly from the earth, without notice or preparation for the movement. It never gave the rider any warning of its intention by rising to its leap. Therefore the loins must have been defective, although the animal was endowed with extraordinary power, which alone could have enabled it to endure the frequent repetition of so unnatural a proceeding. However, the person who was seated, during a hard ride across country, on the top of a "roach back," and was indulged with numerous "buck jumps" during the morning's amusement, although he should invariably be the first in at the death, does by no means present to the author's mind an object deserving of any man's envy.

Neither a long nor a short backed horse is, necessarily, desirable. All depends upon the strength of those muscles which support the spine; though, all other points being equal, length generally provides a springy seat for the saddle: whereas a short back commonly possesses the greater endurance. A long back, having bulging loins, is, however, infinitely to be preferred to a short back, with deficient lumbar muscles. The mere extent of a part can be no absolute proof in either direction; though, should a choice lie between two carcasses, supposing each to be equally deficient or both to be equally favored, then the short back should be preferred, because all increase of length necessitates a greater strain upon the organs of support.

But the spine cannot be too long, supposing length to be accompanied by a proportionate excess of muscle; for length and strength of course increase speed. The practice, common among the vulgar, of placing the open hand upon the upper part of the abdomen to ascertain the distance of the last rib from the hip-bone, is a silly custom, and can prove nothing but the ignorance of those by whom it is exhibited. A living body should be judged as a whole. One part should be viewed in its relation to another development. No opinion on such a subject ought to be formed upon any solitary test or independent development.

When considering this portion of the subject, the author may be permitted to state, it is a disgrace to the intelligence of the present age that any cart should be built without springs. The weight and the uses of the vehicle are the reasons supposed to necessitate the custom. But reason perceives that the real question is, whether living thews and muscles shall endure the burden, or whether this shall be imposed upon inanimate metal? Reducing the matter to a calculation of pounds, shillings, and pence,—which is the cheaper? Which is the more delicate? Which is easier to repair, or the less costly to renew? Fact pronounces iron to be the answer to the foregoing questions; and sense also declares life has no right to be subjected to that unmitigated labor which Providence has provided a means to alleviate.

The tail is a continuation from the vertebræ. Therefore there is reason why a stout dock or a thick root to the tail should be regarded as a sign of excellence; because the part affords some evidence concerning the stoutness and the muscularity of the spine itself. Or, at all events, such testimony is the nearest approach to positive proof which circumstances permit reason to obtain. Nevertheless, it allows of nothing stronger than an inference; but the position of the tail is more decided. It should originate level with the prolonged line of the back, and should look the thing it is, a continuation of the spine; for, in this position, it necessitates a greater length in the posterior muscles of the haunch, some of which extend from the last bone of the vertebræ almost to the hock. In a body whose power is dependent on contractility, of course length of substance favors the ability to shorten or to contract. In proof of this, animals with the tails "well set on" are commonly remarkable for speed and for activity.

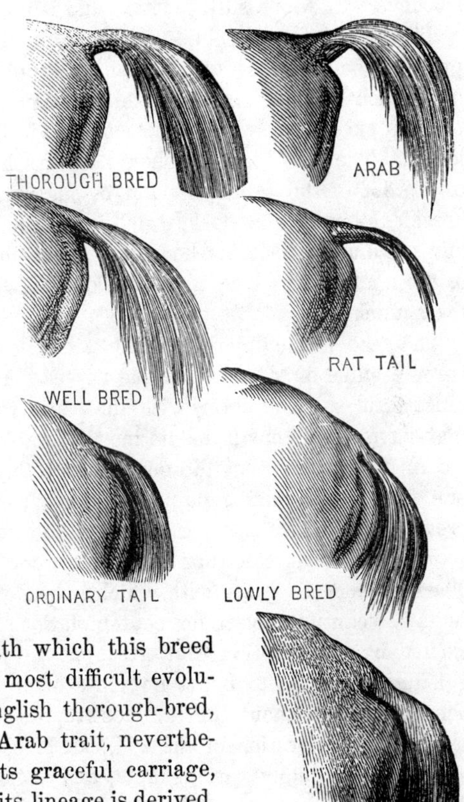

The reader will perceive how much the aspect of the quarters is governed by the position of the tail, when he inspects the illustration which is here submitted to his examination.

The Arab naturally bears the tail erect; and by the rapidity of its motions, together with the power of the organ, an explanation is afforded of the ease and the grace with which this breed of horses can perform the most difficult evolutions. The tail of the English thorough-bred, without emphasizing the Arab trait, nevertheless, by its position and its graceful carriage, declares the origin whence its lineage is derived. A rat tail is a deformity generally disguised in large towns. There exist a wide class of experienced horsemen who assert they never knew a rat tail to spring from a bad body. Why baldness of a particular region should indicate general excellence, cannot be explained; but the author is not prepared to quote a single known exception to this all but universal prejudice, although it may be opposed to reason.

The vast majority of quadrupeds, however, are not conspicuous either for the carriage or the position of the tails. The dock, in the greater number, is compressed between the haunches. The filthy custom of nicking was intended to rectify this position. A portion of the depressor muscle was wantonly destroyed, which of course left the opposing agent with uncontrolled power. Such barbarity, assuredly, made the tail *stick* out. But it injured its utility by damaging its activity. It, moreover, left the situation of the organ without amendment or made it more conspicuous. It was a silly practice, and is now, happily, all but discarded.

The reader, having had his attention directed to the subject, will probably be surprised to notice how seldom horses have tails well set on to their bodies. In short, the position of the tail, if employed as a test for excellence, would cause the majority of quadrupeds to be rejected. The tail, however, should always be observed, not as an absolute proof of the properties, but as suggestive of the breed. The cart horse exhibits a thick dock, which is not remarkable for activity. It has one peculiarity; this is, the extent to which the coat grows backward, or the manner in which the origin of the long hairs is deficient near to the haunch.

The head is the opposite to the tail. In the last, the spinal marrow is represented only by thread-like nerves. In the first, the center of all sense resides. The brain, with the bones that inclose it and the parts that surround it, constitutes no inconsiderable burden. Many structures aid in its support; but the general idea that it is upheld by the vertebræ, is no more than a popular error. The bones of the neck rather prevent the muscular force dragging the head backward, or limit the action of those agents, than actually support any portion of the weight. The ease and the grace with which a head, well set on, is carried, presents a beautiful object for contemplation; our admiration should be excited by a perception that, great as the weight may be, it is so exquisitely poised as to inflict no sense of oppression upon the creature. The chin can, without effort, almost repose upon the chest: the nostril, by the mere operation of the will, can be elevated to the breeze. The motions are equally varied, rapid, and incessant. Each inclination is directed by a purpose; and volition is exercised, without experience of the vast machinery by which the changes are accomplished, although the motions are as active as the power must be great by which they are directed.

The course of the body is, as was before stated, greatly governed by the position of the head. To the inexperienced, the freedom of this part may appear of little consequence; thus, ladies are well known to be the principal perpetuaters of the bearing-rein, although it has for ages been recognized that constant tension will destroy that sensibility of lip by which the course of the animal is now directed. The bit, operating upon a natural mouth, can sway the body during the topmost speed; for by the inclination of the head is the trunk to be rapidly turned.

It is therefore imperative, for the ease and safety of the rider or the driver, that the head should be well set on, and should be carried without sensible restriction. Should the rein be held too tight and a false step be made, or should the foot be placed upon a rolling stone, the quadruped is almost certain to fall; for the rapid motion of the head being impossible, it cannot be used to restore the disturbed balance. The nimbleness which could avoid sudden danger is destroyed by the fashionable want of feeling. It is a matter for surprise that the presence of the bearing-rein is never alluded to when gentlemen seek redress because their vehicles have been damaged. Most horsemen, however, esteem the neck for its appearance, and few comprehend its utility.

Any person can discern the difference which characterizes the necks here represented. The galloway in front has a well-formed neck, although many pretended judges would object that it is too bulky.

THE FORM OF NECK GENERALLY INDICATES THE DISPOSITION OF A HORSE.

Bulk supposes the presence of muscle; therefore a neck, if properly shaped, cannot be too thick. The majority of the cervical motor agents extend either to the trunk or to the fore limbs. The size of the neck, consequently, influences other regions, and confers positive advantage of both strength and activity.

A head well set on is carried in advance of the body only so far as may be necessary to counteract the comparative lightness of the forward structures.

On the other hand, thinness and smallness of neck is one of the peculiar features of emaciation in the horse. It is always seen in the old and in the half-starved quadruped. Hence it may be inferred not to be a sign of vigor in any condition. The observation should be directed to the balance, the ease, and the activity of the cervical region. As respects its bulk, the author never remembers to have beheld an animal with a neck too thick; though, he is sorry to confess, he has witnessed many of man's servitors with this part of the body most lamentably attenuated.

The second horse, in the foregoing illustration, has that form of neck which is commonly seen upon what are called "well bred" and "good horses." It is not incompatible with safety of pace; but it is deficient in beauty of outline or grace of carriage; and it cannot be fully equal to all the uses of a well-formed neck. The chin may be lowered; but it will be at the expense of an effort, and by the unscrupulous employment of the bit or the rein. Such a resort must inflict acute torture, especially as this particular kind of neck is rarely accompanied by breadth of channel or width of space between the branches of the lower jaw.

The inability to lower the head with ease, removes the eye from the ground, and exposes an animal to trip or to stumble, should any sudden inequality be present in the road. The second form is, therefore, preferable to the succeeding neck, which, though possessed of a more graceful crest, yet in the protrusion of the nose indicates that strain upon the muscular system by which progression is accomplished. No force, save that of mechanism, can possibly bring and hold down such a head. This defect exposes the animal to much suffering, renders it liable to fall, makes it very heavy in the hand, and speedily ruins the mouth.

The last horse exhibits the worst form of the group,—or it presents a long neck with the head pointing downward. Such an animal is never safe in harness; but is totally unsuited for the saddle. Creatures thus formed are commonly good tempered, but sluggish. This position of the head should to all, save only the totally inexperienced, characterize a deficiency of nervous energy; and likewise indicate the cost at which pace is maintained, and declare the uncertainty of foot. The neck should never be protruded, save during the exertion of the greatest speed. An animal which habitually assumes this attitude, suggests that an ordinary effort is felt to be a mighty tax upon its capabilities.

The following illustration exhibits a peculiarity of form which the author believes is confined to the heavier breed of draught horses. Such a neck is alone compatible with slowness of pace. It is, however, falsely imagined to denote excessive strength. So far as thickness is concerned, muscle must be present, or adipose tissue must abound; but in length there is a deficiency which necessarily will limit the amount of motor power. In justification of this opinion, may be quoted a well-known fact, that the huge mountains of flesh which parade the streets of London before the brewers' drays, are not remarkable for a power of draught, for a capability of endurance, or for any length of existence.

A BULL NECK.

The ewe-necked horse is one in which every appearance of crest is absent. Such a form may possess length; but it is generally wanting both in depth and in substance. Animals of this formation are generally active, but weakly: other parts are too often characterized by a narrowness of build, which materially detracts from a capability for endurance

THE EWE NECK.

The appearance is, moreover, mean; this is usually rendered more conspicuous by a thinness and a shortness of mane. The shape of the neck is not, however, to be considered only as governing other organs, but is also to be regarded as a consequence of a prevailing absence of development. So may the frequent accompaniment of a vicious disposition be viewed as the result of that feebleness which converts the easiest task into a mighty labor, and of that absence of beauty which can neither kindle the pride nor awaken the fondness of the owner.

Certain supposed judges are greatly prejudiced in favor of a short neck. The characteristic is in some minds associated with the presence of bodily strength; but it cannot be remarkable for denoting the existence of such a quality, because an absence of length must abbreviate the amount of muscular fiber. Shortness of neck, besides suggesting the presence of fat, and interfering with activity, unfits the animal for certain situations. A bull neck, although its possessor inhabited the most luxuriant pasture, would compel the creature to subsist on short commons. *Nags*, however long may be the legs, or short shall be their necks, generally manage to crop the grass, although to do so may cause a constant strain upon the limbs, thus counteracting one of those effects which the run is invariably supposed to realize. Below is inserted an illustration showing the artifice adopted by animals of this description.

THE MANNER IN WHICH A SHORT-NECKED HORSE MANAGES TO FEED OFF THE GROUND.

Having noticed those portions of the spinal column in which the vertebræ are not associated with other bones, or do not enter into the formation of compound parts, it may assist the judgment of the reader if the relative importance of these regions is more particularly descanted upon.

However desirable an arched and lofty crest may be, it is not, when separately considered, any absolute proof of estimable properties. Conjoined with other points, it renders excellence more excellent; but, alone, no deduction should be drawn from it. In many parts of Germany, the horses exhibit beautifully formed necks, bearing luxuriant manes; but in other respects the quadrupeds are lanky, weak, and washy creatures The dock deserves attention, although it can warrant no more than an inference. If it suggests that which other developments equally support, it constitutes a valuable accessory toward a sound opinion; but, by itself, it is of no importance. On the contrary, the loins are absolute proof: their swelling testimony may be trusted, should both neck and tail oppose their evidence. This portion of the body never deceives. It is worthy of all reliance: what it declares must be implicitly received. And, to many minds, it may appear the more deserving of estimation, because full loins are commonly accompanied by a stout dock.

Attached to the neck is the head, which, in the horse, always bespeaks those changes produced by varieties of treatment and difference of climate. The favorite and the companion of the semi-civilized Arab is, by its association with its master, elevated in intelligence as in beauty

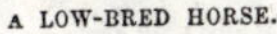
A LOW-BRED HORSE.

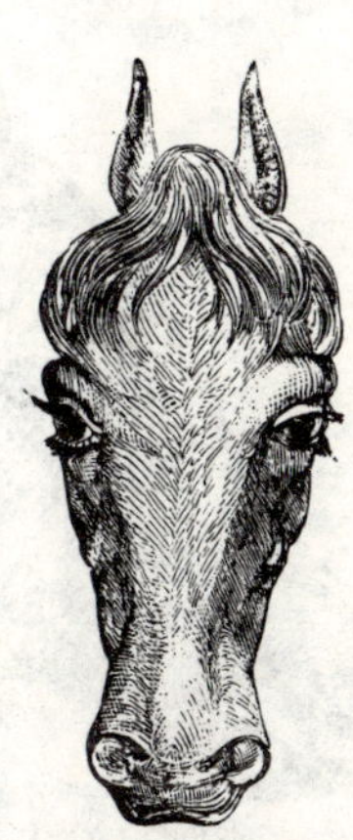
A WELL-BRED HORSE.

The agricultural teamster of this country exhibits, in its expression, the apathy with which it is regarded by its rustic attendant. These are, probably, the extremes of the race. That the reader may recognize the distinction between them, front views of both heads are above shown.

In the Arab, the spectator can hardly fail to remark the distance by

which the eyes are divided. The brow is equally characterized by its length as by its breadth, and constitutes no mean portion of the entire head. In the lowly-bred face, the region of the brain is comparatively small, its width presenting no obvious contrast to the other features. The nostrils are not only compressed, but their margins are thick; while the upper lip is adorned by a pair of abundant mustaches. Some animals the author has beheld with embellishments of this order which would not have disgraced the most hirsute of guardsmen.

The head of a well-bred horse has been frequently described as forming a straight line in its forward margin, when it is contemplated from the side. Such an assertion is generally true; but it must not be received as absolutely correct. Horses have been imported from Arabia with the craniums and the frontal sinuses considerably enlarged. Such a peculiarity is not esteemed a defect by the natives of the East. This fact is established by animals, thus characterized, having been sent to this country as presents for personages of exalted rank. Such developments may not strictly accord with English notions of equine beauty; but the size of the case, in some measure, denotes the magnitude of that which it contains. A large brain can be no detriment to any animal which is partly prized for its intelligence.

BULGING FRONTAL SINUSES.

A CART HORSE, WITH THE ROMAN NOSE

Another peculiarity exhibited by a few English thorough-breds, is the Roman nose, or a prominence of the nasal bones. The trait is, however, less common in the pure Arabian blood than is the previous development. There is a breed of blood horses which exhibit a prominence of the nasal bones, or, in other words, present what is designated as the "Roman nose." This particular shape, however, is with the coarser breeds far from unusual; although in animals of slow work it cannot be esteemed a beauty, it also should not be condemned as a huge defect. The depression of the nasal point may allow less freedom to the nostril; but in a creature whose kind of labor permits slow respiration to be employed, this constitutes no absolute objection; while many quadrupeds of this formation are conspicuous for their high courage and their lively disposition.

The leading or distinguishing characteristic of the thorough-bred horse is its superior intelligence. The stranger hardly has spoken to the creature, before it begins to investigate his personal appearance. It appears to appreciate the words addressed to it, and it responds to any act of kindness which may be lavished upon it. Added to this, is the evident neatness of its formation; the clearness of its various features; the grace as well as the lightness of its construction, united with speaking evidences of strength and of energy. The quadruped appears fit to be the associate of man, and almost seems upon an intellectual level with its master. As we contemplate the lustrous eye, and feel the rush of inquisitive breath, it is impossible not to credit the tales narrated of the creature's affection and of its generosity. We can then sympathize with the love of the Arab for his steed, and sensibly feel that life in the desert would be rendered less desolate by the presence of such a companion.

Yet this elegant quadruped is cast in no arbitrary mould. Its beauty admits of the same variety which is conspicuous in other animated bodies. The ears usually are small, and approximate toward their tips; but they may also be large, and the points may be even wider apart than the roots of the organs. Yet, in every shape, a thinness or a delicacy of the outer walls, a nice arrangement of the internal protecting hairs, together with a fineness in the investing coat, attest to the purity of the parental stock.

A tribe of lop-eared thorough-breds are known to exist upon the English course: this peculiarity, however, is not a distinguishing mark of purity of blood, or a characteristic running throughout the race. The fall of the ear exposes the interior of the organ to the eye of the spectator: that circumstance, no doubt, suggested the removal of the hairs which nature placed as guards before the opening. It is now a common practice, with almost every groom, to *singe* off these hairs with the flame of a candle. Such an agent cannot be safely intrusted to vulgar hands; probably to this foolish custom is owing the deafness which by horses is so frequently exhibited. Any protruding hair the scissors might excise; but as regards the interior of the ear, grooms, had they even a slight acquaintance with physiology, would know that the common Father was actuated by benevolence in all His ordinizations, and therefore hairs have their appointed uses.

GOOD AND ACTIVE EARS. LARGE EARS. EARS WIDE APART. LOW-BRED EARS.

With the ears no corporal excellence is connected, but with the health of this organ the general safety is associated; for the acuteness of the animal's hearing affords no mean protection to the rider. The absolute quietude of the ears indicates that sounds are powerless to excite the organ. Excessive restlessness of these parts suggests that by straining of one sense, the animal is endeavoring to recompense the obscurity of another: that the vision is either lost or imperfect. A lively carriage of the ears expresses a sprightly temper, and generally denotes a kind disposition; whereas one member constantly directed forward and the other backward, is a frequent sign of "vice," or of timidity in its watchfulness.

Near the ear is the seat of another special sense. Many people will pretend to discover the disposition of a horse by the character of the eyes. A restlessness of the globe, the display of any unusual quantity of white, and a perpetual tension on the upper lid are imagined to signify a "vicious" inclination; but, in reality, these traits express only the watchfulness of fear. Such indications are evidences of that suffering which has been experienced; and these traits are consonant with an anxiety to escape the future assaults of brutality. Despair may not be desirable as a companion; but it is not, therefore, to be falsely stigmatized.

A prominent eye, expressive of repose, and not exhibiting an abundance of white, has been pronounced to be declarative of honesty, though certain parties have condemned it as indicative of slothfulness. A quickness or activity, as contradistinguished from a restlessness in the visual organ, is, however, to be desired. The small eye usual with the coarser breed of animals should be avoided, because it is generally accompanied by a heaviness of movement. The retracted or deep-set eye, which displays the organ only partially, which is somewhat angular in figure, and which is commonly spoken of as "a pig-eye," denotes either weakness of the part, or, to the majority of horsemen, will suggest a previous attack of specific ophthalmia. The disease, however, is not, in the author's opinion, hereditary, but is generated by that closeness of abode and that absence of ventilation to which all grooms strongly incline. The present writer has most frequently beheld ophthalmia in full and in perfect organs.

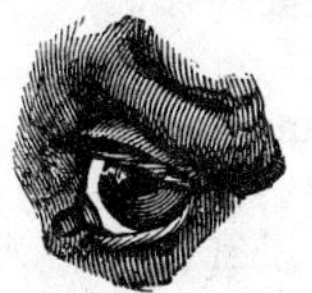

A WATCHFUL AND TIMID EYE.

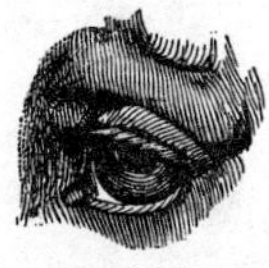

AN HONEST EYE.

A LOW-BRED EYE.

A DISEASED, OR PIG-EYE.

Before quitting the consideration of the face, it is imperative that the mouth and nostrils should be alluded to. In the well-bred horse, these are both large, when compared with the same developments in the animal of a coarser origin. The lips should be smooth, soft, compressed, and suggestive of energy; but they should be without the smallest aspect of ill temper. About them, numerous isolated and long hairs may be located; but there should be no accumulation resembling a mustache, or bearing even a distant likeness to a beard. Such growths are commonly removed by the scissors of the groom; but the palm of the hand, if placed against the muzzle, is certain to ascertain the truth if those things ever have been in existence.

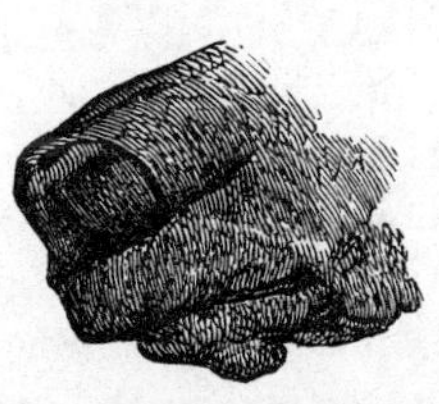

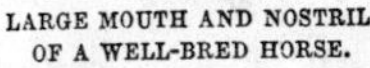

LARGE MOUTH AND NOSTRIL OF A WELL-BRED HORSE.

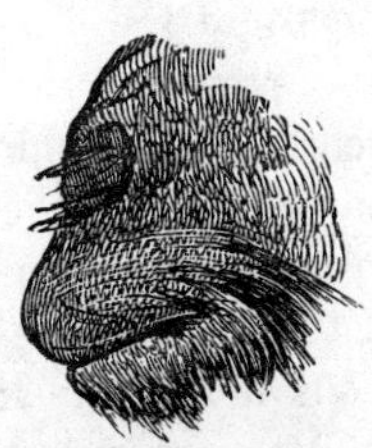

SMALL MOUTH AND NOSTRIL OF A LOW-BRED HORSE.

THE MOUTH AND NOSTRIL OF AN OLD, DEJECTED, WELL-BRED HORSE.

The lowly-bred animal, being chiefly employed for slow uses, has not the need for those ample draughts of air which the faster speed necessitates should be rapidly respired; nor is the mouth declarative of the same determination which marks the lips of the purer blood. The bit is scarcely ever present upon the carter's harness, nor are the mouths of his charges formed to retain this invention. The characteristics of low birth cannot be effaced from the countenance of a quadruped. Age or privation cannot confound the two breeds. The thorough-bred in ruin is not to be mistaken for the teamster. No want, no suffering, no length of years can obliterate the evidence of nobility from the animal of pure descent.

When purchasing a horse, it is always well to examine the angles of the lips. If any sign of induration is remarked, it signifies that the animal has suffered from the abuse of the bit. If on any limited space, however small, a patch of white skin is observed located upon a dark ground, it denotes that "once upon a time" the true skin has been removed from that place, while cicatrix now exists to apprise future purchasers of the fact. If anything like a hardened lump should be felt in this situation, it demonstrates that the quadruped has a hard mouth, and is an obstinate puller, or that it has passed through the hands of an unfeeling master.

In either case, the creature is not a desirable possession. Harshness is not a kindly educator, nor does it beget docility of spirit in the being which is subjected to its exactions. A hard mouth necessitates one of the severest trials which can be inflicted on a horse proprietor. It is painful, every time a change of direction is desired, for the rider to tug at the reins; such a necessity soon destroys every pleasure of the exercise. But a regular puller is always a dangerous servant. Generally it turns out to be a "bolter," and, before running away, will seize the bit between its teeth, when the driver or the rider alike is helpless. Our entreaty to the reader is, to turn his back upon the offer, should he ever be solicited to buy a horse having a damaged mouth.

At this point it is requisite the author should review the various organs which, together, constitute the head. An activity equally removed from stillness and from restlessness, denotes health to be present in all the seats of special sense. These things are of more importance than at first glance is apparent, because such united testimony is the best security as regards the general system. It equally testifies to the soundness of the brain and to the healthiness of the body. When the animal suffers, the perceptions mostly are inactive; when the brain is oppressed, the loss of sense first announces the disorder.

These organs also deserve attention for their own sakes. Man is not gifted with remarkable faculties either in seeing, in hearing, or in smelling. He therefore desires such assistance as the companion of his journey may afford. The value, consequently, of an animal is materially deteriorated by the loss of any of its protective powers. These, when all enjoyed in perfection, assist one another. When any organ is excited, the rest are seldom dormant. Thus when the quadruped perceives in the distance some obscure object, the ears are advanced and the nostrils are inflated. The same general movement is remarked whenever the hearing catches a distant sound, or whenever the scent detects a novel odor. All are conjoined to produce one result; therefore the loss of one cannot be without effect upon the uniformity of action.

As regards the formation of the countenance, an enlarged cranium is no detriment; but the Roman nose sometimes interferes with the capacity of the nostril. When it produces such a result, the peculiarity warrants either a reduction of price or an absolute rejection of the offered sale. In other respects, this make is regarded as of no importance; but it certainly does not add to the appearance of the animal. Horses are generally prized in proportion to their beauty: nor can the author quarrel with such a foundation of judgment, as, in most animals, harmony of figure justifies a belief that excellence of spirit also exists.

The nostrils, however, are associated with the important function of respiration; therefore these organs demand consideration, when regarded apart from the other senses. They admit the air which is inhaled by the expansion of the chest; consequently the dimension of the nostrils allows an inference to be drawn as to the capacity of the lungs. This opinion, however, should be only advanced after the alteration has been noted between their size when at rest and their enlargement when excited. Should no marked variation be produced by the opposite states, then the value of the animal is only to be considered in connection with slow work, as the speed must be regulated by the capability of receiving a quantity of vital air proportioned to the power exerted.

After the capacity has been observed, the nature of the movements of the nasal openings should be noticed. Subsequent to exertion, ease of motion is not to be anticipated; but nothing approaching to spasmodic action should be remarked. The nostrils ought to be regularly expanded: not to fly open with a jerk, or to suddenly enlarge their form, as under the influence of a gasp. A capability of dilatation, attended with an evenness of motion, however fast the movement may be, are the points which should be looked for in the nostrils of a horse,—because the characteristic changes attending inhalation best expose any defect in the respiratory apparatus; for, by such a test, the remotest disposition to become a roarer, or to exhibit diseased wind, is easy of detection.

Connected with the head, every horseman comprehends how much width of channel, or of space between the branches of the lower jaw, is to be desired. The reason why such a form is highly prized in an animal of fleetness or of exertion, is because such an opening allows room for the varied movements necessary for the offices of respiration, or for the change of position imperative in the larynx, which is located near to or within the hollow thus provided. Clear space is of course imperative, wherever rapidity of movement has to be executed. There is also another thing equally desirable. That addition is a full development of the motor power which affects the larynx.

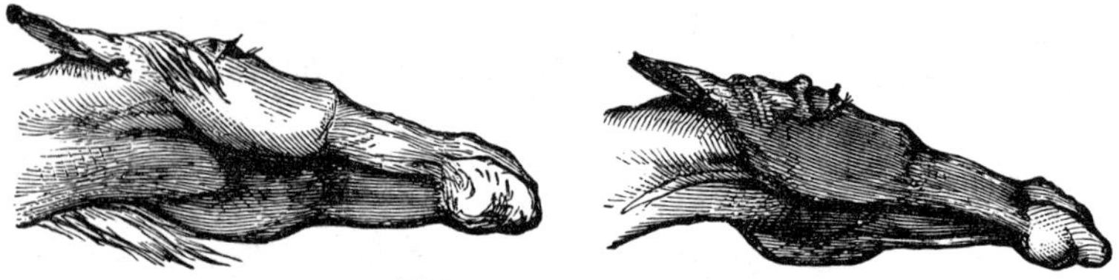

WIDE AND NARROW CHANNELS.

This last point has never been sought for, although the writer has seen it prominently exhibited in some animals. Wherever it has been beheld, the author has confidently pronounced the high character of the quadruped; he has not, in a single instance, been mistaken in his conclusion. The muscles which are attached to the spur process of os hyoides, or to the bone which regulates the movement of the larynx, when well developed, are discernible in the living animal. They form a kind of indication as though nature was half disposed to invest the animal with a

PROMINENT DEVELOPMENT OF THE HYOIDEAL MUSCLES.

miniature dew-lap. They lead the muscles of the neck perceptibly more forward than these agents run in the majority of horses, and in some specimens they may, with a little manipulation, be traced almost to the point of their insertion.

The muscles last alluded to all originate from the trunk, the more forward cavity of which is known as the chest. There is much dispute concerning the best form of the horse's thorax; but such a question can only be decided by the uses to which the animal is to be subservient For instance, below is inserted the illustration of a cart horse with an almost circular chest. Such a form permits the presence of a huge pair of lungs, and favors the increase of weight.

A CART HORSE.

Sufficient oxygen is always present to convert the starch or the sugar of the food into fat: during slow work, enough of atmosphere to vitalize the blood must be inhaled, nor is excessive exertion calculated to materially increase the amount. Where weight is more desired than activity, where propulsion is to be chiefly accomplished by bringing the heavy carcass to bear against the collar, such a make is admirable. All creatures, in which speed is not required, should possess circular chests; for by such a shape the quadrupeds are adapted for the accumulation of fat, and for the performance of slow, of continuous, or of laborious work.

There are, however, numerous animals which are required to possess capability for a "burst;" for the acme of which phrase is embodied in the rush or the closing struggle of the race-course. The creature of speed, therefore, should exhibit rather the deep than the round thorax; for fat is not desired on such an animal. The deep cavity, moreover, admits of an expansibility which is imperative during the extremity of muscular exertion. It is, however, sad to see well-bred animals in and about the metropolis forced to pull carts, for which employment nature has unfitted them. They possess no weight of body with which to move the load. The burden must be propelled by the almost unaided power of the muscles. The limbs, strained by the constant necessity of the position, soon become crippled, while excessive labor causes the flesh to waste; hence the miserable objects which are sometimes witnessed toiling along the thoroughfares of the metropolis.

DIAGRAMS, ILLUSTRATING THE DIFFERENT CAPACITIES OF THE OPPOSITE FORMATIONS OF THORAX.

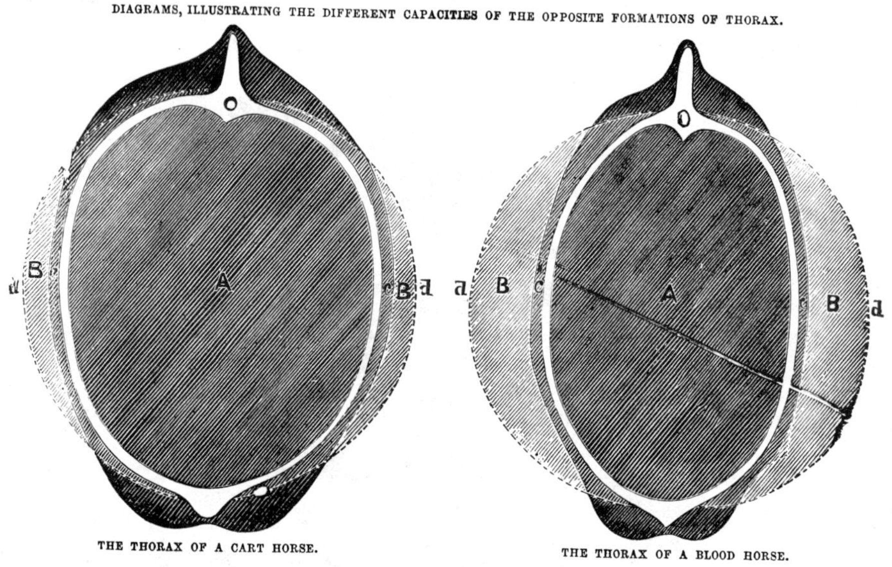

THE THORAX OF A CART HORSE. THE THORAX OF A BLOOD HORSE.

A A. The capacities of the two chests in the quiet condition.
B B, B B. The limits of expansibility in each, when excited.
c c, c c. The outside of the coat in the quiet condition.
d d, d d. The surface of the body in the excited state.

To render the above facts comprehensible to the generality of readers, let it be granted that the lungs of the cart and of the blood horse, when expanded to the uttermost, would occupy the like space. When not excited, or both being of the normal size, the respiratory apparatus of the coarser breed is by far the larger of the two. In the passive condition, the heavy quadruped inhales much more oxygen than is needed to vivify the blood. The excess is, therefore, appropriated by the food and nourishes the frame; hence dray horses have a tendency to become fat. On the contrary, in the ordinary mood, the lungs of the thorough-bred receive scarcely more air than is required to uphold vitality; therefore this kind of quadruped exhibits, as a general rule, no vast disposition toward excessive obesity.

During all quickened movements, however, the action of the lungs and the speed of the circulation are much increased. The impetus given by motion to the vital fluid causes the detention in the lungs to be of a comparatively brief duration. The period of change is shortened; at the same time a larger absorption of the vivifying agent becomes absolutely imperative. The greater depth of chest in the racer admits of a greater change of dimension; then air is inhaled equal to the rapidity of movement. The pace, therefore, can be maintained with comparative ease. But the round form of thorax allows of little enlargement: the demands made by exertion cannot be complied with, and the heavy horse, when hurried, is consequently soon exhausted.

It is not, therefore, the size or dimension of its thorax which fits the steed to the purposes of fleetness. That quality depends on the adaptability of the cavity to the exigencies of excitement; for such purposes, the quadruped with a round chest is not to be preferred. At present there is no instrument by which the motions of the horse's ribs can be accurately ascertained: thus the reader is forced to guess at an alteration which cannot, under existing circumstances, be regarded with that confidence which is inspired by the knowledge of a fact. A quarter of an inch between the enlargement of the ribs in different animals (supposing the other points equal) should more than determine the winner of a race, since the change which takes place in the blood regulates the other properties of vitality.

The belly and the chest are distinct cavities, although there is communication between the organs of each. Thus the great artery which originates at the heart, travels into the abdomen; while the veins which traverse the larger division also penetrate the thorax. Nevertheless, the contents and the uses of each space are generally distinct. The principal agents of the more forward cavity are the heart and the lungs, the thorax being chiefly sacred to the purposes of respiration and of circulation. The liver, the stomach, the spleen, and the intestines are inclosed within the abdomen, the function of this region being engrossed by the offices of appropriation or by those of nutrition.

Most judges admire the horse which presents a belly apparently well filled by its contents. Certainly this appears to be the soundest of the many prejudices which appertain to horse flesh. The shape of the thorax must, in no unimportant degree, regulate that of the abdomen, the two cavities being only parted by a fleshy screen denominated the diaphragm. The herring-gutted quadruped is commonly as deficient in the respiratory as it is wanting in the nutritive functions. Of course this rule is not absolute; but a capacious thorax is required to counteract any absence in the process of nutrition. The animal which rapidly narrows toward the flank generally purges upon work, is commonly of a washy constitution, and usually possesses a bad appetite. Such a retainer will frequently spoil more fodder than it will consume; while the little eaten shall afford less support than the like amount would yield unto the majority of stabled animals.

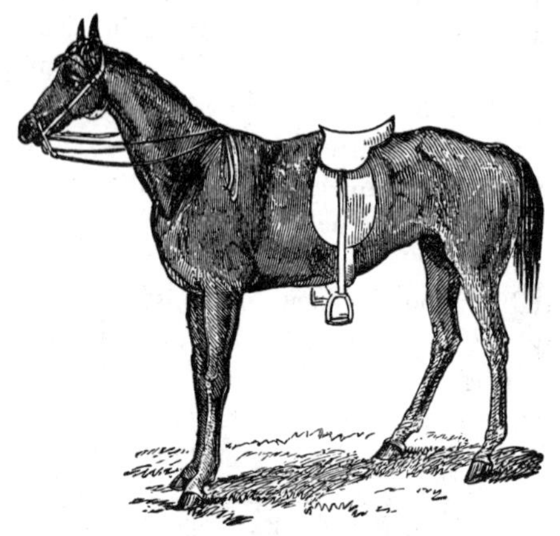

HERRING-GUTTED HORSE.

Horses of the above conformation are soon found wanting in other respects. Narrowing toward the flank being accompanied with deficient quarters, enables them to slip through their body-clothes, and renders it difficult to retain a saddle in its proper situation. The groom may in vain give extra attention to the fastenings; the dwindling form empowers little motion to displace the tightest of girths. The saddle always has an inclination to glide backward; and the rider, when such an occurrence happens, must be placed in no enviable position.

COW-BELLIED HORSE.

Objection even to a greater extent is engendered by the opposite kind of abdomen, or by one which is known as "a cow-belly," or "a potbelly." Animals of this make always seem immatured, as though they had been brought into the world before the proper period, or had been forced to perform hard labor at too early an age: their legs are long; their withers are low; their muscles are mean; their chests are narrow, and their countenances are distorted by a querulous expression. These unhappy creatures possess but little strength for work; if made to travel fast, they are speedily blown. In the stable, they are greedy; when out of it, they are vicious. Many of their faults are to be attributed to disease, the digestive functions being invariably disordered. They are worthless, or are "all too feeble" for harness; while the enlarged belly, when favored by the motion of the limbs, renders retention of a saddle an utter impossibility.

The legs of a horse,—these can hardly prove too short; for brevity of limb is always an accompaniment to depth of chest and proportionably powerful quarters. The long leg always attests to the light carcass; hence the motor agency of the limbs is deficient, while the cavities of respiration and of nutrition are necessarily diminished. A narrow thorax almost enforces low withers and an upright shoulder. The bone of the arm, or the humerus, is pushed into an undue slant by the forward position of the blade-bone, or of the scapula. This compels the front leg to stand too far under the body. Such an arrangement favors neither beauty, speed, nor safety; in fact, it is one of the worst forms which the components of the frame are capable of assuming.

The action of the shoulder-blade, during progression, is upward and backward, or it is drawn toward the highest processes of the withers. Low withers are, of course, opposed to extended motion in such a line. The lessened action of the bone necessarily limits the movement of the structures which depend from it, or the action of the humerus is governed by that of the shoulder-blade. The trivial motion permitted by low withers, therefore, limits the advance of the forearm, the parts being, as it were, tied together. The natural carriage of such a malformation is with the head and neck protruded, so as to favor progression by strain upon the cervical muscles. At the same time the body inclines forward, which throws the limbs backward, or out of their proper situations; and this circumstance accounts for animals of this particular make so frequently encountering "accidents."

A STRAIGHT SHOULDER, SHOWING THE POSITION OF THE BONES.

The gait characteristic of an upright shoulder is very peculiar. A bad forehand is the most common defect witnessed in London thoroughfares.

In the metropolis of the world, it is indeed a rare sight to behold a carriage drawn by a pair of really good animals. The quadrupeds in general use for such purposes are mostly faulty about the shoulders. The forehand is placed upon the trunk in too upright a position. The job master is conscious of this defect. He always endeavors to convince his patrons that such a make is advantageous, where a creature is designed for harness. Possibly the tradesman might succeed in persuading his customers into a false belief, were not prejudice opposed to his suggestions. Ladies admire high action in the steeds attached to their vehicles; this is the kind of step which most of the horses just described are incapable of long exhibiting.

Art or cruelty, however, can partially amend the faulty motion of the limbs. Force the head into an unnatural attitude by the unscrupulous employment of the bit or of the bearing-rein; retain the neck erect, without regard to the cramp induced, or heed of the strain cast upon the muscles,—and the torture, although the life be shortened and the safety of the owner endangered, nevertheless may occasion the feet to be raised during progression. This fact is illustrated in the following engraving

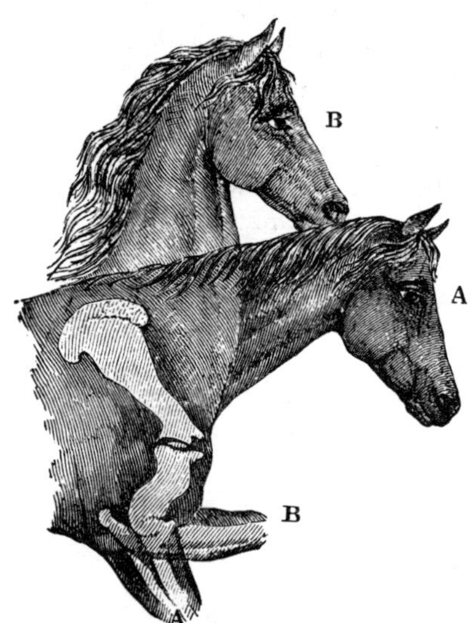

DIAGRAM, SHOWING THE NATURAL ACTION APPERTAINING TO A STRAIGHT SHOULDER, AND ALSO ILLUSTRATING THE CHANGE SOMETIMES OCCASIONED BY THE UNSCRUPULOUS EMPLOYMENT OF THE BIT OR OF THE BEARING-REIN.

The natural mode of going is indicated by the letters A A; the possible change of form is to be seen in the parts distinguished as B B, although the action there depicted certainly displays a most unusual degree of amendment, to induce which must shorten the existence.

Any such improvement is always procured at a vast personal risk; for the head, being raised, partially throws the eyes out of use. It also impedes the circulation, ruins the mouth, distorts the body, and deranges the breathing. All these evils are inflicted to obtain the kind of pace which is never natural, but which closely resembles the sort of step that is characteristic of blindness in the horse. Few of the animals, thus treated, live to descend very low in the scale of equine existence. They mostly perish young; but the reader may recognize them drawing the broughams of gentility, and too often presenting one of the cramped, forced, and uneasy paces which are depicted below; for into such kinds of action all upon service ultimately subside.

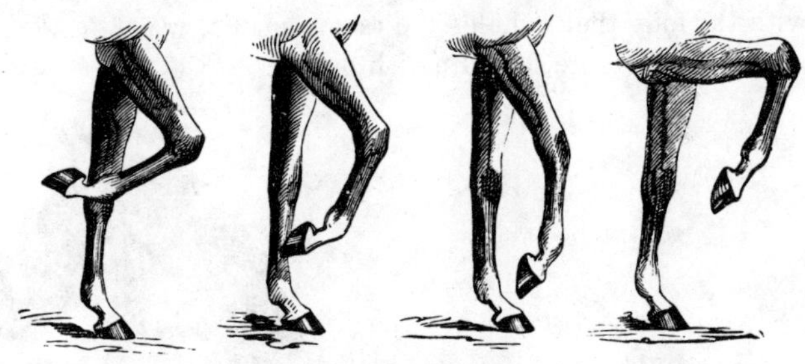

VERY FAULTY ACTIONS.

On the other hand, the animal with a deep chest and with high withers, almost as a necessary adjunct, possesses a slanting shoulder; or, at all events, this probability is favored by that particular formation. Such an arrangement of parts must be accompanied by an upright position of the humerus and the advanced location of the fore limb. This conformation is bettered, materially, by an arched crest and a head "well set on." Unfortunately, these latter points are seldom encountered, the proper disposition of the fore quarter being rarely attended with the last-named grace.

Such horses, however, Stubbs, the animal painter, used to delineate. Either the artist was particularly fortunate in his models, or beauty has been sacrificed in the anxiety to breed other properties. Such horses appear to have been common in England when the racer was compelled to possess endurance, and if report be truth, the last animals exhibited a greater speed than their descendants can display. Hunters were formerly something better than the rejected of the course; they could show a beauty equal to their strength. Creatures with the forehand such as has been described, are not only more pleasant to contemplate, but they are also capable of working with far less exhaustion to the system.

With a front limb of this nature, the movements of the leg are regulated by that of the shoulder. When the blade-bone is drawn upward, the humerus leaves its almost erect position, and assumes a forward inclination. This causes the arm to be advanced, and propels the leg and foot. Thus the movement of a part governs the motion of the whole: a grace or harmony of action is the result. The various components of the member change their relative positions to one another without effort, but with evident intention; all parts of the limb are simultaneously advanced. The work is not cast upon one set of muscles to the injury of another region. A well-made animal is one perfect whole, and formerly was common throughout the land. People may sigh that such quadrupeds are now lost to the nation: this regret, however, does not accord with the folly that upholds the racing mania, which has engulfed the once-prized native breed of English horses.

A SLANTING SHOULDER, SHOWING THE POSITION OF THE BONES.

A SLANTING SHOULDER IN ACTION.

The articulated skeletons which are exhibited in museums present but poor resemblances of the living framework as it is arranged by the hand of nature. In these artificial preparations, the fore limbs are always straight, as are the supports of a kitchen table. But contemplate the living example. The positive perpendicular is never observed. The member abounds in gracefully swelling prominences and admirably poised inclines. The chest may be wide; but the hoofs are placed close together. Such a necessity renders an erect line an impossibility. Try the same rule in another direction. Let a plummet be dropped from the point of the shoulder of a living and well-made animal; it will mark the limit to which the toe is extended when the healthy horse is resting the limb. Such a fact proves the sheer upright form of the member to be an unnatural distortion and a positive impossibility.

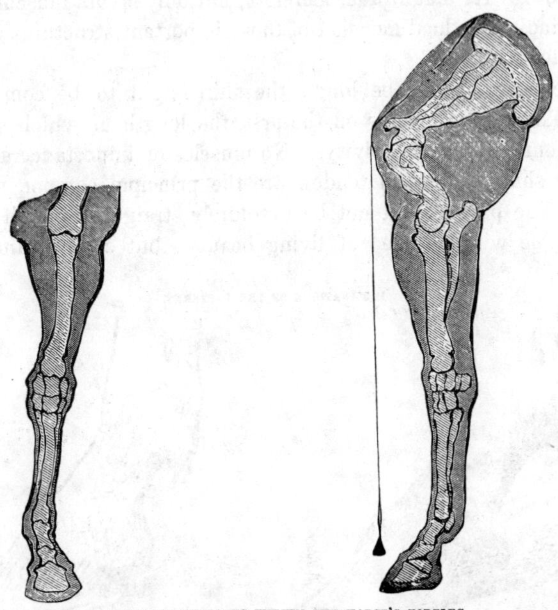

DIAGRAMS OF BONES WITHIN THE HORSE'S FORELEG.

The importance of the shoulder and of the arm bone having been enlarged upon, there remains to direct the reader's attention toward that which in general acceptance constitutes the forearm, as well as the knee, the leg or the shin, the pastern and the foot. Where the limb quits the trunk, it should be characterized by muscular developments, since at this place resides the chief of that power by which the lower portions of the member are directed. The flesh should bulge forth, and cannot be too abundant; for a thin forearm is incompatible with goodness in a horse.

The point of the elbow should be prominently emphasized, as this bone affords a leverage whence many influential muscles originate, and which some of the principal flexor agents directly operate upon. Toward the knee the swelling should gradually subside, leaving upon the surface of the joint a broad, clean, and firm appearance. At the back of the knee there should stand forth, or rather should stick out, an osseous point, the size of which is of every value. Its aspect may not please the inexperienced fancies of the boy; but the uses of this development are, in no little degree, governed by its magnitude. It affords a point of insertion to the short flexors of the limb, as well as gives shelter to the perforans and perforatus tendons in their passage toward the pastern and the foot. Its magnitude, therefore, not only favors muscular action, but also indicates the dimension of those important structures which this bone protects.

The forearm should be long; the shin ought to be comparatively short. The reach depends on the first, the length of which secures an extra amount of motor activity. No muscles of importance are located upon the shin: bone and tendon are the principal components of this region. The part should not be absolutely straight, for such a form is incompatible with all idea of living beauty; but at the same time it

INCLINATIONS OF THE PASTERNS.

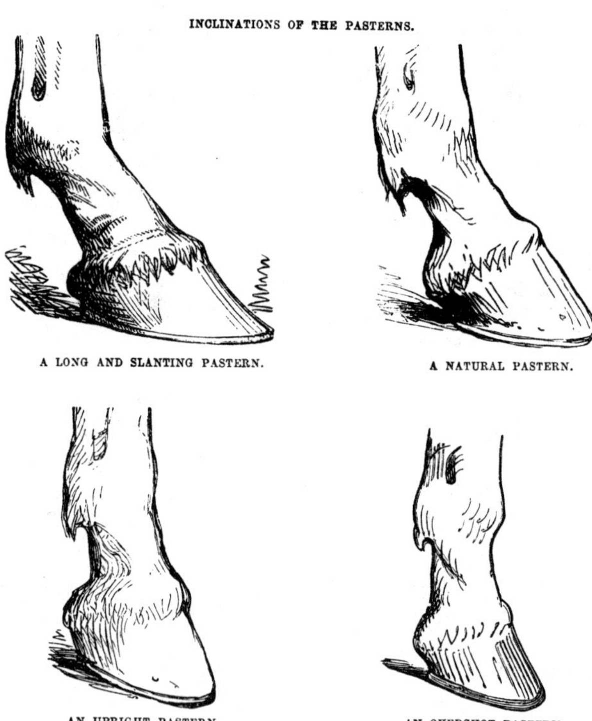

A LONG AND SLANTING PASTERN. A NATURAL PASTERN.

AN UPRIGHT PASTERN. AN OVERSHOT PASTERN.

ought to present no obvious inequalities or sudden enlargements. The bone should be compact, giving to this portion of the limb, when viewed from the front, almost the appearance of being deficient in bulk; but when regarded from the side, the lower part of the leg cannot be too broad; for breadth and strength are here synonymous.

The above rule applies with equal stringency to both legs,—to the hind limb below the hock as well as the more forward member from the knee downward. Each should be thin, when viewed from the front. Neither can well be too deep, when seen from the side. Both should appear solid, and each should feel almost of metallic hardness. The pastern-joint should not present a level surface, when viewed laterally; and as it proceeds downward to join the foot, a graduated enlargement should exist.

Much comment is usually indulged upon the horse's pastern. The degree in which this part may or may not slope, has been authoritatively defined. The reader will best judge of these opinions, by considering the purposes for which the pastern was created. Its intention is to endow the tread with elasticity. The fetlock of a racer, when the animal trots, may be seen to touch the earth every time the weight rests upon the foot: nevertheless, the thorough-bred has, during the contention, to endure the very excess of action. There must, therefore, be something erroneous in the popular judgment which connects weakness with the motion of this part, or no racer could ever reach the goal; and if a quadruped does occasionally break down, the likelihood of such a misfortune is not regulated or to be foretold by the pliability of the pastern-joint. However, that the reader may estimate the value of the prejudice, various pasterns, designed according to the general phraseology, have been submitted to his inspection.

To enable the purchaser to arrive at a sound decision, it is necessary to state that the inclination of this region is governed by the major

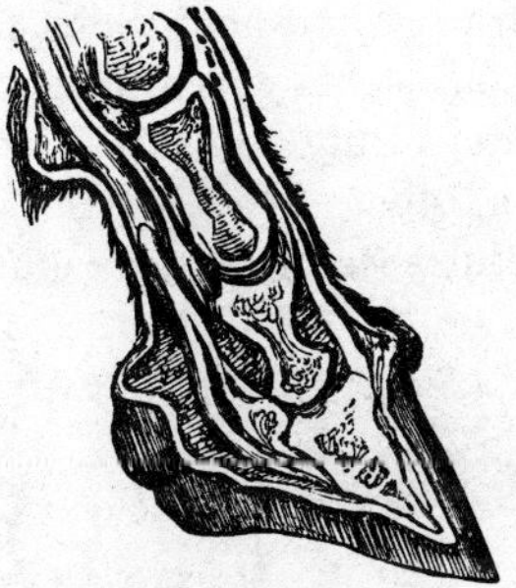

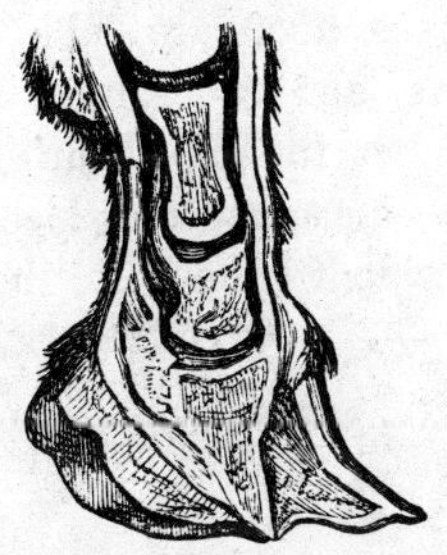

flexor tendons which are situated underneath or behind them. Their slanting, therefore, is regulated by no peculiarity in the forms of the bones themselves, but is controlled by and dependent upon the condition of another structure. A short, upright pastern, if it can bear any evidence at all, testifies to a stubborn and unyielding state of the great flexor muscles, the weight being then thrown upon the osseous supports. The play of the pastern denotes nothing more than the healthy elasticity of the flesh upon the tendon proper to which the osseous structures repose. The bones have no motor power belonging to themselves. The upright and the overshot pastern suggest no change in the more solid frame; but such alterations prove that excessive work has strained the great flexors of the limb, and destroyed the inherent property of elasticity with which every muscle is endowed by nature. The burden being then supported by an osseous pillar instead of an elastic band, of course jar or concussion ensues upon the abnormal change.

Thus, alteration in the natural position of an oblique bone is of great importance to a purchaser; and to judge properly of the pastern-joint, the substance swelling forth beneath the elbow must be regarded. Should this portion of the body be mean or wanting in development, hard work will probably induce it to become rigid, or labor may, ultimately, cause the pastern-joint to shoot forward and out of its proper situation.

The flexor tendon likewise influences another part. The perforans is inserted into the sole of the coffin-bone, or into the bone of the foot. The direction in which the toes point is, therefore, regulated by a substance so far distant that the attempt to connect the two organs may, to the uninformed mind, seem somewhat ridiculous. Yet, the statement being correct, the fact renders the position of the elbow of more importance; for according to the situation of that bone the hoofs will be directed. Thus, an ulna or an elbow which is drawn toward the trunk will be attended with a toe inclined outward. When the bone turns from the body, the forward portion of the hoof is directed inward. When the framework is properly constructed, the hoofs point forward; for horses' hoofs are liable to those derangements which the human foot exhibits, and generally with like results. Only, in man, striking one leg against the other, during progression, is not attended with the unfortunate consequences which such an occurrence often will induce when this accident happens to the quadruped.

INCLINATIONS AND DEFECTS OF THE FEET, AS WELL AS SAMPLES OF ODD HOOFS.

HOOFS POINTING FORWARD. HOOFS POINTING OUTWARD. HOOFS POINTING INWARD.

By the pasterns recently exhibited it will have been observed that the inclination of the bones influences the slant of the hoof. The two structures are so connected one with the other that neither can be independent, for the direction of the pastern, of course, determines the nature of the weight imposed upon the foot. Thus, should the foot receive more than a normal pressure, this circumstance, by throwing the weight upon the bones, occasions the muscles to contract, and produces upright or overshot fetlock-joint. Nevertheless, the hoof is operated upon by other agency. Diseased action will also interfere with the growth of its outward covering. The member may, under such injurious excitement, when long continued, eventually become deformed.

The place of birth also influences the horn. Thus, a quadruped brought up on the fens of Lincolnshire, generally displays a flat sole, a weak, a low, and a slanting crust. The horse whose native land is dry or sandy, mostly exhibits the hoof high in the quarter and thick in its incasement. The creature with feet of the intermediate sort, which a few years ago were esteemed the model form, is generally the inhabitant of a moist, but not of a wet district. The horn, therefore, is indirect evidence of the rearing; and the author has now to consider how far its condition can, by itself, be regarded as a positive proof of any other fact.

There is one defect not generally observed, but which should always be studied in every examination of the feet. It may surprise the reader, when the author declares it to be very far from an uncommon circumstance to encounter a horse with odd hoofs, or with feet of different sizes. Such a peculiarity is totally independent of the defective inclination of the toes, and may be seen in horn of any possible condition, or in feet of any variety of form.

An animal becomes lame in the foot. If the lameness is removed in reasonable time, the affection disappears, and leaves no trace behind it. But let it continue for months, and during such a period the sufferer will throw little or no weight upon the diseased member. The part will be rested. The purpose or function of the organ will be counteracted by the will of the animal. The consequence of long disuse will be a proportionate decrease in size. Upon recovery, the loss of bulk is seldom restored; for if the foot is then employed, so also is the sound one; and the action being equal, of course it does not particularly affect one extremity, but operates on both alike.

The difference in the feet may not be so startling as to enforce attention to the deformity. It is seldom of this nature. Most probably it will require some discrimination to detect it. In the last engraving, the author endeavored to depict the defect as it was generally exhibited. None of the hoofs there delineated positively match, though very probably the reader had not remarked their differences. However, the slightest disagreement is an accepted proof that disease has been present,—at what time, whether recently or long ago, of what nature, whether structural or functional, the examiner cannot tell: he, however, assumes lameness has existed, has endured for some period, and he fears that the organ which has been afflicted may retain a liability to repeated visitations of a similar misfortune.

The so-called model foot is very liable to change, and not less likely to exhibit disease. It is very pretty to look at; but it does not, as a rule, undergo much work without alteration. This opinion, however, must be regarded only as announcing a general law; for though the intelligent Mr. Bracy Clarke puts forth engravings illustrative of the effects which work produces upon the model foot, nevertheless the writer of the present volume has seen hoofs of this description which have, without apparent injury, endured constant shoeing, as well as perpetual battering upon the dreaded London pavement.

The slanting crust, weak heels, and low soles are, however, not to be commended. These are among the worst points which the equine form can present, and they are too commonly the forerunners of sad internal disease, as ossified cartilages, sand crack, pumice foot, etc.

After long reflection, the author must express a preference for the high or the stubborn hoof. When doing this, he is consciously opposing his unsupported opinion against the firmly and repeatedly expressed judgment of his professional brethren. He therefore can ask no man to agree with his decision; but he humbly requests the reader to peruse the grounds of his conviction, before hastily condemning its declaration.

The horse is a native of a dry and an arid soil. Such a region induces that which the inhabitants of this country stigmatize as an excess of horn or an abnormally high sole. This kind of hoof therefore would appear to be natural to the animal: at all events, such a foot must have been general before the invention of iron shoes. Moreover, when the immense weight of the creature's carcass is considered, and the manner in which bearing is increased by speed is also properly regarded, a necessity for the stoutest hoof must be fully apparent.

In addition to the above inferences, the author may advance his own observation, carefully made through a number of years: that all animals exhibiting strong crusts are not, necessarily, cripples; but that the creature with such a development of horn is in consequence less, infinitely less, liable to pedal derangements. The contrary conclusion has been upheld, because most men thought the excess of horn must check expansion, and also severely pinch the internal structures. With regard to the last deduction, all outward developments are produced by and are governed by the inward organs which these shelter. The secreting member may be soft, and the secreted substance may be hard; still, by a wise provision of nature, the tender structure rules the insensitive material which it produces. Therefore the horn cannot press upon or pinch the internal portions of the foot, any more than the skull can compress the healthy brain which it protects.

Then as to the supposed want of expansibility. The hoof may appear stubborn when between the human fingers; but while supporting the body of a horse, it is exposed to the operation of a force altogether greater than any which man is able to exert. The question therefore is not whether the hoof is very yielding, but whether it is so obdurate as to resist the huge weight of the animal when aiding the mechanical force of speed and the vital action of muscular power.

The author, however, while making the above declaration, supposes form to be united with stoutness. Where the heels have become "wired in," and the crust has assumed the upright figure, the internal structures must be in an altered condition, and the points of bearing for the different portions of the limb must be entirely changed. The quarters in the last kind of foot are, frequently, remarkably stubborn. They are rather inclined to crack than to expand. Such parts will not, by their innate elasticity, fly inward on the leg being raised from the ground, and thus regulate the amount of blood which shall be poured into the hoof; neither will they expand when the weight is cast upon the foot, and thus allow free egress to the current which is violently expelled in consequence of the superimposed burden driving the fluid upward.

The upright hoof and narrow heels are, generally, all but unyielding. They have lost their natural function, and the harmony of the whole is destroyed. In consequence, the blood, instead of being expelled from the hoof, cannot escape from the pressure of the bony structures. The vessels within which the fluid circulates are not formed to sustain uninjured so vast a burden. They rupture under the weight; hence this peculiar form of foot is commonly accompanied with corns. Therefore, because corns are a disease, and because disease, being once generated, is not in its course or duration to be prognosticated with certainty, an upright hoof and wired in quarters are decided unsoundness: although stoutness, simply considered, is rather a recommendation than a defect.

The author may not dwell at greater length on this portion of his subject; but those who desire further information may with advantage consult Miles's works upon the horse's foot, which are the best, the cheapest, and the most lucid books upon this topic in the English language. They are written in a style which the most unlettered may comprehend; but when recommending them, the author, in his own justification, may state that the views therein expressed frequently differ from those opinions which are contained in the present volume.

Looking back upon such portions of the frame as have formed the subject of the late remarks, there are certain points which are invariably present in every well-made animal. A very broad, full chest is advantageous for slow work; but for slow work only. Where speed or activity is desired, depth of thorax is indispensable; yet the cavity should not be narrow or the sides flat; while the exterior of the ribs should apparently encircle sufficient space. The general contour should, moreover, excite no idea of fixedness: the part should convey a notion of its capability for easy and for rapid alteration of magnitude.

The abdomen should neither be large nor small. The exhibition of either failing announces a radical defect. The belly ought rather to gracefully continue the line of the chest, than by its protuberance, or the reverse, to enforce its existence specially upon the notice of the spectator. All may be considered right when the form elicits no remark; but when it challenges observation, the fact does not indicate that everything is as the purchaser could desire.

The position and the muscularity of the shoulder are the main points in the forehand. With respect to the limbs, these should leave the body as though they were parts of its substance. They can hardly be too large where they emerge from the trunk; and the forearm can scarcely be too long. The knee-joint should be broad and flat; while the bone which projects forth posteriorly should be well pronounced and evenly situated. The shin should be hard to the touch, and broad, when viewed laterally. The leg should seem straight and strong; the feet standing close together, and the toes pointing in a forward direction, rather than inclining to the outward or to the inward direction.

Such is a general view of organs, all of which are of equal importance. Breathing and digestion are such vital functions, it would be supererogation did the author pretend to point out *their* importance. It may be otherwise with the fore limbs. Their use is not popularly comprehended; those members are exposed to numerous accidents and liable to many diseases. This predisposition is generally explained, by saying they are nearer to the heart than the hind legs are, and the straighter form is more favorable to a descent of the arterial current than is the angularity of the posterior extremities; therefore this portion of the frame is more open to acute affections.

The facts stated are certainly correct. So is the less freedom allowed to the forelegs, by confinement in and fastening the head to a manger in a stall. Such, however, is not the whole truth. There are other causes in operation. The province of the fore limb is to uphold the trunk. Thus, at all times, the member has to support no inconsiderable burden; but when that load is increased by the weight of a rider or is augmented by the drag of the collar, the tug of the shafts, and the generally pendent position of the head, the reader may conjecture the force with which the limb must be driven to the earth, especially during any rapid increase of motion.

The continued battering to which the leg is subjected naturally exposes it to much suffering, which the comparative fixedness in the stable greatly aggravates. As the uses are severe, so are its afflictions painful; and it hazards nothing to assert that very much of the sorrow which visits the animal is dependent upon the diseases or the accidents which are inseparable from these forward supports of the body and of the load.

When, however, the person called upon to exercise a judgment in the purchase of a nag is so new to the subject as to be incapable of forming an opinion, there is one primary test which seldom deceives; and upon the evidence thus evolved the merest tyro is fully qualified to pronounce. Let such a man mount the animal, and, when seated in the saddle, he can surely decide whether he appears to be close upon the neck or placed far behind upon the back. A well-made animal, by the inclination of the shoulder and by the amplitude of the withers, forbids the forward location of its rider; whereas a worthless quadruped, by the lowness of the first dorsal spines and the upright position of the blade-bones, allows the rider almost to rest upon its neck—thereby, because of the greater weight to be supported by the front limbs, increasing the natural liability of the forward members to exhibit disease.

The reason why such a formation should be specially noticed is, upon reflection, made apparent. The hind legs, by their greater motor power, always have a disposition to throw the weight upon the forward member. When this tendency is augmented by the burden on the back, the consequence must be a destruction of any approach to an equilibrium.

The horse's body is, by nature, given four props—one at each corner of the trunk. But when a human load is lodged almost over the fore limb; when the front leg is placed far behind the chest; and when the head swings in advance,—all approach to a proportionate amount of burden is destroyed. The forward extremities then take a position almost in the middle of the substance, a proportionate incumbrance being removed from the posterior extremities. The hind members have less to do, and excessive duty is imposed upon the weaker organs, the motor machine being deprived of safety during progression.

While on the back, the rider should ascertain the shoulders are of equal bulk, or have not suffered injury, and that the trunk is sufficiently developed to afford a secure grip for the thighs of the master. Many animals are so narrow as to necessitate sensible muscular exertion on the part of an equestrian, and thus materially to detract from the pleasure of horse exercise. This matter is the more important, because stoutness of the body allows a fair inference to be drawn as to the substance of the haunches. It is true, no absolute law may therefrom be deduced; but as expectation is warranted, the fact should always be remarked

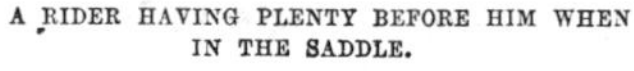

A RIDER HAVING PLENTY BEFORE HIM WHEN IN THE SADDLE.

A RIDER CLOSE ON THE NECK WHEN IN THE SADDLE.

The haunch is that portion of the frame upon which a capability for work is chiefly dependent. This region, therefore, should appear to be the embodiment of strength. It should not seem soft, or invite those pats which inexperienced horsemen are fond of administering to this portion of the body, but the aspect ought rather to suggest firmness and power; for here resides the force which must propel the load or direct the bound. Always choose an animal with good haunches, and invariably regard the position of the tail; as the situation of the dock, when on a line with the back-bone, denotes the greatest possible length, and therefore the largest amount of muscular activity to be present.

Never purchase a horse which is recommended as fully equal to carry your weight; for the dealer who asserts this is, by his interest in the sale, incapacitated from forming a just opinion. But ostensibly appear to seek a horse for a friend—never for yourself—and state the nominal owner to ride at least four if not six stone heavier than the would-be purchaser. There is a saying, that an animal will run away with too light a load; but that assertion is mere nonsense. Most vicious quadrupeds are weakly creatures. The powerful frame is generally united to an even temper. Strength does not endanger the female equestrian, although ladies generally are mounted upon the best-made, the strongest, and the most valuable steeds. Indeed, this argument is never urged, save when a gentleman hesitates to accept a weakly quadruped, or desires to obtain the one which the dealer is not very anxious should be purchased.

In illustration of this subject an engraving is inserted, which represents better-made quarters than are commonly beheld on a native or coarsely-bred animal. But the reader can hardly fail to remark that though the developments are not deficient in width, yet the general aspect rather denotes softness than expresses strength or suggests determination. The tail is well set on for this kind of quadruped; still, the point of the rump-bone is not even indicated. The spectator must guess at its precise location, as he cannot, by the unaided vision, detect its exact situation. Bulk is not absent, yet that which should be its attendant is not prominent. The bones of the leg seem long, but the hocks are not remarkable for size or conspicuous for form. The limbs are not moved with that independence of action which gives to the step of the horse its air of resolution, but they are advanced as though one was timid of proceeding too far without the other.

A COARSE-BRED HAUNCH.

Yet, the inquirer may journey long and travel far before he will meet the equal of the quarters here depicted. The generality of these parts, on the animals of the coarser breed, are much narrower; the tail is seldom encountered springing from a position so near to the level of the spine; while, short as the extent of the posterior muscles may appear in the previous illustration, these are frequently to be seen of more circumscribed dimensions.

In contrast to the foregoing, the accompanying engraving depicts the quarters of a blood horse. In this illustration, symmetry and beauty are equally preserved; but, with these qualities, also are blended other attributes, which ennoble and elevate the object. Strength, power, and determination are impressed upon the image. Every muscle goes direct to the part on which it operates. The posterior line, on being traced from the dock to the leg, does not seem to hesitate between the bone of the member and the stifle-joint. The leg itself is thicker, but its greater substance depends upon the presence of muscle. The hock is cleaner, and uses of the part are better

A THOROUGH-BRED HAUNCH.

characterized. The calcis, as the backward projection is technically termed, stands forth prominently and affords the greater leverage for the motor agents to act upon.

When the quarters of the two breeds are contrasted, the difference is found to be extreme; the pervading attributes of each characterizes the innate qualities of the animal to which the part belonged. The distinctions which divide the two are by these members well indicated. There was, some time back, a loud discussion as to what kind of horse was best fitted for ordinary purposes. The old staging days should have settled such a question; for then fast coaches found the employment of the nobler quadrupeds to their interest. Where slow and heavy propulsion is desired, the coarser animal is infinitely to be preferred. For all the gentler purposes of society, the thorough-bred is, in the author's opinion, to be recommended. Only, these fine creatures should be properly reared; they ought not, as now, to be produced with all the haste of greed, and cast upon the general public when found unsuited to the purposes for which they were generated.

It is offensive, if not painful, to hear persons speak of certain horses as though particular quadrupeds were created only for special uses. A good horse is fit for nearly every purpose; but such an animal is generally employed for the saddle. A thorough-bred, with lofty and well-developed quarters, is too valuable not to be appropriated by the race-course. A blood, with so much bulk and stoutness as to indicate the qualities of endurance rather than of speed, is always destined to become a hunter. Horses of the purer breed are supposed not well suited for gentlemen's hacks. Good animals of this description are only too valuable for common purposes; but no creature is, by its intelligence, its activity, its gracefulness or its beauty, so admirably qualified for the companionship of man as the noblest type of the equine race.

The manner in which the racer trots is asserted to express the action which is natural to all of the thorough-breed. Before the reader agrees to that assertion, he should remember the trot is not a natural pace, nor one which the racer is broken to exhibit. Seen upon the course, the foot evidently moves too near the earth to clear the ruts of most English highways. Yet, as there shown, the motion is not to be despised. During it, at each step the limbs are extended; the reach is admirable, and affords a far better foundation for excellence in a hack than the up-and-down pounding motion which is so highly esteemed by the ignorant.

The greatest possible speed, with the least possible amount of exertion, is secured by the thorough-bred trot. The ground is covered, while the pace is easy and pleasant to the rider. It is very opposite to that which medical gentlemen occasionally recommend as a "hard-trotting horse." A child might sit upon the back of a well-bred steed. The author recollects to have only seen one animal of this description employed as the riding companion of a gentleman. The master (a northern nobleman) was evidently proud of his possession; for the hack abounded in energy and with fire. The life never appeared fresher in a colt; but, on inspecting the teeth, the writer was pleasantly surprised to behold indications which denoted that at least twelve years had been passed. The following illustration will suggest to the inexperienced reader the more striking peculiarities which characterize the well-bred action.

A HACK.

Any quadruped is supposed suited for the collar when it displays points which unfit it for the saddle. A prime saddle horse, however, always makes the best harness animal; only, it is considered too valuable for such a purpose. There is but one law which is absolute with draught horses. In them, the forelegs are pardoned a few faults; but the hind quarters should always be powerful. That is desirable in all quadrupeds; for draught of every kind it is essential; it should never be overlooked, or the want of such a property ever be pardoned.

There is another point of importance. Any gentleman purchasing a draught horse—no matter whether for cart, for carriage, or for phaeton—be it for any kind of vehicle, he should be certain, before the transfer is concluded, that the new possession stands high enough. Nothing looks worse than small horses before a tall carriage. The living power may be in excess—it can hardly appear too mighty—but an inch below the requisite size .gives to the most elegant and the newest of "turn outs" a shabby and a mean appearance. The draught may be light; the horses may not be overweighted; still, no fact or knowledge can reconcile the eye to the general effect, where animals are small for the machine to which they are harnessed.

Of recent years there has been displayed a desire to infuse the Eastern blood into the heavier breed which is native to this country. The desire was commendable; but its gratification has led only to evil. It has enabled the dregs of the race-course to be palmed off upon the public. A thin and lanky offshoot of thorough-bred stock can be of no value. These things should not be bought by gentlemen for any kind of service. The time has come, when it is simple prudence that the public should refuse longer to absorb the cast-offs of the stud farm. No doubt, before the breeding of blood stock became a general practice, the infusion of Eastern fire and activity was a national boon; for a reference to engravings of a few years back exhibits the animal suited only for a plow used as ladies' palfreys. The following copy from a figure, presented in the famous folio work by a former Duke of Newcastle, will give the reader some notion of the kind of horse once chosen to carry the fairest portion of creation in the British isles.

LADY, HAWKING.

From the above illustration, which may be well supposed to embody the height of fashion and the cream of style shortly after the accession of Charles the Second, the reader can imagine the practical knowledge possessed by those writers who speak of James the First as having greatly improved the *native* breed of horses, and quote the benefits conferred upon the national race by the more temperate but equally determined enthusiasm of Cromwell, operating in the same direction.

At this place, the reader must have patience while the method of judging the limbs is pointed out. When the dealer exhibits an animal, the customer's eye always should endeavor to ascertain the bulk or substance of the creature which he is expected to purchase. To do this, let the eye be directed toward the chest, to ascertain if the forelegs are separated by any breadth of thorax, or whether they spring from the body almost from the same point. This decided, a glance may be given to the line of the forelegs; these parts also can be viewed as the gentleman passes backward. Having reached the last situation, he observes if the thighs are large and fleshy, keeping the legs well asunder; also, whether the hocks are rightly placed, are huge, and are cleanly shaped.

Such remarks are important, since the disposition to cut is generally decided by the width of the horse's trunk. Any deficiency in this respect indicates weakness, as well as declares a general unfitness for severe labor. This circumstance being observed, it is usual for the horse to be run up and down the ride. While the limbs are in motion, the spectator should notice the peculiarities of their carriage. A flexion of the front shin to the outer side warrants a belief in the existence of a splint. When the hind limb is not properly flexed, but the toe is allowed to graze the ground, it is a positive proof that the hock is disabled by the presence of a spavin.

A worse evil, however, is, when the forelegs, during progression, crossing each other, the trot becomes a sort of "hand-over-hand" pace. This kind of action is accompanied by "speedy cut," or by a wound made upon one leg, immediately below the knee, with the shoe on the opposite foot. That defect justifies an instant rejection; for such a liability is incompatible with safety, as the blow too often brings the animal and its rider to the earth. The legs being close is the cause of "brushing" or of "cutting,"—a most troublesome defect, which inflicts a wound considerably nearer to the ground than speedy cut.

Before purchase, the hair on the inner side of the legs should be carefully examined. If a cicatrix or a bare spot is discovered near to the seat of cutting; if any paint or coloring matter can be detected upon the part; or if the hair does not lie perfectly smooth upon the place of injury,—have nothing to do with the animal. It is quite true that most fresh and nearly all young horses will cut—others strike only toward the end of a long journey; but it is also true that particular horses, however fresh or however tired they may be, never strike or cut. The quadruped which a gentleman desires, is one that does not contain evidences of a liability to accident or to disease. He wishes for a sound

AN EXAGGERATED VIEW OF A WEAK ANIMAL, WITH DANGEROUS ACTION.

animal; and one disposed to strike certainly cannot, in the author s opinion, be so esteemed. Every man wants a horse for service; but the creature which may at any moment receive a wound that shall incapacitate, assuredly cannot be esteemed a serviceable possession, in any meaning of the words.

While examining the legs, the gentleman should also notice the shoes upon the different feet. If these are rusty, the fact demonstrates that the horse has been wearing wet swabs, and has been long stationary in the stable. The circumstance is suspicious. In horse dealing a justifiable suspicion is always acted upon as an established fact. If the shoes are of rude make and much worn, it looks badly; and though it is no recommendation, it justifies no inference. But if the shoes be thicker at one part than at another; if the horse, being a nag, should wear very high calkins; if the toe be shortened, or one side of the metal is obviously narrowed,—it denotes precautions against clicking and against overreaching: the first being a most audible annoyance, which may lead to the forcible tearing away a fore shoe; and the last causing a fearful, a terrible, and an incapacitating wound upon the heel of the foreleg Also, should the toe of the hind shoe be ground down, while the heel exhibits no obvious wear, the fact demonstrates the existence of a spavin. Either clicking, overreaching, or spavin is legitimate cause for rejection.

The reader, from a perusal of the foregoing remarks, will comprehend a few of the difficulties which beset the purchaser of a horse; and these may warn him, in some measure, of the dangers that surround a person so engaged. The author is a veterinary surgeon, of some experience; but he would be very sorry to buy a steed for himself upon his unsupported opinion. He would always have the animal examined by a professional man ere the purchase was concluded. How greatly, therefore, must the general public stand in need of such protection! Especially when the known hazard of the transaction and the confusion necessarily accompanying a direct personal interest in the business help to confound the intellect and to overpower the judgment!

All persons complain of the roguery that is mixed up with horse dealing. The complaint is just; but it is not just that the public should vent it. It is the general abuse and the inhuman treatment to which animal life is subjected that renders such practices necessary. The cruelty and the roguery are associated as closely as cause and effect. Let the provocative be discarded, and its result, of course, must cease. But no man should blame the conduct which his own deeds have willfully generated. To hurt and to injure a patient and an obedient animal is a positive sin,—a violation of the trust confided by the Creator to the creature. To defraud, in a money transaction, is simply a crime,—an offense committed upon the laws by man established over man. Then, what right has he who violates one of the ordinizations of nature, to point at and to sigh over the person who merely breaks a human institution?

Christianity, if its benefits were exemplified in man's actions toward the creatures living under his dominion, would immediately operate upon society. The horse, under better treatment, would of course not be liable to those injuries and accidents which roguery in the dealer merely endeavors to conceal. There would be no occasion for cheating when the creature exhibited no scar or defect which the seller was interested to hide or to deny. Thus one stain upon the present civilization would be abolished; for, notwithstanding the numerous assertions to the contrary, the author has yet to see the man who practiced dishonesty from a sheer love of iniquity.

The well-to-do may lament the immorality of the class below them; but if gentility would look less leniently upon itself, probably the exhibition of crime might be viewed as no more than the apex of a pyramid whose base is deeply planted in the frailties which are common to general society.

CHAPTER XIII.

BREEDING—ITS INCONSISTENCIES AND ITS DISAPPOINTMENTS.

THERE are very dissimilar kind of horses produced in this country, the breeding of which concerns many different classes of proprietors, and all of which are ushered into this world with most opposite formalities; therefore no author may pretend he is qualified to write about every description of animal, with any air of authority. The person, however, who has long thought upon the subject, and who, by education, is fitted to arrive at a just opinion, may reach a conclusion which, without appealing to the prejudices or interfering with the mysteries of any particular class, nevertheless shall, in its decision, apply with equal force to the entire body.

The writer states thus much, because, though not absolutely without experience, he yet can put forth no pretension to be specially initiated into those practices and tricks which ignorant people suppose to be requisite for the essential regulation of particular affairs. Neither does he aspire to be esteemed a proficient in jockeyship, which the public appear to imagine involves everything concerning the equine race. The following pages are indited by an individual who, fond of the subject, and instructed as a veterinarian, has now attained an age when the mind should be equally above the errors natural to schools and the supersti tious, which appear to be inseparable from general society.

There is one fault which is exemplified with the like strength by all parties who, in England, assume they understand the breeding of horses. Every proprietor, when so engaged, endeavors to render the mare subservient to two or to three distinct uses. All will burn the candle at both ends; then the public sympathizers raise a loud exclamation because such willful extravagance does not specially serve any economical or any useful purpose. Nobody dreams of propagating from an animal until its body has been injured and its vitality has been weakened by services rendered to an exacting master. The results which labor can impress upon a living organism may be observed emphasized upon the manufacturing classes of Great Britain; but much as has been published concerning the cruelty which man can practice on his fellow-man, such inhumanity cannot be compared with the torments which are, openly and without a sense of wrong-doing, inflicted upon the dumb existence that cannot plead its wrongs, and which the social code even permits to be maltreated.

There may be an enactment applicable to extreme cases; but the most acute anguish no statute touches. Where the law is operative, death is always near the extremity which mortal justice condescends to relieve. To prevent extraordinary agony, is not to soften the general treatment. No man hitherto has conceived there can be any outrage committed upon charity by breeding from the body which, through a life of service, had earned a right to rest. But most horse proprietors only "throw up" the animal they intend should perpetuate its race, after strains and pains have rendered longer life a larger misery. Work, in this land, appears with quadrupeds to be esteemed a necessary preparation for "the stud." No one in this country, famous throughout the world for its breed of horses, seems to be endowed with any distant conception of the age which fits the body for the reproduction of its kind; but all appear to imagine the period is any time after the capacity for toil has diminished. What a comment is, by the custom, promulgated upon the Christianity which, after more than eighteen hundred years of doctrine, the inhabitants of many places besides Great Britain may point to in illustration of their belief!

Bodies crippled by too early labor, or carcasses disabled by disease, are generally found among the breeding stud of a modern establishment. The foals of nearly all breeds are injured before the little creatures see the light; it is, therefore, no matter for surprise that a breeding mare is, by the majority of farmers, esteemed to be a losing concern. In the case of blood stock, both sire and dam are submitted to the trainers' processes ere the second stage of equine babyhood has been perfected. Certainly where an amusement is pursued with a reckless defiance of economy, a little longer grace might be accorded to the animals employed to promote it; or where the topmost prize is estimated not by tens but by thousands, it might be prudent to speculate with a little forbearance for such a reward.

Has it never occurred to a nobleman, or to any gentleman, that it might probably be as profitable to keep the most promising foals sacred to breeding purposes; that, simply as a paying speculation, it might answer to do for the course what agriculturists have done for the land,—only with this difference, that whereas one desires bulk, the other should aim at courage, strength, and speed? Animals, if well cared for, and never placed in the trainers' hands, would in all probability bring forth finer specimens of horse flesh than either their parents or their progenitors. These foals, being selected and kept apart until the sixth year, might generate young which should sweep the land; and a stud of "clippers" would, assuredly, prove a pretty private property.

Such a plan includes much more care than is at present bestowed. The author well remembers, some years back, going through the straw yard of a "stud farm," in the depth of a severe winter. The place was covered with mares and their newly-born progeny. Separated only by a few open rails, was a flock of yearlings, whose staring coats and ragged manes told emphatically of exposure and of neglect. This should not be. The animals should, from their birth, be securely sheltered and liberally nurtured. He who first accomplishes this, would most probably convert that which at present is a hazardous speculation into a certain gain.

How far a youth passed in running improves the reputation of some quadrupeds, is well known; but how far it is a good preparation for the offices of paternity, is exemplified by most blood mares and stallions becoming famous through their progeny only after years of repose have mitigated the chronic evils of their early life. Prejudice, however, takes no heed of such teaching; but maintains the absolute necessity of proving both, before sire or dam are allowed to perpetuate their kind. The consequence of this system is shown in the deformed and the misshapen dwarfs which are now ruining the once-prized native breed of English horses.

A huge error also distinguishes the plan adopted by most breeders for the general market. The prevailing opinion discards the compact and close-knit female, in favor of the long-backed and loose-bellied mare, which is praised as a "roomy" animal. But all the supposed advantages of this selection are more than counterbalanced by the food which is consumed during the months of gestation. A grass diet promotes dropsy, besides necessitating so much of the poor and watery nutriment to be swallowed that, before the quantity requisite to sustain life can be eaten, more than the difference of space between the shortest and the most expanded abdomen must be occupied.

The stabled horse employs but a brief period of each day in feeding. The same animal, when turned into the field, nearly occupies both day and night collecting the food needed to satisfy the cravings of its appetite. This difference of habit is not explained away by stating that in the stable only so much sustenance is placed before the quadruped; whereas, when at grass, the produce grows on every side of the creature, which it is always at liberty to consume. Many an animal will not clear the manger; therefore the quantity of food devoured in the field is only to be accounted for by that opinion which justly states grass to be a poor and innutritious sustenance.

The distinction which divides the two kinds of provender is, perhaps, best shown by the condition which each produces. The horse supported by the concentrated nourishment of the stable is commonly, while the natural powers are uninjured, characterized by energy, by firmness of body, and by fineness of limb. Whereas the quadruped is seldom long an inhabitant of the field ere it becomes windy, loose, flabby, dropsical; the walls of the abdomen are unnaturally distended; the digestive canal grows thin and pallid; the belly becomes pendulous with fluid; while worms crowd the intestines and bots cover the lining membrane of the stomach. All this takes place as the consequences which generally follow the act of turning out to grass. The animal in the field commonly performs no work; but when within the stable is rarely idle. Stables are badly victualed, badly ventilated, and almost slaughter-houses to the majority of steeds. Yet in the cold and humid climate of England horses cannot thrive upon exposure. Some few may thus exist in an approach to the wild condition; but these rapidly diminish in stature and soon become very shaggy coated. The sheltered horse, when driven forth, grows dull and

BLOOD MARE AND FOAL.

ragged; its coat stares; the spirit droops; the eye loses luster; the carriage grows mean; the legs fill; and the outcast often experiences such a shock to the system as ruins its utility. While agricultural teams, which are mostly pastured, are not unseldom the victims of numerous diseases, as broken wind, etc.

The common country sire probably is injured from an opposite cause. Its food, during the early months of spring, is generally of too stimulating a nature. These creatures are to be seen led about, very much too fat for the proper performance of their functions. Obesity in other animals does not increase fruitfulness, but rather suppresses its development; and the author can perceive no reason why the heavier horse should be an exception to a rule of almost universal application. Common stallions, as beheld at fairs and markets, are weakened in order to please the ignorant farmers who employ these enervated animals to perpetuate the thews and muscles of the mart for English horses.

ATTENDS AT FAIRS AND ON MARKET DAYS.

From dams suffering under the consequences of an exhausted youth, injured by the consumption of an innutritious diet, and debased by the absence of that care and cleanliness which a northern climate makes imperative, is the common breed of English horses replenished. Stallions, however, afford a convincing proof that abundant food and perfect rest, when unaided, will not impart vigor to a debilitated system. Few racers are famed for their stock, till time, which weakens the powers of the body, has effaced the consequences of early training.

From sires groaning under accumulation of fat, and of course equally pining under deterioration of the muscles, enervated by sloth, excited by stimulants, weakened by age, or with constitutions broken by premature exertions, are the claims of British thorough-breds at present maintained.

What are the results of such a system? Distances have to be shortened. Many start; but few return, contesting the race. Ages have to be altered; while boys have to assume the cap and the whip. Useless weights are sought to suit the failing strength; but more animals break down in the training than come to the post.

Yet racing is maintained, not for the amusement of a few, but *to improve the national breed of horses!* How far does it answer its purpose? Let the public markets testify. A stout hack is a rarity. Such an animal was once all but universal. A brougham horse—one looking fit to pull a house—was formerly to be found in every yard. Now London shall be searched through before the shadow of the original can be encountered; when discovered, the price demanded will be far too heavy for the generality of purchasers. The horse flesh of England is becoming weedy under a forced system. Poor "bloods" are everywhere present. In the sphere to which this breed should be confined, a few foals are retained; but the majority are discarded. Many are born that do not return the first expense which called them into existence. Those rejected are to be seen drawing cabs, carrying riders, pulling carts, and performing every office, which is at once a proof of their utter want of value and the hollowness of the pretense which perpetuates such degradation.

The glut of worthless "bloods" serves to check the raising of the other and the better kind of animals. The refuse of the stud farm being disposed of to the highest bidder, so far keeps down the price of common horses that what are termed serviceable quadrupeds have become scarce throughout the land which once produced them in abundance. Thus blood stock is contaminating the native breed of the country. Even with particular breeds—or with the Cleveland bays—the horses which dragged the cumbrous vehicles of our ancestors are lost to the present generation. Carriages are built lighter; but the animals, being nearly pure blood, lack strength and want substance. They are now a leggy, a washy, a soft species of creature, which gentlemen find it cheaper to hire than to buy; while only by keeping a herd large enough to allow some to be nursed and others to rest, does any person find it profitable to retain these quadrupeds, even though the money paid for three years' loan should double the usual price given for an average pair of such poor and abject deformities.

The consequence is, that many gentlemen drive small horses, while omnibus proprietors, etc. prefer the coarser breeds. People are now aware that the lesser size renders the purchase easier, enables the horses to last longer, while sickness is not only less frequent, but the consumption of fodder is altogether smaller in quantity. Carriages are now built of diminished height and of lighter draught; therefore the expense of such a convenience is in many ways lessened. Indeed, the custom has become so general and has so many advantages to recommend it that dealers cannot afford to trade in Clevelands, the sale and the possession of which quadruped is, by the modern salesman, without a murmur relinquished to the job master.

The entire system must be changed, or, while it continues, men should consult the Calendar only to learn what sire to avoid. The blood stock has been bred too fine: all the properties which formerly distinguished it are now deteriorated. As greyhounds were improved by being crossed by the bull-dog, so does the English racer demand the infusion of little "cocktail" into his lineage. The Jockey Club must not perpetuate the weakness of that animal which this society pretends to conserve. Distances should be lengthened, weights increased, and ages made not to favor the maltreatment of mere foals. Nothing would do more to promote an improvement in the breed of English horses than a stoical determination which should render useless the present abundant crop of "weeds." Sires should be chosen because of their stamina, their make, their thews, their muscles, and their general soundness. The quadruped should be treated naturally; not enervated by first being trained, and then debilitated by being pampered.

At the same time, that excessive obesity which is remarkable in all existing stallions of the ordinary breeds should be avoided; nor should the stimulants now in general use ever be employed. No animal should ever be kept in solitude and in darkness, as though its worth were dependent on the amount of mystery by which it can be surrounded. Such treatment is cruel; therefore it is needless. An entire horse is not, necessarily, a savage, though many, being spirited creatures, are made dangerous by the tricks played upon them and by the restraints to which they are needlessly subjected. In several countries emasculation is unknown. Though in India, native rudeness and European prejudice may engender ferocity, the author can boast of having made friends of animals that had undergone no deprivation; and the memories of such friendships are cherished with something more than the recollections of mere equine gentleness.

To illustrate this subject, the author must be pardoned if he introduces an incident which occurred to himself. He was of middle age when he entered as a student at the Royal Veterinary College. His mind became confused by the new sort of companions which he encountered; by the novel objects which surrounded him; and by the strange kind of knowledge he was required to master. This confusion was the greater, because previous habit in the writer had not rendered him familiar with horse flesh. An animal, therefore, was needed, so that reference might be made to its body for an explanation of the books which the pupil was expected to comprehend. At length, in the corner of a back yard was discovered a lonely, loose box. Inside there was a quadruped; and to this place the volume was daily taken, with various morsels of bread or vegetable. Thus, between feeding, reading, examining and caressing, many an afternoon was most pleasantly whiled away.

It was necessary to indulge in certain intimate familiarities. Sometimes to change the position of the animal, or to finger its lower extremities. When doing this, the author possessed no jockeyship to protect him, neither was he conscious that any protection was necessary. He used to shut himself up with the companion of his studies; and the hours thus spent he now remembers as among the very happiest of his existence.

More than a fortnight's leisure had been pleasantly occupied, when, as the writer was one afternoon stealing to the being which lightened the tedium of his studies, and was in the act of opening the door, a number of fellow-students detected him so engaged. "Mayhew! Mayhew!" the group shouted, as with one voice, "where are you going? Don't open that door! 'Van Amburg' is there! He's a kicker and a biter! You'll be killed! Don't open the door!"

Van Amburg was the name of the thorough-bred racer, which had been sent to the College "for operation," because of its supposed ferocity. Yet I, a novice, had passed many an hour in its society, and assert I could not have desired a more gentle companion. We have often laid long together side by side; or, as I reclined upon the straw, reading, the head would rest upon my shoulder, while a full stream of fragrant warmth would salute my cheek. Still, such a creature, so open to advances, so grateful for little kindnesses, was a reputed savage! Probably its real disposition continued to be maligned, and remains now unknown, save only to him whose ignorance was made happier by a discovery of the truth.

A training stable is not calculated to develop the true disposition of a high-spirited animal. A horse generally retains the character which is earned in such a place. When no longer running, but kept for "service,"—boxed up and chained, debarred from all freedom of motion, highly fed, and *teased* to the performance of his office,—such a creature cannot be good tempered, or long continue very sound. Such usage is parent to many an ailment and to many a disease; but, nevertheless, when surrounded by mystery, the stallion may for years continue profitable to its proprietor. It may be the means of transmitting malformation to its descendants; yet the attendant who could best describe its real condition has, in the money which is always paid to the groom, a direct pecuniary interest to uphold the public ignorance.

The thorough-bred mare fares even worse. The animal may get one or two feeds of corn each day; but its chief support is grass, which crams the viscera without satisfying the appetite or nourishing the body. The creature, when "thrown up" for stud purposes, exchanges an overheated stable for an open shed. From the exhaustion generated by closeness, it has to endure the coldness of all but absolute exposure. The coat is no longer dressed; the mane is left uncombed; the animal gradually turns to a pottled deformity, the resemblance of which may be generally witnessed near to every gipsies' encampment.

All animals which are intended to perpetuate their race should be comparatively young, and only subjected to such easy toil as will repay the difference between the stable and the field. The quadrupeds should be daily groomed, and ought to be supported by fodder of an extra nutritious character. Gentle labor and a warm, loose box will only keep the body in good health. When not required to work, the animal should be left at liberty to roam about a piece of bare pasture, especially during the night, when the flies are not abroad, and when the vision of the horse enables it to move with perfect safety.

This treatment should be continued almost to the time of foaling; when the period is very near, three weeks or a month of perfect rest may be accorded, duration being regulated by the condition of the animal. Rest, however, does not imply that the expected mother is to be turned into a straw yard, or is to be exposed to the inclemency of the season. One month subsequent to birth, the work may be gradually resumed; but the mare and her foal should not yet be made to travel on the high-roads. The little life may, in the fields, safely gambol by its parent's side. The exercise will benefit the youngster, while its eye will become accustomed to the toil with which it will have to be associated hereafter. But the tender hoof of the newly born is not, at the expiration of the fourth week, so formed or so hardened as to endure the grate of the common highways, although the feet may sustain the wear consequent upon moving over meadow land.

The foal, before it saw the light, would be sustained by the good food consumed by its mother; the mare would not, by gentle work, be so lowered as to unfit the quadruped for the offices of maternity. By selecting the jobs to be executed, these need not require greater exertion than would be necessitated by healthful exercise. Thus a suggestion, which to many minds may appear a heartless exaction, being explained, becomes no more than a conservative recreation. Something of the kind is needed, because gestation and lactation naturally dispose to sloth, and half the danger of parturition springs from the debility which idleness engenders.

THE MANNER IN WHICH A MARE MAY EARN ITS KEEP, DURING THE PERIOD OF LACTATION.

To render this subject more easily understood, let the reader ask the family medical attendant who is blest with the strongest child—the wealthy lady, who can afford to repose throughout the day upon a sofa, or the tradesman's wife, who is necessitated to bustle about, and to assist in the lighter portions of the household duties? Or, if a more direct illustration be needed, it is afforded by the contrast presented between the swarming cabin of an Irish laborer and the often heirless mansion of the English aristocrat.

Were such a custom only prevalent as has been indicated, those "stud farms," where mares are taken in and confined in the straw yard, with newly-born foals by their sides, would be thrown out of use. The animal, being daily harnessed, would be constantly inspected. There is always plenty of light employment for one horse, if a farm be kept in order. These odd jobs are now either neglected altogether, or are suffered to accumulate until a wagon-load of rubbish encumbers the soil. To remove such heaps and obstructions from time to time, the mare and a boy might be profitably engaged, doing quite work enough to pay for corn and to recompense for grooming. The necessary handling would prevent that condition of semi-wildness into which too many mares degenerate; while the nature of the labor would not render it profitable for a proprietor of land to keep more than one quadruped for breeding, which is the number that most farmers could find leisure to attend to without neglecting other things.

In the author's opinion, the measures at present pursued in the breeding of horses are altogether wrong. They are expensive in their operations and are deceptive in their results. They seem to be regulated by no consideration for the animal, but shaped to the utter convenience of man. The use of "stud farms" or breeding establishments has increased with the degeneracy of blood stock. The horse is by nature too intimately associated with its master to be profitably reared in flocks, like to sheep or oxen, which, being unsuited for the active purposes of life, and of duller dispositions than the equine race, can thrive on mere tranquillity, increasing in the state of semi-domestication. The horse is gifted with a spirit which refuses to vegetate, to fatten, and to multiply, being content simply with an abundance of provender. Where successful speculation is dependent upon the value of the produce rather than upon the number of foals born, a man may certainly be richer, who shall in two years obtain one prime birth; and he may be much poorer, who is annually the owner of various yearlings, none of which shall be suited to the higher purposes of the breed.

The proper place for the horse is the homestead of the proprietor. It is the servant, and should be the companion of its owner. There is no other living creature which is so entirely blended with man. It is unknown in the wild state,—the flocks of horses spoken of as wild being merely animals which are turned out on uninhabited plains, but which, nevertheless, are strictly private property. The distinguishing mark of wildness—or a tendency to return to a particular color—is lost in this quadruped. Wild sheep and goats are common. Oxen, as an undomesticated race, are largely represented. But on the face of the globe the horse—though the most intelligent and the fleetest of its genus—is not to be discovered unassociated with humanity.

The creature, thus distinguished, merits that the gentleness of civilization should characterize its treatment. During the months of gestation, the animal should be fondled and caressed. Any kindness which may be now lavished upon the submissive slave will be certainly repaid hereafter. The hour is approaching when a familiarity with man may soften restraint, and render less perilous the time of danger. The mare, being more intelligent than the cow, feels more acutely, and does not suffer so apathetically. It is more demonstrative in its behavior; but the generous quadruped will, in the utmost wrench of agony, recognize the step or the voice of one who has been kind, and will even be sustained by the presence of him who has earned its confidence. The animal is by gentleness wooed, as it were, to submission. It learns to associate happiness with the person of its superior; and willingly subjects itself to his assistance. Moreover, there is a depth in nature which humanity has not fathomed, and the indulgences bestowed upon the mother, in some mysterious manner may serve to tame the progeny that is not yet numbered among the host of this world's inhabitants.

Then, following the author's proposed mode of treating a mare, which shall be profitable for brood purposes, let the most promising female foal be destined from its birth for this function. It should never be placed in the hands of a "breaker," or have its back strained by being mounted. The creature should be rather coaxed to toil than coerced to labor; it is astonishing how much more can be accomplished by such means than will be effected by the harsher methods. Subsequent to the fourth year, the quadruped may earn its keep; but it should never be urged beyond that point, and where a difference must exist, the balance should stand in the animal's favor. Only the lightest jobs should be chosen—the mare being treated more like a favorite slave than regarded as the servile drudge, whose exhaustion will tend to the profit of a harsh proprietor.

In this manner the first six years should be passed, when the mare, being matured sufficiently, and uninjured by work, may be put to the destined purpose; similarity—not sameness, but more decidedly not difference—regulating the choice of a sire. In the selection, allow one to amend the faults of the other; but in seeking this, avoid absolute contrast, as the union of opposites is too apt to produce deformity.

When choosing a mare for breeding, endeavor to discard the much which has been printed on this subject. Let compactness of form, strength, and an aptitude for exertion decide the choice. The legs should be stout and short,—declaring bone and tendon to be present. The upper portions of these members cannot be too bulging, thick, long, or muscular. The crest should be highly arched, and characterized by substance; for the movements of the body are much controlled by the muscles of the neck. The shoulder cannot be too fleshy, so it shall slant properly, is firm to the touch, and is situated below withers sufficiently lofty. For hunting or for ordinary purposes, high withers are imperative. For racing they are no recommendation, as lofty action delays speed and lessens the length of stride. The back should be short, save only in the racer. The loins ought to be broad. The hips cannot appear too ragged or be too wide apart, while the quarters must seem large in every direction; nor is it to be considered a fault, should these last parts stand higher than and appear disproportioned to the other regions. Above all, see that the channel is wide, the mouth large, and the nostrils ample.

Do not, according to the prevailing notion, search after a long or roomy trunk. Most people like such a shape, because the carcass which they seek after is wanted to contain, with a foal, the enormous quantity of grass which the animal is forced to consume before life can be sustained. The mare just described is not supposed to live in the field, but to be as carefully tended and as liberally nurtured as the best horse in the stable. It is, during gestation, desirable that nourishment should occupy as little compass as possible; while it should not corrupt the body's natural juices. This last effect is consequent on the consumption of dry fodder. The moisture of the mother's body is abstracted from the fœtus, to soften the harsh and hard food which oppresses the stomach. But when grass is eaten, an excess of water renders that which should support the growth of the future foal weak and devoid of nurture, while it engenders dropsy in the dam, and also compresses the dawning life in its primary home.

When the period arrives, the time occupied by the mare in "foaling" will be short. The cow is usually slow in these matters. The mare is always speedy, and far less patient under pain. Therefore when the signs, which are well understood, declare the time to be rapidly approaching, send immediately for the nearest veterinary surgeon. However, previously ascertain that he is apt in this kind of business; and, above all things, be sure he is a feeling man. A coarse and noisy practitioner is of no service about horses. The words may not be understood, but the manners are quickly interpreted. The quadruped, at this period, wants support, encouragement, and kindness. A harsh command or a threatening gesture may so alarm timidity, in its hour of excitement, as shall retard the event they are intended to facilitate. Severity, however, does not always lead to any immediate result; but it may so flutter the mother or disturb its system as will assuredly be fruitful in after disorder.

Should the animal be properly formed, and have been well selected, but little aid will probably be required; yet it is always prudent to have assistance at hand, as the mare on such occasions admits of no delay. Do not, however, allow the animal to give birth in a field or in the open air. Such may be the prevailing custom; but custom is always a bad leader for a prudent man to follow. Numerous children are born under hedges or in gipsy tents; but, nevertheless, such places are not to be preferred for ladies; and the horse, now under consideration, has not been reared upon a common, or is it one that knows only comfort during the presence of sunshine. Lead the quadruped gently into a thickly littered loose box, having trusses of straw carefully poised against the inner walls of the building.

PREPARING THE LYING-IN CHAMBER.

The proprietor, however, must not be regulated in his measures by any rigid attention to dates. These afford nothing like an absolute rule worthy of being implicitly obeyed. Neither need he be thrown into a fluster, because the mare heaves at the flanks. Such a symptom, when unaccompanied by other signs, merely denotes a passing spasm, which may generally be removed by the following drink. Should the pain not yield, the dose may be repeated in half an hour; for, at this critical period, no bodily disturbance can be without importance. These attacks are said to be produced by drinking largely of cold water, by unexpected excitement, etc.

Drink for heaving of the flanks.

Sulphuric ether	One ounce.
Cold water	Three-quarters of a pint.

Mix. Stir till the ingredients are blended; then give as gently as possible.

The hour of labor being near at hand, a pair of light hobbles should be attached to the fetlocks of both hind legs. This should be done by the person in whom the animal has the greatest confidence, as the near approach of a stranger, at such a moment, is very far from desirable. From each hobble should proceed a stout, short rope, the ends of which should unite with a longer cord. The man whom the quadruped most likes should pass the longer rope through the forelegs, and, taking his position near the head, he should hold the end, not so tightly as to inconvenience the mare, but always so firmly as will be ready for any sudden surprise. Mares are apt to be impatient on these occasions; under the strong tension of agony, they will sometimes "lash out." Should such be the case, the man's strength may not be powerful enough to check the action; but when aided by his voice, it may distract the animal's attention, break the force of the blow, and save the veterinary surgeon from any very serious injury.

PREPARATION FOR THE EVENT.

When the foal is born, let it be received in the arms of the groom, and with care laid upon the straw. This done, all present had better retire, for the mother and its offspring may with confidence be left to nature. There should be no peeping through crevices, for the eye of maternity is cunning at detection. Neither should the slightest noise be permitted around or near to the building, as the nerves are always morbidly excited during this particular period. Silence is a good medicine to quiet a disturbed system. The creature will do well, if left to itself. The cleansing of the foal may be confidently trusted to the parent's affection. All she immediately requires is a pail of milk-warm gruel; three hours afterward, she may accept a meal of prepared food.

THE NEWLY-BORN FOAL.

Should the after-birth not be immediately ejected, resort to no purging; neither adopt any mechanical contrivance to expedite its expulsion. These old methods are altogether wrong. The retention is caused by the weakly condition of the mare, which allows the uterus to remain relaxed. The fittest physic, in such a case, is a quart of strong and sound ale. Give three doses of this medicine, each administered after a lapse of three hours. Should no effect have resulted subsequent to another pause of the like duration, inject into the part a full stream of cold water, permitting the fluid to return unchecked. Continue to do this till a spasm appears; then leave off, for your object is accomplished: the pain announced the viscus has contracted.

Dry the mare; give another pail of gruel; place a feed of softened food in the manger, and leave the creature to luxuriate in that rest which will now be enjoyed.

Animals soon get over such affairs. The foal requires nothing beyond a sheltered abode and its mother's attention. Should, however, the source of the young one's nourishment prove unprolific for more than twenty-four hours, a little skimmed cows' milk, first boiled and then slightly sweetened, being afterward diluted with its amount of warm water, may, if sufficiently cool, be presented. The human hand is inserted into the fluid, and two fingers only allowed to protrude above the surface; these are generally seized upon, the nourishment being easily imbibed by the hungry foal. More than a single feed is seldom needed; even that had better be withheld until evident weakness necessitates its administration.

FEEDING THE NEWLY-BORN FOAL.

Do not bother the mare or be tempted to thwart the course of nature at such a time with the impertinence of ball or drink. All physic should be withheld. The common Parent is very indulgent at such seasons; unless opposed by mortal ignorance, his kindness generally proves the best restorative. However, should the bowels continue decidedly costive, some abdominal irregularity may be suspected, and then a bran mash, into which some softened corn should be thrown, will commonly afford all requisite relief. With regard to the newly born, it is better not to interfere. So the parent be kept in health, the offspring usually has all the medicine it requires. Liberal, not too stimulating diet, a sheltered abode, a dry ground, and a kind proprietor embrace the chief if not all the wants of an animal in this condition.

The mother, after her title is confirmed, should always receive her food out of some vessel, which a man should hold during the time it is consumed. Much good is thus effected by allaying the fear natural to maternity; the person so occupied should carefully abstain from any act which might alarm the anxiety of a newly-made parent. The same individual should not always present the meal; but different people should assume this office, so the animal may be thus trained to regard men as friends, and taught to depend upon the generosity of its superiors. By degrees, the foal should be coaxed to accept morsels from the hand of its attendant; advantage should then be taken to pat and to fondle the timid youngster. The purport of such lessons is quickly understood;

FEEDING THE DAM, AND COAXING THE FOAL TO EAT.

for the horse appears naturally to value, far higher than is its worth, any act of condescension from the appointed master. There seems to exist a yearning toward its custodian, and it is surprising to witness with what persistency the human race repel this instinct. The sole object of man—who should by right of moral appreciation and of intellectual culture subdue, tame, and domesticate the creatures of this earth—apparently being to make his presence dreaded by the lives which long to love and are anxious to serve him.

It is usual to reintroduce the male a few days, generally three, subsequent to delivery. But such a custom is far too saving to be profitable How does man imagine that one poor body is, besides extracting sustenance from grass, to yield milk to the living and to sustain the growth of the future offspring at the same time? It has been well declared that no organ is equally fitted to perform two offices; but surely either of the functions alluded to is a sufficient drag. If the reader has any interested motive for concluding otherwise, the countenances of most women, during the latter stages of pregnancy, and the shout of the pot-boy at the human mother's door, are evidences in favor of the author's correctness. Moreover, to demonstrate how these functions are opposed, a fact of common occurrence, among the lower order, may be mentioned. When failing wages render an increase of family undesirable, it is usual for the married women to suckle the last child even for years, thereby delaying the advent of the next intruder.

To afford the nutriment which shall maintain two growing lives and to support itself, is obviously too great a tax to be readily sustained by one body. The drain must be the greater, because each will demand the more as time progresses; thus the unborn has a portion of its sustenance diverted, while the milk, on which the living foal should be matured, is impoverished by the necessities of the maternal system.

Therefore, when entering upon the speculation of breeding horses, it should be remembered that though a foal is a foal, nevertheless a good and a bad foal are very different beings, when tested by figures in an account book. One good foal, every two years, will pay far better than four bad foals every year; as the eight indifferent creatures may be well sold at £20, whereas a promising produce may be purchased at a very reasonable price if it should be parted with for no more than £50.

When depicting the habits of most breeders, however, it must be recollected that the greater number of mares get no corn. A few receive from their liberal owners a little of the damaged produce of last year's crop; while thorough-breds generally obtain *half* the quantity allowed to most working animals, and to each the grain is always presented dry. The majority of mares are turned out to grass, with the foal running at their sides, and the enlarged abdomens showing that "one off, another will come on," which seems to be a ruling maxim with English breeders. Green herbage has a tendency to induce ascites; such an effect declares the food to be deficient in nourishing properties. The mare, then, while suffering from a most exhausting malady, excited by unwholesome diet is expected to suckle and to breed! The body thus engrossed is, moreover, anticipated to yield its owner a profit. To uphold such a foolish system, there are large establishments scattered over the country; while gentlemen and men of education publicly vent their lamentations, because so senseless a plan does not prove a remunerative amusement!

BREEDING, SUCKLING, AND LIVING ON GRASS.

With the silly method of breeding should also be discarded another general rule, the two regulations evidently forming part of one system. Be the foal healthy or weakly, it is permitted to run at its mother's side only for an arbitrary period. Should the young one be well developed, its good points may, nevertheless, be confirmed by a reasonable enjoyment of the maternal attentions. Often the too early weaning will prove a serious check to the growth. Could man only control his impatience, the settlement of such matters might be left to nature. The pair should not be divided, so long as their company is mutually agreeable. The animals, however, as age advances, should be carefully watched, and the two separated so soon as the mother shows she has received nature's command to stop the supplies.

It is a common occurrence for the breeder to delay "operating" upon the male colt, because the body needs further development. A week or two of early comfort will do more for the future points than will months of delay, after the deficiency is all but confirmed, or when time has given a certain direction to the growth. The author has never beheld any benefit result from these periods of exemption, which are, however, usually granted as a kind of forlorn hope. There is another prevalent custom, which is equally objectionable. All men, in this country, first use the animal which is subsequently to propagate its race. The higher breed is broken, trained, and run, before it is "*thrown*" into the stud. In lower life, the farmer, after having hacked and hunted a creature till existence is worthless and spirit gone, says, over his jug and his pipe, "That ould mare has proved a downright good bit of stuff. I should like to have a foal out of her before she is knocked on the head." So he procures the service of some led horse, and turns the aged animal on to the common, to endure the inclemency of our climate without protection,—"to rest herself," he asserts; but the author declares such food and shelter to be almost starvation. This conduct would seem to be the climax of possible folly! Nevertheless, the farmer acknowledges nothing wrong in his behavior; for he is as bold and as loud in his lamentations as other people, when a weakly foal results from his want of consideration—the blame always being cast upon the sire.

THE OULD MARE.

The foregoing chapter has not been so much an exposition of existing customs, as a consideration how far the prevailing habits reasonably admit of amendment. The views which have been announced may, to many minds, appear as purely theoretical, and, as such, to be deserving of no consideration. But before the reader jumps to such a conclusion, he is entreated to reflect that the period of gestation in the mare occupies nearly the space of an entire year. Having weighed this fact, let him learn the gestative season required by other animals, and determine whether there is any living creature whose capabilities are taxed with an equal severity to those of the equine tribe. At the same time, he should appreciate the circumstance that the offspring of the horse is esteemed only as its body is developed, or is capable of labor; whereas the young of many other creatures are kept for amusement, or valued only as articles of food. Surely, where perfection is the object, a greater patience might be reasonably displayed in the mode of securing its attainment!

CHAPTER XIV.

BREAKING AND TRAINING—THEIR ERRORS AND THEIR RESULTS.

HOWEVER much the English nation may have advanced in civilization, as regards the horse, its habits, its subjugation, and its training, two centuries would appear to have introduced no important change or material improvement. Some minor alterations, undoubtedly, have been adopted; but the benefits conferred upon the animal by such innovations are more than questionable; and these variations seem to have been regulated far more by obedience to the progress of society, than to have been recommended by the slightest sympathy for the quadruped.

A reference to the copper-plate engravings which ornament the old work, in two volumes folio, by William Cavendish, Duke of Newcastle, entitled "*A General System of Horsemanship,*" will demonstrate the present formal mode of sitting in the saddle, which is now regarded as imperative by the military profession, to be no more than the ancient fashion of riding which was common with our ancestry. In language, manners, costume, or in any of the many things which mark a *people's* advance, fixedness has not been allowed to check invention; but, where improvement was most needed, not only to ameliorate the condition of the slave, but to confirm the progression of man, by rendering impossible those sights which degrade and which debase the reasoning faculty, it has apparently been absent. The creature, during these years, has altered in form, and has become milder in character. The spurs and bits of former times are no longer in general use, because these are no longer required. They assuredly were not cast aside from any consideration for the life to coerce which they were employed, although a simple regard for property may have banished such ready instruments of torture and of injury. In justification of the foregoing remarks, the portrait of the Marquis (only of a much reduced size) is inserted on the next page.

The lunging of the existing horse-breaker is obviously nothing beyond that circular practice which constituted the chief portion of equine education with our forefathers. It is in the book just named depicted over and over again, until the image, from repetition, grows tedious. It seems very difficult to understand the useful or rational purpose which this peculiar lesson is now intended to support. Some persons assert it is of much service in taming, as it assuredly must tire, the colt. Others declare it teaches the animal to bear properly on particular limbs. A third party assures us it is of infinite service, because it instructs the young horse in leaning toward the rein, and, by not permitting the eyes to be wholly engaged in directing the feet, it obliges the quadruped to employ "high action."

COPIED FROM THE "SYSTEM OF HORSEMANSHIP" BY THE DUKE OF NEWCASTLE.

The use of the limbs is governed by the natural formation of the body; this last no breaker will undertake to improve. It certainly is assuming too much for any art to pretend it can alter that which nature has decreed. A well-formed creature, although it should never have experienced the breaker's instruction, will, of necessity, exhibit grace in its movements. The action of a badly-made quadruped may be temporarily disguised, but it will permanently retain only the mode of progression it is fitted to exemplify. By forcing a faulty horse to trot in a shallow stream, or by obliging the animal to move briskly with sand bags attached round the fore fetlocks, a badly-made colt often will, for a space, adopt a higher action; but it is always certain that this step, which has been acquired at personal inconvenience, will not be long maintained, when the inducement no longer operates.

But, to take a practical view of the good likely to result from lunging. Horses sometimes are obliged to move in circles: mill horses pass their lives in such educational employment. The only effect produced by this long course of instruction is that the poor victims become sightless. Traveling round and round soon causes giddiness, or induces a determination of blood to the brain. Young animals often stagger when relieved from their monotonous course of lunging duties. Old quadrupeds, we are told, grow used to the motion; but such familiarity is purchased with the deprivation of one "precious sense." This termination is hastened with the rapidity of the movements. Mill horses walk their monotonous rounds; but the breaker, dreading no results, makes the colt trot when describing this, his favorite figure.

LUNGING.

Blood, therefore, rapidly loads and oppresses the brain of the young animal thus abused; and this consequence is the quicker as the pace is more excited, because the circulation is not only faster, but it is also more under subjection to external influences in the young than in the matured. The optic nerves originate from the sensorium, being a direct continuation of the substance of the brain itself; whenever the nervous center is congested, sight is the first sense that suffers, or the first that tells the condition of the organ. Frequent repetition of this result upon the delicate structures of growing life appears to be an antiquated custom, which modern civilization should immediately abolish. It is not prudent in man to hazard the injury of his most valuable possession, when he simply intends to render the animal better suited for his service.

Gentlemen no longer delight to disport on "the grand horse;" neither is it esteemed any part of a liberal education to exhibit an ability to sit in the "high saddle." It is, then, impossible to understand the motive which reconciles the present generation to an injurious form, the intention of which was exploded many years ago. No direct result appears to favor of habit. The people who profess to "break in" colts may vaunt their capabilities; but the author cannot remember the quadrupeds which, by force or cunning, however unscrupulously employed, had been in any degree improved. On the contrary, he has seen several, and has heard of more animals, which are reputed to have been injured by having been improperly "broken."

CIRCULAR PRACTICE. AS ILLUSTRATED BY A FORMER DUKE OF NEWCASTLE.

The horse is the most patient servant intrusted to mortality. Man can only spoil, when he essays to amend the perfection of Heaven's gift.

It is good enough in its natural state. It was sent upon earth with a disposition which adapted it for that position it was destined to occupy. It was created with a spirit that yearned to love, that was happy to serve, and that was proud to obey. Must it not be the fatuity of weakness which tempts mankind to waste the strength, to distort the limbs, and to hazard the sight of their most precious possession, by a senseless adherence to an antiquated form?

Every gentleman was intended to be his own horse-breaker, in the same manner as it is now acknowledged that all men should exercise authority over those families at the heads of which they are placed. The qualifications for such an office many gentlemen may be inclined to dispute; at their investment with such a novel duty many individuals may express unqualified surprise. This, however, is only the announcement of man's want of appreciation for the blessings which surround him. Could humanity exalt its vision, it would perceive in its increased duties the boundless mercies which have fitted it to rule on earth!

The horse is, essentially, the servant of man. The greatest indulgence cannot elevate the quadruped out of its real position. The foal is born to its fetters, happy in the bravery of perfect inexperience. Doubting nothing, but too timid to display much trustfulness. Gracefully pliant in its nature, therefore prepared for subjugation; but soon won to love, thereby fitted for domestication. In fact, the horse is the slave of its reverence and its affection. The breaker injures the quadruped by operating only upon its fears, and by not appealing to its higher or its better qualities. The horse, when not guided by its attachments, is a ferocious savage. It is not prudent in man to treat such a gifted creature as though it were a piece of crude metal, which will bend only to the employment of force; but it would be wiser, did he receive and shelter the youthful spirit prepared by its MAKER to appreciate the rule dictated by a milder impulse than one of brutal severity.

The equine race are rendered capricious or obstinate by injudicious petting; but they are made dangerous and ferocious by the opposite kind of treatment. The animals which are most valuable, or those with feelings most readily kindled, are the quadrupeds which the breaker quickly and irremediably spoils. Thus was poor Cruiser rendered distrustful, and taught to regard all mankind as enemies. The breaking and training inflicted upon the thorough-bred made an impression which no time could obliterate. The animal became dangerous, and continued so till it encountered Mr. Rarey. His gentleness, blended with an ability to instruct, conquered and subdued the rebellious spirit. In its surprise, the creature rose from its bonds to worship and to love forever the being who had overpowered, but had not pained the "man hater." To him it became gentle and familiar as a dog; but toward other representatives of humanity it still was urged by that dread which had been established in its colthood.

The quadruped, being thus susceptible to impressions, of course requires a treatment dictated by wisdom and originating in humanity. No maudlin familiarity must ever be indulged, which may cause the slave to forget it is in the presence of its master. Love delights in humility; but the feelings are traitorous which tempt mortality to assume such a character before its equine dependent. The aptitude for being spoilt pervades all animal life. It is only more strongly marked in the horse than in other creatures. The dog, when too much indulged, loses its affection in its sense of power: it will often snap at the hand which feeds it. The horse requires, at all times, a conviction of authority to restrain its strength. If permitted to indulge its own will,—to stop when the voice says "go on,"—it changes from the most subservient of slaves into the most capricious of masters. Therefore man, in his intercourse with the equine race, should, from prudential motives, never be cruel; but, to anticipate the necessity for punishment, he should remember that nature had created the horse to serve and given it a disposition to obey.

Kindness, however, is essential. When training a racer, excess of fluid is assuredly inimical to condition. But it is not therefore desirable to place the animal where a morbid longing is certain to be generated. That, however, is now always done. The stable is heated with impurity: fever is the consequence. Food is given dry: the raging thirst of disease is thereby aggravated. Still, the trainer laments many of his horses will not eat, while more fail during his efforts to promote their condition. Could he be persuaded to amend his ways, possibly he would have less occasion to sorrow over imaginary misfortunes!

Place the horse in a warm, but airy, loose box. Give the water mingled with the food, or soak the fodder before presenting it. The creature naturally consumes little liquid during health. But if the body be diseased, morbid appetites are excited. Now, condition is the perfection of possible health, and the author only complains because modern training is not calculated to attain the end at which it obviously strives. Therefore, much is ruined and little perfected under the prevailing system. The measures are wrong, simply because they are cruel. They are calculated to provoke resistance rather than win obedience from a simple being. Severity never shows itself so abhorrent as when exercised over the meek and the submissive.

At the same time that man's power may be perfect, it should be as a law of existence: it should be exercised from the hour of birth, not suddenly imposed upon an unbroken spirit which had previously been per mitted to enjoy the wildest freedom. It should govern from the earliest consciousness, not, as now, be plumped upon a young life which has hitherto been permitted to roam, knowing no restraint. The foal should not run entirely free by its mother's side: the colt should not be turned into some handy paddock to feed and grow, till it is old enough "to be wanted:" the life should not exist without a need or a care, until a certain age is attained, when the young creature is to be suddenly parted from its enjoyments, and the happy spirit is to be literally "broken" unto the most servile obedience.

Let the education commence with the birth. Let a man always present the vessel from which the mother feeds. The mare will obey the instinct of appetite; the behavior of its dam will instruct the impulses of her young. At the expiration of a week or two, the semblance of a

CAST BY THE HEAD-STALL.

head-stall may be put on the foal; but this should never be worn when the groom is absent, as animals may cast themselves, by getting the hind hoof entangled when endeavoring to scratch the ear. That part of the body the friction of the straps generally causes to itch; the consequence being almost certain, the result is likewise fatal. Several valuable horses have been sacrificed, through grooms turning the creatures into the field without removing the halters. These last were left on, because the quadrupeds, when thus caparisoned, were more easily caught by an idle domestic. This subject has, in a previous part of the work, been illustrated; but to prevent the inconvenience of a reference to a former page, the engraving was reproduced.

After a space, a cord may be attached, and the young may be held while its parent feeds. Then something like a surcingle may be fixed round the body; such things should be made of strips of cloth or of calico, the intention merely being to indicate those articles which must be assumed hereafter. Subsequently a juicy piece of any root the creature may delight in—of marsh-mallow, of aniseseed, or of liquorice—should be inserted between the lips as a mimic bit, from which should depend two short reins. If these things are properly made and carefully introduced, every addition will be accepted with pleasure as a new ornament. No sense of restraint will interfere with an innocent amusement; but the little animal, conscious of no pain, will soon exhibit gratification when arrayed in the representatives of future fetters.

THE FIRST HARNESS PUT ON A FOAL.

At the same time the hand should be frequently passed over the body, and occasionally carried down the limbs, although nothing approaching a regular grooming can, as yet, be necessary. The fluff of the mane, the tail, the forelock, and the fetlock should, subsequently, be combed out very gently, the attendant taking care to praise the foal during the process, and feigning to feel ecstatic admiration after the performance of each operation. All animal life—even does the truth extend to the birds—is peculiarly susceptible to human flattery; for the German peasant teaches the bullfinch to pipe, by dancing before its cage, playing to the captive, and only pausing after each tune to indulge in the pretense of a most extravagant delight.

The youngster should then be led about a meadow by its tiny reins: when perfect in this lesson, it may be fastened to its mother's head while the mare goes to or from its labor. But it must not be forgotten that a harsh word, hastily spoken, may efface more knowledge than a month of tender tuition can communicate. Gentleness and equanimity are of all value, when the confidence of young existence has to be won; for such a capacity, patience becomes something more than an ordinary virtue. Some shyness or show of resistance must be expected when the little foal finds itself first fastened to its mother's side, near the shafts of a light cart; but this will speedily disappear. The tiny feet should, at length, be raised, and afterward the horn be gently tapped or rapped against. These things should be repeated, till they are submitted to without any evidence of fear having been excited by the liberties. Such preparatory lessons ought to be given before the strength is sufficiently matured to be dangerous.

HANDLING THE FEET.

When the weaning has, by the process of nature, been accomplished, the colt should not be turned out and neglected until a determined time for "breaking in" comes round. It should still be sheltered and nourished at the home, the previous lessons being enforced with greater emphasis as the age progresses, and the animal being taken occasionally to the forge, there to stand among other horses, but not to be shod. From its earliest day, man should appear as the necessary companion to every movement. It will soon learn to follow like a dog; thus it may enjoy a partial degree of freedom. But no weakness should betray its custodian into any resemblance even of over-indulgence, although the little creature will regard its tutor with affection, so he does not by his severity repel its advances.

When, however, the animal is no longer permitted to run by its parent's side, the education ought to assume the character of earnest.

RECEIVING THE FIRST LESSON.

A small snaffle should be attached to a regular bridle; when the youngster is led out to exercise, this harness should be put on. The surcingle should be exchanged for something resembling a saddle; ultimately, a dumb jockey ought to be mounted on the back. Upon the extended points of the last machine, an old hat and a cloth may be affixed. These objects will at first excite terror; but fear not being justified and the colt not being hurt by the dreaded presence, confidence will return. A sack, stuffed with straw, and moulded somewhat into the shape of a man, should then be placed over the dumb jockey. Little stirrups and a pair of representative legs should hang on either side, while, to complete the whole, reins may be fastened to the bit; a portion of these last being formed of India-rubber, for not a few mouths are permanently destroyed by the unyielding tug of the heavy-fisted breaker

All these liberties being permitted, if the instruction has been properly communicated, the pupil will have been rather pleasurably excited than permanently alarmed by the varied progress of its tuition. Such lessons, however, should be daily given, until the colt has attained its second year. It should then be regularly groomed; but nothing weightier than a dumb jockey being placed upon its back before the third year has been completed.

This age being attainded, a very diminutive lad may be put into the colt's saddle; but as boys are too apt to spoil the mouth by hanging back and holding on by the reins, the India-rubber had better be continued, and the jockey instructed not to interfere with the bridle, save when his so doing is necessary to guide the animal. Then the teaching of different paces may begin, the quadruped being always instructed in company with a perfectly trained old horse. All feeble intellects are apt at imitation, and a colt shall readily learn from example what coercion will fail to impart.

By the fourth year, the animal may be placed between the shafts of a very light gig, should its form indicate the creature not to be adapted for the saddle; at first it must be walked about a meadow. When the sound of the wheels is not listened for with evidence of fear, the pace may be quickened. Subsequently a boy may get into the vehicle, while the man remains at the colt's head. Succeeding this, the course should be directed by the driver; ultimately, after a man has for some weeks assumed the office of director, the vehicle may be taken upon the road.

Most harness horses are very imperfectly broken. The education is too hurried, and seems to be considered as perfected whenever the animal will merely take to the collar. The consequence is, there are more bad harness horses to be met with in London than creatures of any other description. Some have all spirit lashed or jaded out of them; these have become "slugs," or the poor wretches are almost dead to command and insensible to the goad. Others are rendered incurable kickers by the treatment to which they have been subjected. A third class are ruined by the unscrupulous use of the reins; and some of these will take long journeys, all the time holding the bit between the teeth. A fourth set are rendered cripples by the unfeeling employment of the bearing-rein, which disables the organs of respiration, and renders the lightest draught a terrible burden, by throwing the work upon the muscles of the limbs, while it compels these agents to contract at a fearful disadvantage.

Those who delight in a lofty crest may accomplish more by attention to the health and diet than by the absence of humanity. The strongest bearing-rein and the sharpest bit cannot exalt the head of a spiritless horse. Clover, tares, beans and peas, by promoting the strength and lending tone to the muscular system, will do more to raise the neck and promote gayety of spirit than the harness-maker can accomplish. Bearing-reins are disgraceful cruelties, and do no more than expose the moral condition or the pecuniary meanness of those parties who employ them,

In corroboration of the importance of the neck as an aid to motion. the reader must pardon the author if he refers to a well-marked circumstance which has hitherto escaped observation. A horse with a thin or narrow neck, measuring from the crest to the wind-pipe, should always be avoided. It denotes bodily weakness, and testifies to an absence of spirit. The cervical region always first exhibits the token of approaching emaciation. If the reader will hereafter test the remark by observation, he will find all poor, exhausted animals, which carry the head as though its weight was oppressive, invariably have the neck much impoverished and altogether attenuated.

In short, a mere catalogue of the evils engendered by the injudicious breaking of draught horses, would occupy more space than the author has at his command. For this reason, the driver of a young animal should never be intrusted with reins made entirely of leather; a part of the length should be composed of India-rubber. Neither should he be permitted to flourish a whip. All severity is but an indulgence of the controller's temper; it is unnecessary with a life which is eager to learn and is anxious to obey. The sound of the voice or the gentlest indication should be sufficient to excite the ability of such a pupil. No one can doubt this, who has beheld its activity of ear whenever the horse is addressed.

After the foregoing fashion the education may be perfected, without allowing any professing brute, under the name of a "horse-breaker," to spoil the temper and to lay the seeds of future disease, by ill treatment of a few weeks' duration. Some years ago the author remembers meeting a man, who must have weighed more than fourteen stone, seated on a side saddle, and having a horse rug dangling about his heels. He was supposed to be "breaking in" a colt, rising three, for a lady equestrian His employer must have been excessively developed, or her representative could only spoil the creature which was, ostensibly, preparing to receive a lighter burden and a more delicate hand. An accident was thus almost rendered certain, whenever the oppressed quadruped should be relinquished to its future mistress.

The matters which have been already pointed out being attended to, and the force having been increased with the growing strength of the colt, the creature, after its fifth year, (if intended for the higher purposes of the saddle,) should be taught to leap. To place a rider on an animal's back and then to expect a bar to be cleared, is very like loading a young lady with a sack of flour as preparatory to a dancing lesson being received. This folly is, however, universally practiced; so is that of teaching the paces, when the quadruped's attention is probably engrossed by the burden which the spine has to sustain.

RISING TO THE LEAP.

Leaping is best taught by turning the horse into a small paddock having a low hedge or hurdle fence across its center. A rider should, in sight of the animal, take an old horse over this several times. The groom, who brings the corn at the meal hour, then goes to that side where the animal is not, and calls, shaking up the provender all the time his voice sounds. The boundary will soon be cleared. When half the quantity is eaten, the man should proceed to the opposite compartment and call again. If this is done every time the young horse is fed, the fence may be gradually heightened; after six months of such tuition, a light rider may be safely placed upon the back.

Instruction, thus imparted, neither strains the structures nor tries the temper. The habit is acquired without those risks which necessarily attend a novel performance, while a burden oppresses the strength, and whip or spur distracts the attention. The body is not disabled by the imposition of a heavy load before its powers are taxed to the uttermost. The quadruped has all its capabilities unfettered, and, in such a state, leaping speedily becomes as easy of performance as any other motion

CLEARING THE FENCE.

Irish horses, all being excellent jumpers, are much esteemed in England. In Ireland, however, the fields are of small dimensions, and gates leading to them are uncommon. It is not unusual for a quadruped to be obliged to clear numerous walls before a certain pasture can be gained. Thus, to leap is rendered a prominent necessity of equine existence, for the steed must either jump or starve. By such a condition of their residence is the Irish breed made conspicuous for that activity which especially excites the admiration of Englishmen. Hunting, moreover, is a favorite pastime with the natives of the sister isle; therefore, while most Irish horses become admirable English hunters, the best of the English breed would be sadly thrown out by a short run in the adjacent kingdom. There can be, however, no reason why an English colt, if properly trained, should not become as fine a performer as the most expert or celebrated of those animals which are generally supposed to be born "fencers."

The seventh year should witness the horse taken into the active service of its master. Too early work, certainly, cripples the majority of animals; but there is not a circumstance of the many, rebuked in these pages, which does not aid powerfully in producing that miserable effect. All the customs about the equine race seem to be antiquated and injurious. An animal is taken up, is cast, is operated upon, is shod, is broken, and is sold often in the course of a few weeks. What a change has to be submitted to! Every incident of life is altered—the creature is suddenly called upon to endure a new existence. Is it a matter for surprise that nature occasionally rebels against so wholesale an innovation? Is it not a proof of the sweetness of the disposition which graces the equine race, that the majority can yield themselves up to the barbarity of such a terrible mutation?

The author does not imagine that any person will immediately delay the breaking of his horse up to the period which has been suggested. To take a colt only every second year, and always allow seven years to pass before the animal is brought to market, would, assuredly, double the present cost; or, in other words, it would displace those animal weeds which now cheapen the price of horse flesh. No proposal generally succeeds in the modern age, in which expense is decidedly ignored. The reader is, therefore, not expected to alter his plans because the present volume has been published. Something, however, will have been gained if the book causes him to question his existing behavior, even though he should not modify his proceedings. A writer, however, is bound to state that which in his conviction is the truth, and to pay no regard to motives of mere expediency. Then, putting probability and expense, convenience and existing arrangements out of the question, let the reader deliberately say, whether very much of what he has read was not right in *theory*.

Then, as regards money expense, this might not be increased; for if the animal would cost twice as much, it would endure under a better system four times as long. The outlay, consequently, reckoned against the years of service, would be smaller; nevertheless, many a decade must elapse before that which the book declares is practically carried out. Still, if a few only are convinced, and none adopt the plans proposed, good will ultimately result; for the *right* must be known before it can be practiced, and man generally, in the end, does that which his better sense has acknowledged to be just. The impulse which urges him to such a course may be resisted; but it will, as a necessity of his existence, at length operate; for by such an irresistible power are thrones upturned, are institutions amended, and all human progress is ultimately controlled.

The animal being educated according to the foregoing description,—not being forced to strain its thews and to distort its limbs before the frame has fairly been perfected, but being gradually brought to the mark of its requirements, and also permitted time to comprehend, before it is lashed to perform—being allowed the benefits of practice prior to being expected to exhibit its accomplishments—being simply treated after a manner that every grade of reason must recognize as just,—would come forth in the full possession of all its natural powers, and would distance the swarm of equine babies which now disgrace the thoroughfares, encumber the field, and ruin the race-course. It would be fitted to carry a man in any manly sport; and it would be able, not being distraught by bodily pains, to sympathize in the pleasures of its rider, and to share the amusement in which he delighted.

One peculiarity, illustrative of the present mode of preparing quadrupeds for exertion, is to be witnessed in most hunting fields. The young gentleman who pays hundreds, perhaps, for his "mount," and whose horse has been long under the trainer's care, is usually "*nowhere*" at the death, although he is at liberty to choose his way and to regulate his pace according to his pleasure; whereas the huntsman, seated on a screw which has been hacked throughout the summer, is generally foremost in the chase.

THE OLD HUNTER AND THE YOUNG STEED.

This seeming inconsistency evidently favors those notions which the author has presumed to promulgate. The wealthy scion of aristocracy usually sits upon the young beauty, while the huntsman generally bestrides the aged animal. The older steed may be of little worth, and its blemishes may be numerous; but it has not been exhausted under a pretense of fitting it to endure; it has been hacked or ridden through the months when the younger quadruped was imprisoned in absolute idleness. The cheaper horse has been in constant requisition to exercise the dogs, etc., and therefore its health has been better preserved than is that of the gentleman's steed, which is either new to the sport, or has recently been taken from the supposed enjoyment of a *summer's* rest.

Training of hunters and of racers, as at present conducted, is neither a strengthening nor a refreshing process. The animal that has recently been relinquished by the trainer, instead of being able to endure extra exertion, is generally debilitated by those measures which were designed to produce a contrary effect. In the first place, three doses of physic, which are given under a belief of their tonic efficacy, are quite sufficient to disable any creature, that, like the horse, is possessed of a very large and a very long digestive track, or which nature, as a protection, had rendered almost safe from the purgative operation of medicinal agents. Before the bowels of the horse can be loosened, the primary effects of poisoning must be established. Aloes is the favorite purgative of the stable; but so nearly related are the quantity which relaxes and the amount which kills, that probably aloes has poisoned more horses than all other drugs in the pharmacopœia.

The reader, to whom such a subject is a novelty, may inquire what the intestines have to do with the muscular action. Supposing such a question possible, the author replies, that although the animal body is made up of numerous parts, and composed of various organs, nevertheless the whole is so united that no part or structure can be diseased, but the whole is affected. The intestinal track is lined with mucous membrane. When this surface is involved, prostration or debility ensues. Cold and sore throat are ready instances of this result; for both are consequent upon small portions of inflamed mucous membrane. Imagine, then, the utter prostration which must ensue upon the morbid excitement of so large a mucous surface as that which covers the digestive canal of a horse. Yet the trainer thrice induces this consequence, under an ignorant conviction that by so doing he confers upon the sufferer extraordinary nervous energy!

Purging is, however, only slightly more weakening than sweating. Perspiration acts differently on different specimens of the same species. One person is nearly always bathed in moisture; another invariably presents a dry skin. This shall hardly be moved without the surface of his body being loaded with copious drops of fluid exudation; that will endure the utmost exertion, grow heated at any employment, but will not sensibly lose a particle by transmission. The trainer, nevertheless, treats all animals alike. He gallops every quadruped submitted to his care, as though the consequence was invariably beneficial. In vain does one horse break down, another refuse its corn, and a third exhibit swollen legs or crippled feet, while a fourth shall be only rendered more lively by the process which disabled its fellows. To sweat is a part of the trainer's system, and all the creatures which he is to train must therefore be violently sweated.

With racers, to these modes of debilitating is united a third,—excessive labor. The horse is tried at its topmost speed. These trials are frequent; although it is a common saying that a horse may be trained until it cannot move, still the practice is continued. The pace is quite as severe as it is in a public race; the weight is usually pretty much the same. It is well known that these trials are often run in less time than the contest for which they are thought to be only a preparation. Notwithstanding the repeated disappointment and the frequent injury induced, such prejudicial experiments are continued, though not in every sphere of training. Men train as prize fighters, but they do not, before entering the ring, engage in numerous pitched battles. There is, assuredly, something wrong when the same law is stringent in one case but is inoperative in another, although both instances are supposed to be governed by the similar regulations.

The trainer of late years has somewhat changed his customs. Formerly, animals, while in training, were taken out of the stable twice each day. Now they are allowed only to smell the air once in twenty-four hours; but the period of labor is lengthened. The pace and the extent of time over which it ranges are important considerations when young life has to be dealt with. No less deserving some reflection is the burden to be carried during such exertion. Last of all, and probably as important as any, is the particular hour during which the natural habits of the colt fit it to sustain extraordinary fatigue.

The trainer's horses, ranged in Indian file, are now abroad from eleven: sometimes they return by twelve; at other occasions it is half-past twelve before the bridles are slackened; but generally one o'clock has struck before the saddles are removed. From eleven to one is the precise period when the sun attains its greatest altitude. At this time, those insect pests which torment the equine race are busy and abroad. It is true, the eye of the animal fits it to encounter the glare of the desert, but instinct disposes the quadruped to roam only when the atmosphere is cool, when all its annoyances have retired, and when moisture hangs upon the earth. The eye can better sustain the effects of light in its excess than the feet—

than the horn of the hoof can endure the results of dryness or the hardness of a baked English clay.

Yet the training horse is housed in stables the temperature of which is oppressive, the foulness of which must be most injurious to the prisoner. It is there shut in stench and in darkness to recruit its strength, and to gain fresh energy to endure further reduction. Exercised, when nature would dispose the animal to rest; forced to submit to a fainting warmth, when instinct would induce the creature to seek the coolest shade; ridden, till it almost fails; physicked, till it reels; and sweated, till the process makes it fear the opening of its stable door,—how is the trained quadruped nurtured? How is it supported, to fortify the body for bearing up against such numerous trials?

It is compelled to consume hard corn and fibrous hay. Water is stinted. The measures just described must generate a raging thirst; but the trainer, according to his system, refuses drink. The contents of the manger must aggravate the dryness of the throat; but the trainer begrudgingly permits the animal to imbibe the contents of the pail. The mode of feeding is productive of other evils. Purging and sweating are excused, as necessary to remove accumulations of fat. Corn and hay are those very substances which induce the accumulation of fat! Then, according to the present trainer's pretended system, one thing does that which another undoes. Whether nature is invigorated by such a process, the reader must decide. But, in the author's opinion, the existing method is a prejudice, which reason condemns, and which man is not justified in compelling any creature to undergo.

All the foregoing customs are, in the author's judgment, decidedly wrong. The stable should be cool—not cold—sheltered and airy. The loose box should be large enough for the limbs to be stretched and for the position to be varied, according to the inclination of the inmate. The kind of equine residence which the writer approves of has already been described; for information upon this subject, the reader is referred to the chapter treating of "Stables as they should be."

The food should not be such as requires stone or steel to comminute it. Horses' jaws are not machines urged by steam, by wind, or by water; but they are only bones acted upon by the contraction of muscular fiber. The exhaustion of a part must, as has been already explained, affect the whole; the exertion of extraordinary power in the head will, therefore, not refresh the limbs. Feed the animal, while being trained, upon softened, not upon watery substances. Do not oblige the body to supply its own moisture, for that is to deprive the system of part of the nourishment which should be devoted to uphold the strength.

As concerns the articles of food, these should not consist of oats and hay, although a portion of either may form a part of the sustenance There are certain substances the nutritive qualities of which are expended in the formation of muscular fiber; other materials are devoted entirely upon the adipose tissues. Among the last prominently stand the favorite provender of the English stable. A little of such nourishment is needed to supply the exhaustion of activity: so much should be presented. Of the other description—as beans, peas, vetches—there is a numerous tribe of legumens or plants, which present their seeds ir pods. Hay should be made of these substances, by the seeds being sown broadcast and mown when only in flower. It is unfortunate that there exists a belief such articles are of too stimulating a nature to form the larger part of the stable diet. That, however, is a point which can only be decided by experiment; and the best proof that no trial of the kind has been made, is afforded by the needful preparation required for its institution being unknown. However, the general custom of maintaining agricultural teams upon green vetches certainly does not countenance the notion that peril necessarily attends the adoption of such a form of diet.

The hours of exercise should be amended. The morning's work should be performed at the earliest dawn, when it is getting light. The evening's labor should take place at dusk—after sunset. The dew will then moisten and refresh the feet; the cool air will brace and revive the spirits. At such hours horses are always full of animation. At midday the creatures incline to repose. The animals, during the greatest heat, congregate under trees, hang the heads, and only by the nervous stamping of the feet or the lashing of the tails, testify to being conscious of the myriads which buzz around them.

No animal should be trained with a weight upon the back. It should be led by a man, mounted upon an older horse. The exercise should never be carried beyond that which is needed to support the health; it cannot possibly be otherwise than injurious, when it is pushed to the point of exhaustion. It betrays the folly of the present system, when we hear a trainer assert that the legs and feet cannot endure the work necessary to promote "condition." Condition could be induced without a single gallop. Trotting—easy motion—is all that is absolutely imperative; only the exercise should continue longer than is at present usual on training ground. A horse thus conditioned would be brought to the post with its energies fresh for the trial—not lamed, nearly crippled, nor thoroughly enervated.

Breaking and training both require serious revision. The first needs to be made level with the improved civilization and gentler habits of the present time; whereas it is now almost that which it has been from the earlier period of authentic record.

No notice is taken of the presence of railways; of the general custom of using fire-arms; of discharging fire-works, or the almost universal habit of gas illumination; not to mention the various strange sights and novel exhibitions which the modern streets and highways frequently display. Accidents, neither few nor far between, are provoked by these things; but the breaker, nevertheless, refuses to acknowledge their existence. He views his duties as perfected, and as needing or admitting of no improvement!

So also the trainer. His system has been only influenced by the evils generated through the customs which he obeys. Beyond the race-course, he sees and acknowledges nothing. Railways bring crowds down to all the great contests; but he still trains his horses to run in stillness and in solitude. Many quadrupeds "shut up," when the people shout: the cause of this conduct the trainer refuses to recognize. Numerous animals only show their qualities after age has familiarized them with the tumult of the mob; still, the trainer can see no intimation in so evident a sequence, although intimately associated as cause and effect.

Then, with respect to aloes. This drug should be discarded altogether. Neither should any of the different nostrums, now common in the stable, be employed. Supposing the abdomen to be larger than is desirable, its amendment should be controlled by condensed diet, and sufficient but easy exercise. An occasional drachm dose of iodide of iron, which medicine is both an absorbent and a tonic, may, at long intervals, be exhibited. Where costiveness prevails, a bran mash or two, with a bundle of green meat, would counteract the symptom. To improve the coat, liquor arsenicalis, in ounce doses, should be administered; for this preparation operates upon the integument, by strengthening the body.

The trainer may exclaim against green meat; but it does not retard condition or generate weakness like aloes, and if employed as a medicine, it is of all importance. Beyond the drugs mentioned, nothing should be given, save under professional advice: the lockers should be cleared of all medicinal agents. Other compounds are not quite abolished; but these should be exhibited only by the veterinary surgeon—the quadruped being physicked as little as possible. When trained after the method which has been indicated, all the dangers of the process would be avoided: the health, not the judgment of any interested individual, would declare whether the instructions had been obeyed, or the orders had been violated. Mystery and impudence would be rendered inoperative, and every animal started for a race should return to the post.

Many of the starters should not, as now, be left, blown, crippled, or exhausted, in the middle of the course.

There is an enemy which the trainer little suspects, but which affects the health and the honesty of his establishment. No regulation can be rigidly carried out, when its adoption is dependent upon the whim and the humor of those undersized lads who lounge about the door of every training stable. These boys are not half employed: they delight to excel each other in "larks," in daring, and in mischief. They are very seldom trustworthy. The reason which causes them to be retained, is the lightness of their bodies. Their duty is to groom and to ride the animals which are placed under the trainer's charge. But the first business is lightened by a series of unfeeling antics; the last is the act which very few of these youths can properly perform. They get into the saddle and manage to remain there; but how far they study anything more than that, is demonstrated by so few of the urchins being promoted to jockeys, for which calling the trainer's stable should be the regular entrance.

Many a horse will refuse to win a race from stubbornness of temper. When the way is clear before it, the racer not unfrequently "shuts up," and cannot be induced to exert its ability or to win. Whence is derived that perversity which loves to thwart the power a slave lives but to obey? It is not natural to the breed or to the tribe. Pass through a flock of yearlings, and the path is interrupted, positively impeded, by a host of velvet noses, each demanding to be noticed. Way is difficult to be made through so much importunate affection! However, walk down the gangway of the two-year old stalls in any trainer's stable, and "'ware horse," "'ware heels," is frequently shouted out, while the excess of white displayed by each animal's eye palpably denotes the reason of the warning.

The trainer may as well break the leg of a colt as ruin its temper. The spirit cannot be right, when the temper, which governs it, is permanently warped. The power to win is of no service, if the inclination to exert it does not also exist. The boys tease and plague the creatures, whose fate is, by the rules of training, not so blissful as to admit of such insults being patiently endured. The act offends, and engenders a desire of resentment, which constitutes the "jolly fun" of the lads. The more excitable a colt may be, the more valuable it is likely to prove to its owner; but in proportion to its value is the animal exposed to the pranks which may ruin its chances in the struggle. These things, of course, are not practiced with the trainer's knowledge; but, nevertheless, they are all but universal, and will become more general if the custom of employing uneducated *boys* is not abolished.

Another foolish practice is the starving all animals when most in need of support. This is common with racers and with hunters. When extra energy is imperative, the trainer, by his conduct, pursues the measure best calculated to destroy all inclination for exertion. The plea urged in defense of such folly is, that a loaded stomach oppresses the breathing. This is true enough; but the evils which result from gluttony do not establish that good only can ensue upon starvation. Let the trainer experiment upon himself, and decide whether a light meal or no meal at all is the better preparation for an extraordinary performance. Many trainers assert that a full stomach rests upon the diaphragm, and thereby is detrimental to the respiration. This is a mistake. The digestive sac is pendent beneath the respiratory agent· a fact which an inspection of the annexed engraving will amply illustrate.

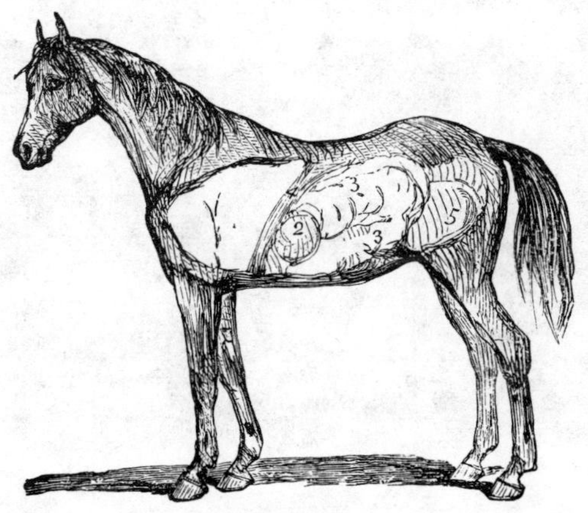

DIAGRAM, TO ILLUSTRATE THE RELATIVE POSITIONS OF THE STOMACH AND OF THE DIAPHRAGM.
1. The lungs. 2. The stomach. 3. The intestines. 4. The diaphragm. 5. The bladder.

If the horse is about to follow the hounds, let a meal of concentrated nourishment be presented. This may consist of a quart of softened malt, or a two-pound stale loaf, moistened with fluid, or a few soaked ship biscuits, or anything of the like nature. This quantity must drive away the pangs of hunger, and the languor attending the sensation; but the author confidently asserts the impossibility of such a repast proving detrimental to the respiration. Then, let every gentleman, who follows the chase, put into each coat-tail pocket a penny loaf. When a check occurs, the rider should dismount, and, having soaked one portion of the bread in any brook or pool, present it to his steed. Such a quantity would be indeed only a snack; but it would be a welcome refreshment. It would serve to repel the approach of inanition, and enable the quadruped to join with spirit in the next "break away."

On the course, excess of weakness has lost many a race. Why should such a system be longer pursued? Why are famishing animals, when prostrated by the want of nourishment, enervated by actual hunger and by thirst, only considered qualified to exhibit fleetness? Is not the idea, when plainly stated, a self-evident fallacy? Nor is it the only error

FED BETWEEN THE BURSTS.

which besets the antiquated customs of the trainer. It is usual to change the shoes, in which the animal is to run, for what are termed "plates," or, in other words, for shoes so light that fearful accidents are reported to have occurred from these inadequate protectors of the hoof. Such things have broken during the violence of the contest. Is there not a foppery in the notion of making a horse's shoe so slight that it shall lose its property of protection, to gain which advantage alone caused the animals to be shod?

All men who have written about the horse agree in regarding the shoe as an evil only to be endured because of its necessity. Its chief injuries are accomplished by fettering the quarters as well as the beels, also by throwing the elastic frog out of use. Upon the action of these very parts of the horse's foot the bound, the spring, and the grace of the animal in no small degree depend. The operation of such organs should, therefore, be of more importance to the thorough-bred than they are to any other description of quadruped. Were these structures never fettered, but the colt left to comprehend their use, its agility would be increased, its stride would be lengthened, and its speed augmented.

The racer chiefly employs the toe to bear weight upon, or this part has to endure nearly all the stress sustained by the hoof while the creature is running. Now, there are shoes known as "tips" which protect the forward horn, but which leave the elasticity of the backward portions of the foot unfettered. This form of shoe is no novelty. It is no crotchet of the author's, puffed into notice by a morbid fancy. It is very humiliating, but it is necessary to make such an acknowledgment, to take from a recommendation all suspicion of the personal or interested motives which are too frequently urged against those who advocate any improvement in stable practice. The author is impelled to make the suggestion simply by his interest in the subject. That the reader may comprehend the difference between the two forms of shoe, and respectively denominated a plate and a tip, the illustrations of each are here reproduced from the article on Shoeing.

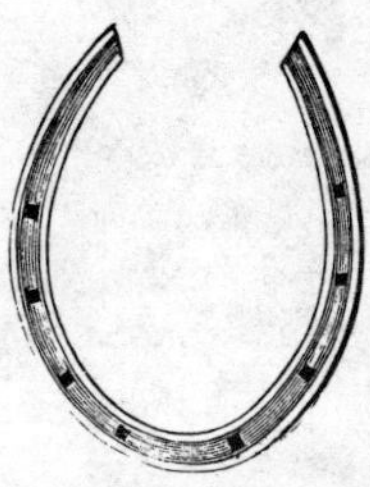

A MODERN RACING SHOE.

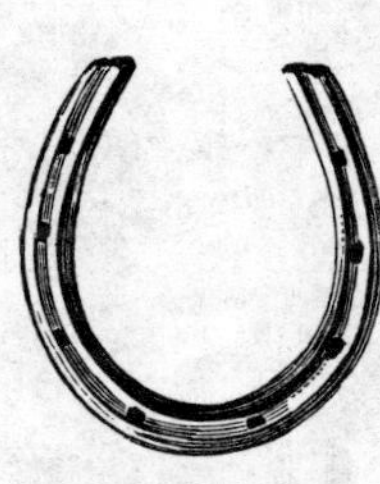

AN ANCIENT RACING SHOE.

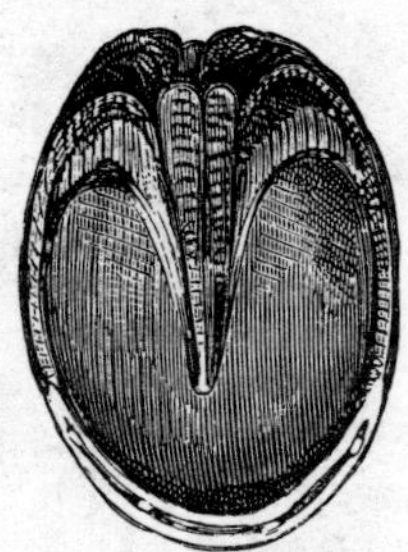

A TIP.

A greater injury is inflicted, however, than has yet been named. Blood horses are often affected with brittle hoofs. This condition of horn renders the nailing on of shoes, even in ordinary cases, a matter of some difficulty. It is a principle with smiths never, if possible, to drive a nail twice into the same hole; and these fastenings being made to pierce the hard outer covering of the wall, the hold is, at all times, in danger of breaking away; but when the horn is abnormally dry or brittle, the nails can scarcely be rendered secure by any possible artifice.

The kind of hoof which prevails among the breed renders it very desirable that the shoes generally worn should never be changed. Tips being of smaller size especially, if a bit of steel were let in upon the toe, if the shoe was formed of the very best metal, as the animal is invariably exercised upon turf, need not be much heavier, if at all weightier, than the present racing plate. Any difference which possibly should exist would, however, be counterbalanced by a healthy condition of horn induced by the greater freedom that must be consequent upon an adoption of the proposed plan; while if a slight additional burden be imposed, that must be much more than counteracted by the new organs to be brought into activity. The frog and the heels, which are now made useless, would lend lightness to the tread, and an ease of motion would thereby be secured.

Another evil is produced by the peculiar notions which the order of trainers have for ages stubbornly adopted, and which gentlemen of education seem to have implicitly accepted. Man himself is not more gregarious than the horse. Men congregate in towns; but it is not unusual

SUMMERED.

to encounter the individual whose delight is solitude. The equine race, when free to exercise a choice, are always seen in flocks; and a solitary animal is never to be met with. Yet it has been found that the severity of eight months' solitary imprisonment cannot be sustained by human culprits. The trainer, however, permits his countenance to radiate under the smiles of benevolence, when he talks of turning an animal into a loose box and of granting the prisoner more than *half a year of rest.* He never appears to think, nor does his employer seem to think for him, whether such a notion be possible. No one, apparently, questions whether stagnation can be a punishment to the living embodiment of muscular activity! We see the heads of quadrupeds, wearing the impress of dejection and looking the images of hopeless misery, hanging over the doors of their cells; but no one reads the lessons which such melancholy spectacles plainly indicate. The language of truth is not understood, and cruelty is perpetuated by ignorance.

When such things are general through the land, is it not justice which has stigmatized England as "the hell of horses?" Does not the heart shudder, as it contemplates the sufferings which have for ages been perpetrated upon the most generous and most self-sacrificing of man's many helpmates? Why doom a quadruped to months of positive stagnation? What is it that converts the intended generosity, where the horse is concerned, into an excuse for actual torture? Why is every act and every intent, when directed to this creature, made to augment and to increase its present load of most unmerited suffering?

Wherefore should the hunter, when the season is over, be shut up or cast aside, as though its life or its feelings were unworthy of consideration? It would be better for the quadruped's health and its happiness, if the attentions to its personal comfort were continued. It would repay the trouble, were it regularly groomed, and fed upon the stable provender. Not turned into a box; its body being, for half a year, uncleansed, and its health being debilitated by a superabundance of green fodder It would thrive better, were it gently hacked by a considerate proprietor. Taken out occasionally, and quietly ridden down the shady green lanes of the neighborhood. Never bustled, but sometimes breathed over an even piece of turf. Ridden always for pleasure, but never saddled when business is to be transacted. Such a life might not allow the groom so much leisure; but it would materially lessen his labors when the hunting season approached. The animal would need but little "*conditioning.*" Improper sustenance would not have induced dropsy; nor would the joints have stiffened by a long period of enforced inactivity.

In conclusion, no horse should be considered fit for general purposes until it has been educated to stand fire,—to hear the rush of sudden noises without alarm, and to remain quiet while a railway whistle is sounded by its rider. Were such things taught, how much misery would be avoided! But the public, as a body, have no faith in goodness, although they profess to believe that the *All-good* is the *All-wise.*

Does it not sound like a fabrication, to say that in the land where many barbarities are openly practiced by the higher orders of society, there should exist a combination, supported by the rich, established to suppress cruelty when perpetrated by the lower classes? The society alluded to should not be abolished. As an institution, it is right. But are the patrons in their proper positions, when punishing cruelty to animals? The highest personage heads both the doings of the race-course and the corporation which professes humanity. But which is worst—the sin which, for its pleasure, tortures the young, or the want which, hardened by adversity, disregards the pangs of the aged? Let the society be continued; but let the race-course also be amended. Render it a rational amusement: let it no longer remain the dominion of vice, upheld for gambling purposes, and maintained by the heartless waste of that life of which man, in gratitude, should assert his right to be the natural protector.

CHAPTER XV.

CARRIAGES—THEIR COST, THEIR MAKE, THEIR EXCELLENCES, AND THEIR MANAGEMENT.

THE following particulars are derived from the highly respectable establishment of Edwin Kesterton, (late Horn,) a well-known firm which transacts business at No. 93 Long Acre. The writer is directly indebted for the facts now stated to the generosity of Mr. John Ronald, the gentleman to whose intelligence is intrusted the conduct of the before-named business. If an extended observance, assisted by years of experience, can lend value to information, certainly Mr. Ronald may advance a good plea to be heard when speaking upon such a topic. And the editor cannot forbear expressing a profound sense of personal obligation for the unreserved and satisfactory manner in which all statements were communicated, and unhesitatingly submitted to the writer's discretion. In short, Mr. Ronald's mode of communicating his knowledge speedily gained the confidence of his listener; but as individual characteristics cannot be embodied in a written declaration, the circumstance is only mentioned, to assure the reader that the following details are worthy of his acceptance and deserving of his consideration.

Carriages are of various kinds; they differ very widely as to cost. Every maker will manufacture every variety which may not be under the protection of the Patent Office. Certain houses, however, may be famed for a certain description of conveyances,—as that of Tilbury for the gig, which is known by the name of its inventor.

The following statement of charges is to be regarded only as a probable approximation to the cost of those articles which are specified. Nothing assuming the form of a definite figure could be named, because the orders given by gentlemen are so essentially opposite. Thus one may be contented with a simple crest or two; but another will insist that his vehicle shall display the fullest heraldic adornments. Such differences in taste regulate the extremes which divide the charges made for the same description of article when furnished by two equally respectable manufacturers.

The gentlemen who profess Herald painting are remunerated according to the time occupied, the amount of work done, and the elaborateness of the design which has been executed. The scale may, to the uninitiated, appear to be gifted with a great power of expansibility; but this quality must reside in every form of art. Heraldic painting demands extreme exactitude; for no liberty is allowable in this practice. Every thing is strictly defined. All examples must be rigidly followed. Consequently, such a pursuit must be no inconsiderable tax upon the memory, while occasionally it necessitates the most laborious research. Such qualifications, moreover, should be paid for, when exercised merely for the gratification of another.

To convey a rough idea of the expense of heraldic ornamentation, it may be stated that two simple crests painted on a gig might, probably, be executed for fifteen shillings. Coats of arms—such as were usually seen on the panels of carriages—begin at two guineas; but the more elaborate embellishments of this description—even should they demand no research and require no particular skill—cannot be executed at a less cost than eight or ten guineas. State vehicles, however, generally abound in fanciful adornments. These have exceeded, for heraldic painting alone, four or sometimes five hundred guineas. Such a sum has been paid for the time, the labor, and the talent bestowed upon a single carriage which, when thus embellished, could be seldom used!

The foregoing figures possibly may surprise most readers; but there are several circumstances to be considered as tending to justify such charges. In the first place, the community of Heraldic Painters are few in number; and the uninviting character of their studies, with the prolonged probation to be undergone before the novice is permitted to practice the art, will probably prevent the body from ever becoming a large association. Then, the employment of the proficients is very much regulated by fashion, which does not, at present, appear disposed to favor the display of family honors. The pursuit, when regarded by itself, may be liberally recompensed. Yet it is not an every-day necessity; but, being once finished, the work will probably endure for years, while the vehicles upon which the resources of the art are most expended are not articles of general use. Few heraldic painters, therefore, accumulate fortunes; but the great majority live to repent having adopted that which the reader may have felt inclined to regard as an extravagantly remunerated calling.

Also, connected with the carriage builder's trade is a still smaller body of industrious and of deserving persons known as Coach Draftsmen. These are the artists who labor upon those neat and picturesque drawings which are always submitted for the approval of that gentleman who may order a new vehicle to be built.

The primary requisite for such a profession is firmness, combined with extreme delicacy of touch; an eye capable of appreciating the nicer rules of art, united to a mind fully endued with the elements of grace, or with that flow of line which is inseparable from all elegance of design. None of these qualities can be dispensed with in the person who embraces the pursuit. Much of the drawing is, no doubt, executed according to measure and to rule, or is purely mechanical; but the qualities which alone can fit an artist for eminence in his peculiar calling are assuredly governed by something very different from and far higher than the patient employment of the compass.

Prior to considering the cost attending the manufacture of various vehicles, it may be proper to state some of the reasons that render an admirably built carriage apparently so expensive. While this is being done, the reader is requested to remember that the present time has frequently been designated as that of competition. Artificers are said to have become too numerous for all the members of any trade to live by the practices of honesty. The people following a particular business are reported to be more than half employed in cutting one another's throats. We are told that no sooner does the tradesman establish a thriving traffic, than another starts an opposition, and under-sells him.

Certainly there is no realizing those snug profits which our fathers talked about having secured, during the termination of the last and the beginning of the present century. Carriage builders are not few in number, neither do they constitute a close society. They are numerous as a trade, and each member of the calling is eager to transact business. Still, the prices are not lowered by the spirit of competition. A good article is yet worth nearly the same money which it has always cost; and the patience of the reader is earnestly requested while an attempt is being hazarded to explain the cause of so prominent a peculiarity.

Before a carriage can be properly built, the conjunction of many distinct callings is imperative. They must all work together, and should all be actuated by harmony of spirit. The various parts are almost innumerable; but each must be adjusted with the minutest nicety. To collect, to retain, and to practice a body of men in such united labor to a common end; to entice artisans, who can exhibit the perfection of their crafts, to relinquish all idea of individuality or of independence; and to induce such people to blend their efforts or to allow only one spirit to actuate a large society,—is no mean undertaking. Yet this must be accomplished; nor is that all, for such contrary elements must be retained, each mutually assisting the other.

As the proprietor succeeds in accomplishing this object, so will be his success in the coach building business. Let the reader, however, understand that a good set of workmen is not the only necessity required for this business. The tradesman must be himself distinguished by the loftiest of human attributes. He must be also willing to sink his individuality in his pursuit, and must be ambitious only for a general result.

The coach builder works with very expensive woods, the original cost of which is materially increased by the lengthened periods that these articles have to be kept before being used. The time required to season thoroughly a piece of timber, for the choicest of ordinary trades, would be altogether insufficient for the coach builder's purposes. Wood must not only be seasoned, but it must be rendered so perfectly hard or dry as shall make shrinking or warping, even in the slightest degree, totally impossible.

Such a necessity compels the coach builder to keep a large stock of the timber which he employs. This wood, when introduced to the workshop, must be in a state of the utmost perfection. It must be possessed of the greatest strength and the most approved hardness which its fiber is capable of exhibiting. Those characteristics can only be attained where the material is particularly fine in grain. Of course, such a quality makes the substance specially retentive of that moisture which circulated throughout every product of the vegetable world. This last property gives rise to the necessity which obliges every log to be so long kept before the tradesman dare have the wood admitted within the precincts of his established manufactory.

The tools employed to cut such timber must needs be of exquisite temper, and of course are equally costly to purchase. Moreover, the simple cutting of wood almost as hard as metal is not sufficient. The workmen must be capable of adapting the various parts so closely that these shall, when put together, possess the strength of one entire piece. The several junctures must be imperceptible either to sight or to touch; the different portions must fit as though they grew together. No amount of jolting, no possible shaking should cause the work to yield even a hair's breadth. Should the carriage be injured, though of course the paint must be damaged, nevertheless the frame should remain firm. Every part of the vehicle should be formed to endure the rudest treatment; should be able to sustain, uninjured, the long rattling over the roughest of country roads. Unless his products can bear such usage, no tradesman need write "*Coach Builder*" subsequent to his name.

The tools sold to carriage builders are quite distinct from those manufactured for the cabinet-maker or the joiner. The first articles are known by different names, and are kept as a distinct class of superior goods. An ordinary chest of such tools, possessed by every average journeyman, could not be purchased under thirty, or probably forty pounds.

This price, in order that it may be justly appreciated, must be regarded in connection with the class of men to whom it refers; also it must be considered in association with the facts—that workmen provide their own tools, and that each man is confined to one particular species of toil; that the members of every shop often borrow and as frequently lend; and that every tradesman is educated to adopt various resources Thus one instrument is often compelled to serve several uses.

An ordinary carriage builder can generally command two guineas a week. That sum, however, does not fairly represent the earning of all workmen, when viewed as members of one body. Most clever artificers will not engage by the period; but they prefer to be paid by the piece. A person of no more than average talent, when employed at piece-work on the ordinary run of jobs, can gain from two to three guineas by six days' toil. Thus every man in the trade has a direct stimulus to improvement, the higher wages being a constant spur to excite the work-people, none but the better sort of whom are engaged on the more remunerative labor.

Then, of the many trades which the coachmaker employs, each must be the perfection of its order. The upholstery must not be merely tacks or tacking. All must be sewn with the stoutest thread, and nailed with an intention that it should never loosen. The smith's work must be forged with an exactitude which is little expected in the general sphere of the anvil. The painting and the varnishing must be carried to the refinement of possible finish. In short, the best of many opposite callings must be united before a carriage manufactory can be instituted.

The business which necessitates the junction of such adverse kinds of perfection, of course cannot be conducted cheaply. The climax of ability is a commodity which will always command a ready sale, and for which, in every market, there is never a lack of bidders. He who wishes to obtain it, must not, therefore, haggle about remuneration; but be prepared to meet its demands with liberality. That circumstance, taken in conjunction with the expensive nature of all the materials he employs, disables the coachmaker, who is anxious to do justice to his patron and to himself, from producing a cheap article.

A full dress coach or chariot, such as once were the only conveyances permitted to approach St. James's Palace on a Drawing Room day, cannot be properly made for a less sum than four hundred guineas; if the taste of the customer should be very fastidious, either article may cost seven or even eight hundred guineas. A state carriage must be charged for according to its adornments, which can almost be carried to any extent.

The state carriage which was built to order for a particular monarch had solid silver let in upon its exterior; while the ground was composed of the choicest colors, overlaid by the most exquisite decorative painting.

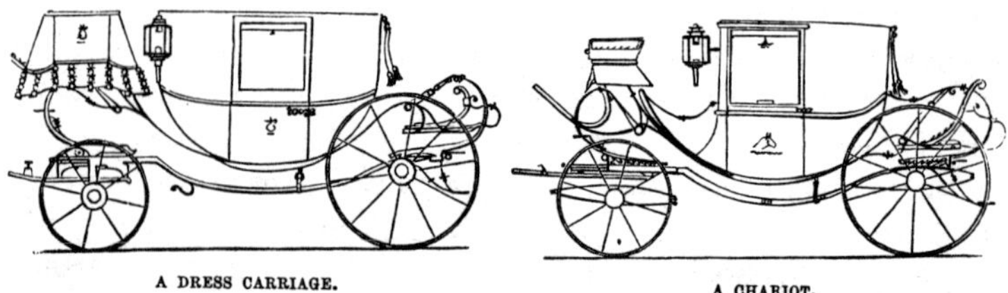

A DRESS CARRIAGE. A CHARIOT.

The charge for this toy was seven thousand guineas. The Sheriffs of London, however, manage to ride in a state carriage at a more economical rate. Their vehicles are commonly hired for the year of office; and the expense is only varied by that amount of adornment which each new dignitary may please to command. The ordinary charges are seldom lower than eighty guineas, and are rarely higher than one hundred and sixty guineas.

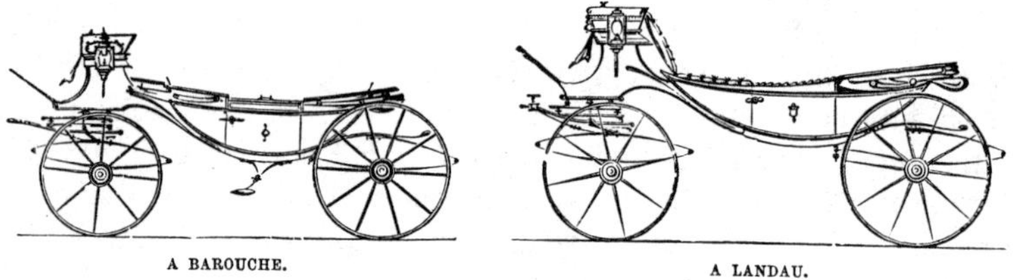

A BAROUCHE. A LANDAU.

A neatly-built step-piece barouche is certainly an elegant conveyance, though, at the present moment, hardly so popular as it was a few years ago. Vehicles, like most other things, are subject to the arbitrary dictates of fashion, and this circumstance renders the coachmaker's stock, which must at all times be costly, particularly hazardous. However, the risk which is inseparable from the character of the trade must be covered by the profit account when the books are balanced. A good barouche is an expensive luxury; since this conveyance cannot be manufactured under one hundred and sixty guineas, while it may, without much extravagance, be easily made to cost two hundred and twenty guineas.

The landau, which has now become almost the exclusive property of the ladies, is even more expensive than the barouche. But with this fact it may be necessary also to state that the landau requires to be especially well built, and must be highly finished in every part It ought to be particularly light in appearance, and so nicely balanced upon its springs that, though perfectly firm, the touch from a finger nevertheless could set the body in motion. Such properties necessitate the very best workmanship which can be procured, even in the carriage trade. Consequently, this kind of conveyance cannot be properly raised for a less price than two hundred guineas; but as the feminine taste appears to be more cheaply satisfied than are the masculine desires, the cost of an ordinary landau seldom rises above two hundred and fifty guineas.

A CARRIAGE WITHOUT C SPRINGS. A BROUGHAM.

A coach without the circular springs, or C springs, as they are commonly called, and also wanting a dickey or seat behind, is now manufactured according to various patterns. This kind of conveyance is, at present, frequently encountered in the streets of London. Of course, it is difficult to name the price of an article which is generally built in accordance with some arbitrary command, and which is not governed by any acknowledged regulation. The cost, therefore, can only be controlled by the time, the labor, and the materials which are expended in the construction; but this may be roughly calculated at something between one hundred and ninety and three hundred guineas. Such, however, are light and pleasant carriages, sufficiently roomy to ride at ease in, and not difficult to propel. They are rapidly ascending on the scale of public favor.

Broughams seem to be made of various forms: some vehicles bearing this name are very little better than the more cleanly order of street cabs. But such a brougham as no gentleman need be ashamed to own, or need blush to see his crest emblazoned on, should be built for one hundred and thirty to one hundred and eighty guineas. These vehicles have been much improved of late. They were formerly manufactured of a weight which was a severe tax upon the strength of one horse, and they were at once vulgar both in appearance and in size. The draught has been greatly diminished, while the aspect has been so far improved as to advance a claim to elegance. Those proprietors who still cling to a brougham which can accommodate more than two persons usually have the equipage drawn by two small horses. The carriage, thus propelled, looks showy, and is moved with perfect ease.

A mail phaeton may occasionally be seen driven through the park. But this form of vehicle is not now so much used as it was a few years ago; but when well appointed, it certainly has a most aristocratic appearance. Few ladies, however, like to ride in such a conveyance, unless they occupy a seat in the front compartment, and are accompanied by the husbands, who are driving. Such a prejudice consigns half of this carriage to the servants, while the length of the phaeton renders its draught so heavy as to necessitate the employment of two horses. Custom, therefore, makes these vehicles expensive to the proprietors, although the first cost is not so large as the style suggests. One hundred and forty guineas or one hundred and sixty guineas will generally cover the purchase of the mail phaeton.

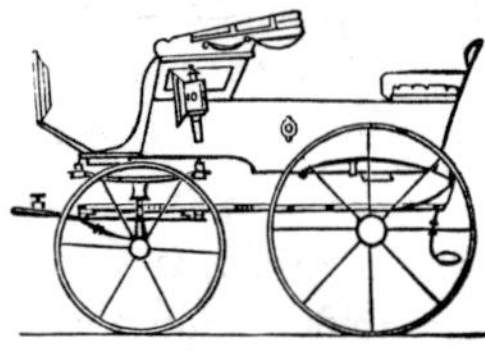

A MAIL PHAETON.

A FOUR-WHEELED DOG CART.

The four-wheeled "dog cart" has lately come into general use. Such conveyances possess a more gentlemanly, and have an infinitely less dangerous appearance, than the two-wheeled "turn outs" bearing a similar designation. When driven with a pair of spirited horses, they may proceed at almost any pace with perfect ease and safety; running very light, yet affording ample accommodation for every portion of the load, and looking the perfection of a sporting "concern." They are, moreover, when compared with the sums at which the more showy properties of most carriages are purchased, not to be esteemed expensive. A good article of this description can be bought for seventy guineas, and the most elaborated seldom costs more than one hundred and twenty guineas.

Gigs of different denominations are mostly of one price. This figure ranges from forty to seventy guineas. It matters not the shape, whether it be a Stanhope or a two-wheeled dog cart, the expense is pretty much the same. The last form of vehicle is now coming into very general use; but when fully loaded, it appears dangerous, and is a severe tax upon animal strength when driven at the rate which most drivers seem to prefer. Hence the obvious origin of the four-wheeled dog cart, which, when harnessed to a pair of horses, is free from those objections that the original form of this conveyance invariably suggested.

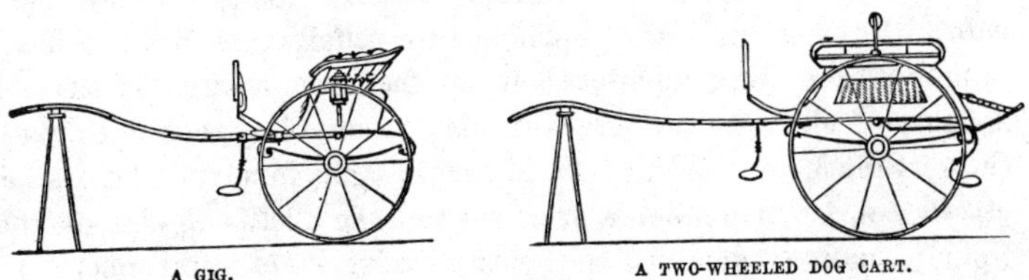

A GIG. A TWO-WHEELED DOG CART.

A well-built carriage is, consequently, a rather expensive convenience; but, unfortunately for the honest tradesmen, few persons are qualified to advance an opinion upon the conveyance. The reader, therefore, must accord his indulgence while the author endeavors to explain the points which characterize a well-manufactured article. In the first place, the wheels should revolve without perceptibly varying from the line which they indicated when the carriage was stationary and the tires were viewed from behind. They should not, during rotation, incline either to the right or to the left, for if they, when in motion, alter even a hair's breadth from such a line, it is proof positive that the wheels are faulty. They should move slowly and quickly without making the slightest sound: they should glide noiselessly over all even surfaces, and with no more audible disturbance than is unavoidable, they should travel, at the most rapid pace, over the roughest highway.

The body should be poised so evenly as will answer to the gentlest force, and be readily swayed by more violent action; but however excited it may be, the body should never lean to either side, and, the impetus being arrested, it should speedily become stationary. All the parts should be firmly united. When violently urged, the movements should elicit no creaking; the steps should not jingle; the windows should not rattle; and, above all, when the outlets are shut, a person inside should be incommoded by no perceptible draught.

That time may not injure such properties, the coach-house should be warm, should be well aired, and should be perfectly dry. Damp is ruinous to the paint, to the ornaments, and, in short, to every part of a conveyance. As the most used carriage must be a greater number of hours within its house than it can possibly be abroad, so for the larger portion of its existence is it exposed to the operation of those enemies (when any exist) which will be silently destroying. The length of time which a vehicle improperly housed may endure, will of course greatly be dependent upon the amount of evil with which it has to contend; but only a moderate degree of moisture will so speedily tarnish as shall necessitate restoration at least twelve months prior to the usual season for that renovating process.

A good coach-house should neither by door nor by window communicate with the stable. Such openings are usually present in most London buildings, and are evidently allowed either from thoughtlessness or from a greater feeling for the servant's convenience than regard for that which the servant is engaged to keep in order. The fumes of the stable principally consist of ammonia or of the volatile alkali. These emanations, from manure made pungent by the exclusion of atmospheric air, are very insidious in their effects, and are much more destructive than either of the fixed anti-acids, potash or soda.

Most coachmen are aware that the employment of soap, in any form, is injurious to paint and to varnish. Soap, however, is a salt, or consists of an alkali, which is neutralized or combined with a fatty acid. Still alkali, even in this shape, should not be applied to any conveyance. The idea of dissolving potash or soda in water, and then employing the liquid to cleanse the family carriage, appears to be so preposterous as to be rejected even by the ingenious ignorance of the stable. But a single application of the last agents would do less damage than the long exposure of a vehicle to the more penetrating fumes of gaseous ammonia.

Another subject of much importance to the carriage interest—but one not generally considered by the majority of proprietors—is the kind of water with which the stable is supplied. Coachmen commonly think to counteract the ill effects of bad water upon the horses, by exposing pails filled with the liquid, for some hours, within the tainted interior of the stable. But the fluid is more likely to become foul from the impurities which it can there absorb, than for the action of ammoniacal gas to amend the properties or to correct the evil qualities of the liquid.

Hard water, especially that which is impregnated with a solution of any mineral substance, is equally prejudicial to the health of animals and to the beauty of vehicles. Such should never be employed in any stable. Soft water or river water is alone suited for either purpose. Pipe water, or water which has traveled far in leaden tubes, is frequently impure; while pump or well water should always be avoided.

This may to many readers appear a trivial matter to be so energetically enforced; but as all the comforts of life are only secured by attention to those particulars which surround existence, certainly the pocket of the master is concerned in the conditions to which his carriage is exposed.

Many gentlemen, however, will permit the servants to ruin the best-made carriage, and then blame the builder, because his work is capable of being abused. When the family returns home at midnight, after the necessities of the horses have been attended to, the vehicle should be thoroughly sluiced with cold water, so that not a speck of dirt remain clinging to the paint. At whatever hour the residence may be reached, this operation should never be neglected. The free and copious employment of fluid floated over the varnish is imperative, and (as will be explained hereafter) prevents serious damage.

There is no occasion, at so late a period, when extreme hours have probably indisposed the servants for exertion, that the carriage should be regularly cleansed with brush, mop, and pail; but a large watering-pot, kept ready for such uses, will, in a very brief space and without much trouble, pour forth a steady stream of liquid, and float off the loose fresh mud by the simple action of gravitation. This done, the superabundant moisture will have run off the varnish, which was first sluiced, and the surface may be roughly dried with a sponge. All being accomplished, the coachman may safely delay his regular routine of duties until he rises on the following morning.

The reason which necessitates a carriage to be immediately washed, whenever it returns home soiled, is quickly stated. If wet mud be permitted to continue and to dry upon the surface, a white, opaque spot will afterward indicate the place to which the dirt adhered. Moreover, a vehicle which is invariably left in its coat of filth until the following morning, always requires repainting and revarnishing twelve months, and very often two years, before the general period for restoration, when the opposite and the more careful measures are adopted.

Should a carriage have to wait the convenience of its master, it should never rest in the full blaze of the sunshine. Where a choice is possible, the careful servant always withdraws into the shade. It is even worth while that pride should so far sacrifice its feelings as to sanction such a precaution; for the cool shadow is not only more pleasant for the horses, but is infinitely better than the extreme of glare and heat for the conveyance to which the animals are harnessed.

The excess of light causes the varnish to crack, and removes the gloss from the smartest vehicle. The smooth and the highly polished surface suffers; this, of course, injures the deeper structures. Should the carriage have been purchased from an honest builder, there is small danger of any degree of warmth affecting the main structure; but if the custom of standing in the sunshine is sanctioned, the paint will not last longer than three years, while, even for that period, the effect will not be good; since the cracks in the varnish serve as gutters wherein soil will accumulate.

The well-built body of a regular carriage should remain together while three sets of wheels are used up. The arbitrary dictates of fashion, however, interfere with the economy which was, formerly, generally observed. Few, save the titled or the old aristocratic families, at present keep what once was the recognized build of every private carriage. The conveyances now manufactured for the moneyed and the respectable classes are built according to no common model; but the forms are moulded by the dictates of most arbitrary caprice. The article therefore which, when it was newly built, excited surprise and kindled emulation, shall, before it has existed eight years, provoke contempt, as a lumbering concern altogether behind the spirit of the age. Consequently, the duration being limited, (and a set of wheels being calculated, with ordinary work and care, to last four years,) not many of the lighter and more novel vehicles can be used for a longer period than suffices to wear two-thirds of the stated number.

A set of wheels hardly ever cost the same price, when made for vehicles of different descriptions. A brougham and a carriage both possess four wheels; yet the charges made for each kind are very opposite. The wheels proper for a carriage cost fourteen or twenty guineas; whereas those which are fittest for a brougham can be made for ten guineas. Then, again, the gig requires only two wheels; but the pair are generally sold at six guineas. These variations are regulated by the extent of the circumference, the substance necessitated, and by many particulars which the reader can readily imagine. Wheels are, therefore, somewhat expensive; a fresh supply is rendered the more costly, because the newness of one part makes imperative the renovation of the whole; although some persons avoid such a consequence by having the wheels and the body of a carriage of different colors. However, such piebald affairs always betray the intention, and the idea of exposing a personal meanness has, hitherto, prevented the practice from being generally adopted.

The good and the careful coachman can only display the value of his services when there is no stint of those appliances which are imperative for the proper exercise of his calling. It is always necessary that the master's economy should afford no ready excuse for neglect of duty in the servant. This is important, because no domestic, excepting the groom, has such valuable and such perishable property intrusted to his discretion. Paint and varnish are not enduring commodities. Most London houses are redecorated every third year; with all care, a carriage will appear respectable but one term longer.

For the proper discharge of his duties, the coachman requires three sponges and three leathers for the body of the vehicle. One sponge to cleanse the coarser dirt from the carriage; another to remove any lingering soil; while the third serves to render the surface somewhat dry, previous to the employment of the leathers. For the wheels a setter, or a machine to raise them from the ground, cannot be dispensed with · a mop and a pail to remove the dirt; a brush to cleanse the angles; also sponges and leathers to thoroughly purify or polish the surface—all are needed. There should also be a superior brush for the lining; and another brush, with an additional leather, to brighten the brass or plated ornaments upon the exterior.

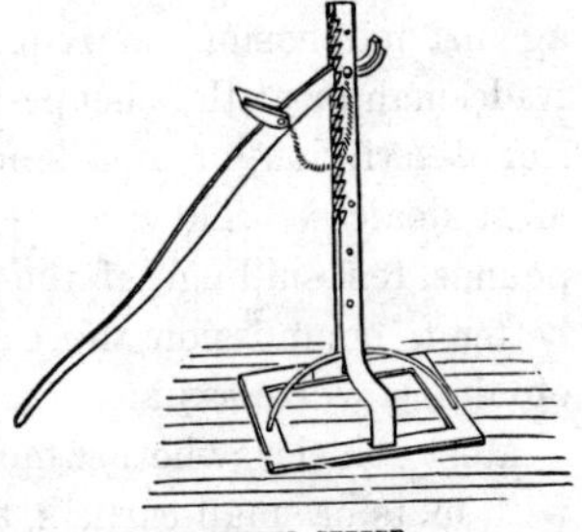

A WHEEL SETTER.

To polish the last, no preparation excels prepared chalk, when mixed with soap and water. It thoroughly removes every impurity, without sensible wear of the substance to which it is applied. In this last particular, it possesses an immense advantage over the gritty pastes sold for the purpose of polishing metals; for this material acts chemically and mechanically on such surfaces. The prepared chalk may, moreover, be purchased at every chemist's, the charge commonly being a shilling for the pound; while the other ingredients are found in every household.

In one respect, few servants are sufficiently careful. They imagine whitening and other filths are indispensable when glass is to be cleaned. The prejudice originates in ignorance; for glass requires nothing except two leathers, or a sponge and a leather, to render it perfectly bright. The first article should be merely moist, the intention being to loosen or to remove the superficial dirt. After this has been accomplished, the dry leather is brought into play to cleanse and to polish the metal. By such an easy and so simple a resort are prevented those accumulations round the edges of windows, and the soiled condition of the frames which disgrace too many carriages, and which certainly would generate no regret if rendered altogether impossible.

The lining does not need so much care as might be imagined. Unless the weather be hot and the roads very dusty, it will hardly require more than a single brushing. A brown holland cover for the interior has become general; but such a thing, when soiled, should never be sent to the family washerwoman. The article may come home washed, starched, and ironed to perfection; but in these processes it is sadly stretched and pulled out of shape. The holland never sets well afterward, and very speedily requires the cleansing to be repeated.

The proper method, and not the dearest in the end, is to return such things to the carriage-maker, by whom such matters are understood; the article will be returned cleansed and calendered, looking like new material and with no part strained or stretched till it does not fit into its relative situation.

When speaking of cleaning, it may be as well to caution the reader against purchasing the requisites for cleaning his carriage of the nearest tradesman or at the cheapest shop. Such goods should all be of a superior description, or of a kind which is not encountered in the stock of most dealers. They cannot be purchased for a less sum than three pounds ten shillings, if the quality is to be excellent; and it is always better to commission the carriage builder to procure them than to risk obtaining worthless articles.

Most vehicles, whether mounted upon two or four wheels, are furnished with mats or small carpets, though the nature of these articles are better represented by such things being designated "rugs." These "rugs" are commonly of two sorts: one kind being known as "Brussels," the other being termed "pile." The last, of any figure, always strike the beholder as not having been specially made for the situation which the article occupies. The Brussels are not open to the same objection, having an ornamental center, surrounded by a complex border. However, the coachman should always carefully attend to the rug every morning; because, as the pavement has to be crossed every time the passenger leaves or enters the conveyance, that upon which the feet rest is more likely to be soiled than any other portion of the interior.

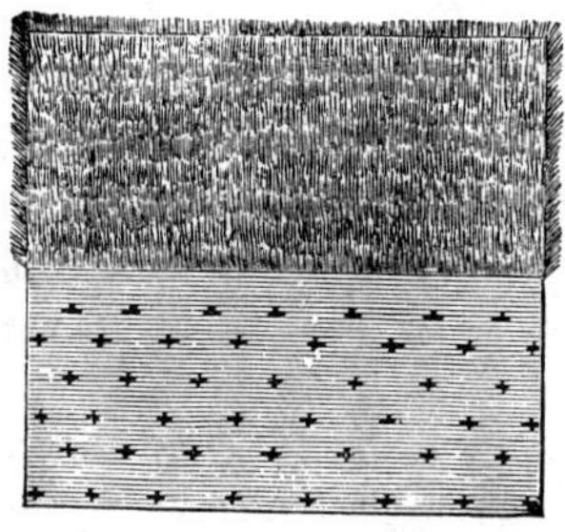

A PILE AND A BRUSSELS CARRIAGE CARPET PLACED TOGETHER.

Moist mud upon the surface of the rug should never be interfered with. The soil should invariably be permitted to become dry prior to its removal being attempted. Then the offending patch is more quickly displaced by rubbing the sides smartly together, or by passing a clean besom briskly but not heavily over the place, than by those numerous gentler measures which occupy more time in performance and are more wearing in their operation. All dirt being removed, no further brushing is required; but the rug, after having been beaten against any door post, (but that of the stable,) may be replaced in the carriage. All rugs should be similarly treated, and should be always removed every morning; because grit will necessarily accumulate upon the floor, and thus cause much more wear than can be occasioned by the feet alone.

As concerns those things which the wheels require, the coachman should observe three matters, which are all specially important: screwing on the box or the central cover; oiling the axletrees; and perpetually noticing the wear which the tire, or the marginal rim of metal, undergoes. With regard to the box, that should be screwed until the wheel turns steadily, evenly, and pleasantly. Should sensible effort be requisite to put the wheel in motion, the necessity for force is proof positive that the box has been screwed too tightly, or that it has been made to press too hardly against the wheel, which it should merely help to retain in its position. Such a compression, acting upon all four of the wheels, will increase the draught threefold, the action being the same as a break when it is applied to check the perilous downward progress of any vehicle.

Inferior axle-trees soon wear with the friction of the wheels which rotate upon them. Colins's (expired patent) are, perhaps, the best; though the choice is somewhat extensive, and there is no article of this description which does not possess some merit. When the box will not screw steadily, and the case-hardening of the axle has worn off, the wheel is not, as many persons imagine, imminently dangerous; but its rotation becomes uneven, and the motion of the carriage is rendered less pleasant to the rider. The greasing or the oiling of the wheels, when the work is of the ordinary duration and character, is performed sufficiently often, if done once in three months. Quicker progression necessitates more constant attention; and the axles of a conveyance driven notoriously fast had better be inspected every week.

Coachmen are not commonly negligent concerning such particulars. Neglect, however, would cause the grease to assume a solid form, and impede the motion. This effect causes an extra drag upon the collars of the horses; and gentlemen, when the vehicle moves slowly, should, upon reaching home, see that the axles are properly greased, and the boxes are not screwed too hardly.

The tires will sometimes outlast the wheels; but all depends upon the distance covered, the weight drawn, and the pace at which the vehicle is driven. Some gentlemen—especially medical gentlemen in full practice—will wear through a set of tires in eight or nine months, when the orders given are to move fast, and four changes are required to get through the daily visits. However, no person should risk riding in a carriage when the tires become perceptibly thin or loose.

Small lamps are a mistake. Diminutive lanterns may in some eyes look prettier during daytime; but when they are used, the confined space does not allow the amount of oxygen to enter the interior which is required to support the flame. The consequences are, diminished brilliancy and an abundance of smoke. The glasses become speedily soiled and the reflectors deadened. A lamp of sufficient size is not without its recommendations, as, even in daylight, it lends purpose and dignity to the vehicle which it adorns. At night it will nourish the flame, and cause the reflectors to shine forth with almost dazzling effulgence.

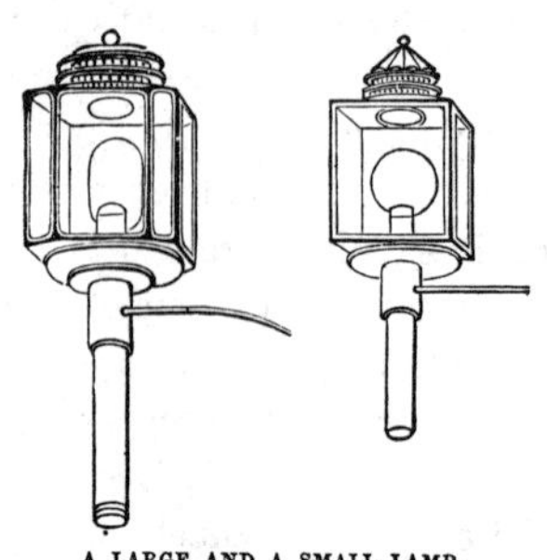

A LARGE AND A SMALL LAMP.

That it may do this, however, it is imperative the proper kind of candles be consumed. Of candles, there are two kinds sold for carriages. One, which is the cheaper, is a composition that soon softens under the combined effect of confined heat and strongly reflected flame. The light is not bad, but, nevertheless, is far from brilliant; while the want of an essential property makes the candle dear, even when purchased at a lower price. The other light is the old, stout, wax candle, which, if procured from a respectable dealer, will burn brightly, and scarcely be affected, with regard to firmness, after the longest night journey has terminated.

The carriage, when in the coach-house, should be covered and protected from soil by a large brown holland envelope. Under such a protection, it is usually placed with every door and window closed. The consequence is, that too many vehicles strike cold when entered, and communicate to the passenger a damp or musty smell. The interior is foul with imprisoned air; and custom conserves the moisture natural to confinement. The appendage suggestive of luxury is thus rendered a dangerous possession.

The brown holland covering will exclude the dust. Always, therefore, leave the windows wide open whenever the carriage is in the house. The atmosphere of such a locality should be warm and dry. It will sweeten the interior, within which four people may have been seated and breathing for upwards of an hour on the night before, when the rain fell in torrents. It will freshen up the padded linings, and the mistress will be grateful for the care which the coachman has bestowed upon her comfort.

The owners of carriages are not sufficiently careful when engaging the stable attendant. They often will, if there be a vehicle to look after, without hesitation hire a *groom* to perform the duty. When this is done, the gentleman infers that the man who can dress horses must necessarily comprehend everything that concerns the carriage to which horses are harnessed. Such an inference is certainly not warranted by fact. A good groom professes to understand only horses; and servants of this description are the coachmaker's aversion. It would assuredly be better for many parties could proprietors condescend to exercise a little more caution in this particular; as a capable dependent alone ought to be created potentate over all the contents of the stable.

All that essentially concerns a carriage having now been stated, the subject, as the reader will have perceived, is not remarkably difficult to understand. A few questions, therefore, put to the candidate for a situation, would speedily elicit whether the applicant comprehended the duties of that office which he aspired to undertake. Ignorance can by its misdoing prove quite as harmful as the most designing malice. Much money and no little vexation would be spared could gentlemen practice a reasonable precaution before trusting in the discretion of a stranger.

It was formerly a rule among the trade to allow five per cent. every year off the employer's bill as a gratuity to the servant. This custom was general, not only with the carriage builder, but with all persons who had dealings with the stable. It even extended to those whose services were only occasionally retained, involving the veterinary surgeon, the shoeing smith, etc. The reason upon which such a habit was based being a desire to bribe the coachman, that he might damage what the trades-people would be required to repair; or, at all events, it was a fee commonly paid, hoping it would encourage the extravagance which it was the master's interest to restrain. "The *good old days*," however, are past! Most carriage builders have learned, from experience, their best interests are promoted not by the fragility, but by the enduring quality of those articles which they supply. Most proprietors also know how long a sound conveyance should endure, as well as what ought to be the average cost for repairs.

The more respectable houses, even now, certainly give trifling presents to the deserving domestics whom they encounter; but such presents are bestowed rather to induce care than to encourage willful damage of the manufacture, for the tear and wear of which the donor is responsible. In proof of this, the head of an establishment may frequently be seen walking about, restless with pleasurable emotions, when a vehicle which was built by his house shall last a month or two over the regular period for renewal; and the servant would therefore find he had embarked in a losing speculation, who should damage his master's property with the intent of increasing his occasional gratuity.

CHAPTER XVI.

SADDLERY, HARNESS, AND STABLE SUNDRIES—OF WHAT THESE CONSIST; THEIR APPLICATION AND THEIR PRESERVATION.

THE ensuing particulars were communicated by Mr. Thomas Sainsbury, Junr., the skillful foreman to a well-known and old-established firm — Messrs. Gibson & Co., of Coventry Street, Leicester Square. Proceeding from so trustworthy a source, the information cannot otherwise than merit implicit confidence; for when descanting on the above subject, the author, being anxious to state only facts, deemed it better to seek instructions from an established tradesman rather than to employ such knowledge as he himself possessed; since, not being acquainted with every branch of the business, his opinions must necessarily be more or less speculative, or based upon probabilities. Having enjoyed the benefit of Mr. Sainsbury's unreserved communications, the writer rejoices at the resolution which he had formed; and can only tender his sincerest thanks to Messrs. Gibson & Co. for the extreme liberality they have evinced throughout the transaction.

Saddlery and *harness making* are two distinct branches of one occupation. Saddlery strictly implies only that furniture which fits a steed for the uses of its rider. Harness making signifies the manufacture of those trappings which are employed upon animals of draught. There are, also, other subdivisions recognized by the trade; but on the present occasion these need not be particularly enlarged upon.

Many men are expert at either kind of manufacture; but the best workmen are those who devote themselves to one particular branch of the trade. Such can only find remunerative employment with the masters who can afford to keep an artisan constantly employed at the work in which he excels.

Saddlers justly complain that a horse cannot be accurately fitted when the animal is fresh from a dealer's stable. A good saddle should be so exquisitely adapted to the body on which it is placed as scarcely to be moved, even by the action of the limbs. A tradesman approaches perfection, therefore, in proportion as his trappings cleave to the trunk for which they are manufactured. Such a desideratum necessitates that a precise measurement should be taken. Not only is length and breadth required, but the curves or shape of the body are also needed. The material employed by saddle-makers to ascertain such particulars is equally simple and effective. It consists merely of a narrow slip of pliable sheet-lead, about two feet long, and doubled in the center, like a pair of compasses. Such a material will preserve the outline of that body on which it may be compressed, and is sufficiently solid to retain any indentations made upon its substance; thus it possesses those attributes which to the saddler are essentials.

With such an article, the shape of the barrel, the sweep of the shoulders, and the hollow of the back can be accurately moulded, while even particulars can be ascertained; for lead demands little pressure to assume the figure of any substance over which it is bent, and will subsequently remain sufficiently fixed to permit of the lines, which have been modeled, being traced upon a sheet of paper. This process should always be observed; but when a saddle has to be made, it does not constitute the "be all and the end all" of the tradesman's duty. The tree, or the wooden base of the future article, should invariably be tried on the horse before the furnishing is proceeded with, because a saddle cannot possibly be perfect when the foundation of the structure shall prove defective, and any error is more easily corrected before the article be further complicated.

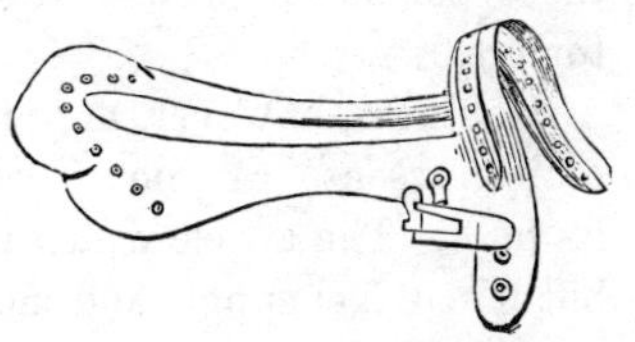

A SADDLE-TREE WITH THE SPRING STIRRUP BAR ATTACHED.

Nevertheless, it is obvious folly to have a saddle or a harness fitted to a quadruped while the body is loaded with fat, as the majority of horses are when fresh from the dealer's yard. At first no part should be accurately adjusted, but margin should be allowed for those subsequent alterations which are always imperative. After three or four months the dealer's "make up" usually subsides. Then each article will require to be overlooked, and may be amended to the animal's form, which probably will be preserved after it has been taken into regular work.

The choice of leather is of primary importance to the manufacturer of, and to the dealer in, equine furniture. After the goods are made up. no man, excepting he be a regular workman, can possibly form an opinion concerning the material of which it is composed. Certain tradesmen, not of questionable respectability, are in the habit of ticketing cheap articles to entrap chance customers. The dealers, however, do not always *know* the precise nature of the trash which they become the means of circulating They, nevertheless, must guess its character, for it is bought of the scamps who, shut out from all honest employment, exist by practicing upon the ignorant, or by pandering to the selfishness of the reckless portion of society.

The fellows purchase faulty leather. This, when made up, necessarily has the under surface concealed; it then requires a sharp and an educated eye to detect the nature of the fixed and highly polished material. The men, however, are fully aware that, with most gentlemen, stoutness is the test of quality. The prejudices of the general public are therefore propitiated, only the well-known shops being solicited by the peculiar order of workmen now under consideration. It is a common trick with the fraternity, before using, to line the flimsy stuff which they employ. This artifice is practiced as a bait to catch the notorious weakness of those persons in whose parsimony they find their most profitable customers.

Stoutness, however, may frequently deceive, even where excellence is really present. A good piece of leather is not always characterized by its bulk. The article which possesses the greatest strength may be thin, but it will feel supple and mellow to the hand. A skin of such a nature may confidently be trusted to wear. Persons, however, who are not educated to understand these qualities, would do well to avoid the showy harness which, in leading thoroughfares, is stuck prominently forward, and is very low in price. This generally fails when stress is put upon it. A fair proportion of all accidents reported spring from that cause, a common form of which is snapping of the reins when these are subjected to more than ordinary tension. Such things are either cut from unsound leather, or made of imperfectly manufactured material, or the furniture of the harness is designedly deficient in some most essential quality.

By the furniture of harness is strictly implied that portion which is of metal, and which is always added to the leather before the fabric is completed. The best metallic ornaments are a London product, and are always forged or cast, but never stamped. The best quality of iron alone should be used for such a purpose. Recently a very superior article has been adopted by the trade. This is made of the metallic combination known as German silver. That substance was, when first brought under public notice, far too brittle to be employed by the harness-maker; but late improvements have endowed it with a strength and a tenacity equal to that exhibited by the very best Swedish iron.

After the furniture has been shaped, it has to be plated. It is as a plated article that German silver is most valuable. The butler's pantry is characterized by greater delicacy than commonly distinguishes the stable, though, in both places, goods the same in kind may have to be operated upon. When the thin coating of silver is removed, of course the substance upon which it is overlaid must be exposed. The duration of a modern ornament cannot be accurately stated; but when the chief body was of iron, the contrast presented by the coarser metal and the silvered surface rendered repeated renewals unavoidable: whereas the integrity of the superficial layer is not so important when the bulk, both in color and in aspect, is a fair imitation of the more precious investment. For this reason, Messrs. Gibson always recommend the use of plated German silver, which, if a trifle dearer to the purchaser, proves in the end the most economical, besides being a superior article from the commencement.

Buckles are of much use, as these allow the harness to be adjusted; but no buckles can adjust that which is not properly made. The tightening or loosening of a strap may improve the set; but a suit of well-constructed harness should be so accurately proportioned as to fall into its proper place without the aid of manual strength or the repeated alteration of the various fastenings. When harness does not fit, the collar either pains the shoulders or the saddle galls the back. An animal cannot progress steadily when its attention is engrossed by bodily suffering. The sight is no longer employed to guide the steps. The foot is incautiously placed upon a stone; the steed stumbles over the first inequality; or, the mind being excited by pain, any object may alarm or startle the quadruped. The animal is blamed, and has been destroyed because of such accidents; whereas the real cause of the mischief was a badly-made set of cheap harness, which was probably worn for the first occasion, and which the owner may have journeyed forth specially to display.

Such mishaps should caution the public always to have the trappings of a horse made for the quadruped; or, at all events, altered by a proper tradesman, before allowing them to be employed. The difference of cost between the ready-made article and the goods which are manufactured to order is not more than a third of the outlay; while the products of any respectable house will, upon an average, last twice as long as, and need infinitely less repairing than, the rubbish which is sold "cheap." Therefore, by true economy, by durability, and by safety, the public should be urged to a particular selection.

The gentleman, however, who contemplates "starting his horse," must not conceive the expenditure has terminated with the purchase of the animal. There are stables to rent and a groom to hire. Then there is the building to provide and to furnish; a saddle and a bridle to procure; with a set of harness and a vehicle to obtain. Rent and servant necessitate no immediate outlay. Hay, oats, and straw may possibly be acquired upon short credit; but stable furniture, saddlery, harness, and

32

vehicle should be paid for on delivery; otherwise more than a fair percentage for time and for money may be added to the account.

The articles requisite to furnish a stable are rather numerous; certainly they are somewhat expensive. Because of that circumstance, everything should be purchased of the stoutest kind and of the best quality. On no account should the servant receive extra wages to supply such necessaries. The man, when making such an agreement, of course contemplates a profit, and, as he concludes the bargain, calculates how few accessories he can contrive "to get along with." The smaller the number the greater must be the pecuniary gain. The horse is, therefore, inconvenienced, if not tortured, by certain processes being accomplished with inefficient instruments, the grooming being performed rather to please the master's eye than to conduce to the comfort of his animal.

The consequences of such an arrangement are, the gentleman is cheated, the horse is maltreated; while the only gainer by the transaction, should he be suddenly discharged, of course carries away the many et ceteras he has been paid to provide. The stable is in a great measure stripped of its furniture. The new-comer may not enter upon his situation immediately. A helper, who must in the interim be engaged, will not feel disposed to adopt any artifice for the convenience of his employer.

FULLY CLOTHED.

Moreover, the new servant may agree to certain conditions, without comprehending the outlay these involved. Grooms, when they enter upon a fresh situation, seldom possess cash in any abundance; therefore, several expedients are imperative, each of which implies the imperfect performance of some necessary duty.

Supposing one horse only to be kept, stable furniture embraces—*clothing.* Of this, the first cost of the blanket kind certainly is the lowest; but the sort denominated "kersey" last much the longer period and therefore must, in the end, prove by far the least expensive. The animal's clothes consist of several pieces, each being known by a distinct name: as, quarter-sheet; breast-piece; hunting-piece; pad-cloth; hood; body-roller, and knee-caps.

To these are added a moderate sized and coarse blanket or horse rug for the night, as well as a night roller to fasten it upon the body.

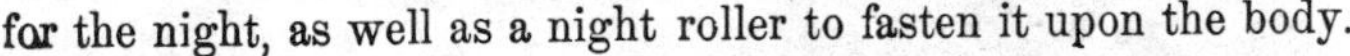

NIGHT CLOTHING.

Among the stable furniture, which is more directly employed about the horse, ranks the head collar, the manger log, and the manger rein or the rope rein. Of which last, the leathern fastening is not much the dearer; while in appearance, in utility, and in wear, it will be found altogether the superior.

Of articles required by the groom for use, are the scraper; the hoof picker; the curry-comb; the dandy, or dandruff brushes and water brushes; combs; straight and crooked scissors for trimming the mane and tail; sponges; bandages for the legs; cloths; leathers; a rack chain; the pillar reins; the exercising bridle; hard and soft brushes for cleaning harness; a burnisher; a brush to clean the bit; an oil pan and a brush; a dung basket; pails and forks. All these articles, that they may survive the usual treatment of such things, should be supplied by some reputable tradesman.

SOME OF THE ARTICLES REQUISITE FOR THE GROOM'S USE.

The above goods, being designed to endure hard wear, should each be of the best possible quality. More order than is commonly observed ought to be maintained in the arrangement of the stable. A place should be allotted for every article when not in use. That this may be accomplished, stables should be built with better accommodations for storing than it is customary to provide in such erections. Bottles, jars, and implements are now thrust into any ready corner; the interiors of these places consequently present a littered appearance; but such an aspect is unavoidable, when there exists no receptacle where such articles might be placed until again required. There is now no help for the nuisance: forks, brooms, pails, and boxes must incumber the gangway, since the architect never provides a situation where such properties might be more safely lodged.

Another essential should be attended to by every gentleman who values the condition of his horse, the comfort of his stable, or the preservation of those accessories with which the last-named place must be stocked—this is, the temper of the servant. Some people favor a strange prejudice, which asserts irritability and industry are frequently associated. Anger, however, does not open the heart to sympathy, and its habitual display assuredly unfits its victim for the exercise of authority.

Evil passion will render a servant disobliging, and cause him to become an expensive retainer. The manner in which the failing will act upon the groom may not be very apparent to the reader, therefore his indulgence is requested while the author proceeds briefly to explain the matter.

Nothing can possibly be more extravagant than passion. It is heedless of consequences, and destruction is its delight. The author formerly knew a gentleman who used to indulge in the most violent fits of unbridled temper. He made his home miserable, and a moderate income was sadly crippled by expenses resulting from gusts of constitutional irritability. The last consequence, it is melancholy to relate, alone induced thoughts of amendment. When this individual, in later life, became conscious that what he termed his cloudy mood threatened to darken his intellect, he would retire to some solitary apartment: there, he would station himself before a looking-glass, and begin simpering and blandly talking to his own image. He would then tear or break something, generally a wooden or a paper match, and, having thus gratified that which he named his destructive impulse, after a few more antics would return, all smiles, to the bosom of his family, exclaiming, "Thank Heaven! It's all over now!"

But the great majority of grooms, imbued with the pride of ignorance, cannot afford to acknowledge a failing. Conceit makes them rather lend strength to an affliction by striving to conceal its existence. The master may never discover, if he cares not to search for, the truth. But the servant is necessarily empowered with absolute control in the stable. The implements speedily are damaged; certain duties are either neglected or imperfectly performed; the horse loses its fat; the coat never looks well; the eye becomes restless from the natural timidity of the animal being perpetually awakened. Nothing promotes thrift in a quadruped like the placidity of its attendant; whereas the constant alarm excited by the habitual anger of its superior is inimical to that glossy outside and blooming aspect in which the larger number of horse owners so much delight.

The groom, in most situations, is greatly trusted with valuable property. In a large stable the cost of the trappings alone would form no inconsiderable possession to a needy man. There must be either saddlery or harness. There is no one to overlook the treatment of either. Such articles are expensive, and each is composed of numerous complications. Harness for one horse consists of a bridle, of a collar, of a pad, of a martingale, of reins, of traces, of a breeching or of a loin strap, of a crupper, etc.; all of which should be solidly and well constructed. The whole should be formed of the very best leather, for any defect in this furniture may be fruitful with the greatest danger. Hence the advantage of dealing with a maker whose warranty represents more than a wordy inducement to purchase; and hence the necessity for care in the servant to whom such perishable property is intrusted.

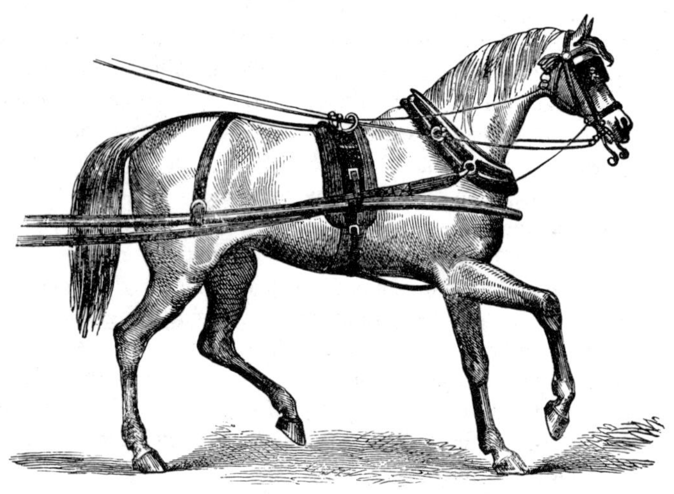

GIG HARNESS WITH KICKING-STRAP.

For the gig horse, a set of harness, if embellished with plated ornaments, is generally charged about thirteen pounds. For a pair of carriage animals, the harness possessing similar adornments will commonly cost nearly thirty-three pounds. If brass is preferred in the place of plated goods, a slight reduction is the result. Yet even the foregoing figures do not include crests and other fanciful items, which are invariably paid for as extras, since no estimate could possibly embrace articles concerning the size, the number, and the elaboration of which the tastes of scarcely two individuals perfectly agree.

The harness for a brougham is generally more expensive than that sold for the gig. Extra strength is required, and where work and leather are concerned, of course strength represents money. The trappings also should be more showy and more embellished when intended for a servant's use. Most gentlemen prefer the animal they control should be so caparisoned as to attract no attention. This feeling causes the difference in price. Ornamentation, where the horses are to be adorned, of course necessitates expenditure, though the degree in which the last quality shall be exhibited necessarily depends on the taste of the proprietor.

Carriage harness, however, is viewed as the perfection of its particular craft. It is astonishing how nice is the adjustment required, and how perceptible any fault or deficiency becomes to the least observant spectator. The carriage may be new, the liveries of the smartest kind, but unless the harness be excellent, the general effect will be deteriorated The pace of the horses is rendered uneven, the coachman becomes nervous, and the vehicle is not drawn smoothly onward when any sensible defect exists. Gentlemen cannot imagine how much danger is hazarded by the endeavors often made to procure an expensive article at less than a fairly remunerative price.

FULL SUIT OF BROUGHAM OR PHAETON HARNESS.

Harness is thus expensive because its uses demand excellence in every part. It is subject to daily trials; it must be manufactured to sustain perpetual tests as well as to endure constant supervision. A good set of harness should wear eight or ten years, although during the lengthened service repeated repairs must be expected. The mendings, or perhaps the partial renewals, will of course grow heavier as the age of the material increases. If done by piece-work, the repairs will average from one pound to four pounds yearly; but if a contract be entered into with the maker, the terms usually are from thirty shillings to two pounds per annum; the agreement dating from the commencement of the wear.

The endurance of such things, however, is greatly governed by the uses to which they are subjected, and by the manner in which they are treated. When harness is seldom at home, of course it wears faster than when it is rarely or is moderately employed. The industry and habits of the person who looks after the articles have also to be considered. Some lazy men will ruthlessly wash the leather in a pail of water and afterward hang it upon the most convenient paling to dry in the sun shine. Such a proceeding will prove quickly ruinous: harshness is in duced; all suppleness is destroyed; a disposition to crack is engendered; while the plated ornaments speedily become tarnished.

The proper method of cleaning is, to employ as little water as possible. A moist sponge, well soaped, may, when very much soil exists, be quickly passed over the surface, but each part should, without loss of time, be immediately dried after the dirt is removed. All the mud having been thus obliterated, the several pieces should be most carefully gone over again with a dry cloth, so as to absorb any possible moisture which, during the first cleansing, may have escaped notice. In fine or during dusty weather, no fluid is necessary, nor should the employment of any be suffered. A pail of water will, doubtlessly, save labor; but the servant's leisure, which is thereby secured, is a severe burden upon the master's income. A good brush, not too hard, but one having springy hair, will soon remove all dry impurities; and with that the harness, when not made moist by the road or rendered wet by exudation from the animal's body, should always be cleansed.

A FULL SUIT OF CARRIAGE HARNESS.

This being done, apply Harris's jet-black oil, but not thickly; enough has been laid on so that the application lies upon every portion of the surface. No long time need be allowed for the oil to dry in; but the first piece is generally ready to receive the next application by the time the last part has been properly finished. Then apply a little of the compo., which being polished to a lustrous black, the entire process is perfected by a final wash of Harris's harness fluid.

The appearance will be longer preserved when harness is cleaned after the foregoing directions, while its lasting properties are not injured by the process. Instead of being deteriorated every time it is cleansed, the leather is nourished, its strength and its aspect being renovated. The plated ornaments, of course, are not alluded to in the above instructions; to polish these, some prepared chalk, fine brushes, finer than are generally employed, and a wash leather are imperative.

An inefficient groom is, perhaps, more readily detected by his manner of cleaning harness than by any other stable operation. Practice alone confers aptitude in handling the various pieces. Use enables the different articles to be rendered smart without staining the flesh or soiling the dress of the operator. When the servant is new to the occupation, particular portions are invariably scamped; others get more than the requisite attention. Certain of the ornaments are left with the crevices full of powder, while some parts are wholly neglected; but, above all, the linings to the various pieces are always smeared and impressed with dirty finger-marks. A good groom apparently will not trouble himself to avoid such errors, but, when he has finished, each portion is equally clean, while the insides are untainted and free from the smallest soil.

The linings should be cleansed in the same manner as the other parts, only the blacking and the polishing are unnecessary. In most situations, leather is employed to cover the under surface; where this substance is present, no beating is then required. Where cloth is used, as in the lining of a saddle pannel, this should be daily beaten with a small cane, and subsequently brushed till all hairs and dust are removed. The bad servant invariably strives to hide his laziness under a pretense of excessive zeal for his master's interest. When ordered to attend to the lining of his harness, he will endeavor to escape from the command by pleading the wear which attends the constant friction occasioned by continual beating and by perpetual brushing.

A collar placed on the horse should be firm, falling easily into its proper situation. It is stuffed with straw or flock, and is lined with leather. That the lining may not be stretched and that the stuffing may not be hardened in parts but may feel equally firm upon every portion of its inner surface, the article should never be used when moist, even in the remotest degree. When removed in a wet state, it should be dried either in the sun or before the kitchen fire, prior to again being taken into service. When doing this, of course the nature of the material should be considered; it should only be exposed to such a heat as will cause the moisture to evaporate, and if that end can be attained by a brisk current of air in a shady place, such a situation is to be very much preferred to any natural or to any artificial warmth.

The collar should pass into its situation without requiring the force which careless grooms seem to delight in exerting, or ignorant servants, possibly, may regard as necessary to the proper fulfillment of their duties. Any violence, when daily repeated, must eventually damage the horse's appearance by removing hair from the prominences of the head, and by causing the naturally placid countenance of the animal to assume a worn or a ragged expression. The collar should be turned when put over the face, the widest part of the opening being passed over the ears. When the head is through, and before the article proceeds lower than the topmost portion of the neck, it should be righted, or the pointed part should occupy the most elevated situation; after which it is slid down upon the shoulder.

The collar, when fitted to the neck, should sit firmly and closely. The bearing should be equal and even, because the entire draught is from the collar; in proportion as the bearing is accurately distributed, so the weight will be easily propelled. Some people have endeavored to render the collar more steady by attaching the traces to hames with double eyes. The hames are the metal rods which repose upon the

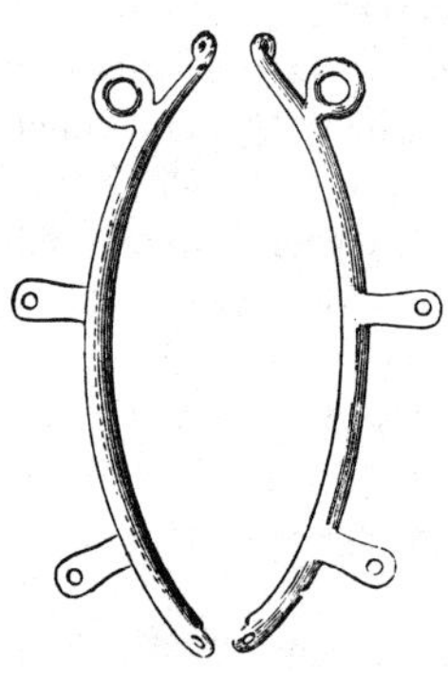

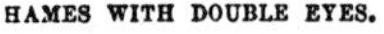
HAMES WITH DOUBLE EYES.

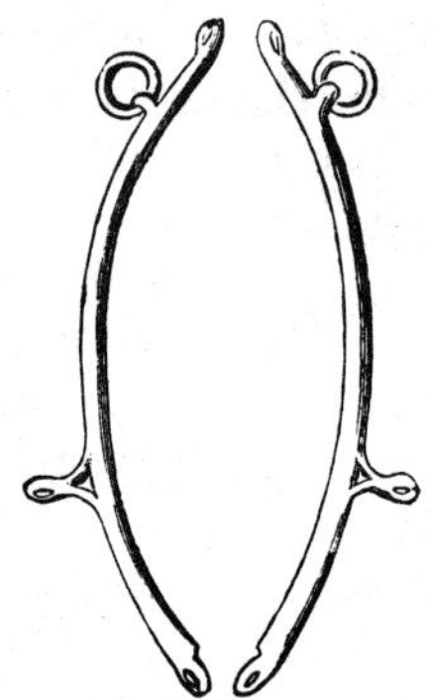

A SCROLL-EYED HAME.

collar; the eyes are circular spaces which permit the traces to be united to the hames. Though double fastenings may occasion the force to seem better distributed along these rods, the effect must operate rather upon the spectator's mind than upon the substance it is meant to render stationary. If a line is drawn from the point where the trace should end, and equidistant from those places to which the two bands are attached, the real seat of bearing will prove not to have been changed by the angularity of the fastenings, but will either remain confined to its original situation, or it may act only on one fastening to the exclusion of the other. That which is known as a scroll eye, however, is more elegant than the plain attachment, and on account of its smartness deserves to be preferred.

A breast-collar, when the circumstances permit a free exercise of selection, should never be adopted. It may, in the eye of inexperience, look prettier; but it goes directly across a part of motion; it drags against the muscles, which, being loose in structure, are not made to endure continual pressure. Moreover, the cartilage of the chest moves with each respiration; any force operating from without, therefore, cannot but oppose this normal action. Besides, the chief component of the chest, the terminations of the ribs, which are inserted into the sternum, are also cartilaginous. Now, cartilage is highly plastic, and readily assumes strange shapes, as is seen by the larynx when distorted by the bearing-rein. (See "Illustrated Horse Doctor," pp. 108, 109.) Whereas, when the collar bears against the shoulder, it is supported by solid bone, as firm and as compact as can be found in most structures throughout the body.

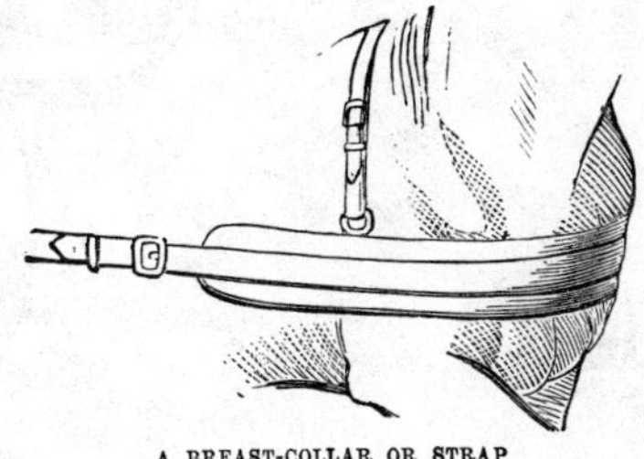

A BREAST-COLLAR OR STRAP

However, when accident or disease makes it impossible to continue the employment of a collar, the breast-strap, although in itself an evil, becomes the only substitute.

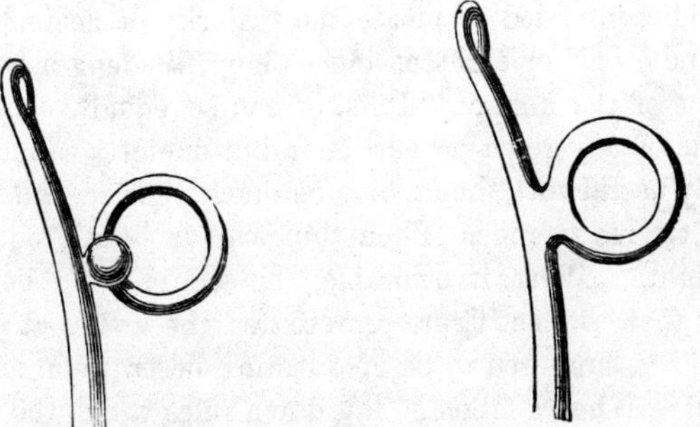

A MOVABLE AND A FIXED RING FOR THE REINS TO PASS THROUGH.

There is connected with the hame a simple arrangement, about which neither gentlemen nor makers are always sufficiently particular. The reins are supported in their proper position by passing through a ring or ferret, which is generally fixed upon the hames. Should the horse, thus caparisoned, accidentally fall, the loop, being immovable, is either bent out of all shape, or, more probably, it is broken short off by the weight of the prostrate animal. It may be replied, that horse collars are not, when manufactured, made to be violently driven against stones. The writer does not contradict the assertion; but when a hinge will not interfere with the aspect, and, by yielding to pressure, will guard against a possible mischance, the little extra labor which the addition would require assuredly could not be better expended.

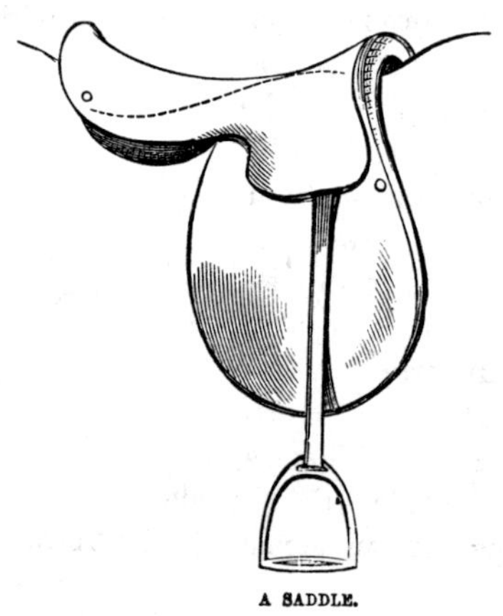

A SADDLE.

The principal portions of the harness having been considered, some thought must now be bestowed upon the chief essentials of saddlery. A good saddle, intended to please the majority of horsemen, should be seventeen and a half or eighteen inches long, the length being regulated by the shape of the animal. It is, of course, equally easy to manufacture a saddle of any given proportions; but one of a sound working and a thoroughly useful sort should not be much shorter, and should weigh from ten to twelve pounds. Such things have been produced of seven pounds weight. Were it desirable, the saddle could be made much lighter even than the last figure represents; the article at present under consideration is supposed to be of a lasting description, and not of the fanciful kind. When gentlemen lay down rules which the manufacturer is to observe, they should remember that the tradesman, who merely carries out his employer's ideas, and is not permitted to obey his own convictions, is no longer responsible for results.

A broad seat is generally preferred. This should not be so wide as to disable the grip of the rider; but it ought to be of no greater dimensions than will allow a firm hold to be taken by the fleshy part of the thigh. Every saddle has two girths, but all girths have not three straps These should always be present; because if one strap should break, another is ready to supply its place. It vexes most keen sportsmen, near the termination of a hard run, to lose a good place because, strained by the accelerated action of the horse's lungs, a girth strap shall, when excitement is at its height, give way.

To avoid so irritating an accident, the hunting or the Melton girth is now commonly employed. This consists of a broad webbing, which is tightened by two straps, one at either margin. Over the main girth there runs a narrower length of the same material, which is kept in its situation by passing through two loops upon the principal binder. The narrower webbing is fastened by means of the third or central strap. Thus, should one of the fastenings of the chief girth yield, or even should both be forced from their holds, the saddle will not necessarily be displaced, as there is always a supernumerary guard in attendance ready to officiate as the representative of its incapacitated principals.

CRUPPER, MELTON GIRTH, AND MARTINGALE.

Cruppers are generally discarded. These appendages have occasioned terrible sores, and are of no actual utility to the retention of the saddle; for the withers should prevent that convenience from moving too forward. A martingale is occasionally used; but if the animal be rightly formed for its purposes, and has been carefully broken in, the head should be carried properly without necessitating compulsion. The mouth is soon injured and loses its sensitiveness when a tight rein is constantly in requisition to bring the muzzle into its proper situation. When the lips are subjected to perpetual pressure it can hardly be anticipated that the steed can obey the slightest movement of the rider's hand. Most people are vexed when obliged to tug and haul every time it is desired the animal should deviate from the direct course.

Once the spring stirrup was hailed as a marvelous invention and an indispensable part of every good saddle. This was designed to release the foot of a rider who had lost his seat. Such things were very pretty toys. They acted beautifully in the chamber when first taken out of paper, but, when exposed to use, these elegant precautions soon got out of order. Dirt would work into the joint and would interfere with the mechanism, which thus became useless at the very time its services were likely to be required. After a hard gallop the joint could not be otherwise than clogged, especially when the run was across country. Therefore the spring stirrup has been displaced in public estimation by the spring bar. This last is the newer and the less costly provision, the spring being attached to the bar which supports the stirrup leather.

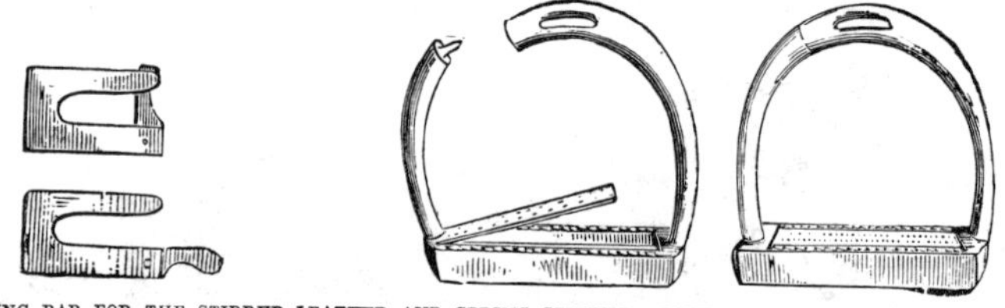

SPRING BAR FOR THE STIRRUP LEATHER AND SPRING STIRRUP. BOTH BEING EXHIBITED DURING REST AND WHEN IN ACTION.

The situation where the machinery is lodged protects it from dirt, from wet, or from dust, being doubly sheltered from all such intrusion. It is covered by the skirt of the saddle, and is likewise shielded by the thigh of the rider. The article thus placed is removed from the operation of that objection which has thrown the spring stirrup into disuse. The purpose of both inventions is equal, being exactly similar. When the rider was unseated, the stirrup was *intended* to yield before the drag of the imprisoned foot. When the horseman is thrown, the smallest traction *does* occasion the spring bar to act, and the leather is released, the limb forcing the stirrup iron and the leather to quit their relative situations.

The stirrup iron was formerly made of various shapes, each of which was imagined to possess some special advantage. At present, however, the public appear to disregard peculiarities of form in such articles, and to pay no attention to those contortions concerning which our forefathers were so extremely precise. It is now considered quite sufficient if the stirrup iron afford a firm rest to the foot of the rider, if it be not disposed to glide away from the pressure of the boot, and if it be as light as possible, but nevertheless possesses the strength necessary for its purposes. All these intentions are embodied in a plain, three-barred stirrup iron, which presents an ample surface of bearing, while, being slightly roughened upon its upper surface, it is readily retained by pressure; but for the strength of the article the respectability of the salesman must afford the only possible guarantee.

Also appended to the saddle is an adjunct frequently of no inconsiderable utility in the field. It is comparatively of modern invention, and is known as the hunting breast-plate. One extremity is attached by means of a hold to each side of the saddle, near to the pommel. The straps proceeding thence are short, and soon unite, when the medium of junction proceeds to the chest. The two leathers, one from either side, are there joined to a single strap, which, after passing between the fore-legs, is finally attached to the girth. The intention of this addition is to retain the saddle in its proper situation, an object not always easy to accomplish even with this provision, as high withers and violent muscular exertion naturally incline to its backward movement.

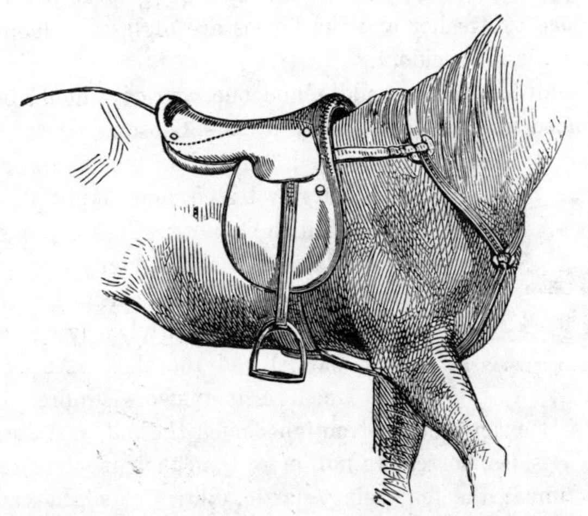

A HUNTING BREAST-PLATE.

The breast-plate, for the full development of its use, necessitates much care in the groom when caparisoning the quadruped. The two short upper straps, on which all stress must center, join directly under the windpipe. Because of this all parts necessitate the most accurate adjustment; where a breast-plate is used, the servant should particularly notice the position of the girth when securing the fastening. If the leather should be loose or even slack, the backward motion of the saddle will of course dispose the two side pieces to assume the straight line, or it will force their junction upward as well as render its pressure more stringent. The consequence will be, the strap must press upon the trachea and blood-vessels; the animal may be choked, and the hunting of one day spoiled, even should the rider and his horse ultimately escape all injury.

The upper reins of the martingale are sometimes made to spring from the center fastening of the breast-plate. But the use of the martingale is to force the head downward. To do this requires a firm hand and a straight rein, which consequently pulls the restraining strap of the breast-plate upward, and thus destroys the purpose of the last invention. The two articles are, in their uses, perfectly distinct; such things cannot be profitably blended. The martingale is designed to counteract an upward traction. The fastening of the breast-plate should drag only in the downward line, whereas the head strains in the contrary direction. When a martingale cannot be dispensed with, one should be worn totally distinct and separate from the breast-plate. It is, however, always desirable to join the meet with as few floating gear as possible; since, when the pace grows hot and the fences are high, such loops are little better than baits for accident.

A good addition to the saddle, and one no rider should be without, was introduced into this country by Messrs. Gibson. It was originally used in India, where its utility was largely tested, and amply proved by the British cavalry. This improvement consists of a felt under-pannel; which is made of such dimensions as to be perfectly concealed when lying between the pannel and the skin. As an adjusting medium it answers admirably. Should the saddle not exactly fit, the motion chafes the felt, and does not gall the body. Besides, horses are not, more than their masters, of the same size at all times; the felt, being elastic, allows of slight variations in bulk without imperiling the safety of the proprietor.

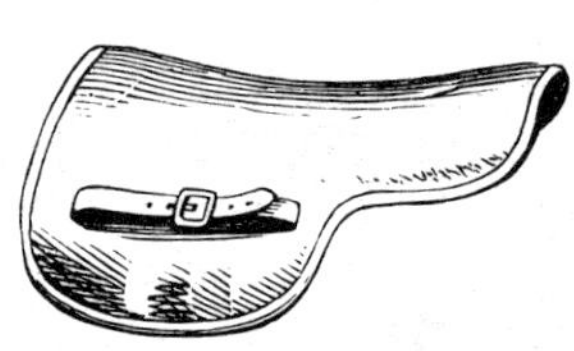

FELT UNDER-PANNEL.

The felt under-pannel should always be used whenever a side-saddle is employed; it renders the adjustment more easy, and makes it more secure. Such an advantage cannot always be attained, even with the extra girth, with which all side-saddles should be provided. Every possible care ought to be exercised that the seat of a lady's saddle may be rendered firm; because, as the make throws the bearing upon the near side, and the fixedness of the position must incapacitate the lady for freedom of action, therefore any movement of the saddle is likely to be attended by serious consequences.

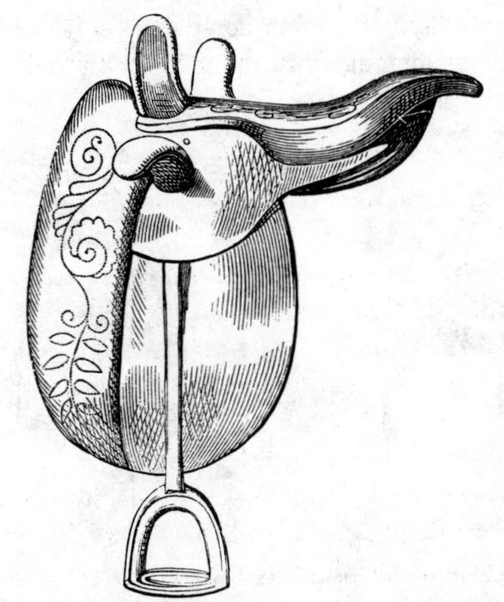

A LADY'S STIRRUP WITH THE KNEE CRUTCH AND THE VICTORIA STIRRUP.

For the foregoing reasons, the maker should bestow the greatest attention upon the shape of the saddle-tree; no artifice should be neglected that is calculated to render the side-saddle more fixed upon the horse's back. The seat should be longer as well as broader than is usual in those articles which are manufactured to sell quickly and to look prettily. It should be covered with soft, unpolished leather, and be quilted, so that its partial roughness and trivial inequalities may present a more secure and an easier seat for the fair equestrian.

Every aid would, however, be useless, were it not for the crutches. The female rider must cast her bearing upon the near crutch; hence horses, when forced to work under an ill-made side-saddle, often suffer terribly, and exhibit as the consequence severe examples of fistulous withers. Experience has proved that the off crutch is of small service, save as it may confirm the confidence of the lady; although, by rendering the leg more stationary, it is in reality calculated to increase her danger. Its utility lies in calming the timidity of the horsewoman; for the instant a horse gets into motion, the bearing is entirely toward the near side; therefore most modern saddlers, although they dare not remove the useless crutch, have its height materially diminished.

The third or knee crutch is a comparatively recent improvement. It offers a point for pressure to the left knee, or of bearing for the stirrup leg. It is of every service, enabling the lady to retain a firm seat. During the perils of leaping it prevents the lighter weight of the female body being, by the violence of the motion, so shaken as to lose all hold upon the upper crutches. Thus, in some degree, it compensates for the advantage that gentlemen enjoy in the grip which their position enables them to take of the saddle.

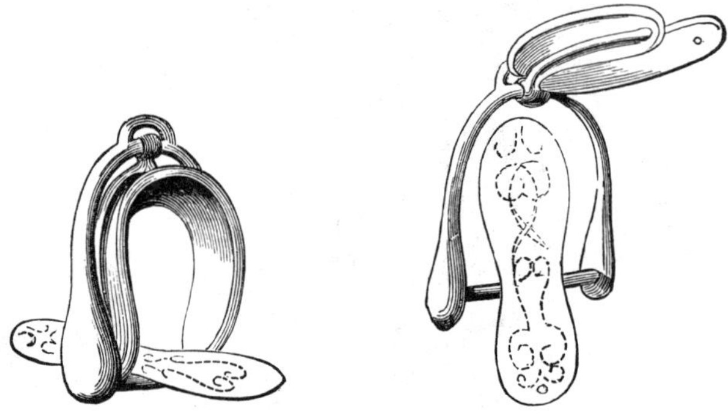

THE LADIES' PATENT STIRRUP. EXHIBITED AT REST AND IN ACTION.

The slipper was the favorite stirrup in use with the side-saddle a few years ago. Its adoption then was all but universal, and so at the present time is its rejection. The Victoria stirrup, or an iron of the shape which is adopted by Her Majesty, now engrosses public patronage; it being generally employed, with the addition of the previously noticed spring bar.

The patent stirrup for ladies is not liable to those objections which were urged against the spring stirrup, when employed for the saddles of gentlemen. The habit protects the machinery, which is not therefore exposed to the intrusion of mud. Its action is almost certain; but, should it not answer the occasion, the next invention, when employed with the foregoing provision, would probably set the malice of "luck" at defiance.

The following should also be appended to every lady's saddle. Male equestrians may esteem the spring bar to afford the gentle sex sufficient protection. However, where there is a possibility of question, no expense ought to prevent the more fearful rider from being guarded by the latest additions, which may promise even the remotest chance of security. The common spring bar rarely fails to act; but, on particular occasions, it has retained the stirrup leather. The patented improvement shown on the next page appears to provide against such an accident, and when employed with the stirrup represented in the previous engraving, it assuredly affords an almost certain immunity from those accidents which each is assumed to render an impossibility.

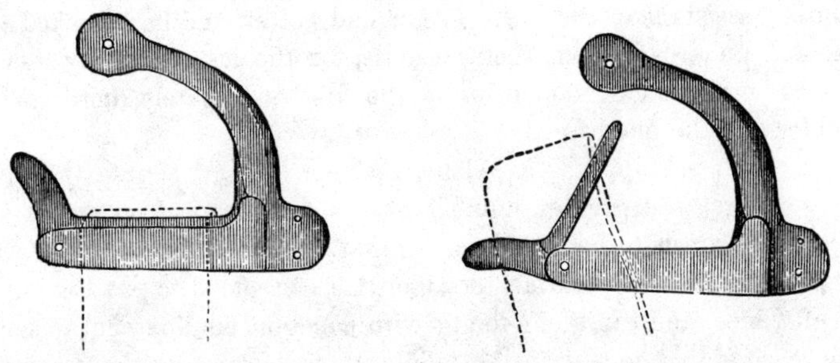

PATENT SAFETY SPRING PRESSURE STIRRUP BAR. DEPICTED AT REST AND IN ACTION.

The dotted lines indicate the relative positions of the stirrup leather.

No lady's saddle should be used without being accompanied by the hunting breast-plate; for nothing which might possibly increase security should in that case be neglected. For the last reason, also, a felt underpannel should never be absent; because firmness of seat lends assurance to the rider, and because the provision prevents that unsteadiness which is known to provoke one of the worst evils to which the horse is exposed.

Saddles are covered by what the public denominate pigs' skins, but which the trade, aiming at a distinction without being able to indicate a difference, persist in calling hogs' skins.

These are always procured from the currier in large lots when purchased at first hand; but they are a hazardous article to buy. Out of two hundred, of which a parcel shall consist, there may not be more than two dozen really sound skins; therefore no tradesman has hitherto been able to establish a reputation for dealing in so uncertain a commodity. The wholesale merchant, consequently, knows but few customers Established houses alone can afford the requisite outlay to obtain goods of so notoriously uncertain a character. From the larger parcels the best specimens are carefully selected by the first buyer; the remainder are cast upon the retail market, and are distributed among the numerous class of trades-people, whose limited capital does not allow them to speculate with the articles which they employ.

A good saddle is recognized by the accuracy of the fit. When let fall upon the back, it at once finds the proper situation. There it remains stationary and firm before a girth is fastened. When the maker, having brought home a new article, finds occasion to interfere with the groom, shifts about the saddle, and concludes his performance by tugging at the girths before he requests the employer to feel how firmly the new production is located, it is always an evil omen. The saddler, supposing the groom to be competent to his position, should never be suffered to volunteer assistance; the horse owner had better ride bare-backed than be seated on a badly-constructed saddle, for the last is hardly less unpleasant to a good horseman, while the first is infinitely more safe for the rider and the quadruped.

A good fit presupposes excellent workmen, and of course the larger houses attract the greater number of such artificers, because in such shops men expect to be employed on that particular branch of work in which each excels. Such masters, likewise, can afford to pay the highest rate of wages, and can alone tempt with constant employment. Add to these reasons that money in the saddlery and harness trades commands rather more than its just influence, being able to select the pick of every market, and it must be apparent how many advantages the established firm enjoys over the ordinary beginner, who has to struggle against the lack of pecuniary ability, against a want of regular customers, and against those difficulties which are peculiar to his calling.

Hogs' skins are easily cleansed by washing quickly with a little soap and water; but washing and drenching are not here regarded as representing the same process. Water is not beneficial to leather of any sort, therefore as little fluid as will accomplish the object should be used; the more speedy the operation the better. It should be concluded by a clean cloth immediately wiping the surface quite dry. This finished, a sponge damped with good milk should be passed over the exterior; the saddle then should be hung up (not before the fire or in the sunshine) to expel the moisture. The more seldom, however, this process is adopted the better; consequently, it is only to be recommended upon urgent necessity.

Bridles, and every strip of harness which bears the slightest resemblance to a rein, should be cut only from the best, the strongest, and the choicest of English leather. Struggling tradesmen do not all possess the ability, however powerful may be the desire, to exercise selection in this article. Some have sent forth reins made of so faulty a material as stood exposed the moment it encountered the glance of a practical or an educated eye. The head-piece, requiring shorter straps, may possibly be cut from a partially imperfect hide; but for the reins, length and toughness are essential. The merest crack will, with constant wear, become a fissure; and no horseman can foretell the moment when personal safety shall depend upon the power which he shall be able to exert through the reins.

A fair proportion of the injuries which happen to riders or to drivers are aggravated by faulty reins. A contest arises between a restive horse and an intemperate master. The contest, which from the earliest period alarmed timidity in the animal, has just excited the man, when the reins fly asunder. The scared quadruped finds itself suddenly released. The creature understands nothing of the cause; but the first impulse natural to fear is to fly from the presence of the power against which it has been struggling. Whenever the horse displeases its master, pain inflicted by whip, bit, or spur generally ensues as a natural consequence. It is from such torture that the poor life endeavors to escape. Motion increases its terror as the unshackled being dashes blindly onward. An accident is the probable result. The coroner and the jury assemble; a verdict, which all approve, is formally delivered; but no one thinks of inspecting the reins to discover the real cause of injury.

Reins should always be attentively examined. If good, they look pleasant to the eye, and are yielding to the touch. Any roughness, harshness, or hardness denotes the presence of defective leather. It may not break to-morrow or the next day, but before long the rein will separate. The slightest indication of a crack will gradually become an extensive division. Messrs. Gibson have often been honored with commands to export reins, the foreign leather being harsh and inelastic, therefore feeling unpleasant to English hands; but more frequently the natives of this country are afraid to employ reins exhibiting innumerable cracks, everywhere displaying the roughness which should not exist, and being totally deficient in the suppleness which ought to be abundantly present.

When reins are intended for the use of ladies, their character should be unexceptionable. Many girls, before they have conquered the seat, depend, in no slight degree, upon the reins for retaining their positions in the saddle. They of course understand nothing about saddlery. They accept anything which is offered; but the sudden snapping of the reins always terrifies the steed, while it greatly alarms the gentle being on its back, whose fears are increased by finding herself instantaneously deprived of a support on which her inexperience had depended. Ladies' reins, being made lighter, should be cut from better leather than those intended for gentlemen; if there be a possible choice, it should be accorded to the weaker party. Some horsewomen like the reins and the head-piece to be formed of rounded straps. Thus made, they cer

A LADY'S BRIDLE.

tainly have a lighter and a more graceful appearance; but Messrs. Gibson do not recommend such a form of bridle to those ladies who delight in mounting and in subduing high-spirited animals.

Martingales are generally complained of as troublesome appendages when added to the trappings of either the saddle or of the gig horse. These articles, however, can be so manufactured as to lend a dignity to the quadrupeds which run before carriages; though, where a martingale is used, the bearing-rein becomes unnecessary, since both restraints aim at the same object. Perhaps of the two, the martingale is the better, because, while obliging the head to be held in the proper position, it enables the coachman, by slackening the reins, to rest the muscles of the neck when the vehicle pauses. The martingale certainly requires the better driver, and imposes the greater exertion upon him who drives, the latter circumstance being likely to interfere with the digestive serenity of most servants.

There is, however, one species of martingale, without which few ladies' saddles appear to be fully equipped. Some animals necessitate no restraint to improve the carriage of the head, but these, nevertheless, acquire a habit of throwing the muzzle suddenly up and of jerking the foam from the lips into the face of the rider. This propensity communicates no pleasure to the person who occupies the seat. It generally causes the equestrian to lower the head whenever the quadruped evinces a disposition to exalt its countenance; such being the precise moment when the human vision is of double value; for the eye of the horse, being direct heavenward, can then take no cognizance of earthly objects; hence the great need for the guidance of the rider.

A FRENCH MARTINGALE.

To correct this, the French martingale, which consists of a single strap, is attached to the nose band. The band passes over the nasal bones, and under the forward part of the lower jaw. To the lowest part of this band the French martingale is fixed. The operation is obvious. The horse, by raising the head, causes the martingale to act on the bridle: the nostrils are compressed; the breathing is interfered with; and, as the quadruped resents the slightest hinderance to its respiration, the fruitless effort to indulge an obnoxious habit is relinquished, so that the annoyance of the tightened nose band may be avoided. French martingales, which were once largely in use, are now never employed with a gentleman's saddle, although they have not been discarded by equestrians of the gentler sex.

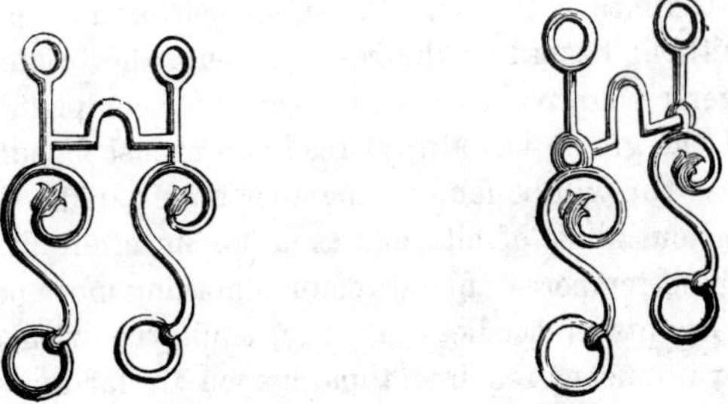

BITS USUALLY ATTACHED TO LADIES' BRIDLES.

The bits which accompany the ladies' bridle are more fanciful in shape, and more ornamental in appearance, though hardly so heavy as the articles manufactured for the use of gentlemen, because the generality of ladies seldom resort to this instrument of positive torture: indeed, these severities seem to be losing their attractions over the harsher natures. Many men, however, employ them; most regard a bridle as incomplete without a bit; but very few are so fond of the restraint as to order it to be sewn to the head piece.

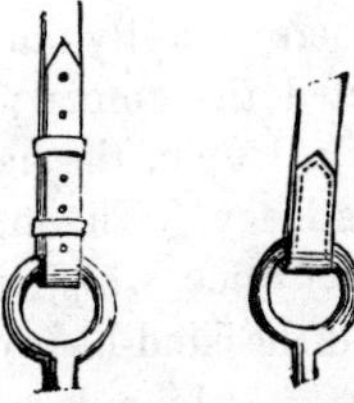

BUCKLED AND SEWN ON.

A bit permanently attached certainly appears lighter, and necessitates the employment of less obvious force, though at the same time it must be more acute when in operation. Nevertheless, it is to be doubted whether one foot passenger out of ten thousand would notice the only peculiarity for which such an arrangement is to be commended. Moreover, every animal does not require the exertion of extraordinary power; while the irremovable character of the bit is not without attendant disadvantages. The article can no longer be changed at pleasure. A rider may grow to dislike the constant employment of one form of coercion. The animal's education may not need the perpetuation of such severity; the temper may improve, or the steed may accommodate itself to the personal peculiarities of its proprietor; or the quadruped's mood may change, for horses, like their masters, are swayed by strange influences, and are sometimes impelled by eccentric impulses.

When the metal has to be washed, cleaned, and polished, should the bit be sewn to the head piece, the leather cannot be removed during the processes. Water is not beneficial to a leathern material; therefore the bit must either be imperfectly renovated, or the head piece must be soiled during the requisite labor demanded for the purification of its adjunct. These annoyances are avoided when the bit is made to take on and off by the means of a buckle. Each part can then be properly attended to without hazard to the rest. Should the bridle not appear clean, the owner recognizes a legitimate cause for complaint; but when the bit is fixed, the groom has always ready an excuse for idleness, while the consequent wear will be found altogether more rapid.

There are various kinds of bits, and each has its admirers; but a well-broken and a good-tempered animal requires nothing more powerful than a snaffle. Restraints of needless severity, employed with extravagant exertion, are by no means required, though such are far too general with the great majority of professed horsemen. The animal is spoilt by such tuition. It is educated to understand nothing but coercion; whereas gentleness and firmness combined can accomplish much more than brutality can compel.

There is a well-known tale, which, being illustrative of this subject, may here be aptly quoted. A farmer, intending to break a colt for sale, mounted the animal; but hardly was he in the saddle before the ears were laid upon the neck, and the frame rendered rigid by the presence of obstinacy. The intention of the attitude was recognized by all; but offers of stick, whip, or spur were as stubbornly rejected. "No, no, no," replied the kind-hearted proprietor to the proposal of such favorite persuaders. "Jane, lass! bring I the afternoon's mug and pipe." These were discussed. Another pipe was filled and exhausted, without the honest fellow descending to earth. Then the colt was invited to proceed; but the humor of the quadruped continued unaltered; accordingly it remained stationary, with the master on its back.

"Father! tea is quite ready," cried Jane, peering from the kitchen window. "Bring it here, lass, for I shan't get down!" was the response. The tea was brought and partaken of. The day was drawing toward its close, and the air was becoming cold. "I should not mind having my great-coat, a pipe, and a glass," shouted the farmer. Everything was brought, and the man endeavored to make his position comfortable; but apparently took no heed of the creature beneath him. "For," he observed, "if I could strike, the colt could fling and prance; so it might not be certain which would master; whereas, while I be quiet, I've the best on't."

Supper was eaten where the tea had been swallowed: the master showed he was resolved, unless the colt moved, to pass the night in the saddle. The animal became uneasy, and shifted about; but without progressing until some time after the clock had struck eleven. Then the colt was suddenly disposed to progress. "Whoy!" shouted its master, "you have stayed so long to please yourself, now remain a little longer to pleasure I!"

At length the rider was disposed to move, but in an opposite direction to that which the colt was inclined to travel. The animal was also willing to trot briskly, but the farmer would sanction nothing faster than a walk. Accordingly, the pair slowly moved five miles out, and trotted five miles home. Then the quadruped was placed before an empty manger, and left, tired and hungry, to its night's meditations on the evils of disobedience. The above narrative, of course, concludes by stating that the animal proved docile "forever afterward."

The obvious intention of the above is to discourage the employment of force. The strongest man cannot physically contend against the weakest horse. Man's power reposes in better attributes than any which reside in thews and muscles. Reason, alone, should dictate and control his conduct. Thus guided, mortals have subdued the elements. For power, when mental, is without limit: by savage violence nothing is attained, but the man is often humbled through a conviction of defeat

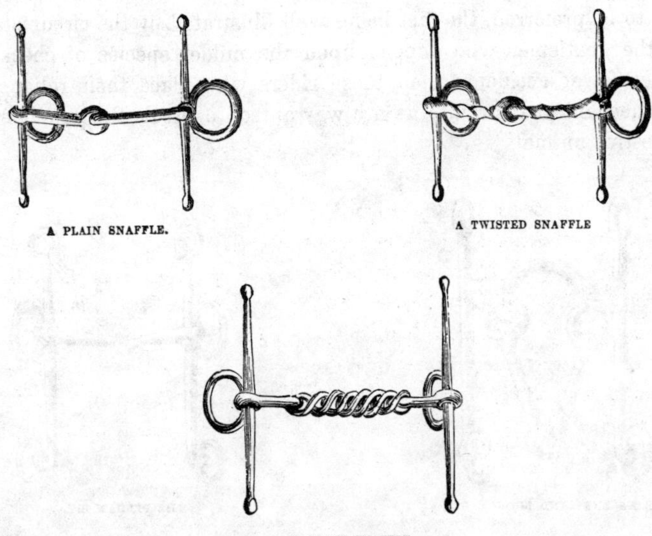

A PLAIN SNAFFLE.

A TWISTED SNAFFLE

A CHAIN SNAFFLE.

Every species of bit is evidence of a human mistake, and the wrench which it can exert is only the measure of the error. Many valuable animals are annually ruined, under a prejudiced notion about subduing a stubborn spirit. The horse is born submissive. It by nature acknowledges the superiority of man. When the animal refuses to obey, the disobedience only expresses the creature's ignorance of the desires of its master; or declares the presence of some more potent influence than human authority. In either case, patience is the best remedy. Let the rider be passive until the slow understanding of the quadruped comprehends his pleasure; or until a sufficient pause has destroyed the spell by which the servant was enthralled. Pat the neck; speak encouragingly to the alarmed timidity. Then gently walk the fearful life a few steps. In shorter time, with less trouble and with far greater safety, will such measures restore composure, than violence possibly can compel submission; upon recovery, the acknowledgment of the master's sway will be revived and strengthened by that sense of gratitude which, in animals, reason is powerless to pervert.

The snaffle is the gentlest indicator which the bridle possesses. It is generally sold in two forms—either plain or twisted. The latter supposed improvement renders its action upon the lips more sharp, the sharpness being proportioned to the fineness of the twist. The chain snaffle is, however, still more terrible in its operation, and is certainly better calculated to punish than to guide. A plain snaffle is, therefore, much to be preferred, the fact being well illustrated by the circumstance that the gentlemen who depend upon the milder species of check encounter fewer accidents than those riders who place their reliance in such mechanical restraints as are warranted to break the jaw-bone of any restive animal.

THE HACKNEY AND BIRDO BIT.

THE PELHAM BIT.

The mildest of the many bits in general use is called the "Hackney." It is a curb bit and birdoon, having a double reined bridle. The last instrument is, however, gradually being superseded by the "Pelham bit," which is capable of creating terrible agony. This restraint riders commonly employ with double reins; but it can be used with a single head piece. In general it is manufactured smooth or plain, but it also can be twisted to any desired degree of severity.

The "Hanoverian bit," like the majority of imported inventions, is a terrible exaggeration of the worst properties that once were thought sufficiently powerful. Its nature is best expressed by the phrase "hard and sharp," which it has almost solely appropriated. A horse cannot grasp this novelty in its teeth, and thus render futile an unscrupulous master's efforts to punish. "The Hanoverian" enables a rider to continue the agony which may have driven a sensitive creature to the confines of madness. As the sides are movable at pleasure, it is esteemed to be an admirable check for a pulling quadruped.

THE HANOVERIAN BIT.

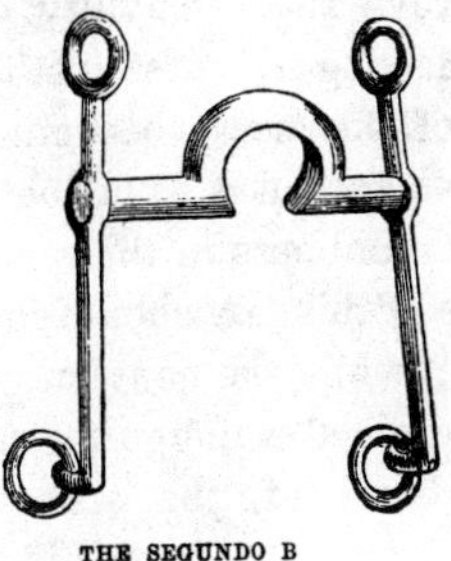

THE SEGUNDO B

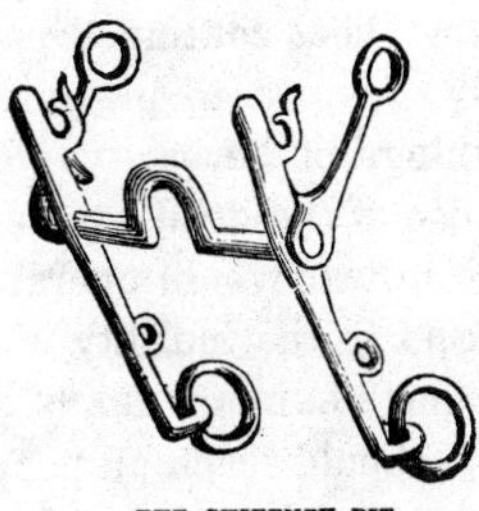

THE CHIFFNEY BIT.

Should none of the foregoing embody the desires of some desperate horseman, there remains another, which is an ugly thing to be put into a living mouth; it is called the "Segundo bit," and is the most barbarous of all the cruelties in general use. It is manufactured of three sizes; the longest of which enables any Christian gentleman to inflict the most lively torture upon the meekest of living creatures.

The "Chiffney bit" was once highly esteemed, and, assuredly, was fully equal to its pretensions; but it seems lately to have sunk low in public favor. The "Sliding Mouth bit" is the last invention of this kind. It is thought to operate beneficially upon animals which are employed in harness. The mouth piece is reversible, having a rough and a smooth side, and it is much approved of, because it professes to afford the horse something for the mouth to play with.

The actions of the dumb, however, are easily mistaken. Anything which pains the angles of the mouth, whether it should be a roughened bit or a tight bearing-rein, will provoke the horse to toss the head into the air. This motion is regarded by most persons as evidence of spirit, and as signifying a playful disposition; but it is in reality an effort to relieve for an instant the tension which drags against the lips. Another action which gratifies the majority of spectators is to behold a steed move the lips which are whitened with foam. Foam, however, only indicates the presence of thirst, and the reader will, upon reference to "Scald Mouth" in the previous volume, discover that rapid labial motion is not, in the horse, characteristic of amusement.

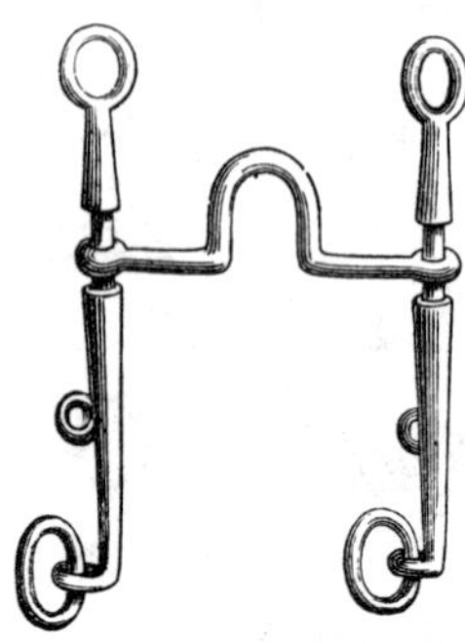

THE SLIDING MOUTH BIT.

Bits of all sorts are decided mistakes, and the blunder is the greater as the restraint becomes the more severe. The occasional employment of such things is highly dangerous; their perpetual use destroys the sensibility of the mouth. That continued pain should deaden feeling is a wise institution, kindly ordained to prevent the sensibilities of this world becoming the playthings of barbarity. Nature protects her creatures from the incessant use of the goad by causing it to provoke numbness in the region on which torture would operate. The knowledge of this law should instruct mankind in the inutility of habitual severity; while the conviction that the same TENDER PARENT has, in madness, ordained a refuge for sudden agony, should teach all people not to lash the horse into that state which can alone render it truly dangerous.

INDEX.

A.

PAGE

Abnormal condition of horn induced by the present mode of nailing 99
Absence of the groom watched for... 255
Accidents are more rare since mutilation is less common............. 381
might be avoided by masters being more gentle............ 263
occasioned by injudicious breaking................................. 460
Accomplishments which fit to take charge of a dealer's yard......... 368
According to the position of the elbow so the hoofs must incline.. 412
Action natural to a slanting shoulder 408
necessitated by a straight shoulder................................. 405
often witnessed before private cabs in London..................... 407
Actions of the dumb are likely to be misinterpreted...................... 271
Active animals are always disliked in the stable......................... 215
Activity constitutes the horse's pleasure........................... 206
Adapted for speed and exertion...... 19
Additional bonds only provoke additional struggles.................... 228
Advantage of, and peculiarities of the new slipper shoe............. 111
Advantages and disadvantages of all horns to give drinks with........ 74
of the tin bottle........................ 75
Advantages of having the stable well regulated.............................. 339
of nailing the new shoe to the toe 113
of shoeing racers with tips 473
Advantages secured by adopting the Arabian mode of nailing......... 105
secured by movable mangers........ 191
Advice to purchasers......................121
Affections of the horse.................... 201
Aftermeath, or rowen..................... 174
Age ought to be accurately observed 147
renders the jaw-bone thin and narrow.................................... 153

PAGE

Ages have produced no change in the horse's treatment............ 223
Agony is evinced by a "kidney dropper," when the spine is pressed 269
Air-passages, the, can alter their dimensions.......................... 25
All animals are spoilt if too greatly petted................................ 453
in the same stable are subjected to the same usages................ 288
creatures play with food when not hungry 213
feeding and drinking compartments should rest upon the ground................................... 310
hands should help the groom when the horse is exhausted........... 348
horses are fully worked during the fourth year..................... 150
horses do not consume the like quantities of food................. 197
needful security assured by open trevises in private stables........ 306
Alteration in the nippers consequent upon old age......................... 136
Alterations are made to suit the declining breed of horses........... 432
in the incisors........................... 159
Aloes, the retention of this medicine within the body..................... 165
become hard by keeping............. 57
Aloes cannot be given to some horses 56
often kill............. 56
the purgative of the stable......... 54
very uncertain in its action........ 55
Always choose a horse having good haunches.................................. 418
see the horse led out of the stable 278
Ambulatory, an, anticipates the necessity of mounting in the stable 310
Anatomical considerations............ 18
Anatomists, were horses extinct, could tell their characters from their bones.............................. 17
Ancient Arabian shoe..................... 95
Anecdote, about breeding horses..... 429

Anecdote concerning swerving in the horse... 291
illustrative of the evils generated by the present mode of exercise 303
of a jibbing horse... 284
of the author and Van Amburg... 434
to illustrate kicking... 272
Anger excited by the colt's restlessness... 209
Angular prominences are upon the grinding surface of the new molar tooth... 156
Animal, an, at five years old, pronounced to be in its prime... 153
not fitted for the saddle, is said to be suitable for harness... 421
Animals roll when their hair is uncomfortable... 230
after being conditioned are often passed by hacks... 464
are beaten when master complains of waste... 213
are guided by their experiences... 264
are incapable of conjecturing consequences... 264
are said to eat their own heads off 367
brought to market at three years old... 146
drink less, having water at command... 314
having ewe necks are generally weak... 391
knowing no future, act on their experiences... 218
love most those who instruct them 283
may be deeply diseased, and therefore called "vicious"... 271
the, are secondary to household duties in genteel families... 327
when procured, become members of the purchaser's family... 379
Apparatus for steaming the horse's food... 186
Appearance, the, of horses is the strongest evidence against modern stables... 231
Appliances needed to cleanse a carriage... 488
Arab horse, the, conforms to no arbitrary mould... 395
Arabian mode of fastening the horse's shoe... 100
Arab tail is well set on, active, and powerful... 387
Arnica lotion used for rick of the back... 275
Arrangement in the components of the teeth... 157
of the gutters within stables... 298
Art cannot amend a natural development... 450
Ascertain, to, if the horse has been properly groomed... 340
Aspect of the mouth materially changes after the first year... 138
At grass, horses enjoy free communication... 307
Attempted cures of jibbing are uncertain and expensive... 283
Attends at fairs and on market days 431
Attend to the heels on the following morning... 352
Author's plan of nailing... 105
suggestions should be tried for their own sakes... 297

B.

Back-bone of the horse... 382
Backing on to the gangway... 278
the horse out of the stall, supposes the spine to be injured... 278
Back of the stables... 317
the, as seen from above... 381
the, is often injured... 275
the, is supported by eighteen ribs on either side... 40
Bad hay and corn commonly given to horses... 179
Bad hay often cut into chaff... 177
Bad qualities of the cow-bellied horse... 404
Balling, blistering, firing, and bleeding in veterinary practice... 85
Balling irons, common form of... 62
improved form of... 62
only of use to timidity or inexperince... 60
Professor Varnell's newly invented 62
Balls, arguments in favor of... 73
caustics often employed in large doses with... 58
commonly intrusted to grooms 54
horse, how made... 54
how prepared... 57
how moulded before delivery... 58
how to administer... 63
quiet mode of giving... 67
the form of... 58
the swallowing of, should be watched for... 68
Barouche and landau... 482
Bars or open trevises admit of equine familiarities... 307
Battering and fixedness aggravate the weakness of the fore limbs. 417
Beans, bad sample of... 188
Egyptian... 188
Egyptian, free from objection... 188
English, are too astringent... 188

Beans, English field, unwholesome when new 187
good and bad sample of, contrasted with each other 187
should be steamed 188
Beard is sometimes present on good oats 180
Bearing-rein, the, interferes with the use of the head 389
Beating the horse in a stable is dangerous 209
Beauty in horses generally coincides with excellence of spirit 399
Be brief in your inquiries in the dealer's yard 374
Bed, a, is uncomfortable when not horizontal 257
Beer recommended for the horse with a sensitive skin 290
Behavior of grooms requires amendment 338
to be exhibited toward dealers 373
Bell, a, connected with the grooms' cottages, enables assistance to be summoned 325
Benefits derived from having a stock of frosted shoes 127
secured by a new mode of nailing 105
Better division of work for the horse 342
have no carriage than one kept in a damp shed 324
Bird, the, returns to its cage, and the horse seeks its stable 251
Birthday of all horses arbitrarily fixed by the Jockey Club 146
Bishoped teeth 134
Bishoping easily detected 134
described 134
Bit, the Pelham, its recommendations 522
the Hackney and birdoon 522
the Hanoverian 523
Bits attached to ladies' bridles 519
buckled and sewn on 519
Blackguards who sell horses are not horse dealers 138
Black mail is exacted by most grooms 329
Blacksmith's forge, a, during frost 127
Bleeding can, its form and use 88
fleam, described 89
horses should be blinded before 91
lancet not recommended for 89
not necessary in many cases 87
strange love of 86
was formerly fashionable 85
Blistering and firing often united 78
a stable right through 80
often resorted to, to please the owner 80
Blistering oil should be procured of a chemist, and diluted 82
oil should be quite clear 82
ointment is made with old flies 82
omnibus horses 81
Blisters and oak bark proposed for rick of the back 275
and the firing iron counteract each other 78
are at present too powerful 78
only of late years have been reduced in strength 78
Blood horses draw weight by strain upon the muscles 401
can should be pressed against the neck 91
if cold, and exposed to the air, becomes oxygenated 24
mare and foal 430
stick depicted 90
when cold, has lost its living properties 245
Bloods want an infusion of a little cocktail 433
Body, horse's, beautiful when skinned 45
the, anatomically considered 17
the, should be judged of as a whole 386
Boiler-house between the gig-house and first loose box 321
Bolting commonly ensues after a fit of jibbing 280
through the stable door 239
Bone bears the burden when the body descends a slope 253
Bones, character of the animal pronounced by 17
of the fore extremity, how retained in their places 42
of the spine described 38
of the forelegs, their action is regulated by the shoulders 408
Bones, the, of the leg do not uphold each other 408
Boy picking hay 172
Boys should not be employed to lead horses through stable doors 240
the, about training stables are not trustworthy 470
Bracy Clark's jointed shoe, remarks on 118
Bray of the donkey and neigh of the horse, how produced 47
Brain, the, becomes congested by moving in circles 451
Branch drains also oppose the ingress of rats 300
Branches of the lower jaw contract with age 136
Bran mashes, how to prepare 55

Bran mashes, more gentle and more safe than aloes.................... 55
Breaches of stable decorum by young horses.............................. 207
Bread, given to horses in Germany, might be used as food............ 195
Breaker, the, operates only on the fears of the colt...................... 453
Breaking and training................ 449
begins at three years old............ 147
loose.................................. 217
should be gradually enforced from the earliest age...................... 455
Breaks are not often publicly used to exercise horses in 304
Breast collar-strap.................... 507
Breathing life treated as it were an inanimate chattel................... 200
Breeders should take example from the agriculturists.................. 428
Breeding, its inconsistencies and its disappointments 427
of horses is at present altogether wrong 437
suckling, and living on grass..... 446
Bricks and mortar are valueless in comparison with horse flesh..... 298
Bricklayer's trowel likened to the teeth.................................. 158
Bringing the sole near to the ground, danger of........................... 102
Brittle hoof............................ 99
Brougham horse, a..................... 371
Brougham or phæton harness......... 503
Brushing or cutting about the pastern joint.............................. 121
Bulk is not always an assurance of strength.............................. 419
merely distends and injures the stomach.............................. 177
Bull neck, a............................. 391
Bustle hails the appearance of a stranger in the stable............ 204
Buy a young horse by the teeth as regards age......................... 164

C.

Calkins destroying the even bearing of the foot... 109
in the slipper shoe made by thinning the quarters.................. 111
Can, bleeding, its form and use...... 88
blood should be pressed against the neck.............................. 91
horses have aristocratic predilections................................. 215
Capacity of most doors to stables... 235
Capital and tact required to job carriages successfully................ 368
Carriage, a, without C springs, and a brougham......................... 483
harness, a full suit of....... 504
horses are not kept by the London dealers........................... 367
houses are always large enough... 233
the treatment required for, when in its house.......................... 492
Carriages................................ 477
congregate on wet nights before fashionable mansions............. 323
Carrying round the food to the stables 192
Carters sit upon the loins of young horses.............................. 265
Cart horse, a........................... 401
with a Roman nose.................. 394
horses are not formed to trot...... 273
have long mustaches............. 394
Cartilago nictitans..................... 36
its special use and action........... 36
Carts should never exist without springs............................... 386
Cast in the stall......................... 231
under the manger.................... 259
Cause of chink of the back is the greed of proprietors.............. 273
Cause of odd hoofs in the horse...... 413
Causes of cutting....................... 121
which increase the liability of the foreleg to injury................... 416
Caustics dangerous as internal medicine................................. 59
Cavity of the pulp in the molar teeth 157
Ceiling of stables, how it is formed 316
Certain steeds snap and bite when being dressed too violently...... 289
Channel diminishes with age 136
Character and color of upland hay 173
lowland hay......................... 173
Cheap harness is generally dangerous 496
horses are not to be bought in London 359
Cheapness is not economy when buying oats......................... 182
Chiffney bit, the........................ 523
Child, a, might sit the thoroughbred trot.............................. 421
Chink of the back...................... 266
Circular chest, the, good for slow work 401
exercise............................... 452
motion induces blindness........... 451
Clark, of Edinburgh, his old shoe preferred to new inventions..... 121
Classic mind, the, recognized the signification of the horse........ 242
Clean saddle, how to................... 516
Cleaning harness, the proper method of................................. 504

Cleansing and cooling with hot and cold water 349
an exhausted horse 348
an unclipped horse 347
Clearing the fence 462
Cleaveland bays are a dangerous property 368
Clinches are more secure when made upon the toe 114
Clicking or forging common toward the end of a long journey 124
Clipped horse, a, is a deformity 346
Clipping and singeing 343
induce many terrible disorders 344
Clock-loft and lumber-room above the sheltered space 320
Closing the wound after having bled the horse 92
Clothes and saddle cannot be retained on the herring-gutted horse 404
Clover hay, first crop of 174
second crop of 175
Coal-cellar 319
Coaxing the foal to feed 444
Coax the horse when giving medicine 78
Collar-rope is bitten through without design 216
Collar-strap disfigures the neck and mane 218
Colt at three years may cut sixteen teeth 149
Colts are wayward creatures 207
Comminution of the food described 155
Common form of horn employed to administer drinks 74
Common sense is alone necessary to understand horses 524
Common stallions are generally led through the country 431
Comparison between the wild and domesticated horse 201
Complex calculations required of the horse dealer 362
Composure returns only when the rug is destroyed 287
Compound soap liniment recommended for rick of the back 275
Condition of horses referred to 432
of stable windows generally 315
of the blood explains the diseases of the foot 246
Conduct of most drivers when the horse bolts 293
Conjunctiva, nature and distribution of 35
Consequences of being cast in the collar-rope 224
of being cast under the manger 259
of too much paring, miscalled disease 106
Contents of the abdomen and thorax 403
Continued standing is a bad symptom 352
Contraction of the jaw-bones forces the teeth into the mouth 158
Contrast between a three-year old and a bishoped sixteen-year old mouth 135
between the permanent and milk incisor teeth 160
Cooking food for horses no novelty 193
Copers esteem a kidney dropper a valuable horse 269
the, always flurry a horse when pretending to show it 277
Corner incisors first cut at nine months old 141
milk incisors, being shed, announce five years old 153
Corns are natural to upright hoofs 415
Corn promotes fat 187
should be crushed on the premises 184
when crushed, requires further preparation 186
Corpora nigra, present in the horse and camel 31
Cost of a separate house for the groom would be fifteen pounds per annum 333
of horse flesh is much increased by hard food 166
Coughing, its danger during the administration of a drink 75
provoked by raising the head 76
Countenance during a fit of jibbing 282
Countersinking for driving nails 113
Course of the food, how arranged 28
Covered ride round the stable 302
Cow-bellied or pot-bellied horse, the evils of 404
Cribbing induced by confinement and indigestion 205
Crime is the climax of social frailty 426
Crowded forges prevented by laying in a stock of frosted shoes 127
Cruel imprisonment 201
Cruelties undergone at three years old 148
Cruelty and roguery are associated 425
cannot promote development 164
is practiced to coerce the jibber 280
of rasping the hoof to fit a small shoe 131
of the present mode of breaking in 141
resorted to after bleeding 94
sometimes changes the action of the straight shoulder 406
unintentionally inflicted on all horses 168
Cruiser and Mr. Rarey 453

Crusta petrosa.......... 157
is endowed with a limited power of growth.......... 158
Cures proposed for cutting from exhaustion.......... 122
Curry-comb should be abolished..... 337
Curveting and lunging are alike in their influences.......... 449
Customers are protected by the author's recommendations.......... 378
should be better suited than pleased.......... 364
Custom of the drivers attached to the former fly wagons.......... 265
Cutting away the horny sole.......... 103
often produced by exhaustion...... 123

D.

Damp stables are equally costly and dangerous.......... 322
Danger consequent upon the internal use of caustics.......... 59
of casting the entire weight upon the wall.......... 103
of coughing during the giving of a drink.......... 75
of getting the hind leg beyond the post of the stall.......... 230
of gorging on dry wheat.......... 169
of standing in the manger.......... 209
Dangers of racing plates.......... 114
of the present method of nailing.. 100
Darkness does not incapacitate the horse's eye.......... 32
Date is apt to deceive the breeder... 440
Dead donkeys not rare.......... 47
Dealers buy with a view to certain purchasers.......... 375
do not show all their stock to every chance customer.......... 138
generally possess one or two blood-weeds.......... 369
horses are exercised in front of the house windows.......... 304
take much trouble to buy horses.. 359
visit horse fairs and breeders of stock.......... 364
will not submit a horse of known unsoundness to a veterinary examination.......... 378
Deformity consequent on neglect of the hoof.......... 102
Deglutition described.......... 29
Degree of motion permitted in the stable.......... 202
Deluging with water does not please the horse.......... 346
Dentine.......... 157
Depth of the lower jaw in the young horse accounted for.......... 157
Deranged stomach denoted by fastidious and by voracious appetite.......... 196
Detailed description of the surface-gutters of the stable.......... 299
Development of the hyoideal muscles 400
Diagrams of the opposite formation of thorax.......... 402
Difference between fullering and countersinking.......... 113
between man and horse in their lodging.......... 233
in the food of man and horse when in training.......... 170
of head in a one and a two-year old 144
Different articles eaten by horses ... 166
forms of pasterns.......... 410
kinds of ears.......... 396
kinds of snaffles.......... 521
Digestion deranged by modern stables and present food.......... 196
of the horse is frequently impaired 342
Disease in the horse is exposed to the conjectures of ignorance.... 285
Discovered in the morning with the head under the manger.......... 258
Dishonest dealers always demand a written warranty.......... 365
Disposition of the horse should be studied.......... 77
Dock, the, should be regarded as a continuation of the back-bone.. 386
Domesticated animals generally live on prepared food.......... 167
horse is very old by its thirtieth year.......... 165
Donkey, the, belongs to the equine race.......... 46
Donkeys natural to the sandy desert 48
have to toil after man's day of labor has ended.......... 51
prejudices concerning, tend to their misery.......... 51
serve only the poor.......... 49
the loins of, uphold riders.......... 51
thrust into any hole for the night. 49
work before the master begins to labor.......... 50
Do not coax a tired horse to feed.... 351
Do not punish the horse for jibbing. 281
Doors of stables should fold, or be divided through the center...... 307
open on to the ambulatory.......... 307
size of, according to Professor Stewart.......... 235
Double coach-house.......... 319
Doubt as to the weakness of a hollow back.......... 384
Down in the hip.......... 237

Drag on the clinches the consequence of the thin heel shoe.... 120
Draught horses require high and good haunches.................... 421
Draughts in crowded stables enable the horses to live.................. 81
Draughtsmen, their qualifications... 478
Dress, a, carriage and a chariot...... 482
Dressing the heels...................... 353
the horse 340
Drinking, the manner of, explained. 71
Drinks or draughts, a form of horse physic 68
danger of administering........... 69
generally objected to.............. 68
reasons for these objections........ 68
sometimes poured down the nostril...................................... 69
the objection to so giving medicine 73
usual mode of giving................ 74
Driving a nail too fine 100
Dry fodder prematurely wears down the teeth 133
Drying the heels........................ 350
Dryness affects the nature of the horse's food 171
Dusk, and at ten o'clock, duties of... 341
Duties of the night-watcher.......... 325

E.

Each groom should lead two horses to exercise 306
Earning its keep during lactation... 436
Early and late is the best time for exercise. 466
Ears, different kinds of 396
Eastern elevation of the contemplated stables........................ 325
Education, modern, makes men knowing and not good............ 198
should commence with birth 455
Effects of living upon grass in the field 430
Egyptian beans are mild and sweet.. 188
Eight months' solitary imprisonment is not rest............................ 475
Eight o'clock duties 340
Employers should be blamed for the groom's debasement.............. 330
Employment of the drawing knife a necessity 106
Enamel 157
English mode of paring the foot..... 102
thorough-bred tail approaches to the Arab 387
Entire horses are not necessarily savages 433
Entreaty not to credit the possibility of a "vicious animal"........... 294
Equine race, the, are treated as creatures without habits or instincts.................................... 241
Estimable qualities of hollow-backed horses 384
Even man's generosity causes the horse to suffer 475
Every gentleman his own horsebreaker.................................... 453
Everything in the stable yields tribute to the groom 330
Evils of long nights to horses and to grooms 198
of modern stables................... 200
Ewe neck, an............................. 391
Exaggerated view of a weakly animal with dangerous action 424
Examine the angles of the mouth before purchasing................ 398
Excellence of the racer's action in the trot 420
Excessive weakness has lost many a race 472
Exchanges, with horses, are very expensive 373
Excited horse, mouth of an........... 288
Excitement ensues upon first sniffing the pure air 334
prevented by rapidly and silently distributing the food 312
Exercise, during training, is given at mid-day 466
can be given in all weathers under the ambulatory 303
Exhausting labor renders bleeding unnecessary 87
Exhaustion in youth is a bad preparative for the stud-farm 428
Expense of feeding the horse, how increased................................ 193
would not be increased by proper treatment 463
Experiments, uselessness of, as a test for medicine......................... 60
Experiment, testing the effects of a thick and of a thin covering..... 344
Explanation of the doctor's difficulty 303
of the term "May bird" 364
of the word "nicking"............ 387
Expression of the ears................. 396
Extended view obtained by mounting into the manger 210
Extravagance of hard food........... 166
Extreme age rare in the horse........ 88
Eye, the, is a certificate of the horse's origin.................................... 30
Eyes, the, of the horse are much exposed to injury 291
various sorts of....................... 397

F.

Fœtus, the, is injured by the mother being sucked while breeding.... 445
False nostrils, situation, nature and uses of.............................. 25
Fancy is most active in the weakest intellects.............................. 227
Fangs of the milk teeth are absorbed 160
Farmers, the, idea of a breeding mare 447
Fat is laid on, although lameness exists in the foreleg.............. 243
is promoted by the food—horses are sweated to remove fat....... 467
Faults inseparable from stables...... 233
Fearful change takes place when a horse is "thrown up" to breed. 435
Fed between the bursts................ 472
Feeding of the grazing and the stabled horse............................ 429
the mare.............................. 455
the newly-born foal................ 443
Feeling, instincts or inclinations of the horse are never heeded...... 198
Feet of farm horses are generally sound.................................. 246
of thorough-breds generally bad.. 115
Felt under-pad.......................... 512
Few gentlemen's stables are supplied with the best grain......... 181
grooms live in the house........... 327
horse dealers die rich............... 367
horses reach their thirtieth year.. 155
human beings should be exposed to the groom's temptations.. ... 330
tails are well set on................. 387
Fleam, the, as made to be struck by the hand............................. 89
the, is preferable to the lancet.... 89
the, described as used for bleeding 89
Field (newspaper) description of roughing, from..................... 129
Fifth molar present by the second year.................................... 145
Fired, sometimes, and blistered after it................................. 78
Fire has been kindled under a jibbing horse.............................. 281
First crop of clover.................... 174
drops of blood taken from the forefoot are cold.................... 243
lessons in breaking should commence with the foal.............. 141
permanent tooth appears at one year old............................. 142
the, harness put on a foal.......... 456
Fittings needed for the interior of a carriage............................. 490
of the sheltered space.............. 320
Five-feet wide doors do very well for sleepy animals..................... 237
Flattery is much relished by all lower life............................ 456
Flesh is only another name for muscle.. 381
Flexor muscle, the, influences the direction of the foot.............. 412
Flooring of the proposed stables described.............................. 298
Foal first nips the grass when four months old......................... 141
one fortnight after birth........... 139
the, may accompany the mare in her work............................ 436
Foals are generally crippled before they are born....................... 428
should be taught to regard men as friends........................... 444
teeth at birth.......................... 139
Folly of docking......................... 380
of employing blisters to the legs.. 79
of ornamental scroll work instead of plain bars......................... 306
of tying a horse by its head to the manger........................... 225
Food.. 168
for the foal if the mare's milk is tardy.............................. 443
not thoroughly digested when presented dry........................ 165
of horses is contaminated in modern stables......................... 318
proper for an exhausted horse..... 347
should be proportioned to the animal's fatigue........................ 351
the greatest of many evils under which horses suffer............... 169
when too abundant is wasted...... 212
Foot, the, perspires through the horn 353
Foreleg over the collar-rope.......... 221
Forelegs in the manger................ 208
Forelimb is not a straight pillar..... 409
the, is joined to the trunk by muscle...................................... 41
Forge, horse's dread of................ 109
strange custom of charging different prices in......................... 110
the state of the, during a sudden frost.................................. 127
Formation of the soil of stable...... 301
Former shoes, unsuit for modern use 96
Form of thorax which is best suited for slow and for fast work...... 402
the, of a mare for breeding........ 438
Four fully-grown permanent incisors only denote three years of age.................................... 147
miles an hour is a fair exercising pace................................... 305
or five o'clock duties................ 341
permanent incisors in each jaw announce four years old......... 152

Four "roomy" stalls may be converted into three loose boxes.... 332
Fourth molar is the first permanent tooth.. 142
year, at the, the horse should be taught to leap 416
Four-year olds are thought to need no indulgence 151
Four-year old colt may be placed between shafts 459
Fracture of the haunch disqualifies for a gentleman's service 238
Freedom is naturally desired by the horse 220
Freemasonry, the, which exists between steed and rider 372
French martingale, the use of 518
revolution, the nobleman and Bastile 252
Frequent change of shoes injures the feet of thorough-breds 473
Friction, when brisk, warms more than slow walking exercise 352
Frog and sole injured by the wedge-heeled shoe 119
Front of the new stable has no intermediate rails 319
teeth appear to be but temporary. 145
teeth stick out like spikes at thirty years of age 167
Frosted shoes worn out in three or four days 128
Frosting or roughing as generally performed 128
Fullered shoe 113
Full loins are generally associated with a stout dock 393
set of horse clothes 498
Fuzzy tail disappears at one-year old 143

G.

Gangway, the, should be kept clean 338
General complaint of the roguery of horse dealers 425
mode of leading the horse out of the stable 236
view of the shoulder and foreleg.. 416
Gentlemen like the springy seat afforded by a young spine 146
should respect their station when treating with dealers 378
when ignorant of horse flesh, should not attempt display 370
Gentleness and caution requisite when trying a fresh horse 372
should be displayed during a fit of jibbing 282
Gentle riding and proper grooming would sustain condition 475
German silver makes the best ornaments for harness 496
Gestation is opposed to lactation 445
Get up 351
Gig, a, and a two-wheeled dog cart.. 485
Gig harness and kicking-strap 502
house 319
Girths of saddles generally considered 509
Giving a horse a quart of malt liquor 347
out macerated food 191
Glycerin and rose-water removes scurf 290
wash, the mode of applying it to the skin 337
Gnawing the manger rail the result of long captivity 204
Good bridle, the characteristics of... 517
feeders are too commonly sluggish animals 352
form, a, generally requires little aid in foaling 439
horse, the, is good for every purpose 420
oatmeal, how to recognize 178
oats display no vast difference in size 180
reach, a, in the trot, a valuable quality in a hack 420
saddle, a, should fall into its proper place 515
shoes are spoiled by being roughed 128
Gowing's, Mr., mode of giving a ball 65
its advantages and defects 66
Graced with the sweetest manners, sells the horses 362
Grass, horses are generally shod with tips when out at 116
suggests the food of the horse 20
the natural food of the undomesticated horse 133
Great muscular power is necessitated to move the head 388
Greenhorns disliked by the regular dealer 373
Green meat and mashes are better than aloes 469
Grooms 327
conceive the horse injures them... 222
display the union of innocence and knowingness 354
doing house work generally neglect the stable 355
flog the horse for standing in the gutter 257
generally manage their nominal masters 229
imagine the foot to be a mystery.. 353
like fat in horses 212
like the horse to have hard meat.. 193

Grooms never regard cutaneous sensitiveness as a disease........... 285
pretend to comprehend impossibilities........................... 355
pride themselves upon being "*close*"........................... 355
regard see-sawing as a fearful "vice"........................... 205
report effects, and never hint at causes........................... 229
ride as they please when exercising horses........................... 303
singe the hairs inside the horse's ears........................... 395
should not ride when exercising horses........................... 306
Groom's room is situated over the boiler-house........................... 324
idea of a horse's long imprisonment........................... 211
secret mixtures are the originals of patent food........................... 196
Ground plan of the proposed stables 321
Gruel is proper for an exhausted horse........................... 351
Guess only at the age after the fifth year........................... 163

H.

Hair should never be inclosed in the wound after bleeding............. 93
Hairs from oats are felted together in the stomach........................... 183
on the oat........................... 182
Half an acre of close grass should be attached to each loose box...... 309
Hames with double eyes............. 506
Handling the feet........................... 457
Hand-over-hand pace, the, is bad... 423
Hard food must be a tax on the muscular system........................... 467
provender wears the teeth and shortens the life........................... 165
substances derange the horse's digestion........................... 186
Hardships undergone at three years old........................... 148
Harness and food are benefited when separated from stables............ 317
and stable sundries........................... 494
for the young........................... 456
horses are usually imperfectly broken........................... 459
Hat, the, should be removed before a horse is led out of the stable.. 240
Haunch-bone is often broken by striking against the door-post.. 238
Haunches, the, will express the qualities of the horse........................... 419
Hay, aftermeath........................... 174
clover, first crop........................... 174
second crop........................... 175
from legumens might cost more, but would be better........................... 189
heated........................... 175
loft, the, should be over the coach-house........................... 333
lowland........................... 173
musty........................... 176
promotes fat........................... 189
should be sorted before it is placed in the rack........................... 171
upland........................... 172
weather beaten........................... 176
Head, carried straight out is ungraceful and unsafe........................... 390
the, must be retracted before the horse can rise........................... 260
the, by its movements inclines the body in certain directions........ 380
the, denotes the treatment of the horse........................... 393
Health suffers from improper food.. 169
Heaped manger unsuited for a famished horse........................... 178
Heat and impurity naturally provoke cuticular irritability........ 224
and moisture correct the unwholesomeness of food............ 190
Heaving at the flanks........................... 440
Heavy animals were formerly used for gentle purposes........................... 422
carts having long reins are injurious to the horse's spine........ 273
Heels are left unprotected if the shoeing is neglected........................... 106
Herald painting—how its charges are regulated........................... 478
Herbs, when dried, retain their properties........................... 171
Herring-gutted horse, the disadvantages of........................... 403
High-spirited horses are the most troublesome when confined...... 215
stubborn horn the author prefers in the horse's foot........................... 414
Hind hoofs enjoy a freedom denied to the forefeet........................... 244
legs, the, have a tendency to increase the burden of the fore limbs........................... 417
Hinge of the spine for rearing....... 44
Hobble the hind legs of a mare...... 441
Hogs' skins are seldom perfect...... 515
Hollow-backed horse........................... 383
cavity at the toe of the slipper shoe 111
Home, a, for a horse is not the same thing as a home for a man...... 298
Hoofs are spoiled by roughing during frost........................... 128

Hopeless struggle of mankind........ 200
Horn for giving drinks, common form of........................ 74
improved form of..................... 74
of the hoof described............... 98
whalebone and wood are best for stable instruments........ 336
Horse auction marts deal largely in unsound horses 277
a, when sold should suit the purchaser 361
dealers.............................. 357
dealers are alive to the value of their stock 379
dealers generally occupy the same place at successive fairs.......... 365
is intended to run unshod over grass land............................ 116
is very choice when eating grass. 170
its disposition should be studied... 77
lowers the head to feed and drink.................................. 170
the, cannot turn in its stall without twisting the back............. 279
the, has embraced its position..... 252
the, has not changed with the mutation of society 449
the, squatting suddenly like a dog denotes a kidney dropper........ 267
knowledge is not a mystery........ 524
Horses when they speedy cut are liable to fall, as though shot.... 423
should be taken into use with bodies uninjured...................... 463
are always blamed for human carelessness 234
are by grooms credited only with evil qualities..................... 216
are furnished with the means of self-injury.......................... 262
are inclined to rest at mid-day.... 468
are often captives for many days in the stall...... 211
are put to the greatest exertion at five years of age.. 153
are seldom dressed when brought home late 230
are starved when confined to small stables............................ 81
body still beautiful even when the skin is removed.................... 45
can protrude their heads through the half-opened doors 308
can see in comparative darkness.. 228
dread the forge..................... 109
eating from the ground, require no hay-rack 310
eat various substances in different countries.......................... 194
have no right to do as they like with their lives 207
Horses have perished from all four feet being blistered................ 78
have to sleep on slanting pavement.................................. 256
having wide hips and large thighs very seldom cut.................... 122
intended to breed should be tenderly nurtured....................... 435
lower the head while drinking..... 76
must feel their captivity 202
should be exercised on the premises.................................. 304
slide backward on the slanting pavement 259
the, painted by Stubbs, are lost to the present generation........... 407
their rest broken by the inclination of their beds 257
which kick when the foot is in the stirrup are often quiet when mounted 272
clothes generally much too short.. 350
Horse flesh is being ruined by the race-course 432
Hot-water pipes traverse the proposed stable....................... 322
How grooms contrive to spend so much money........................ 329
to examine for kidney dropping .. 268
for the signs of cutting....... 423
to feed a famished animal.......... 178
to feed a hunter.................. 471
to feed the mare and foal.......... 443
to make good gruel................. 178
to macerate food.................... 190
to procure good oats................ 182
to recognize a bishoped tooth...... 134
Human child not a man when the permanent teeth appear.......... 152
Humanity in purchasers would destroy roguery in dealers......... 425
Hunters, as a rule, are not kept by the London trade............ 369
must be over four years old........ 146
Hunting breast-plate 511

I.

Impaling the foot on a projecting nail......... 101
Imperfect vision renders a horse dangerous........................... 293
Importance of warmth to the horse.. 322
Impossible to convince most grooms. 220
to make the teeth declare a horse older than it really is............. 168
Imprisonment engenders eagerness to breathe the fresh air 237
Improvement has not reached the jail of the horse 297

Impure air, sameness of food, and confinement generate disease.... 243
residence, an, generates a morbid craving........ 329
In cavalry stables, horses are separated by bales........ 307
Incisor teeth are not employed in the stable........ 167
Incisors, the, which denote a three-year old........ 147
Inclination of the feet of horses..... 412
Incline of the superficial gutters.... 301
Inferior margin of the jaw still thick at four years old........ 151
oats possess the longest hairs...... 183
specimens of oats commonly adulterated........ 179
Injury done by boys who hold your honor's horse........ 124
occasioned to the crust of the hoof by nailing........ 100
often done by the laws of the Jockey Club........ 146
or blemish is feared by dealers as much as death........ 366
Inquiry into the conduct of colt and groom........ 209
Instinctive acts in man........ 295
Instruction properly imparted does not strain the body........ 461
Interior of the stable should be colored green........ 316
In the end, it is cheapest to act justly 331
field, horses rest with the hind legs highest........ 247
stable, horses stand with the fore-feet highest........ 248
Inward soft organs govern the hardest outward secretions........ 118
Irish horses are famed as good fencers........ 462
Itching and scratching rank as vices in the stable........ 223

J.

Jaw-bone becomes thin and narrow with age........ 153
in early life, is full and round at the lower margin........ 142
Jaw, the, of a two-year old intimates approaching change........ 145
Jealousy regarding a choice colt..... 376
Jibbing first alluded to........ 280
is as common now as it was formerly........ 286
is equine epilepsy........ 280
most common in heavy and in harness horses........ 282
Jobbing requires skill in placing horses........ 368
Job-masters assert the straight shoulder is the best for harness purposes........ 406
the, terms of........ 368
Jockey Club, folly of its laws........ 146
further alluded to........ 163
Jolly fun of the trainer's stable...... 470

K.

Keep the stableman to his duties.... 355
Kettle, a two-gallon, wanted in every stable........ 178
Kicker, a, and a biter........ 434
Kickers often stand quiet when mounted on the opposite side... 273
Kicking in the night........ 227
"Kidney dropping" is esteemed a terrible "vice"........ 266
Kidneys, the, are not concerned in what is termed "kidney dropping"........ 270
Kiln-dried oats, to detect........ 185
"Kim ovare"........ 336
Kindle an opposite emotion and fear is destroyed........ 293
Kindness preferable to any mechanical restraint........ 61
is especially remunerative when bestowed upon the mare........ 437
is responded to even when consciousness is partly lost........ 283
Kinds of horn composing the wall of the hoof........ 98
Know your own wants before a dealer's yard is entered........ 373
Konisberg oats........ 180

L.

Labial action often mistaken in the horse........ 524
Lachrymal gland........ 35
Lad, a, should be allowed in every stable........ 332
Ladies flushed from the ball-room often sleep in damp carriages... 323
patent stirrup........ 514
Lady, the, and the magistrate........ 164
Lady's palfrey in the reign of Charles the Second........ 422
side-saddle........ 513
bridle is generally light........ 517
"Lampas" explained........ 157
Lamps, large and small, for a carriage........ 492

Large lungs favor the increase of weight.... 401
nostrils and mouth show breeding in a horse.... 397
stables are generally well managed.... 332
Lying on the gangway.... 261
Lead liniment softens the exudation after blistering.... 84
Leanness of hay-fed horses accounted for.... 189
Leaping, how it should be taught... 461
Legitimate horse dealers, all have private yards.... 358
as a body, are honorable men.... 360
Legs, lower parts of the, contain no muscles to stimulate.... 82
of the horse highly sensitive.... 79
Legumens, sown broadcast and reaped, form a better kind of hay.... 189
Length of back is of no separate importance.... 386
Let no man talk about a "vicious horse".... 295
Licking the manger, an endeavor to make employment.... 204
Life is fixed to no one condition.... 371
Light draught horses can best dispense with muscular loins.... 383
generally stops the kicking in the night.... 227
should always be present in the stable.... 228
work need only exercise the mare 436
Lining of harness is soiled by bad grooms.... 505
Liquid which drains from steamed food is a nutritious drink.... 186
Liquor arsenicalis is good for the skin.... 290
Load, the, being delivered, the heavy cart is trotted back.... 273
Locality for the proposed stable.... 319
Lofty crest, a, is best induced by proper food.... 460
Loins, the, are without bony support 382
cannot be too large or muscular.. 382
transmit the force of the haunches 382
the spines of, and of the sacrum, point different ways.... 44
Long and short legs, the value of each.... 405
Loop, a, of string, used instead of a twitch.... 75
Loose boxes eighteen feet square... 298
would cure many "vices" of the stable.... 222
shoes, perils of.... 101
Low-bred haunches express weakness.... 418
Lower jaw becomes sharp with age. 136
Lowland hay.... 173
Lunging.... 451
Lungs, capacity of, illustrated.... 19

M.

Mail phaeton, a, and four-wheeled dog cart.... 484
Malt liquor, horses soon grow fond of.... 347
Man alarms the horse by needless cruelties.... 263
alone has conceived a life without a pleasure.... 206
and horse supposed to change positions—the result.... 206
could not create the perfection which he injures.... 44
is not more gregarious than the horse.... 474
is not more humane than formerly 381
is to blame for the horse's stable conduct.... 211
neglects the life which cannot be repaired.... 234
not fitted to exert absolute authority.... 80
and horse are not a match in strength.... 521
Man's fingers, a, cannot test the expansibility of a horse's foot.... 415
responsibility, how evaded.... 53
senseless adherence to antiquated forms.... 452
Manger, the, rope fastens the head immediately under the opening to the hay-loft.... 310
Manner of judging the limbs.... 423
of using the blood can.... 92
Manners, the, requisite in a horse dealer.... 361
Many animals are ruined in the breaking.... 452
animals become restless when clothed for the night.... 286
artisans, conjunction of, to form a carriage manufactory.... 479
grooms also expected to act as gardeners.... 327
horses are unable to pass through a stable door with calmness.... 239
houses have doors far larger than any stable.... 235
horses lamed by the wedge-heeled shoe.... 119
muscles of the haunch rise close to the dock.... 387
smiths will profess to cure clicking.... 125

Many things must change before present customs alter............ 331
Mare, a, generally hardly treated ... 445
Marks of the teeth are unworthy of dependence........................ 137
Macerating box for food.............. 190
Mastication a compound process..... 155
Master and groom like a quiet stable 203
May bird................................. 364
Medicine, the less the better during training.............................. 469
Melton girth and martingale......... 509
Men desire only to know the physical necessities and capabilities of the horse... 199
who know nothing of such matters, order the building of stables 234
Meshwork of veins, a, lies under the secreting membrane of the hoof.. 245
Method of treating the newly-born foal..................................... 443
Midst noise and bustle the horse dealer must be calm.............. 361
Might not Egyptian beans be grown in England?....... 188
Miles's works on the horse's feet recommended........................ 415
Miniature dewlap a good point....... 400
Minor operations........................ 53
Mistake, the, of a summer's rest..... 464
Mode of dressing a wet horse........ 349
of distributing food to restless horse.................................. 312
of fastening the Arabian shoe..... 100
of sitting the horse in the olden time.................................. 450
Model foot, the, is not good in the author's opinion..................... 414
Modern Arabian shoe.................. 95
carriages are fraught with danger to the upper classes.............. 323
mode of nailing......................... 97
stables as they may be adapted.... 332
stables invite accidents............. 262
Molars are not level in aged horses. 154
Molar teeth are not all of one size or the like form..................... 155
tooth of an aged horse.............. 159
Money does not constitute the entire price of a good horse............. 375
is saved by encouraging habits of regularity........................... 318
paid to the job-master............... 369
sunk in stables is most remunerative.................................. 298
More bonds do not destroy the desire to be free........... 220
important portion of the groom's duties.................................. 343
Morning exercise should begin the day's work.......................... 340
exercise, the, is essential to the master's safety..................... 334
Most corn-chandlers do not keep the heavier oats......................... 182
horsemen do not comprehend the utility of the neck................. 389
masters only know their horses through the groom's report...... 222
people who buy and sell horses are cheats............................ 357
well-bred horses have stubborn necks.................................. 390
Mother's milk, allowed to the young, best secures development......... 446
Motion and sensation of the hind limbs depend on the spinal cord 270
of the quarters aids the pedal circulation.............................. 114
Mounting a horse is a good test for its excellence..................... 417
Mouths, large, small, and dejected.. 397
Movable and fixed ring................ 507
manger.................................. 191
Movement of the feet is regulated by the condition of the body....... 126
Mr. Lupton's recommendation of White's method of roughing... 129
Mr. Percival rode an animal shod with tips on the London stones. 116
Mucous membrane, when inflamed, greatly weakens..................... 465
Much would be gained if the reader only acknowledged the writer right in theory..................... 463
is learned by watching the groom lead a horse out of the stable... 278
the same now as in the seventeenth century...................... 449
Muscles exist in pairs................ 253
how these operate upon the eye... 33
the, of mastication force the venous blood to the heart............ 23
Musty hay................................ 176
Mysterious conduct of grooms........ 335

N.

Nags are now more ridden by others than by their masters............. 334
Nails, reasons for driving into the toe 113
Natural process of drinking described................................. 70
diagram, of............................ 71
Nature does not obey the laws of the Jockey Club...................... 146
has allowed vacant spaces to exist so as to preserve the beauty of the head.......................... .. 27

Nature pauses after the first year ... 144
should decide the period of lactation ... 446
Nature's toil regulated by density of structure ... 151
Nearly every man will sell his unsound horse ... 269
Nearness to the heart does not explain want of sensation in the foreleg ... 243
Necessity for ascertaining the customer's desires ... 363
Neck, the, generally indicates the disposition ... 389
Neglected foot of the ass ... 102
Never buy a horse said to be equal to your weight ... 418
decide upon the first trial of a horse ... 373
enter the stable where horses are kicking ... 227
finger the horse you mean to purchase ... 372
leave the animal before the bleeding is finished ... 92
lose sight of the horse you contemplate buying ... 279
mount a strange nag in a crowded locality ... 272
purchase a horse without a veterinary examination of it ... 425
Newly, the, born foal ... 442
New shoe, the, has many recommendations ... 114
Nibbling the wood-work induced by enforced idleness ... 204
Nicking was a senseless barbarity... 380
Night before the horse fair ... 359
clothing ... 499
the horse can see as well in, as the cat ... 32
watcher, a, enables the food to be better distributed ... 325
Nine o'clock duties ... 341
Nippers is a misnomer when applied to the front teeth of the stabled horse ... 167
only inspected to ascertain the age 137
No accident should teach a horse doors and pain are associated... 308
instrument formed of steel or iron should be permitted in the stable 335
jockeyism can foretell the attack of kidney dropping ... 266
man can know all about the breeding of all animals ... 427
means can eradicate the evils of stables while pavement slopes... 251
muscles present on the shin ... 410
one would purchase, did horse dealers speak the truth ... 360
No teeth no horse ... 133
unknown undividual can pick the dealer's stock ... 375
wild horses are known to be in existence ... 437
Northern extremity of the stables divided into three small rooms.. 317
Nose alone breathed through ... 3[illegible]
Nostrils, the, indicate the dimensions of the lungs ... 399
Novel use made of the manger ... 210
Noxious atmosphere, a, compels the resort to stimulants ... 329

O.

Oatmeal, good, described ... 180
Oats are a most extravagant feed for horses ... 194
are often moistened to increase their bulk ... 185
best Scotch ... 180
English feed ... 185
English, from Canadian seed ... 180
Finland black ... 184
first class Swedes ... 181
hair calculus ... 183
Irish, bleached ... 184
kiln dried Danish ... 184
Konisberg ... 180
light and heavy ... 182
magnified English ... 183
magnified musty ... 189
new Irish feed ... 181
Petersburg ... 180
Scotch, second quality ... 184
should be always bought by weight ... 181
when musty are covered with fungi ... 189
Observe that both shoulders are of the same bulk ... 417
the eating capabilities of horses.. 354
Objections to drinks ... 73
Odd feet are evidences of former lameness ... 413
feet are not uncommon among horses ... 413
Ointment, blistering, is made with refuse flies ... 82
Old English shoe ... 96
hunter and young man's steed ... 464
One failing, the, of horse dealers ... 360
kind of jibber stops suddenly and backs ... 284
lateral incisor in both jaws declares a four-year old ... 151
prime foal in two years may be better than four bad every year 445

One-year old, a, worked as a matured animal.... 143
Open railings are becoming general. 307
railings should partly form the partitions to loose boxes.... 307
the stable doors during the night. 309
Order the groom to peep during the night at the horse which is too tired to eat.... 352
Original habitat of the equine race. 34
Ould, the, mare.... 447
Over-indulgence ruins the horse.... 454
Oxyen, different quantities of, inhaled by different horses.... 402

P.

Pace natural to blindness is induced by fixing the head with the bearing-rein.... 407
Pad grooms, their weight, their qualifications, and their duties.. 334
Pail, a clean one, should be kept in every stable.... 178
Pain consequent upon eating the stable diet.... 169
expressed by any peculiarity in progression.... 103
from strain on the ligaments occasions inveterate kicking.... 271
merely increases timidity.... 293
Panic acts on horses as on men.... 226
Paring the foot.... 102
Parts affected in "kidney dropping" 270
Passion an evil quality in a groom.. 500
Pastern bones repose upon the back tendons.... 43
play of, in thorough-breds, proof of elasticity in the entire body. 115
the, are regulated by the flexor tendons.... 411
the, should be judged by the swelling beneath the elbow.... 412
Patented food, only the groom's secret largely acted upon.... 166
Patent foods.... 196
safety-spring stirrup bar.... 510
trace shaft recommended in spinal disease.... 276
Pattern of grating to put over gutters.... 300
Patience is more than a virtue in a teacher.... 457
Pay a fair price for good a horse.... 375
Peculiar features of the fore limb... 409
Peep, a, into a dealer's yard.... 305
Peril of turning horses to graze without removing the halters.... 225
Perils attending fright in the stable.. 209
of modern coach-houses.... 323
Period of gestation in the mare.... 448
Permanent incisors come up in the same canals as the milk teeth occupied.... 159
molars are not perfected when cut 156
Perspiration implies cuticular activity.... 345
when excessive, greatly weakens the body.... 465
Perversity of the old agricultural mind.... 447
Petersburg oats.... 180
Physic and its administration.... 53
Pinning up subsequent to bleeding.. 92
Pitiable "vice" in horses.... 254
Place of birth, the, also regulates the kind of hoof.... 413
the, is cleared before the stable flooring is disturbed.... 249
two powerful men to prevent the jibber bolting.... 283
Plan of hot water service.... 322
Points, their importance and their development.... 379
made to screw on to shoe, a good substitute for roughing.... 129
of the blood haunches.... 419
Portrait of a one-year old.... 143
Position of the bones in the straight shoulder.... 405
of the foot casts the weight on different structures.... 253
Posterior limbs have no motion or sensation during a fit of kidney dropping.... 267
Precautions necessary after bleeding 93
necessary when bleeding the horse 90
Prejudices concerning blisters.... 80
Prejudice concerning the ears of a horse.... 282
declares in favor of a short neck.. 392
Preparation for scurfy skin.... 337
Prepared horse skin boot is the best application for cutting.... 123
Preparing the lying-in chamber.... 440
for the event.... 441
Present mode of shoeing is a failure. 104
Presents, occasional, to servants.... 493
Price, the, of most carriages.... 477
Pricking the foot when nailing.... 100
Pride, the, of the trade.... 360
Prime horses are often bought on speculation by dealers.... 376
Prisons should be built to resist the captives' utmost exertions.... 219
Probable result of a man enduring the horse's doom for one week.. 206
Profit and loss of a dealer's establishment.... 366
Proper mode of preparing stems for food.... 177

Proper treatment would be far the cheapest in the long run.......... 222
Properties of the horn forming the wall of the hoof.................... 98
Proposed stables are not to be measured by existing buildings. 297
Prolonged action is better than excessive labor......................... 468
Protect the points of flexion before blistering............................ 83
Proved, that the horse cannot be vicious.............................. 264
Provision against the ravenous feeding horse............................ 312
Prudence is banished by joy when the horse is leaving the stables.. 237
Puller, a, is always a dangerous servant................................. 398
Pumping action necessary for the circulation of the foot............ 246
Punish the smith who injures the hoof to fix on to it a small shoe. 131
Pupil of the horse's eye not circular 31
Purchases necessary when the horse is started............................ 497
Pure breeds often have bulging, frontal sinuses...................... 394
Purpose of the pastern joints......... 411

Q.

Qualifications of the author to descant on breeding.................... 427
Quarrels are provoked by narrow doorways............................ 236
between horse and driver generally end fatally................. 264
Quarters, hind, the seat of propulsion.................................... 45
Quarters of the hoof are left free by nailing the new shoe to the toe. 114
Quiet method of giving a drink...... 77
mode of giving a ball................ 67
Quietude and darkness do not dispose the horse to sleep........... 311

R.

Racers, when training, undergo excessive labor........................ 466
generally are old before their stock becomes famous............ 431
inhale more air during rapid motion.................................... 403
Racing men and bumpkins, their conduct contrasted................ 144
Racing plates.............................. 115
are dangerous shoes during the struggle............................ 472
Railroads not opposed to the breed of horses............................ 18
Rats enter stables through ordinary gutters............................ 300
Rat tails are said to denote good horses................................. 387
Rayment's, (Mr. C.,) his oatmeal recommended........................ 178
Rebound or spring of the racer improved by the present mode of shoeing.............................. 115
Recapitulation of certain points in the horse.............................. 416
Receiving the first lesson.............. 458
Reflection needed to comprehend the requirements of the horse....... 200
Regular horse dealers avoid flats.... 363
Regulations to be observed at feeding time.............................. 191
Reins, the necessity of good leather for................................. 517
for foals should be partly of India-rubber............................ 459
Remedies for a scurfy skin........... 290
for clicking............................ 126
for cutting............................ 122
for wounds and abrasions.......... 231
Repeated blows on one spot, evil of, when bleeding...................... 91
Requisites for the groom's use........ 500
indications of a well-built carriage.................................. 485
Respect is felt toward a person who can state his wants to a dealer. 374
Rest depends upon digestion......... 311
generally good for pedal annoyances.................................. 126
is imperfect when taken standing. 260
Restless eye, a, denotes timidity...... 396
Restlessness induces the collar-rope to be bitten........................ 215
Results of deranged digestion......... 196
Retention of the placenta............... 442
Rick of the back........................ 264
disables a horse as a wheeler or to endure excessive strain....... 275
is severe in heavy horses............ 273
often leads to fracture of the spine 276
or chink of the back is common, but little understood............. 266
Ride, to, is not necessary in a good groom................................. 333
Rider, the, and the head destroy the equality of weight on the limbs. 417
should understand the appearances of the healthy eye......... 290
swings on elastic life when seated on the back.......................... 41
Ridiculous to talk of a horse being "vicious"............................. 263
Rising to the leap........................ 461

Roach backs are common on the Essex marshes........ 384
generally spiteful........ 384
have been used as hunters........ 385
Rolling occasions the hind leg to get beyond the post of the stall..... 230
Roof consists of two parts........ 314
of the ambulatory, how supported and drained........ 302
the, described........ 314
Room for the night-watcher is supplied with comforts........ 325
Rooms at back divided from the stable by a stout wall........ 316
Roomy mares are a mistake........ 429
Roots are relished by horses........ 195
Roughing, as generally performed... 128
Rough-riding is practiced at three years of age........ 147
Rounded incisors would prevent the animal biting the grass........ 289
Roundness of the jaw's lower margin during colthood........ 142
Rowen hay........ 174
Rules for selecting a sire........ 438
Running away........ 294

S.

Sacrum, the, is one bone in the adult 38
Saddle-tree, a, with spring stirrup-bar attached........ 495
Saddlery and harness........ 494
Safety is sacrificed by the violent use of the bearing-rein........ 407
Sameness of diet deranges the digestion........ 195
of provender induces cutaneous irritability........ 286
proves vice to be induced by disease or by instinct........ 295
Sand in the eye, the horse protected against........ 35
Savage horse, how to render quiet... 60
Scene witnessed at Holloway........ 294
Science has demonstrated the mews is an unhealthy abode........ 328
and practice unite in estimation of the loins........ 383
Scotland, the ass does not breed in.. 49
Scratching the ear often fixes the hind pastern in the collar-rope. 224
Screw shoe, folly and inhumanity of. 118
Scroll-eyed hames........ 506
Seated shoe........ 117
Second crop of clover........ 175
Secretions, though hard, are governed by the inward soft organs 118
Section of a superficial gutter........ 299
of the proposed stables........ 324
See-sawing, or weaving, in horses... 205
Segundo bit, the........ 523
Senses, the special, assist one another........ 398
Serious accident to a cavalry officer. 272
Servants exaggerate the master's behavior........ 202
Seven o'clock duties........ 339
Seventh year, the, should witness the active service of the horse........ 462
Several diseases are almost peculiar to the rich........ 323
Severity endangers man's property in the horse........ 255
Sharp-pointed nail heads no effectual substitute for roughing........129
Shedding of the temporary molars.. 156
Shelter and nurture are requisite for all young horses........ 429
Sheltered ground between the gig and coach houses........ 320
Ship biscuit proposed for horses' food........ 195
Shoe is displaced by growth of horn 106
is wide enough if it supports the wall........ 104
Shoeing........ 95
blamed for all the changes in the foot........ 101
Shoes act injuriously by confining the foot........ 472
the, should be observed at the time of purchase........ 424
Short-necked horses cannot rest the limbs when at grass........ 392
horses feed badly in the field........ 392
Sides of the ventilator can be opened or closed at pleasure........ 315
Sight should be obscured during the act of bleeding........ 91
Sights of London streets........ 199
Signs of old age in the horse........ 136
Situation of the cistern........ 313
Six o'clock duties........ 339
Size and requirements of stable doors........ 307
of less import than form of thorax. 403
Skeletons in museums are never correct........ 408
Skin and lungs sympathize with each other........ 344
Slanting floors pervert the intentions of bone and tendon........ 251
hoofs are very bad........ 414
pavement causes horses to stand across the stall........ 254
shoulder, the benefits of........ 408
Sliding mouth bit, the........ 524
Slight movements excite the attention of a stabled horse........ 203
Slipper shoe, first mention of........ 111

Sloping pavement, a, extends from the front of the ambulatory..... 319
Sloth not favorable to paternity...... 437
Slow consuming boiler employed to warm the stables.................. 321
Small animals are preferred for their working capability................ 433
stables do not generally kill because they are draughty 81
Smallness of neck shows debility... 389
Snares which surround the groom... 330
So-called "incapacitating vices"..... 263
Society forces horse dealers to employ fiction......................... 360
the, for preventing cruelty to animals................................ 476
Soft palate, some of the uses of...... 28
Sole is removed by the shoeing smith and the veterinary surgeon...... 104
made to bear some pressure........ 104
Some English thorough-breds have Roman noses 394
substitute should be found for a stud groom.......................... 335
Southern end of the proposed stable. 319
Space, the, above the horses should be free to the roof.................. 332
Spasmodic inhalation denotes defective respiration 399
Special senses, the, should be noted as testifying to the health of the body.................................. 398
Speedy cut often causes a fall........ 121
warrants instant rejection......... 423
Spinal cord, the, is injured when "kidney dropping" occurs...... 269
Spine, how the bones of are united.. 39
sinks and rises in the living horse 383
the, of a horse is delicately organized............................ 265
the base of the skeleton 38
Spring bar and spring stirrup........ 510
Squatting on the haunches is an unnatural position in the horse.... 267
Stable implements are terrible weapons..................................... 318
pails are not suited to contain a horse's drink....................... 314
the, cannot be well managed by one pair of hands.................. 339
is relinquished to the servant...... 335
the only one known to the ass..... 48
new, will be thrice drained........ 301
Stables are inadequate prisons for horses 219
not proportioned to the horse's size.................................... 225
opposed to the habits and instincts of horses.......................... 247
the last considered when houses are planned 233
Stables as built—are they the best possible?.......................... 252
are paved with Dutch clinkers..... 249
as they should be.................... 297
do not require a blaze of light.... 229
in many families, are regarded as lumber lofts 220
promote the decomposition of urine.................................... 249
should be as clean as dairies 316
Stablemen suffer most from present customs................................ 226
Stagnant misery is personified in the horse................................... 243
Stallions are generally too fat........ 431
Standing in the manger............... 208
while it sleeps 260
Starvation is injurious before exertion 471
Starved, horses are, when confined in small stables........................ 81
Steeds are worn out serving more than one master....................... 334
Steel inserted at the toe of the clip shoe.................................... 120
Stewart's stable economy.............. 234
Stiff back reduces the horse's value. 278
Stick, blood, depicted.................. 90
Stomach small and well situated..... 20
Stout horn is required in the hoof of a horse.................................. 415
Stranger, a, has entered the stable.. 204
Strange substances eaten in stables. 196
Straw figure should be placed on the colt's back.............................. 458
worthless as food 177
Striking a horse when passing through a door is dangerous.... 238
Strong feet are not necessarily liable to disease 414
Submissive, the, are the abused...... 234
Substance is absent in the present breed of horses 432
Substances which do not nourish are not food.................................. 193
Suburban grooms generally live in the house... 328
Suburbs, the, are often disturbed by the thud of a trotted cart......... 274
Successful dealers are conceited...... 377
Sudden agony makes horses kick when mounted........................ 271
Suffering experienced at three years 148
Sulphur on oats, to detect............. 185
Summered.................................. 474
Summer's coat, advent of, is delayed by clipping.......................... 344
Supposed places of the groom's residence during certain periods.... 329
Supply of water, how arranged...... 313
Swerving is a mild form of shying.. 292

T.

Tails as denoting breed 387
Tail, the, acts as the rudder of the body 380
Take everything coolly when in a dealer's yard 374
Tale, a, illustrative of patience 520
Tapidum lucidum, its uses in the horse's eye 32
Tares are good food 189
Tax, a, is demanded on all that enters or leaves the stable 330
Tearing the clothing 287
Teeth 133
  at advanced periods 161, 162
  at birth 139
  cannot be positively interpreted after the fifth year 163
  one fortnight old 140
  three months old 140
Telescopic nature of the horse's eye. 33
Temporary loose box 356
  molars, peculiarity in the shedding of the 156
Tempting position of the manger 210
Tendon cannot sustain pressure 254
Ten o'clock duties 341
Terrible consequences of thoughtlessness, or of parsimony 262
Terror is never removed till the horse's spirit is broken 240
  is dangerous as the place of its exhibition is circumscribed 255
  mistaken for "vice" 109
Test for "kidney dropping" 268
Thickness of neck not an objection 389
  jaw caused by young teeth 142
Things needed to dress a sensitive horse 289
Thin heeled shoe pointed the toe upward, and did harm 120
  neck accompanies emaciation 460
  stomachs often taken from the bodies of old horses 178
  walls, difficulty of nailing a shoe on 100
  web to the seated shoe 117
  ear denotes goodness of breed 395
Thinning the sole. 103
Thirst, a consequence of dry food 167
Thorough-bred quarters express determination 419
Three purgatives cannot promote strength 465
  quarter shoe 116
Time should be allowed for nervousness to subside 240
  the, occupied in foaling is short 439
Times when the horse feeds 197
Timidity flies from any danger 281
Tips afford all the protection the racer's foot requires 473
Toe is cut and burnt when the horse shoe has a clip 108
  reasons for fixing nails into 113
Toes, the, in the forefeet point upward in the stable 243
  the, depressed in the gutter cause a luxurious sense of ease 256
To fly from danger is an instinct in the horse 295
  make gruel properly 178
Tool-house at the back of stables 318
Tools necessary for White's mode of roughing 130
  the, employed for carriages 480
Too many classes swindle when horse dealing 269
Tooth, its component substances 157
Torture is a favorite mode of cure with grooms 287
Town grooms inhabit impure rooms over the stables 328
Trainer's, the, stables are foul 467
Training and running are bad preparations for paternity 429
  folly of the present system 187
  necessary for young horses from the country 366
  spoils the tempers of many colts 470
  stables do not develop the true disposition of a horse 434
Treading on an upright nail 101
Treatment for jibbing 283
  for kidney dropping 268
  for rick of the back 275
  of the ass reprobated 47
  of the blood stallion 431
  of the heels when dirty 350
  proper for the blood mare 435
Troughs are empty while the cistern contains some water 321
Tuition should be daily till the second year 459
Turkish slipper, likeness to 102
Tushes are affected by age 161
  are uncertain teeth in the horse 150
Twitch, a, generally kept 74
Two chains and a collar-strap are employed on some horses 217
  kinds of cutting 121
  men meeting on a hill do not retain their relative positions 254

U.

Uncertain which shoe will prevent clicking or forging 125
Unclothing the beauty 376

Undulating pavement affords every kind of standing ground 299
Unfitness of horses for captivity... . 203
Uninitiated, the, greedy for bargains......... 277
Unnecessary, bleeding is............... 93
Upland hay................. 172
the only good hay...................... 176
Upright pasterns denote hard work has strained the flexor muscles. 411
Urine, on exposure yields ammonia. 249
stagnates in the gutters............. 249
Use of the mane and tail................ 380
Uses of the different components of the teeth.............................. 158
of the false nostril.................. 25
of the harness-room 317
of the sheltered space............... 320
to which stable doors are subject...................................... 236
Usual applications, the, check the hoof's perspiratory functions ... 353
explanation, accounting for the weakness of the fore limbs....... 416
length of horse cloths................. 350
method of cleansing the heels..... 346
Utter darkness excites timidity...... 226

V.

Valves aid the circulation when opposed to gravity..................... 245
in the veins of the leg............... 244
of jugular veins only act when the head is depressed............. 22
Various people buy and sell horses 257
substances are interposed between the ends of bone.................. 42
Veins so arranged as to prevent congestion if feeding off the ground 21
Ventilation secured by having the doors in parts........................ 308
Ventilator roofed with stout glass... 315
Vertebræ, the, are the base of the skeleton............................... 380
Vetches, on which agricultural teams live, indicate no danger in beans 468
Veterinary examiners too often neglect the spine....................... 277
profession composed of imperfectly educated men 73
Vicious horses are mostly weakly creatures............................... 418
View extended by mounting on to the manger........................... 210
Voice, the, is sufficient goad for a willing animal....................... 460

W.

Walking a horse is more than simply moving.................................. 124
through the stables and physicking the stock......................... 377
essential to the horse's foot........ 246
Wall of the hoof......................... 98
the, is struck during darkness..... 258
Warranties are of no value........... 370
Waste of present feeding.............. 193
Wasting the hay 212
Watch the action while the horse is being run along the ride 423
Water, its importance in the stable.. 486
should be freely employed.......... 338
should only be applied to the heels after special permission.......... 352
troughs described...................... 313
Weakly or healthy foals now suck only the same time 446
Weakness is not the accompaniment of the racer's elastic pastern.... 411
Weariness cannot promote thrift..... 249
induces the horse to play with its needless corn......................... 213
Weaving is an effort to promote the circulation of the foot............ 250
or see-sawing in horses............. 205
Web slants in the seated shoe......... 117
none to the slipper shoe............. 111
the, of the shoe serves to retain stones 103
Wedged-heeled shoe, danger of 119
Weeds of the blood stock.............. 422
Weight should not be put on horses during training 468
the, of the head is not felt during health 388
Well-bred, the, and coarse-bred heads contrasted...................... 393
Wetting the heels most injurious.... 346
What occasions horses to kick by night? 228
Wheels, how long these should last.. 488
how to use and understand......... 491
When a part of the frame moves, all parts are agitated.................... 150
buying, procure a horse rather too strong than strong enough...... 374
gentlemen meddle, the dealer exults..................................... 372
the foal quits its dam, breaking should commence 458
Where the fore limb quits the trunk, muscle should abound 409
White horses are generally old...... 136
Why a carriage should be cleansed from mud 487
breeding does not pay 428

Widest, the, of modern stable doors are too narrow.................... 238
Width of channel testifies to the breathing capability.............. 399
Wild animals are not caged like the horse.................................. 202
horses nowhere exist................ 37
Wind sucking caused by stables...... 205
Windpipe capable of contraction..... 26
Winter's frost always takes horse proprietors by surprise.......... 126
Winter shoes are best made in summer............... 126
Wintry perspirations, probable cause of 343
Wipė the oil off after blistering...... 83
Wired-in hoofs are bad................ 415
Wisp and brush are abused........... 342
Withhold all medicine from the breeding mare 442
Wolves' teeth are of no importance. 143
Work demands more support than grass affords...................... 138
when not excessive, benefits health 435
Worked too early......................... 19
Worst cheat, the, in horse flesh 357
Wound, precautions necessary after bleeding............................. 93
Written warranties seldom required by the honest dealer............... 365
Wrongs inflicted on horses 199

Y.

Yew clippings poison horses.......... 171
Young animals are purchased by the London dealers 366
horses are put in the chains as teamsters............................ 265
horses should be from birth set apart for their future uses....... 438